Life Histories of North American Nuthatches, Wrens, Thrashers and Their Allies

by Arthur Cleveland Bent

Dover Publications, Inc., New York

ADVERTISEMENT

The scientific publications of the National Museum include two series, known, respectively, as *Proceedings* and *Bulletin*.

The *Proceedings* series, begun in 1878, is intended primarily as a medium for the publication of original papers, based on the collections of the National Museum, that set forth newly acquired facts in biology, anthropology, and geology, with descriptions of new forms and revisions of limited groups. Copies of each paper, in pamphlet form, are distributed as published to libraries and scientific organizations and to specialists and others interested in the different subjects. The dates at which these separate papers are published are recorded in the table of contents of each of the volumes.

The series of *Bulletins*, the first of which was issued in 1875, contains separate publications comprising monographs of large zoological groups and other general systematic treatises (occasionally in several volumes), faunal works, reports of expeditions, catalogs of type specimens, special collections, and other material of similar nature. The majority of the volumes are octavo in size, but a quarto size has been adopted in a few instances in which large plates were regarded as indispensable. In the *Bulletin* series appear volumes under the heading *Contributions from the United States National Herbarium*, in octavo form, published by the National Museum since 1902, which contain papers relating to the botanical collections of the Museum.

The present work forms No. 195 of the *Bulletin* series.

ALEXANDER WETMORE,
Secretary, Smithsonian Institution.

Published in the United Kingdom by Constable and Company Limited, 10 Orange Street, London W. C. 2.

This Dover edition, first published in 1964, is an unabridged and unaltered republication of the work first published in 1948 by the United States Government Printing Office, as Smithsonian Institution United States National Museum *Bulletin 195*.

International Standard Book Number: 0-486-21088-X
Library of Congress Catalog Card Number: 64-24413

Manufactured in the United States of America

Dover Publications, Inc.
180 Varick Street
New York 14, N. Y.

CONTENTS

INTRODUCTION

This is the sixteenth in a series of bulletins of the United States National Museum on the life histories of North American birds. Previous numbers have been issued as follows:

107. Life Histories of North American Diving Birds, August 1, 1919.
113. Life Histories of North American Gulls and Terns, August 27, 1921.
121. Life Histories of North American Petrels and Pelicans and Their Allies, October 19, 1922.
126. Life Histories of North American Wild Fowl (part), May 25, 1923.
130. Life Histories of North American Wild Fowl (part), June 27, 1925.
135. Life Histories of North American Marsh Birds, March 11, 1927.
142. Life Histories of North American Shore Birds (pt. 1), December 31, 1927.
146. Life Histories of North American Shore Birds (pt. 2), March 24, 1929.
162. Life Histories of North American Gallinaceous Birds, May 25, 1932.
167. Life Histories of North American Birds of Prey (pt. 1), May 3, 1937.
170. Life Histories of North American Birds of Prey (pt. 2), August 8, 1938.
174. Life Histories of North American Woodpeckers, May 23, 1939.
176. Life Histories of North American Cuckoos, Goatsuckers, Hummingbirds, and Their Allies, July 20, 1940.
179. Life Histories of North American Flycatchers, Larks, Swallows, and Their Allies, May 8, 1942.
191. Life Histories of North American Jays, Crows, and Titmice. January 27, 1947.

The same general plan has been followed, as explained in previous bulletins, and the same sources of information have been utilized. The nomenclature of the 1931 Check-list of the American Ornithologists' Union and supplements has been followed.

An attempt has been made to give as full a life history as possible of the best-known subspecies of each species and to avoid duplication by writing briefly of the others and giving only the characters of the subspecies, its range, and any habits peculiar to it. In many cases certain habits, probably common to the species as a whole, have been recorded for only one subspecies. Such habits are mentioned under the subspecies on which the observations were made. The distribution gives the range of the species as a whole, with only rough outlines of the ranges of the subspecies, which in many cases cannot be accurately defined.

The egg dates are the condensed results of a mass of records taken from the data in a large number of the best egg collections in the country, as well as from contributed field notes and from a few published sources. They indicate the dates on which eggs have been actually found in various parts of the country, showing the earliest and latest dates and the limits between which half the dates fall, indicating the height of the season.

The plumages are described in only enough detail to enable the reader to trace the sequence of molts and plumages from birth to maturity and to recognize the birds in the different stages and at the different seasons.

No attempt has been made to describe fully the adult plumages; this has been well done already in the many manuals and State books. Partial or complete albinism is liable to occur in almost any species; for this reason, and because it is practically impossible to locate all such cases, it has seemed best not to attempt to treat this subject at all. The names of colors, when in quotation marks, are taken from Ridgway's Color Standards and Nomenclature (1912). In the measurements of eggs, the four extremes are printed in bold-face type.

Many who have contributed material for previous volumes have continued to cooperate. Receipt of material from nearly 500 contributors has been acknowledged previously. In addition to these, our thanks are due to the following new contributors: Earl Brooks, F. C. Clayton, J. D. Cleghorn, Roland C. Clement, Clarence Cottam, E. M. S. Dale, David E. Davis, Russell S. Davis, Richard J. Eaton, Mary M. Erickson, Albert K. Fisher, Robert Fredericks, John F. Freeman, Herbert Friedmann, Russell K. Grater, Hugh M. Halliday, Samuel A. Harper, Donald M. Hatfield, Harold Heath, Catherine A. Hurlbutt, Ruth B. Inman, H. R. Ivor, L. A. Kosier, Gordon M. Meade, Loye H. Miller, Mrs. D. M. Morrison, H. R. Meyers, A. L. Nelson, Norman A. Preble, W. F. Rapp, Jr., Richard Reade, J. W. Slipp, Bruce P. Stiles, William A. Taylor, W. Bryant Tyrrell, Stephen Waldron, J. Dan Webster, James B. Young, and Francis Zirrer. If any contributor fails to find his or her name in this or some previous bulletin, the author would be glad to be advised. As the demand for these volumes is much greater than the supply, the names of those who have not contributed to the work during the previous ten years will be dropped from the author's mailing list.

Dr. Winsor M. Tyler rendered valuable assistance by reading and indexing, for these groups, a large part of the literature on North American birds, and he contributed three complete life histories. Dr. Alfred O. Gross and Robert S. Woods contributed two each; and Dr. Mary M. Erickson and Alexander Sprunt, Jr., contributed one each.

Egg measurements were furnished especially for this volume by the American Museum of Natural History (Dean Amadon), Griffing Bancroft, the California Academy of Sciences (Robert T. Orr), Charles E. Doe, James R. Gillin, Wilson C. Hanna, Ed. N. Harrison, Turner

E. McMullen, the Museum of Comparative Zoology (Ruth B. Inman), the Museum of Vertebrate Zoology (Margaret W. Wythe), Laurence Stevens, George H. Stuart, 3d, and the United States National Museum.

Our thanks are also due to William George F. Harris for figuring hundreds of egg measurements and for sorting over and arranging a mass of egg dates. Through the courtesy of the Fish and Wildlife Service, the services of May Thacher Cooke were obtained to compile the distribution and migration paragraphs. The author claims no credit and assumes no responsibility for this part of the work.

The manuscript for this bulletin was completed in August 1942. Contributions received since then will be acknowledged later. Only information of great importance could be added. Since this manuscript was first compiled, 18 new forms have been admitted to our Check-list by the A. O. U. committee. Their life histories are included in those of other forms of the species. The reader is reminded again that this is a cooperative work; if he fails to find in these volumes anything that he knows about the birds, he can blame himself for not having sent the information to—

THE AUTHOR.

LIFE HISTORIES OF NORTH AMERICAN NUTHATCHES, WRENS, THRASHERS, AND THEIR ALLIES

ORDER PASSERIFORMES (FAMILIES SITTIDAE, CERTHIIDAE, CHAMAEIDAE, CINCLIDAE, TROGLODYTIDAE, and MIMIDAE)

By Arthur Cleveland Bent

Taunton, Mass.

Order PASSERIFORMES

Family SITTIDAE: Nuthatches

SITTA CAROLINENSIS COOKEI Oberholser

WHITE-BREASTED NUTHATCH

PLATES 1–4

CONTRIBUTED BY WINSOR MARRETT TYLER

HABITS

The white-breasted nuthatch is a droll, earnest little bird, rather sedate and unemotional. He is no great musician and seems to lack a sense of humor. He has none of the irrepressible fidgetiness of the house wren, none of the charming happiness of the song sparrow; he appears to take life on a matter-of-fact level. He is short-necked, broad-shouldered, sturdy, quick and sure in his motions, suggesting an athlete, and as we study him on his daily round, as he hops up and down over the bark, we see that he is an athlete with marked skill as an acrobat, like the tumbling kind, as much at home upside down as right side up.

It is a characteristic pose of the nuthatch, perhaps unique among birds, to stand head downward on the trunk of a tree with the neck extended backward, the bill pointing straight outward from the bark.

Spring and courtship.—If we have had a male nuthatch under our eye through the winter, either a bird roaming through a bit of woodland or one visiting our feeding station daily, we notice, as spring approaches, a change in his behavior: he begins to sing freely at all times of day, whereas previously he sang sparingly and only in the morning

1

hours. At this time his deportment toward his mate changes also. All through the winter the pair has lived not far apart, feeding within hearing of each other, but the male has paid little attention to his mate; in fact, on the food shelf he has shown dominance over her; but now in the lengthening, warmer days of spring he becomes actively engaged over her comfort. A real courtship begins: he carries food to her and places it in her bill, he stores bits of nut in crevices of bark for her convenience, and he often addresses his singing directly to her. Standing back to her, he bows slowly downward as he sings, then in the interval before another song he straightens up, then bows as he sings again. The songs come with perfect regularity over and over again and can thus be recognized even in the distance as the courtship song.

We may imagine what a changing color scheme is presented to the female bird, if, as his song invites her to do, she glance his way—the black of his crown and his rough raised mane, then the blue-gray of his back, then the variegated black and white pattern of his expanded tail, then, perhaps, at the end of his bow, a flash of ruddy brown. At other times he approaches the female more aggressively, strutting before her with stretched-out neck and flattened crown, a pose of intimidation.

The change from the passive behavior of the winter months to active courtship takes place in New England early in April and indicates the advent of the nesting activities.

Nesting.—Speaking of eastern Massachusetts, William Brewster (1906) says: "The favorite breeding haunts of the White-bellied Nuthatch are ancient woods of oak, chestnut or maple where the trees are of the largest size and more or less gone to decay." In these surroundings the bird commonly builds its nest high up in a tall tree, either in a natural cavity or in an old woodpecker's hole, or, in an orchard, it may make use of a knothole in an apple tree.

Edward H. Forbush (1929) states that nuthatches sometimes nest in a cavity excavated by the birds themselves in decayed wood. Such instances, however, must be of rare occurrence, for William Brewster once told me that he had never known of a case.

Mr. Bent (MS.) describes a nest "about 30 feet from the ground near the top of a large crooked swamp maple that stood near the end of a strip of woods on a private estate. The cavity was a rotted-out crevice in a nearly horizontal branch. The opening was too narrow for me to insert my small hand and had to be enlarged. The nesting material consisted of a small handful of soft fur that looked like rabbit fur, but nothing else; the cavity was very small and not over a foot deep."

Thomas D. Burleigh (1931) says of the bird in the mountainous regions of central Pennsylvania:

This species is one of the most characteristic birds of the scattered short stretches of woods in the open valleys, one pair at least, frequently two, being found in each one. Nesting is well under way by the middle of April, and by the latter part of that month or the first of May these birds are incubating full sets of from seven to nine eggs, the last being actually the commoner number. The nests are invariably in knot holes in the trunks of the larger trees, varying in height from 15 to 50 feet from the ground, the cavity itself being 6 to 8 inches in depth, and usually 6 inches from the entrance. The nests are substantial matted beds of soft shreds of inner bark and rabbits' fur, with rarely a little wool, cow hair, and chicken feathers. But one brood is raised each year.

Francis H. Allen says in his notes for April 18, 1942: "My attention was called by low-pitched notes of indeterminate character. I found a pair acting in a strange manner about a bird house on the side of a tree. Besides feeding or going through the motions of picking food from the bark, they spent much of the time in wiping the bill from side to side—that is, the right side and left side of the bill alternately in rapid succession over and over for a considerable period of time in each bout. It was like the swinging of a pendulum in its regularity. The male did most of this, but the female also took part. A courtship rite was suggested, though it was not accompanied by any form of display. It was so regular and so long continued that I do not think it could have been merely for the purpose of cleaning the bill, though it may have started in that way and have been continued by imitation and as a sort of play."

William Brewster (1936) writes thus of the birds nesting in Concord, Mass.:

There is a round hole about 3½ inches in diameter 60 feet above the ground in our big elm, in which a pair of Flickers reared their brood 6 or 7 years ago. It has since been occupied at all seasons by gray squirrels. I have seen three animals enter and leave it within a week. Yet this morning about 8 o'clock a pair of White-bellied Nuthatches were building a nest there. The female did most of the work and performed it with remarkable rapidity. She would run out on a large branch, pry off a scale of bark 5 or 6 inches long, take it into the hole and almost instantly reappear and go after another. The male occasionally got one and simply *poked* it into the hole, without entering himself.

Of the several accounts in the literature of nuthatches breeding in bird boxes the following is an example, showing also the bird's method of obtaining rabbit fur for the lining of its nest. Lucien Harris (1927), of Atlanta, Ga., writes:

I saw a pair of White-breasted Nuthatches carrying strips of bark into the soap box. Often they would carry strips larger than themselves. They were very industrious and paid no attention to us. The birds used the bark to cover the entire floor of the box and the layer was about half an inch in thickness. They then proceeded to collect little pellets of dried earth and lumps of mud which was scattered thinly over the bark.

After this preliminary they started on the nest proper, which they placed in a back corner of the box. The nest was saucer-shaped and constructed of small twigs, grasses and rootlets.

Then, as if not quite satisfied, this unique pair discovered a dead rabbit—one that had been dead for some time—and proceeded to line the nest proper, as well as the rest of the box, with rabbit fur, so that when completed the box smelled more like a buzzard's domicile then a nuthatch's home. Brer' Rabbit's fluffy tail held a conspicuous place in the middle of the box.

The habit of taking hair from dead animals may be the birds' usual procedure, for Edward H. Forbush (1929) says: "Mr. Maurice Broun tells me that he saw one come down from a tree and hop along the ground until it reached a dead squirrel from which it plucked a bunch of hair nearly as large as its own head."

Helen Granger Whittle (1926) gives a record of a pair mated for 2 years. She says: "In the Bulletin for October, 1925, I reported a pair of Nuthatches (*Sitta c. carolinensis*) which had remained together a winter and a summer, and which had brought a family of young to our Peterboro [New Hampshire] station in July 1925. These parents have been under observation for another year. They have now spent at least two winters and two summers constantly in each other's company, and they have raised two families which we know about. Keeping 'tabs' on these birds has been simplified by the fact that both are banded on the left tarsus. All our other Nuthatches have been banded on the right tarsus."

Eggs.—[AUTHOR'S NOTE: All the nuthatches lay large sets of eggs, and the white-breasted nuthatch is perhaps the most consistently prolific; it lays 5 to 9 or even 10 eggs to a set, but the extremes are uncommon; 8 seems to be the commonest number. In a series of 15 sets in the J. P. Norris collection there are 2 sets of 5, 1 of 6, 3 of 7, 7 of 8, and only 1 of 9.

The eggs are usually ovate or short-ovate and have very little gloss. The ground color is usually pure white but often creamy white and sometimes pinkish white. They are prettily and usually heavily marked with bright reddish brown, "ferruginous," "cinnamon-rufous," "hazel," or "vinaceous" and sometimes with a few spots of pale lavender or purplish drab. The markings are often thickest at the larger end; some eggs are evenly sprinkled over the whole surface with fine dots of pale brown.

The measurements of 40 eggs in the United States National Museum average 18.8 by 14.3 millimeters; the eggs showing the four extremes measure 19.8 by 15.0, 17.3 by 13.0, and 18.3 by 15.2 millimeters.]

Young.—The young birds when they leave the nest look very much like their parents. In Mr. Bent's nest there were "two females and three males, showing the same sex characters as the adults. They were nearly grown and fully fledged; they could not fly much, but could climb perfectly."

Dr. Arthur A. Allen (1929) states that the incubation period is 12 days and that both parents incubate the eggs and feed the young for 2 weeks after they have left the nest. He says that the young birds do not return to the cavity to sleep, but "cling upside down to the trunk of a tree beneath a projecting branch."

In Dr. Wilbur K. Butts's (1931) experience, "the male Nuthatch does not assist in incubation. He does feed the female while she is on the nest. * * * Both sexes feed the young."

Plumages.—[AUTHOR'S NOTE: All the nuthatches are peculiar in having a juvenal plumage that closely resembles the adult nuptial plumage and in which the sexes are distinguishable by the same characters as in the adult (see pl. 2). In the young male the black of the pileum and hind neck is duller than in the adult and less sharply defined against the gray back, and the edges of the greater wing coverts are more or less gray. The young female is similar, except that the pileum (front half of the crown) is deep plumbeous-gray instead of black; the hind neck is dull black. Otherwise, young birds of both sexes are much like their parents.

Dr. Dwight (1900) says that the first winter plumage is "acquired by a partial postjuvenal molt, in July, in Florida, which involves the body plumage and wing coverts, but not the remiges nor rectrices, young birds and adults becoming practically indistinguishable."

Adults have a complete postnuptial molt in July.]

Food.—The nuthatch feeds on insects as well as on nuts, acorns, and other vegetable matter. Waldo L. McAtee (1926a) gives thus an excellent summary of its diet:

The White-breast has been observed to feed freely on beechnuts, to devour acorns and hickory nuts, to take maize from cribs, and to be very fond of seeds of sunflowers. These observations point to a fondness for mast which is characteristic of the nuthatch tribe. During the winter months nearly all of the food is mast, while through the spring and summer, much animal food is taken, often to the full capacity of the bird's stomach.

This is derived chiefly from the ranks of beetles, spiders, caterpillars, true bugs, and ants and other small hymenoptera. Besides these some flies, grasshoppers, moths, and millipeds are eaten. Among the insect food items known to have a detrimental relation to the forest are nut weevils, the locust seed weevils (*Spermophagus robiniae*), round-headed wood borers, leaf beetles, tree hoppers, psyllids, scale insects, caterpillars, and ants. The White-breast has been observed to feed also on larvae of gall flies, eggs of plant lice and of fall cankerworms, oyster scale (*Lepidosaphes ulmi*), and upon larvae of the gypsy moth and forest tent caterpillars. * * *

In the long run, the White-breast, no doubt, destroys a large number of forest pests, and while not so valuable as some of the more highly insectivorous birds, still deserves protection.

The birds are fond of suet, as everyone who maintains a feeding station knows. William Brewster (1936) gives this scene of a pair caching this delicacy:

The pair of Nuthatches came regularly to the suet, oftenest in the early morning. I watched them closely for half an hour this morning [March 17, 1911]. The male was digging out pieces up to the size of a large pea and carrying them away to store them in crevices in tree trunks and behind scales of loose bark. He took them to different trees and in all directions, usually going about 100 yards. Whenever the female was with or near him, he invariably employed her to carry off and *cache* the morsel. She took it from him without hesitation and flew, as he did, in various directions, chiefly to apple trees in the orchard. Curiously enough, he would not permit her to touch the main store of supply from which he was drawing. Whenever she attempted to do so, he attacked her quite viciously and drove her away. Yet the next moment he would give her the small pieces that he had just extracted.

Edward H. Forbush (1929) states: "Several ornithologists have doubted that they ever break nuts of any kind. There is credible testimony however to support the statement. Dr. C. W. Townsend says that he has twice observed the habit." Dr. Townsend (1905) continues: "On one occasion, when the bird was disturbed, it flew off with the acorn into which it had thrust its bill. Their object was probably to obtain the larvae within."

Those of us who have fed nuthatches at our window ledges and have watched them feed at arm's length have had ample proof that the birds do crack and swallow pieces of nuts. I have frequently had a bird take a bit of nut meat from my hand and swallow it, or, if it were too large, take it to the corner of the shelf, as to a cranny of bark, and split it, and I have watched a bird crack open a cherry stone.

Prof. O. A. Stevens (MS.) writes: "When they first appear in the fall, we have often fed them squash seeds, which they cache with great industry. I have at times watched an individual bird take six or seven seeds in succession in different directions, hunting for suitable places in trees, shingles, and other parts of houses."

Behavior.—The white-breasted nuthatch spends most of his day hopping over the bark of the trunks and main branches of large trees, generally moving head downward toward the ground. Francis H. Allen (1912) points out an advantage in this procedure, saying: "I suspect that by approaching his prey from above he detects insects and insect-eggs in the crevices of the bark which would be hidden from another point of view. The Woodpeckers and the Creepers can take care of the rest."

Edward H. Forbush (1929) explains how the downward progress is accomplished. He says: "They seem to have taken lessons of the squirrel which runs down the tree head first, stretching out his hind feet backward and so clinging to the bark with his claws as he goes down; but the nuthatch having only two feet has to reach forward under its breast with one and back beside its tail with the other, and thus, standing on a wide base and holding safely to the bark with the three fore claws of the upper foot turned backward it hitches nimbly down the tree head first." A photograph in Bird-Lore, vol. 31,

p. 424, seems to corroborate this statement. However, I once had under observation for weeks a nuthatch that had lost his entire left foot, the tarsus ending in a stump, thickened at the end, and in spite of his deformity, he was able to clamber over the branches, both large and small ones, and even to hang head downward, clinging to a small branch with his single foot.

Sometimes a nuthatch will hop down to the very base of a tree and then continue on over the ground. Here the bird looks strange enough, accustomed as we are to see it in reversed position, as leaning forward it jumps or leaps along, reminding us not a little of a frog. Edward H. Forbush (1929) tells of "a pair that spent an entire forenoon going over the chips left under a large tree from which the loose bark had been scraped. The birds picked over this material very thoroughly in their search for insects and insects' eggs."

The tameness of the white-breasted nuthatch, or the lack of suspicion it shows toward human beings, is remarkable. With a little patience a bird may be induced to feed from our hand, especially if we are indoors and reach out through an open window to the food shelf where it is accustomed to feed. There are many such records in the literature. A striking example of trustfulness is related thus by E. M. Mead (1903), who while outdoors in Central Park, New York, fed a bird for two successive seasons: "So fearless is she that she will take food from my lips, shoulder or lap. Even an open umbrella over my head has no terrors for her. Although she manifested some annoyance at the appearance of the camera within 2 feet of us for more than an hour, during which time 12 exposures were made, still she repeated all her little tricks, not only once, but several times."

The bird displays remarkable agility in the air, on the bark of trees and small branches; it can catch a falling nut in midair, or scramble downward over the bark and overtake it, and it can hang upside down, swinging from a tiny branch. A. C. Bent (MS.) mentions a bird that ran down a swaying rope, "always head downward, and scolded me within 2 feet of my face."

Charles L. Whittle (1930) reports a banded bird known to have reached the age of 7½ years.

Wilbur K. Butts (1927), after making a careful investigation of the feeding range of marked white-breasted nuthatches, remarks: "In the course of the study it soon became apparent that each pair did not wander freely about, but had a definite, restricted, though fairly large feeding range." This accords with the experience I had with a male bird which visited my feeding shelf daily, with one short interlude, for over a year. Butts (1931) gives the following interesting summary of a subsequent study of the bird:

1. All or nearly all the individuals of the Nuthatch found at Ithaca were permanent residents. There is no evidence of any migration in this locality.

2. Each pair of Nuthatches had a definite feeding territory throughout the year. 3. The size of the territory in the winter was about 25 or 30 acres in wooded country and apparently about 50 acres in semiwooded country. 4. They ranged over an approximately equal area during the nesting season, though it was not necessarily the same area. 5. Feeding stations had no effect on the feeding range of the Nuthatch. 6. Feeding stations should be about one-fourth of a mile apart for the Nuthatch. 7. The nest is built in or near the winter feeding territory. 8. Besides the mated pairs which have established territories there are a number of wandering birds. 9. In case of the disappearance of one member of a mated pair, its place may be taken by one of these wandering birds. 10. Nuthatches may nest in the same hole for successive seasons. 11. The large size of both winter and breeding territories is apparently not caused by inability of the birds to find sufficient food in a smaller area. They are able to obtain plenty of food quite near the nest. The feeding of the young birds is apparently not such a severe task as it is commonly supposed to be.

Francis Zirrer, of Hayward, Wis., writes (MS.): "The families stay together until about the end of November, as up to that time the old birds are still occasionally feeding the young, which at first are somewhat reluctant to come to the feeding table. Later, the old males usurp the table and chase, or try to chase, all others away. They tame readily, come to the hand for food, but know perfectly well the difference in size of the food; they will come, pick the first piece, but seeing a larger piece will pause a little, drop the first one and take the largest. If no food is on the table, they will come to the window, or visit the woodland dweller at his place in the woods, where he works at his winter supply of fuel, often a considerable distance from home; and there is usually no rest until he returns to the cabin and fills the table with a fresh supply of food. They become so used to a certain person and his call that they will, if within hearing distance, come and follow long distances through the woods. Met in the woods during the breeding season, often more than a mile away, they will come at the call and sit on the hand, head, or shoulder. Of course, it is advisable to carry something in the pockets, which one used to such things usually does. As a rule, they are quite fearless, even bold; during the nesting season of the goshawk, which nested several years a few hundred yards from the cabin, the bold little imps inspected fearlessly the limbs and trunk of the nesting tree, apparently not fearing the fierce raptores a few feet or yards away."

Voice.—Most of the notes of the white-breasted nuthatch bear a decided resemblance to the human voice; they seem to be spoken or whistled. A song, for example, may be likened to a man whistling to a dog—a regular series of about six or eight notes, sometimes more, sharply accented, striking the same pitch, each with a slight rising inflection. The pitch is commonly D next but one above middle C. When a bird is singing near at hand the voice loses some of its whistled quality and becomes full, resonant, almost mellow. The song has been variously rendered into syllables such as *hah-hah-hah*, *tway*, *tway*, *what, what, too, too,* and *whoot, whoot.* These renderings represent the song heard from different distances, and all of them suggest it somewhat. Occasionally the pitch of the song falls slightly at the end; sometimes the pitch undulates in slight degree; and rarely the bird crowds 20 or more rapid notes into a song of normal length.

Some years ago I had a male nuthatch under close observation where I could hear it practically every day for a full round of the seasons. The following quotation (W. M. Tyler, 1916) gives a summary of his notes:

The Nuthatch sings every month in the year; even on the coldest days of January he occasionally sings a few times in the early morning—I have heard the song when the temperature was zero;—in February songs are more frequently heard, but singing during this month is still irregular. The chief singing period is from the first of March until the last of May; during these 3 months the male sings continually. June is a month of comparative silence (I have only five records of song); in July and August songs are heard almost as infrequently as in winter, and during the last 4 months of the year singing is still rarer. In winter, singing is confined to the early morning hours,—soon after sunrise—and even during the spring it is rare, before the first of April, to hear a Nuthatch sing in the afternoon. In autumn an occasional song is heard in the warmest part of the day.

In addition to his songs, our Nuthatch utters five different notes: (1) The simplest of these, and by far the most frequently used note of his vocabulary, is a high, short syllable, quietly pronounced, much aspirated, sounding like "hit." This note is given when the bird is perched and when he is in the air, both by a solitary bird and by the pair when they are together. It is both a soliloquizing and a conversational note and is associated as a rule with a calm mood. (2) The well-known ejaculation "quank," a call at certain distances remarkably suggestive of the human voice, is often employed when the bird seems excited. At such times the note is delivered with much vigor; on other occasions it is apparently used as a call between a pair of birds. This note and the "hit" are the only notes I have heard from the female bird. The "quank" call is very often doubled and is frequently extended into a loud, rattling chatter. As in the case of the song, the "quank" appears very much rounder, fuller and more resonant when heard near at hand. At short range it has a rolling "r" sound. (3) A low-toned "chuck" is sometimes addressed to the female. (4) On several occasions I have heard the male bird utter a growl (deep in tone for a bird) as he dashed in attack at a Sparrow. (5) A note which I have heard but rarely is a long, high whistle with a rising, followed by a falling inflection. Our word "queer" recalls the note which bears a decided resemblance to one of the Pine Grosbeak's piping calls. The note has a ventriloquial property, appearing to come from a distance when, in reality, the bird is close by. I heard this note several times in late February and early March, generally between songs in the early morning.

Francis H. Allen says in his notes for May 9, 1939: "From a pair feeding in trees I heard a note that was new to me often repeated. It was a soft, two-syllabled note that might be rendered *k dӑăp.* Sometimes I saw that it came from the female, and I never was sure that I heard it from the male. The note was at least as high-pitched as the familiar *tüt,* which the birds also uttered frequently. Twice I say

the male feed the female.   The feeding was accompanied by a faint
little rapid chatter that was new to me.   The *k dăăp* note was so different from the ordinary calls of the species that I did not suspect a nuthatch as the author when I first heard it."

Field marks.—The white-breasted nuthatch is a small, thick-set bird
with a pearl-gray, unstreaked back, shining black crown, and black-
and-white wings and tail.   The side of the head is white, without an
ocular stripe, and the bill is long, straight, and dark.   It is the largest
of our nuthatches and does not resemble the smaller species closely in
plumage.   Its confirmed habit of hopping downward over the bark
of tree trunks distinguishes it readily from the warblers, kinglets, and
other small avian frequenters of woodland.

Enemies.—The white-breasted nuthatch is one of the species victimized by the cowbird, but cases are apparently rare, for Dr. Herbert
Friedmann (1934) says: "I knew of three instances before; now another one has come to my attention, a set of six eggs of the nuthatch
and one of the Eastern Cowbird, collected May 5, 1912, at State College, Pennsylvania, by R. C. Harlow."

R. W. Williams (1918) gives this lively description of an attack of
two red-headed woodpeckers upon a nuthatch's nest and young:

Bright and happy days for the birds, old and young, ensued, until one morning
before breakfast (May 9) two Red-headed Woodpeckers arrived on the scene and
inspected the box.   I did not attach much significance to this and contented
myself, before leaving for my office, with frightening them away by vigorous ges-
ticulations and by small sticks thrown at them.   These methods seemed to suffice
for the time.   Later in the day, however, I received a message that the Woodpeckers were enlarging the entrance and possessing the box, throwing out the
young Nuthatches—three having already been cast to the ground—and altogether
evicting the parents, which, grief-stricken, were looking on from nearby stations.
The red-headed ruffians were at the box when I reached home that afternoon
but they disappeared at my approach.   I procured my gun and took a position
from which I would be sure to reach them if they returned.   I had not long to
wait.   One of them alighted at the entrance of the box.   I fired and the bird
fell to the ground directly under the box.   Both of the Nuthatches flew to the
base of the tree and, clinging there within a foot of the ground, regarded the
Woodpecker for more than a minute, with exhibitions of keen satisfaction and
exultation.

I found another of the young Nuthatches dead a few feet away from the tree.
None of the young birds was mutilated to any extent, from which circumstance it seems probable that the Woodpeckers were not in quest of food, but
distinctly bent on mischief.

Harold S. Peters (1936) mentions two flies, *Ornithonica confluenta*
Say and *Ornithomyia anchineuria* Speiser, which have been found
in the plumage of this bird.

Fall and winter.—As we have seen above, no prominent migration
of the white-breasted nuthatch has been noted.   P. A. Taverner and
B. H. Swales (1908) report from Point Pelee, Ontario, Canada:

"This species, though met with on nearly all visits, has never been very common. Usually a few scattered individuals have made the day's record. Our date of greatest abundance was October 14, 1906, when 10 were listed. * * * Our fall dates are conflicting, but seem to indicate that migrants arrive irregularly from the last of August to the middle of September."

The nuthatch, as we know him best, is an autumn and winter bird. We meet him hopping about the leafless trees, settled in some woodland, generally in the company of his mate. Here through the whole winter he remains in a domain that he has established as his winter quarters, and where he roosts in some sheltered cavity. He often appears to be alone, but if we listen we may hear his mate answering from a distance his little piglike, grunting call. Thus the pair keeps in touch, and when, drifting through the woodland, they meet and feed in close proximity, they exchange salutations back and forth with their soft, conversational *hit, hit*. The chickadees and creepers often join them for a time, all three species, with sometimes a downy woodpecker, searching for food in the same trees, until the more restless birds flit onward and leave the nuthatches alone again.

DISTRIBUTION

Range.—Southern Canada to southern Mexico.

The white-breasted nuthatch ranges **north** to British Columbia (150-mile House) ; Alberta (Swift Current Rapids and Beaver Hills) ; Saskatchewan (probably Prince Albert) ; Manitoba (Lake St. Martin, Kalevala, and Winnipeg) ; Ontario (Sudbury and Ottawa) ; Quebec (Montreal) ; New Brunswick (Grand Falls) ; Prince Edward Island (North River) ; and Nova Scotia (Pictou). From this line the white-breasted nuthatch is found in every State to the Gulf coast and **south** in Mexico to Veracruz (Las Vigas) ; Puebla (Mount Orizaba) ; Guerrero (Chilpancingo) ; and Baja California (Victoria Mountains).

The white-breasted nuthatch is not truly migratory, but apparently it sometimes withdraws in winter from the northernmost part of its range and from the higher altitudes. On the Atlantic coast it is found in some parts of the Coastal Plain more in winter than during the breeding season.

The above outline applies to the species as a whole. At least seven races are recognized within our area, and additional ones in Mexico. The southern white-breasted nuthatch (*S. c. carolinensis*) occupies the southeastern zone from North Carolina and Tennessee southward. The eastern white-breasted nuthatch (*S. c. cookei*) occurs in the northeastern part from Manitoba eastward and south to Virginia and eastern Kansas and extending to central Texas. The Rocky Mountain nuthatch (*S. c. nelsoni*) occurs from northern Montana to northern

Mexico and from the western edge of the plains west to western Montana and Wyoming, eastern Nevada, and central Arizona. The Inyo nuthatch (*S. c. tenuissima*) occurs from British Columbia to northern Baja California, and from western Montana and Wyoming to the Cascades of Oregon and Washington. The slender-billed nuthatch (*S. c. aculeata*) occurs from the western side of the Sierra Nevada to the Pacific coast and from central Washington southward. The Mexican white-breasted nuthatch (*S. c. mexicana*) ranges from the Chisos Mountains of southwestern Texas through the highlands of Mexico. The San Pedro nuthatch (*S. c. alexandrae*) occurs in the pine belt of the Sierra San Pedro Mártir, Baja California. The San Lucas nuthatch (*S. c. lagunae*) occurs in the Cape district of Baja California.

Casual records.—A specimen is recorded to have been taken at Churchill, Manitoba, previous to 1845; the species was observed at the Forks of the Albany River, Ontario, on September 2, 1920; one was observed at Kamouraska, Quebec, on May 3, 1934, and one seen in Gaspé County, Quebec, on July 9, 1924.

Egg dates.—Arizona: 9 records, April 22 to May 28.

California: 56 records, March 21 to June 29; 28 records, April 6 to May 17, indicating the height of the season.

Colorado: 12 records, May 13 to June 25.

Florida: 8 records, March 15 to June 11.

New York: 15 records, April 29 to May 30.

Oregon: 9 records, April 19 to June 24.

Pennsylvania: 11 records, April 21 to May 29.

Wisconsin: 5 records, April 29 to May 11.

SITTA CAROLINENSIS CAROLINENSIS Latham

FLORIDA NUTHATCH

PLATES 5, 6

HABITS

This southeastern race of the white-breasted nuthatch has a rather wide range in the Lower Austral Zone of coastal South Carolina, Georgia, and Florida, along the Gulf coast to Louisiana, and up the Mississippi Valley to southeastern Missouri, Kentucky, and southern Illinois.

W. E. D. Scott (1890) in describing this subspecies (under the name *atkinsi*) gave as its characters: "Average of wing, as compared with northern birds, 0.20 in. smaller in males, 0.15 in. smaller in females. Bill relatively much longer and slenderer. Light markings of tipping of the coverts and quills of the wings decidedly narrower. A little less white in the tail. In the female birds the *black* of the top of the head and nape is *pronounced*, and it is difficult to distinguish the sexes easily, and in some cases impossible, by the color of these parts. * * * The variation in the Florida form is mainly in the direction of the western subspecies *aculeata*, but the bill is less attenuated; the gray of the secondaries is purer, and there are other minor differences of coloration."

He says that this nuthatch was not common around Tarpon Springs, where his type was collected. I cannot remember having ever seen a white-breasted nuthatch on any of my trips to Florida and have no reference to it in my notes, though I have traveled over the State rather extensively. A. H. Howell (1932) refers to it as "a fairly common resident in northern and middle Florida; casual in southern Florida." Apparently, it occurs in southern Florida only in winter. He says that it is "found chiefly in open pine forests, and its nests are said to be placed in pine stubs on tracts that have been cut and burned over." H. H. Bailey (1925) refers to it as a resident the year round, in northern and central Florida, "breeding sparingly."

According to Arthur T. Wayne (1910), the range of this subspecies should be extended northward into the coast region of South Carolina. "for the birds that are resident on the coast are certainly much nearer *atkinsi* than typical *carolinensis* of the interior of the State." Breeding adult females that he collected "had the whole top of the head, as well as the nape, deep black," the well-marked character of *atkinsi*. He says of its haunts: "This nuthatch is by no means common and a forest of from one hundred to three hundred acres seldom contains more than three or four pairs. The birds frequent wooded land, showing a preference for mixed pine woods; but I have also found them in the largest swamps, where they are generally in pairs, never congregating in small flocks like the Brown-headed Nuthatch."

Dr. H. C. Oberholser (1938) refers to it as "an uncommon permanent resident," in Louisiana, and says: "It is an inhabitant of woodlands, orchards, and other cultivated areas, shade trees about houses, and in fact even the parks and streets of the towns and cities."

Nesting.— Mr. Bailey (1925) says that, in Florida, "they prefer the natural cavities of the several species of oaks and other hard-wood trees in which to place their nest of bark-fiber, fur and hair; though occasionally they may use the old cavity of the smaller woodpeckers." S. A. Grimes has sent me several photographs of nesting sites of this nuthatch, taken in Duval County, Fla. (pls. 5, 6). One of these nests was in a natural cavity, a long, narrow slit, in the trunk of a longleaf pine; others were in dead or living pines, and one was in a cypress.

In South Carolina, Wayne (1910) remarks that the nest is hard to discover, as we all know; he found only three nests. His first nest was in an abandoned hole of the red-cockaded woodpecker, in a living pine tree 20 feet from the ground, and a set of five eggs was taken from it on March 18, 1903. He took another set of five eggs, the second set of this same pair, on April 6; this nest was in an old hole of the downy wood-pecker, 35 feet from the ground in a dead pine. His third nest was in a natural cavity of a red oak, about 45 feet above the ground, from which he took another set of five eggs on March 31, 1904.

Dr. Oberholser (1938) says that, in Louisiana, "occasionally the bird excavates its own home, and it is also fond of using nesting boxes or bird houses, even close to a dwelling."

M. G. Vaiden (MS.) reports a nest that he found near Rosedale, Miss., on April 12, 1926; the nest was in a dead willow, some 8 feet up, in a natural cavity; it was "composed of feathers, some grass and decayed hair and skin of a squirrel."

Eggs.—Five seems to be the usual number of eggs found in the nest of the Florida nuthatch. Perhaps more or fewer may occasionally make up a set. These are practically indistinguishable from the eggs of the northern white-breasted nuthatch, though some that I have seen are somewhat more heavily marked. The measurements of 40 eggs average 18.3 by 14.3 millimeters; the eggs showing the four extremes measure **19.6** by 15.0, 18.7 by **15.3, 17.1** by 14.5, and 18.1 by **13.4** millimeters.

I can find nothing peculiar in any of the other habits of this nut-hatch, which probably do not differ materially from those of its northern relative. Maynard (1896), however, states that the "males utter a singular song which consists of a series of low notes which partly resemble those of the Carolina Wren and partly those of the Tufted Tit. The birds when giving this odd lay appear very restless, and fly from tree to tree without pausing anywhere." This may be a courtship performance.

SITTA CAROLINENSIS NELSONI Mearns

ROCKY MOUNTAIN NUTHATCH

HABITS

In the Rocky Mountain region, from southern Alberta southward into northern Mexico, and from the eastern base of the Cascades and the northern Sierra Nevada eastward across the Rocky Mountains, we find this large and well-marked race of the white-breasted nuthatches.

Dr. Mearns (1902a) describes it as the "largest known form of *Sitta carolinensis.* Bill large and rather stout, with contour of maxilla convex rather than straight above. Coloration dark. Under parts washed with gray and fulvous or fawn color, but less strongly so than in *Sitta carolinensis mexicana* Nelson and Palmer. * * * In addition to its larger size, this form may be separated from the eastern bird by its darker coloration, the back being more nearly slate color than plumbeous, and the color pattern of the tertials as in *Sitta carolinensis aculeata,* from which latter its larger size, stouter and differently shaped bill, and the gray and fawn color instead of pure white under parts distinguish it. In *nelsoni* the white of the tail-feathers is more extended than in other forms, and, excepting *mexicana*, the fawn color of the sides and abdomen of the young is more intense than in the remaining subspecies of *Sitta carolinensis*."

This is the form that we found to be fairly common in the Huachuca Mountains, in southern Arizona, up to about 7,000 feet, where we saw it occasionally and found one nest. Mr. Swarth (1904b) says that it is "resident throughout the mountains, though most abundant in the higher pine regions. During the cold weather it is quite common in the oaks along the base of the mountains, but though a few breed there, the majority of them ascend to a higher altitude in the summer."

In New Mexico, according to Mrs. Bailey (1928), it "is found in summer mainly from 7,000 to 8,000 feet. Few species are so strictly confined as this to a definite belt of altitude." In fall it wanders sometimes below but mainly above its breeding range. In Colorado, Sclater (1912) says that it "is a common resident throughout the year, being found chiefly among the foothills and in the piñon and cedar zone in winter, and at higher elevations, nearly up to timber line, in summer, but it has been found breeding as low as 5,300 feet at Littleton near Denver." In extreme northeastern California, in the Lassen Peak region, Grinnell, Dixon, and Linsdale (1930) found the Rocky Mountain nuthatch resident in the "higher coniferous forests." They observed it in yellow pine, white fir, and lodgepole pine. Aretas A. Saunders (1921) says that, in western Montana, it "breeds in coniferous forests in the Transition, Canadian and Hudsonian zones, showing preference for yellow pine forests in the Transition, about the foothills of the mountains, or for white-bark pine in the Hudsonian."

Nesting.— Grinnell, Dixon, and Linsdale (1930) found a nest, on May 21, 1925, on the west side of Eagle Lake in the Lassen Peak region, "in a water-killed pine stub on the lake shore." They report another nest "in the stub-forest near Eagle Lake Resort. It was one and one-half meters up in an old woodpecker nest hole on the southeast side of a stump three meters high." The birds were feeding young at the time, June 12, carrying in food "at intervals sometimes as short as one minute. * * * Much of each bird's time was spent in flying into the air and catching flying insects."

Rev. P. B. Peabody (1906) published some photographs of unusually low Wyoming nests of the Rocky Mountain nuthatch; in one case, in a low, rotten stump in an open space, "the bottom of the nest was but a few inches above the ground; and the cavity but about 9 inches in height. The entrance was very irregular; and the cavity still more so. It appeared to have been made a year previous; apparently by Chickadees. The containing nest was beautifully made; and the blackish hair of which it mostly consisted made delicate contrast with the pearl-white eggs." He says that, ordinarily, "the material that surrounds the eggs is a strange conglomerate; made up, in greater part, of disintegrated pellets ejected by birds of prey or voided by coyotes. It is most interesting to note; that this material seems to be irregularly added at all times after the first choice of the home. Material is often brought to the nest as late as mid-incubation time."

Frank C. Willard (1912) says that, in Arizona, "nine out of ten nests are in oaks, the balance usually in pines though a sycamore or madrone is occasionally selected. A natural cavity with a long narrow opening is generally elected. The nest is a mass of assorted fur and hair of various animals, skunk and squirrel fur, cow and deer hair predominating. I have also found rabbit fur and bear's hair in their nests. Enough is used to completely fill the bottom of the cavity and come up a little on the sides." He mentions a nest in a pine stub on the summit of the main ridge of the Huachuca Mountains, altitude 8,450 feet, one in an oak near the summit, and a nest in a dead stub of a sycamore in the bed of a canyon, altitude 5,200 feet. "One brood, only, is raised in a season. The same nesting site is sometimes used year after year, though vermin in the nest frequently cause them to select a new location the next season." The only nest that we found, while I was with him, was 18 feet from the ground in a big blackjack oak, at an elevation of about 7,000 feet in the Huachucas; it was in a natural cavity in which the base of a limb had not entirely rotted out; the bird had entered through the cracks in the rotted wood and had a fresh set of five eggs on May 12, 1922. The nest consisted of a great mass of rabbit's fur, mixed with pieces of inner bark and bits of straw.

Eggs.—Mr. Willard has found as few as three heavily incubated eggs and as many as six, but apparently the set most commonly consists of five eggs. These eggs are practically indistinguishable from those of the eastern white-breasted nuthatch. What few eggs I have seen are more lightly marked, but Mr. Peabody (1906) mentions some heavily marked eggs; I infer therefore that the eggs probably show all the normal variations common to eggs of the species. The measurements of 40 eggs average 18.9 by 14.2 millimeters; the eggs showing the four extremes measures **21.1** by 14.3, 20.2 by **14.8**, **17.3** by 14.2, and 18.5 by **13.2** millimeters.

Behavior.—In most of its habits and traits the Rocky Mountain nuthatch does not differ greatly from its eastern relative, though its voice is thinner and weaker. It does not seem to gather into flocks, as the pygmy nuthatch does, and is almost always seen singly or in pairs, though Swarth (1904b) says that "a single one may occasionally be seen in a flock of Pygmy Nuthatches or Chicadees." The members of the pair are much devoted to each other; the male feeds the female on the nest; and the pair travel about together in winter, keeping in touch with each other with their quaint calls.

SITTA CAROLINENSIS ACULEATA Cassin

SLENDER-BILLED NUTHATCH

PLATES 7, 8

HABITS

The first of the western races of the white-breasted nuthatches to be described is a well-marked subspecies and is found on the Pacific slope, west of the mountains, from southern British Columbia to northern Baja California. Ridgway (1904) gives the following very good description of it: "Similar to *S. c. carolinensis*, but gray of back, etc., darker (about as in *S. c. atkinsi*); black central areas of greater wing-coverts much less distinct; black areas on inner secondaries also much less distinct, as well as more restricted, that on outer web of second tertial usually with posterior extremity acuminate-pointed instead of rounded; under parts more purely white; bill averaging longer and relatively more slender, and toes shorter; adult female with black of hindneck broken by dark gray tips to the feathers and concealed white spots."

Its haunts are in the coniferous forests of the mountains from 4,000 to 9,400 feet, among the yellow pines on mountain slopes, and in the oaks of the higher foothills. Grinnell, Dixon, and Linsdale (1930) say of its haunts in the Lassen Peak region: "This race of white-breasted nuthatch had its metropolis entirely within the 'blue' vegetational area, in the western end of the section; that is, the birds collected and found upon comparison to belong properly to the subspecies *aculeata* were all from points west of the western edge of the 'green' coniferous timber. The trees they most frequented were blue oak, valley oak, digger pine, and, along stream courses, cottonwood."

W. E. Griffee tells me that, "in western Oregon, the slender-billed nuthatches are commonest in the oak-covered foothills, but nowhere are they really abundant."

Nesting.—There is nothing in the nesting habits of this nuthatch that is different from those of the other races of the species. In the Lassen Peak region, Grinnell, Dixon, and Linsdale (1930) found a nest in "a cavity 5 meters above the ground in a broken lower limb of a living blue oak. The tree stood near the bottom of a small ravine. The nest opening was on top of, and at the end of, a limb which extended nearly horizontally from the main trunk for at least 3 meters. The site was found by tracing the course of the male as it carried food to the female at the nest." Two other nests were found in oaks; one was "in a natural cavity below a knot hole two meters above the ground on the east side of a large, partly living blue oak"; the other "was in a cavity below a crack in a large limb of a valley oak, and it was at least fifteen meters above the ground."

In the Yosemite section, according to Grinnell and Storer (1924), the slender-billed nuthatch "ordinarily makes use of abandoned woodpecker holes for nesting sites." They found two such nests; the first "was 9 feet above the ground in an old hole of the White-headed Woodpecker in a broken off and barkless Jeffrey pine stump"; the second nest was in another old hole of the same species of woodpecker, and was 7 feet from the ground; the interior of this hole had been enlarged by the nuthatches to a diameter of over 5 inches, and was filled to within 7½ inches of the top, with deer and chipmunk hair and feathers from various birds.

W. E. Griffee writes to me of a nest that he found near Portland, Oreg., that was in a natural cavity only 3½ feet up in a small ash tree. "The bottom of the cavity, which was about 6 inches in diameter, had a heavy layer of grass and moss, and on top of that at least 2 inches of rodent fur and a few feathers."

Incubation.—From the observations of the ornithologists quoted above, it seems evident that the female alone performs the duties of incubation and remains on the nest for long periods at a time. Referring to the second nest, mentioned above, Grinnell and Storer (1924) write:

The female was on the nest and as she refused to leave even during the hubbub incident to enlarging the entrance, the observer had to lift her from the nest in order to examine the eggs. She seemed to be in a sort of lethargy and did not struggle until actually taken in hand. That the bird had not left the nest for some time was evident from the quantity of excrement which was accumulated in the cloaca. The condition of this female, the food supply which the male of the first nest had been seen to take to his nest, and the further fact that only males had been noted abroad for some days previously, led to the belief that in this species the female alone carries on the duties of incubation and that she remains upon the nest continuously for a greater or less period of time, during which she is fed by the male.

Fred Evenden writes to me that he saw a male feed its mate in the nest 18 times between 2:30 and 3:49 p. m.; the female came out of the hole only once and perched on a stub for a moment.

Eggs.—The slender-billed nuthatch has been known to lay 5 to 9 eggs, but oftener 6 or 7, though sets of 8 are fairly common. The eggs probably show all the variations common to the species, but what few eggs I have seen have been sparingly marked with small dots. The measurements of 40 eggs average 18.5 by 13.9 millimeters; the eggs showing the four extremes measure 20.0 by 13.5, 17.3 by 15.0, and 16.5 by 12.2 millimeters.

Behavior.—White-breasted nuthatches are not, as a rule, gregarious; they are almost always seen singly or in pairs. But a remarkable story of communal roosting at night is told by Dr. G. V. Harvey (1902). One winter evening he saw 29 of these nuthatches come singly to an old dead yellow pine, alight upon a knot, and vanish into a large crack in the trunk. "At no time during all the lodgment of these 29 birds, did 2 arrive at the same time, nor was there a variation in the time of the appearance of any 2 birds of more than 30 seconds." He does not state the exact time, which was probably only a few minutes before sunset, for these and other birds have a remarkable sense of time, which is almost uncanny.

This wonderful faculty is well illustrated by an observation, or series of observations, made by Dr. S. F. Blake (1928), on the regularity with which a slender-billed nuthatch went to roost under the tiles of the roof of a band stand at Palo Alto. "His hour of retiring, usually just before the sun disappeared, corresponded in a general way with the decrease in the length of day." On nine occasions, from June 29 to August 26, the time varied from 10 minutes to 25 minutes before sunset, and on only four occasions was it more than 20 minutes. "On two occasions, two nuthatches were seen together near the band-stand, but only one was ever seen to enter a tile."

Voice.—The voices of the western races of the white breasted nut-hatch seem to differ somewhat from the well-known calls of our eastern bird. Ralph Hoffmann (1927) calls the note of this one "a sharp nasal *keer, keer,*" and says further: "When two birds are working together, they utter a low *quit quit.* A high *quer* is the alarm note about the nest. In early spring and summer the male repeats a mellow *too too too,* like the blowing of a little trumpet; this song is generally given from a twig, an unusual perch at any other time." Grinnell and Storer (1924) describe this spring song as "a mere monotonous repetition of a certain two syllabled word: *cher-wer, cher-wer, cher-wer,* etc."

Dawson (1923) says that it has a variety of notes "all distinguished by a peculiar nasal quality." One he mentions, *quonk, quonk, quonk,* or *ho-onk, ho-onk,* might remind us of the call of the eastern bird; but he says that "all the notes of the Slender-billed Nuthatch have a softened and subdued character as compared with those of the eastern bird."

SITTA CAROLINENSIS TENUISSIMA Grinnell

INYO NUTHATCH

HABITS

If the slender-billed nuthatch has a slender bill, this more recently described form from the Panamint and White Mountains of California has a much slenderer bill; hence the appropriate name *tenuissima.*

Although originally described from a series of 21 specimens, collected in the above-mentioned mountains, in Inyo County, Dr. Grinnell (1918) suggested that it "is likely to be found to extend north along the western rim of the Great Basin at least to Fort Klamath, Oreg." This prophecy has been partially fulfilled by A. J. van Rossem

(1936) who collected 13 specimens of this nuthatch in the Sheep and Charleston Mountains in Nevada and says that it "was found in every type of coniferous timber above 8,000 feet. Until the middle of August the birds ranged up to 10,500 feet in the bristle-cone and limber-pine forests, but after the first cold weather the higher altitudes were almost deserted. On August 19, I saw but one nuthatch above 9,500 feet and on the 21st none above 9,200 feet, although on both dates they were common, chiefly in yellow pines, between 8,000 and 9,000."

Dr. Grinnell (1918) gives, as the diagnostic characters of the Inyo nuthatch: "Similar to *Sitta carolinensis aculeata* from west-central California, but bill much longer and slenderer, size larger, back of darker tone of gray, and flanks paler; similar to *S. c. nelsoni* from southern Arizona, but bill much slenderer, and sides, and lower surface generally, whiter.   *   *   *   In some respects this race is intermediate between the Rocky Mountain form and that of the Pacific coast region, but in the extreme slenderness of bill differs from either."

Nothing peculiar is mentioned about its habits.

The eggs of the Inyo nuthatch are probably similiar to those of other races of the species. J. Stuart Rowley has sent me the measurements of a set of seven eggs, which average 19.2 by 13.4 millimeters; the eggs showing the four extremes measure **19.97** by **13.16**, 19.23 by **13.68**, and **18.71** by 13.38 millimeters.

SITTA CAROLINENSIS ALEXANDRAE Grinnell

SAN PEDRO NUTHATCH

HABITS

Dr. Joseph Grinnell (1926) described this race and named it in honor of Miss Annie M. Alexander, who sponsored the expedition to the San Pedro Mártir region of Baja California, where this decidedly local subspecies was discovered. It seems to be confined to the Transition and Canadian Zones in the San Pedro Mártir Plateau, between latitudes 30° and 31°30', and at altitudes of 6,000 to 8,500 feet, a very narrow range. It is widely separated from the San Lucas nuthatch by "some 600 miles of forbidding country"; and there seems to be a wide gap between it and the slender-billed nuthatch of California.

Dr. Grinnell (1926) gives as its characters: "General features of size and coloration as in *Sitta carolinensis aculeata*, but differs from this race in much longer wing, tail, and bill, in much broader rectrices, in greater proportion of white on rectrices, in broader white-tippings to inner primaries, and in slightly darker color-tone of dorsum." He says further: "These modifications in the flight equipment of the nuthatches of the San Pedro Mártir plateau, it may be suggested, have been developed as a result of long existence in the very open type of forest there prevalent; the individual trees are far apart as compared with the forest stands in which White-breasted Nuthatches live in Upper California. This necessitates more extensive flights from tree to tree in the usual course of foraging; and numerous studies have shown that 'sharpness' as well as length of wing and length of tail vary in direct correlation with extent of flight, whether in migration or in day-by-day foraging."

SITTA CAROLINENSIS LAGUNAE Brewster

SAN LUCAS NUTHATCH

HABITS

The San Lucas nuthatch was described by William Brewster (1891) as "similar to *Sitta carolinensis aculeata*, but with the wings and tail shorter, the black on the tips of the outer tail-feathers more restricted." These characters are slight, but constant. The race was not recognized at first by the A. O. U. Committee, but the fact that it lives in a restricted habitat, near the southern tip of Baja California, and the fact that it is separated from its nearest relative, in the San Pedro Mártir region, by some 600 miles of unsuitable terrain make it seem worthy of recognition, as an isolated race.

Of its distribution and haunts, Mr. Brewster (1902) writes: "The St. Lucas Nuthatch is probably confined to the higher mountains south of La Paz, where it was first detected by Mr. Belding in 1883. To Mr. Frazar, however, is due the credit of collecting a sufficient series of specimens to bring out the slight but nevertheless very tangible differences which distinguish it from *aculeata*, to which Mr. Belding very naturally referred it. Mr. Frazar met with it only on the Sierra de la Laguna, where, at all seasons, it is a rather common bird inhabiting the pine forests at high elevations."

Specimens collected by Frazar, early in May, were incubating; but he evidently found no nests; and, so far as I know, no one else has.

SITTA CAROLINENSIS MEXICANA Nelson and Palmer

MEXICAN WHITE-BREASTED NUTHATCH

In naming and describing this form, Nelson and Palmer (1894) write: "The White-bellied Nuthatches from the mountains of south-central Mexico present certain characteristics by which they may be distinguished from either of the two recognized forms of the United States. The Mexican bird has a beak averaging rather smaller than that of *Sitta carolinensis* from the eastern United States. With this character it combines the color of the dorsal surface and dark markings on tertials of *S. aculeata*, and differs from both northern forms in having only the chin and throat pure white—the rest of the lower parts in the present form being washed with a distinct ashy shade, heaviest on the flanks and posteriorly."

Its range was not fully known at that time, but it is now known to include the highlands of Mexico from Oaxaca to Nayarit and southern Chihuahua, north to the Chisos Mountains, Tex. *Sitta carolinensis oberholseri* Brandt is now regarded as a synonym of *mexicana*.

SITTA CANADENSIS Linnaeus

RED-BREASTED NUTHATCH

PLATES 9–11

CONTRIBUTED BY WINSOR MARRETT TYLER

HABITS

The red-breasted nuthatch is a happy, jolly little bird, surprisingly quick and agile in his motions. He has the habit of progressing over the bark of trees like his larger relative, the whitebreast, but his tempo is much more rapid, and he extends his journeys more frequently to the smaller branches. Here he winds about the little twigs out to the end, among the pine needles, moving very fast—up, down, and around—changing his direction quickly and easily, seeming always in a hurry to scramble over the branches. He is more sociable, too, than the larger bird, and when a little company is feeding together they keep up a cheery chatter among themselves. We find them at their best when gathered in the northern forests at the close of summer. Then they give their high, tin-whistle note, *kng*, back and forth on all sorts of pitches, varying its inflection, ringing unheard of changes on this simple call, and when they are together thus, they use also a squealing note—a very high, nasal, little piglike or mouselike squeal— and a short explosive *kick*, or a rapid series of *kicks*. The effect of these notes, given by a dozen birds as they chase one another about, is very jolly. The little birds seem so happy, animated, and lively and their voices have such a range of expression that they almost talk—a playful gathering of talkative, irrepressible, woodland gnomes.

Spring and courtship.—Cordelia J. Stanwood, of Ellsworth, Maine, noted (MS.) that a male bird she had watched during winter appeared with a mate in March. "Five years later," she says, "another red-breasted nuthatch wintered at 'the sign of the suet', and he also selected a mate in March, and so that it would seem that *Sitta canadensis* chooses his helpmeet early in the season. However, even in years in which the birds winter here in goodly numbers, the nuthatches are not common until April or May. Then in their favorite evergreen woods their merry pipings fill the land. They tap all over each dead tree to find suitable nesting quarters. Undoubtedly they start nest holes in many trees before they find one that is exactly adapted to their needs. One season I followed for many days a pair that nested in a beautiful tract of mixed woodland. I saw them attempt to excavate a cavity in four or more trees before they found the site that best suited them."

Ora W. Knight (1908) says: "I have quite good reasons for believing that they remain mated for more than one season and that mated birds remain in each others company all the year, rarely associating with others in flocks, while it is the young birds of the year, as yet unmated, that mingle in flocks with others of their kind as well as related species."

Of the bird's courtship apparently little is known. On one occasion I saw a hint of it. A male strutted before a female in a manner similar to the courting pose of the white-breasted nuthatch. The pose was maintained but a moment or so and was accompanied with some rapid chippering notes. It consisted of a spreading and lowering of the wings and a spreading of the tail. There was, too, I think, a slight bowing downward and forward of the whole body.

Gordon Boit Wellman (1933) records a courtship flight which he observed on April 6, 1932, in Sudbury, Mass. He says:

Mrs. Wellman and I were approaching the end of the garden, when a bird flew out of a red cedar and, with incredible speed, zigzagged through the bare limbs of a large old apple tree. After two or three circular turns in this erratic manner through the branches, it dived back into the cedar. Neither of us, although we stood just in front of the tree, had the slightest idea what the bird was; immediately the flight was repeated, leaving us as much mystified as before. No eye could follow the tremendous speed and sharp turns; it seemed impossible that any bird could do it a second time and avoid striking the irregular branches of the apple tree. A third flight followed in 2 or 4 seconds and consisted of a shorter performance: this time the bird stopped suddenly on a small branch of the apple tree and we saw that it was a Red-breasted Nuthatch. Almost at once a second *Sitta canadensis*, a female, joined the first and the two began investigating holes in the old apple trees of the garden. During the flight there were no notes from the male; later, when the two birds were together, the usual call notes were given intermittently.

Nesting.—The red-breasted nuthatch usually excavates a cavity for its nest in a rotton stub or branch of a dead tree. Sometimes, however, it makes use of an old woodpecker's hole, and it has been known to breed in bird boxes.

Manly Hardy (1878) speaks thus of nests found in Maine:

[One] was in a white-birch stub some 10 feet from the gound; the entrance was 1½ inches wide by 1¼ deep. The hole ran slanting for 3 inches, and then straight down for 4 inches more. [Another nest] was in a poplar stub some 12 feet from the ground. Hole 1½ inches by 1 inch, slanting down 4 inches, and then 4 inches straight down. * * * Near both the nests were other holes not so deep, probably used for one of the birds to occupy while the other is sitting, as is the case with most Woodpeckers. Both nests were composed of fine short grasses and roots. I notice that in making the hole the bird makes a circle of holes round a piece about as large as a 10-cent-piece, and then takes out the piece of bark entire. I have one nest which has near it a piece circled in this manner, but not removed.

Walter Bradford Barrows (1912) says: "It does not seem to restrict itself so closely as does the White-breast to the natural cavities of trees, but often, perhaps most often, makes use of a deserted woodpecker's hole, in which it builds a nest of soft materials."

Charles W. Michael (1934), pointing out "the difference in habits in the same species of bird in different sections of its nesting range," says:

Here in Yosemite Valley it has been my experience that the Red-breasted Nuthatches (*Sitta canadensis*) never occupy old nests of any sort. Each year the birds of a pair working in turn excavate a new nest-hole. Often they dig two, or three, or possibly four prospect holes before finally deciding on the one that is to be the nest-hole of the season. Most often they choose to work in the dead wood of a living cottonwood. The second choice of tree is the Kellogg oak, but I have also watched a pair of birds drill a nest-hole in the dead stub of a yellow pine. In one case the same pine stub was used two different seasons, but instead of using the old nest-hole, which appeared perfectly good, the birds quite ignored it and drilled out a fresh hole.

I have seen nests of the Red-breasted Nuthatch as low as 5 feet above the ground and as high as 40 feet from the ground. The average height of the nest-hole above the ground is probably close to 15 feet.

Henry S. Shaw, Jr. (1916), gives this account of a pair of birds that successfully reared a brood of young in a bird box at Dover, Mass.:

On April 10, I noticed a female Red-breast carrying nesting material into one of my bird-boxes. This is a Berlepsch box, size No. 2, made by the Audubon Bird House Co., of Meriden, N. H. The entrance hole is 1⅛ inches in diameter, and the box, which is made of yellow birch, is placed in a white birch tree about 7 feet from the ground. It was put up in the hope of attracting Chickadees.

I did not see the male Nuthatch at work until April 16, when I observed him carrying shreds of bark which he pulled from the trunks and limbs of red cedars (*Juniperus virginiana*) growing nearby. Examination of the box after the nesting season showed that the nest was composed exclusively of this material, the box being filled to within an inch or two of the level of the entrance-hole. The male usually left his load at the hole, without entering, and I suppose that the material was put in place by the female inside.

William L. G. Edson and R. E. Horsey (1920) report a similar nesting in Monroe County, N. Y., in a bird box "placed on an Electric-wire pole in the midst of thick hemlocks."

It is an apparently invariable habit of the red-breasted nuthatch to smear with pitch the entrance of its nesting cavity. All the descriptions of nests mention this peculiarity, whether the nests are in hard wood, pines, or bird boxes. In the northern woods the birds use the pitch of the balsam fir and spruce; farther south they use the pitch of pine trees. The pitch as a rule is generously laid on, often all around the hole. In Mr. Shaw's nest noted above the pitch was added progressively during the nesting season, and Thomas D. Burleigh (1921) says, writing of the bird in Montana: "The birds continue to carry pitch to the entrance of the nest from the time the nest is first begun until the young have flown. * * * On June 16 I found a nest containing almost fully grown young that was but 2 feet from the ground in an old rotten stub and during the 15 minutes that I watched the birds they made seven trips to the nest, carrying each time not food but pitch which they carefully smeared on any wood that was exposed within several inches of the entrance."

William Brewster (1938), writing of a nest found near Lake Umbagog, Maine, says: "This nest was finished today but contained no eggs and had but little pitch. Both birds, however, were there, and both were *bringing pitch* and plastered it on the bark below the hole. I watched them a long time. They brought it on the tips of their bills in little globules, alighted against the lower edge of the hole, and then tapped it on in various places as low as they could reach, but without shifting their foothold." Of another nest in the same region he says: "Nest in red maple stub over water; tree very rotten; height about twenty feet; hole on west side about two feet from top. A quantity of pitch, which my guide pronounced unmistakably *spruce*, about the entrance and inside its tunnel. Stub standing in five feet of water twenty yards from the shore."

W. Leon Dawson (1923) writes: "Canadian Nuthatches nest at any height, and their lack of consideration in this respect accounts for much of our relative ignorance. I located a nest, in Seattle, in a nearly limbless live fir tree, at a height of 120 feet. Obligations to a growing family forbade attention to details. On the other hand, a nest taken near Tacoma on the 8th of June, 1906, was found at a height of only 7 feet, in a small fir stump. * * * The wood of the last-named nesting stub was very rotten, and the eggs rested only 4 inches below the entrance. The nest-lining, in this instance, was a heavy mat an inch in thickness, and was composed of vegetable matter—wood fiber, soft grasses, etc.,—without hair of any sort."

Eggs.—[AUTHOR'S NOTE: The red-breasted nuthatch lays ordinarily 4 to 7 eggs; probably 5 or 6 eggs make up the usual set. The eggs vary from ovate to rounded-ovate, and have very little or no gloss. The ground color is pure white, or more rarely pinkish white or creamy white. They are sometimes heavily and sometimes sparingly spotted, or finely dotted, with bright reddish brown, such as "ferruginous," "hazel," "cinnamon-rufous," or "vinaceous," and some darker shades of brown. As a rule they are very pretty eggs. The measurements of 50 eggs in the United States National Museum average 15.2 by 11.9 millimeters; the eggs showing the four extremes measure **17.0** by 12.5, 15.2 by **12.7, 14.2** by 11.2, and 15.2 by **11.1** millimeters.]

Young.—As with most young birds that spend their nest life hidden away in cavities, we know little of the development of nestling nuthatches. After their emergence, however, we note a rapid increase in strength and activity. Some years ago I watched four young birds that had left the nest 5 days before. They were in a white pine a hundred yards from the nest, and they moved about easily, sometimes hanging back-downward from the branches. They did not venture out to the ends of the twigs among the needles (as the parents did for food) but remained not far from the trunk. Although the young birds picked at the bark of the branches, I could not be sure that they gathered any food for themselves.

We get a hint of the rapidity of the development of very young nuthatches from the account of Florence K. Daley (1926), who reared in a cage some young birds from the time when they were "not more than a few days old" until they could care for themselves. She fed them on bread and milk, water, and "Song Restorer" and after 2 weeks was able to liberate them safely.

In the opinion of Cordelia J. Stanwood (MS.), who has studied the nesting of the bird extensively at Ellsworth, Maine, the young red-breasted nuthatches leave the nest 18 to 21 days after hatching. F. L. Burns (1921) gives the period of nestling life as 14 days or more, and the incubation period (1915) as 12 days.

Plumages.—[AUTHOR'S NOTE: The natal down of the young red-breasted nuthatch is dark gray. In the juvenal plumage the sexes are distinguishable, the young males resembling the adult males and the young females resembling the adult females, but all the colors are duller. There are faint black edgings on the back, the black portions of the head are much duller, the white superciliary stripe, chin, and sides of the head are speckled with black, and the underparts are pinkish buff, deepening to pale cinnamon on the crissum.

A partial postjuvenal molt begins late in July, involving the contour plumage but not the wings and tail. This produces a first winter plumage which is practically adult, the back being a darker, bluish gray, the pileum (in the male) glossy black, the white portions of the head without black speckling, and the underparts more richly and deeply colored.

Adults have a complete postnuptial molt, mainly in July. There is no spring molt, but considerable wear and fading make the spring plumage almost as pale as that of the juvenal.]

Food.—Waldo L. McAtee (1926a), summarizing our knowledge of the food of the red-breasted nuthatch, says: "Unfortunately we know very little about the food of this species. It is very fond of the seeds of pines, spruces, and the like, which it takes in lieu of the larger mast favored by the White-breast. The animal food is known to include beetles, hymenoptera, and spiders, and among forest pests it has been observed to feed on the ribbed pine borer (*Rhagium lineatum*). No doubt the Red-breast does its modicum of good to compensate for the tree seeds which it draws from a store which usually is superabundant."

Ora Willis Knight (1908) speaks of the diet thus:

Their food consists of about the same run of insects' eggs, insects and larvae as is eaten by the White-breasted species. They greatly relish the seeds of fir, spruce, and pine and in winter can generally be found feeding in a region where trees of these species have seeded abundantly the past season. They deftly pry open the scales of the cones, insert their bills and obtain the seed. Maple seed are sometimes eaten by them. They will also eat bits of rotten apple, suck sap from the bleeding stumps of trees, take their share of bits of suet or meat exposed and on a pinch eat seed of dock and other weeds which protrude above the snow.

C. K. Averill, Jr. (1888), emphasizes their fondness for the seeds of the black spruce, writing: "In the Northern Adirondacks I noticed that the Red-bellied Nuthatches seemed to be feeding exclusively on the seeds of the black spruce. After that I watched them for a number of days, and although they were abundant, I did not see them feeding on anything else. Alighting on a bunch of cones at the extremity of a bough, the Nuthatch would insert its bill between the scales of a cone and draw out a seed. Then flying to a horizontal bough nearby it would detach the wing which adheres to each seed, letting it fall to the ground, swallow the seed, and fly back for another."

Richard F. Miller (1914) describes the bird feeding in beds of giant ragweed during the fall migration in northeastern Philadelphia, Pa. He says: "A remarkable feature, to me, about the occurrence of this little *Sitta* here during that fall, was their habit of frequenting water courses fringed with dense growths of giant ragweeds (*Ambrosia trifida*), in which they sought food on the thick stems, petioles and leaves, often feeding close to the ground. I always regarded this nuthatch as a denizen of the forest and its occurrence in these weedy growths surprised me. They exhibited no fear as I entered the weeds, and if I kept quiet, they fed fearlessly within close proximity of me, often only a yard away."

Edward H. Forbush (1929) states that they "fly off into the air after flying insects or search about in the long grass for them" and P. M. Silloway (1907) speaks thus of this habit: "The red-breasted nuthatch (*Sitta canadensis*) at times acts like a real flycatcher. Just now one alighted on a tree-trunk near me, and while investigating the bark crevices, twice he flew out from the trunk, captured a flying insect dexterously in the air, and returned to his gleaning on the bole."

Cordelia J. Stanwood (MS.) watched from a blind a pair feeding their young in the nest. She says: "They came and went constantly; sometimes caterpillars dangled from their beaks, at other times their bills bristled with crane-flies or moths. Once a bird carried in a large white grub, at another time the larvae of a spruce bud moth, and still again spruce bud moths themselves."

William Brewster (1938), speaking of a nest in northern Maine, says: "Quite regularly at intervals varying from 10 to 15 minutes the male came to it with a bill full of insects—large, gauzy-winged Diptera they looked like."

O. A. Stevens, of Fargo, N. Dak. (MS.), writes to Mr. Bent of his experiments in feeding a female nuthatch. He says: "To facilitate observations, I feed finely chopped nuts in a block on top of the window shelf. Three holes in the block allow comparisons of different foods. Black walnuts are by all means preferred, but peanuts are quite acceptable and constitute the usual fare. English walnuts and pecans rank high, the harder almonds and hazelnuts below peanuts. Curiously, the soft, oily Brazil nut, which would seem suitable, rates low. It is interesting that the birds adopt so readily foods that they could not have known before.

"In feeding, nuthatches are untidy, spearing into the supply and scattering the crumbs about. A striking feature of their feeding is that they never use their feet as chickadees do continually, but always wedge a large piece into some crack while they pick it to pieces. In one full day's observation when sunflower seed, walnuts, and peanuts were available, I did not see this nuthatch take any sunflower seeds although the chickadees were taking them freely."

Francis H. Allen (MS.) says: "On August 22, 1929, a warm, still day when flying insects were probably plentiful, I found many red-breasted nuthatches perched on the tops of spruce trees on Grand Manan and flying out and catching insects after the manner of fly-catchers." He saw one in West Roxbury, Mass., catching flies in October, once from an apple tree and then from the top of a larch. He also saw one flying frequently to the ground under a hemlock and back into the tree or a shrub, "where he evidently ate or disposed of what he had picked up. He was probably getting hemlock seeds, the tree being full of cones. He seemed to be making a business of getting his food in this way."

Behavior.—Besides scrambling over the trunks and branches of trees in the true nuthatch fashion, this little bird, as we have seen, makes excursions out into the air to capture flying insects, and not infrequently visits the ground where it hops about or bathes in a little pool of rain-water or melted snow. Theed Pearce, in a note to Mr. Bent, mentions "a habit, when perched on a small branch, of flirting or wagging its tail and back part of its body from side to side. This was seen on March 23, and so suggests a form of display."

Dr. Charles W. Townsend (1913) describes thus the behavior of five birds which alighted on a steamship:

Five of this species, one adult, the others immature, came on board the steamer in a fog and remained on board two days. They were extremely tame and crept about the deck, and on the ropes and spars, sometimes within a few inches of the passengers. One alighted on the coat-collar of a sailor as he was lighting his pipe, and another on my shoulder as I stood on the bridge. I put my hand near the adult Nuthatch on the rail and he picked at my finger; then he flew into the captain's cabin and gathered insects from the window. There were many small dead moths on board that seemed to be particularly relished. I noticed two Nuthatches on the chains of the smoke stack undisturbed by the constant vibrations, and, what is still more surprising, by the deafening steam fog-horn that was blown at frequent intervals within a few feet of them.

The habit of flying straight into the nest hole is mentioned by two observers: Charles W. Michael (1934) says: "When feeding small young the parent nuthatch dives on the wing directly into the nest-hole," and William Brewster (1938) remarks: "She usually flew in, without so much as touching her feet to the edge of the hole."

William Brewster (1886) speaks thus of the bird in the Black Mountains of North Carolina in summer: "In the balsams of the Black Mountains, from about 5,000 feet to the top of the main ridge (6,000 feet), this Nuthatch was more abundant than I have ever seen it elsewhere. Whenever I stopped to listen or look around its whining, nasal call was sure to be one of the first sounds that came to my ears, and often three or four different birds would be heard at once. They were usually invisible—high in the tops of the matted evergreens, but I occasionally caught sight of one hanging head downward at the end of a branch, or winding up the main stem of the tree." Walter B. Barrows (1912) calls attention to the bird's habit of storing seeds "in the punctures made by the Sapsucker in various species of trees."

Francis H. Allen watched 14 of these nuthatches moving in and out of the conifers near his house, in September, of which he (MS.) says: "At first I saw one perched on the tiptop of each of two neighboring Norway spruces. They kept up a constant piping and flicked their wings continually—that is, partly spread them. Later others appeared and all performed likewise. When they flew from tree to tree, it was with an irregular flight. This was probably a species of mock courtship."

Francis Zirrer (MS.) writes to us: "At the feeding table they fight and angrily chase one another away. They are great hoarders, which trait occasionally leads to amusing incidents. The woodpeckers, especially the hairy, watch the hoarding with interest, and, as soon as the nuthatch leaves to get another piece, fly to the place and appropriate the morsel. This lasts sometimes for quite a while until the little bird gets wise and flies away scolding."

Voice.—Of the two commonest notes of the red-breasted nuthatch one is a short, faint little note, heard only when the bird is near. It is suggested by the word *hit*, pronounced emphatically in a whispered voice, and is used, apparently, as a conversational note, exchanged between a pair of birds or among the members of a flock. To my ear it is indistinguishable from the corresponding note of the whitebreast. The other commonly heard note is a far-carrying, nasal cry with the quality of a blast on a tiny tin trumpet. This note varies greatly in length, sometimes being drawn out into a long whine; it may be repeated in a very rapid series, or delivered in a slow, regular, deliberate measure. Often written *yna*, although *kng* suggests the nasal quality better, it corresponds evidently to the sharply pronounced *kank* of the whitebreast. The other notes of the bird, and there are many of them (see below), may be regarded, perhaps, as variants, uttered under different stresses of emotion, from these two main themes.

The question as to what is the song of the red-breasted nuthatch has been ably considered and convincingly answered by Francis H. Allen (1932). He says:

As the true song of the Red-breasted Nuthatch (*Sitta canadensis*) seems not to be generally known and never to have been fully described in the books, it seems worth while to put on record in "The Auk" as adequate a description as I can give of the song as I have heard it this spring of 1932. I have heard the song many times between March 27 and May 14 of this year from a bird near my house in West Roxbury, as well as on two occasions from two other birds in other places in eastern Massachusetts. The song when I first heard it (March 27) was so strongly suggestive of that of the White-breasted Nuthatch (*Sitta carolinensis carolinensis*), yet so different in tone, that though I could not at the time follow up the bird to identify it, I had little doubt that it was a Red-breasted Nuthatch. On April 6 I heard the song again and was then able to connect it definitely with *Sitta canadensis*, for I saw the bird in the act of singing. After that and up to the time when the bird left us, presumably for his breeding-haunts farther north, I heard the song frequently, and I never had any difficulty in distinguishing it from that of its white-breasted cousin, which I also heard nearby not infrequently. The song resembles the familiar *wa-wa-wa-wa*, etc., or *what-what-what-what*, etc., of the other species, but it is more rapid and higher-pitched and possesses a reedy quality unlike the smooth, liquid tone of the other.

And he adds: "To my ears the note repeated is not at all the familiar 'nasal *hank*' of the call-note but a much softer note that is not particularly nasal."

Aretas A. Saunders (MS.) speaks of the song thus: "Only once have I heard anything from this bird that one could call a song. At Flathead Lake, Mont., July 1914, a bird called, day after day, a long *yaaaaa yaaaaa yaaaaa*, just like its usual voice in quality, but much prolonged, usually three *yaas* in succession, and then a short pause. The sound was so persistent that it became monotonous and almost irritating. I found the bird sitting on a twig beside a stub with a hole in it (apparently its nest), with its head up in the attitude of song as it called."

Harrison F. Lewis (MS.) sends to Mr. Bent the following comprehensive list of the notes he has heard the bird utter: "(1) The common, well-known *yna yna*, *yna*, *yna*. (2) *Zeee*, *zeee*, *zeee; zeee*, *zeee*, *zeee*, like the notes of a katydid. This is used by the male when scolding an intruder near the nest, and when chasing a rival. (3) *Biddy-biddy-biddy-biddy*, etc., the notes being run off quite fast in long series, with brief pauses between the series. This is also a scolding note of the male. (4) A long trill, like the song of a toad. This was uttered by the male when chasing his mate. (5) A loud, prolonged twitter. This was uttered by the male while near his mate. (6) A fine *it, it, it, it,* etc. I have recorded this for the female only. (7) An inquiring little *eh? eh? eh?* This was uttered by both sexes when I was offering them suet, and they were near me, but were not quite sure whether or not they should trust me. (8) A *peep, peep, peep,* etc., like the note of a young bird begging for food. This was uttered by the female, when she, with fluttering wings, sat on a limb near where the male was eating suet, but I could not see that either bird paid any particular attention to the other at this time. (9) A true song, which I have heard but once, viz, about 6 o'clock on the morning of March 26, 1920, near Quebec, P. Q. It consisted of the ordinary loud *yna, yna,* given *very* fast in short series, or runs, almost trills. It was much like the early morning singing of the chipping sparrow, the notes being uttered about as rapidly in each brief series, and the individual series being of about the same length, but the intervals between the series were a little longer in the case of the nuthatch. Singing continued for 2 or 3 minutes, while another red-breasted nuthatch twittered excitedly in a nearby tree."

Bradford Torrey (1904), in this pretty passage, lets us hear, through his ears, the sound of the nuthatches' voice in a New Hampshire forest: "There is seldom a minute when, if I pause to listen, I cannot hear from one direction or another the quaint, homely, twangy, countryfied, yet to me always agreeable voice of Canadian nuthatches. At frequent intervals one or two come near enough so that I see them creeping about over the trees, bodies bent, heads down, always in search of a mouthful, yet keeping up, every one, his share of the universal chorus." And later: "On all sides the little nuthatches were calling to each other in their quaint childish treble."

Field marks.—The red-breasted nuthatch is a trim, stylish-looking little bird; the dark line through the eye adds a distinction to its appearance that the whitebreast lacks; the blue-gray, black, and tawny coloring makes a pleasing artistic combination, and the diminutive tail supplies a piquant effect.

Enemies.—Although this nuthatch is exposed to the vicissitudes that beset most small birds, it is an abundant and widely spread species. Doubtless its quickness and agility as well as the protection that thick evergreen growth affords render it comparatively safe.

Joe T. Marshall, Jr. (1942), lists a red-breasted nuthatch as having been found in a pellet of the spotted owl.

Fall and winter.—As autumn draws near, those of us who live near the Atlantic seaboard to the south of the Canadian forests are on the alert to detect the earliest sign that the red-breasted nuthatches have left their northern homes and are on their way to visit us. For in any year they may move southward in fall, or they may elect to remain in the north through the winter, their movements depending, apparently, on the state of the cone crop. We begin to look and listen for them early in August and, if it is to be a nuthatch year, we have not long to wait before we hear the little trumpet call and see the tiny birds romping and rollicking through the woodlands.

They are very common near the seacoast, especially during the early days of the flight. I remember that Dr. Charles W. Townsend and I found many of them in 1923 gathered in the little patches of pitch pines scattered among the Ipswich sandhills, and William Brewster (1906) speaks of them on their first arrival as occurring "on barren points or islands along the seacoast, where they may be started in beds of beach grass or watched climbing over the surfaces of lichen-covered boulders and cliffs."

William Dutcher (1906) gives an account of an extensive flight in New York State thus:

During a vacation spent on Fire Island Beach, New York, in September, a remarkable migration of these birds was observed. Point o' Woods is a cottage settlement, on the barrier beach, at this point about 1,000 feet wide, between the ocean and Great South Bay, which is here eight miles wide. The soil is sand-covered with a rank growth of weeds of various kinds, low bushes, scrub-oaks and small pines. On the night of September 20, it was very damp, with a moderate southwest wind and a number of showers. On the morning of the 21st the wind still continued southwest, very moderate, with a temperature of 74° at 7 a. m. During the night there must have been a great flight of Red-breasted Nuthatches, for they were seen on the morning of the 21st in large numbers. They remained all that day, although there seemed to be a steady movement to the west, which here is the autumn direction of migration. During the night of the 21st, we had more showers, and on the 22d, the wind was strong southeast, with some rain. There was a large migration of small birds during the night, as the bushes were full of Towhees, Cuckoos and Kingbirds, and the Red-breasted Nuthatches were more numerous than the day before. They outnumbered the sum total of all the other small migrants. On the 23d, large numbers of them still were in evidence, but not so many as on the 22d, and on the 24th only a few were seen.

The flight covered three days—21st to 23d—while on the 24th the stragglers brought up the rear, a lone laggard being seen on the 25th. At the height of the migration, Nuthatches were seen everywhere,—on the buildings, on trees, bushes, and weeds and even on the ground. They were remarkably tame and would permit a near approach; if the observer were seated they would come within a few feet of him. They crept over the roofs and sides of the houses, examining the crevices between the shingles; they searched under the cornices on the piazzas and in fact looked into every nook and corner that might be the hiding-place of insects.

Every tree had its Nuthatch occupant, while many of them evidently found food even on the bushes and larger weeds. On a large abandoned fish factory at least 50 of these birds were seen at one time. The proprietor of one of the hotels told me that five of the birds were in his building catching flies, they having come in through the open doors and windows.

L. B. Potter (MS.) thus writes to Mr. Bent of a conspicuous flight in western Canada: "In the fall of 1919 in this district [of Eastend, extreme southwestern Saskatchewan] I witnessed a most remarkable invasion of red-breasted nuthatches. The little birds could be seen anywhere and everywhere, outside and inside farm buildings, among the sage brush in open country, as well as in the woods."

Swales and Taverner (1907) report the bird very common in the fall of 1906. They say: "September 1 to 3 they were common at Point Pelee, and still more so from the 15th to the 22d, and October 15 vast numbers were seen there. They were everywhere, in the hard woods, hanging head downwards from the tips of the long branches, in the orchards, creeping over the trunks, and in the red cedar thickets; but by far the largest numbers were towards the end of the Point on the edge of a waste clearing where every dead and dry mullen stalk had several of their little blue forms upon it. There seemed to be hundreds in sight at one time."

Winton Weydemeyer (1933) speaks of the winter range of the bird in Montana thus:

My observations on the range of the Red-breasted Nuthatch in winter have been limited to Lincoln County; but over the rest of the adjoining area described above its habits are probably similar. In winters when the birds occur as commonly as in summer, they may be found locally in all the forest types which they frequent during the breeding season, showing the same preference for fir-larch woods in the Transition zone and heavily-forested high valleys and basins in the Canadian zone. During winters when most of the nuthatches have migrated from the region, a few remain throughout the season in the Hudsonian and upper Canadian zones, even when they are entirely absent from the Transition and Canadian zone forests of the lower valleys and foothills.

DISTRIBUTION

Range.—Central Canada to southern United States. The range appears to be divided into two discontinuous regions, as from Saskatchewan to Texas it occurs only as a migrant or stray. It is a bird of the coniferous forests, and it is possible that this gap between the two ranges may be bridged in the northern forest from which no records are at present available, since it occurs as an uncommon migrant through southern Saskatchewan.

Breeding range.—In the west the species ranges **north** to southern Alaska (Chitina Moraine and Skagway, probably breeding); Yukon (junction of the Pelly and Lewes Rivers, and Squanya Lake); southern Mackenzie (Fort Simpson). **East** to southern Mackenzie (Fort Simpson), Alberta (McMurray and Camrose); and south through the mountains to eastern Wyoming (Laramie); Colorado (Breckenridge and Fort Garland); and southeastern Arizona (White Mountains, Mount Graham, and the Santa Catalina Mountains). **South** to southeastern Arizona (Stata Catalina Mountains); and California

(Bear Lake and Point Pinos); **West** to California (Bear Lake and Point Pinos) and northward through the Sierra-Nevada and Cascades of Oregon and Washington to British Columbia (Kispiox and Atlin); and Alaska (Chitina Moraine).

The eastern range is **north** to Manitoba (Echimamish River and Knee Lake); central Ontario (Moose Factory); Quebec (Godbout and the Mingan Islands); and Newfoundland (Cape St. George and possibly St. Anthony). **East** to Newfoundland (possibly St. Anthony); Massachusetts (Gloucester and Canton); New York (Orient, Adirondack and Catskill Mountains); and south through the mountains to North Carolina (Roan Mountain and Mount Mitchell). **South** to North Carolina (Mount Mitchell), and Tennessee (Cosby Knob); northeastern Ohio (Mentor); northern Michigan (Wequetonsing and Douglas Lake); and Wisconsin (Pine Lake). **West** to Wisconsin (Pine Lake and Perkinstown); Minnesota (Duluth and Clear Lake); and Manitoba (Elk Island, Lake Winnipeg, and Echimamish River).

Winter range.—The species sometimes occurs in winter almost as far north as it breeds. It winters fairly regularly **north** to southern British Columbia (Vancouver Island and Okanagan Lake); Saskatchewan (one in December at Cumberland Lake); Manitoba (Lake St. Martin and Winnipeg); Quebec (Montreal and Godbout); and Nova Scotia (Antigonish). **East** to Nova Scotia (Antigonish) and the Atlantic coast States to North Carolina (Raleigh). **South** to North Carolina (Raleigh); Tennessee (Chattanooga and Memphis); casually northern Florida (Fernandina and Pensacola); rarely Louisiana (Monroe and Bienville); Texas (San Antonio, Knickerbocker and El Paso); New Mexico (Carlsbad); and southern California (Redlands and Santa Barbara). **West** to California (Santa Barbara and Redlands) and the Pacific coast to British Columbia (Vancouver Island).

Spring migration.—Late dates of spring departure from the winter home are: Georgia—Dalton, April 28. Mississippi—Bay St. Louis, April 1. Texas—San Antonio, March 25. North Carolina—Raleigh, April 25. Virginia—Lynchburg, April 30. District of Columbia—Washington, May 20. Tennessee—Nashville, May 14. Kentucky—Bowling Green, May 4. Ohio—Oberlin, May 29. Indiana—Notre Dame, May 23. Illinois—Chicago, May 15. Missouri—St. Louis, May 18. Iowa—Keokuk, May 13. Kansas—Topeka, May 3. Nebraska—Omaha, May 8.

Early dates of spring arrival are: Massachusetts—Amherst, March 28. Vermont—Burlington, March 27. Maine—Ellsworth, March 15. New Brunswick—Scotch Lake, April 1. Quebec—Cap Tourmente, April 28. Ohio—Cleveland, March 1. Ontario—London, March 14. Indiana—Indianapolis, March 7. Michigan—Grand Rapids, March 13. Iowa—Iowa City, March 12. Wisconsin—Madison, March 26. Minnesota—Minneapolis, March 26. South Dakota—Yankton, April 14. North Dakota—Fargo, April 28. Colorado—Denver, March 10. Wyoming—Laramie, May 2. Montana—Missoula, March 24. Oregon—Pinehurst, March 2. Washington—Tacoma, April 10. Manitoba—Aweme, May 6. Saskatchewan—Regina, April 30. Alberta—Glenevis, April 15. Mackenzie—Fort Simpson, April 17. Alaska—Egg Harbor, May 17.

Fall migration.—Late dates of fall departure are: Alberta—Glenevis, October 10. Saskatchewan—Eastend, October 1. Manitoba—Aweme, November 27. Washington—Pullman, October 2. Oregon—Portland, November 17. Montana—Fortine, October 26. Wyoming—Laramie, October 20. Colorado—Walden, October 4. North Dakota—Fargo, October 25. South Dakota—Aberdeen, October 29. Minnesota—Minneapolis, October 29. Wisconsin—Racine, November 15. Iowa—Cedar Falls, November 18. Ontario—Guelph, November 15. Michigan—Sault Ste. Marie, November 11. Quebec—Montreal, October 8. Nova Scotia—Sable Island, November 5. Maine—Unity, November 28. Massachusetts—Marthas Vineyard, November 13.

Early dates of fall arrival are: Wisconsin—Madison, August 28. Nebraska—Lincoln, September 4. Kansas—Manhattan, October 4. Iowa—National, September 9. Missouri—St. Louis, September 4. Illinois—Glen Ellyn, August 29. Indiana—Indianapolis, September 15. Kentucky—Lexington, September 17. Tennessee—Nashville, October 7. Ohio—Canton, August 29. District of Columbia—Washington, August 22. Virginia—Salem, October 1. North Carolina—Chapel Hill, October 4. Georgia—Atlanta, October 11. Alabama—Greensboro, October 4. Florida—Fernandina, November 1.

Casual records.—One was observed near Churchill, Manitoba, on August 4, 1934; Bermuda Islands, a specimen was taken previous to 1884. On Guadalupe Island, Baja California, there is a small resident colony, quite isolated from other breeding areas, as it has never been recorded on the mainland of Baja California.

Egg dates.—California: 10 records, May 13 to June 13.

Maine: 14 records, May 20 to June 21.

Nova Scotia: 7 records, May 5 to June 5.

Washington: 14 records, April 30 to June 25.

SITTA PUSILLA PUSILLA Latham

BROWN-HEADED NUTHATCH

PLATE 12

HABITS

The above name is now restricted to the northern race of the brown-headed nuthatch, with a range entirely north of the Florida boundary;

it breeds along the Atlantic slope as far north as southern Delaware, in the Gulf States as far west as eastern Texas, and up the Mississippi Valley as far as eastern Arkansas and southern Missouri.

Its favorite haunts are in the pine woods, especially in the more open parts and in the clearings and burnt-over areas, where it finds a number of old stumps in which to excavate its nest; but it is found also to some extent in mixed forests of pines and hardwoods and in some of the small cypress swamps in such woods. M. P. Skinner (1928) says that, in North Carolina, he has found it "on the trunks of loblolly pines, long-leaf pines, shrub oaks, gums and hardwood trees of various kinds."

Dr. Eugene E. Murphey (1937) says that, in the middle Savanna Valley, it "prefers open pine woods and deadenings and seems to have a particular fondness for large pines which have been riven by lightning. Within the last 15 years, many areas of impounded water have been created, some for power, others for fishing, with the resultant death of the trees where the water level has been raised. In a short time the bark falls from these trees leaving a denuded, decaying trunk which seems to be most attractive as a nesting site. Six nests were found so located in a pond of not more than fifty acres in extent in Richmond County, Georgia, 1920."

Nesting.—The brown-headed nuthatch builds its nest in a tree, stump, or post, which apparently is usually, if not invariably, partially or wholly excavated by the birds themselves. I can find little evidence that it occupies old holes of the woodpeckers, but it may enlarge a natural crevice or cavity. The height from the ground varies from 2 to 50 feet, wherever it can find the right conditions; but most of the nests recorded have been far below the higher figure, nearly all of them at less than 10 feet above ground. A preference seems to be shown for pines or pine stubs, often fire-blackened stumps, and for dead trees. Nests have been found in a dead apple-tree stump, a birch stub, a pear tree, an ash tree, and probably in several other kinds of trees. The cavity is usually excavated to a depth of from 6 to 9 inches, uncommonly more or less. This is sometimes filled with only dry grasses and weed stems, but more often with strips of inner bark, chips of wood, wool, cotton, strips of corn husks, and perhaps a few feathers; the leaves of pine seeds are favorite nesting material and are found in many nests, sometimes forming the entire nest. Frequently the nest hole is excavated in a fence post, a gate post, or a telegraph or telephone pole.

Nesting begins early; both birds take part in excavating the holes; and often several holes are started before one is finally selected for the nest. Mr. Skinner (1928), in the sandhills of North Carolina, on March 16, 1927, "found a pair industriously digging in the dead stub of a small gum tree standing on the shore of a small lake. This stub was 12 feet high and 8 inches in diameter, and the birds were at work 8 feet above the ground. The digging bird (and only one worked at any one time) worked in all positions, but really preferred to hang head downward from the trunk above the hole; even when working in this position, it did not touch its tail to the bark, except accidentally. This Nuthatch gave its strokes like a woodpecker, but slower and at a rate of about 50 strokes a minute for at least 30 minutes. Then its mate came and relieved it. Although these birds were small, their digging strokes were powerful and could be heard quite a distance, perhaps as much as 200 yards, and had a rhythmical beat."

C. S. Brimley (Pearson, Brimley, and Brimley, 1919) made some notes on the time required by four pairs of brown-headed nuthatches to make and line their nests and lay their eggs: "The first pair I noted had finished digging out the hole and had commenced to line it on March 22. Sixteen days later the nest contained four fresh eggs. Pair No. 2 had just begun building on April 16, and in 10 days more the nest was finished and fresh eggs laid. Pair No. 3 worked for 22 days on one hole, and when I then lost patience and broke it out to see what they had done, they had not even started to line it. They then commenced on another stump, and in 22 more days had the excavation completed, lined, and three eggs laid. Pair No. 4 dug a hole, lined it, and laid three eggs in 13 days."

Arthur T. Wayne (1910) says that, in South Carolina, "the hole, which is excavated by both sexes, ranges from 6 inches to 90 feet above the ground, and is generally dug in a dead pine stump or tree, though sometimes a fence post is used. * * * The nest is constructed chiefly of the leaf-like substance in which the seeds of the pine are enclosed, and I have often wondered at the infinite number of trips the birds make in carrying, one at a time, these soft and delicate pine seed-wings."

Charles R. Stockard (1905) writes thus of the nesting habits of this nuthatch in Mississippi:

In the old pine deadenings of Adams County this small bird was found nesting in considerable numbers. They dug their own burrow but it was a badly botched affair, nothing about it suggesting the even smoothness of a woodpecker's hollow. The Nuthatch makes a small entrance through the bark of a dead snag, then usually, rather than burrow into the stump itself, they scooped out an irregular cavity by removing the soft wood that generally lies just under the bark. This burrow ran a crooked course but generally extended 10 or 15 inches below the entrance. In this cavity they placed a nest of soft fibers, moss, cotton, and wool. The burrows were usually only a few feet from the ground but one was found 12 feet up. * * * On one occasion when the bark was pulled away exposing a nest while the female sat upon it, she could not be made to leave until pushed off with my finger.

Eggs.—Nests of the brown-headed nuthatch have been reported to contain as few as three eggs and as many as nine, but the prevailing numbers are five or six, most commonly five. The eggs are ovate or rounded-ovate in shape, and they have practically no gloss. The ground color is usually white, but sometimes light creamy or buffy white. They are usually more heavily or more profusely marked than are the eggs of other nuthatches and are often very handsome. The markings may consist of fine dots evenly distributed, or small spots or blotches more or less concentrated about the larger end; rarely the ground color is largely obscured by the heavier markings. The prevailing colors of the markings are various shades of reddish brown, "ferruginous" or "cinnamon-rufous"; some eggs are quite heavily blotched with "chestnut"; and some show underlying spots or small blotches of various shades of lavender or "plumbeous." The measurements of 50 eggs average 15.5 by 12.3 millimeters; eggs showing the four extremes measure **16.7** by 12.6, 15.2 by **14.2, 14.1** by 12.3, and 16.6 by **11.4** millimeters.

Young.—The period of incubation is said to be about 14 days, and Wayne (1910) says that both sexes share this duty; the male sometimes calls the female off the nest while she is incubating. According to Mr. Wayne (1910), only one brood is raised in a season. Both parents help to feed the young in the nest and for some time after they leave it, while they continue to travel about in the tree tops in family parties. Dr. Francis Harper (1929) describes such a family party as follows:

About 5 p. m. on April 10 I noticed a number of Brown-headed Nut-hatches among some pines in an old field. Presently three or four of them huddled together a couple of feet from the tip of a long limb 35 feet from the ground. The limb was well provided with twigs and needles. Then a couple of others began visiting those lined up on the limb and feeding them. I was astounded to realize that fledglings were abroad thus early in the season. Sometimes the adults passed over the food from a perch on the same level, but about as often as not they clung to the under side of the limb in acrobat fashion and fed the youngsters from below.

By degrees several more came and lined up on the limb, till there were finally six, if not seven, all touching each other in close array. Some faced in one direction, some in the other. They kept up a gentle, musical twittering. The adults often gave their loudest call (a nasal, twanging *knee-tnee; knee-tnee-tnee*) as they searched the pine cones, limbs, and trunks for food. They also gave, while so engaged, a much lower, conversational note: *pik*. Once in a while one of them would hammer some piece of food on a limb, in the manner of one of the larger species of nuthatches.

Up to about 5:30 p. m. the old birds fed the youngsters assiduously, returning every half minute or so. Then, when the latter were pretty well quieted, though the sun had scarcely set, the old birds disappeared for some minutes. Eventually they returned, but did not go to the young ones, merely feeding industriously in the adjacent trees. All this was so like a human family, where the babies are given an early supper and put to bed, after which the parents can attend to some of their own wants.

I waited till after 6 o'clock to see if the adults might not join their brood, but apparently that was not their intention. * * * It seemed strange that a hole-nesting species should roost thus in the open.

Aretas A. Saunders tells me that, at a nest he watched in Alabama, "both parents fed the young, each showing its individuality by approaching the nest from a different direction than the other. They carried insects in their bills, but only a few measuring worms could be identified. They removed excreta from the nest and carried it away."

Plumages.—I have seen no very young nestlings of this nuthatch. The juvenal plumage is fully acquired before the young birds leave the nest. In this plumage the young bird is similar to the adult, but the coloration is duller and paler. The brown of the head and neck is grayer, or nearly all gray, and the white nuchal patch is indistinct or obsolete; the greater wing coverts are edged with pale brownish buff; the white in the tail is less extensive; and the underparts are more extensively and more deeply washed with brownish buff. After the postjuvenal molt, in summer, the young bird becomes practically indistinguishable from the adult.

Adults have a complete postnuptial molt, beginning in July, after which in fresh plumage, the brown of the head is darker, and the underparts are more extensively and more decidedly buffy than in spring birds; these colors fade more or less before winter. The sexes are alike in all plumages.

Food.—I can find no very extensive analysis of the food of the brown-headed nuthatch. The bird is mainly insectivorous, searching diligently in the crevices of the bark on the trunks and branches of the pines for its food, even out to the tips of the twigs and among the needles. It forages, also, on many other kinds of trees, old stumps, fence posts, telegraph poles, buildings, or anywhere else that it can find insects or spiders hidden in nooks and corners. It seems to be especially fond of pine seeds, fragments of which are generally found in such stomachs as have been examined.

Arthur H. Howell (1924) says that "10 stomachs from Alabama examined in the Biological Survey contained remains of beetles, bugs, cockroaches, caterpillars, ants and other Hymenoptera, scale insects, and fragments of pine seeds." Dr. H. C. Oberholser (1938) states that, in Louisiana, "the food of this bird consists chiefly of insects, which include moths, grasshoppers, beetles, many of these injurious kinds; ants, caterpillars, and scale insects; also pine seeds and spiders." These, like all the other nuthatches, are very useful protectors of the trees and do no damage of consequence.

Behavior.—Unlike the rather solitary red-breasted species, the brown-headed nuthatch is a decidedly sociable bird. During most of the year, except when the pairs are busy with their nesting activities, these nuthatches are almost gregarious; family groups or small parties of them may be seen trooping through the tree tops, chattering in friendly conversational tones, but each one apparently intent on its own vocation. They seem never still but are always full of life and restless activity. In their behavior they remind me of the red-bellied nuthatch, as they forage through the upper branches out to the ends of the terminal twigs, often hanging head downward from a bunch of pine needles. Like all the nuthatches, they are expert at creeping either up or down the trunks, often in an inverted position, or at exploring the under sides of branches. Mr. Skinner (1928) says: "In all this climbing, they move by short hops, generally with their bodies turned a little to one side or the other, and they may turn after going a few feet with their bodies turned one way, so that the other side is then uppermost. Occasionally, they perch crosswise on a twig and may rest motionless for some time in such a position.

"These little birds are very tame and friendly. When in pairs, they are devoted to each other. * * * Generally, they fly from tree to tree with a gently undulating flight, but with strong and rapid wing-beats."

Voice.—The voice of the brown-headed nuthatch is quite unlike that of either of the northern nuthatches and has been variously interpreted. There is a familiar nuthatch quality in the ordinary *cha, cha, cha,* or *cah, cah, cah,* or the short *pit, pit;* we know what kind of a bird to look for when we hear it coming to us from the tree tops in the lonesome pine barrens.

Mr. Skinner (1928) writes: "Perhaps these nuthatches do not 'talk' as much as some others. Yet, I have heard them utter a sweet little 'pri-u, de-u, de-u,' quite like a song, in the mating season. They also have a number of chirps and kissing notes, and a 'dee-dee-dee' comparable to a Chickadee's note. A lively twitter is the call of one Brown-headed Nuthatch for its mate."

Dr. Chapman (1912) says: "They are talkative sprites, and, like a group of school children, each one chatters away without paying the slightest attention to what his companions are saying. When feeding they utter a liquid, conversational *pit-pit,* a note which is accelerated and emphasized as the birds take wing. At intervals, even when the individuals of a troop are quite widely separated, they all suddenly break out into a thin, metallic *dee-dee-dee* or *tnee-tnee-tnee.*"

William Brewster (1882b) calls their usual utterance *"whick-whick-whee'e'é whick-whicker-whicker."* And Nathan Clifford Brown (1878) writes: "While busily in search of food they have a subdued, conversational chatter which almost exactly resembles the notes usually uttered by the Goldfinch when similarly employed. Rather curiously, the two species have another call in common: the most frequent cry of the Nuthatch is remarkably like the Goldfinch's meditative *béyr-béh*,—indeed, I have sometimes mistaken one for the other. Both sexes of the present bird have several other call-notes, all of which are characterized by a certain reedy harshness rendering them quite unlike the usual utterances of the two Northern species of the genus."

Field marks.—This small nuthatch could hardly be mistaken for the larger white-breasted species, and it is so plainly colored that it could easily be distinguished from the more conspicuously marked red-breasted nuthatch.

Winter.—The brown-headed nuthatch seems to be a permanent resident even in the more northern portions of its range; in North Carolina, Mr. Skinner (1928) found "no variation in numbers during the winter or the migration seasons of other birds." I can find no evidence of migration elsewhere, and apparently the birds remain all winter in or near their breeding haunts, with only limited wanderings into neighboring open spaces, or occasionally into the trees of villages and towns. They are much in evidence in winter, when they are associated in bands of from half a dozen to two dozen birds, made up of one or several families. These jolly bands of active playful birds are interesting to watch, as they chase each other about, almost never still, as if too full of energy and vitality. At this season they often join the loose gatherings of kinglets, titmice, pine warblers, bluebirds, and small woodpeckers that are roaming through the woods in winter, though such associations are probably due more to chance than to intent.

DISTRIBUTION

Range.—Southeastern United States; nonmigratory.

The brown-headed nuthatch breeds **north** to Arkansas (Newport); southeastern Missouri (possibly Ink, Shannon County); northern Mississippi (Iuka); northwestern South Carolina (Spartanburg); eastern Virginia (Amelia and Petersburg); eastern Maryland (Queen Annes County); and southern Delaware (Seaford). **East** to the Atlantic coast and Bahama Islands (Great Bahama). **South** to southern Florida (Royal Palm Hammock) and the Gulf coast. **West** to eastern Texas (Houston) and Arkansas (Newport).

The entire species as above outlined is divided into three subspecies or geographic races. The typical brown-headed nuthatch (*S. p. pusilla*) occupies all of the continental range except Florida, where the birds have been described as the gray-headed nuthatch (*S. p. caniceps*). The birds of the Bahamas are a separate race.

Casual records.—Several were seen near Keokuk, Iowa, in May 1893; a specimen was taken at St. Louis, Mo., on May 6, 1878; a specimen was obtained at Elmira, N. Y., May 24, 1888; while one was observed closely at Haddonfield, N. J., during the winter, about 1876.

Egg dates.—Georgia: 22 records, March 11 to July 20; 11 records, March 24 to April 11, indicating the height of the season.

Florida: 19 records, March 4 to May 10; 10 records April 2 to 14.

North Carolina: 19 records, April 4 to May 29.

Texas: 5 records, March 8 to April 18.

SITTA PUSILLA CANICEPS Bangs

GRAY-HEADED NUTHATCH

HABITS

The brown-headed nuthatch of peninsular Florida has now become the gray-headed nuthatch, not because it has grown gray with old age, and not because its head is very decidedly gray at that, but because the keen eyes of its describer have noted this and other minor differences. Outram Bangs (1898) gives it the following subspecific characters: "Size smaller than *S. pusilla pusilla;* bill larger; top of head much lighter brown, the feathers tipped and edged still lighter —often grayish; loral and post-ocular streak dark brown, in marked contrast to color of top of head; white spot on nape usually less extensive; under parts slightly darker, more plumbeous."

The gray-headed nuthatch is recorded by Arthur H. Howell (1932) as "an abundant resident in northwestern Florida; moderately common in the central and southern parts." It has been taken at least as far south as Miami. Its home is in the extensive open pine forests of the State, known as the "flatwoods." The northern tourist, seeking a winter sojourn in Florida, rides in the southbound train for hour after hour with nothing to see from the car window but apparently endless miles of uninteresting flat pine barrens, until he wearies of the monotony. He does not appreciate the intriguing vastness of these almost boundless flatwoods; nor does he admire the stately beauty of the longleaf pines and the picturesque charm of the Caribbean pines. Only the naturalist fully appreciates them, for "there is a nameless charm in the flatwoods, there is enchantment for the real lover of nature in their very sameness. One feels a sense of their infinity as the forest stretches away into space beyond the limits of vision; they convey to the mind a feeling of boundless freedom. The soft, brilliant sunshine filters down through the needle-like leaves and falls in patches on the flower covered floor; there is a low, humming sound, something mimicking the patter of raindrops, as the warm southeast wind drifts through the trees; even the loneliness has an attraction," as so well expressed by Charles Torrey Simpson (1923).

One may wander for many miles through these parklike woods, along the winding, grass-grown cart roads, but he never seems to get anywhere, as the trees seem to lead him on indefinitely; he may turn aside occasionally to examine the thicker vegetation about a stagnant pool, or to explore the more abundant bird life in one of the few scattered "cypress heads"; or in some wide open space, he may flush the stately sandhill crane from a larger grassy pond. But the three characteristic birds, which one finds everywhere in the flatwoods, are the red-cockaded woodpecker, the pinewoods sparrow, and this little nuthatch. The woodpecker climbs upward on the trunks of the pines; the sparrow flushes suddenly from any one of the many clumps of saw palmetto that carpet the forest floor and almost as suddenly drops out of sight into another patch; and the nuthatch may be seen climbing upward, downward, or sidewise, in true nuthatch fashion, on the trunk of a pine; or, perhaps more often, a little troop of them may be seen foraging in the tree tops and advertising their presence with their gentle twittering.

There is not much more to be said about the habits of the gray-headed nuthatch, which do not seem to differ materially from those of the more northern race. The eggs are indistinguishable. The measurements of 28 eggs average 15.0 by 11.8 millimeters; the eggs showing the four extremes measure **16.1** by 12.1, 15.8 by **12.8, 14.1** by 11.2, and 14.4 by **11.0** millimeters.

The following account is contributed by Frederick V. Hebard:

"This race seems to be valid, since it is distinguishable in life from the brown-headed nuthatch with comparative ease, although their habits seem the same. The range is stated to be 'Peninsula of Florida' (A. O. U. 1931), but the nesting form in southeastern Georgia is unquestionably gray in crown color and within the size limit of this race. Comparatively limited records indicate that the gray-headed withdraws into Florida in cold winters and is replaced to a limited degree by the brown-headed nuthatch. In warm winters the species is so much more common that this range withdrawal may not then take place. In all years our little friend will be present by the middle of February and nest-building commences shortly thereafter. During the winter this species is usually seen 20 feet or more above the ground either in family flocks, flitting from pine tree top to pine tree top, or less commonly inching up or down a pine tree trunk. During nesting season they are usually seen from 20 feet down, but as soon as nesting is over they seem to return to the tree tops, returning earthward only to fill one of their feeding stations in a rotting sapling with acorns for the nesting season or perhaps to associate with other species in a bird wave (cf. Murphey, 1937) of which they do not seem to be an integral part. These waves seem to result from animation of insect life in damp, warmish weather after a chill. This results in true commensalism in such species as the Carolina chickadee, tufted titmouse, ruby-crowned kinglet, and black and white and orange-crowned warblers, which I consider integral parts of bird waves, and in an apparent but unreal commensalism, since they feed at another table, of such species as the downy and red-cockaded woodpeckers, phoebe, and brown or gray-headed nuthatches."

Nesting.—"My three nest records," continues Mr. Hebard, were all less than 5 feet from the ground, but John W. Burch considered this unusual, as he has generally found them 4 to 20 feet up. I did see nest-building commencing in a 6-foot-high fence post on February 26, 1942, along the May Bluff road in Charlton County. Other records are:

1. Nest found April 14, 1942, in Camden County in a dead pine stump 4½ feet high, with an undetermined number of young.

2. Nest found April 23, 1942, in Charlton County in a charred pine stump 3 feet high, with young almost ready to fly. The nest hole was so deep that the nest was not over 20 inches from the ground. When examined on May 13, 1942, the nest was empty except for great numbers of creamy-white pinfeathers. This nest was composed of strips of cypress bark, unmatured pine mast, one or two strands of Spanish moss, and an unidentified wool-like substance that may well have been an insect nest.

3. Nest found April 12, 1942, in Camden County, containing one egg about a foot down the top of a 4-foot pine fence post. From May 13 to 16, this nest contained three well-grown young whose mouths were always open when observed. On July 1, this nest was found covered by an incompleted bluebird nest.

It is extremely interesting to compare this with what has been written about the same race 40 or 50 miles away (Grimes, 1932) : "A brown (-gray)-head was noted working on a newly started nest hole in a pine stump on February 20. Others were found from time to time, the two latest probably being second-brood nests—one May 16 with four large young, the other May 18, with an undetermined number of nearly fledged young."

SITTA PYGMAEA PYGMAEA Vigors

PYGMY NUTHATCH

HABITS

The type race of the pygmy nuthatch is now restricted to a very narrow range in the Transition Zone of the coast region of California, from San Luis Obispo County to Mendocino County.

A. J. van Rossem (1929) says that "the color characters distinguishing *pygmaea* from *melanotis* * * * are more brownish pileum and nape, combined with a relatively indistinct ocular streak which is never prominent and in extreme cases so nearly concolor with the head as to be almost indistinguishable."

Grinnell and Linsdale (1936) say that this subspecies, which was named from specimens collected at Monterey, "is restricted quite closely to the southern portion of the humid coast strip," as mentioned above. They further state:

[It] "lives commonly in the same habitat, the coniferous forest, with the Santa Cruz Chestnut-sided Chickadee; and it does so, therefore, compatibly. Our observations show the niche occupied by the nuthatch to be essentially different. While the two birds have about the same forage beat and cruising radius, often indeed seen closely associated, the nuthatch seeks (at least in the season of greatest food scarcity) static insect food in crevices of dry cones, twigs, and smaller branches in the subperipheral parts of the trees, and it uses its specialized digging tool (the bill) to dislodge or uncover these insects. In other words, the nuthatch has a food source beyond the usual reach of the chickadee. And then, too, with suitably rotted boles of trees available, it digs its own nesting cavity; it does not tolerate the chickadee.

Nesting.—The same observers write:

The breeding season for this species [in the Point Lobos Reserve] was a long one, with a prolonged period of preparation. As early in the spring as February 18, there were signs of pairing in this bird. In an excited flock in a pine, one individual was seen feeding another. Later, on several occasions, a male (?) was seen to feed its mate.

Actual excavation at a nesting site was noted first on March 20. Just before noon, a nuthatch was digging 15 feet up on the west side of a 25-foot pine stump. It left the cavity, barely started, but returned again in 5 minutes. More than a month later, on April 24, a nuthatch, then out of sight, was still digging at this cavity. * * *

Thirty-eight occupied nesting cavities were found, all of them in pines or dead remains of pines. The sites selected were high ones, averaging 30 feet above the ground and running as high as 60 feet. Only seven nests were found lower than 20 feet and only one under 10 feet. Sometimes the excavation was started at some crevice or break already existing in the tree, but more often, and especially when the wood was partly decayed, it was started on a plain surface. Once a cavity started by a hairy woodpecker was deepened and occupied by a pair of nuthatches. * * *

The bluebirds were the most serious competitors of this species for nest sites, and in several instances, in which the entrances were of sufficient size, they temporarily or even permanently ousted the smaller birds from a cavity. Nearly always in such cases the nuthatches had been the excavators, but the larger birds seemed usually to be the aggressors. At one stump where nuthatches were digging only 2 feet below a bluebird's nest, there were alarm notes and activity when the bluebirds were near. The nuthatches usually retreated, but they sometimes kept on working.

The birds at one nest showed great excitement when a hairy woodpecker came near. Chickadees were competitors of close to nuthatch size. Once one was seen pursued by a chickadee, and at another time one was chasing a chickadee. In general, however, these two species avoided one another by nesting at wholly different levels. One pair of nuthatches which was feeding young chased away a male linnet and, later, a violet-green swallow, from the vicinity of the nest.

Mrs. Amelia S. Allen tells me that in fall these nuthatches "wander through the lower valleys where their chattering notes betray their presence in the tops of the trees among the cones. At Inverness, in Marin County, they are much at home among the Bishop pines, and at Carmel, in Monterey County, among the Monterey pines."

The eggs of this subspecies are indistinguishable from those of the following form. The measurements of 40 eggs of the present race average 15.4 by 12.1 millimeters; the eggs showing the four extremes measure **16.3** by **12.8, 14.5** by 12.3, and 14.7 by **11.2** millimeters.

DISTRIBUTION

Range.—Southern British Columbia to southern Mexico.

The pygmy nuthatch breeds **north** to southern British Columbia (Cawston, Penticton, and Newgate). **East** to southern British Columbia (Newgate); western Montana (probably Belton and the Beartooth Mountains); Wyoming (near Laramie); Colorado (Estes Park, mountains west of Boulder, Golden, and Fort Garland); possibly northeastern Oklahoma (Kenton); New Mexico (Sangre de Cristo, Capitan, and Sacramento Mountains); southwestern Texas (Guadalupe Mountains); and Veracruz (Las Vigas). **South** to Veracruz (Las Vigas); Puebla (Mount Orizaba and Río Frío); Morelos (Huitzilac); and Michoacán (Mount Tancitaro). **West** to Michoacán (Mount Tancitaro); Jalisco (San Sabastián); Baja California (Sierra San Pedro Mártir and Laguna Hansen); California (Mount Pinos, Monterey, Point Reyes, and Inglenook); Oregon (Pinehurst and Warm Springs Reservation); Washington (Seattle and Mount Baker); and British Columbia (Cawston).

The pygmy nuthatch is not migratory, but it does wander about some in winter, at which time it has reached western Nebraska.

The distribution as given is for the entire species, which has been divided into four subspecies or geographic races within our limits. The pygmy nuthatch (*S. p. pygmaea*) occurs in the coast region of California from Mendocino County south to San Luis Obispo County. The white-naped nuthatch (*S. p. leuconucha*) breeds from Riverside and San Diego Counties, Calif., south through the San Pedro Mártir Mountains, Baja California. The Nevada nuthatch (*S. p. canescens*) occurs in the Charleston and Sheep Mountains in southern Nevada. The black-eared nuthatch (*S. p. melanotis*) occupies the Rocky Mountain region from southern British Columbia southward to New Mexico and Arizona, and possibly Sonora, and the Sierra Nevada in California.

Egg dates.—Arizona: 9 records, May 7 to June 6.

California: 89 records, April 17 to June 27; 45 records, May 16 to June 3, indicating the height of the season.

Colorado: 22 records, May 13 to June 19; 11 records, May 22 to June 12.

Oregon: 17 records, May 3 to June 21.

SITTA PYGMAEA MELANOTIS van Rossem

BLACK-EARED NUTHATCH

PLATE 13

HABITS

Up to the time that this race was separated, in 1929, all the pygmy nuthatches of the western United States were supposed to belong to the type race. The species is widely distributed and was always known to all the earlier writers as the pygmy nuthatch, *Sitta pygmaea pygmaea*. But *melanotis*, as now recognized, is the most widely distributed and the best-known race and must be given the most consideration here, even if the new name is not always used.

A. J. van Rossem (1929) gives as the subspecific characters of *melanotis:* "Similar in size to *Sitta pygmaea pygmaea*, but top of head and nape decidedly darker and more slaty (less brownish); streak from bill through eye broader and often nearly black, contrasting strongly with the white or buffy white malar region. Differs from *Sitta pygmaea leuconucha* in decidedly smaller size and very much darker coloration."

It occupies the entire Rocky Mountain region, from southern British Columbia and northern Idaho south to the Mexican boundary, and west to eastern Washington, eastern Oregon, the Sierra Nevada, and the San Bernardino Mountains of California. Mr. van Rossem (1929) says that "in southern California, intergradation with *leuconucha* is very gradual and birds from the extreme southern Sierras, Mt. Pinos, the San Gabriel and San Bernardino Mountains are definitely larger than northern Sierra and Rocky Mountain series."

The black-eared nuthatch is a mountain bird, breeding in the Transition Zone at elevations from 3,500 to 10,000 feet in various parts of its range. Its distribution seems to coincide very closely with that of the yellow pine, where it is generally common and often really abundant. In the San Bernardino Mountains, Dr. Grinnell (1908) found it "most numerous in the lower Transition zone, in the Jeffrey and yellow pine belt." It is doubtless found to some extent among other species of pines, though the yellow-pine belt seems to be its favorite breeding ground. In the Huachuca Mountains we found it very common in the pines above 8,000 feet and up nearly to the summit, where the open growth of pines ended at about 9,000 feet. It reaches about the same altitudes in Nevada and Colorado; and, in New Mexico, Mrs. Bailey (1928) says: "The Pygmies are characteristic birds of the Transition Zone yellow pine belt, following it on steep hot slopes to the extreme upper limit of the zone, sometimes as high as 10,000 feet."

According to Grinnell and Linsdale (1936) it is resident "along the west flank of the Sierra Nevada, at altitudes of 3,500 to 6,000 feet, according to slope exposure and other factors."

W. E. Griffee tells me that "the black-eared nuthatch, like the short-tailed chickadee, is found throughout the pine forests of eastern Oregon." According to Fred Mallery Packard (MS.), of Estes Park, Colo., "in spring and fall, small bands of pygmy nuthatches wander through the yellow pines, calling noisily; but they scatter during the nesting season and are seldom heard then. Nests have been found, between June 5 and 18, at 8,200 feet, and it is certain that they nest well into the Canadian zone. There is a vertical migration, sometimes to the plains."

Nesting.—It was on the summits of the Huachuca Mountains that I made the acquaintance of the tiny black-eared nuthatch, then known as the pygmy nuthatch. On these summits at elevations between 8,000 and 9,000 feet, above the steepest slopes, the surface of the ground was nearly level in some places, or rolling in gentle slopes in others. It was covered with a fine parklike, open forest of tall pines of two or three species that towered skyward to heights of 80 or 100 feet. Scattered through this forest were a number of tall dead pines and lower stubs. Here, on May 7, 1922, many of the nuthatches were already paired and were busy with their preparations for nesting. The nesting holes were easy to recognize, as little circular openings, usually near the tops of the dead pine stubs and often under the stump of a branch. One nest that we investigated was 30 feet from the ground in such a situation, but no eggs had been laid in it. Another, similarly located, was not examined, as we were apparently too early. My companion, Frank Willard, returned to this locality on May 30 and collected three sets of eggs of this nuthatch, consisting of six, seven, and eight eggs, respectively; the nests were all in dead pine stubs, 20, 40, and 50 feet above ground; the depth of one cavity, evidently excavated by the birds, was 10 inches; the nest lining consisted mainly of "pine bud hulls," with a few feathers.

Nests are not always placed at such heights above ground. In the San Bernardino Mountains, at about 7,000 feet elevation, Dr. Grinnell (1908) found a nest "in a rotten pine stub eight feet above the ground. The cavity seemed to have been excavated by the birds themselves. Two blows on the stub brought out the setting bird, which at once disappeared. After a while what proved to be the male nuthatch made his appearance with an insect in his mouth, an indication that the male feeds the female on the nest. The nest was a felted mass of rodent fur and plant down. There were seven slightly incubated eggs."

Irene G. Wheelock (1904) writes:

At Lake Tahoe a hollow post several feet out in the water held a nest of these gray midgets, the entrance being a crevice scarcely large enough for a mouse. Both birds worked busily carrying feathers into this crevice until it seemed there must be at least a peck of them tucked away inside. Although I stood in a boat with hand resting on the post not a foot from their doorway, they came and went as unconcernedly as if no one were within miles of them. * * * Another nest found, June 14, ten feet from the ground in a dead pine was also entered through a crevice; the birds displayed the same fearlessness, going inside with food, while the bird-lover stood on her horse's back and tried to make the opening large enough to admit a friendly though curious hand. The brave little bird would light on the trunk just above the nest hole, and, running quickly down, dodge in when the fingers of the investigator were pulling at the crevice.

Another nest near Lake Tahoe is reported by Claude Gignoux (1924), in "a hole about 10 feet from the ground in an upright post. * * * The nest, entered by a small, irregular orifice, was in a decayed portion of the pole, where excavation was easy. * * * The pole in which the nest was placed stood at the junction of two board walks, not over 20 feet from an occupied cottage. People were passing every few minutes, workmen were repairing a drain and board walk within 100 feet, and automobiles were being repaired, moved about, and their engines raced by mechanics, within 50 or 75 yards. The adult birds were so intent upon their duties [feeding their young] that none of these activities disturbed them."

There is a set of eggs in the J. P. Norris collection taken from a deserted woodpecker's hole, one from a hole bored by the birds in a cottonwood tree, and another from "under loose bark on a dead tree". Probably any suitable cavity that is available may be occupied.

From the mountains northeast of Silver City, N. Mex., J. S. Ligon wrote to Mrs. Bailey (1928) in April 1919, as follows: "I watched two of these little fellows laboring at a nest hole 18 feet up in a dead pine. One was inside, making the noise of a woodpecker. I watched the performance for about 10 minutes, during which time it made three trips out to the entrance to fling the chips and dust to the wind with a quick shake of the bill. It came out apparently to rest and the other went quickly in, and after it had hammered a little, came up with its cuttings, flinging them away and quickly returning. On the 18th or 19th, it seemed that all the Pygmies, as if by general order, were working in nest holes."

Mr. Griffee writes to me that the nests of this nuthatch, in eastern Oregon, "usually are in ponderosa pine snags. The larger snags, after being dead for several years, have a layer of punky sapwood, 3 or 4 inches thick, and deep season checks which need only a little enlarging to serve as entrances to nesting cavities. Since the entrances are irregular in shape, being 1 to 1¼ inches wide by 1¼ inches or more high, and usually 10 to 25 feet up, they are not at all conspicuous. The bottom of the nesting cavity is usually about 8 inches below the entrance, and in some cases it is so small that a family of six or seven young nuthatches must find it very cramped quarters. The lining, often scanty, is of shreds of bark, bits of cocoons or of wool, and a few feathers."

Eggs.—Pygmy nuthatches may lay anywhere from four to nine eggs to a set; the smaller numbers are unusual, and most of the sets consist of six to eight eggs. They vary in shape from ovate to short-ovate and have practically no gloss. The ground color is pure white, and they are usually unevenly and rather sparingly sprinkled with fine dots of reddish brown or brick red, "hazel," or "vinaceous-cinnamon"; some eggs are more heavily spotted about the larger end, rarely elsewhere, with these colors or "chestnut." Eggs of this species do not show so much variation as those of some of the other nuthatches, and are not so handsomely marked. The measurements of 40 eggs average 15.3 by 11.9 millimeters; the eggs showing the four extremes measure 16.3 by 11.4, 15.0 by 12.5, 14.2 by 12.2, and 15.2 by 11.1 millimeters.

Young.—I can find no definite statement as to the period of incubation, which is probably about 14 days. Perhaps both sexes share in this duty, but the fact that the male is known to feed the female on the nest indicates that she probably does most, if not all, of the incubating. Both parents feed the young in the nest and for some time after they leave it. Mrs. Wheelock (1904), at the nest she watched, noted that "both male and female were busy hunting some sort of white larvæ that they obtained from an old stump. The adults did not swallow these, but carried them in their bills—which convinced me that the nestlings were at least five days old."

Mr. Gignoux (1924) writes:

Both parent birds were engaged in the task of carrying what appeared to be flies, worms, and white grubs, and both birds were often in sight at the same time. The first visit was recorded at 2 : 26 in the afternoon and by 3 : 27 the birds had made 24 calls, carrying food each time. At this rate the adult birds were making over 300 trips a day. The longest interval between visits was 8 minutes, the shortest was half a minute. The parents did their foraging in nearby pine trees and well up from the ground, from about 50 to 80 feet or more high. The insects were thrust into the bills of the young the instant the parents arrived, without the slightest delay, and the old birds were off for more, now and then stopping a second or so to remove material from the nest. * * *

During the days on which I watched the birds, foraging was done in a group of about 20 large pine trees. The flights were always direct from near the nest to and from these pines. I measured what seemed the distance of these trees from the nest and estimated that 150 yards was the average round trip and that the total distance traveled each day was approximately 30 miles.

Mrs. Wheelock (1905) tells of another nest, not those referred to above:

In this case there were newly hatched young in the nest; and, as the adults went inside to feed them not more than two feet from my eyes, I was able to see perfectly that the food was carried in the throat. Of course this could only mean regurgitation; but not until the third day could I get at the nestlings to examine the crops. The contents consisted of larvae of insects and ant eggs, all partially digested. On the fifth day the examination indicated the presence of fresh or unregurgitated insect and grass food. On the sixth day most of the food given was fresh, but on two occasions the adults visited the nests with no visible supply in the bills. No record was kept of this brood after the sixth day. Two other broods of this species were recorded at the same place and with practically the same results.

J. Eugene Law (1929), while studying the behavior of a pair of these nuthatches, noted that "when a fecal sac was brought out, it was not dropped in flight but was carried out and left attached to some high limb. One particular limb of another tree received it on more than one occasion that I saw. After depositing the feces the bird wiped and rapped its beak on the limb vigorously." He also relates the following:

One day as Dr. Tracy I. Storer and I stood near, a parent, grasping with its beak, seized a nestling by the shoulder, and after a rough tussle pulled the chick out and let it go fluttering to the ground. There, after a rest, during which parental solicitude obviously urged action, the fledgling fluttered along the ground directly to the base of a huge live pine near-by and began to climb. A yard or two at a time, intervalled by long rests, it finally worked up the trunk to the first limbs, some 50 feet. The astonishing thing was that the fledgling elevated itself up trunk mainly by rapid fluttering of its wings while keeping the body axis parallel with the perpendicular tree trunk, all the while pawing the bark furiously with its feet. Progress was slow, dangerously near no progress, it seemed.

After the young have left the nest, they travel about in a family party until they learn to shift for themselves. These parties later join in larger flocks, made up of several families, and roam through the tree tops during fall and winter.

Plumages.—Ridgway (1904) says that young pygmy nuthatches in juvenal plumage are "similar to adults, but pileum and hindneck gray, only slightly, if at all, different from color of back, and sides and flanks pale buffy brown or brownish buff instead of gray." Apparently, after the postjuvenal molt in August, old and young birds are practically indistinguishable. Adults have a complete postnuptial molt beginning about the middle of July and lasting through most of August; I have seen adults in fresh plumage as early as August 20. In fresh fall plumage the colors are richer and darker, the under parts decidedly buff, and the pale spot on the nape is partially concealed with gray tips.

Food.—Prof. F. E. L. Beal (1907) examined only 31 stomachs of the California races of the pygmy nuthatch and found the food to be divided into approximately 83 percent animal matter and 17 percent vegetable. The largest item of animal food was Hymenoptera, mostly wasps with a few ants, amounting to 38 percent of the whole. Hemiptera came next, 23 percent; "a large proportion of these belong to the family Cercopidae, commonly known as spittle-insects, from the fact that they develop inside of a froth-like substance resembling saliva produced in summer upon grass and various plants and trees. While none of these insects have yet become pests, there can be no doubt that collectively they do considerable harm to plants, as sometimes they are very abundant and subsist entirely upon their sap." Eighteen out of twenty stomachs from the pine woods of Pacific Grove "contained remains of Cercopidae, and six were filled with them. The average for the 18 stomachs is a little more than 76 percent of all the food." Beetles of various families formed about 12 percent of the food, caterpillars 8 percent, and spiders 1 percent. "The vegetable portion is made up almost entirely of seeds, of which a majority are those of conifers, as was to be expected from the habits of the bird."

A few other items have been mentioned by others. R. C. Tate (1925) adds, from Oklahoma, moths, pine nuts, and grasshoppers. Junius Henderson (1927) quotes from Professor Aughey's first report that "four Nebraska stomachs averaged 23 locusts, 4 other insects and four seeds each."

Most of the pygmy nuthatch's food is obtained in the topmost branches of the pine, where it climbs over and under the branches and out to the outermost twigs and among the pine needles. But it also forages on the trunks in true nuthatch fashion, looking for hidden insects, or resorts to the ground to pick up insects and seeds. It can crack the pine nuts with its strong little bill and pick out the seeds. It has been seen darting out into the air after flying insects, or fluttering in front of the terminal twigs of the conifers to pick off insects while poised in the air.

Behavior.—As may be seen from some of the above quotations, pygmy nuthatches are tame, confiding little birds, showing great confidence in human beings or being quite oblivious to their intimate presence; and they have even been known to pursue their nesting activities close to those of humans, apparently unafraid. Their behavior is much like that of their near relatives, the brown-headed nuthatches of the southeastern States; like them they live mostly in the tree tops in merry little parties; they are even more gregarious than their eastern cousins. Except when the pairs are busy with their family affairs, these little birds are almost always seen in small flocks, which increase greatly in size during fall and winter. Mr. Swarth (1904b) says: "During the migrations they seem to form a sort of nucleus for other birds to gather around, and are usually accompanied by a number of migrating warblers, vireos, etc. Many of them [in Arizona] remain in small flocks up to the middle of May, though others may be seen at work at their nests in some old stump early in April; so by the time the last of them are paired off, those that first went to work are nearly ready to appear with their broods, and there is consequently hardly any time when Pygmy Nuthatches are not to be seen in flocks."

These flocks of sociable little birds are full of incessant activity, as they drift through the tree tops in loose formations, twittering constantly to keep in touch with each other, reminding one of the flocks of bushtits that travel in a similar disconnected way through the shrubbery, yet definitely associated. In some ways, too, their behavior reminds one of the titmice or kinglets, especially in their feeding habits.

J. Eugene Law (1929) has published an interesting paper on the climbing technique of this nuthatch, well illustrated with photographs showing the specialized use of the feet. He says: "Down-tree progress for a nuthatch seems to be a series of sidling hops or drops. While the bird is moving, its body rarely, perhaps never, parallels the axis of the tree, and at each pause one foot is usually apparent, clinging up-trunk, its grasp transverse to the axis of the tree. When the bird stops, its body may turn so that the body and head point directly downward, and even then there is always that foot up-trunk holding on while the other foot holds the body out from the tree. * * * It is obvious, if we think a minute, that in this position the function of the up foot is to cling by the toes, while that of the down foot is to support. * * * The sole of the lower foot is depressed against the trunk while that of the upper foot is free." All these points are well shown in his photographs, with the feet widely spread in all crosswise or head-downward positions.

Very little is known about where and how birds spend their nights. Night roosting of passerine birds has been observed in only a few instances for very few species. From what little has been seen, we might infer that hole-nesting birds may prefer to roost in such cavities, though other methods of roosting have been observed. Mrs. A. H. Jones (1930) watched a family of black-eared nuthatches, in Colorado, go to roost for several nights in a bird box made of slabs and attached to the trunk of a large yellow pine. They came regularly each night at about 6:45, entered the box, and apparently spent the night there. But they were not allowed to enjoy this comfortable retreat very long before a house wren appeared one morning and tried to take possession of the box. For a few nights the nuthatches were able to drive out the wren, but eventually the wren secured a mate and filled up the box with twigs, which the nuthatches were unable to remove, and the nuthatches had to give it up.

Voice.—Pygmy nuthatches are noisy birds, and their notes are quite different from those of other nuthatches; especially noticeable is the entire absence of the familiar *yank-yank* of the white-breasted species. Ralph Hoffmann (1927) describes it very well as follows: "They call to one another incessantly with a high staccato *tĭ-dĭ, tĭ-dĭ, tĭ-dĭ,* which becomes a rapid series of high cheeping notes when a number are together, and in spring is combined with a vigorous trill. As they fly they utter a soft *kit, kit, kit.*" Robert Ridgway (1877) thought that "the notes of this species greatly resemble in their high pitch the 'peet' or 'peet-weet' of certain Sandpipers (as *Tringoides* and *Rhyacophilus*), but they are louder and more piercing."

Field marks.—The pygmy nuthatches can be easily distinguished from the other two western nuthatches by the absence of the conspicuous black caps of the white-breasted and red-bellied species. It is much smaller than the former and slightly smaller than the latter. Its coloration is dull, and the black line through the eye and the white spot on the nape are not very conspicuous, except at short range. Its very short tail, its jerky flight, and its habit of crawling over trunks and branches mark it as a nuthatch.

Fall and winter.—These are the seasons of most conspicuous activity and the greatest concentration into large flocks. As fall approaches the little family parties join with other families, adding to their numbers as the season progresses, until the flocks increase to as many as 50 or 100 birds. As these great flocks travel through the woods, they may occupy several trees, but, like the flocks of bushtits, they keep in touch with the general throng with their ceaseless chatter, and the main flock moves along. Associated with these flocks there may be a few white-breasted nuthatches, chickadees, titmice, warblers, or creepers, or perhaps one of the smaller woodpeckers, all intent on their own affairs, but on peaceful terms. The woods seem alive with the merry parties, in which the shrill notes of the nuthatches are most conspicuous.

In winter the nuthatches retreat more or less from the higher altitudes in which they nested, and drift downward, Mrs. Bailey (1928) says as low as 4,000 feet in New Mexico. They descend to some extent from the pine belt and may be seen foraging among the evergreen oaks, or in the juniper and pinyon belt, at this season. But at the first hint of spring they move up again into their beloved yellow pines.

SITTA PYGMAEA LEUCONUCHA Anthony

WHITE-NAPED NUTHATCH

HABITS

This nuthatch was originally described as a local race, living in the higher parts of the Sierra San Pedro Mártir in Baja California, but it is now also recognized as the resident form in the southern counties,

Riverside and San Diego, in California. A. J. van Rossem (1929) remarks: "*Leuconucha* in typical form occurs only south of the Lower California boundary. Birds from north of that point are somewhat intermediate toward *melanotis*, but a good series from the San Jacinto Mountains demonstrates clearly that *leuconucha* extends to that range."

A. W. Anthony (1889), in naming it, says that it "differs from *S. pygmaea* in larger bill, grayer head, more conspicuous nuchal patch and whiter underparts. Compared with the other races, *leuconucha* is characterized by largest size, particularly of bill; paler, more ashy coloration of the upper parts, and least buffy underparts. I can not agree that the amount of white on the nape is of diagnostic value."

Mr. Anthony (1893) called the white-naped nuthatch "the most abundant species on the San Pedro Mártir mountain; found everywhere in the pines. Upon our arrival May 5 this species was mating; noisy little companies of five or six to a dozen were seen chasing one another through the pines, chattering and calling from daylight till dark; although dozens of nests were discovered all were practically inaccessible. A favorite location for the burrow was on the under side of a dead branch, well away from the trunk of a large pine, and from twenty-five to a hundred feet from the ground."

The eggs of the white-naped nuthatch are apparently indistinguishable from those of the other races of the species. The measurements of 23 eggs average 15.7 by 12.0 millimeters; the eggs showing the four extremes measure **16.3** by 12.3, 16.0 by **12.4, 15.0** by 11.7, and 15.4 by **11.6** millimeters.

SITTA PYGMAEA CANESCENS van Rossem

NEVADA NUTHATCH

Mr. van Rossem (1931) described this local race of the pygmy nuthatch as "exactly resembling *Sitta pygmaea leuconucha* Anthony of northern Lower California in pale, ashy gray coloration, but size, particularly of bill, decidedly smaller. Similar in size to *Sitta pygmaea melanotis* van Rossem of the Rocky Mountains, but coloration paler and more ashy throughout, particularly on the head. Measurements of the type, which was selected as showing the racial average in size and color, are: wing, 64.0 mm.; tail, 34.0; culmen from base, 15.0."

He gives the range as "Charleston and Sheep Mountains, extreme southern Nevada, where resident in the yellow pine association from 7,000 to 8,500 feet," and says: "The series of 11 *canescens* are all in relatively fresh fall plumage, indeed seven of them had only just completed the annual moult at the time of collection. The color characters are, therefore, true ones and not the result of wear or fade. * * * The Lower California race, *leuconucha*, the only one resembling *canescens* closely in color, measures on the basis of 10 adult males from the San Pedro Martir Mountains: wing, 68.0 mm.; tail, 36.0; culmen from base, 18.2."

Family CERTHIIDAE: Creepers

CERTHIA FAMILIARIS AMERICANA Bonaparte

BROWN CREEPER

PLATES 14, 15

CONTRIBUTED BY WINSOR MARRETT TYLER

HABITS

The brown creeper, as he hitches along the bole of a tree, looks like a fragment of detached bark that is defying the law of gravitation by moving upward over the trunk, and as he flies off to another tree he resembles a little dry leaf blown about by the wind. As he climbs up the tree, he is feeding, picking up tiny bits of food that he finds half-hidden in the crevices of bark along his path. In his search he does not work like the woodpeckers, those skilled mechanics whose work requires the use of carpenter's tools, the drill and chisel. The creeper's success depends on painstaking scrutiny, thoroughness, and almost, it seems, conscientiousness. Edmund Selous (1901), speaking of the European tree-creeper, a bird close to ours in habit, uses the exact word to show us the creeper at work. "His head," he says, "which is as the sentient handle to a very delicate instrument, is moved with such science, such *dentistry*, that one feels and appreciates each turn of it."

Spring.—The creeper is rather a solitary bird as we see it in its winter quarters and in spring on the way northward to its summer home. We often find it, to be sure, feeding near chickadees, nut-hatches, and golden-crowned kinglets, but there seems to be no close association between it and the other members of the gathering. The creeper pays little or no attention to the birds about him and by no means always follows them in their wanderings.

There is little change in his behavior as spring advances; he is the same calm, preoccupied searcher he has been all through the winter, but before the close of March he may, on rare occasions, sing his delicate song. When we hear it—a strangely wild song for so prosaic a character—we, who live not too far from the creeper's northern forests, suspect that the singer may have a mate, or is attempting to acquire one, and if the song continues into May, and if the bird frequents a locality where the trees are broken, burned, or dying, we shall do well to look about for a nest, or the preparation for one, because the bird often breeds well to the south of its normal range, provided that the surroundings are favorable for nesting.

Ordinarily we meet but one creeper, or at most two, in a woodland of moderate extent, but Dayton Stoner (1932) states: "During May 1929 season, when the brown creeper was unusually common in several districts on the south side of Oneida Lake [New York], I often came upon small groups of three to six individuals in the woods, all within a few yards of one another. Perhaps not another individual would be seen for an hour or even during the entire morning. This apparent concentration of birds within localized areas led me to believe that a more or less concerted movement was taking place and that the species traveled in loose groups, not close enough to be termed flocks."

Courtship.—The creeper's courtship appears to consist of a display of agility in the air. Once in a while we see a bird launch out from a tree and at top speed twine around it close to the bark, then dart away and twist around another tree, or weave in and out among the surrounding trees and branches. He has thrown off his staid creeper habits and has become for the time a care-free aerial sprite, giving himself up, it seems, to an orgy of speed, wild dashes, and twists and turns in the air. But after a round or two, back on the bark again, he resumes his conventional routine and becomes once more a brown creeper.

Chreswell J. Hunt (1907) describes a somewhat similar excursion through the air, associated with the pursuit of another creeper. He says:

It was on March 9, 1904, * * * that I saw two Brown Creepers engaged in this game of tag. In my experience the Brown Creeper always alights near the base of a tree trunk and then works upward, his course being a spiral one—he travels round and round as he climbs upward. In the pursuit I speak of this same program was carried out, only instead of climbing up the trunk the birds would fly up. They alighted near each other upon the tree, then number one would take wing and fly upward, describing one or two complete spirals about the trunk and again alight upon it with number two following in close pursuit. To travel in a spiral course seemed to be such a well formed habit that they could not get away from it. It was not simply a chance flight, for I saw it repeated again and again.

Nesting.—There is a bit of interesting history in regard to the nesting of the brown creeper. Alexander Wilson (Wilson and Bonaparte, 1832) says: "The brown creeper builds his nest in the hollow trunk or branch of a tree, where the tree has been shivered, or a limb broken off, or where squirrels or woodpeckers have wrought out an entrance, for nature has not provided him with the means of excavating one for himself." He says nothing, however, about the nest itself. Thomas Nuttall's (1832) remarks on the situation of the nest consist, as usual, in a rephrasing of Wilson's report, but Audubon (1841a), while obviously copying Wilson in speaking of the situation of the nest, adds that he himself has found nests, saying: "All the nests which I have seen were loosely formed of grasses and lichens of various sorts, and warmly lined with feathers, among which I in one instance found some from the abdomen of *Tetrao Umbellus.*"

Many years later, with the idea of setting right a long-standing error of the older ornithologists as to the situation of the creeper's nest, Dr. Thomas M. Brewer (1879) published an article in the spring of 1879 in which he says:

In "North American Birds" [i. e., Baird, Brewer, and Ridgway, 1874] it is said to breed in hollow trees, in the deserted holes of Woodpeckers, and in decayed stumps and branches of trees. This statement is rather legendary than positively ascertained, and I am now inclined to somewhat modify this opinion, the more so that I learn from Mr. Dresser that the European *C. familiaris* usually places its nest between the detached bark and the trunk of a large tree. This exactly describes the situation of the nest found in Grand Menan, and of six or seven other nests since identified and described to me. All of these nests have been in just such situations and in no other. Instead of this being exceptional, it is probable that this is our Creeper's most usual mode of nesting, and that this is one of several reasons that unite to make this nest one so rarely discovered.

The hint contained in this article aroused the interest of William Brewster (1879), who, in the following spring, searched the region of Lake Umbagog, Maine, for creepers' nests and in the fall published an account of his investigations. "During former seasons," he says, "I had wasted much valuable time in sounding old Woodpecker's holes and natural cavities about places where the birds were evidently nesting; but, with the right clew at last in my possession, I succeeded on this occasion in finding quite a number of nests." The following description of a nest is a good example of those he found:

The tree selected was a tall dead fir, that stood in the shallow water just outside the edge of the living forest, but surrounded by numbers of its equally unfortunate companions. Originally killed by inundation, its branches had long ago yielded to the fury of the winter storms, and the various destroying agents of time had stripped off the greater part of the bark until only a few persistent scales remained to chequer the otherwise smooth, mast-like stem. One of these, in process of detachment, had started away from the trunk below, while its upper edges still retained a comparatively firm hold, and within the space thus formed the cunning little architect had constructed her nest. The whole width of the opening had first been filled with a mass of tough but slender twigs (many of them at least 6 inches in length), and upon this foundation the nest proper had been constructed. It was mainly composed of the fine inner bark of various trees, with an admixture of a little *Usnea* moss and a number of spiders' cocoons. The whole mass was firmly but rather loosely put together, the different particles retaining their proper position more from the adhesion of their rough surfaces than by reason of any special arrangement or interweaving. The general shape of the structure necessarily conformed nearly with that of the space within which it was placed, but a remarkable feature was presented by the disposition of the lateral extremities. These were carried upward to a height of several inches above the middle of the nest, ending in long narrow points or horns, which gave to the whole somewhat the shape of a well-filled crescent. In the centre or lowest part of the sag thus formed was the depression for the reception of the eggs—an exceedingly neat, cup-shaped hollow, bordered by strips of soft, flesh-colored bark and lined with feathers from Ducks and other wild birds. The whole was fastened to the concave inner surface of the bark-scale rather than to the tree itself, so that when the former was detached it readily came off with it.   *   *   *

With respect to their general plan of construction, all of the eight nests which I have examined were essentially similar. Indeed, the uniform character of the nesting-sites chosen by the different pairs of birds was not a little remarkable. Thus, in every single instance that came under my observation, the nest was placed on a balsam fir, though spruce, birch, or elm stubs were often much more numerous, and frequently presented equally good accommodations. Again, in no instance did the tree resorted to retain more than three or four pieces of bark, while oftentimes the scale that sheltered the nest was the only one that remained. The height varied from 5 to 15 feet, but this particular was perhaps sometimes determined more by necessity than by any individual preference, as I noticed that when several equally suitable bark-scales occurred on the same tree, the lowest was invariably the one taken. In one such case the nest was so low that I could easily look into it by standing up in my boat. As before indicated, the size and shape of the different structures varied with that of the cavities in which they were placed. When the space between the bark and trunk was very narrow, the foundation of sticks was entirely dispensed with, the nest being then entirely composed of bark. Of the five examples now before me, only two are feather-lined, the remaining three being simply finished with shreds of the reddish inner fir-bark of a somewhat finer quality than those which make up the outer part of the structure. The most striking feature of all is the prolongation of the upper corners, already described. In one extreme specimen these horns rise four inches above the central cup that contains the eggs. They are, perhaps, designed to act as stays or supports, as they are firmly attached to the rough inner surface of the bark which sustains the nest.

The experience of Dr. Brewer and Mr. Brewster proved satisfactorily that creepers build their nests behind bits of loosened bark, yet there remained a good record by Professor Aughey, who in 1865 had found a nest in a knothole. Brewster (loc. cit.) investigated this record and explains it in this way:

Were it not for Professor Aughey's testimony we might fairly be inclined to suspect that all our earlier accounts of this Creeper's nesting were either founded upon hearsay or were purely fictitious. But we have this gentleman's satisfactory assurance that in Nebraska the Creeper does sometimes nest in holes in trees. Being desirous of obtaining further particulars regarding the nest mentioned by him in his paper on "The Nature of the Food of the Birds of Nebraska," and referred to by Dr. Brewer in the April Bulletin, I wrote to Professor Aughey on the subject, and the following is an extract from his very courteous reply: "In reference to *Certhia familiaris*, it is certain that in Nebraska, where its favorite position for nesting under scales of loose bark is in some localities difficult to obtain, it makes a nest in knot-holes. I have found two other nests in such places,—one in June 1877, between Bellevue and Omaha, on the Missouri Bluffs, in a box-elder tree; another in June of the present season on Middle Creek, 4 miles from Lincoln, also in a box-elder. I have also found several in the ordinary positions where old cottonwoods or elms abounded. It is therefore my conviction that this method of nesting in knot-holes was inaugurated because of the scarcity of the ordinary positions. I could not find any tree near by where a nesting-place under bark could have been obtained in these instances of nesting in knot-holes."

The records of Macoun and Macoun (1900) may perhaps be accounted for in the same way. They say: "Have taken several nests at Ottawa, always in deserted woodpecker's holes."

A creeper's nest presents an odd appearance when it and the bark to which it adheres firmly are removed from the tree. In shape it is like a loosely hung hammock or a new moon, the horns built high up at the sides of the nest, which seems to hang suspended between them. The structure bears a striking resemblance to those little windrows that we see on a forest path after the passing of a summer shower when the flowing water has pushed along the loose twigs, leaves, and pine needles and has left them lying in long, curved heaps, crescent-shaped like the creeper's nest.

The nest is apparently built entirely by the female bird, but her mate often brings in nesting material and delivers it to her. I quote from my notes (Winsor M. Tyler, 1914) taken as I watched a pair building a nest in Lexington, Mass., in 1913:

When we first came upon the pair, the female was making long flights from the nest. She brought in bits of bark and some fuzzy material (fern down or caterpillar webbing). We saw her collect also bits of bark from nearby trees. Twice at least the male brought material and delivered it (bark or dead wood) to the female who was in the nest cavity. The female made half a dozen long flights, returning every 2 minutes. Then she flew eight times in the next 10 minutes to a very small dead white pine a few yards away and returned each time with one or more fine twigs. Often after returning with a twig 6 inches long, she had some difficulty in forcing it through the entrance hole. She was wise enough, however, to turn her head so that the twig might slip in end first. Once, when she brought in a beakful of fern down, the material kept catching on the rough bark and tripping her up, but by bending her neck backward she was able to hold the stuff clear of the mark. In her trips to the little dead pine, the Creeper always alighted on the slender trunk, but in order to reach the terminal twigs she had to hop out on the smaller branches. Sometimes, when these were very small, she perched crosswise upon them; often she crawled around them,—her back to the earth. When perched, her tail hung straight downward, like a Phoebe's or a Brown Thrasher's when he sings. She broke off the twigs by tugging at them while perched or while fluttering in the air * * *.

The use of both the fern down and the webbing is, I believe, to bind the twigs together and to hold the nest to the bark, against which it rests. In the first nest site, if it had not been for this adhesion, the nest would have fallen to the ground of its own weight, for its base was unsupported. * * *

The female flew to the nest with a bit of bark (2½ × ¼ inches) then pulled from the protruding base of the nest a piece of bark and took it into the cavity. Five minutes later she (or her mate) crept again to the base and pulled off a bit of bark which she carried within. The economical habit of using material twice (first for the foundation and later for building the nest proper) is apparently a common practice. We saw it again and again.

Verdi Burtch (MS.) points out that the extensive killing of trees furnishes brown creepers with many sites suitable for nesting. He says: "In the very cold winter of 1903 or 1904, with water 2 to 3 feet deep in Potter Swamp, New York, the ice froze to such a depth that hundreds of trees were killed. A few years later, the bark below the water line came off, and the bark higher up split and, curling inward, made ideal nesting sites for the creepers. This was the condition in 1906 and 1907, and the creepers were quick to take advantage of it."

A similar condition prevailed in eastern Massachusetts about 1913, following an invasion of gypsy moths.

In addition to such fortuitous nesting sites as those mentioned above, there are other stations far to the south of the creeper's normal breeding range where the bird finds surroundings adapted to its nesting requirements. For example, Kennard and McKechnie (1905) found several nests in inundated white cedar swamps near the town of Canton, Massachusetts, and Dr. Arthur P. Chadbourne (1905) found a nest containing young in a similar swamp in Plymouth County, Mass. He remarks: "The conditions which determine the distribution of the Creeper in this region, are apparently a very moist, humid atmosphere, dense evergreen growth, through which the sun penetrates with difficulty, and considerable extent of wild woodland which is not disturbed by man throughout the nesting season."

Arthur Loveridge (MS.) found two deserted nests, each holding three eggs, behind the shutters of a cabin on an island in the Belgrade Lakes, Maine.

Eggs.—[AUTHOR'S NOTE: The brown creeper lays four to eight eggs to a set, most commonly five or six. They are usually ovate in shape, with variations toward short-ovate, or more often toward elliptical-ovate. The ground color is generally pure white but sometimes creamy white. They are usually more or less sparingly marked with small spots, fine dots, or mere pin points; the larger spots are often concentrated in a ring about the larger end, in which case the rest of the egg has only a few fine markings; some eggs are nearly immaculate. Shades of reddish brown predominate in the markings, such as "hazel" or other bright browns, but darker browns, such as "Kaiser brown" or "liver brown," are not rare. I have seen one unusual set that was heavily marked with these darker browns in large blotches three-sixteenth of an inch long.

The measurements of 40 eggs in the United States National Museum average 15.1 by 11.8 millimeters; the eggs showing the four extremes measure 15.8 by 12.2, 15.5 by 12.7, and 13.7 by 10.7 millimeters.]

Young.—The nestling creeper has not far to go to reach his native bark, and in 13 or 14 days after hatching he is ready to undertake the short journey. The following note tells of a brood that I (1914) watched on their first day after leaving the nest:

The young birds left the Concord nest early on June 4 (possibly June 3). At 8 a. m., two were clinging, 30 feet from the ground, to the trunk of a living white pine tree which stood not far from the nest. One or two more were on another pine trunk. The little birds were extremely difficult to find by reason of their small size, their distance from the ground, their inconspicuous color and especially because each took a station in the dark shadow immediately below a horizontal limb. Here they remained motionless for many minutes. Later, two young birds, one following the other, moved upward by feeble hitches and perched or squatted close to the trunk in the right angle formed by the limb. In hitching over the bark, they moved almost straight upward and whenever I saw them as a silhouette against the sky, and could thus determine the point, they did not use their tails for support. The shortness of the young Creeper's tails gave to their bodies a rounded, unbird-like outline and, with their short, stubby bills of wide gape and their squatting position on the upright bark they suggested tree-toads in no small degree. Like most young birds after they leave the nest, the fledgling Creepers were more noisy than they had been the day before. They announced their whereabouts to their parents with a note not previously heard—a high sibilant call, "*tssssi*," or sometimes clearly divided into two syllables thus: "*ts-tssi*." The voice was very slightly tremulous and, although the pitch and delivery of the notes were decidedly Creeper-like, they suggested to Mr. Faxon and me a flock of Cedarbirds.

William Brewster (1938) states that the young birds "when held against the trunk of a tree instantly crept upwards using the short tail precisely in the manner of the old bird." Dayton Stoner (1932) speaks of the young creepers thus:

Below the nest, the bark clung firmly to the tree, but above, it bulged out so that it formed a canopy for the nest beneath which the young birds might have taken their first lessons in climbing.

As I stood viewing the situation in general and the young birds in particular four of them climbed into this covered space and, as I attempted to capture them, made a short flight into the surrounding vegetation. A little later I saw an adult feeding one of the youngsters clinging to the side of a tree. The young one did fairly well in its first attempts at climbing in the open, but seemed to have some difficulty in clinging to the smooth bark of the maples and moved about on these trees until it came to a little ledge of bark where it appeared more comfortable.

Cordelia J. Stanwood (MS.) estimates the incubation period as about 11 or 12 days.

Plumages.—[AUTHOR'S NOTE: The young nestling is sparsely covered on feather tracts of the upper parts with dark gray down, which later adheres to the tips of the juvenal plumage. This first plumage is much like that of the adult, but the colors are paler and duller and the plumage is softer and looser; the streaks on the head and back are broader and less sharply defined and tinged brownish; the rump is paler russet, and the wing coverts are edged with pale buff; the under parts are buffy white, flecked on the chin, throat, and sides with dusky.

A partial postjuvenal molt, beginning early in August and involving all the contour plumage, wing coverts, and tail, but not the rest of the wings, produces a first winter plumage which is practically indistinguishable from that of the adult. Dr. Dwight (1900) says of this plumage: "Similar to previous plumage. Above darker, the rump much rustier, the crown and back with white shaft streaks, wing covert edgings whiter. Below, silky white, the crissum faintly cinnamon; tail olive-brown on the inner webs, Isabella color externally, a faint barring discernible, the middle pair of rectrices more broadly and less distinctly barred than in the juvenal plumage."

Adults have a complete postnuptial molt in August. Fall birds are usually darker, more suffused with buffy, especially on the flanks and under tail coverts, and the white wing markings are tinged with buffy white. Spring birds are somewhat faded above and dingy white below.]

Food.—Speaking of the food of the brown creeper, W. L. McAtee (1926a) says:

The bird must have a close and important relation with forest insects, but unfortunately studies have not yet been made that disclose the details of its food habits. However, we know that it devours weevils, leaf beetles, flat-bugs, jumping plant lice, leaf hoppers, scale insects, eggs of katydids, ants, and other small hymenoptera, sawflies, moths, caterpillars, cocoons of the leaf skeleton-izers (*Bucculatrix*), pupae of the codling moth, spiders, and pseudoscorpions. It takes only a little vegetable food, chiefly mast. Most of the insects the Brown Creeper is known to feed upon are injurious to trees and we may safely reckon this small but very close associate of trees as one of their good friends.

Dayton Stoner (1932) remarks: "Most of the insects taken are highly destructive; and many of them and their eggs, and immature stages as well, are so small as to be overlooked by the majority of arborial birds. That this bird is a valuable ally of the forester and horticulturist cannot be doubted."

Francis H. Allen sends us the following note: "When feeding on the ground or on hard snow, as it occasionally does, it hops with the legs far apart and the body resting back on the tail, or apparently so. The bird in this rather pert attitude looks very different from the demure and rather humdrum creeper we usually see on the tree-trunk."

Behavior.—We think of the creeper as always climbing upward over the bark in a straight or spiral course until, after reaching a fair height on the trunk, he drops to the base of another tree to ascend it in like manner. This is his ordinary way of feeding, but he often varies it. We may sometimes see him take a short hop backward to re-investigate a crevice in the bark, or take a hop sideways to broaden the field of his research, and, as we have noted under "Nesting," a bird may visit a slender branch and even perch on it, and he may also hitch along the underside of a horizontal branch, his back to the ground. Dr. Arthur P. Chadbourne (1905) speaks of a bird making "a horizontal run sideways and most decidedly crablike," and A. Dawes Du-Bois (MS.) notes the action of a creeper thus: "He proceeded up the tree for a while, but soon began to search the branches, usually working outward from the trunk to the tip, and then flying back to the base of another branch. He seemed more at home on the under side of a limb than on top of it, for he went over the top only occasionally; evidently most of his food is to be found on the under side."

O. A. Stevens, of Fargo, N. Dak., in a letter to Mr. Bent, describes the behavior of creepers at his feeding station. He says: "From all our observations we feel that they are slow to change their habits. In the early winter of 1941–42, three birds appeared in the tree near our window shelf and repeatedly worked up the tree past suet, nuts, and doughnuts where other birds were feeding, but rarely paid any attention to the food. After a time they came to the window shelf and ate the chopped peanuts regularly. It was amusing to see them swallow pieces as large as a millet seed. Once I saw a creeper pound a larger piece of suet against the tree.

"Dr. W. J. Breckenridge of Minnesota told me that the creepers were fond of peanut butter put in holes of a stick. I prepared such a stick and hung it in the tree. The first results were disappointing. Once a bird sampled it and went on up the tree wiping his bill every few hops. A week or two later they were seen to visit it frequently, remaining for some little time. One day when I took it down, they looked for it repeatedly. The tree stands some 10 feet from the window shelf. In coming to the shelf, the birds always work up the tree to the level of the shelf or higher, watch to see if the coast is clear, then drop as if to reach the side of the house below, but rising to alight on the shelf. They never come *down* to the shelf as most birds do. Frequently they eat a little snow from the tree; occasionally they walk out from the base of the tree on the ground. When they drop to a lower part of the tree, they always seem to fall off their perch and flutter, insectlike for a few moments."

The brown creeper is not a shy bird as we meet it during its migration; it doubtless sees few men on its breeding grounds in the northern forests. Clarence M. Arnold (1908) relates the following instance of the bird's disregard of man:

While walking along a wide wood-path I stopped to observe a mixed flock of winter birds in the trees nearby. There were Chickadees, Golden-crowned Kinglets, a Downy Woodpecker and a Brown Creeper, the latter being the first I had seen this season. For this reason, and also because this species is much rarer than the others, I was watching it closely through my field glass, standing almost motionless in the center of the path; meanwhile, it flew to the base of a chestnut tree about 50 feet from me, and hitched its way up the rough bark. It had reached the lowest branches, about 20 feet from the ground, when suddenly it left the tree and darted straight at me, and, to my amazement, alighted on the left leg of my trousers, just above my shoe, in front, evidently mistaking the black and gray color for the bark of a tree.

Arthur C. Bent (MS.) gives another example of the fearlessness of a bird on her nest. He says: "Hersey and I had been watching a pair of creepers in a pine grove, mixed with a few other trees, partly swampy. Today we found the nest 17 feet up under a loose slab of bark on a large dead white pine. The female bird could not be driven off the nest by rapping the tree or shaking the loose slab; Hersey had to poke her off."

Mrs. A. L. Wheeler (1933) reports the roosting of creepers on the porch of her house. She says: "For the last two winters I have been having some Brown Creepers clinging to the rough stucco in the entrance of our front door. Last winter there were two of them. They came about 4 o'clock, seldom later; they would fly to the bottom, then climb to the top, and 'snuggle' close together in the corner. I put a protection near, to keep the cold wind off them, but they would not come near until I removed it. They paid no attention to persons passing through the door, although they were within easy reach."

One winter afternoon at dusk I saw a creeper settle, evidently for the night, about 6 feet from the ground on the rough bark of a big white-ash tree. A cat was watching the bird and started to climb up toward it. When I drove the cat away, the creeper moved farther up the tree and settled again on the bark.

Some years ago I spent many hours observing the breeding activities of a pair of creepers. I append a quotation from my notes taken at the time (Winsor M. Tyler, 1914):

In watching a pair of Brown Creepers about their nest, whether they are building, incubating their eggs, or feeding their young, one is soon impressed by an air of happiness and calm which pervades the active little birds. From the behavior of many birds, one comes to associate the finding of a nest with anxiety expressed in various ways—with the nervous panic of the Warblers, the Robin's hysterical apprehension, the noisy complaint of the Crow and even with the polite uneasiness of the gentle Field Sparrow. The Brown Creeper, however, although doubtless observant, does not seem to look upon man as a danger; he continues his work uninfluenced, I believe, by close scrutiny. Happy and calm, even under observation, the Creepers appear preoccupied in their work and the comradeship of a pair is very pretty to see. The male shares with the female her interest in the progress of the nest; even although he knows nothing of nest building he collects material and offers it to his mate. Ever ready to assist, he feeds the female while she builds and while she is sitting and, after the young are hatched, he is no less industrious than she in caring for their needs.

Francis Zirrer sends us the following note: "In April 1941, a farmer nearby called my attention to some little brown birds that climb trees coming nightly to a hollow beam, at the end of his barn, that protrudes about 2 yards from the building to within a few feet of several pine trees, part of a considerable grove of pines, into which the farm buildings are set. According to him the birds come every night, enter the opening at the end of the beam, and remain there for the night. With a long pole, and standing on a ladder, I was able to touch the beam, which has such small entrance that it is hardly noticeable from the ground, 25 feet lower. It was quite dark, but upon the touch with the pole, the birds at once began to come out, some flying to the trees nearby, others climbing around the beam or upon the walls of the barn. This, however, was enough, the birds were not molested further. We waited awhile, but it was too dark already, and we could not see whether the birds returned. Next evening, however, we were there earlier, and had the satisfaction to know that the disturbance of the previous night was apparently forgotten; altogether 11 birds entered the beam, but it took quite a while, and much moving in and out, flying back and forth, and climbing around the beam, nearby wall and trees before everybody was settled for the night."

Frederick V. Hebard writes: "This familiar creeper, so common in the Thomasville-Tallahassee region, is absent or extremely rare in southeastern Georgia, except in times of extremely dry weather. Its nearsightedness is nowhere better illustrated than in our tangled branches and river swamps where, instead of dropping to the base of a tree after having reached the top of a nearby one, it drops only to the point where the trunk emerges above the underbrush."

Voice.—How seldom we should see the creeper if he did not sound his little note! Yet what a faint little note it is, the shortest, lightest pronunciation of the letters *ts*. He utters it as he climbs upward over the bark and as he flits downward to the base of the next tree. He often gives also a longer, more characteristic note, which may be suggested by the letters *zi-i-i-it*, a long, high, ringing note, but not loud, apparently broken into minute syllables so that it has a quavering effect. This note resembles the sound made by a small steel chain which, held by the end and let fall, tinkles into a little heap. A third note, more rarely heard, is a whistle, exquisitely pure, exceedingly high, and, if it were not so tiny, piercingly sharp. It may be given as a single long whistle or in a series of three or four shorter whistles. This note is clearly not a modification of the song, for it is used in the winter months and is not delivered with the cadence of the true song; it is, perhaps, a whistled form of the *zi-i-i-it* note.

The song of the creeper, heard rarely during migration, but commonly on the bird's nesting grounds, is one of the gems of bird music. Most often a phrase of five notes, a dactyl and a trochee, it is a simple, modest little strain, but it is delivered with such delicacy and daintiness and in a tone so pure and sweet that when he sings we feel we are listening to a delightful bit of verse.

Aretas A. Saunders (MS.) says of it: "The song of the brown creeper is rather rarely heard. I hear it once in several years in the spring migration in April. On the breeding grounds the song evidently continues till the middle of July or later. It is short, weak, and very high-pitched. The pitch varies from the A above the highest note on the piano to the E above that. Most of the songs begin with a rather long note followed by one or two shorter notes that are a third lower in pitch, and these notes are repeated immediately, the six notes constituting the entire song. This may be varied a little by dropping one or two of the short notes or varying the pitch, but a majority of creeper songs are built on this plan."

Frank Bolles (1891) gives a word of praise to the creeper's song. He says: "While watching and admiring these gay survivors of the winter [two butterflies and a moth], we heard a brown creeper sing. It was a rare treat. The song is singularly strong, full of meaning and charm, especially when the size of its tiny performer is remembered."

Field marks.—The brown creeper is a tiny bird not much over 5 inches long and nearly half of his length is taken up by his long tail. He is brown on the back, faintly streaked with pale gray, and beneath he is pure white. His beak is long, needle-sharp, and bent downward in a long curve. His wings, rather long for so small a bird, make him appear larger when he opens them in flight.

Enemies.—William Brewster (1936) describes the pursuit of a creeper by a northern shrike. He says:

When I first saw him he was in hot pursuit of one of the Brown Creepers and both birds were about over the middle of the river and scarce a yard apart. The Creeper made straight for the big elm which stands at the eastern end of the bridge. When he reached it, the Shrike's bill was within 6 inches of his tail, but he nevertheless escaped, for an instant after the two birds doubled around behind the trunk the Shrike rose to the topmost spray of the elm, where he sat for a minute or more, gazing intently downward, evidently watching for the Creeper. The latter, no doubt, had flattened himself against the bark after the usual practice of his kind when badly frightened and he had the nerve and good sense to remain perfectly still for at least *10 minutes.* My eyes were no better than the Shrike's, for it was in vain that I scanned the trunk over and over with the greatest care. Feeling sure, however, that the Creeper was really there, I waited patiently until at the end of the period just named he began running up the trunk, starting at the very point where I had seen him disappear. It was one of the prettiest demonstrations of the effectiveness of protection coloration that I have ever witnessed.

Bradford Torrey (1885) tells thus of the defensive response of a creeper to the scream of a hawk:

It was the last day of my visit, and I had just taken my farewell look at the enchanting prospect from the summit, when I heard the lisp of a brown creeper. This was the first of his kind that I had seen here, and I stopped immediately to watch him, in hopes he would sing. Creeper-like he tried one tree after another in quick succession, till at last, while he was exploring a dead spruce which had toppled half-way to the ground, a hawk screamed loudly overhead. Instantly the little creature flattened himself against the trunk, spreading his wings to their very utmost and ducking his head until, though I had been all the while eying his motions through a glass at the distance of only a few rods, it was almost impossible to believe that yonder tiny brown fleck upon the bark was really a bird and not a lichen. He remained in this posture for perhaps a minute, only putting up his head two or three times to peer cautiously round.

Fall and winter.—The earliest brown creepers that come down into southern New England in fall find the woods almost silent and deserted. The jolly little summer residents have mostly begun their journey southward, and few migrants from the north have arrived thus early— only the vanguard of the blackpoll flight and the earliest juncos. It is sometimes in the first half of September when the first creepers quietly and almost unnoticed appear on their winter quarters, before the trees have dropped their leaves, and when the first frost may be a month away, yet they bring us long in advance the first hint of winter. During their migration, we often see the creepers on the trees bordering the streets of our towns, in our city parks, almost anywhere where there are large trees, but for the winter months they settle in woodlands or in the trees of large estates.

Speaking of the creeper on Mount Mitchell, N. C., Thomas D. Burleigh (1941) says: "Unlike the preceding [red-breasted nuthatch] this species, while it nests in the fir and spruce woods at the top of the mountain, invariably retreats to the valleys in late fall and has never been found above an altitude of approximately 4,500 feet during the winter months."

Mr. and Mrs. Arthur Argue had a very unusual experience on October 31, 1944, at Newburyport, Mass., near the seacoast. Mr. Argue writes: "Walking toward Pine Island [a wooded area in the marsh] we observed 20 brown creepers. The birds were climbing up the sides of buildings, up telephone poles, and fence posts as well as trees. Proceeding to Pine Island we found 30 more creepers. Here they were on trees and rocks and even on the ground. One bird alighted for a moment on my trouser leg."

DISTRIBUTION

Range.—The greater part of the Northern Hemisphere; in America, from southern Alaska and southern Canada to Nicaragua.

Breeding range.—In America the breeding range of the brown creeper extends **north** to southern Alaska (Tyonek and the Kenai Peninsula); northern British Columbia (Flood Glacier, Nine Mile Mountain, and Hazelton); central Alberta (Glenevis and Camrose); southern Manitoba (Winnipeg); central Ontario (Kapuskasing, Cobalt, and Ottawa); southern Quebec (Rouge River Valley and Grand Greve); and Newfoundland (Stephenville). **East** to Newfoundland (Stephenville and Makinsons Grove); New Brunswick (Bathurst); Nova Scotia (Advocate); Massachusetts (Essex County and Mount Graylock); and in the mountains south to North Carolina (Grandfather Mountain). **South** to western North Carolina (Grandfather Mountain); Tennessee (Mount Guyot); northern Michigan (Beaver Islands); Minnesota (St. Paul); eastern Nebraska (Omaha and Lincoln); Wyoming (Wheatland); south through the Rocky Mountains of Colorado (Estes Park and Fort Garland); New Mexico (Taos and Cloudcroft); the highlands of Mexico (Arroyo del Buey, Durango, and Tizayuca, Morelos); Guatemala (Volcán de Fuego and Tecpam); to Nicaragua (San Rafael del Norte); and southern California (Strawberry Valley and Mount Wilson). **West** to California (Strawberry Valley, Fort Tijon); principally in the mountains of California (Yosemite Valley and Mount Shasta); Oregon (Rogue River Valley and Portland); Washington (Mount Rainier and Bellingham); British Columbia (Queen Charlotte Islands); and Alaska (Tyonek).

Winter range.—The winter range extends **north** to southeastern British Columbia (Comox, Chilliwack, and Okanagan Valley); North Dakota (Grafton and Fargo); Minnesota (Minneapolis); Ontario (Ottawa); and Nova Scotia (Pictou). From this line brown creepers are found in winter south through all the States to the Gulf coast, northern Mexico (Chihuahua); and southern California (Victorville and Whittier).

The range as outlined refers to the entire species in America, which is broken up into seven Check-list races with additional races resident in Mexico, Guatemala, and Nicaragua.

The typical race (*C. f. familiaris*) is confined to the Old World. The eastern brown creeper (*C. f. americana*) occurs from the eastern edge of the Plains, Manitoba to Nebraska eastward, south to Pennsylvania. The southern creeper (*C. f. nigrescens*) is the bird of the southern Appalachians from West Virginia to North Carolina and Tennessee. The Rocky Mountain creeper (*C. f. montana*) occurs from southern Alaska (Cook Inlet), central British Columbia, and in the Rocky Mountains south to Arizona and New Mexico. The Mexican creeper (*C. f. albescens*) ranges from southern Arizona south to Nayarit and Zacatecas, Mexico. The Sierra creeper (*C. f. zelotes*) is found in the Cascades and Sierra Nevada from British Columbia and northern Idaho south to the San Jacinto Mountains of California. The Nevada creeper (*C. f. leucosticta*) is apparently confined to the Charleston and Sheep Ranges of southern Nevada. The California creeper (*C. f. occidentalis*) is found along the Pacific coast from Sitka, Alaska, to Monterey County, Calif.

Spring migration.—Late dates of spring departure from the winter home are: Florida—Pensacola, March 24. Georgia—Athens, April 1. South Carolina—Spartanburg, April 17. North Carolina—Charlotte, April 17. Virginia—Lynchburg, April 15. District of Columbia—Washington, April 24. Pennsylvania—Pittsburgh, May 8. New York—New York, May 10. Massachusetts—Boston, May 16. Arkansas—Tillar, April 4. Tennessee—Nashville, April 17. Kentucky—Danville, April 22. Missouri—Columbia, April 26. Illinois—Chicago, April 28. Indiana—Indianapolis, April 25. Ohio—Oberlin, May 9. Ontario—Toronto, May 24. Iowa—Sioux City, May 9. Wisconsin—Madison, May 10. Texas—Somerset, April 1. Oklahoma—Oklahoma City, March 18. Kansas—Onaga, April 28. Nebraska—Lincoln, May 8. South Dakota—Mellette, May 6. North Dakota—Fargo, May 7.

Early dates of spring arrival are: New York—Albany, March 16. Massachusetts—Boston, March 16. Vermont—Rutland, March 16. Maine—Ellsworth, March 19. New Brunswick—St. John, April 24. Quebec—Montreal, March 18. Illinois—Chicago, March 18. Indiana—Indianapolis, March 5. Ohio—Painesville, March 12. Michigan—Sault Ste. Marie, April 10. Ontario—Toronto, April 4. Iowa—Sioux City, March 18. Wisconsin—Madison, March 27. Minnesota—Minneapolis, March 28. South Dakota—Yankton, March 18. North Dakota—Fargo, March 29. Wyoming—Wheatland, April 1. Montana—Great Falls, April 28. Manitoba—Winnipeg, April 17. Alberta—Glenevis, April 4.

Fall migration.—Late dates of fall departure are: Alberta—Belvedere, October 22. Manitoba—Aweme, October 22. Wyoming—Wheatland, October 27. North Dakota—Fargo, November 6. South Dakota—Faulkton, November 15. Minnesota—St. Paul, October 22. Wisconsin—Racine, November 4. Michigan—Lansing, November 28. Ontario—Ottawa, October 25. Iowa—Keokuk, October 26. Quebec—Quebec, November 23. New Brunswick—St. John, October 8. Maine—Portland, November 6. Vermont—St. Johnsbury, November 17. Massachusetts—Boston, November 20. New York—New York, November 14.

Early dates of fall arrival are: North Dakota—Fargo, September 29. South Dakota—Faulkton, September 18. Nebraska—Hastings, September 28. Kansas—Lawrence, October 1. Oklahoma—Norman, October 17. Texas—Commerce, October 30.

Casual records.—A specimen was taken on Mount McKinley, Alaska. October 21, 1907; and there is a single breeding record for extreme southeastern Missouri. In the Bermuda Islands a specimen was taken from a group of three or four seen on November 24, 1870.

Egg dates.—California: 33 records, April 16 to July 8; 17 records, May 19 to June 11, indicating the height of the season.

New York: 36 records, May 5 to July 18; 18 records, May 17 to May 26.

Ontario: 12 records, May 23 to June 11.

Washington: 39 records, March 27 to July 15; 20 records, May 5 to May 31.

CERTHIA FAMILIARIS NIGRESCENS Burleigh

SOUTHERN CREEPER

In naming and describing this subspecies, Thomas D. Burleigh (1935) says that it is "similar to *Certhia familiaris americana*, but crown and upper half of back distinctly darker, the prevailing color being fuscous black rather than sepia; primaries darker and approaching clove brown; tail more grayish (hair brown); russet of rump darker; underparts grayer."

He gives the distribution as follows: "Breeds in the Canadian Zone of the southern Appalachians from Pocahontas County, W. Va. (Cranberry Glades), to the Great Smoky Mountains in western North Carolina and eastern Tennessee; winters at a lower altitude in this same region."

Burleigh says further: "This southern race of the brown creeper is easily distinguished in fresh winter plumage by the lack of brown on the crown and the upper half of the back. In worn breeding plumage this character is somewhat obscure, but the color of the tail, hair brown rather than pale brown as in *Certhia familiaris americana*, is readily diagnostic, as are the darker primaries. Breeding birds taken in June and July are so badly worn that accurate measurements could not be taken, but apparently there is no appreciable difference in size in the two eastern races."

This subspecies is based on the study of 13 specimens taken in the above-mentioned localities.

CERTHIA FAMILIARIS MONTANA Ridgway

ROCKY MOUNTAIN CREEPER

PLATE 16

HABITS

The Rocky Mountain creeper enjoys the widest distribution of any of the western races of the species. The 1931 Check-list states that it "breeds in boreal zones from central Alaska (Mt. McKinley), central British Columbia, and southern Alberta south in the Rocky Mountains to Arizona and New Mexico." Its summer range is at high altitudes in the mountains in the coniferous forests. In New Mexico, according to Mrs. Bailey (1928), it breeds mainly at altitudes ranging from 7,500 to 9,000 feet; after the breeding season the birds were noted as high as 12,000 feet on Pecos Baldy; but it evidently drifts down to much lower levels in fall and winter. Dr. Mearns (1890) found it no lower than 6,500 feet in the Arizona mountains, where he found it "an abundant summer resident of the spruce, fir and aspen woods of high altitude, ranging to the timber line; much less common in the pines, to which it descends, however, in winter, when it is also occasionally seen in the cedars and piñons of the foot-hills, or in the deciduous timber along the streams in the valleys." In Colorado, W. C. Bradbury (1919) found it breeding at an altitude of nearly 11,000 feet, almost up to timberline. Fred M. Packard writes to me from Estes Park, Colo.: "Pairs of these birds are scattered throughout the conifer forests of the park, the principal nesting habitat being in the Canadian and Hudsonian Zones. Between August and early October a number descend into the Transition Zone, some reaching the plains. Their upward migration is in April."

Nesting.—The nesting habits, and apparently all other habits of the Rocky Mountain creeper, are similar to those of other races and need not be repeated here. Mr. Bradbury (1919) gives the following measurements of a nest that he found in Colorado: "The extreme dimensions of the nest, including foundation, are: Top to bottom, 7 inches; width, 5 inches. While the nest itself was 3 inches deep and 4 inches broad in one direction, the restrictions due to its location confined it to a breadth of 1½ inches in the other direction. In fact, so limited was the space that the bark itself comprised one side of the cup, the latter being 1½ by 2 inches at the rim and 1½ inches deep."

Eggs.—The eggs of this creeper are indistinguishable from those of the other races. The measurements of 20 eggs average 15.9 by 12.3 millimeters; the eggs showing the four extremes measure **17.0** by 12.5, 16.5 by **13.0**, **15.2** by 12.2, and 15.5 by **11.1** millimeters.

Winter.—Frank L. Farley, of Camrose, Alberta, tells me that numbers of these creepers spend the winter in the spruce woods on the Battle River, south of Camrose. He has never seen them foraging on any trees but spruces, nor has he ever seen them there in summer, and on only one or two occasions as migrants.

CERTHIA FAMILIARIS ALBESCENS Berlepsch

MEXICAN CREEPER

PLATE 17

HABITS

This is a Mexican subspecies that extends its range into the United States for only a short distance into southern Arizona, with one record, probably of a straggler, into extreme southwestern New Mexico.

We found the Mexican creeper fairly common in the pine forests of the Huachuca Mountains, above 8,000 feet and near the summits. The keen ears of my companion, Frank C. Willard, frequently heard the faint wiry notes of the birds, but I could not hear them and they were not easy to see, except when they flew from one tree to another. Numerous dead pines in this region offered attractive nesting sites.

This subspecies differs from the other North American races in being darker above and pale brownish gray below, white only on the chin and throat, and with a chestnut, rather than a tawny, rump.

Nesting.—On more than one occasion we spent considerable time following a Mexican creeper about among the dead and living pines near the summit of the Huachuca Mountains, for we knew that eventually the male would call the female off the nest to feed her. Twice the male came near what proved to be the nesting tree, and twice we saw him feed the female; but it was not until the second time that we were able to trace her path back to the nest. She went into a little hole in a big piece of loose bark that hung under a branch, about 35 feet from the ground and near the top of a scraggly dead pine.

The foundation of the nest, which was firmly attached to the bark, consisted of dry pine needles and a few fine twigs; the cup of the nest was well made of fine strips of inner bark and it was profusely lined with feathers. Mr. Willard made the difficult climb to this nest (pl. 17) and secured a set of five fresh eggs on May 15, 1922.

Another set of five eggs was taken, in the same locality on May 30, from a similar nest placed behind a big slab of loose bark on a large dead pine, but only 6 feet above the ground.

Eggs.—I have seen as many as six eggs and as few as four in sets of the Mexican creeper. These are similar to the eggs of other creepers, though what few eggs I have seen are of the finely speckled type. The measurements of 26 eggs average 15.3 by 11.8 millimeters; the eggs showing the four extremes measure 16.4 by 11.4, 14.1 by 12.2, 13.9 by 11.4, and 14.7 by 10.9 millimeters.

Young.—Referring to the Huachuca Mountains, Swarth (1904b) writes: "About the middle of July young birds began to appear, and they seemed more abundant at this time than at any other. As with many other species breeding in the higher parts of the range, a downward movement began about this time, and though never descending to the foothills, in the late summer Creepers were found scattered all through the upper part of the oak belt. The juveniles seem to be attended by their parents for a long time, for up to the first week in September, when young and old were practically indistinguishable in size and general appearance, the families still clung together, and the old birds were seen continually feeding their offspring."

This creeper seems to be only a summer resident in Arizona.

CERTHIA FAMILIARIS ZELOTES Osgood

SIERRA CREEPER

PLATE 18

HABITS

Dr. Wilfred H. Osgood (1901) described this form from specimens collected in the southern Cascade Mountains of Oregon and the Sierra

Nevada of California, but its range has since been extended north-ward to southern British Columbia and northern Idaho, and south-ward to the San Jacinto Mountains of California.

The characters given by the describer are: "Similar to *Certhia f. occidentalis* but colors more dusky and less rufescent; rump decidedly contrasted with rest of upper parts; similar to *Certhia f. montana* but much darker; light centers of feathers on head and back much re-duced." In this race, the rump and upper tail coverts are between "chestnut" and "hazel," whereas in *montana* these parts are "cinna-mon-rufous." In *occidentalis* the color of the rump blends into that of the back, while in *zelotes* and *montana* the colors of these parts are sharply contrasted. Dr. Osgood says further: "This subspecies has generally been included under the name *occidentalis* but it seems to be more similar to *montana* and its characters might be considered intermediate between those of these two. They are perfectly constant throughout its range, however, so that the form is easily recognizable."

In the Lassen Peak region in summer Grinnell, Dixon, and Linsdale (1930) found the Sierra creeper above 3,300 feet, where it breeds. "The range of situations through which the brown creeper feeds is indicated by the following list of trees, on the trunks or limbs of which individuals were observed: valley oak, live oak, blue oak, digger pine, yellow pine, white fir, incense cedar, lodgepole pine. Deciduous trees predominate within the winter range of the creeper, while coniferous trees predominate in the territory occupied in summer."

In the San Bernardino Mountains, in southern California, Dr. Grinnell (1907) found the Sierra creeper more numerous than he had ever seen it elsewhere. "While observed from an altitude of 5,600 feet in the Santa Ana Canyon to as high as 9,500 feet, above Dry Lake, on the north base of San Gorgonio Peak, yet the creepers were most abundantly represented in the canyons from 6,000 to 7,500 feet. This belt of abundance was also the belt in the Transition Zone where the incense cedar (*Libocedrus decurrens*) is conspicu-ously represented."

Nesting.—Referring to his experience in the San Bernardinos, Dr. Grinnell (1907) writes:

Although the majority of the nests found were on cedar trunks, one was on a Jeffrey pine, and at least five were on silver firs. In the latter cases the trees were dead and rotting, for it was only on dead trees that the bark had become loosened and separated enough from the trunk to afford the nar-row sheltered spaces sought by the creepers for nesting sites. But the huge living cedar trunks furnished the ideal situations. For the bark on these is longitudinally ridged and fibrous, and it frequently becomes split into inner and outer layers, the latter hanging in broad loose strips. The narrow spaces behind these necessitate a very compressed style of nest. A typical nest closely studied by me may be described as follows:

The material employed externally was cedar bark strips one-eighth to one-half inch in width. This material had been deposited behind the loosened bark until it packed tightly enough to afford support for the nest proper. The bark strips extended down fully a foot in the cavity, and some of them protruded thru the vertical slit which served the birds as an entrance.,

The main mass of the nest consisted of shredded weathered, inner bark strips of the willow, felted finest internally, where admixed with a few small down-feathers. This nest proper was 6 inches wide in the direction permitted by the space, and only 1¾ inches across the narrow way. The nest-cavity was 1⅛ by 2¼ inches, so that the sitting parent probably always occupied one position diametrically. * * *

Myself and companions examined fully 30 nests, easily discovered after we once learned how to find them, and of these I should judge the average height to have been 6 feet. In other words the majority could be at least touched by the hand as we stood on the ground. One nest was only 3 feet above ground.

Nests have been reported from other localities in similar situations, behind loose strips of bark on cedars and pines, which are the characteristic nesting sites of the species. Emerson A. Stoner (1938), however, reports a decided departure from the usual rule. He found a nest, in Solano County, Calif., in "the end of a badly decayed laurel stub, 4 feet high and 5 inches in diameter. * * * The nest was open to the sky in the hollow tip of the decayed stub about 6 inches down in the hole, the inside measurement of the cavity being approximately 3 inches in diameter. The nest was of fine, thread-like bark strips, matted with feathers and decaying wood dust. I recognized one of the feathers as that of a Steller Jay, and several were from a Horned Owl. The nesting stub was so badly decayed that it would have snapped off with very little pressure."

Eggs.—As a rule, the eggs of all the western subspecies of the brown creeper are similar in number, shape, and coloration to those of the eastern race. Dr. Grinnell (1907) describes two sets of eggs, nine in all, taken in the San Bernardino Mountains, as follows: "The ground-color of the eggs is pure white. The markings are elongated in shape lengthwise of the egg. The brightest markings are burnt sienna, the tint varying from this towards vinaceous as the depth of the markings in the shell substance increases. The darkest markings average 1 millimeter in diameter, while the vinaceous ones vary down to mere points. The markings are most crowded around the large end of the egg-shells, and radiate from this pole in lesser numbers towards the opposite pole."

The measurements of 40 eggs average 15.1 by 11.4 millimeters; the eggs showing the four extremes measure **16.1** by 12.2, 14.7 by **12.2**, **14.0** by 10.9, and 15.0 by **10.0** millimeters.

Young.—Irene G. Wheelock (1904) writes:

Only 9 [?] days are required to hatch the small eggs, and the naked nestlings squirm and wriggle like so many pink mice in the cosy nest. They are slow in feathering, not being fully covered until 15 days old, and even then the down shows through the feathers in hair-like patches. According to the best of my observations with a powerful field glass, they are fed by regurgitation until 4 days old. After that a visible supply of insect food is given them. Their first journey from home is a creeping about on the bark of the nest tree, to which they cling desperately, aided by their sharp little tails. Instinctively they pick at every crevice in the bark, and soon become so business-like about it that they are quite independent of the adults and of each other.

The plumage changes, food, behavior, and voice of the Sierra creeper are all, apparently, similar to those of the other western subspecies and not very different from those of the eastern race.

Winter.—Although permanently resident throughout the year in the Transition Zone of the mountains, the Sierra creeper to some extent wanders down into the foothills and into somewhat different environments in winter. In the Lassen Peak region, Grinnell, Dixon, and Linsdale (1930) found it "present in winter on the western slope down to the lowest altitudes. * * * Although seen usually in rather thick woods, creepers sometimes were found, as at 7 miles east of Red Bluff on December 30, 1927, on the trunks of small, far-separated blue oaks. In winter single creepers were sometimes seen moving along with flocks of feeding bush-tits and kinglets."

John G. Tyler (1913) writes: "The winter of 1910–11 was remarkable for the number of unusual visitants among our avian friends, that appeared in the vicinity of Fresno. By no means the least interesting of these were the little creepers, which occurred quite numerously in the willow trees that border some of the larger ditches, and doubtless elsewhere as well."

CERTHIA FAMILIARIS OCCIDENTALIS Ridgway

CALIFORNIA CREEPER

HABITS

The California creeper occupies the long coastal strip from Sitka, Alaska, to Monterey County, Calif., living in the Canadian and Transition Zones. Whereas the other western races of the brown creeper are mountain birds, during the breeding season at least, this coastal race seems to live and breed at much lower levels, even almost down to sea level. In California it breeds in the great redwood forests, and from there down as far as the Point Lobos Reserve, where Grinnell and Linsdale (1936) found it nesting in the pines. There "a slight preference was shown for the thicker stands of trees, especially where there were old trunks, but this bird followed other species even out among scattered young trees; probably the whole area of pines was covered."

D. E. Brown showed me some of his favorite collecting grounds near South Tacoma, Wash., in which the California creeper was breeding quite commonly, together with several other interesting birds such as Oregon and chestnut-backed chickadees, western golden-crowned kinglets, and Audubon's warblers. It was a large tract of smooth, level, prairielike country that supported a fine open growth of large cedars, two or three species of firs, and a few scattering oaks.

Ridgway (1904) called this the tawny creeper, an appropriate name, also used by others. He says that it is "similar to *C. f. zelotes*, but browner and more suffused with tawny above; wing-markings more pronouncedly buff; under parts more buffy (about as in *C. f. americana*)."

Nesting.—In the locality referred to above, near South Tacoma, Mr. Brown showed me a new nest of the California creeper, which he had found building; it was not over 3 feet from the ground, under a piece of hanging bark on a small, dead oak. This is the locality in which J. H. Bowles tried his interesting and successful experiment of providing artificial nesting sites for these birds. As he (1922) says, he "selected trees with very smooth bark, or else cut the bark down smooth, and nailed against them bark shelters 15 inches or more in length, and 3 or 4 inches in width, leaving a space inside of about 3 inches between the bark and the tree. This inside space will, of course, be tapering towards the bottom, but creepers require a considerable depth for their nests, which are started by a large foundation of twigs, on top of which is built the nestcup of soft bark, feathers, etc."

Prof. Gordon D. Alcorn (MS.) adds the following specifications: "This bark nailed at a convenient height against a vertical tree was furnished with a leaning bark roof and bark floor. With a pocket knife we carved an entrance on each side immediately beneath the roof. The creepers apparently did not care whether the site was natural or not, but they did appear to be rather particular about the entrances. They demanded two. If but one was present, the birds rejected our offering."

Dawson (1923) says that "from a line of, say, 35 or 40 traps he gathers an annual vintage of 5 or 6 sets of creepers' eggs. It is only fair to add that the birds profit in the long run by this arrangement for they are allowed to raise second broods undisturbed throughout an area which offers no other shelter."

Mr. Bowles writes elsewhere (1908) :

Nest building commences about the third week in April, either an oak or a fir being selected for the purpose. The only exception I have ever known to this was one bird that I had watched until it disappeared under a strip of bark fully 60 feet up in a giant cedar. * * * The nest is placed, as a rule, from 2 to 20 feet above the ground, tho the majority that I have seen were under 10 feet. * * * In its composition the nest has a groundwork of twigs, the size of which depends entirely on the dimensions of the space between the bark and the main trunk of the tree. Sometimes only a scant handful is sufficient, while in one nest the twigs would have filled a quart measure to overflowing. Slender dead fir twigs, from 4 to 8 inches long, are almost invariably used, and this must frequently be a most arduous piece of business. Twigs have to be thrust into the crevice until the first dozen or so lodge firmly, then the rest is easy. In every nest quite a little mound of twigs is found on the ground below, showing how persevering the little architects must have been in the face of repeated failure. Probably they consider such twigs as unsuitable; at any rate it never seems to occur to them to pick up a twig when once it has fallen. Scattered amongst this network of twigs is always a little green moss and a considerable amount of down taken from ferns, willows and cotton-woods. What purpose these serve, beyond ornamentation, must be known only to the birds themselves. On top, and firmly embedded, is the egg cup of the nest, which is composed of a thick felting of fine strips from the inner bark of the cedar, with occasionally a few feathers.

Dawson (1910) tells of a nest that contained, in the cup alone, "cowhair (red and black and white), feathers, horsehair, moss, fine bark, macerated weed-stems, chips, fir needles, bits of white cloth, ravelings, string, cocoons, spider-egg cases, catkins, moth-wings, and vegetable fiber." This was a very unusual collection of material.

S. F. Rathbun sends me the following very good description of a nest of the California creeper, found near Tacoma, Wash., on June 2, 1912: "The base of the nest was entirely of bits of bark and rotten wood, this being merely a mass of material lying at the bottom of the space behind the bark. On this was very uniformly placed dry hemlock and fir twigs, these being of a length that conformed perfectly to the spaces remaining at each side of the nest proper, many of these twigs being bent to accomplish this; generally their ends projected upward with the tips curving somewhat beneath; and among these twigs were many flat, thin pieces of inner fir bark and a little rotten wood. What may be called the nest proper was entirely of plant fibres of a grayish color, finely shredded and very soft, this having the appearance of wool, as it was very elastic; and this material was firmly bound on its inner surface by a few horsehairs. It was not carelessly built in any way, but was neatly and carefully put together, and, unlike some others of its kind, substantially built."

Eggs.—Creepers' eggs are all about alike and show similar variations. Those of this subspecies are no exception to the rule. The measurements of 40 eggs of this race average 15.5 by 11.9 millimeters; the eggs showing the four extremes measure **16.7** by 12.4, 16.2 by **12.5, 14.0** by 11.2, and 14.6 by **11.1** millimeters.

Food.—Professor Beal (1907) writes: "Only seven stomachs of the California creeper were available for examination, but they confirm the good opinion observers have formed of the habits of this bird. Like the titmice and nuthatches, the creeper is an indefatigable forager on the trunks and branches of trees, and the food it obtains there is of the same nature—that is, small beetles (many of them weevils), wasps, ants, bugs, caterpillars, and a few spiders.

"Of the seven stomachs examined, only one contained vegetable food,

and this had only 19 percent of seed, too much digested for identification."

Grinnell and Linsdale (1936) saw one "fly out 12 to 15 inches and
catch a flying insect."

Winter.—All through the winter, California creepers wander about,
mostly in pairs or singly, but often associated with the merry little
bands of chickadees, titmice, nuthatches, and kinglets. But they always seem absorbed in their own affairs, diligently searching for their
food on the tree trunks; their association with other species is probably
due to a community of interest rather than to a desire for company,
for creepers are not especially sociable.

CERTHIA FAMILIARIS LEUCOSTICTA van Rossem

NEVADA CREEPER

In naming and describing this local race, Mr. van Rossem (1931)
says: "Among the North American races of *Certhia familiaris* this
is the palest and grayest. Dorsally the coloration resembles, in the
absence of brown tones, *Certhia familiaris albescens* Berlepsch, but
is much paler and the streaks are pure white instead of pale gray.
Ventrally *leucosticta* is clear pure white, tinged on the flanks with
pale gray and on the under tail coverts with pale clay color.

Van Rossem gives the range as "Transition and Alpine Zones in
the Sheep and Charleston Mountains, Clark County, Nevada."

"The five specimens," he says, "on which the new form is based
are uniform in characters and bear little resemblance to *Certhia
familiaris zelotes* Osgood of the Sierra Nevada, or to *Certhia familiaris montana* Ridgway of the Rocky Mountains, with good series of
both of which races they have been compared. In the relative amount
of white on the dorsal surface there is close agreement between
leucosticta and *montana*, but while in *montana* light brown tones
prevail, *leucosticta* is ashy and practically colorless dorsally except on
the rump."

Family CHAMAEIDAE: Wren-tits

CHAMAEA FASCIATA PHAEA Osgood

COAST WREN-TIT

HABITS

The coast wren-tit is the northern race of this California species.
It occupies the humid Transition Zone on the Pacific coast of Oregon,
from the Columbia River southward to the vicinity of the northern
boundary of California. Like many other races of that humid coast
strip, it is the darkest race of the species. Ridgway (1904) calls it
the dusky wren-tit and describes it as similar to the ruddy wren-tit,

its nearest neighbor on the south, "but still darker, the back, etc., deep sepia brown, the pileum and hindneck nearly clove brown, the general color of under parts deep vinaceous-cinnamon or fawn color, with streaks on throat and chest broader (those on throat nearly black)." Evidently the colors of the different races of this species become progressively darker and richer as the range extends northward.

Bernard J. Bretherton (Woodcock, 1902) says: "This species is only met with on a strip of land lying directly along the ocean. Its range is inseparable from the Manzanita bush, and, as far as I know, Yaquina Bay is the limit of its northern range, and it is not found anywhere in our state east of the Coast Range."

Dr. Mary M. Erickson (1938) has contributed such a full and interesting life history of the type race, *Chamaea fasciata fasciata*, that there is practically nothing to be added on the habits of this subspecies and very little on the habits of the other races.

There are four nests of this wren-tit, with sets of four or three eggs each, in the Thayer collection in Cambridge. One was placed in a maple bush, one in a salmonberry bush, one in a huckleberry, and one in a myrtle bush. They are all neat and compactly woven baskets, deeply hollowed and with the rims curved inward at the top. They are made of a variety of plant fibers, weed stalks, and weed blossoms, bound together with strips of grapevine bark, fine grasses, cattle hair, and spider webs; the lining consists of still finer grass and much horsehair or cowhair. One nest has considerable green moss worked into the rim. Externally they measure about 3 inches in height and about the same in diameter; the inner cavity is about 2 inches in diameter at the top and about 1½ inches in depth.

The eggs are indistinguishable from those of the other races of the species. They vary in shape from ovate to short-ovate and have only a slight gloss. The color varies from "pale glaucous blue" to bluish white, and they are immaculate. The measurements of 24 eggs average 18.6 by 14.1 millimeters; the eggs showing the four extremes measure 21.4 by 14.0, 17.8 by 14.7, 17.4 by 14.3, and 17.8 by 13.5 millimeters.

CHAMAEA FASCIATA RUFULA Ridgway

RUDDY WREN-TIT

HABITS

Farther south along the coast of California, from Del Norte County south to Santa Cruz County, in the humid coast strip, is the range of the ruddy wren-tit. This race is not so dark as the coast wren-tit, but it is darker and more richly colored than the type race, Gambel's wren-tit, of the San Francisco Bay region. Ridgway (1904) characterizes it as "similar to *C. f. fasciata*, but more richly colored, the general color of under parts deep pinkish cinnamon or dull vinaceous-cinnamon, the upper parts darker and browner (back, rump, and upper tail-coverts bistre or sepia)."

Apparently what has been written about the habits of the neighboring type race would apply equally well, in most respects at least, to the subspecies. I can find nothing in the literature to indicate anything peculiar in its habits. Its rich coloring is probably due to its humid coast habitat.

There are two sets of eggs with nests of this wren-tit in the Thayer collection in Cambridge. One nest, containing three eggs, was placed against the trunk of a fir tree among some azaleas, at Eureka, Calif. The other nest, taken at Sonoma on May 17, 1895, contained five eggs; this nest is similar to nests of the coast wren-tit but is somewhat less bulky and made of finer materials, with many spider nests on the exterior, and lined with very fine grass and hair; it measures 2½ inches in height and 3 inches in diameter, externally; the inner cavity is 2 inches in diameter and 1¾ inches in depth.

The eggs are indistinguishable from those of the other wren-tits. The measurements of 35 eggs average 18.3 by 14.3 millimeters; the eggs showing the four extremes measure **21.0** by 14.8, 19.9 by **15.0, 16.6** by 14.3, and 18.4 by **13.8** millimeters.

CHAMAEA FASCIATA FASCIATA (Gambel)

GAMBEL'S WREN-TIT

PLATES 19–21

CONTRIBUTED BY MARY M. ERICKSON [1]

HABITS

The wren-tit is a bird that many do not have an opportunity to know, since it represents a monotypic family and its range is restricted to a narrow belt along the Pacific coast from south of the Columbia River down into Baja California. It is principally a bird of the wind-swept brushland of the immediate coast at the northern end of its range, but in California it is found everywhere west of the Sierras in the extensive chaparral belt or in the brushy margins of the forests and streams. Even in the area in which it occurs it is better known by its voice than by its appearance. Casual visitors to the chaparral ask what bird makes the loud-ringing call that may come from the distant ridge or with surprising suddenness from within the nearby bushes. But even if one knows it is nearby it is not easy to see this dweller of the brushland, for it rarely leaves the endless expanse of twigs within the leafy crown to come into the open at the top or to the ground below. If one has the time and patience to wait nearby, its own curiosity will often bring it within view. With practice one can glimpse them, but it is never easy to see them clearly or follow them for any distance.

[1] Derived largely from Erickson, "Territory, Annual Cycle, and Numbers in a Population of Wren-tits," 1938.

The subspecies under consideration, which lives along the coast from San Francisco Bay south to southern Monterey County, I watched intensively for four years. Most of the work was done in a small canyon containing 16.7 acres of brush near Berkeley, Calif. In this canyon nearly all the wren-tits were banded and marked so that they could be recognized as individuals.

Spring.—The wren-tit is classified as a permanent resident, and this residency is of the most restricted sort. Individuals probably rarely go more than a few miles from the place of their birth. Adults that have once nested spend most of the remainder of their lives on the half to two and a half acres of brushland used during the first nesting. In spring, then, the wrentit population is essentially static. Pairs are established on breeding territories, many of them with the same mate on essentially the same territory they have held a year or more. Individuals that have died have been replaced by a male accepting a new mate from among the young-of-the-year or a widowed female joining a bereaved male or a young male establishing himself. All suitable ground is held by one pair or another. A few individuals, either unable to secure a territory or mate, or for some reason not ready to do so at the normal time, wander through the territories of established individuals and are driven from one to another by them. However, vacancies that may occur are quickly filled from the ranks of these wanderers.

The activities of the pair at this time, as they are all the year except during the breeding season, are concerned with finding food for themselves and defending their territory. The pair are constantly together as they work through their segment of the limitless chaparral hunting for food. They keep in touch with each other by frequent calls. The male often pauses to sing, and echoing calls are given by other males. If a jay perches nearby, they scold it. Occasionally they pause to rest or preen. If their movements bring them to the margin of their home area or territory, they usually turn back and continue the endless search for food. If they continue until they reach the extreme limit of their territory or go into the margin of the adjoining one, they are invariably met by the owners of this area and a boundary dispute occurs. The fighting that takes place is never prolonged or violent, and the infringing pair soon retreat to their own area and both pairs continue to forage. Rarely, an individual seeking to establish itself may invade the territory and is persistently harrassed by the owner as long as it remains, or possibly, if the territory is unusually large, the owner will relinquish part of it to the newcomer.

Courtship.—Courtship activities of a pair so constantly hidden are not easily observed. Pairs seemingly are originally formed by a female joining a male that has, or is establishing himself on, a territory. Two birds of the year, which I believe are a male and a female, are often seen together during fall and winter, but these seem to be transitory attachments, and the female will leave such a male to join an established one.

I once observed what appeared to be the establishment of a male on a territory and his acquisition of a mate. In a patch of brush that had not been occupied on the previous days, a young banded male was observed in the morning between 7:30 and 9 o'clock. During this time he went from the upper end to the lower and back to the upper, and except for a few brief intervals sang on an average of 5 times a minute—approximately 450 utterances. When he was at the top the second time, his calls were low and of poor carrying quality, but here a second wrentit was heard and glimpsed for the first time. The two moved down the the slope again. I heard no sounds except a single song and a *krrr* answer, but low notes would not have reached me. About 9:30 the pair were lost in the lower part of the territory. At 11:30 I looked for them again and found them behaving as any established pair would behave.

What actions take place as the pair first meet were never seen in the field. When a female was put into a cage containing two males and a female, the subsequent rapid movements of the four birds were exceedingly difficult to follow. The actions of the original female were mainly hostile. Lightning advances and retreats occurred between the two males and the new female, accompanied by a variety of soft musical and harsh notes as well as those common during disputes. The frequency of these chases decreased markedly by the end of the day, and soon the new female acted as the typical mate of one of the males.

Most of the time there is little activity to indicate that two birds are mates except their constant companionship. They forage together, they frequently preen each other, they rest on the same perch during the day, and they roost together at night. Their interest in each other moves toward a peak, as shown by sexual flight and special versions of the song as they build the nest, and it reaches its climax in coition on the days the nest is lined. In sexual flight the female continually hops or flies away from the male as he approaches, so that a rapid chase takes place. Posturing was never observed, but it may occur, since it would be difficult to observe it.

Once mated, the pair remain together as long as both are alive. Of the pairs I knew, five existed at least three years and a sixth for 2½ years. Six pairs were together for 2 years and may have existed prior to or after my knowledge of them. Only five pairs were known to have lasted only 1 year. When a pair was broken up, one or both members of it disappeared completely and presumably must have been killed, though this was only definitely known to be true in 1 of 17 cases.

Nesting.—The nest is placed in one of the bushes that make up the chaparral home of the species. It is usually not in a continuous dense mass of brush, but at its margin where a rock outcrop, less in height than the brush, or a trail or clearing makes a break; or if the chaparral is sparse the nest may be in any small bushy plant. I have found nests in coyotebush (*Baccharis pilularis*), artemisia, hazelnut, stick monkeyflower, and poison oak. Mailliard (1902) and A. H. Miller (MS.) have found them in live oaks, and Ray (1909) in an alder. In chaparral where other plants dominate, other shrubs are used.

From the nature of the habitat, the height of the nest above ground usually cannot be great and averages 18 to 24 inches. The lowest that I found was 12 inches, the highest 42 inches. The nests in trees mentioned above were 12 and 15 feet up.

Support, both under and at the sides of the nest, is usually found in a group of horizontal or vertical twigs built into or lashed to the nest. Occasionally a crotch of larger limbs is used. The nest is placed so that leafy twigs screen it from view on all sides.

The nest, a compact cup, is built by both members of the pair. It is begun by stretching a cobweb network between the twigs that are to form the support. Then coarse bark fibers are introduced, sparingly at first, until a saucerlike platform from ½ inch to 1½ inches thick and about 4 inches in diameter is formed. Fine bark strips are then placed on the outer rim until a deep cup is formed. Throughout the construction of the platform and cup, masses of cobweb are stretched over and interwoven with the bark fiber to bind it together and hold it in place. Cobweb is also stretched over the rim until it becomes smooth and firm. Finally a lining of fine round fibers is inserted in the cup, and tiny bits of lichen may be, though are not always, fastened to the outside. The type of bark used depends largely on the type of brush nearby. I have seen them strip bark from the dead or weathered branches of old-man sage, lupine, snowberry, thimbleberry, ninebark, baccharis or coyotebush, cow parsnip, and elderberry. The lining was often taken from the outer coat of the bulb of the soap plant, but fine grasses or hair are also used. Abandoned nests are a common source of material for later nests. The difficulty of finding nests makes the case uncertain, but I believe only one nest is worked on at a time, though a nest may be left incomplete and another begun.

The nest, though it may be the center of the birds activity for upward of a month, is not necessarily near the center of the territory. Of 47 nests that I observed, 60 percent were near the margin rather than the center. Successive nests of the same year or succeeding years may be near together or widely separated. The male often sings within 25 feet or less of the nest as he goes to it or leaves, but with equal frequency from other parts of the territory.

Eggs.—The number of eggs in a set is usually four, but sets of three are not infrequent and sets of five occur occasionally. There is some evidence that the smaller sets are laid by the younger females or early in the season and the larger sets by older females or late in the season. The eggs are usually laid early in the morning on successive days. They are oval and of a uniform pale greenish blue. There are no markings of any kind and the surface is dull. A single brood of young is reared each year, but if the eggs or nestlings are destroyed, the birds will lay as many as four or five sets during the nesting season, which at Berkeley lasts from March to July.

[AUTHOR'S NOTE: The measurements of 40 eggs average 18.1 by 14.5 millimeters; the eggs showing the four extremes measure **19.6** by **16.0, 16.3** by 14.2, and 17.8 by **12.7** millimeters.]

Incubation.—The incubation period was 16 days for three sets of eggs that I observed and was probably the same in two other cases. Newberry (1910), however, observed a nest in which the eggs hatched in 15 days. The adults spend at least some time on the nest after the second egg is laid, but in all cases that I observed, continuous incubation began on the day the next-to-the-last egg is laid; hence usually on the day the third is laid. In the nest watched by Newberry a lapse of 3 days occurred between laying and the beginning of incubation.

During the days of incubation the activities of the pair follow a set pattern. The female incubates at night. About 20 minutes after sunrise (the wren-tit is a relatively late riser) the male sings from his roosting perch. The female responds with her call, and both often repeat them. In 10 or 15 minutes the male comes to the nest bush, and when he is within a few inches the female leaves. Her first action is to stretch thoroughly, then in a few moments she is off in search of food. In 15 or 20 minutes she returns, and when she is close to the nest her mate leaves. He sings almost at once and frequently while he is foraging and patrolling his territory and as he approaches the nest again. Similar exchanges continue throughout the day though the shifts gradually lengthen to 45 or 60 minutes during midday and again shorten toward sunset. Finally when the female returns to the nest within 30 minutes or less of sunset no more changes occur. The male sings often as dusk approaches, and his last songs come from near or on the roosting perch.

Young.—The eggs of a set hatch within a period of 24 hours. In two nests that I observed, two eggs hatched early one morning, a third later in the day, and a fourth the following morning. During the first 35 days the young are constantly brooded by one or the other of the adults except for the brief moment when one leaves and the other feeds before settling on the nests. Older young are left uncovered for short intervals during the warm parts of the day and may not be brooded at all the last few days before fledging.

Food is brought on each return of the adults at intervals at 15 to 30 minutes when the adults are brooding and of 5 minutes or less when the young are older. The food, which is carried in the bill and is often a conspicuous mass of green larvae, is placed in the mouths of one or more young while the parent perches on the rim of the nest. At first there is usually some for each of the three or four young, later only one or two receive food at each visit. The first to raise its head if only by a fraction of a second, is served first. One receiving no food will continue to hold its head up, and often the adult rapidly and repeatedly thrusts its bill into the upturned throat. There is probably no regurgitation of food, for the bill and throat of the adult seem quite empty. The slight jar caused by the adult landing on the nest or nearby twigs is the signal to the young that a meal is at hand. The adults seem to have no specific calls to their young. The fecal sacs are eaten by the adult, if it remains on the nest, or are carried away, if it does not brood.

The young are naked at hatching. By the third day many of the feathers show as slight irregularities on the surface. By the fifth day the feathers show as slight ridges, with the tips protruding above the surface of the skin, and the resting posture is upright rather than on the side. By the tenth day the young when huddled in the nest seem completely covered but the feathers do not actually cover the apteria until the twelfth or thirteenth day. At this age the young stand up in the nest, stretch, preen, vibrate their wings, and give a faint food call.

On the fifteenth or sixteenth day after hatching, the young leave the nest. On two occasions of which I have record, they left before 7:30 on the fifteenth day. One family was evidently frightened from the nest when only 13 or 14 days old, and two of the three young survived. The brood that Newberry watched all left the nest explosively at 1:30 on the sixteenth day. Twice that I know of, one of the young remained in the nest several hours or a day longer than the others. At the time the young leave the nest, the body is well covered, but the wing feathers are not fully grown and the tail is scarcely an inch long. The iris is white as in the adult.

The first day out of the nest the young are easily located by their frequent calls. They remain perched most of the time. If forced to move they progress by a series of short hops accompanied by probably useless fluttering of the wings, but they are not sure-footed and if hurried often fail to gain the intended perch and scramble desperately to gain a footing and recover their balance. I was able to catch and band two such families. By the following day the young respond to the alarm note of their parents with frozen silence, and it is next to impossible to locate them. They also move with such facility that they cannot be taken. By the fifth day they move with as much skill and ease as the adults. By the time the young are 30 to 35 days old they are probably securing some food for themselves, but still beg from and are fed by their parents. A week later they scold as do the adults. By the time they are 9 or 10 weeks old they are no longer dependent on the adults and wander or possibly are driven, from the adults' territory.

Plumages.—The young at hatching are without down and the only vestige of a down plumage that ever develops is the 2- to 3–millimeter neossoptiles on the tips of the rectrices.

[AUTHOR'S NOTE: Ridgway (1904) says that the young are "similar to adults but texture of plumage looser, color of pileum and hindneck less grayish (concolor with that of back) and that of under parts duller and grayer." A small young bird in my collection, of the subspecies *henshawi*, in juvenal plumage, fits the above description, except that the under parts are more buffy than in the adults, "pinkish buff."

The postnuptial molt of adults, and apparently the postjuvenal molt of young birds, occur mainly in August, though some young birds may molt earlier in the season. I have seen adults in worn plumage up to August 10, others that were still molting on September 10, and still others that had nearly or quite completed the molt on September 3.]

Food.—The wren-tit's diet consists of insects, which are taken all the year but in great abundance during spring and summer, and small fruits, which are taken when available, principally during fall and winter. F. E. L. Beal's (1907) study of 165 stomachs shows that, of the 48 percent of vegetable food taken, 36 percent consisted of elderberries, snowberries, coffeeberries, twinberries, blackberries, and the fruit of poison oak. The poison-oak berries, which remain in an edible condition on the bushes for a long time, made up a fourth of the diet from August to February. I have seen all of these fruits eaten and in addition thimbleberries, huckleberries, and toyonberries. The insect food that Beal found to make up 52 percent of the food consisted of 23 percent ants and small wasps, 10 percent beetles, 8 percent caterpillars, 7 percent bugs, principally scales, 2 percent spiders, a few flies, and in one case each the remains of a grasshopper and a woodcricket. I successfuly kept wren-tits in captivity on a diet consisting of mixtures for soft-billed birds, banana, cottage cheese, lettuce, bread crumbs, and occasional live insects and wild berries. The young are fed principally on caterpillars, spiders and their cocoons and eggs, leafhoppers and other bugs, and small beetles. I have also seen adults come to a feeding table and get bread crumbs to feed their nestlings and fledglings.

The wren-tit finds its food principally on the bark surfaces, and to a less extent on the leaves and fruiting stems. Rarely they go to the ground. Not infrequently an individual flies up and hangs inverted while hunting among the leaves of live oaks for larvae, as a bushtit or titmouse might do. A few times individuals hovered at sticky monkey flowers. Once one caught a small butterfly which flew near, snipped off its wings, and swallowed the body.

Small objects, such as most of the insects and poison-oak berries, are swallowed whole; large ones are broken up. After obtaining a large morsel, the wren-tit resorts to a twig, places the object under one foot, and pulls off small pieces with its bill. Snowberries and thimbleberries are regularly handled in this way, elderberries sometimes. The berry is pecked until the skin is broken, and then pieces are pulled off and swallowed. Seeds met with are discarded, though the large flesh-coated seed of poison oak is swallowed and later disgorged. Large bread crumbs were held with the foot, or small pieces were broken off with a quick shake of the head.

Wren-tits drink water when it is available either from pools or the drops of moisture that collect on the leaves, but in much of their range they appear to do without water for periods of several weeks.

Behavior.—A wren-tit's habitat is such that most of its movements are a series of hops or flights of a few feet from one twig to the next. Individuals do not cross open spaces of even 30 or 40 feet readily or frequently. The longest flight I observed was about 150 feet over open grassland, but such flights are unusual.

Care of the plumage, which involves the usual preening and bathing, has two features of special interest. Preening is usually done by the individual's working over the feathers with its bill, or where the bill cannot reach, with its foot. Not infrequently, however, the members of a pair or family preen one another. The activity is usually limited to the region of the head but sometimes includes the feathers of the back, sides, breast, and crissum. The method is always the same: the bill is thrust into the feathers and a single one is manipulated between the mandibles from the calamus to the tip of the vane. Bathing in puddles when they occur near bushes includes the usual bobbing and splashing, but the plumage is moistened by a series of momentary dips rather than one long one. Rain- or fog-moistened brush is perhaps a commoner source of water for bathing. Birds move about in the leafy crowns, brushing and bumping against the wet leaves until their plumage is well dampened, and then the customary shaking and preening take place. Once a bird was observed to dust-bathe.

I observed the roosting habits in both cage and wild birds and found that the pair, and presumably a family, roost together. A pair sit side by side, facing in the same direction and so near together that they appear as a single ball of feathers from which tails, wings, and feet protrude—an appearance that is not accidental but is produced by fluffing, spreading, and interlacing the body feathers to such a degree that when the heads are turned to the outside and buried under the scapulars a single ball remains without so much as a line of separation. This arrangement of the feathers is an active process involving both movements of the feathers by the muscles that control them and manipulation of them with the bill. Usually the birds sit so low that the body feathers touch the perch and partly conceal the toes, but sometimes the bodies are well above the perch and then one can see that the inner leg of each bird is drawn into the feather mass and the weight supported on the outside leg. The angle of the leg to the body suggests that the two birds are braced against each other. In the wild the roost is a horizontal branch within the crown of a bush. The same roost is used frequently but not necessarily on successive nights.

The fighting between adjoining pairs that takes place during boundary disputes rarely deserves the name. The head feathers of the contestants are raised, the long tail cocked sharply up, the body crouched and tense. Each bird eyes its opponent and shifts its position or perch as if sparring for an opening. One or more may utter a staccato *ter ter* or a continuous *pit*. This action may go on for only a moment or for 15 minutes or longer. If it is prolonged one bird may fly at the other, but the latter makes a quick shift and is a foot or two away when the attacker reaches the empty perch. This continues as the opponents move rapidly through a bush, or along the boundary or back and forth across it. Sometimes the pursuer becomes the pursued. Rarely, the combatants fly at each other and momentarily flutter through the brush or on the ground, bills clicking and wings striking. Eventually one pair, usually the invaders, works back toward the center of its territory, and the other soon does likewise. The defending male usually sings, the invader sometimes does.

Wren-tits are persistent in scolding the California jays, which enter their territory during the breeding season. When a jay is discovered the pair circle or follow it, constantly hopping about and uttering a krrring sound until the jay moves on out of their territory. The jays seem quite indifferent, but I found this habit useful in two ways. One was in marking the territory of a pair by where they began and ceased to scold jays. The other was to attract marked birds I wished to identify to a given point by putting up a mounted jay. This ruse worked only for a short time, but it did enable me to learn the identity of several individuals.

Various actions of the wren-tit disclose the approximate location of the nest, though in my experience the nest is not easily found. An intruder near the nest is scolded persistently and vigorously with a krrring note, which becomes intenser as one nears the nest and decreases as one moves away from it. During the incubation period patient watching and listening should indicate the point from which the male sings as he goes to the nest and as he leaves. In either case, a search of the likely bushes in the region so indicated may reveal the nest. Finding the nest by watching adults carrying food is comparatively easy in this species. I never found that a random hunt through the bushes paid dividends.

The reaction of a wren-tit on a nest to an intruder varied in my experience. If the approach is quiet, the wren-tit usually remains on the nest until the hand is brought within a few inches. Then it silently slips off into the surrounding brush. Here it may remain quiet or it may scold. Sometimes the song or *pit-pit* call is given. Twice I was successful in painting a spot on the tail of an incubating bird. Three times birds with young exploded from the nest and fluttered and tumbled through the brush rapidly vibrating their wings, but these cases were the exception.

A wren-tit rarely, if ever, deserts eggs or young. Several nests I found in the early stages of construction were subsequently completed and used. Others were not, though there was no direct evidence that my discovery caused the desertion. One pair continued to incubate although work on a nearby trail pulled the nest into an exposed position at the top of the brush.

Voice.—The wren-tit is best known by its song, a series of loud-ringing whistlelike notes all on the same pitch and given at decreasing intervals until they run together into a trill. Grinnell (1913) recorded it as *pit—pit—pit—pit—pit-tr-r-r-r-r*. Slight variations occur. A common one is an increase or decrease in the number of "*pits*". Another, peculiar to a few individuals, is a short *tr* note at the end of the trill. Other variations of quality and rhythm and slight change in pitch and duration occur. The song is usually given while the bird is hidden within the leafy crown, but it may be given by a bird on a semiopen perch at the top of a bush. It may be given repeatedly from a single perch or as a momentary interruption while a bird is foraging. The singing posture is alert, the head raised, the tail tilted upward. The entire body, especially the throat and tail, vibrates in rhythm with the notes.

The full song is given throughout the entire year and is characteristic of the male. Many times I have identified the member of a marked pair that was singing, and only once was it the female. She gave it a few times while her mate was fighting with a neighboring male. From my experience I believe that, except during a territorial dispute, the bird giving the song may be assumed to be the male. The song appears to have a double purpose. It is used as an announcement of territorial possession. One male sings, a neighbor sings, the first repeats its song, and so on until most males are echoing the song. The male often sings as he advances to drive an intruder out of his territory. It also serves as a call or answer to his mate as will be described below.

What might be considered another variation of the song is actually a distinct call. It is similar to the song in quality, intensity, and pitch, but all the notes of the series are given with the same rhythm, so that it does not end in a trill. As compared with the song, it might be written as *pit—pit—pit—pit—pit—pit—pit*. The number of notes in the series is usually 7 or 8 but may be only 2 or more than 15. The individual notes are sometimes more a *peeka, pita,* or *peet*, and the intensity is more variable than that of the full song. This call is used mainly by the female but is also used by the male and is a call to the mate. Innumerable times I have heard the full song given first and answered by this one, or the reverse is just as frequent. Often the calls alternate three to six times, or they may even be given simultaneously. Such calls and answers may be heard at any time of day and throughout the year and seem to give the location of one to the other, as one of the birds frequently goes to the other. Sexual excitement may also play a part as variations of these calls, variously recorded during field work as *pit-tr-tr-tr-tr*, *perrrrrrrt*, musical repeated *trrr* or weak *pit* followed by accented *trrrr*, are heard on the days when the pair is completing a nest and sexual flight or copulation is taking place, though neither of these acts is invariably accompanied by this song.

Sometimes the response to the loud-ringing call of either the male or female is a faint burring note, *krrrrrr*. This short note is given at intervals as a pair forages and seems to keep the two near together.

A similar but louder accented *krrrr*, often repeated three or four times, is an alarm note. It is given as the bird disappears in the brush when it is startled. It is often given by a trapped bird or by another bird that is circling the trap.

A loud continuous *krrrr* that may be kept up for minutes on end is a scolding or mobbing note. At intervals it may be interrupted, only to start again with equal vigor. The bill is held slightly open, and the whole body vibrates as the sound is produced. The bird is in constant motion, shifting from one perch to another and following or circling the disturbing factor, usually a jay. The same note was used to mob a sharp-shinned hawk. Once a snake appeared to be the cause. The same sound was often given when I was near the nest.

A squealing note, *scree* or *schree*, was heard a few times.   Three or four times it was given when I reached into a trap to take the bird in my hand or when I was banding it.   The same sound was heard during fights between individuals kept in cages, once by a bird fighting bill to bill with another, and once by a male when another attacked it. It appears to be a note of fear, defeat, or submission.

During boundary disputes between established pairs, a series of low staccato notes, which I have recorded as *pit' pit' pit'*, *tut' tut'*, or *peeka*, is commonly given, often by several birds at once.

The first songs of the young may have the full ringing quality of the adults, but often they are thin, weak, and tremulous.   The trill that terminates it is frequently more prolonged and has a warblerlike quality.

Field marks.—An outstanding field character of the wren-tit is its long tail tilted up at an angle from the body, rounded at the tip and narrow at the base.   Other characteristics are the general grayish brown of the back and the cinnamon-brown of the underparts, its relatively long legs, the way it remains hidden within the brush, and the fact that two are invariably seen together.   If one is near enough the white iris may be seen.   The songs and calls are distinctive and easily learned.

Enemies.—The destruction of eggs and young by natural causes is high.   Of 24 nests found before or soon after the set was completed, young were fledged from only 10.   Wren-tits recognize jays as a source of danger to their young, and with reason, for both Mrs. A. S. Allen (MS.) and I have seen the jays take eggs and young from nests. Other enemies of the young and adults are probably those common to most small species.   Dr. A. H. Miller found the remains of two wren-tits in the pellet of a horned owl.

Fall and winter.—As already indicated, the adults remain in pairs on their territories during fall and winter.   Their activities continue on a relatively uniform level and serve to maintain themselves, their companionship, and their territory.   They are constant companions, forage together, keep track of each other by calls, preen each other, sleep together, and may rarely show sexual excitement to the degree of attempting copulation.   They are relatively tolerant of the wandering young and are themselves occasionally found a little distance beyond their usual boundaries, but the male sings regularly and both defend the territory from aggressive invasion.

The young, on the other hand, tend to wander during the early fall. Of 46 banded young reared in the canyon where I watched intensively, only one was seen or trapped after it was nine weeks old, though unbanded immatures were common.   One of my banded young when nine weeks old was trapped half a mile from its original home.   It is at this time that wren-tits are seen in the shrubbery of dwellings. How far they wander is difficult to say, but I doubt if it is more than ten miles. Soon after this period of wandering, the young tend to remain in one place, usually with a companion of the opposite sex. Sometime in the course of the winter, certainly by March, it ceases to be satisfied with merely a place to forage and a casual companion. If a male, it tries to acquire a territory; if a female, it seeks an unmated male with a territory. Most but not all are successful. Once established it will, usually, survive on its territory for 5 years, but it may persist for as long as 10 years.

DISTRIBUTION

Range.—Oregon to Baja California.

The wren-tit is found **north** to northwestern Oregon (Astoria). **East** to western Oregon (Astoria, Rogue River Valley, Gold Hill, and Medford); central California (Hornbrook; the western slope of the Sierra Nevada, Yosemite, Walker Pass, Kern County, and the San Bernardino Mountains); and Baja California (east base of the Sierra San Pedro Mártir and Aquaita). **South** to Baja California about latitude 30° (Aquaito). **West** to the Pacific Ocean, Baja California (San Quintín, San Ramón, and San Telmo); California (San Diego, Santa Paula, San Francisco, and Humboldt and Del Norte Counties); Oregon (Newport, Tillamook, and Astoria).

The range as outlined is for the entire species, which has been divided into six subspecies or geographic races. The coast wren-tit (*C. f. phaea*) is found in the humid coastal region of Oregon from the Columbia River about to the California line; the ruddy wren-tit (*C. f. rufula*) occurs in the humid coast belt of California south to San Francisco Bay; the intermediate wren-tit (*C. f. intermedia*) is found in the San Francisco Bay region, except the coastal strip north of the Golden Gate, south to Santa Clara County; Gambel's wren-tit (*C. f. fasciata*) occurs in the coastal strip of Monterey and San Luis Obispo Counties; the pallid wren-tit (*C. f. henshawi*) is found from the Rogue River Valley of Jackson County, Oreg., and in the foothills and valleys of interior and southern California, and along the coast from Santa Barbara County to about the Mexican boundary; the San Pedro wren-tit (*C. f. canicauda*) is found in northwestern Baja California, south to about latitude 30°.

Casual records.—A pair were collected at Klamath Falls, Oreg., on November 7, 1912; an individual was observed in July 1937, 10 miles north of Kelso, Wash.

Egg dates.—California: 118 records, March 1 to July 2; 45 records, May 1 to May 22; 35 records, March 10 to April 6.

CHAMAEA FASCIATA INTERMEDIA Grinnell

INTERMEDIATE WREN-TIT

Although this subspecies was originally described and named nearly 50 years ago, it has only recently been recognized in the twentieth supplement to our Check-list (Auk, vol'. 63, p. 431, 1946).

Dr. Joseph Grinnell (1900) described it as follows: "Back and upper tail-coverts, sepia, shading into hair brown on nape and top of head. Lores and small spots on upper and lower eye-lids, pale gray. Throat and breast, cinnamon-rufous, fading posteriorly into pale vinaceous-cinnamon on middle of belly. Feathers on breast, with faint dusky shaftstreaks. Sides, flanks and lower tail-coverts, brownish olive. Under wing-coverts and axillars, pale vinaceous-cinnamon. Wings and tail, clove-brown, the feathers with slightly paler edgings."

This subspecies is clearly intermediate between the dark northern race and the pale southern form. Whether it is wise to recognize intermediate forms in nomenclature is open to serious question. We have no reason to think that it differs materially in any of its habits from other races of the species. Its eggs seem to be indistinguishable from those of the species elsewhere. It has only a limited range in the San Francisco Bay region, except the coastal strip north of the Golden Gate, and southward to Santa Clara County.

CHAMAEA FASCIATA HENSHAWI Ridgway

PALLID WREN-TIT

PLATE 20

HABITS

The pallid wren-tit is the most widely distributed race of the species. The 1931 Check-list gives its range as the "Upper Austral Zone of the foothills and valleys of interior and southern California from Shasta County south, and along the coast from Santa Barbara County to the Mexican boundary."

Living as it does in an arid environment, it is also the palest of the California races. Ridgway (1904) describes it as "similar to *C. f. fasciata*, but decidedly paler, the back, scapulars, rump, etc., grayish brown (deep hair brown), the pileum and hindneck brownish gray (nearly mouse gray or deep smoke gray), and general color of under parts varying from very pale grayish buff to buffy ecru-drab or pale vinaceous-buff, fading to nearly white on lower abdomen." He remarks in a footnote that "occasional specimens from the southern coast district are nearly as deeply colored beneath as true *C. fasciata*."

In spite of its interior habitat, the haunts of this wren-tit seem to be similar to those described under Gambel's wren-tit, for Grinnell and

Storer (1924) write of its haunts in the Yosemite region: "The regular niche of the Pallid Wren-tit is in the foothill chaparral, beneath the crown-foliage of the brush plants and so usually not more than 5 feet from the ground. Fully nine-tenths of the bird's existence is passed in this shallow zone. Occasionally wren-tits are to be seen up in oaks or other trees growing amid or close to the brush, while now and then a bird will be noted on the ground, momentarily. But the three essentials for the bird's life, food, shelter from enemies, and safe nesting sites, are afforded in largest measure in the chaparral itself."

Nesting.—The same writers located a nest of this wren-tit 7 feet above the ground, much higher than is usual, "in the spray of terminal foliage of a slanting greasewood stalk."

Wright M. Pierce (1907) found a nest of the pallid wren-tit in San Antonio Canyon, elevation about 4,500 feet, near Claremont, Calif. He describes it as follows:

It was situated among thick branches and near the top of a scrub oak bush perhaps two and a half feet up, and is a gem of bird workmanship, composed, as it is, of bleached weed fibres such as fine grasses, an abundance of soft plant down, a little weed bark, and fine hairy threads of bark of the yucca plant, with a few wider blades of grass intermixed and woven about thru the whole thick-walled structure. A thick mass of horse hair makes the lining. To more firmly bind and hold together the nest, which even without would have been unusually strong and serviceable, these ingenious little birds used cobwebs as an outer covering to make their house doubly strong. The dimensions of the nest are: Depth, outside, 5 inches; inside, 2 inches. Diameter, outside, 4 inches; inside, 2 inches.

This seems to be an unusually large nest in outside dimensions.

There are two nests in the Thayer collection in Cambridge, taken near Escondido, that were placed about 2 feet up in sagebushes; fine strips of sage bark and some of the sage blossoms were used in the construction, which must have helped to conceal the nests.

This seems to be the only one of the wren-tits that has been recorded as a victim of the dwarf cowbird; Dr. Friedmann (1934) reports only three cases of such parasitism.

The eggs of the pallid wren-tit are similar to those of the other races of the species. The measurements of 40 eggs average 18.0 by 14.1 millimeters; the eggs showing the four extremes measure **19.4** by 14.3, 18.3 by **14.7**, and **16.8** by **13.4** millimeters.

CHAMAEA FASCIATA CANICAUDA Grinnell and Swarth

SAN PEDRO WREN-TIT

HABITS

This is the southernmost of the wren-tits, living in northwestern Baja California, from the United States boundary south to about latitude 30.

In describing this race, Grinnell and Swarth (1926) give, as its distinguishing characters—

pale colored as regards plumage, more so even than its nearest geographic relative, *henshawi*, hence the palest colored of the forms of *Chamaea fasciata*. The differences distinguishing *canicauda* from *henshawi*, though slight (hardly appreciable in badly worn plumage) are, it seems to us, notable in being of a different sort from those distinguishing *henshawi* from *C. f. fasciata*. In the latter case, while *henshawi* is much paler than *fasciata*, they are both *brown* tinged birds. In *canicauda* the browns are almost eliminated. The cinnamon of the underparts is extremely pale, the middle of the belly being nearly white, the upperparts, whole head, wings, and flanks are slaty, while the tail is deep slate. In *canicauda* the bill and feet are unequivocally black; in all the other races of *Chamaea* the bill and feet are more or less tinged with brown—"horn color."

A. W. Anthony (1893), while exploring the San Pedro Mártir Mountain, found this wren-tit "common along the lower slopes of the mountain and not rare in the highest altitudes where it nests in the scrub oak and Manzanita."

The measurements of 7 eggs in the P. B. Philipp collection average 18.5 by 14.3 millimeters; the eggs showing the four extremes measure 20.4 by 14.0, 17.6 by 14.8, and 17.3 by 14.2 millimeters.

Family CINCLIDAE: Dippers

CINCLUS MEXICANUS UNICOLOR Bonaparte

DIPPER

PLATES 22-24

HABITS

From northwestern Alaska and northeastern British Columbia southward to southern California and New Mexico, the dipper, or water ouzel, enjoys a wide distribution throughout the mountain ranges of western North America as far east as the eastern foothills of the Rocky Mountains, wherever it can find clear, cool, rushing mountain streams, with waterfalls, cascades, rapids and quiet pools, among which it loves to dwell, and to which it is strictly confined. Our bird differs from the type of the species, now understood to be mainly confined to Mexico and Central America, in paler coloration with the head and neck less decidedly brown, though not entirely free from this color, hence the name *unicolor*.

The dipper lives at different elevations in various parts of its range, where it is permanently resident, but obliged to seek the lower levels when winter freezes the upper reaches of the streams. Nelson (1887) found it "at the headwaters of the Yukon," as well as "along the shores of Norton and Kotzebue Sounds, where the small streams flow into the sea." We saw only one pair in the Aleutian Islands, on an inland mountain stream near a little waterfall at Unalaska, not much above sea level; Lucien M. Turner (1886) says that it is not common in these islands, but is a permanent resident.

We found it at Ketchikan, Alaska, on the stream that dashes down from the mountains just back of the town, and on the coast of British Columbia, not far from salt water. In the Yellowstone Park, M. P. Skinner observed it at levels ranging from 5,300 to well above the 8,000-foot level. Grinnell and Storer (1924) record it in the "Canadian and Hudsonian zones at altitudes of from 2,000 to 10,000 feet, and is continuously resident, even under the rigors of the Sierran winter, up as high as water remains open," in the Yosemite region. In Colorado, according to Sclater (1912), it ranges from 5,000 feet up to timberline at 11,500 feet. And Mrs. Bailey (1928) records it in New Mexico as low as 7,000 and as high as 11,600 feet. The American dipper seems to reach its southern limits in Arizona; we saw one in Ramsey Canyon on April 13, 1922, and Swarth (1904b) saw one in the same place in the Huachuca Mountains on August 4, 1902. We explored the lower portion of Sabino Canyon, at the southern end of the Catalina Mountains, but saw no dippers there. Charles T. Vorhies (1921), however, found a pair on two occasions in this canyon, eight or ten miles up from the mouth of the rocky stream; he thought they were probably resident there.

No better account of the American dipper has ever been written than John Muir's (1894) chapter on the water ouzel; I cannot do better than to quote freely from it, as it covers the ground most beautifully. Of its characteristic haunts, he writes:

Among all the countless waterfalls I have met in the course of ten years' exploration in the Sierra, whether among the icy peaks, or warm foot-hills, or in the profund yosemitic cañons of the middle region, not one was found without its Ouzel. No cañon is too cold for this little bird, none too lonely, provided it be rich in falling water. Find a fall, or cascade, or rushing rapid, anywhere upon a clear stream, and there you will surely find its complementary Ouzel, flitting about in the spray, diving in foaming eddies, whirling like a leaf among beaten foam-bells; ever vigorous and enthusiastic, yet self-contained, and neither seeking nor shunning your company. * * * He is the mountain streams' own darling, the humming-bird of blooming waters, loving rocky ripple-slopes and sheets of foam as a bee loves flowers, as a lark loves sunshine and meadows.

But the water ouzel, as I prefer to call it, is not wholly confined at all times to the mountain streams and waterfalls. Several observers have seen it on the shores of lakes, or feeding in them at considerable depths.

Taylor and Shaw (1927) observed several birds "on the quiet waters of the Tahoma Creek beaver pond," on Mount Rainier; and "water ouzels were frequently seen swinging low over the water near the shores of Reflection and Mowich Lakes, apparently as much at home as in the cascading creeks below."

Referring to Yellowstone Park, Mr. Skinner (1922) writes: "Only once have I seen one away from water and then he was flying over the quarter mile stretch between two streams. I have seen them on streams not more than two feet wide in the fir forests; along ditches, if the water be but clear and running; and occasionally, in November, along a ditch watering a barn yard. They live about beaver ponds."

Courtship.—Clyde E. Ehinger (1930) watched a pair of dippers flying down a stream, keeping close together, and acting in a manner that seemed to suggest mating antics. He says:

A typical incident of the kind was noted on February 6. A smaller and lighter colored bird—which I believe to have been a female—was observed spreading and fluttering her wings and closely following the bird which was singing. At times she would run rapidly toward him, with head lowered, wings extended and in rapid motion. These charging motions were repeated again and again, the male however, apparently giving but scant heed. It seemed quite obvious that the advances—at the time—were mainly made by the female, although the male gave vent to ardent bursts of song when the female flew to or past him. It seemed as though the little lady gave expression to her feelings chiefly by means of muscular movements and attitudes while her admirer expressed his passions by means of sweet melodies.

Nesting.—The water ouzel builds a beautiful and unique nest, unique in structure and unique in location. The characteristic location, and probably the usual location under primitive conditions, is close to and almost in its beloved mountain stream, often far from the haunts of man, sometimes under a waterfall hidden by the falling torrent, sometimes fully exposed to view on a rock in midstream, but more often on some narrow ledge on the face of a rocky cliff among mosses and ferns, where it is beautifully camouflaged and constantly wet with flying spray or mist. Muir (1894) describes it very well as follows:

The Ouzel's nest is one of the most extraordinary pieces of bird architecture I ever saw, odd and novel in design, perfectly fresh and beautiful, and in every way worthy of the genius of the little builder. It is about a foot in diameter, round and bossy in outline, with a neatly arched opening near the bottom, somewhat like an old-fashioned brick oven, or Hottentot's hut. It is built almost exclusively of green and yellow mosses, chiefly the beautiful fronded hypnum that covers the rocks and old drift-logs in the vicinity of waterfalls. These are deftly interwoven, and felted together into a charming little hut; and so situated that many of the outer mosses continue to flourish as if they had not been plucked. A few fine, silky-stemmed grasses are occasionally found interwoven with the mosses, but, with the exception of a thin layer lining the floor, their presence seems accidental, as they are of a species found growing with the mosses and are probably plucked with them. * * *

In choosing a building-spot, concealment does not seem to be taken into consideration; yet notwithstanding the nest is large and guilelessly exposed to view, it is far from being easily detected, chiefly because it swells forward like any other bulging moss-cushion growing naturally in such situations. This is more especially the case where the nest is kept fresh by being well sprinkled. Sometimes these romantic little huts have their beauty enhanced by rock-ferns and grasses that spring up around the mossy walls, or in front of the door-sill, dripping with crystal beads.

Nests are not always placed on rocks; several have been reported as built among the upturned roots of fallen trees, near or over the water. Mrs. Wheelock (1904) reports one that "was located on a smooth granite boulder that rose from the white foam of the American River in the Sierra Nevada. Resting half on the rock and half in the stream was a fallen tree trunk, and under the shelter of this on the slippery rock the Ouzel had woven his little moss nest, kept fresh and green by the spray that dashed over it."

Since man has invaded some of the ouzel's mountain haunts, the birds have learned to use man-made structures, little daunted by human activities in the vicinity. A number of nests have been observed under bridges that were in regular use. Such nests were built against or upon the girders or the supporting beams, often close up to the planking; the nest in such a situation had to be made to fit the available space; sometimes there was not room for the usual dome, which, of course, was not needed for protection; an occasional bridge nest may be entirely open at the top, like a phoebe's nest. Dean Amadon tells me that he found a dipper's nest, in Wyoming, that was under a bridge on a main improved road; it was 4 feet above the water on top of a supporting beam. Nests have been found under bridges in villages. Two rather remarkable cases of such familiarity with civilization have been recorded. Many years ago, Dr. Cooper (Suckley and Cooper, 1860) wrote:

I found a nest of this bird at a saw mill down on the Chehalis river. It was built under the shelving roots of an immense arbor-vitae, which had floated over and rested in a slanting position against the dam. The floor was made of small twigs and bare, the sides and roof arching over it like an oven, and formed of moss projecting above so as to shelter the opening. This was large enough to admit the hand, and the inside very capacious. It contained half-fledged young. The old birds were familiar and fearless, being accustomed to the noise of the mill and the society of the men, who were much interested by their curious habits. They had already raised a brood in the same nest that summer.

In a small village in Modoc County, Calif., Charles L. Whittle (1921) traced a water ouzel to its nest in a wooden lean-to, or shed, in the rear of the village bank, built of brick. "As close inspection as possible revealed the bird's somewhat bulky nest placed on a horizontal timber near where it joined a rafter and close against the end of the shed. The nest was placed directly over and some 8 feet above the water," which flowed swiftly under the shed.

Nest-building seems to be performed mainly, if not wholly, by the female in a most ingenious manner. This is fully described in some extracts from the notebooks of Denis Gale, published by Junius

Henderson (1908), to which the reader is referred, as his account is too long to be included here.

Aretas A. Saunders tells me that, in Montana, "some dipper nests, built on rocks, are without a bottom or lining, the eggs being deposited on the rocks, the nest being merely a roof, side walls and the usual front entrance, made of woven moss."

Samuel F. Rathbun refers in his notes to a dipper's nest in an unusual location:

It was placed on the sloping top of a stump, and at a height of three feet above the surface of a small, swiftly running stream in the mountain foothills. There was a cavity of some size in the top of the stump, and this was completely filled with a mass of fresh moss, some of which had been worked into the under side of the nest proper to aid in its attachment. The whole affair resembled a roughly-shaped ball of green moss on the top of the stump, which was in plain view in an open spot just within the water's edge. But since there was a considerable growth of moss on the side of the stump, it helped to make the mass of moss less noticeable.

Mr. Saunders writes to me of another well-concealed nest: "There was a small waterfall about 2 feet high and near it I saw a dipper with food in its bill. There was moss on the rocks all around the fall, but I saw no nest. Then the bird went to a vertical wall of moss near the fall, and evidently fed young. When it had gone, I investigated and the moment my hand touched the wall of moss several young popped out of a hole in the moss into the pool below the fall. The nest, from external appearance, was merely a hole in the moss wall, back of which there was a niche in the rock."

Eggs.—The American dipper lays from three to six eggs in a set, usually four or five. These are ovate in shape, sometimes slightly elongated and often somewhat pointed at the small end. They are pure, dead white and entirely unmarked. The measurements of 50 eggs average 25.9 by 18.5 millimeters; the eggs showing the four extremes measure 28.5 by 19.1, 26.2 by 19.5, 24.0 by 19.0, and 25.0 by 17.0 millimeters.

Young.—According to J. A. Steiger (1940), "the female alone covers the eggs during incubation, and about the thirteenth day hatching occurs. * * * After about 18 days of rapid growth, the fledglings file from the crowded nest. Amidst raucous calling, the experimenting young follow the creek. Flying at short distances, the parents entice their charges from rock to rock, seeming to encourage them to greater and braver acts."

Dr. A. H. Cordier (1927) built a platform within 6 feet of a water ouzel's nest, from which the following observations were made: "The female did most of the feeding. * * * On one occasion when my head was within 18 inches of the nest, the female lit on the face of a slick rock 3 feet from the nest, but only for a second. She had in her beak a small rainbow trout, which she delivered to one of the young birds. Although there were four young birds, at no feeding did I see more than two gaping mouths protruding from the nest's entrance." The feeding visits of the male "were about 1 to 10 as compared with those of the female," and Dr. Cordier continues:

The female fed about 8 times per hour. The male fed oftenest between 10 and 2 o'clock, at which time the combined feeding visits averaged 12 per hour. I noticed that the male made most of his visits to the nest while the female was brooding. She entered the nest by crawling over the young birds, turned about within the nest cavity and remained far back in the nest. At such times when the male made his visits, she remained in the nest, the young birds protruding their heads from beneath her breast to receive food from the male. * * *

The birds are extremely cleanly in their habits. As the interior of the nest was often inspected, any excrement found adhering to a straw or piece of moss was carefully picked up and carried away. The young birds when defecating turned the tail toward the nest entrance and with a well marked expulsive effort shot foecal mass 4 to 6 inches from the nest. These masses were always enclosed in a membrane. Many of them rolled unbroken down the rocky incline into the water and were carried down stream. Those remaining were picked up by the female and removed. * * * One bird only was fed at a feeding visit.

Probably two broods usually are raised in a season under favorable circumstances throughout most of the dipper's range, though this is hardly likely in the more northern regions. The young are much more precocial than are the young of other passerine birds. They seem to know instinctively, as soon as they leave the nest, how to run, climb, dive and swim, or flutter along the surface of the water; they soon become as much at home in the water as their parents.

Claude T. Barnes has sent me the following interesting account: "On July 24, 1930, while I was in City Creek Canyon, near Salt Lake City, Utah, at an altitude of about 6,000 feet, it was my rare good fortune to see a water ouzel feeding its young. Sitting idly beside the noisy stream, I first heard a continuous cry, which resembled somewhat the stridulation of a locust, yet more, in its lusty character, the squeal of a mouse, distinct above the brook's purling and extended for three or four minutes at a time. Puzzled, I waited until the cause appeared; a young water ouzel, nearly as large as its mother, hopped to a stone on the opposite bank, constantly making the crying sound, which I thought now similar to the noise of a fighting hummingbird. The mother ouzel was ahead, wading the stream, diving occasionally into the water, and busying herself with the finding of worms and grubs. As she did this the young bird cried, watched her, followed her, flipped its wings, and, every few moments, made the characteristic bob of the species. Finally the mother got a grub; and, as if aware of the fact, the little one began violently to agitate its wings and to cry more greedily for its dinner. The mother ouzel flew to it, placed the grub in its mouth, and indifferently went to work again. Satisfied for the moment, the young one dipped its head into the water, ceased crying, and rested, only to become apprehensive about the mother's progress away, and to renew its crying and watchful following. For the most part, it kept close to the edges where the water was but an inch or so deep and protruding stones were numerous, though, now and again, it flew a few yards across an inconvenient bend. Away they went down stream, around a bend, out of sight."

Mrs. Amelia S. Allen has sent me an interesting note on the feeding of a young ouzel. The mother (?) "alighted near the young bird and tried to place a fat insect in its beak. The baby dropped it. The mother picked it up, flew across to a dead branch that sloped down to the water, dipped the insect into the water, then flew back to the youngster. Again he fumbled. The mother picked up the insect again, flew across to the same branch, walked along it to the edge of the water, dipped the insect in and returned to the baby. At last the insect was swallowed."

Fred Evenden, Jr., sends me the following note: "After a while I moved in close again to the nest while both parents were gone. I remained motionless, but even then they detected me when they returned. The female returned alone and hopped around on a rock in midstream and then flew to the water's edge about 3 feet from me. Then she went to the rock in midstream and gave what must have been an alarm note, for almost immediately her mate came upstream and they talked to each other and then both of them defiantly took it upon themselves to scold me. I left the spot for I didn't want to keep them from bringing food to their young. This alarm note I mentioned went this way. Several short and high notes with a rasping trill at the end. The female gave this call twice."

Plumages.—I have not seen any small nestlings, but Mr. Steiger (1940) says that "from the first, the young Ouzel has a complete coat of down."

This down becomes a necessary protection by the time that the young bird takes its first plunge, at an early age, into the cold water.

In the juvenal plumage, the young bird is somewhat like the adult, but paler generally, and the under parts are suffused or mottled with very pale buff or buffy white; the chin and throat are mainly white; and the greater wing coverts are narrowly tipped with grayish white. This plumage is worn through the summer and into September; I have seen a bird in juvenal plumage as late as September 6. I don't know how extensive the postjuvenal molt is, but it evidently involves the contour plumage at least.

The first winter plumage of the young bird is similar to that of the adult, with perhaps a little more white on the underparts.

Adults have a complete postnuptial molt in July and August; I have seen adults in fresh plumage as early as August 20. Ridgway (1904) says that fall and winter adults have the "feathers of nearly all under parts more or less distinctly (always narrowly) margined with whitish, the larger wing-coverts and tertials (sometimes also secondaries, innermost primaries, and rectrices) also narrowly margined at tips with white, a narrow whitish mark on each eyelid, and the bill horn brownish."

Food.—The water ouzel obtains most of its food in, on, or under the water of the streams on which it lives. It is very fond of the larvae of the caddicefly, for which it probes around and under the small stones on bottom; there it also finds water-bugs, water-beetles, the larvae of other insects, aquatic worms, and other forms of animal life that live in such places. John Muir (1894) writes attractively:

He seems to be especially fond of the larvae of mosquitoes, found in abundance attached to the bottom of smooth rock channels where the current is shallow. When feeding in such places he wades up-stream, and often while his head is under water the swift current is deflected upward along the glossy curves of the neck and shoulders, in the form of a clear, crystalline shell, which fairly incloses him like a bell-glass, the shell being broken and re-formed as he lifts and dips his head; while ever and anon he sidles out to where the too powerful current carries him off his feet; then he dexterously rises on the wing and goes gleaning again in shallower places.

Mayflies, caddiceflies, and other insects often drop into the pools, or the quiet reaches of the stream, or are washed down over the waterfalls; under the waterfalls are favorite feeding places; and, on the more quiet surfaces, the ouzel swims like a duck, using its feet as paddles, or flaps along the surface with the help of its wings, and picks up the floating insects, if it can do so before the trout rise to snap them up. Under the overhanging banks, under logs, or under the shelter of rocks and stones, where trout fry or other small fish are hiding, it seeks such finny prey. Often fish as much as 2 or 3 inches in length are captured, taken ashore, and killed by vigorous beating; some of these escape, and others, too big to swallow, are abandoned.

In cold weather, or high up in the mountains, the dipper has been seen to pick up frozen insects from the ice of lakes, or from snowbanks after the manner of rosy finches. Junius Henderson (1927) makes the surprising statement, on the authority of Prof. Aughey (1st Rep. U. S. Ent. Comm., 1878), that dippers "have been observed catching locusts" in Nebraska. J. A. Steiger (1940) says that "at times they make water cress and other aquatic flora part of their diet."

Unfortunately for the dipper's welfare, it is too fond of the spawn and small fry of salmon and trout, and it is tempted to feed on them freely when and where they are easily available. This habit has made many enemies for the dipper among sportsmen and especially among the managers of fish hatcheries. The damage done to wild salmon and trout by this bird is probably not serious under natural conditions, for these fish are known to lay vastly more eggs than can ever hatch, many eggs eaten by the dipper are known to be infertile, and vastly more fry are hatched than can possibly survive; I have seen it estimated that, if all fish eggs hatched and the fry grew to maturity, the oceans would soon be packed solid full of fish. Furthermore, the spawning grounds of both salmon and trout are mainly in waters not often frequented by the dippers, as these birds live mainly on the rapid mountain streams rather than on the slower valley streams and spawning grounds where they are rarely seen.

Under the artificial conditions prevailing at fish hatcheries, it is a different story; here the dippers undoubtedly do considerable damage. J. A. Munro (1924) made a study of the relation of the dipper to fishing interests in British Columbia and Alberta; I offer a few quotations from his report. The manager of the Skeena River hatchery offered the suggestion that "if naturally it eats a few salmon fry and ova, it will balance this by eating ova and fry of the salmon enemies." The Banff hatchery reported that "during the winter of 1921–22 not less than 10,000 advanced Cut-Throat trout fry were taken from the ponds and destroyed by these birds." In summing up all the evidence that he gathered, Mr. Munro said that "it will be noted that little evidence has been presented in reference to their consumption of spawn and this is evidently not considered serious by the fishery officials. * * * The destruction of fry is perhaps a more serious offence but we have little evidence that this takes place to an alarming degree under natural conditions, the complaints having reference to the destruction of artificially propagated fry after they have been placed in the retaining ponds. It has been noted that these small fish swim continually along the shores of the ponds, seeking an outlet perhaps, and so fall an easy prey to Dippers, Kingfishers or other birds that may be attracted to this bountiful supply of food. * * * The practice of shooting these birds in order to protect the fry has not had the desired effect," as new birds come in to take the places of those that are shot. "The obvious remedy is to screen the surface of retaining ponds with fine mesh wire netting. This will adequately protect the fry and render it unnecessary to destroy a song bird of high aesthetic value."

A. Dawes DuBois writes to me: "Mr. Baigrie Sutherland, then forest ranger in the Flathead National Forest for the district having its ranger station at Belton on the Middle Fork of the Flathead River, told me on the 24th of August, 1915, that he saw a water ouzel eating fish offal which he had thrown into the edge of the water."

Behavior.—It is indeed strange that a land bird, a song bird, and one so closely related to the wrens and the thrushes should adopt so many of the habits of the grebes and the ducks, for it is an expert diver and a good swimmer. Its feet are not webbed, of course, but its legs and toes are long, and its flexor muscles are very strong, enabling it to hold firmly to the rocks and stones against a strong current, to climb over the slippery rocks, or to swim fast enough for its purposes. The water ouzel is also well equipped otherwise for aquatic life, as pointed out by Grinnell and Storer (1924):

The covering of feathers on the body is thicker and denser than in either the thrushes or wrens, to which the dipper is closely related. Also, the ends of the feathers are somewhat more loosely formed, as in many of the true water birds, and this seems to help in keeping the plumage from soaking up water. Each nostril is covered by a movable scale, obviously to exclude water when need be. The oil gland at the upper base of the tail is about ten times as large in the dipper as in related land-dwelling birds of equivalent size, and the bird makes frequent use of the product of the gland to dress its feathers. The stout but tapered form of the body, the short tail, the short rounded wings, and the stout legs and feet all would seem to be of advantage to a bird living along and in swiftly moving waters.

The flight of the ouzel cannot be better described than in the following quotations from Muir's (1894) charming account:

The Ouzel, born on the brink of the stream, or on a snag or boulder in the midst of it, seldom leaves it for a single moment. For, notwithstanding he is often on the wing, he never flies overland, but whirs with rapid, quail-like beat above the stream, tracing all its windings. Even when the stream is quite small, say from 5 to 10 feet wide, he seldom shortens his flight by crossing a bend, however abrupt it may be; and even when disturbed by meeting some one on the bank, he prefers to fly over one's head, to dodging out over the ground. * * *

The vertical curves and angles of the most precipitous torrents he traces with the same rigid fidelity, swooping down the inclines of the cascades, dropping sheer over dizzy falls amid the spray, and ascending with the same fearlessness and ease, seldom seeking to lessen the steepness of the acclivity by beginning to ascend before reaching the base of the fall. No matter though it may be several hundred feet in height he holds straight on, as if about to dash headlong into the throng of booming rockets, then darts abruptly upward, and, after alighting at the top of the precipice to rest a moment, proceeds to feed and sing. His flight is solid and impetuous, without any intermission of wing-beats,—one homogeneous buzz like that of a laden bee on its way home.

Mr. Skinner's (1922) account of its flight is only slightly different: "Only once have I seen one away from water and then he was flying over the quarter mile stretch between two streams. * * * The flight is direct and the wing beats are very rapid for 100 feet, then the Dipper coasts along 10 feet with the acquired momentum before taking up its wing strokes again. * * * A bird will come flying down one stream, turn an acute angle at the mouth of a second stream, and then go buzzing merrily up it after flying three times as far rather than cross the neck of land between the two streams."

Dippers are solitary birds and are usually seen singly, rarely in pairs, except during the breeding season, and very rarely as many as three or four together unless it be a group of parents and young. Muir (1894) once watched three of these birds—

spending a winter morning in company, upon a small glacier lake, on the Upper Merced, about 7,500 feet above the level of the sea. * * * The portion of the lake bottom selected for a feeding-ground lies at a depth of 15 or 20 feet below the surface, and is covered with a short growth of algæ and other aquatic plants,—facts I had previously determined while sailing over it on a raft. After alighting on the glassy surface, they occasionally indulged in a little play, chasing one another round about in small circles; then all three would suddenly dive together, and then come ashore and sing.

The Ouzel seldom swims more than a few yards on the surface for, not being web-footed, he makes rather slow progress, but by means of his strong, crisp wings he swims, or rather flies, with celerity under the surface, often to considerable distances. But it is in withstanding the force of heavy rapids that his strength of wing in this respect is most strikingly manifested.

Dr. James A. Henshall (1901), who had some good opportunities to watch ouzels in the clear waters of trout hatchery ponds, writes: "I have seen them plunge into the water, while flying, and continue their flight under the surface for the length of the pond. I have also seen them dive, like kingfishers, from the top of the drain boxes into the water. Then again, I have observed them leave the shore and swim away on the surface like so many ducklings."

Opinions differ as to how long an ouzel can remain under water; I have seen it stated as 10 seconds; Dr. A. H. Cordier (1927) noted one-half minute as the longest he had observed; Muir (1894) *implies* that it can remain under 2 or 3 minutes, but he probably made a wild guess at it!

Some observers claim that ouzels do not use their wings in swimming under water, but most of them now seem to agree that they do; certainly it hardly seems reasonable to think that they could progress rapidly enough or swim strongly enough with feet that are so poorly adapted for swimming. I believe that they not only can enter the water flying but also can come out of it flying.

It seems strange that a bird that spends so much time in the water and in flying spray should be in need of a bath, but Mr. Skinner (1922) has seen one plunging into the water with the evident purpose of bathing; he has seen one stand in shallow water and flutter its wings in true bird-bath fashion; and he says that "on early winter mornings, sun-baths are the regular thing. One cloudy morning I noted a Dipper do the next best thing—warm himself and bask luxuriously in the steam from some cooled geyser water that was still much warmer than the keen, winter air. While swimming on the water, a Dipper goes along nodding his head quite like a miniature rail, or a coot. In many ways Dippers suggest wrens. They are small and quick; they often perk up their short tails at a steep angle; and they are forever exploring every nook and cranny of their domain."

The water ouzel usually alights on rocks or snags in the mountain streams, but it has been known to alight occasionally in trees near its habitat. Dr. C. Hart Merriam (1899) says: "One afternoon just before dark (6 o'clock) I was surprised to see an ouzel fly up into the dead top of a tree, light on a branch, and climb up several feet on the trunk with his short tail hanging straight down, after the manner of a woodpecker."

Late one afternoon, Mr. Ehinger (1930) found one of the birds singing "at the foot of the steep bank where they had previously been seen to disappear under the shelving sod and roots." This suggested a nightly roosting place, and "a little careful investigation confirmed this fact as two of the birds at dusk, retired under the cover and did not reappear."

Everyone who has seen a dipper must have noticed one of its characteristic habits, from which its name may have been derived. When perched on a rock or snag it is almost constantly dipping, nodding, or bobbing, or teetering. It has also been called the "teeter bird." But it is not really a teetering like that of the spotted sandpiper, nor is it really nodding, for there is no downward nod of the head or up and down movement of the tail. It is a strictly vertical movement of the *whole body*, accomplished by bending the long legs to a crouching position and then raising them to a high standing position; this produces a perpendicular movement of the body, up and down, for a distance of an inch or more, and is quite different from such movements in other birds. This dipping is rapid, often at the rate of from 40 to 60 times a minute, or about once a second. Mr. Steiger (1940) suggests that, as the dipper "does not seem to have one consistent call note for its mate," as the noise of rushing torrents often makes its voice difficult to hear, and as its sombre coloring offers no very conspicuous recognition mark, we may "interpret the dipping as an effective device for communication. This bobbing serves as a wig-wag, drawing the attention of the mate, or, when used by young, to draw the attention of parent birds. The logic of this explanation finds support in two behavior patterns. Flush the Dipper and you will note repeatedly that upon alighting again the dipping will be more frequent. Each time the bird takes a new location, this increased dipping is striking. It is also clear that older birds do not resort to dipping so frequently as the young."

Notwithstanding the fact that the dipper prefers to live in the mountain solitudes, far from the haunts of man, it is a tame, confiding species, if not molested. It seems indifferent to our presence; if we sit quietly on a rock beside the stream, even one of its favorite perching places, and do not move a muscle, it may alight beside us, gaze at us intently with its large, liquid eyes for a moment, and then flit away to another rock and begin to sing; several observers have had such

108 BULLETIN 195, UNITED STATES NATIONAL MUSEUM

an experience. John Muir (1894) saw one "cheerily singing within reach of the flying chips" from a man that was chopping wood on a river bank. "On the lower reaches of the rivers where mills are built, they sing on through the din of the machinery, and all the noisy confusion of dogs, cattle, and workmen." This does not mean that the ouzel does not need protection, or that it can adapt itself to civilization, for it is slowly disappearing from some of its former haunts where its living conditions have been altered, and it may eventually find a suitable habitat only in some national park or other protected reservation.

A striking habit of the water ouzel, which has caused considerable discussion and difference of opinion, is the frequent winking of either the nictitating membrane or the upper eyelid, which has a narrow border of short, white feathers. Some contend that the wink is produced by the membrane, and some say that it is the eyelid that produces it. As a matter of fact, I believe that it may be produced by either feature of the bird's anatomy at different times. Grinnell and Storer (1924) say: "The nictitating membrane or 'third eyelid' is whitish in the Dipper, and, when drawn backward across the eye, as it is frequently when the bird is above the water, can be seen at a considerable distance. This membrane probably is drawn over the eyeball when the bird is working beneath the surface of the water." I cannot agree that this last assumption is correct; this membrane is translucent, but not transparent, and would probably impede rather than help the bird's vision where it would need it most; even the unaided human eye can see under water; and I doubt if the trained eye of the dipper needs this protection.

Mr. Ehinger (1930), "being at very close range noted particularly the winking of the white-edged eyelids and the flash of the third lid or nictitating membrane. When the bird was facing me the winking seemed simultaneous with both eyes; when but one eye was turned toward me the nictitating membrane *seemed* to flash out from different portions of the eye and at times as though it came from the outer canthus."

Dr. Cordier (1927) collected considerable evidence on this subject, to which the reader is referred, and made some thorough, close-up observations, which seem to throw considerable light on the subject, and from which I quote as follows:

My observations leading to these conclusions were made at a range of 4 feet to 18 inches from the bird, extending over several hours each day for several days. The winking in this bird was performed by the action of the nictitating membrane and not by the upper eyelid. The upper eyelid has a well defined white margin. From beneath this, the membrane was flashed in a downward direction in rather an oval shape, extending to the lower border of the cornea. The moving pictures show this membrane very distinctly. The movement is seen to come from above downward, *nearly the horizontal width of the upper eye-*

lid. When the bird was in the shadow of the nest cavity, with my eyes within 18 inches of it, I could see the membrane very plainly as it frequently flashed across the eye ball. * * * The true lids in most birds move up and down, the winker moving horizontally. The Water Ouzel is an exception in so far as the movement of the winker [nictitating membrane] is *nearly vertical.* In no bird can the upper eyelid be made to close and open with the speed of the nictitating membrane. According to the record made by the moving picture camera, there are five frames, or individual pictures, impressed on the film at each flash of the membrane. This represents about one-third of a second to each wink.

* * * On one occasion Mr. Sandahl pressed the button of the camera exactly at the time the bird winked. This picture shows the extent of the membrane's action from above downward. It also shows the membrane as an oval covering of the eye and not a straight line as would be the case if made by the upper eyelid.

The membrane is called into action to clear the cornea of the watery mist while the bird is near the spray and splashes of falls and rapids. This was beautifully illustrated while the female was in the nest brooding. The flashes of the membrane could plainly be seen. The spray from the nearby falls, with the changing air currents could be seen to enter the nest and with each gust of moistened air, the membrane was called into action with increased vigor to brush aside the watery vapors from the cornea. This was performed independently of the white margined upper eyelid. The slow eyelid action is in part controlled by volition; the quick action of the membrane is brought about by an unconscious reflex demand.

Each pair of ouzels establishes and defends a definite territory on its home stream, from which trespassing ouzels are driven.   As a rule, such territorial rights are respected, but sometimes the invading bird is attacked and forced to retire.   During the nesting season and when broods of young have to be fed, such territories are quite extensive and the nests are placed a mile or more apart; Dr. Cordier thought it unusual to find two nests within a mile.   But when winter closes some of the upper reaches of the mountain streams, the birds have to become more concentrated at lower levels, and perhaps half a dozen birds may be found within a mile or two.   Dawson (1923) mentions finding as many as 37 within a distance of two miles.   Even then, though the territories are shorter, they seem to be fairly well maintained.

Voice.—The water ouzel is a beautiful singer, singing persistently and almost constantly during most of the year and in all kinds of weather.   The song period is at its lowest ebb during the molting and low-water period in August and September, but as soon as winter snows have begun to replenish the mountain streams, early in winter, it begins to build up and the flood tide of joyous music is reached early in spring, mingling with the roar of rushing torrents, and generally to be heard above the music of the cascades.   John Muir (1894) pays the following glowing tribute to the song of the ouzel:

As soon as the winter clouds have bloomed, and the mountain treasuries are once more replenished with snow, the voices of the streams and ouzels increase in strength and richness until the flood season of early summer.   Then the torrents chant their noblest anthems, and then is the flood-time of our songster's

melody. As for weather, dark days and sun days are the same to him. * * *
Indeed no storm can be more violent than those of the waterfalls in the midst
of which he delights to dwell. However dark and boisterous the weather, snow-
ing, blowing, or cloudy, all the same he sings, and with never a note of sadness.
No need of spring sunshine to thaw *his* song, for it never freezes. Never shall
you hear anything wintery from *his* warm breast; no pinched cheeping, no
wavering notes between sorrow and joy; his mellow, fluty voice is ever tuned
to downright gladness, as free from dejection as cock-crowing. * * *
What may be regarded as the separate songs of the Ouzel are exceedingly difficult of description, because they are so variable and at the same time so confluent. * * * Nearly all of his music is sweet and tender, lapsing from his
round breast like water over the smooth lip of a pool, then breaking farther on
into a sparkling foam of melodious notes, which glow with subdued enthusiasm,
yet without expressing much of the strong, gushing ecstasy of the bobolink or
skylark.

The more striking strains are perfect arabesques of melody, composed of a
few full, round, mellow notes, embroidered with delicate trills which fade and
melt in long slender cadences. In a general way his music is that of the
streams refined and spiritualized. The deep booming notes of the falls are
in it, the thrills of rapids, the gurgling of margin eddies, the low whispering of
level reaches, and the sweet tinkle of separate drops oozing from the ends of
mosses and falling into tranquil pools.

After the above beautiful words of worshipful praise, it seems
almost a sacrilege to say anything more about the voice of the ouzel,
but a few call notes, not included in Muir's account, are worth mentioning. An alarm note, a sharp *jigic, jigic*, is mentioned by Ehinger
(1930) and by others. Grinnell and Storer (1924) write: "The call
note is short and rather burred, uttered singly when the dipper is
'jouncing' on a rock, or given in rapid series when the bird takes to
flight. One of our renderings of it is *zit, zit, zit*, * * *; another
bzeet, or extended to *bz-ze-ze-ze-ze-ze-et*. It is quite different in character from the song, and resembles in general character the call note
of the cañon wren." Claude T. Barnes writes to me that one he was
watching "flew to a wet stone and uttered a single note, *cheep*, but in
a few seconds more it flew upstream uttering a chatter like *cheep a la
la la*, the characteristic notes of the species when flying along a brook."
He also mentions a protesting chatter, "which sounded like *ching,
ching, ching, ching, ching, ching*, uttered more rapidly than I could
count the notes and with a thin, tinkle-like sound, as of a large fishing
reel clicking. I could hear it distinctly above the roar of the fall. The
note was repeated six times in each song or scold, whatever it was."

Mr. Rathbun tells me that "under favorable conditions many of the
notes of this bird's song carry a long distance. On quiet mornings and
when the lake was calm, more than once I heard the song coming
from the far side of the lake which was more than a mile away."

Enemies.—Mr. Steiger (1940) writes:

Its natural enemies are many. The water snake, mink, marten, the skunk,
weasel and other stream-frequenting animals continuously prey upon the mother

and young. Since they build their nests on the ground they are endangered by more predators than are the tree nesters.

Natural selection has developed a remarkable protection for the female Dipper and her brood. During the nesting period and while the young remain dependent, they give no body odor. As most ground-traveling predatory animals depend primarily upon their keen sense of smell, they are in this way effectively disarmed. The survival struggle has made the Dipper's enemies expert hunters, and they acquire an uncanny knowledge of the birds' habits; thus, though protected in this way, destruction is an ever present menace.

The pollution of the streams by refuse from mills and by drainage is doubtless destroying some of the dipper's food supply, and driving them farther and farther back into the mountains. Some are driven out by too congested settlements, and many hundreds of them are shot at fish hatcheries. They are too much beloved, as cheerful companies along the lonely brooks, to be molested by the trappers and the appreciative anglers.

Fall.—Fred M. Packard tells me that, in Estes Park, Colo., "the adults and fledglings remain at the higher altitudes until September; then most of them begin to descend into the lower zones for winter. Stragglers migrate as the upper waters freeze, and some will winter in the park, if the larger streams remain partly free of ice."

Winter.—The dipper is a hardy mountaineer, indifferent to cold and impervious to it. His thick, downy underwear and his coat of dense feathers keep the cold out and the heat in. He lives all winter as far north, or as high up in the mountains, as he can find any open water. And he sings as freely perched on a cake of ice, or in an icy cavern along the shore, as he does from a rock in his summer haunts. Dr. Nelson (1887) had several brought to him "in midwinter from the head of Norton Sound, during a cold period when the thermometer registered as low as 50° at Saint Michaels, and they must frequently endure a temperature of −60°, or even lower, since in the interior the cold is almost invariably much more severe than along the coast. On the Upper Yukon it is also a resident, whence the fur traders brought me wintering specimens."

Farther south the dippers are forced to retire from the higher parts of the mountains, as the streams freeze and are covered with snow; then they become more crowded on the lower reaches of the streams or rivers, or resort to the shores of open lakes. At that season they often wander even beyond the foothills. Frank L. Farley, of Camrose, Alberta, tells me that he has "several records of its appearance on rapid creeks in the ranching country west of Innisfail, at least 50 miles distant from the Rockies." And Laurence B. Potter, of Eastend, Saskatchewan, writes me that he has sight records of the dipper "on the swift flowing creeks that form the headwaters of the Frenchman River."

A fitting closing is this winter picture, drawn by Muir's (1894) matchless pen:

One mild winter morning, when Yosemite Valley was swept its length from west to east by a cordial snowstorm, I sallied forth to see what I might learn and enjoy. A sort of gray, gloaming-like darkness filled the valley, the huge walls were out of sight, all ordinary sounds were smothered, and even the loudest booming of the falls was at times buried beneath the roar of the heavy-laden blast. The loose snow was already over five feet deep on the meadows, making extended walks impossible without the aid of snowshoes. I found no great difficulty, however, in making my way to a certain ripple on the river where one of my ouzels lived. He was at home, busily gleaning his breakfast among the pebbles of a shallow portion of the margin, apparently unaware of anything extraordinary in the weather. Presently he flew out to a stone against which the icy current was beating, and turning his back to the wind, sang as delightfully as a lark in springtime.

DISTRIBUTION

Range.—Alaska to Guatemala; nonmigratory.

The dipper is found **north** to northern Alaska (Kobuk River Valley, tributaries of the upper Atlatna River, and Eagle); central Yukon (Forty-mile, Ogilvie Range, and the forks of the Macmillan River); northern British Columbia (Atlin and Fort Halkett); Alberta (Athabaska River, about 150 miles northwest of Stony Plain, and Edmonton). **East** to Alberta (Edmonton and Calgary); Montana (Glacier Park, Belt Mountains, and Bozeman); Wyoming (Wolf, Sundance, and Laramie Mountains); South Dakota (Black Hills); Colorado (Gold Hill, Golden, Manitou, and Wet Mountains); New Mexico (Sangre de Cristo Mountains, Taos, and Ruidoso); Chihuahua (Cerro Prieto); alpine region of Veracruz (Jalapa and Río Blanco); Puebla (Mount Popocatepetl); Oaxaca (Oaxaca); and Guatemala (San Mateo, Los Arcos, and Tecpam). **South** to Guatemala (Tontonicopam and Tecpam). **West** to Guatemala (Tecpam and Barrillas); Oaxaca (Oaxaca); Mexico (Temascaltepec); Chihuahua (Pinos Altos, Chuhuichupa, and Pacheco); Arizona (Huachuca Mountains, Santa Catalina Mountains, Salt River Wildlife Refuge, Oak Creek, and Grand Canyon); the Coast Range in California (San Diego County, Carpenteria, San Francisco Bay region, and Hoopa Valley, Humboldt County); Oregon (Trail and Tillamook Bay); Washington (Vancouver, Olympic Mountains, and Bellingham); British Columbia (Vancouver Island and Graham Island, Queen Charlotte Islands); and Alaska (Sitka, Kodiak Island, Unalaska Island, Nunivak Island, and Kobuk River).

The range as outlined applies to the entire species, which has been divided into three subspecies or geographic races. The typical race, the Mexican dipper (*C. m. mexicanus*), occurs from the Huachuca Mountains in Arizona to southern Mexico; the dipper (*C. m. unicolor*) is found in Alaska, Canada, and the United States; the third race is found in Guatemala.

Casual records.—An individual was watched closely in May 1891, on the White River, Sioux County, Nebr.; and a specimen was collected June 2, 1903, at Wauneta, Chase County, Nebr.

Egg dates.—Alberta: 8 records, April 14 to June 28.

California: 30 records, March 23 to June 26; 16 records, April 18 to May 20, indicating the height of the season.

Colorado: 20 records, April 4 to June 10; 10 records, May 9 to May 31.

Oregon: 6 records, April 18 to June 7.

CINCLUS MEXICANUS MEXICANUS Swainson

MEXICAN DIPPER

Discovery in the Field Museum in Chicago by Emmet R. Blake (1942) of a specimen of this type race of the species, collected by George F. Breninger in the Huachuca Mountains, Ariz., on May 28, 1903, entitles this form to a place on our list. Until recently our North American form, *C. m. unicolor*, was supposed to extend its range in the mountains of California, Arizona, and New Mexico approximately to the Mexican border. Evidently these, and other extreme southern mountain ranges, have also attracted several other Mexican forms, as they lie close to the border and have formed a natural pathway into the United States.

The Mexican dipper is darker than our more northern bird; its head and neck are deep sepia brown, whereas in our northern bird the head and neck are more grayish brown, and the whole plumage is paler.

Family TROGLODYTIDAE: Wrens

TROGLODYTES AËDON AËDON Vieillot

EASTERN HOUSE WREN

PLATES 25–27

CONTRIBUTED BY ALFRED OTTO GROSS

HABITS

There are two recognized forms of the house wren, the eastern, *Troglodytes aëdon aëdon*, and the western, *Troglodytes aëdon parkmanii*. Oberholser (1934) in a revision of the North American wrens has adopted Wilson's name *domestica* because it "seems" to antedate Vieillot's name *aëdon* by which the bird has long been known. The less rufescent birds inhabiting the region from Michigan, Indiana, Kentucky to West Virginia, western Pennsylvania, western New York, and Quèbec and occurring as a migrant farther east are described as a new form with the name *Troglodytes domestica baldwini*. For the present at least it seems best to adhere to the nomenclature of the 1931 A. O. U. Check-list: As far as this life history account is concerned the subspecies are of minor consequence, and what is generally true of one will also apply to the other subspecies.

One of the earliest recollections I have of birds is a pair of energetic little house wrens that built in a rustic box placed inside an open porch of our Illinois home. These little brown birds (unknown by name to me at that time) had an intriguing fascination, with their constant going and coming with flitting upcocked tails, their innumerable visits to the nest with food to satisfy their clamoring young, their chattering vibrant songs, and their saucy scoldings when I ventured too near; all those early experiences have left indelible and pleasurable memories. For similar reasons the house wren has gained countless human friends who cherish the presence of these birds as tenants about their homes.

Unfortunately, individual house wrens, especially those inhabiting populated areas, have displayed too much aggression for *Lebensraum* in their relations to other birds. This Nazi trait has brought them into disfavor by persons who now hold a strong prejudice against this attractive and useful bird.

The house wren because of its depredations on the nests, eggs, and young of other birds has been hailed into court where notable witnesses both for and against his character have taken the stand. The controversy raged during the twenties as evidenced by the numerous articles and communications published in the ornithological journals. Sherman (1925) in a spirited article, "Down with the House Wren Boxes," took a venomous stand against the wren. She reviews at length the statements made by numerous observers, of the destructive tendencies of the house wren especially toward those species that come into direct competition with it, through their nesting in the same environment. Miss Sherman's paper stimulated the writing of many of the articles for and against the wren that followed.

Chapman (1925) in an editorial on the wren controversy stated in part as follows:

The day that I returned from Florida I found the House Wren here to greet me. * * * The bubbling music which springs so uncontrollably from his quivering throat is too characteristic a part of the season's chorus to be spared. The box which has been hanging so patiently on my grape arbor would be but a sad reminder of past joys if it should not again be animated by his bustling little body.

Tried in a court of men and he no doubt would be convicted of the charges made against him; but a court of Wrens would dismiss the case and commend the culprit. Purely as a matter of justice which verdict should we take?

Should we judge Wrens by their standards or by ours? That we may insist that they conform to our standards is quite a different matter. * * *

The so-called nature-lover who takes his own standards, personal likes and dislikes afield with him, is apt to find quite as much to condemn in animal, as in human life. Nature attracts us primarily because she is natural. It is the wild not the tame animal which appeals to us; and we want it to exhibit the traits which have won for it a place among competitors. * * *

The House Wren has become abundant with our help and through the exercise of the instincts which have made it a successful species. But is there any reason why we should call him a criminal? As a matter of fact we are the guilty ones. Inspired by the best of motives and encouraged by those in authority, in an excess of zeal we have embarked on a campaign in the behalf of hole-nesting birds without perhaps stopping to think just where it will lead us.

McAtee (1926b) reviewed the evidence from the standpoint of an economic ornithologist in his article "Judgment on the House Wren." He writes in part as follows:

Recently the relations of the House Wren to other birds have been fully discussed in our ornithological journals. The Wren has had its supporters as well as defamers, but few on either side have taken a justicial view of the controversy. The evidence that House Wrens sometimes destroy the eggs and otherwise interfere with the nesting of other birds is indisputable, but it is not so positively realized that this is only one of the factors we must take into consideration in forming a judgment (in the technical sense of the term) on the economic value of the species.

Many birds are so free from special vices or virtues that their economic status is decided upon the basis of their food-habits alone. Were this true of the House Wren, the species would receive a very high appraisal, for it is almost exclusively insectivorous, and that, too, in chiefly commendable directions. * * * The House Wren is as worthy of approbation as any of our birds on the score of its food-habits. It has a better rank in this respect than most of the species whose eggs it occasionally destroys. Egg- and nest-destruction by the Wren is of local, not general, occurrence and the remedy should be local. It is simple to eliminate bird-houses that only Wrens can use, a measure to be applied in places where serious depredations have been noted, or to close temporarily, or reduce in number, houses that have proved bases for sporadic marauding. Most problems in economic ornithology resolve themselves into local irregularities of bird-behavior, and the wisest treatment in almost every case proves to be that adapted both in kind and degree to local needs.

The relations of the house wren to other birds make him a much more interesting even though it be a less desirable personality. His aggressions toward other birds have not been recently acquired but constitute an old and well-established trait. His behavior is evidence of his superior intelligence in the battle of the survival of the fittest. He is activated to secure and dominate a definite area during the reproductive season for the sake of his own preservation. For this reason this small enterprising midget making his way in the world often against superior odds deserves our respect rather than our condemnation. If man upsets the balance of nature by his interference, for example by erecting too many nesting boxes, then man alone is to blame for the conditions which prevail in certain localities.

Spring.—The first arrivals of the house wren make their appearance along the southern limits of the breeding range during the latter part of March, but it is not until the middle of April that they become common. Certain individuals remain on the southernmost wintering grounds until the second week of April. In Florida a series of 8 years of records of birds last seen in the spring range from April 12 to April 22, an average date of April 17. The first house wrens arrive in New England and a corresponding latitude in the Midwest during the last week of April or early in May, but it is not until the middle of the month that the nesting activities are in full swing. At Hillcrest, Ohio, according to Kendeigh (1941), who made observations on the time for beginning of the nesting activities of 186 males and 165 females, "The median date for all the males to begin nesting activities is May 11, although the median date for the *first* male activity is May 1, and for the *latest* male to begin activity * * * is June 22. Females average later, the corresponding three dates being May 20, May 11, and July 1." Kendeigh continues:

Although first-year birds may be among the first to arrive in late April and early May, adults of two or more years of age make up a far greater percentage of the migratory population at this time than they do later in the season. Females arrive about 9 days later than the males.

Adult males that have previously nested almost invariably return to the same territory that they formerly occupied, or they establish a new territory adjacent to it. The return of adult females to their former nesting areas is almost as regular.

With young birds hatched the preceding season, there is a marked tendency to scatter in all directions, although they occur in greatest relative numbers in the vicinity where they were hatched.

Territory.—As soon as the male appears on the breeding ground his arrival is announced by the territory song. The male isolates himself and establishes himself in a definite area. Territory is important as a means by which birds become paired and mated and an insurance for adequate nesting sites and food supply. According to Kendeigh (1941)—

the process of courtship and mating can scarcely be separated in the house wren from the phenomena of territory, as they are so vitally interwoven and intrinsically related.

Territory is established and defended chiefly by song. * * * The "territory song" of the house wren is but little different from the "nesting song," and both songs announce to other birds that the territory is occupied. [The territory song is also an advertisement of the male's presence to females, and of inducement to the female to enter a particular male's territory in preference to the territory of some other male.]

The presence of a female is a distinct incentive to song. The male will give his territory song over and over again, day after day, in a purely mechanical manner until a female comes into view. Not really until then does he show emotional excitement. The song is given more energetically, the mating song is interspersed and males from adjoining territory may tune in. Competition between two males in adjoining territories becomes most vigorous when an unattached female enters the area. * * * The male whose song is most stimulating to her ears would seem to have the advantage.

In addition to song, territories are also defended by the wren's assuming threatening postures sometimes accompanied with scolding, chasing, or physical combat.

Kendeigh says:

In the establishment of nest-sites, house wrens may destroy the nests, eggs, or young of the same or different species, or even the adult birds. Although there is considerable individual variation in this aggressive behavior, it tends to be most intense during years when the total house wren population on the area is highest. * * *

Territories in the Hillcrest area average 1.0 acre * * * in size. * * * The size of the territory varies inversely with the size of the house wren population and does not exert a limiting influence on the total numbers of the species in the area until it approaches the minimum compressible limit. The adult birds restrict their intensive daily activity to limited parts of the territory but eventually cover the entire area. * * *

The successful mating of two birds of opposite sex appears to depend on their physiological and psychological readiness, their ability to stimulate each other sexually, the location and character of the territory [and] nest-site together with the nest foundation begun by the male, and finally their freedom from other activities.

Territory is maintained throughout each breeding period and breeding season, although there may be some decrease in activity as nesting progresses. This continuance of territory may be correlated with the tendency toward polygamy manifest in the male, with the use of the same territory for later matings, and it may also involve the need for a constant and readily available source of food and for freedom from annoying intruders. Primarily, however, the territorial behavior is most closely linked with the acquiring of a first mate. There is no evidence that territory is maintained at any other than the breeding season of the year.

Courtship.—With the arrival of the female an ardent courtship begins. They have an extensive repertoire of songs and call notes, which are used for various occasions and for purposes of intercommunication. Both males and females have a habit of quivering their wings when excited, which is most pronounced during the mating process but is evident also when the birds are disturbed or scolding. The position of the male's tail is also a good indicator of the degree of his excitement. During ordinary singing it is kept lowered, but when his courtship song is intensified, or at times when he is scolding, the tail is tilted upward. During copulation it is vertical or tilted forward at an acute angle.

Much excitement is manifested during the inspection of available nesting sites, some of which have already been selected and partially filled with sticks by the male. The female has opinions of her own resulting in violent domestic controversies that intersperse their passionate courtship antics. The female may refuse the nest proffered by the male; sometimes she may accept the nesting box but disapproving of the nesting material or the way it was arranged by the male proceeds to throw it out stick by stick. Both birds do their part in the building of the final nest, but the male spends more time singing and guarding the nesting territory.

After the female is busily engaged with her incubation duties the activities of the male are less important since all he does is to sing rather mechanically. Occasionally he spends his time carrying sticks into some nearby box in the pretense of building a new nest, and while doing so he sings his courtship song. In fact, the building of the extra nest has been thought to be one of the manifestations of his peculiar courtship. While so employed he often acquires a second mate while the first is still busy with household duties.

Nesting.—The house wren stands out preeminently as one of the most eccentric of our birds in the choice of its nesting site. In fact, its choice of a nesting place exhibits such extreme variation that it is difficult to select one that can be considered typical.

The primitive environment of the house wren was the woodlands and its nesting site the natural cavity of some tree or stump. The nest is seldom exposed, but generally the requirements of the wren demand an enclosure that conceals the nest on all sides except the point of entrance. These birds have readily adapted themselves to the environment of man reaching a state of semidomesticity. They have availed themselves of houses constructed for their special use or lacking these they have built their nests in various contraptions incidentally provided either inside or outside of buildings. They are not particular and are just as apt to accept an old rusty can in a garbage heap as they are a neatly painted house set in the midst of a beautiful flower garden.

Innumerable curious nesting places have been reported, a few of which will serve to illustrate their infinite variety. At a sanctuary located on Wallops Island, Va., 24 empty cow skulls found bleaching on the island were hung up or lodged in the trees and shrubbery. Almost immediately 23 of the gruesome skulls were occupied by house wrens, who were quick to accept these unusual nesting boxes (Forbush, 1916). There are several instances where house wrens have built their nests inside the large paper nests of hornets or wasps that were attached to private or public buildings. Before adding nesting materials the interior of the insect nests were excavated by the industrious birds. This relationship between wrens and wasps was reversed in one instance as illustrated by a photograph taken by R. E. Hart (1941) on the campus of Keuka College, New York. A wren house was taken over by a swarm of wasps and was completely covered except for a small part of the roof, with successive layers of paper layed down by the insects.

It is not uncommon for the wren to make use of the nests of other birds. At Loring, Va., a pair of wrens built in a deserted barn swallow's nest. At Laanna, Pike County, Pa., Burleigh (1927) writes of a nest containing seven eggs which was in a robin's nest on a ledge above a pillar of a porch. Here the cavity had been deepened and a few twigs and feathers added, but these were not noticeable a short distance away. He found another nest in a barn swallow's nest lodged against a beam in the roof of a barn. Here again the cavity had been deepened and a few twigs and feathers added. Both nests were new and apparently had been appropriated from the rightful owners. Angus (1934) reports finding five young wrens in a phoebe's nest under a bridge, and in this case no nesting material had been added by the wrens. Wilbur F. Smith (1911a) relates a strange partnership in which wrens and English sparrows built a nest in a bird house, the sparrows starting first. Both the sparrow and wren layed eggs that were incubated by the English sparrow. Though wrens are ordinarily antagonistic toward bluebirds and tree swallows, they have been known to occupy different compartments of the same martin house and exist in apparent harmony.

Not only do wrens occupy nests of other birds built in boxes or natural cavities or those in the protection of buildings but also they have appropriated nests built in open situations. Schwab (1899) writes of a pair of wrens that occupied the deserted nest of a Baltimore oriole hung 20 feet from the ground in one of the outermost branches of a large sugar-maple tree. Two other cases of wrens occupying oriole nests have come to my attention; hence the above case is not unique. At Bay of Erie, Pa., a pair of wrens departed greatly from their nesting environment when they selected a kingfisher's nesting hole in a sand bank. This nest contained young when discovered (Sennett, 1889). Still another unusual nesting site in relation to other birds was that of a pair of wrens which built in the deeper interstices of an osprey's nest located on Plum Island, N. Y. (C. S. Allen, 1892).

Other interesting nesting sites of the house wren have been in a fish creel or watering pot hung on the side of a shed or fence, rusty tin cans in garbage piles, old threshing machines and other farm machinery, in tin cans, teapots, and flowerpots left on shelves of sheds, in a soap dish, in old boots and shoes, and even in a bag of feathers. Outdoors they have been known to nest in the nozzle or main part of pumps, in the hat or pockets of a scarecrow, in an iron pipe railing, in a weathervane, in holes in a brick wall or building, and in a coat hung up at a camp site. One pair of wrens built their nest on the rear axle of an automobile which was used daily. When the car was driven the wrens went along. Even under these most unusual circumstances the eggs were successfully hatched (Northcutt, 1937).

The individual wrens have one trait in common in that these energetic creatures strive to fill the container they select with nesting material.   Regardless of its size it is usually well filled except for a narrow passageway leading to the comparatively small nesting cavity that contains the eggs or young.   This trait is probably one that has developed through the protection the birds derive by keeping out certain intruders.   This fact is often considered in the construction of wren nesting boxes by cutting an entrance large enough to admit the tiny body of the wren but too small to admit the passage of competitors the size of an English sparrow or a starling.

The bulk of a house wren's nest is generally composed of relatively long and coarse twigs and sticks and grass.   According to Godard (1915) if the wrens are given a choice of dry and green sticks they select the dry dead sticks and reject the green ones.   The nesting cavity is usually lined with finer and softer materials such as feathers, hair, wool, spider cocoons, and catkins.

McAtee (1940a) analyzed the materials in 33 complete or partial nests found at the Bureau of Plant Industry Experiment Station located near Glen Dale, Md.   His report is as follows:

Foundations included (in the number of nests indicated): twigs (33), feathers (16), chestnut spikes (13), wool (12), leaves (7), cord (6), and weed stalks (5). Materials used in fewer instances were: rootlets, red-cedar bark, cotton, grass, chestnut shell, paper, a large fragment of snail shell, exoskeletons of milleped and sowbug, and a spider cocoon. The twigs were characteristically coarse and included some up to 8 inches in length and a few that were branched. Rose twigs with plentiful thorns were frequently employed, and in a few cases callow young were raised in such nests with little or no cushioning to protect them from the spines. The twig bases of nests were often from 4 to 6 inches deep. Flecks of wool and cotton were scattered through the twig bases to no conceivable purpose. The lining of the 33 nests included grass in 19 cases, hair, chiefly horsehair, in 16, feathers in 13, and rootlets in six. Other items were red-cedar bark, chestnut spikes, weed stalks, and grass. The material in one nest, loosened up in the process of analysis, filled a 2-gallon bucket.

The house wren may use other than the traditional nesting materials. Mrs. Gilbert Drake (1931) describes a nest built in a chicken house in West Park, N. Y., that consisted largely of small pieces of rusted chicken wire.   A nest observed by Helen P. Williams (1931) was made up entirely of metal consisting of rusty bent nails, double-pointed tacks, and pieces of wire.   An analysis made of a nest found at Ames, Iowa, by Harriet C. Battell (1925) was made up of the following rubbish: "52 hairpins, 68 nails (large), 120 small nails, 4 tacks, 13 staples, * * * 10 pins, 4 pieces of pencil lead, 11 safety pins, 6 paper fasteners, 52 wires, * * * 1 buckle, 2 hooks, 3 garter fasteners, and 2 odds and ends."   Goelitz (1918) reports finding a nest made up entirely of rusted pieces of wire.   In fall a tangle of rusted chicken wire was thrown behind a shed, and the following spring a pair of house wrens in search of nesting material found that the wire would break easily into pieces just suited for the purpose. The birds used this wire to the practical exclusion of all other usual materials.

The house wren has the habit of frequently building dummy or extra nests, a trait common to other members of the wren family. Many of these nests are built by the male prior to the arrival of the female in the spring, but a mated male may use its superfluous energy in building extra nests in the neighborhood of the one where his mate is incubating the eggs. Even if a male is unsuccessful in obtaining a mate, he may continue to build several nests during the course of the season. The nests built by the male are crude structures, and it is probable that some of the curious nests made of rusted wire nails and other metallic material previously described are to be attributed to the work of the male. In central Illinois I observed both members of a pair of wrens build three complete nests in different boxes before selecting one for final occupancy.

Mrs. Daisy Dill Norton (Forbush, 1929), of Lewiston, Maine, reports a case in which an unmated female built a nest in a bluebird house. It went through all the manifestations of a maternal wren with a family in prospect. She allowed no birds on her house or near the nest and was ready to do battle with anything that appeared regardless of size. The wren remained until the end of August, and in all this time Mrs. Norton never saw another wren, nor did she hear the song of the male. After the wren left, the box was taken down, and inside was found an exquisitely built nest containing 12 (sterile) eggs. From these observations it is apparent that the nesting instinct is strongly developed in both the male and female house wren.

One cannot watch a pair of wrens in their repeated attempts to get long unwieldy sticks through a narrow box entrance scarcely large enough to admit their tiny bodies without being greatly impressed by their dogged persistence, energy, and skill. At first the wren, especially if it is a young individual, may attempt to enter a nesting hole with the beak grasped at the center of a long twig, but very quickly through trial and error it learns to thrust one end of the stick through the opening and then to inch it along with the beak until well inside the nesting box. After the technique is mastered it is not unusual for them to add four or five such sticks during the course of a minute. In a single day they may accumulate a mass of sticks several inches in depth, and in 2 or 3 days the entire structure is completed and ready to receive the eggs.

Eggs.—The number of eggs in complete sets varies from 5 to 12, but the range in numbers is usually 6 to 8 in the vast majority of nests. Harlow (1918) in reporting on 47 nests of the house wren found in New Jersey and Pennsylvania states that the average set was 6 or 7 eggs, but in his series there was a range from 5 to 8 eggs in complete

sets. Baldwin (Baldwin and Bowen, 1928) found that of 21 pairs
that had two broods that he had under observation, the average was
6 eggs for the first and 5.5 eggs for the second brood. Of 19 pairs
known to have but one brood the average number of eggs laid was
6.3 per female.

Birds may be classed as determinate with respect to egg production
when they lay a definite number of eggs in a set and indeterminate
when they can be induced to continue laying by egg removal. Cole
(1930) found that if eggs, presumably from the same female house
wren, were removed daily, the bird layed an unusually large number of
eggs. Detailed measurements he made revealed that the length of the
eggs increased in general to a certain point, then rested, then increased
to a second high point, then rested, and for a third time increased to
a high point; following this there was a downward trend. Thus there
appeared to be four cycles, separated by rest periods. It is suggested
that the process of incubation may react on endocrine glands to cause
cessation of egg production.

The eggs vary from short-rounded-ovate to oval in shape. The
ground color is white, usually with a vinaceous tinge. They are
thickly speckled with minute dots of brownish red or cinnamon-brown,
which are often so dense as to conceal the ground color giving the
entire egg a uniform salmon-colored or reddish-brown cast. The
color is deepest at the rounded end, and in many eggs there is a wreath
of spots concentrated around this end of the egg. The eggs vary in
their long diameter from 0.58 to 0.70 inch and in their short diameter
from 0.46 to 0.53 inch. The average dimensions of 100 eggs are
0.64 by 0.50 inch. The measurements of 50 eggs in the United States
National Museum averaged 16.4 by 12.7 millimeters; the eggs showing
the four extremes measure 18.3 by 13.2, 15.8 by 15.5, 14.7 by 12.2, and
16.3 by 11.7 millimeters.

The house wren has two distinct breeding periods. The first, according to Kendeigh (1940), who has made very extensive observations
at the Baldwin Bird Research Laboratory, Cleveland, Ohio, begins in
the middle of May and lasts until the end of June; the second begins
late in June and lasts to the middle of August. Egg-laying occurs
most regularly during the first 2 weeks of each period, but occasional
sets may be deposited at any time. One egg is laid each day during the
egg laying period until the full complement of eggs is completed.
Certain observers have credited the house wren with as many as three
broods in a season, but these cases are unusual, and it is extremely
doubtful whether three broods are ever successfully reared.

Young.—The incubation period of the house wren is 13 days. The
egg temperatures in the nest of the house wren according to Kendeigh
fluctuate between 33.9° C. and 36.9° C. The temperature of 35° C.
may be considered the temperature at which incubation to hatching is

normally accomplished in 13 days. Based on the rate of gaseous exchange the most favorable incubation temperature for rapid development falls between 35° and 37.8° C. On the basis of Kendeigh's computations, if we take into account the total amount of oxygen absorbed and assume the respiratory quotient to be 0.72, development at a controlled temperature of 37.8° C. would require only ten days, while at 32.2° C. it would require 18 days. Temperature is an important factor in determining the length of incubation. Reports by different observers present a variation in the length of the incubation period from 11 to 15 days, but this discrepancy can be explained in part through the lack of proper consideration in the factors involved and especially through the lack of accurate determination when incubation actually starts.

Baldwin and Kendeigh (1927) made a detailed study of the behavior of nesting house wrens, including their attentiveness and inattentiveness. Their information was obtained by direct observations and from continuous records secured by the use of special apparatus involving the principle of thermoelectricity to determine the presence or absence of the birds from the nest. It seems desirable to quote their statements at considerable length.

The differentiation between the periods of attentiveness when the bird is actually engaged in nesting activities and the periods of inattentiveness when it is feeding or resting is best developed with the female for it is she who is most active in the reproduction of the species.

After the female becomes mated with the male, she soon begins to carry in lining for the nest, the rough part of which has been begun or finished by the male some time previous. The female, however, does not carry nesting material into the box continuously for long at a time, getting her food at odd moments when she is looking for material. On the contrary, she works assiduously at building the nest for a period of a few to several minutes, and then goes off and hunts actively for food for herself, only to come back when this period is ended to carry more material for another stretch of time, and so on. While building her nest she is not concerned with looking for food. Likewise, when she is away looking for food she does not concern herself with nesting duties. She usually spends a great deal longer time away from the box than at the box during this phase of her nesting activities.

The same holds true for the days during which she is laying her set of eggs. Her inattentive periods are usually much longer than her attentive periods, although she comes to the box at regular intervals throughout the day. As her set nears completion and the duties of incubation approach, the inattentive periods gradually shorten, and the attentive periods not only lengthen but become more numerous.

The day on which the eggs hatched the activities during the early morning started at the normal rate. However, at one nest studied, beginning at 7:11 her record indicates considerable uneasiness.

The reason for this became apparent when at 7:35 the first young bird was found to have just broken out of the shell. All of her eggs hatched during the rest of the day. The number of her attentive and inattentive periods during the day was 82, although the average number per day during the incubation period had been only 43½. This unusual restlessness, however, was exceptional, since our records for other females are much steadier.

The female during the next few days gradually resumed her normal rate of activity. During the next 6 days when she spent considerable time brooding the young, the periods of attentiveness averaged about 13⁸⁄₁₀ minutes and her periods of inattentiveness about 4⁶⁄₁₀.

When both adult birds were busy from morning till night with the feeding of the young, periods of attentiveness and inattentiveness still were the rule. The adults would feed the young several times in succession and then take a short period off when they would get some food and rest for themselves. Sometimes they would feed the young repeatedly and rapidly nine, ten, or more times before they would stop. Then again the number of feedings per period would be only three or four, or in many cases, but one. Usually the number of feedings per period averaged higher in the morning than in the heat of the day.

Baldwin (1921), through his exhaustive banding operations at Cleveland, Ohio, has shown that house wrens are not permanently mated. Not only do they change mates from season to season but also they shift mates between the two nesting periods of the same season. His banding records indicate also that the house wren breeds the season after hatching when it is one year old. Out of 156 wrens banded during the 5 years between 1915 and 1920, 10, or 6⅔ percent, returned either to the same or to other nesting boxes on his premises. In more recent banding results Kendeigh (1941) reported a 75 percent return ratio of adults. Baldwin observed the details of the life history of seven different nests of which the following is typical: The nest was started on July 4 and completed 2 days later, July 6. The set of eggs was completed on July 13 and hatched on July 26, an incubation period of 13 days. The young left on August 10 after spending 15 days in the nest. The total cycle required 36 days.

Col. S. T. Walker, of Milton, Fla., made the following detailed observations of a pair of nesting house wrens (Ridgway, 1889):

I was sick at the time, and watched the whole proceeding from the laying of the first stick to the conclusion. The nest was placed in one of the pigeonholes of my desk, and the birds effected an entrance to the room through sundry cracks in the log cabin.

Nest begun_____ April 15th.
Nest completed and first egg laid_____ April 27th.
Last egg laid_____ May 3d.
Began incubation_____ May 4th.
Hatching completed_____ May 18th.
Young began to fly_____ May 27th.
Young left the nest_____ June 1st.
Total time occupied_____ 47 days.

The time spent by the young in the nest, as reported by various observers, varies from 12 to 18 days. Burns (1921) states the complete nesting cycle of the house wren is 35 to 45 days, whereas Bewick's wren and the chickadee require 52 to 53 days.

Baldwin and Bowen (1928) state that out of 104 nests under observation at Gates Mills, Ohio, 86 broods were successful. "The total number of eggs laid by all females under observation was 581. Of these 424 or about 73 percent hatched, and 390, or about 67 percent left the nest as normal young. The remaining 33 percent perished at one stage or another."

The instincts of the house wren are so strongly developed in certain individuals that curious situations sometimes occur. Mrs. Bridge (1911) reports a single pair of birds nested on her premises, but two nests were constructed, one in a gourd and the other in a birdhouse. When the young were hatched the brood in the birdhouse were fed by the male alone but the young in the gourd were fed by both members of the pair. The inference is that after the female laid both sets of eggs she incubated the eggs in the gourd while the male took care of those in the box.

Kendeigh (1941) records cases of multiple nesting as follows:

Although the female ordinarily remains with the young until they become independent, there is a tendency towards the end of the first period when the nestlings are being cared for in the box for the female to begin preparations for a second brood. She may inspect other boxes either of the same male or of other males in different territories. If acceptable, mating may occur very soon, nest-lining inserted, or even egg-laying begun before she is through caring for her first brood. It is but a small step to actual desertion of the first brood by the female in order to start a second brood that much sooner, but desertion does not ordinarily occur without provocation. When the female leaves, the male will ordinarily care for the young alone. He mostly stops singing and applies himself assiduously to the task of hunting food for his offspring. However, he does not brood nor does he stay in the box at night. If the female deserts before the young have acquired self-regulation of their body temperature, death usually follows, but after a week's development, the male is often able to bring them off successfully.

It has been observed that house wrens that for some reason or other fail to raise a brood of their own and sometimes individuals that do not succeed in obtaining a mate will satisfy the urge for caring for offspring by feeding the adults or young of other species. Hills (1924) reports a case in which a house wren fed the adults and young of grosbeaks as well as a family of English sparrows. His account is as follows: "The female Grosbeak was on the nest and a House Wren was bringing small caterpillars to her, which she took from the Wren's beak and fed to her young. At first it seemed to me as though the Wren was liable to be cited as co-respondent, but soon the male Grosbeak came and relieved his mate on the nest, yet the Wren continued to come with food which the male Grosbeak likewise received and fed to the young. * * * Both of the Grosbeaks sometimes themselves ate the Wren's offerings, in place of feeding them to their young. The Wren made more trips to the nest than both Grosbeaks combined." After the young grosbeaks left the nest the wren persisted in feeding them directly. A few days later this same wren was observed feeding a family of English sparrows.

There is evidence that polygamy may be practiced among house wrens. Kathleen M. Hempel (1919) gives an account of two families of wrens that were served by one male. The lone male carried food to both females during the course of incubation and assisted in feeding each of the broods of offspring. John W. Taylor (1905) cites a similar case at St. Paul, Minn., in which a male wren carried food to two nests, one located in a stump and the other about 60 feet away in a birdhouse. Metcalf (1919) writes that he had eight house-wren nests on his place at Foreston, Minn., but at no time did he observe more than two males.

After the young leave the nesting box in which they were reared, they seldom return, but many observers have reported seeing the entire family brood rounded together by the parents, at the end of the day, to roosting places. These places may be other nesting boxes, a platform provided by an unused robin's or chipping sparrow's nest, or the dense foliage of a pine tree or shrub. Such roosts may be used for a week or more before the family disperses and the young assume a more or less independent role. Usually the adults remain with their young about 12 or 13 days, and for the first part of this period the parents feed the young practically everything they receive. During the last few days of this period they acquire the ability to hunt food for themselves, and the parents spend less and less time with them. Finally, when the young are able to take care of themselves, the relationship of parent to offspring ceases and becomes that of individual to individual.

Plumages.—The natal down is sepia brown in color. This first plumage is very scant, being represented in typical specimens by not more than 25 neossoptiles or down feathers. Of these there are five on each side of the crown and four on each side of the occipital region. On the back of the bird there are three on each side and usually a single one at the posterior end of the median line.

The down undergoes disintegration by wear and abrasion in the nest, and by the time the young are ready to fly only a few filaments remain attached to the tips of the juvenal feathers. The juvenal plumage of the house wren is described by Dwight (1900) as follows: "Above, Prout's-brown, russet tinged on the rump and deep grayish sepia on the pileum, sometimes faintly barred. Wings and tail Prout's-brown, darkest on the wings both with wavy, dusky barring, the palest areas on the outer primaries. Below, including sides of the head, dull grayish white with dusky mottling, washed strongly with russet on the flanks and crissum. Orbital ring dusky buff. Bill and feet buffy sepia-brown, becoming darker." The juvenal plumage differs from that of the adult in the blackish mottling of the breast, but these markings disappear with the postjuvenal molt.

Boulton (1927) has presented a detailed and exhaustive study of ptilosis of the house wren in which his general conclusions are as follows:

The first appearance of feathers and the sequence of their development in the various regions follow in definite pre-determined order, constant for any one region but varying among different regions.

Development usually begins at one side or end of a region and spreads progressively over it until growth is completed.

In at least one case (primaries), development begins in the middle of the region and proceeds simultaneously toward each end.

In another case (Ventral Tract), there are two centers of development. One appears in the middle of the tract and spreads both posteriorly and anteriorly. The other starts in the inter-ramal region and spreads backward until it meets the anterior portion of the other development center. In the Spinal Tract is found a somewhat parallel case.

The feather sheath, after emerging from the skin, has no function and its rate of disintegration is primarily correlated with the amount of abrasion to which it is exposed.

The growth of feathers appears to be retarded until the second week of nestling life, but, to a large extent, this is actually due to the fact that development is going on beneath the skin during the first week and is often overlooked, while the rupture of the feather sheath and consequent exposure of the feather during the second week makes growth appear more noticeably.

According to Dwight (1900),

the first winter plumage is acquired by a partial postjuvenal moult, beginning late in August, which involves the body plumage and wing coverts, but not the rest of the wings nor the tail. The young and old become practically indistinguishable. [This plumage is] similar to the previous plumage but darker and grayer with faint barring above, the wing coverts, chiefly the lesser with whitish spots; below whiter without mottling, the throat and sides obscurely barred with pale drab, the flanks and crissum boldly barred dull black which is bordered with russet.

First nuptial plumage acquired by wear, excessive by the end of the breeding season, which brings out the barring more conspicuously and makes the bird grayer and paler, especially below.

Adult winter plumage acquired by a complete postnuptial moult in August. Practically indistinguishable from first winter, perhaps averaging grayer with darker wings and tail.

Adult nuptial plumage acquired by wear as in the young bird. * * * The sexes are alike and the moults correspond.

Albinism and melanism, which occur frequently in many families of birds, is apparently rare in the Troglodytidae. Ruthven Deane, who gave this subject a great deal of attention, knew of none and emphasized the absence of these plumages in certain families, including the Troglodytidae. He offered no explanation for its absence. In a search through the literature I have failed to find a single record of an albinistic or a melanistic form of the house wren. Hence these phases of plumage in this species are remarkable for their rarity if not their absence.

Wetmore (1936) counted the number of contour feathers in various passeriform birds including two house wrens. A male secured on June 11, 1933, weighing 13.3 grams had 1,271 contour feathers, the latter weighing 0.6 gram. Another male, obtained on July 9, weighin 11.5 grams, had 1,178 contour feathers weighing 0.7 gram.

Poole (1938) in studying the ratio of wing area to weight and the effect of this ratio on flight, determined the wing area of a house wren weighing 11.0 grams to be 48.40 square centimeters. The wing area per gram is shown to be 4.40 square centimeters. As a means of comparison it is interesting to note that in the case of the loon, a poor flier, there is the ratio of only 0.56, while that of Leach's petrel, which spends much of its time in flight, has a ratio of 9.47.

Temperature.—Kendeigh and Baldwin (1928) made an exhaustive series of temperature readings of the house wren in connection with their study of temperature control. For this work they used specially devised thermometers and thermocouples.

The average temperature of wrens during the first day after hatching is 98.6° F. This gradually increases with the age of the young, and by the time they are 15 days old the average temperature is 106.7° F. According to these authors:

The body temperature of young house wrens vary several degrees during the first few days out of the shell, but by the time they are ready to leave the nest their temperatures are not only higher but distinctly less variable.

The development of a resistance in young house wrens against cold follows the sigmoid growth curve. This development of temperature resistance is due primarily to the mass of body increasing faster proportionately than the external dissipating surface, to the development of a feather covering, to the development of an internal dissipating surface probably under nervous respiratory control, and to the production of heat in the metabolism of the bird. * * * No efficient resistance against extreme heat is developed in young house wrens, although the rapid respiration from the lungs and air sacs probably serves toward this end.

According to Kendeigh (1934) the standard temperature of adult house wrens taken at complete rest and without food in the alimentary tract is for the males 104.4° F. (40.2° C.) and for the females 105.0° F. (40.6° C.). He says further:

These values are fairly constant under various conditions, but may be lowered at night when the bird is inactive and without food for several hours. * * * Emotional excitement, muscular activity, extremely high air temperature, and the digestion of food cause a rise in body temperature, while starvation and extremely low air temperature produce a decrease. * * * Under natural conditions a slight correlation exists between variations in average bird and air temperatures from day to day; but the variation in the average bird temperature may amount to only a few tenths of one degree while the average air temperature may vary 20° F. (11.1° C.) or more. Even this slight correlation may not be a direct one but dependent upon variations produced in the amount of activity of the bird from day to day.

* * * Under certain experimental conditions, the body temperature of a house wren has been lowered to below 75° F. (23.9° C.) yet the bird recovered when it was placed for a short time in a warm incubator. A body temperature of 71° F. (21.7° C.) is, however, lethal.

High air temperatures become significant only when they get as high as 93° F. At air temperatures above this degree the resistance time of the birds decreases, body temperatures may rise, the general metabolism is abnormally disturbed, and the normal reproductive behavior interfered with. Birds have upper limits of temperature tolerance as well as lower limits, and these seem to be effective in controlling distribution.

Food.—As far as its feeding habits are concerned, the house wren may be considered entirely beneficial to the interests of mankind. The food is almost all animal life, the small amount of plant material found in stomach examinations being purely incidental and taken in the course of capturing insects poised on the vegetation. Much of our knowledge of the food habits of the house wren is based on field observations, but the most precise information we have has been derived from the detailed analyses of the stomach contents of individuals collected in all sections of the distributional range of the species.

According to Beal (1897), 98 percent of the food is made up of insects or their allies and only 2 percent is vegetable matter. One-half of the food consisted of grasshoppers and beetles, the remainder caterpillars, bugs, and spiders. The examination of 68 stomachs of house wrens, reported in a later publication, by Beal (Beal, McAtee, and Kalmbach, 1916), substantiated the above findings. The largest four items taken in order of their amounts are bugs, grasshoppers and related forms, caterpillars, and beetles. The bugs, made up chiefly of stink bugs, negro bugs, and leafhoppers, constituted 29.34 percent of the food. Grasshoppers, crickets, and locusts are represented in the food throughout the season and aggregate 17.61 percent of the food. Moths and caterpillars, including such forms as cabbage worms and gypsy moths, make up 13.9 percent, and beetles trail closely in amount at 13.8 percent. Ants are eaten to the extent of only 8 percent of the yearly food, but during March they are more significant, being represented in that month by 22.67 percent. Bees, wasps, and flies are taken in smaller amounts; evidently these types of insects are left for the fleeter flycatchers and swallows. Spiders are very acceptable and are captured every month in the season. The latter are found by the inquisitive wrens while searching and exploring under piles of lumber or brush, stone walls, hollow logs, outhouses, and sheds. Only a mere 3 percent of the insects eaten can be considered useful as enemies of destructive species of insects.

In addition to the above-mentioned items of food, small numbers of millipeds, ticks, lice, aphids, snails, and small crustaceans are sometimes included in the diet. There is no evidence in the examination of stomach contents that the wren eats fruit or other farm products, thus placing it high in the group of our beneficial birds.

The nestlings are fed very frequently and consume enormous quantities of food. Judd (1900) made field observations of a brood of three wrens that were housed in a cavity of a locust tree at Marshall Hall, Md. The nest with its family was transferred to a baking-powder can nailed to a trunk of a tree to facilitate the observations. In the course of 4½ hours the mother wren made 110 visits, during which she delivered 111 insects and spiders. Among those identified were 1 white grub, 1 soldier bug, 3 millers (Noctuidae), 9 spiders, 9 grasshoppers, 15 mayflies, and 20 caterpillars. On the following day similar observations were made from 9:35 a. m. to 12:40 p. m., during which time the young were fed 67 times. The food included 4 spiders, 5 grasshoppers, 17 mayflies, and 20 caterpillars.

Jones (1913) observed a pair of wrens feeding their young for a period of 65 hours, during which there were 667 visits to the nest, 560 by the male and 107 by the female. "There were 637 [641?] pieces of food brought"—161 geometrid larvae, 141 leafhoppers, 112 young grasshoppers, 56 bugs, 42 spiders, 29 crickets, 10 moths, 5 ants, 4 miscellaneous, and 81 pieces unidentifiable; and 29 visits were made without food.

McClintock (1909) observed a wren feeding her nestlings considerable numbers of blue-bottle flies. Sometimes the flies were stripped of their legs and wings, but oftener they were fed intact.

Perhaps a record for number of feedings by an individual wren in one day is that of a male bird observed by Clara K. Bayliss (1917) at Macomb, Ill. The pair of wrens nested in a bird box nailed to a disused poultry house. The female disappeared, probably killed, after the brood of seven was hatched. On June 26, when the young were 12 days old, the lone male bird, during a continuous all-day watch from 4:15 a. m., the time of the first feeding, until 8 p. m., when activity ceased, made 1,217 visits to the nest with food. During the hour from 9:15 to 10:15 a. m. the bird made a record of 111 visits to the nest, or an average of nearly two visits for every minute.

Similar observations by various other observers confirm the large number of visits made to the nests by the adult birds, indicating that enormous quantities of food are consumed by the young. Indeed the young as well as the adults spend the major part of their daylight hours in the serious business of feeding.

Stevenson (1933) has shown that the stomachs of the young are consistently larger than those of the adults and has proved the greater food-carrying capacity of young birds over adults. Through a large series of measurements he has found that the average length of the intestine of a house wren one day old is 4.2 centimeters, and by the time it is 11 days old it reaches a maximum of 12.5 centimeters. He finds the value obtained by dividing the length of the intestine by the body weight decreases from 2.80 at the time of hatching to 1.31 at 11 days. There is a gradual decrease in this proportion with increasing age until the birds become adults. Tests indicate that food passes through the entire alimentary tract in approximately 1½ hours, and thus the food supply must be constantly replenished. Stomachs examined at all hours of the day reveal that they are seldom empty and indicate that food is taken repeatedly even though the stomach already contains food.

Hervey Brackbill (MS.), of Baltimore, Md., has attempted to ascertain the source of the food brought to the nestlings. He carefully watched the adult bird during 152 feedings to determine the places of its foraging. The parent flew out of sight on 107 occasions, but in 45 instances he was able to follow the bird to its hunting grounds. On 21 of the trips it went to the ground, a clipped lawn, wild land covered with tall grass and weeds, and the gutter of an asphalt-paved road. Twenty times it secured the food from a tree, one time climbing up the trunk of the nest tree after the fashion of a brown creeper to pick off a moth. It resorted to a bush three times, and once it hawked its prey by flying out in a swift loop from the nest tree.

Voice.—The loud clear song of the house wren is one of the dominant characteristics of its striking personality. The Chippewa Indians, who were keen observers of nature, fully recognized this trait as revealed by their name for the house wren: *O-du-ná mis-sug-ud-da-we'-shi*, meaning a big noise for its size (Cooke, 1884).

The scolding or alarm note of the house wren is a harsh, grating chatter, but the song is a burst of melody, a rather loud, hurried, strenuous, bubbling outpouring—shrill, ecstatic, and difficult to describe or to translate into written words. It is a varied song, but to human ears it is not musical or nearly so appealing as that of its relative, the Carolina wren. The persistent repetition of its nervous energetic outbursts has after a time a tendency to tire the listener.

Dr. Winsor M. Tyler, in correspondence, writes of the song as follows; "The house wren's song is a simple little smooth-running strain, a common form begins with a chatter of rapid notes and then, without pause, runs down the scale in a cascade of seemingly doubled notes. The syllables *tsi-tsi-tsi-tsi-oodle-oodle-oodle-oodle* suggest it somewhat. It varies in form a great deal in minor details and is often full-bodied in tone of voice, but it is practically always delivered with the customary gush and tiresome reiteration. When disturbed, and it takes little to disturb a house wren, the bird bursts forth with a sharp, tense chatter of the Baltimore oriole, or with a long series of nervous fidgety chip-notes."

In correspondence from Aretas A. Saunders, he presents an excellent analysis of 55 records he made during his extensive study of the songs of the house wren. His remarks follow: "While the song of the house wren is very variable, it most frequently consists of a series of very rapid notes, the pitch rising at the beginning, falling toward the end, with a sudden increase in loudness on the highest notes in the middle of the song. There are commonly groups of three to eight repeated notes on the same pitch. Some of the songs contain trills, but the majority do not. Twelve of my 55 records contain one or more trills, that is, places where the notes are so rapid that the single notes cannot be counted. With these 12 records omitted, and six others that are unusual and all from the same bird, the remaining 37 records average 16 notes per song, the least being 11, in five records, and the most 23 in only one.

"The pitch of my records ranges from D''' to B''' and a great majority have the highest and loudest notes on A'''. The average song ranges from about two and a half tones from the lowest to the highest note. The greatest range of any one song is four tones, and the least one and a half. One unusual song is not considered, since it is all one pitch and therefore has no range. The songs of my records range from 1⅖ to 2⅗ seconds in length. The rapid notes seem to be about eight per second in most cases."

Hervey Brackbill (MS.), of Baltimore, Md., has observed the house wren sing during the course of its flight. He states: "During May I saw a house wren burst into song on the last 2 or 3 yards of a 50-yard flight from tree to tree, completing the song without interruption after alighting. Again, one or two that were keeping close company several times continued songs while flitting from branch to branch, and once this bird began a song about a foot from the finish of a 5-yard flight."

At the height of the singing season the song is repeated with an amazing frequency. In one timing of the song of a male of a pair that nested in a box on an Illinois farm, the full song was repeated three to four times every minute and at one time totaled five times during the course of one minute.

The house wren begins its singing at an early date even before its departure from its winter to its summer haunts. Kopman (1915) writes that it sings freely for 3 weeks or more in its winter retreats of Louisiana before leaving on its northern migration.

Early in the spring one may find a house wren singing a song that is an irregular indefinite jumble of notes, only slightly or not at all suggestive of the usual song of the species, which has been referred to as a "primitive" and by others as an "abnormal" song. Saunders (1929b) relates an interesting experience with a house wren singing these abnormal songs at Fairfield, Conn., as follows:

[The] song was like that of no bird with which I am familiar. In fact the bird possessed nine different songs, no one of them normal, although one or two had a wrenlike suggestion in them. One began with five long, loud whistled notes, a little suggestive of some notes of the cardinal. Another began with two such notes and two others ended with a single note of this character. One was a series of slurs and somewhat suggested a Swamp Sparrow. Another in form but not in voice, was like a Song Sparrow song, yet no one of these songs suggested any of these birds clearly enough as to make me think them imitations. All these songs were recorded between June 4th and 17th, after which the bird disappeared. When I first heard this bird I had not the slightest idea what species was producing the song.

The song of some birds ceases or deteriorates with the completion of the set of eggs and the beginning of incubation, but in the case of the house wren the full song is continued with great frequency even when the young are being fed. Saunders (1929b) has presented an interesting interpretation of this continued singing from the standpoint of function. During the early part of the breeding season it serves as a territory song, but later when the young appear it acts as a stimulus in prompting the young to a feeding response. Saunders writes as follows:

Many have undoubtedly observed the incessant singing of the male House Wren when feeding young and the habit of approaching the nest with a bill full of insects and singing just before entering the door, without dropping any of the insects. This explains why the bird has this habit. The song at that time does not differ materially from the territory song of earlier spring but it is no longer a territory song, but a stimulus for the young. According to my own observations during the early nest life of the young House Wrens, the male gathers the food and the female stays in the nest with the young, probably brooding, the male passing the food to her at the entrance. Later, when the young are older and need no stimulus, but need a greater quantity of food, both parents gather food and feed the young.

According to correspondence received from A. D. DuBois, the notes of the male, at the time when the wrens had young, changed to a shorter simpler strain consisting principally of two tones: a succession of high notes followed by a succession of low notes.

The song of the house wren is continued to a time well beyond the nesting season. The bird is in full song until the last week of July and then tapers off into August, but it continues to sing during most of the month and has been heard as late as November 5. Evans (1918), a florist at Evanston, Ill., left the door of his greenhouse open in the fall. A house wren entered, and in the evening the song was heard. The bird remained all winter, and the song was delightful in zero weather of January. These late songs, however, are different, often exhibiting a decided change in quality and volume when compared with the territory song. Likewise, the song has none of the spontaneity and vigor of the spring song; rather it is a low rambling warble. They are abnormal songs resembling those that are sometimes heard early in spring. Likewise there comes at this time a correlated change in the behavior of the birds. They no longer cling to the vicinity of human habitations and are more apt to be found inhabiting the rocks and shrubs of wild and unfrequented localities.

Albert R. Brand (1938) has made recordings of numerous bird songs on film, a medium from which sounds can be studied objectively. Such a film reveals a picture of the number of vibrations per second that determines the pitch of sound. He has found that the average pitch of passerine bird songs is 4,280 vibrations, or a quarter of a note higher than C_7, the highest note on the piano keyboard. The approximate mean of the notes of the house wren is 4,100. The highest note in its song reaches 7,125, while the lowest is about 2,050 vibrations per second.

In the table below are Brand's determinations of the pitch of the song of the house wren placed alongside those of the crow, which has a low-pitched voice, and those of the black-polled warbler, a bird with an extremely high voice. This table will serve to facilitate a comparison in the pitch of these three very different songs.

	House Wren	Crow	Black-polled Warbler
Approximate mean	4,100	1,500	8,900
Highest note	7,125	1,650	10,225
Lowest note	2,050	1,450	8,050

Enemies.—As is true with many birds, the house wren is host to a number of external parasites. Peters (1936) lists five species as having been found on the house wren: Two lice, *Menopon* sp. and *Philopterus subflavescens* (Goef.), and three species of mites, *Dermanyssus gallinae* (Deeger), *Liponyssus sylviarum* (C. & F.), and *Trombicula whartoni* Ewing. While the presence of lice and mites is not usually fatal to the birds, heavy infestations are very annoying and may prove harmful especially to the nestlings, which have no means of ridding themselves of the pests.

Baldwin (1922) cites a specific example in which there was a lone house wren in a nest that received all the food and attentions of the adult birds. This nestling, instead of growing rapidly in size and weight, as might be expected, was far below normal, greatly undernourished, and a miserable skinny-looking specimen. This condition prevailed until a heavy infestation of lice was discovered and a poultry-louse killer applied on the twelfth day. After that there was some improvement, and a considerable gain in weight was noted.

No records of internal parasites and diseases of the house wren have come to my attention, but doubtless a thorough examination of many specimens would reveal them.

Nests of the house wren have been found by Mason (1936) to be infested by the larvae of the blood-sucking fly *Protocalliphora splendida sialia*. These larvae have been found to be very destructive to the young of such box-nesting species as the bluebird and tree swallow. The nests of the wren are less favorable for the parasites, but even so they have proved to be an important factor in the mortality of nestling wrens. This has been found to be especially serious when the infestations are accompanied by other unfavorable conditions such as bad weather, and lack of food which tend to lower the resistance of the young. These flies are not known to be carriers of diseases, but, when present in sufficient numbers in a bird's nest the larvae often suck enough blood from the young birds to bring about their death.

In the examination of 39 nests of the wren a total of 201 larvae and puparia were found. A secondary parasite, which serves as a natural check on *Protocalliphora*, is the chalcid *Mormoniella*, and it is thus desirable to give this little fly every opportunity to increase in numbers. When heavy infestations of the blood-sucking fly *Protocalliphora* occur, it is important to clear the nesting boxes after the young are four or five days old.

It is well within the range of possibility that pests such as *Protocalliphora* have been an important factor in the local disappearance of the wren in sections of New England where the English sparrow has shouldered most of the blame.

Spiders hatched from egg sacs carried into the nests with sticks sometimes prove a menace to the wrens. Hathaway (1911) gives an account of a pair of wrens that were driven away by spiders. His story in part is as follows:

About a week after I missed the delightful song, so I started to investigate. Rapping on the stub no bird appeared, and I soon saw that the edges of the hole were alive with small spiders. I took the stub down and examined it, and found the nest swarming with these spiders. The birds in building the nest had used small twigs entirely and had thickly stuccoed them with the white egg sacs of a species of spider, that had hatched before the wren had deposited her own eggs, and instead of making a home for her young, she had unwittingly gathered together a fine family of spiders and provided them with a well-sheltered retreat.

Cats rank as enemy No. 1 of the house wren. Since these birds nest about human habitations, especially on farms, where cats are common, they fall prey to them oftener than do species of birds nesting in remote localities. Cats are especially destructive to young when they leave the nest prematurely. Reports of adults' falling victim to cats are common, but young are always in imminent danger of the ravages of these bird destroyers. I vividly recall seeing a cat seize two young wrens in rapid succession when a brood of seven were startled from the nest before some of them were able to fly well. The unfortunate youngsters landed on the ground where a prowling cat was poised for action.

Errington (1935) reports finding the remains of house wrens in the stomach contents of red and gray foxes; hence individuals inhabiting places remote from the houses of man are also subject to prey by predatory mammals. Wrens are also preyed upon by predatory birds such as owls; Fisher (1893) reports finding the remains of a house wren in the stomach contents of a screech owl, and Errington (Errington et al., 1941) found three wrens in the pelletal remains of the horned owl.

While the house wren is notorious for its aggressions toward other birds, sometimes the tables are turned and it is driven away by huskier intruders. Henderson (1931) reports that Carolina wrens nest in boxes at his home, located near a heavy forest at Greensburg, Ind. Although house wrens attempt nest-building on his premises, they have been completely driven out by the Carolina wrens. The same can be said for Bewick's wren in the southwestern section of the range of the house wren, although in some localities the situation is reversed. In the past the English sparrow has offered the severest competition. Indeed, the scarcity of the house wren in certain sections of its range, especially in New England, has been attributed to this persistent and audacious marauder. Knight (1908) states that the house wren was a common bird near Bangor, but at the advent of the English sparrow the species began to diminish about 1885 and none have occurred there since 1887. Similar conditions prevailed in Massachusetts. In recent years since the marked decrease in English sparrows the house wren is coming back and is now nesting in sections where for years it was virtually extirpated.

Other birds have had their innings with the house wren, and even the midget of a hummingbird may spend its wrath on it when occasion arises. Hervey Brackbill (MS.) submits the following interesting experience: "One late August day I came upon a wren under attack by a ruby-throated hummingbird. Scolding, the wren was hopping and flitting from one place to another close in to the two main stems of a small locust tree while the hummer—apparently unable to follow it through the twigs directly—darted in at it from the outer edge of the tree, then shot back out again to strike in through some other opening at the wren in its new position. The hummer made half a dozen thrusts within the next few minutes; then the wren apparently found a safe spot. The hummer perched for a while, in near the heart of the tree, then flew off."

Snakes are not a common enemy of the house wren, but the following experience of Hunter (1935) is interesting: "Last spring on one of my nature rambles at West Point, Ill., my attention was drawn to the nest of a pair of House Wrens   *   *   *   by the alarm notes of the owners. Upon making an investigation I found it necessary to remove a Garter Snake   *   *   *   from the nest, while the process of digesting five young wrens continued uninterrupted."

Wasps, bumblebees, fields mice, red squirrels, and chipmunks have also been cited as troublesome to nestling house wrens.

Friedmann (1938) has reported two cases in which the house wren has been host to the eggs of the parasitic cowbird. The character of the usual nesting site of the house wren is such that they are seldom imposed upon by these molothrine visitors.

Sometimes man unwittingly becomes an enemy of the house wren by spraying vegetation to kill insect larvae that are eaten by the wrens. Hoffman (1925) writes as follows: "For three successive years the House Wrens have abandoned their nests in the writer's yard when their young were partly grown. The dried remains of the nestlings were found when the nest boxes received a cleaning in the fall. At the time that the nests were abandoned the currant bushes had become infested with the small green currant worms and had been dusted with finely powdered arsenate of lead. It was shortly after the old birds were observed carrying the arsenate-covered worms to their nests that they disappeared and were not seen again."

Philp (1937) reports that house wrens among other birds were blackened by smudge made during a cold wave to protect fruit from a threatening frost. The carbolic acid in the crude-oil vapor that covered both their food supply and their plumage was not enough to prove fatal to the birds, but Philp states the birds were so saturated with the greasy oily deposit that they could not regain their normal colors until the following molt.

During migration fatalities frequently befall the house wren when it flies into lighthouses and tall city buildings. Overing (1938) reports that a house wren was killed by flying against the Washington Monument, thus sharing the fate of many other species of birds. Sometimes wrens are carried out to sea by storms: Sprunt (1931) states that a house wren came aboard a ship when it was well out to sea off Cape Lookout, N. C. It crept under the winches and about the mooring bilts for the better part of an hour.

Fall.—In September the house wren, as we know it as a tenant in our nesting boxes during summer, undergoes a marked change in behavior, in song, and in plumage. At this time it deserts the environment of man and resorts to the deep recesses of the woodlands, where it skulks among the tangled underbrush making its presence more difficult to detect. The song as previously noted may continue, but it undergoes considerable modification. Its plumage is grayer and darker than the garb worn in summer. Little wonder that Audubon thought the bird he observed at this season to be a different and a distinct species, which he described as the wood wren.

In New England and in most of its summer range the last house wrens remain until the middle of October, but the majority of them have departed for their winter quarters in the Southern States before this time. A few may linger until the first week of November. On November 5, 1941, one was seen and heard singing at Kingston, R. I., and another was observed on November 7, 1938, at Amherst, Mass., a record for the last-seen house wren in that region. According to A. H. Howell (1932), the first house wrens reach their haunts in Florida during the last week of September or the first week of October. His earliest two records are of one seen at Oxford on September 26, 1928, and one at Orlando on September 27, 1909.

Concerning the house wren in its winter haunts Chapman (1912) writes:

It has been claimed that the name of the House Wren is a misnomer, because in the South during the winter these birds are found in the forests miles away from the nearest habitation. This, however, is owing to circumstances over which the House Wren has no control. He is just as much of a House Wren in the south as he is in the north; you will find a pair in possession of every suitable dwelling. The difficulty is that in the winter there are more House Wrens than there are houses, and being of a somewhat irritable disposition, the House Wren will not share his quarters with others of his kind. Late comers, therefore, who can not get a snug nook about a house or outbuilding, are forced to resort to the woods.

A. H. Howell (1932) writes of the house wren in Florida as follows: "This little wren, well known in the North as a conspicuous inhabitant of orchards and dooryards, loses most of its familiarity while resorting in the South, and during the winter months frequents palmetto thickets and brushy tangles in the hammocks. Here the birds are shy and for the most part quiet, but as spring opens one may occasionally hear snatches of the bubbling song, which on the breeding grounds is a nearly continuous performance." In Alabama, Howell (1924) states that the house wren "is quiet and rather shy, frequenting low bushes and weed patches in the fields." Of the bird in Louisiana Oberholser (1938) writes: "It frequents much more commonly the forests, thickets, and swamps, where it skulks about among the undergrowth, and is sometimes difficult to observe. * * * It is seldom found in flocks, but most of the birds move singly or in pairs."

Kendeigh (1934) concludes in his study of the role of environment in the life of birds that—

The northward distribution of the eastern house wren during the breeding season appears to be limited primarily by low night temperatures for which the shortening of the daily periods of darkness does not entirely compensate. The southward distribution appears to be primarily controlled by high daily maximum temperatures and competition with the Bewick wren, *Thryomanes b. bewicki* (Audubon). The eastward limit of the breeding range is determined by the Atlantic Ocean, while a decrease in relative humidity and precipitation may be directly or indirectly concerned in the westward transition from the eastern to the western subspecies of the house wren. Other factors are of uncertain or secondary importance.

The wintering area of the eastern house wren is limited on the north by low night temperatures combined with long daily periods of darkness, short daylight periods, low intensity of solar radiation, snow, and lack of available food. On the east, the wintering area is limited by the Atlantic Ocean, on the south by the Gulf of Mexico, and on the west by much the same conditions, perhaps, that are effective during the breeding season.

The southward migration of the eastern house wren in the autumn is necessary for the continued existence of the species, while the northward migration in the spring avoids unfavorable breeding and existing conditions in the south. By migrating south in the autumn and north in the spring, the bird maintains itself in a more nearly uniform and favorable environment throughout the year. The regulation of migration as to time is controlled in the spring by rising daily maximum and night temperatures and changing relative proportions daily of light and darkness. In the autumn, decreasing temperatures particularly at night, longer nights and shorter days, and, for some species, decreasing food supply are most important.

DISTRIBUTION

Range.—Southern Canada to southern Mexico.

Breeding range.—The house wren breeds **north** to southern British Columbia (southern half of Vancouver Island, Chilliwack, and 150-mile House); northern Alberta (Vermilion, McMurray, and Lesser Slave Lake); southern Manitoba (Duck Mountain and Lake St. Martin); central Ontario (Lake Abitibi); southern Quebec (Quebec); and New Brunswick (Fredericton and Grand Falls). **East** to New Brunswick (Fredericton); casually to Nova Scotia (Wolfville); and south through the Atlantic Coast States to North Carolina (Beaufort and Salisbury) and western South Carolina (Greenwood). **South** to South Carolina (Greenwood); Kentucky (Harlan); northern Oklahoma (Tulsa and Enid); southern New Mexico (Cloudcroft and Silver City); Arizona (Tombstone and the Huachuca Mountains); and northwestern Baja California (Sierra San Pedro Mártir). **West** to northwestern Baja Balifornia (Sierra San Pedro Mártir); western California (Santa Barbara, Palo Alto, and Berkeley); Oregon (Pinehurst, Elkton, and Portland); Washington (Vancouver, Shelton, and Bellingham); and British Columbia (Courtenay). It may breed rarely in the uplands of Mexico, as specimens have been taken in the breeding season, but as yet no nests or young have been reported.

Winter range.—The house wren in winter is found **north** to southern California (Los Angeles, San Bernardino, occasionally to central California); southern Arizona (Tucson); northeastern Texas (Bonham and Corsicana); southern Louisiana (Jennings and Port Allen); Alabama (Autaugaville); and the coast of South Carolina (Cape Romain). **East** to South Carolina (Charleston and Port Royal); and Florida (Daytona and Miami). **South** to Florida (Miami and Long Pine Key); along the Gulf coast to southern Mexico, Veracruz (Tres Zapotes); Oaxaca (Huajuapam); and Guerrero (Chilpancingo).

West to Baja California (Cape region), and southern California (San Diego, Los Angeles, and San Bernardino).

The above distribution applies to the species as a whole, which has been divided into three subspecies. The eastern house wren (*T. a. aëdon*) breeds from New Brunswick southward east of the Alleghenies. The Ohio house wren (*T. a. baldwini*) breeds from Michigan to central Quebec south to Kentucky and western Virginia. The western house wren (*T. a. parkmanii*) breeds from Wisconsin and Illinois westward. It is impossible at this time to break down the winter range by races; in fact, it seems more than likely that there is considerable overlapping.

Spring migration.—Late dates of spring departure from the winter home are Florida—Daytona Beach, April 28. Georgia—Macon, May 1. North Carolina—Raleigh, May 4. Louisiana—New Orleans, April 18. Texas—San Antonio, May 14. Arkansas—Helena, April 27.

Early dates of spring arrival are: North Carolina—Raleigh, April 20. Virginia—Lynchburg, April 11. West Virginia—Bluefield, April 14. District of Columbia—Washington, April 11. Pennsylvania—Pittsburgh, April 21. New Jersey—Elizabeth, April 16. New York—New York, April 19. Connecticut—Fairfield, April 22. Massachusetts—Springfield, April 22. Vermont—Burlington, April 22. Maine—Waterville, May 6. Quebec—Montreal, May 8. Ohio—Oberlin, April 23. Indiana—Indianapolis, March 29. Illinois—Olney, April 15. Ontario—Toronto, April 2. Michigan—Ann Arbor, April 25. Iowa—Des Moines, April 21. Wisconsin—Milwaukee, April 10. Minnesota—Duluth, April 27. Kansas—Manhattan, April 6. Nebraska—Omaha, April 16. South Dakota—Yankton, April 17. North Dakota—Bismarck, April 18. Colorado—Denver, April 20. Montana—Billings, April 23. Manitoba—Winnipeg, April 23. Saskatchewan—Indian Head, April 14. Alberta—Camrose, May 9. Arizona—Tombstone, April 1. California—Santa Barbara, March 17. Oregon—Corvallis, April 7. Washington—Seattle, April 12. British Columbia—Victoria, April 11.

Fall migration.—Late dates of fall departure are: British Columbia—Okanagan Landing, October 6. Washington—Spokane, September 25. Oregon—Weston, November 10. California—San Francisco, November 4. Alberta—Edmonton, October 7. Saskatchewan—Qu'Appelle, October 1. Manitoba—Aweme, October 5. Montana—Big Sandy, October 12. Colorado—Colorado Springs, October 14. North Dakota—Fargo, October 6. South Dakota—Sioux Falls, September 29. Nebraska—Lincoln, October 27. Kansas—Onaga, October 2. Minnesota—St. Paul, October 6. Wisconsin—Madison, October 2. Iowa—Iowa City, October 2. Missouri—Columbia, October 9. Michigan—Grand Rapids, October 13. Ontario—Ottawa, September 30. Illinois—Urbana, October 1. Indiana—Fort Wayne, October 11. Ohio—Columbus, October 17. Quebec—Quebec, October 6. Vermont—St. Johnsbury, October 2. Massachusetts—Boston, October 18. Connecticut—Hartford, October 14. New York—Rochester, September 21. New Jersey—Elizabeth, October 30. Pennsylvania—Berwyn, October 20. District of Columbia—Washington, October 23. West Virginia—Bluefield, October 13. Virginia—Lexington, October 6.

Some early dates of fall arrival are: North Carolina—Piney Creek, September 3. Georgia—Athens, September 15. Florida—Pensacola, October 6. Arkansas—Delight, September 23. Louisiana—New Orleans, October 8. Texas—Corpus Christi, October 7.

Some light on the individual migrations of house wrens may be gathered from the following records of banded birds: Banded at Katonah, N. Y., September 14, 1937, and taken at Palma Sola, Fla., November 18, 1937; banded at East Lansing, Mich., May 17, 1937, recovered at Rockledge, Fla., May 11, 1938; banded at Notre Dame, Ind., June 13, 1931, recovered at Moultrie, Ga., December 11, 1931; banded at South Bend, Ind., June 20, 1930, and caught at Ardmore, Ala., January 18, 1931; banded at Zion, Ill., July 10, 1931, and killed near Baxley, Ga., November 1, 1931.

Casual records.—The house wren has been recorded casually at Kispiox, British Columbia, where a specimen was collected on June 2, 1921; and at Fort St. John where one was observed June 18, 1943; at Fort Simpson, Mackenzie, on May 20, 1904; one observed near The Pas, Manitoba, on September 26, 1942; another observed near Churchill, Manitoba, on June 21, 1944; and at Kamouraska, Quebec, it was recorded for the first time on June 19, 1939.

Egg dates.—California: 119 records, April 11 to June 26; 65 records, May 1 to May 20, indicating the height of the season.

Colorado: 22 records, May 26 to July 10; 12 records, June 3 to June 15.

Illinois: 32 records, May 10 to July 27; 14 records, May 10 to May 30; 10 records, June 5 to June 20.

Montana: 12 records, June 5 to June 30.

Ontario: 13 records, May 29 to July 23.

Virginia: 13 records, May 15 to July 10; 6 records, May 21 to May 29.

TROGLODYTES AËDON PARKMANII Audubon

WESTERN HOUSE WREN

PLATE 28

HABITS

Audubon (1841a) named this wren after his friend Dr. George Parkman, of Boston, considering it a distinct species. It has since been shown to intergrade with the eastern house wren. Its range includes most of the western United States and southern western Canada. It differs but little from the eastern bird, averaging only slightly larger, but being decidedly paler and grayer, with the back and scapulars more distinctly barred with dusky.

Its habits are so similar to those of its eastern relative that nearly all that Dr. Gross has contributed in his full life history of the eastern house wren would apply equally well to the western race. It seems, however, that the western bird is a little less domestic in its taste, less of a dooryard bird, or rather more of a woodland bird than our familiar eastern house wren. It does, of course, frequent the haunts of man, but seems to be more often found away from them in woodlands. The difference may be more apparent than real, for much of the western house wren's range is thinly settled, but where it *does* come in contact with civilization it becomes less primitive and adapts itself to the new surroundings.

In the western mountain ranges, it is often found breeding in the forested regions up to 10,000 feet, or nearly up to timberline. In the Huachuca Mountains, Ariz., we found it breeding commonly in the coniferous forests, from 7,000 feet upward. Mr. Swarth (1904b) says: "Upon their arrival in the spring, the first being noted on April 8th, they were distributed over all parts of the range, but soon withdrew to the higher altitudes to breed; nor did they descend again when the young were out of the nest, as so many species similarly placed, did."

In southwestern Saskatchewan we found this wren very abundant in the timber belts along the creeks, where it was the commonest and most ubiquitous bird and one of the most persistent singers; it apparently had not yet learned to frequent the ranches. Late in May they were evidently just mating, as the males were chasing the females about and paying them courtship; I saw a female perched on a fence post, with quivering wings, while her ardent lover hopped along the rail toward her, with wings and tail spread and head thrown back, pouring out a rich flood of rapturous song.

Nesting.—The western house wren is no more particular about its choice of a nesting site than is its eastern relative; many and varied are the nooks and crannies in which it seems satisfied to build its nest; any old cavity almost anywhere seems to suit it. In North Dakota we found a nest in the hollow of a dead branch on an old stump of an elm, just above a larger hollow containing an occupied goldeneye's nest, and almost under an occupied nest of Krider's hawk; another nest was found in a bank swallow's burrow.

In the timber belts along the streams in Saskatchewan we found many nests in the hollows in the boxelders and poplars. In the Huachuca Mountains, in Arizona, we found one nest in a pigeon-hole case in a deserted house in an abandoned mining camp; and my companion chopped out a nest in a knothole in a large oak, about 30 feet from the ground; both of these were at an elevation of about 8,000 feet. F. Seymour Hersey mentions in his Manitoba notes a nest that was built in the skull of a moose, with horns attached, that was hung up in a tree back of an Indian's house.

The commonest and most primitive nesting sites are in natural cavities or crevices in stumps, or in fallen or standing trees, including old woodpecker holes; such sites are usually at no great height above ground, generally below 10 feet; heights of 20 or 30 feet are unusual. The highest nest I find recorded is reported by Grinnell, Dixon, and Linsdale (1930) in the Lassen Peak region: "The bird carried twigs to the top of one of the tallest of the dead yellow pine stubs of that vicinity, fully fifty meters above the ground. The bird each trip moved upward by a well defined route, flying from limb to limb as though moving up a staircase. By the time the wren reached the nest in a crack at the top of the stub, the observer on the ground could scarcely trace its movements." They found two other nests that were ten meters up in similar stubs, as well as others at more normal heights.

Nests have been found in cavities in rocks and crevices in caves. Ridgway (1877) mentions some interesting nests, observed in Nevada: "One nest was placed behind a flat mass of a small shrub (*Spiraea caespitosa*), which grew in moss-like patches against the face of a cliff. Another one, and the only one not concealed in some manner, was built in the low crotch of an aspen, having for its foundation an abandoned Robin's nest. It consisted of a somewhat conical pile of sticks, nearly closed at the top, but with a small opening just large enough to admit the owner. Including its bulky base, the total height of this structure was about 15 inches."

About human habitations bird boxes are eagerly accepted where these are available; otherwise, any nooks or crannies on or in buildings are used, or any tin can, box, pail, crate, empty stove pipe, or old hat or coat left hanging in a shed will do. Some such interesting nests have been described. Dr. W. W. Arnold (1906) shows a photograph of a huge nest: "A shallow box afforded the foundation of the nest, which was constructed of the smaller twigs of the scrub oak and built into the form of a pyramid. Many of the twigs were forked and skillfully locked together, forming a very rigid structure, 12 inches wide at the base, 5½ inches across the top, and 16 inches high."

The nests are constructed mainly of small sticks or twigs, or rather more accurately, this material is used to fill up, or to attempt to fill up, the cavity adopted; in some cases an immense amount of such material is brought in, sometimes enough to fill a bushel basket. The lining consists mainly of feathers, often in great profusion and of many colors.

Many nests contain more or less snakeskin, and some are largely lined with it. Dix Teachenor (1927) reports that out of 30 nests of western house wrens examined by him and Harry Harris, near Kansas City,

Mo., 19 contained cast snakeskins, or about 63 percent of those examined.

Miss Maude Merritt (1916) gives an interesting list of material which a male wren brought into a bird box and mixed with the usual assortment of twigs: One hat pin, 1 buckle, 10 bits of chicken wire, 2 stays, 3 fasteners, 1 unidentified, 3 paper clips, 1 staple, 1 brass ring, 2 toilet wires, 6 collar stays, 2 oyster-bucket handles, part of a mouse trap, 67 hair pins, 38 bits of wire, 5 safety pines, 3 steel pins, 22 nails, and 3 brads. The female refused to accept the nest and departed; I don't blame her.

While we were studying birds at Lake Winnipegosis, Manitoba, my companion, F. Seymour Hersey, watched a house wren carrying nesting material through a knothole in a shed where it was building a nest. She worked at it industriously; her time from leaving the nest until returning with more sticks varied from 25 to 35 seconds, though once she was gone a minute and 10 seconds. She had considerable difficulty at times in forcing the twigs through the small hole. Often the twig would drop from her bill, when she would pick it up and try again; one twig, about 8 inches long, was dropped and picked up five times before she succeeded in getting it through the hole. He placed some duck feathers near the hole, thinking she might use them, but she carried them away and dropped them at some distance.

Eggs.—The western house wren lays about the same number of eggs as the eastern bird, and the two are similar in size, shape, and markings. The measurements of 40 eggs in the United States National Museum average 16.3 by 12.6 millimeters; the eggs showing the four extremes measure 17.7 by 12.7, 17.3 by 13.3, 14.7 by 12.2, and 17.3 by 11.2 millimeters.

Young.—Practically all that has been written about the young of the eastern house wren would apply equally well to the western subspecies, but there are a few items of interest that are worth adding here. Mrs. Amelia S. Allen (1921) gives the following list of food that was fed to a brood of eight young during a period of 1 hour, 10:20 to 11:20 a. m., on June 15, 1921, at Berkeley, Calif.: 5 ladybugs, 4 crane-flies, 5 large and 4 small beetles, 2 wireflies, 1 lacewing, 1 leafhopper, 5 crickets, 1 grasshopper, 1 butterfly, 1 moth, 1 milliped, 1 grub, and 1 unknown; there were 33 feedings, with an average interval between feedings of 14 minutes and 32.7 seconds for each nestling.

Dr. J. G. Cooper (1876) tells a remarkable story of a pair of wrens, with no other wrens within a quarter of a mile, that used the extra nest, built by the male, to raise a second brood simultaneously with the first! As soon as the first nest was finished, the male began to build another. "The female rarely assisted in this work, though I occasionally saw both there, and in due time the second nest was finished. Soon after the young in the first nest were hatched, and although needing much attention, the old birds still frequented the new nest, and I began to suspect that one of them was sitting on eggs there. This suspicion was soon verified by hearing the young, and seeing them fed. In this case each parent must have been sitting at the same time on a nest, perhaps taking turns, during the week that elapsed before the first hatching."

Young wrens are known to return to their nest to roost at night for a while after leaving the nest. Miss Morritt (1916) tells of a brood of four young wrens that, on the second evening after leaving the nest, were escorted by their mother to an empty catbird's nest in a syringa bush, where they spent the night. "The entire family of four young ones returned with the mother each evening for 14 days. On the fifteenth evening one of the young wrens was missing; on the next evening two did not return." On the evening of the seventeenth day the one remaining young refused to remain in the nest; it flew away and never returned. The mother bird never roosted in the catbird's nest, and her roost was not discovered.

Food.—The food of the western house wren agrees so closely in its general character with that of the eastern bird, that what has been reported on the food of the latter will illustrate very well the food of the former. Prof. Beal (1907) examined only 36 stomachs from California, of which he says that "animal matter, consisting entirely of insects and spiders, formed 97.5 percent, and vegetable food 2.5 percent. Beetles, as a whole, amount to about 20 percent; caterpillars, aggregating 24 percent, are taken in the earlier months of the year; and Hemiptera, amounting to 33 percent, are eaten chiefly in the last of the season. Grasshoppers amount to about 5 percent, and different insects, mostly ants and other Hymenoptera, aggregate 15 percent."

The western bird is evidently just as beneficial in its food habits as its eastern relative. About the only useful insects that it destroys are the coccinellid beetles, or ladybugs, and it destroys no fruit.

I cannot find any evidence that it has the harmful habit of destroying the nests or eggs of other birds, of which the eastern bird has been so often accused. It is seldom imposed upon by the western races of the cowbird; Dr. Friedmann (1938) records only two such cases; the entrance to its nest is generally too small for the cowbird to enter.

Fred Mallery Packard sends me the following note from Estes Park, Colo.: "House wrens arrive in the park early in May, to become the most abundant songster of the pines and aspens through the Transition and Lower Canadian Zones. They sing during the nesting season, which starts early in June; and some sing to the end of July, when most of the young of the second brood are fledged. They appear to depart early—late in August and early in September—but there is one October record."

OHIO HOUSE WREN

According to Dr. Oberholser's (1934) description, this subspecies is similar to the eastern house wren, "but upper parts darker, much less rufescent (more sooty or grayish) ; the sides and flanks less rufescent (more grayish) ; rest of lower surface more grayish (less buffy)." He says that "this is the darkest of the forms of *Troglodytes domesticus*. It is always less rufescent than *Troglodytes domesticus domesticus*, but it has not only a dark sooty phase of plumage, but also a lighter, more grayish phase that more approaches *Troglodytes domesticus parkmanii*. This latter phase is apparently not to be regarded merely as a manifestation of intergradation, since it appears in all parts of the range of *Troglodytes domesticus baldwini*."

It breeds from central Quebec, southeastern Ontario, and Michigan south to Kentucky and western Virginia. It migrates in fall and winter to southern Texas and Florida.

APACHE WREN

HABITS

While they were in Arizona, in 1945, Dr. H. C. Oberholser and Dr. Herbert Brandt wrote enthusiastic letters to me about their discovery of a new bird, its nest, eggs, and young, that would be an addition to the North American list. But I had to wait some time before they gave me the full particulars, which have now been published. The bird that they discovered was a Mexican species of wren, which they found to be commoner than expected in a region where more ornithological work has been done than in any other section of Arizona. Previous workers, including the writer, had overlooked it because of its resemblance to the well-known house wren, to which it is quite closely related. While Frank Willard and I were collecting in the Huachuca Mountains, on May 28, 1922, we took a set of six eggs that we supposed belonged to a western house wren; the nest was about 30 feet from the ground in a knothole in a large oak at about 7,000 feet elevation; we noticed that the eggs looked different from house wren's eggs, being more sparingly marked, as described by Dr. Brandt; the eggs went into Mr. Willard's collection, and I do not know where they are now. Perhaps we missed the chance to make this interesting discovery!

In naming this wren as a new subspecies, in honor of Dr. Charles T. Vorhies, of the University of Arizona, Dr. Brandt (1945) describes it as "similar to *Troglodytes brunneicollis cahooni* Brewster, from the plateau of northwestern México in the states of Sonora and Chihuahua, but duller and more grayish (less buffy) particularly on the under parts." He gives as its range "the Huachuca and Santa Rita mountains of Arizona and southward for an undetermined distance."

Dr. Brandt (1945) gives the following interesting account of its discovery and its nesting habits:

At an elevation of some 7,200 feet, in one of the main defiles of Major John Healy's Carr Canyon Ranch, in the Huachuca Mountains, on June 6, 1945, I detected a feathered flash leaving the opposite side of a large ash when I "squeaked" and scraped its rough bark. This tree was growing at the stream-bed, so I climbed the adjacent abrupt slope, to a level of the upper half of the tree.

Before long the bird appeared and nervously entered a natural cavity, which proved to be its nest, but quickly departed. The next time it returned, I was able to obtain a good view of it with 8-power glasses, and, although it had the general behavior and appearance of a House Wren, yet there was a decided buff stripe above the eye.

His familiarity with the song of the eastern house wren enabled him to recognize a difference in the song of this bird, and so they decided to investigate further. As the nest was 16 feet from the ground in the main trunk of a solid tree, it was necessary to postpone further work on it until the next day with the proper equipment.

The next morning, June 7, Nelson Carpenter, with boldness and extreme difficulty, chopped through the 10-inch living trunk to the nest, and removed five incubated eggs, which appeared about a third smaller and more sparingly marked than those of the House Wren. Meanwhile, Lyndon Hargrave skillfully collected both shy parents, and we realized that we had an avian find. Doctor Oberholser at once pronounced the birds Cahoon's Wrens (*Troglodytes brunneicollis cahooni*), a most remarkable memory feat, as he had not studied this Mexican species in nearly 40 years.

A second nest of this bird I discovered on June 8, several miles away in another canyon of the range, also at an elevation of 7,200 feet. Its presence was suspected as the result of a male's singing, and later a bird was seen entering a natural cavity in a tall, upright branch of an ash, 35 feet up, which proved to be in a position too unsafe to climb. * * *

All nests discovered were situated at an elevation of between 7,000 and 7,300 feet, in well-wooded canyon bottoms of the Transition Life Zone, and were in a region where the Western House Wren was absent, although higher up the latter is not uncommon. Below 6,000 feet, Baird's Wren (*Thryomanes bewickii eremophilus*) is often encountered.

Since the above was published, Dr. Brandt has sent me a reproduction of a photograph, showing the nest and five eggs, and specimens of a pair of adults and four young of different ages of the Apache wren. On the back of this is printed the following description of the nest: "The nest was in a small cavity of an ash tree and was a cozy cradle of colorful bird feathers, placed on a bed of pine needles. The eggs are more like the warbler tribe than those of the House Wren, and are smaller than the latter."

TROGLODYTES TROGLODYTES HIEMALIS Vieillot

EASTERN WINTER WREN

PLATES 29, 30

HABITS

Although the winter wren breeds in suitable localities in some of the northern States, from western Massachusetts to central Minnesota, and as far south in the Alleghenies as northern Georgia, it is usually found there in only limited numbers. To many of us it is known only as a migrant, a furtive little mite, the smallest of its tribe, creeping mouselike about our wood piles or brush heaps, under the overhanging roots of trees along some woodland stream, or under the banks of marshland ditches. To see it, or rather to hear its tinkling, rippling song, to best advantage, we must visit its summer haunts in the cool, shady northern forests, where the sunshine hardly penetrates, where rotting stumps and fallen tree trunks are thickly covered with soft mosses, where dampness pervades the atmosphere near babbling woodland brooks, and where a luxuriant growth of ferns springs from the accumulation of rich leaf mold to nearly hide the forest floor. Here it finds a safe retreat from prying eyes, where its dark color, diminutive size, and retiring habits make it hard to find, until we hear its remarkable voice announcing its presence.

Henry Nehrling (1893) says that "in the Alleghenies where our most magnificent shrubs, rhododendrons, mountain laurel or kalmias and different azaleas fringe the streams and brooks and often cover whole mountain sides, lending to them an indescribable charm, this bird appears to take up its abode everywhere."

Even on its breeding grounds this wren is sometimes seen in more open places; William Brewster (1938) has seen one among large boulders at the very edge of the water at Lake Umbagog and among the tall grass on the lake shore.

Spring.—The winter range of this wren is so extensive, from New England to Florida, and the birds are so widely scattered at that season, that the spring migration is not conspicuous. Those that spend a short winter in the Southern States start early to join their companions that have wintered farther north. There is a gradual and a leisurely northward movement, as the birds drift along from bush to bush, through one gully after another, through woodland underbrush and windfalls, along the edges of swamps, and along old stone walls, always under cover where possible. Only when they come to some wide stream or open space must they spread their tiny wings and speed across.

They mostly pass unobserved, until we hear the fine silver thread of their delightful music and stop to seek them out. They follow close on the heels of retreating winter, waiting not for the full flush of springtime, and reach their breeding grounds in southern Canada fairly early in April, often while the ground is still frozen or covered with snow, and are soon singing merrily in their woodland haunts.

Miss Cordelia J. Stanwood (MS.) writes of the arrival of this wren in Maine: "About the middle of April, when the blossoming willows look like yellow flames amid the somber sprout growths and the last snow wraith has slowly transformed itself into a tinkling rill, the winter wren, the Spirit of the Brooks, is abroad. No one who has heard him sing will dispute the right of the little red-brown bird to this appellation."

Nesting.—I have never been fortunate enough to find a nest of the winter wren in its typical northern haunts, but I believe I have seen the only nest ever recorded in southeastern New England. Although this has already been recorded by one of the two men that were with me at the time (Hathaway, 1913), it seems worth while to describe it and its immediate surroundings, which, though out of its normal range geographically, were evidently suitable and congenial.

On May 24, 1908, Harry S. Hathaway, John H. Flanagan, and I were exploring the southwestern corner of Kingston Swamp in Rhode Island, searching especially for nests of the waterthrushes. This is a large, heavily wooded swamp; the portion that we visited was covered with a heavy, primeval deciduous forest, a cool and shady retreat, the dense foliage of the large trees shutting out the sunlight; the atmosphere was cooled by a steady flow of clear, cold spring water, about ankle deep nearly everywhere and in many places nearly knee deep; the current was perceptible all over the swamp, and in many places it was quite swift. The principal tree growth consisted of maples and swamp white oaks, many of which were of very large size; there were also many red oaks, beeches, white and yellow birches, ashes, a few solitary white and yellow pines, and some fine specimens of hollies. There was an undergrowth of saplings and shrubs, with numerous brakes and other ferns in the drier spots. The shade and dampness produced the conditions that the winter wren seems to require.

We had found a nest of the Louisiana waterthrush in the lower right corner of the upturned roots of a large fallen tree; the exposed roots were 5 or 6 feet in diameter, and the tree in falling had left a hole full of water more than knee deep. While we were photographing this nest, we were surprised to see a winter wren hopping about near the tree, with food in her bill. We withdrew to watch and soon saw her go to the same root and enter a small cavity, that we had not noticed, in the soil adhering to the roots. The nesting cavity was about 3 feet above the water in the upper left corner of the root and only 4 feet from the nest of the waterthrush. Here was a bird of the Carolinian fauna and one of the Canadian fauna nesting in the same stump, each near the extreme limit of its range! Furthermore, only a few yards away was an occupied nest of the northern waterthrush, a most interesting combination.

The front of the cavity, in which the wren's nest was built, was completely filled with sphagnum moss, green but partially dry; the nest was made of soft grasses, reinforced with weed stems, fine twigs, and rootlets; it was lined with white hair, which we concluded must have come from a white-tailed deer, several wisps of which we found hanging in the woods. The nest contained six young, which we thought were about a week old. We saw the bird come to the nest again and feed the young with a large white caterpillar, while we were within 15 feet of her. Then she cleaned the nest and flew off with a white sack of excrement.

The upturned roots of fallen trees offer favorite nesting sites for these wrens, for when the tree falls the roots carry up with them large quantities of earth, in which many convenient cavities may be found. All six of the nests recorded in Owen Durfee's notes from northern New Hampshire were in upturned roots. Among 35 nests of which I have descriptions, 18 were in the upturned roots of fallen trees, evidently a favorite choice. Seven nests were recorded as in or under rotten stumps, or under the roots of trees; in such situations the nests are well concealed, for old stumps and roots are usually covered with a luxuriant growth of moss, which matches perfectly the material with which the outer part of the nest is made; the small entrance hole is not easily seen and the nest resembles any other mossy mound. Verdi Burtch has sent me a photograph of a nest that was concealed in the roots of a tree overhanging a gully bank.

Although the nests are usually placed on or near the ground, well concealed, some few have been reported in other situations. There is a set of eggs in my collection, taken by E. H. Montgomery in Labrador from an old hole of a woodpecker, 8 feet from the ground. F. H. Kennard mentions in his notes a nest that was "placed in a roll of bark on the side of a huge yellow birch, about 5 feet from the ground." Ora W. Knight (1908) says that the nests are "sometimes suspended from the branches of a spruce or fir tree even as high as ten feet from the ground. While these tree nests are more frequently the 'mock' nests, they sometimes lay in one of these and rear their brood." Harry Piers (1898) found a nest near Halifax, Nova Scotia, in an unusual location: "It was simply a cavity in moss, *in situ* upon the face of a rock close to the shore of a small lake. This moss *was constantly satu-rated with water* which trickled from a bank above and slowly flowed over the stone on which the moss grew." Baird, Brewer, and Ridgway (1874) mention a nest, found by William F. Hall in Maine, that was "built in an unoccupied log-hut, among the fir-leaves and mosses in a crevice between the logs. It was large and bulky, composed externally of mosses and lined with the fur of hedge-hogs, and the feathers of the spruce partridge and other birds. It was in the shape of a pouch, and the entrance was neatly framed with fine pine sticks."

The nests are all much alike in construction; there is usually a base of fine twigs and coarse mosses, on which a bulky nest of various green and yellow mosses is built, reinforced with a few fine twigs of spruce or fir; the interior is well lined with the soft feathers of various birds and the fur of any mammal that is available. Knight (1908) gives the measurements of a nest before him as "outside from top to bottom 7 inches; depth of cavity inside 2 inches; diameter of entrance hole 1 inch; diameter of interior of nest 1¼ inches; from bottom of entrance hole to bottom of nest outside 4 inches; diameter of nest outside 4 inches." This was evidently a long and narrow nest; the size and shape of the nest varies considerably as it must be adapted to the cavity it has to fill; but it is always a large nest for so small a bird; and always the entrance on the side is only just large enough to admit the little owner. Like some other wrens, the winter wren builds false nests, decoy nests, or extra nests, supposed to be built by the male; these are usually not lined.

Eggs.—Four to seven eggs may constitute the set for the winter wren, but five or six are commoner. They are usually ovate in shape, less rounded than those of the chickadees, which they otherwise somewhat resemble. They are clear white, with small spots and fine dots of pale reddish brown, "cinnamon" to "hazel," which are distributed more thickly, as a rule, near the larger end. Some eggs are very sparingly marked with the finest of dots, or are nearly immaculate. The measurements of 40 eggs average 16.7 by 12.5 millimeters; the eggs showing the four extremes measures 17.8 by 12.7, 16.7 by 13.0, 15.2 by 12.7, and 15.7 by 11.9 millimeters.

Young.—The period of incubation for the winter wren does not seem to have been definitely determined, though it is probably the same as for the English bird, 14 to 16 days. Whether both sexes share this duty seems to be unknown also, but this is not surprising as it is so difficult to distinguish the sexes in life. Early and late breeding dates suggest that sometimes two broods are reared in a season.

William Brewster (1938) writes: "A brood of young scarce able to fly came about the camp this forenoon [Aug. 31]. They kept calling to one another as they dodged in and out among the fallen logs uttering a fine, wiry *tree-e-e* something like that of the small spotted thrushes. When I disturbed and scattered them they *chirruped* at me in soft tones. This chirrup is unlike any other bird call that I can remember.

I think it is peculiar to the young as the *tree-e-e-* certainly is. An old bird with this brood called *tick, tick*."

Perley M. Silloway (1923) says of the behavior of the young: "It is interesting to watch these youngsters when disturbed. They scatter like young Bob-whites, some crouching in the sparse ground cover, while others may seek higher shelter. One was noticed clinging to the bare bark near the base of a large tree, like a growth on the bark, silent and watchful, seeking to avoid detection while the adults were scolding forcibly under cover near by and trying to draw the brood from the threatened danger."

Miss Stanwood has sent me some very elaborate notes, based on her extensive observations on two nests of the winter wren, from which the following information has been gleaned. Apparently the male takes no part in building the nest, in incubating the eggs, or in feeding the young while they are in the nest, though he encourages his mate by singing his most glorious songs in the immediate vicinity. He frequently approaches the nest in full song, calls the female off the nest and feeds her; he may, also, occasionally feed her while she is on the nest. He, apparently, assists in the care of the young after they leave the nest and while the family keeps together for some time.

The female feeds the young at frequent intervals; a large number of observations indicate that the young are usually fed at intervals varying from 2 to 5 minutes but often as frequently as once a minute; rarely the intervals between feedings were as much as 10 or 15 minutes. The feedings continue from dawn to dusk but are most frequent during the early morning hours. The food given to the young, as far as could be determined, consisted of moths, including spruce-bud moths and tan geometrid moths, craneflies, cutworms, caterpillars of various kinds, numerous small insects, and spiders. The female removes the fecal sacs as often as necessary, until the young are large enough to back up to the nest entrance and shoot their excrement over the edge. She broods the small young occasionally for periods of 2 or 3 minutes.

At one nest the young left when they were about 19 days old. "They had a soft, abrupt *zee* food call, which was very pretty and uttered constantly." They traveled about in a loose family party, often passing close to the observer but paying no attention to her.

Plumages.—The natal down, with which the nestling is only scantily covered on the dorsal feather tracts, is between "drab" and "hair brown"; in a young bird, about half grown, that I took from the nest referred to above, the last of this down still persists on the crown, where it is more than a quarter of an inch long. On this bird the juvenal plumage was well out, on the dorsal and ventral tracts; on the former it is "russet," barred with dusky, on the flanks "sayal brown," and on the breast pale buff, barred or mottled with dusky; the wing feathers were just beginning to break their sheaths. Dwight's (1900) description of a bird in full juvenal plumage is similar, but he adds: "Wings darker and tail ruddier, both duskily barred, alternating on the outer primaries with pale buff, the coverts with whitish terminal dots. * * * Flanks and crissum deep russet. Orbital ring and faint superciliary line dull buff."

A partial postjuvenal molt occurs, beginning about the middle of August, involving the contour plumage and the wing coverts, but not the rest of the wings or the tail; in the first winter plumage adults and young are practically indistinguishable. Adults have a complete post-nuptial molt in August but apparently no spring molt. The sexes are alike in all plumages.

Food.—The winter wren is almost wholly insectivorous, and it is especially useful in consuming many of the woodland insects and their larvae which are more or less injurious to our forests. W. L. McAtee (1926a) writes: "Vegetable food is of practically no interest to the winter wren; the bird wants flesh and its choice of meat most commonly strikes upon such creatures as the beetles, true bugs, spiders, caterpillars, and ants and other small hymenoptera. By contrast grasshoppers, crickets, crane flies, moths, millipeds, and snails are minor items of food, and dragon flies, daddy-longlegs, mites, pseudoscorpions, and sowbugs are merely tasted. Forest insects consumed are bark beetles and other weevils, round-headed wood borers, leaf beetles, leaf hoppers, plant lice, lace bugs, ants, sawflies, and caterpillars."

Arthur H. Howell (1924) says that, in the South, "the bird has been known to capture boll weevils." And E. H. Forbush (1929) writes: "The winter wren feeds along the banks of streams, frequently pecking at something in the water, and sometimes in its eagerness to secure its prey, it immerses the whole head. It may thus secure water insects. Miss Mabel R. Wiggins informed me that at East Marion, Long Island, N. Y., on October 20, 1918, winter wrens were feeding on the berries of the Virginia juniper or red cedar."

Behavior.—The winter wren is a secretive little mite, the smallest of our wrens with the exception of the short-billed marsh wren. Because of its retiring habits, it is often overlooked and is probably more common than most of us realize, for it does not advertise itself in the tree tops or pose to pour out its delicious song from some conspicuous perch as so many songsters do. We must look for it, if we would find it, in its lowly retreats near the ground, in the tangles along old stone walls, in the brush piles, and about fallen trees, prostrate logs, and wood piles. But it is really not shy and often quite indifferent to human presence. If we sit or stand quite still near its retreat, we may see it hop up to some twig near us, perhaps within a few feet of us, bobbing or bouncing up and down, flirting its short tail, and eyeing us inquisitively, but fearlessly. Edward J. F. Marx (1916) tells of one that actually alighted on the side of his coat while he was standing motionless, clad in a brown suit; it may have mistaken him for a tree.

Taverner and Swales (1908) write of one that made itself familiar on their last day in camp at Point Pelee: "This last day one fellow became much interested in our tent and camping equipment. It explored the former several times thoroughly, searching every crevice. It examined our methods of packing, and sampled the crumbs of our commissary, gleaning from the cracks of the table, and seemed generally pleased with himself and us. Finally it flew to a neighboring brush pile and scolded us as we took down the tent and piled the things into the wagon."

Although this wren may approach us fearlessly of its own free will, it is another matter for us to find it in its sylvan retreats. Its glorious song may lure us to catch a glimpse of the singer, but as we push our way through the forest tangles, the voice seems to retreat before us; it leads us on, now here now there, but it always seems to come from somewhere else, and we are lucky if we catch a fleeting glimpse of the little brown bird.

One seldom sees a winter wren in open flight, but Wendell Taber (MS.) was favored with the following observation: "The bird was in a clump of catbrier at the top of a bank that shelved rapidly about 20 feet down to the Ipswich River. Ultimately the wren rose up in the air, but instead of heading inland and flying low it went out over the river and downriver until lost to view, flying at an altitude of 35 to 40 feet above the river and marshes. Shortly after the wren had attained its maximum height and started downriver, a bird came and pursued it until both were out of sight. The latter bird was not identified but was assumed to be a redwing." This was on April 30, which suggests that the wren was probably on migration; the redwing may have been chasing what it mistook for a marsh wren, with which it is not on good terms.

Taber (MS.) and Richard Stackpole "watched a winter wren that seemed to have a regular route it covered. We were facing the open door of a barn. The narrow end of the barn was only a few feet to the left of the door and a brook paralleled the narrow end. We would see the wren disappear behind the barn, come out the open door, fly to its right to the brook, work the few yards down the brook, disappear behind the barn, and come out the open door again. The wren did this several times."

Voice.—The winter wren owes most of its charm and much of its claim to fame to its wonderful voice. Its charming song is a marvelous performance for such a tiny bird. To hear it coming from the shady depths of the northern forests is a delightful surprise, almost startling amid the silence of those dark sylvan aisles. Its variety is entrancing; the full rich song fairly bursts upon the ear with a tinge of nature's wildness; and again, at close range we hear the soft whisper song, a subdued rendering of the same trills and cadences; we cannot place the singer, the music seems to come from everywhere, but we stand amazed and thrilled.

Bradford Torrey (1885) writes: "The great distinction of the winter wren's melody is its marked rhythm and accent, which give it a martial, fife-like character. Note tumbles over note in the true wren manner, and the strain comes to an end so suddenly that for the first few times you are likely to think that the bird has been interrupted. * * * The song is intrinsically one of the most beautiful."

Rev. J. H. Langille (1884) refers to it: "Copious, rapid, prolonged and penetrating, having a great variety of the sweetest tones, and uttered in a rising and falling or finely undulating melody, from every region of these 'dim isles' this song calls forth the sweetest woodland echo. It seems as if the very atmosphere became resonant. I stand entranced and amazed, my very soul vibrating to this gushing melody, which seems at once expressive of the wildest joy and the tenderest sadness."

Aretas A. Saunders (1929b) analyzes the song as follows: "There is usually a long trill in the middle of it, which is followed by a short note of lower pitch. I found that the majority of the songs were of three parts, the first ending with the trill and its short note; the second was a repetition of the first; and the third, a sort of termination in which there were usually no trills. The notes follow each other so rapidly that it is hard to catch them all, but there are often 30 to 50 notes, in addition to the trills, in a single song."

Albert R. Brand (1935 and 1938) made careful studies of the songs of many birds by recording bird sound on motion-picture film, giving us much valuable information on the subject. He found, on his two records of the winter wren's song, that the length of the song varied from 6.72 to 7.17 seconds, as against less than 2.5 seconds for the song of the song sparrow; the wren's song contained from 106 to 113 separate notes, compared with 35 or 36 for the sparrow. "Two songs of the Winter Wren studied under the microscope show that an average of 16 distinct notes with a corresponding number of distinct stops were produced each second" (1935). He also found that the wren's song is very high in frequency, or pitch, exceeded only by the grasshopper sparrow and a few other birds, mostly warblers. The grasshopper sparrow, with one of the highest notes recorded, has an average frequency of 8,600 cycles, or vibrations, per second and a maximum of 9,500. The winter wren has an average frequency of 5,000 cycles and a maximum of 8,775 in its highest note. Out of some 55 birds that he lists only 12 have a higher average frequency than the winter wren.

The active song period of the winter wren extends through spring and through much of summer, up to the first week in August or later.

It is rarely heard singing on the fall migration, or even in winter. In its breeding haunts it sings all day and occasionally into the evening. In addition to its song it has a variety of chirping notes or alarm notes, which have been recorded as *churp*, or *chick*, or *crrrrip* by different observers. Saunders (1929a) says: "Its alarm note may be written 'trrip' or 'tree'. Another note has been written 'quip-quap'."

Since the above was written, Mr. Saunders has sent me the following additional notes on the song: "The song consists of warbles, rapid notes, and trills interspersed in a great variety of ways. Every song I have recorded contains at least one trill and commonly two or three. Only one contains more than four, but that one contains eight. In 13 of my records the song ends on its highest note, often terminating in a series of rapid notes, so high that they lose their sweet quality and become squeaky.

"My records show the lowest-pitched note to be D′′′ and the highest G′′′′, a range of two tones more than an octave and extending 3½ tones higher than the highest note on the piano. The average song ranges 3½ tones, but some only 2 tones and one 13 tones, going one-half tone over the octave in range.

"The great majority of songs are 8 seconds long, or very near it. I have one of nine seconds, and several shorter ones, the shortest being five seconds. But even this one is considerably longer than most bird songs, if we except the long-continued singers. Songs often contain short pauses. Some of them, however, according to my ear, are continuous throughout, while others contain two or three pauses and others 20 or 25."

Wendell Taber tells me that he "watched a winter wren singing. At first the bill is open and moves somewhat, then the bill is stretched unbelievably wide open, and the full last half, or more, of the song pours out with all its many variations of notes, during which period the bill remains motionless."

Francis H. Allen (MS.) mentions two notes of the adult, a *chrrrr* with a rising inflection, and a call, or alarm note *chut* very suggestive of the song sparrow's familiar note, but repeated once or twice, whereas the sparrow's is single; he calls the note of the young *chi-chi-chi-chi*, etc., "suggesting a miniature belted kingfisher."

Field marks.—The winter wren and the short-billed marsh wren are the smallest wrens, both among the smallest of birds in eastern North America, but the former is much darker and has a much shorter tail, which is often carried erect or even pointed forward, and the light line over the eye is not very conspicuous. The bobbing habit of the winter wren is characteristic.

Enemies.—Mr. Forbush (1929) reports the following incident, which seems rather unusual; he says: "Mrs. Mary P. Hall writes that on September 30, 1926, she saw several winter wrens very much excited about something. They hardly noticed her, and as she came near she saw a chipmunk running with a bird in its mouth. The little squirrel sprang from the stone wall and went up a tree, dropping the bird as it did so. She picked up the victim, a winter wren."

Fall and winter.—This little wren may have derived its name from the fact that a few hardy individuals venture to spend the winter in the northern States and even occasionally in southern Ontario. During mild winters they manage to make a fair living in the more sheltered places, but in severe winters many of them may perish from hunger and cold, especially when their meager food supply is buried under a blanket of deep snow. Mr. Forbush (1929) says that their dead bodies are found occasionally under piles of lumber or wood. Dr. John B. May told him that, at his summer camp in New Hampshire, "on two different occasions winter wrens entered his camp buildings through knot-holes in the walls, and, unable to find their way out again, perished, their shriveled bodies being found in the buildings the next spring."

In January 1871, Mr. Brewster (1906) "found one in Waltham (Mass.), that had taken up its abode in an old, disused barn which it entered by means of a conveniently placed knothole and from which it made short excursions in search of food along a neighboring wall."

Most of the wrens, however, migrate southward during the fall. We look for them in Massachusetts during the first cold weather in October. At this season they are often seen in the more open places and in some unexpected situations. They are occasionally seen about houses and gardens in towns and villages, and they even wander into the cities. I have seen one in my yard in the center of the city of Taunton, within a hundred yards of brick buildings. And Mr. Brewster (1906) reports one that was discovered, on October 15, 1899, "crouching in the shelter of one of the massive granite columns which support the front of the Boston Custom House."

In the southern Alleghenies there is a downward migration from the coniferous forests on the mountain tops late in fall. Referring to Mount Mitchell, in western North Carolina, Thomas D. Burleigh (1941) says of the winter wren: "Breeding abundantly in the thick fir and spruce woods at the top of the mountain this hardy little bird lingers in the fall until winter blizzards force it to a lower altitude. The first hint of milder weather sees its reappearance, so for 10 months out of the average year it can be found on the higher ridges. Exceptional winter will influence its movements to a certain extent, but it can invariably be seen on Mt. Mitchell from the latter part of March until the middle of November, and has been recorded there as early as February 6, 1931, and as late as December 6, 1932."

Dr. Eugene E. Murphey (1937), writing of its haunts in the

middle Savannah Valley, says: "In many places throughout the valley, cypress and hardwood have been logged out, leaving behind scattered deciduous trees and a vast array of stumps about four feet in height which are overgrown with matted vines and brambles and a fairly thick growth of ground-loving and creeping plants, including many ferns. Here the Winter Wren spends his sojourn."

M. G. Vaiden, of Rosedale, Miss., writes to me that this wren seems to be from "fairly to very common here during winter in suitable localities, such as dry open woods." Throughout the other Gulf States and northern Florida, the winter wren frequents mainly the brushy woodlands and is very quiet and retiring in its habits. While Arthur H. Howell (1924) was hunting geese on an island near Muscle Shoals, "one of these little wrens also spent the day there, dodging about in a pile of brush and running in and out of a log pile. He scarcely moved 10 feet all day and often came within 3 or 4 feet of" Mr. Howell's face without showing any signs of alarm.

DISTRIBUTION

Range.—In America from just north of latitude 60° south almost to the southern limits of the United States.

Breeding range.—The winter wren breeds **north** to Alaska (Aleutian Islands, Pribilofs, and Kodiak Island); southern Mackenzie (Great Slave Lake); southern Manitoba (Hillside Beach); northern Ontario (Lac Seul, Moose Factory, and Lake Abitibi, probably); southern Quebec (upper St. Maurice River and Godbout); and Newfoundland (Bard Harbor). **East** to Newfoundland (Bard Harbor and Nicholsville); Nova Scotia (Halifax and Seal Island); northern Massachusetts (Winchendon); Rhode Island (Kingston); New York (Adirondack and Catskill Mountains); and through the mountains to northern Georgia (Brasstown Bald). **South** to northern Georgia (Brasstown Bald); western Maryland (Accident); northern Michigan (Douglas Lake, Blaney, and Palmer); northern Minnesota (Onamia and Cass Lake); northwestern Montana (Flathead Lake); northern Idaho (Coeur d'Alene); and southern California (Portersville). **West** to California (Portersville) and north through the Sierra Nevada and the coastal ranges of California, Oregon, Washington, and British Columbia to Alaska (Aleutian and Pribilof Islands).

Winter range.—The winter range is discontinuous. The western range extends **north** to southeastern Alaska (Craig and Juneau casually); and southern British Columbia (Comox and Okanagan Landing). **East** to southern British Columbia (Okanagan Landing) through western Washington (Olympia and Camas); western Oregon

(Beaverton and Sweet Home) ; and the Sierra Nevada in California. **South** to southern California (Santa Barbara and San Dimas Canyon) ; and **west** to the Pacific Ocean.

The eastern section of the winter range extends **north** to southeastern Nebraska (Hastings and Omaha) ; central Missouri (Warrensburg and St. Louis) ; Ohio (Toledo and Cleveland) ; southern Ontario (Toronto) ; Connecticut (Hartford) ; and Massachusetts (Taunton). **East** to Massachusetts (Taunton and Woods Hole) ; and through the Atlantic coast States southward to Florida (New Smyrna). **South** to central Florida (New Smyrna, Orlando, and casually to St. Lucie) ; the Gulf coast to eastern Texas (Giddings and Victoria). **West** to eastern Texas (Giddings and Bonham) ; eastern Oklahoma (Caddo) ; eastern Kansas (Clearwater and Manhattan) ; and eastern Nebraska (Hastings).

The above range applies to the entire species in North America. It has been broken up into 10 subspecies or geographical races. The eastern winter wren (*T. t. hiemalis*) breeds from southern Alberta and Minnesota east to the Atlantic coast and south to West Virginia. The southern winter wren (*T. t. pullus*) occurs in the southern Appalachians from Virginia to Georgia. The western winter wren (*T. t. pacificus*) breeds from Prince William Sound, Alaska, east to northern Alberta, and from central California east to the Rocky Mountains. Six races have been described from Alaska: the Aleutian wren (*T. t. meligerus*) on Attu at the extreme western end; the Kiska wren (*T. t. kiskensis*) on Kiska and Little Kiska Islands; the Alaska wren (*T. t. alascensis*) on the Pribilof Islands; the Tanaga wren (*T. t. tanagensis*) on Tanaga and probably adjacent islands; Stevenson's winter wren (*T. t. stevensoni*) on Amak and Amagat Island; the Unalaska wren (*T. t. petrophilus*) on Unalaska, Amaknak, and Akutan Islands; the Semidi wren (*T. t. semidiensis*) on the Semidi Islands; and the Kodiak wren (*T. t. helleri*) on Kodiak Island.

Spring migration.—Some late dates of spring departure are: Florida—Orlando, March 10. Georgia—Athens, April 14. Mississippi—Biloxi, April 16. Louisiana—New Orleans, April 7. North Carolina—Raleigh, April 21. Virginia—Lynchburg, April 20. District of Columbia—Washington, May 1. Maryland—Hagerstown, April 10. Tennessee—Knoxville, May 1. Kentucky—Bowling Green, May 3. Pennsylvania—Pittsburgh, April 20. New Jersey—Elizabeth, April 29.

Early dates of spring arrival are: Pennsylvania—Harrisburg, April 5. New Jersey—Elizabeth, March 5. New York—Plattsburg, April 1. Vermont—Woodstock, March 30. Maine—Presque Isle, April 17. New Brunswick—Scotch Lake, March 29. Nova Scotia—Wolfville, May 3. Quebec—Quebec, May 6. Ohio—Columbus, March 30. Indi-

ana—Lafayette, March 17. Illinois—Chicago, April 8. Ontario—
Toronto, April 6. Michigan—Sault Ste. Marie, April 15. Iowa—
Davenport, March 31. Wisconsin—Sheboygan, March 25. Minne-
sota—Minneapolis, April 5. South Dakota—Faulkton, April 10.
Manitoba—Winnipeg, April 19. Montana—Fortine, April 23. Brit-
ish Columbia—Okanagan Landing, March 16.

Fall migration.—Late dates of fall departure are: British Columbia—Okanagan Landing, November 9. Montana—Fortine, October 9.
South Dakota—Faulkton, October 5. Minnesota—St. Paul, October
18. Wisconsin—Madison, October 30. Iowa—Sioux City, October 5.
Michigan—Sault Ste. Marie, October 11. Ontario—Ottawa, November 1. Illinois—Glen Ellyn, October 25. Indiana—Fort Wayne, October 29. Quebec—Montreal, October 27. New Brunswick—St. John,
October 12. Maine—Dover, November 5. Vermont—Rutland, October 29. Massachusetts—Boston, November 4. New York—Ithaca,
October 20. New Jersey—Morristown, November 3. Pennsylvania—
State College, November 23.

Early dates of fall arrival are: Maryland—Hagerstown, September
10. District of Columbia—Washington, September 25. Virginia—
Lexington, September 28. North Carolina—Chapel Hill, September
23. Georgia—Atlanta, October 12. Florida—Pensacola, October 20.
Missouri—Columbia, October 8. Kentucky—Lexington, October 1.
Tennessee—Nashville, October 14. Oklahoma—Oklahoma City, No-
vember 5. Louisiana—New Orleans, October 24. Mississippi—Biloxi,
October 21.

Casual records.—The winter wren has bred once in Wyoming: a
nest containing two young ready to fly was found in the Freezeout
Hills on July 15, 1897; birds were seen west of Fort Collins and in
Estes Park, Colo., in July 1896, but no evidence of breeding was found.
This species was seen in the Sacramento Mountains of New Mexico in
September 1902 and at Coony, N. Mex., on December 26, 1889, the
only records for the State; in Arizona there are three migration records, two in April and one in October, and one of a specimen taken
about 35 miles north of Fort Verde on January 6, 1887. It is an
uncommon winter visitant to southern Utah, specimens in Zion Canyon
on January 1, 1936, and February 1, 1942.

Egg dates.—Alaska: 11 records, May 20 to July 23.

California: 29 records, March 20 to July 19; 15 records, April 20 to
May 12, indicating the height of the season.

Labrador: 5 records, June 28 and 29.

New Hampshire: 8 records, May 14 to May 21.

Ontario: 11 records, May 18 to June 18.

Washington: 19 records, April 15 to June 22; 10 records, April 22
to May 9.

SOUTHERN WINTER WREN

Thomas D. Burleigh (1935) discovered and named this wren. He says that it is similar to the eastern winter wren, "but decidedly darker and less rufescent above, the underparts lighter brown, with the vermiculations of the abdomen and flanks heavier; wing longer; bill smaller and more slender." It breeds, he says, "in the Canadian Zone of the southern Appalachians from western North Carolina (probably Virginia), to northern Georgia, occurring in winter at a lower altitude in this same region."

"This southern race of the winter wren," continues Burleigh, "can always be easily recognized in either sex by its distinctly darker upperparts, a characteristic common to other birds limited in their distribution to this general region. Even in worn breeding plumage this character is at once evident."

The subspecies description is based on eight North Carolina specimens, five from Mount Mitchell, two from the Great Smoky Mountains, and one from Rocky Knob.

TROGLODYTES TROGLODYTES MELIGERUS Oberholser

ALEUTIAN WREN

HABITS

The 1910 Check-list treated the Alaska wren, of the Pribilof Islands, and the Aleutian wren, of the western Aleutian Islands, as two distinct species and listed both as specifically distinct from the winter wrens from other parts of North America. A thorough study of all the Old World and New World forms of the genus *Nannus*, by Dr. Harry C. Oberholser (1919), has demonstrated that all the North American forms of this genus are only subspecifically distinct; furthermore, he claims that these, and all the Old World forms as well, are all subspecies of the Old World species *Nannus troglodytes*. The framers of our 1931 Check-list evidently do not agree with this latter concept, but they do list all the North American forms as subspecies of *Nannus hiemalis*.

The Aleutian wren (*Troglodytes troglodytes meligerus*), the subject of this sketch, was formerly supposed to inhabit all the western Aleutian Islands, from Attu to Kiska; but now Dr. Oberholser (1919) restricts this name to the wrens of Attu Island and possibly the neighboring Agattu Island; and he names three new races for Tanaga, Kiska, and Unalaska Islands. He says that the Aleutian wren "is one of the most deeply colored of the North American forms and is apparently a well-differentiated race."

We found wrens of this species on all the islands we visited in the Aleutian Chain, from Unalaska on the eastern end to Attu in the west. It was one of the pleasantest surprises of our trip to find these delightful little songsters on these wholly treeless islands, where the only cover was the few stunted willows that grew in the sheltered hollows, or the piles of loose rocks along the shore; they seemed quite out of place in such surroundings, so different from the shady forest haunts of the closely related eastern winter wren. We found them first in an inland rocky ravine along the bed of a cool mountain stream and again in a grassy valley where there were a few scattered rocks on which they could perch and pour out their rich songs, adding a rare charm to this cheerless wilderness. But, most surprising of all, we often heard the glorious, bubbling song of the winter wren coming from the bleak, bare, rocky shores, where loose rocks and boulders were piled in confusion at the bases of the cliffs, washed by cold ocean spray and often enveloped in dense, chilly fogs. Here he sits and sings his thrilling, soulful song, perched on the pinnacle of some damp rock, or the branch of some drifted snag, buffeted by the gales that sweep down from snow-capped mountains, or drenched by frequent rain and snow squalls, all too prevalent in that wretched climate. He must have a brave and cheerful heart under his tiny coat of thick plumage.

A. H. Clark (1945) writes: "The lively bubbling trill of the winter wrens, the smallest of the Aleutian birds, is a characteristic bird note of the islands. These vivacious and pert little creatures are common, always keeping close to the sea, along the high rocky shores or in the lower portions of the valleys, where their surprisingly loud and clear notes betray their presence. These wrens are variable, and several different local forms are recognized in the Aleutian population."

Nesting.—We did not succeed in finding a nest of any of the wrens of the Aleutian Islands, but Lucien M. Turner (1886) says: "Mating occurs early in May or late in April. Nidification begins immediately. The nest is placed in a crevice in the face of a cliff or amongst the large tussocks of wild rye or other grasses. The nest is large and well built; coarse grasses and roots form the foundation, and as the nest nears completion smaller grasses are selected. The interior of the nest contains few feathers of various species of birds. The walls of the nest are well carried up, and in some instances form a partial roof over the nest, leaving a hole in one side as an entrance. Five to nine eggs are laid; they are pure white in color."

He says further, as to their habits:

They remain on these islands during the entire year. * * * Their food consists of insects, and occasionally a few seeds will be found in their crops. * * * Their note is a prolonged twitter of several modulations and repeated at short intervals. When surprised, or when they come upon an object that excites their curiosity, a rapid and long rattle is sounded as an alarm, soon to be answered by a second bird. These two keep up the sound until all the Wrens within hearing assemble to investigate the cause. As many as a dozen will surround the object, and approach so close that the outstretched hand might capture them. The least motion, however, disperses them so quickly that one wonders where they have disappeared. They, at these times, hide under the stalks of the weeds or grass. * * * At the approach of winter the bird becomes very familiar, and is frequently found on the window-sills searching for insects. On one occasion I heard a gentle tapping at my back window; as I had frequently heard the same noise, I carefully drew the curtain partly aside, and saw a Wren endeavoring to obtain a fly that was inside of the pane of glass. The bird did not appear to be disturbed by my presence.

The above account is based on observations made on various islands in the Aleutian Chain, from Unalaska westward, and must not be construed as applying especially to the wrens of Attu Island. The observations were made before the species was subdivided as it is now.

TROGLODYTES TROGLODYTES KISKENSIS (Oberholser)

KISKA WREN

HABITS

In naming this wren, Dr. Oberholser (1919) described it as similar to *meligerus*, the preceding form, "but wing, tail, and tarsus shorter; upper parts lighter, less rufescent (more grayish) brown, and posteriorly more uniform (less distinctly barred); lower parts more deeply ochraceous, and posteriorly somewhat less heavily barred with blackish." The eight specimens from Kiska Island, on which this subspecies is based, exhibit individual variations which suggest intergradation with both the Attu Island bird and the Unalaska bird.

Most of the wrens of this race that we saw on Kiska Island were living on the shore of Kiska Harbor. A high, rocky cliff, on which a pair of Peale's falcons were evidently nesting, rose above a narrow beach strewn with masses of broken rocks and boulders, with scattered tufs of long grass growing in some places among the rocks. Pacific eiders were nesting among these tufts of grass, pigeon guillemots had their eggs hidden far under the rocks, and on a grassy slope some Aleutian song sparrows were singing songs reminding us of home. Here the wrens were darting in and out among the rocks, climbing over them, or perching on their tops to sing, often bobbing up and down in true winter-wren fashion. Their songs were much like those of the eastern winter wren, but it seemed to me that they were louder and richer; perhaps they sounded more beautiful by contrast with their bleak surroundings, the rocky background, the pounding surf, and the cries of sea birds.

TROGLODYTES TROGLODYTES ALASCENSIS Baird

ALASKA WREN

PLATE 31

HABITS

This race of the winter wren group is now supposed to be confined to the Pribilof Islands, on St. George and St. Paul Islands. The type, which was obtained by Dr. Dall on the former island, was an immature bird in its first plumage.

Dr. Oberholser (1919) describes this race as similar to the Kiska bird, "but wing and tail longer; bill decidedly, tarsus and middle toe without claw somewhat, shorter; upper parts darker, more rufescent; lower parts rather more deeply ochraceous, and posteriorly with narrower, less deeply blackish bars." It seems to be subspecifically distinct from *all* the birds of the Aleutian Islands, including Unalaska.

Dr. Nelson (1887) wrote: "One of the most peculiar facts in its history is its abundance on the island of St. George, which is about 180 miles north of the Aleutian Islands, whereas, on St. Paul Island, only 27 miles distant from St. George, and apparently suitable in every way for its presence, there is not a single record of its occurrence; and Elliott states that he searched carefully for it during his residence at that place." This statement could not be made truthfully today, for specimens have since been taken on St. Paul Island. We failed to find it there, but our stay was very limited; we failed to find it on Walrus Island in the same group, where we made a more thorough investigation of its wonderful bird life.

More recently, Dr. Harold Heath (1920), who spent the greater part of May and the first half of June 1918 on St. George Island, has added much to our knowledge of this wren and its habits. As to its distribution on these islands he says: "Until recent years the wrens of the Pribilof Islands were strictly limited to the island of St. George. In 1915, however, six individuals were observed by Dr. Hanna on St. Paul Island, and of these, three were secured. None, so far as I now recall, have since been noted there, but in the summer of 1918 a considerable number were seen on Otter Island, a small body of land 4 miles to the southward."

In a still more recent paper, Preble and McAtee (1923) state that Mr. Hanna took two of his specimens on St. Paul Island on October 29, 1914, and the third on May 16, 1915; he also reported that, during 1915, George Haley saw 11 individuals on Otter Island, that they have since become well established there, and that they bred there in 1916, 1917, and 1918. These authors conclude:

It seems likely, therefore, unless the species meets with a reverse on Otter Island from some cause, that it will in time become regularly established as a breeder on St. Paul, and that, therefore, the likelihood of the species surviving will be strengthened.

During the winter of 1916–1917 St. George was visited by an unusual number of gyrfalcons, which preyed upon the wrens and rosy finches to such an extent that they were almost extirpated. G. Dallas Hanna states that in May 1917, he found not over six pairs of wrens during a trip made entirely around the island. Since then, however, as elsewhere detailed, the species has become at least fairly common again and has even spread to the other main islands, previously unoccupied.

Nesting.—It was many years after the discovery of the Alaska wren that its nesting habits were fully described by a competent naturalist. Earlier accounts were based on reports by the natives or on nests and eggs collected by them. The earliest account came from Dr. Elliott Coues (1875) ; he quotes from the manuscript notes of Henry W. Elliott, who spent parts of 3 years on St. George Island, as follows: "Its nest is built in small, deep holes and crevices in the cliffs. I have not myself seen it, but the natives say that it lays from 8 to 10 eggs, in a nest made of soft, dry grass and feathers, roofed over, with an entrance at the side to the nest-chamber, thus being of elaborate construction."

The attempts of various naturalists, who visited the island during subsequent years, to find the nest of this elusive bird were not successful until 1918, when Dr. Heath (1920) made a special effort to solve the problem and succeeded in finding over 16 nests. He has given us the following full account of the nesting haunts of the Alaskan wren, the difficulties to be encountered in hunting for the nests, and a description of the nests:

Throughout the summer at least, these diminutive creatures confine their activities to the perpendicular cliffs and the adjacent boulder-strewn beach where they prove to be more than usually inconspicuous, for several reasons. In the first place their brownish coats harmonize almost perfectly with the weathered basaltic rock and the encrusting lichens, and this, together with their habit of slipping along the face of the cliff by very short flights, or moving mouse-like through the grass, or entering crevices of the cliff or beneath the beach boulders to appear again several feet distant, renders it most difficult to follow their movements for many minutes together. Also, during the month of May and the first half of June—the length of my sojourn on St. George Island— the weather was anything but ideal. Rain, dense fogs, or at least heavily overcast skies, with piercing winds and a temperature of not over 50 degrees, placed a heavy tax on one's powers of endurance and eyesight. Furthermore, the almost incessant incoming and outgoing stream of least, crested and paroquet auklets interpersed with kittiwakes, puffins and murres, and the movements of these species on the cliffs, produce a bewildering effect which tends to blot out minor details. * * *

At the outset be it known that the male is almost utterly useless when depended upon to disclose the presence of the nest, until after the young are hatched. In carefree fashion he explores the cracks and crannies of the cliffs for half-frozen bugs and flies, or repairs to a commanding position at the upper margin of the cliff, where he delivers himself of his unoiled song; or tiring of this he flies a quarter of a mile or so along the coast to sneak back a few minutes later to the same old stand. In three instances only, have I seen the male fly to the neighborhood of the female or the nest during the building or incubation period, and his stay in every case was of brief duration.

During this time the female may or may not be in evidence, and if discovered her activities are usually found to be essentially the same as her mate. If so— and an hour's watching will generally settle the matter—it is economy of effort to postpone the search for the nest until the morrow.

However, if the female is in the midst of house building, no better time can be found to locate her nest for, in spite of intruders, even at a distance of a few feet, she works with feverish activity and with a directness of flight that can scarcely escape the observation of even an untrained eye.

Nevertheless, this period of construction is frequently interrupted by flights to the beach or along the cliff in search of insects, or for a period of song on some lofty point, or she too may dash out of sight far up the coast to return after a period of from 5 to 30 minutes.

Another favorable time for the location of the nest is during the incubation period. Four nests under observation showed that the female remains upon the eggs, whatever the character of the day or the stage of incubation, for a period ranging from 18 to 21 minutes. She then feeds from 2 to 5 minutes. Here also her flight is relatively direct, in marked contrast to her usual journey along the cliffs, and is unmistakable after a brief experience. The recorded habits of several other birds indicate a fairly definite daily program during the breeding season, but, so far as I know, none are so timed to the minute as the Alaska Wren.

All of the nests discovered in 1918 were in the faces of cliffs anywhere from 25 to 100 feet in height, and were placed at elevations varying from 8 to 100 feet. The spot chosen may be a crevice between shattered blocks of rock, or in a small blowhole in the ancient lava flow, or, more frequently, underneath banks of moss where rain and frost have excavated cavities of tidy size. In three instances the nesting site had been chosen the year before, the new nest being built upon the remains of the old one. In my experience the nest is never hidden far beneath the general surface of the cliff. Of 12 nests described in my field notes 4 were plainly visible, while the others were merely concealed by an overhanging fringe of grass or moss or by a few small shattered scales of rock. Four other nests were placed in cracks at a considerable elevation and in overhanging cliffs that effectually prevented a close examination.

The nest of the Alaska Wren is indeed a work of art, with the materials composing it bearing a definite relation to the nature of its surroundings. Generally speaking, it is a globular, more or less bulky affair with the entrance at one side. When situated in a lava bubble or in cavities where the adjacent rock is relatively dry, it usually consists of an external sheath of moss, thick or thin, according to the size of the space to be filled. Where the soil inclines to be soggy the roof alone is built of moss (at least in three instances) to absorb the moisture and prevent its precipitation upon the sitting female. Farther down, at the sides of the nest, it rests upon a meshwork of grass and roots that not only drains away the water from above, but permits of rapid drying. To determine the correctness of this theory a nest of this type was brought in from the field, and was left overnight under the slow drip from a water tap. The next morning the mossy roof was soaked and the grassy base adrip, but not a drop of water had made its way into the interior. * * *

The lining of the nest forms a heavy feltwork of which delicate roots and fine filamentous lichen form the chief constituents. With these are usually associated the feathers of the least auklet (and other birds to a less degree), fox hairs, and in late years, the hair of the reindeer.

There is a nest in the Thayer collection in Cambridge, which I have examined. It was collected by E. C. Crompton on St. George Island on May 20, 1922, taken from a crevice in the rocks of a cliff on the seashore, about 20 feet up. It is quite bulky, being made mainly of dry grasses and weed stems, mixed with green mosses and lichens and a few feathers; it is lined with small feathers and very fine white hairs. These white hairs were probably from the bleached-out winter coat of the blue fox; those examined microscopically by Dr. Heath proved to be from this source.

Eggs.—The six eggs that came with the above nest are ovate and have very little gloss. They are pure white; some are nearly, or quite, immaculate, but most of them are sparingly sprinkled, mainly about the larger end, with fine pinpoints of the palest brown.

The earlier reports by natives that this wren lays as many as 10 or 12 eggs should not be taken seriously; probably the natives were careless or could not count accurately. Dr. Heath (1920) says: "In the majority of the nests examined this year the number of eggs laid is 7. Six may be the complement. * * * A young, intelligent native boy told me that he had examined several wren's nests during the past 10 years, and had never found more than 7 eggs or young." He says that the eggs "are more or less peppered with reddish dots." The eggs in his photograph all show these markings plainly (pl. 31). The measurements of 34 eggs average 17.0 by 13.2 millimeters; the eggs showing the four extremes measure **19.0** by 13.7, 18.0 by **14.0, 14.0** by 13.0, and 17.1 by **12.2** millimeters.

Young.—Dr. Heath (1920) writes: "A nearly as I can judge from one pair of wrens, the period of incubation lasts 11 days, and the young in this same nest were fed for 22 days. The incubation period seems too short and the altricial period too long. When the eggs are hatched the male abandons his usual haunts, and with his mate collects insects from foggy morn to yet more foggy eve. When this brood is dismissed a second one may be reared the same season. In 1918, for example, E. C. Crompton, Government agent on St. George, reported to me the discovery of a nest that was left by the young about the middle of July. During the following week the female deposited a second set of eggs."

Plumages.—Ridgway (1904) says of the young: "Essentially like adults, but brown of upper parts more rufescent, flanks and under tail-coverts less distinctly barred (bars sometimes obsolete), and feathers of under parts more or less distinctly margined with brown or dusky." Nelson (1887) says that the young "may be distinguished from the adult by a smoky brown shade on the sides of the head, chin, and throat, and a brighter rusty-red on the back, especially on the rump. In the adults the bill is longer and proportionally slenderer, and the faint, light superciliary line is better marked."

As far as we can tell from the scanty material available, the molts are apparently similar to those of the eastern winter wren.

Food.—Preble and McAtee (1923) write:

Of the 11 stomachs of Alaska wrens available 9 were examined some time ago by less discriminating methods than those at present in use, and it is only possible, therefore, to indicate the nature of the food in very general terms. The sustenance was entirely animal and included the following groups:

Amphipods, 24.1 percent; two-winged flies (partly Borboridae), 24.1 percent; beetles (including ground and rove beetles), 14.3 percent; bugs (Hemiptera), 13.2 percent; caterpillars, 12.9 percent; and Hymenoptera, 11.4 percent.

A recently examined stomach contained the following items: Six beetles of the sexton-beetle family (*Lyrosoma opaca*), 12 percent; rove beetles (*Olophrum fuscum* and 2 *Liparocephalus brevipennis*), 3 percent; three small parasitic wasps (including *Phygadeuon* sp. and *Plesignathus* sp.), 1 percent; remains of dung flies (*Scatophaga* sp.) and perhaps other flies, 74 percent; one mite of an undescribed genus of the family Gamasidae, trace; and amphipod remains, 10 percent.

Another stomach, lately examined, taken October 29, 1914, contained remains of 24 or more rove beetles (Staphylinidae), 70 percent; 4 beach beetles (*Aegialites debilis*), 19 percent; 1 other beetle, 1 percent; and a few flies, 10 percent.

Behavior.—The behavior of the birds during the breeding season has been described by Dr. Heath above. Mr. Elliott's notes, quoted by Dr. Coues (1875), say that "the male is very gay during the period of mating and incubation, flying incessantly from plant to plant or rock to rock, singing a rather shrill and very loud song, and making, for a small bird, a great noise."

Winter.—The destruction of these wrens by gyrfalcons in winter has been referred to above. Mr. Elliott told Dr. Nelson (1887) that "during exceptionally severe winters on the island of St. George, large numbers of these birds die of exposure, so that only the hardiest among them survive. But the rapidity with which they multiply brings their numbers up to the former standard in a very few seasons."

TROGLODYTES TROGLODYTES TANAGENSIS (Oberholser)

TANAGA WREN

HABITS

Dr. Oberholser (1919) has given the above name to the wrens of Tanaga, Adak, and Atka Islands in the Aleutian Chain. The subspecies description is based on nine specimens, collected on the above islands, mostly by the members of our expedition in 1911. He says that it is similar to the Kiska bird, "but wing somewhat longer; upper parts more rufescent and rather lighter, especially on the lower back, rump, and upper tail-coverts; posterior lower parts on the average less heavily barred, and with the bars less blackish; the entire under surface averaging lighter and somewhat more ochraceous." He says that it is nearest to the bird of the Pribilof Islands, "but its bill is much longer and its upper parts lighter."

On Atka Island we found the birds in a sheltered, grassy hollow with a few rocks scattered through it, and in rocky ravines and gulches, where it was in full song. On Adak Island they were on the rocky shores of the Bay of Waterfalls. They doubtless occur in both types of habitat on all of these islands. Their habits are evidently the same as those of the other island subspecies.

TROGLODYTES TROGLODYTES PETROPHILUS (Oberholser)

UNALASKA WREN

HABITS

Dr. Oberholser (1919) gives this new name to the wrens found on Unalaska Island and the neighboring islands of Amaknak and Akutan. On the basis of 15 specimens from these localities, he describes the new subspecies as similar to the Pribilof bird, "but wing shorter; bill longer; upper parts lighter, much more rufescent; lower parts decidedly paler, and posteriorly with narrower and lighter bars."

We noticed nothing different from the habits of these wrens elsewhere in the wrens we saw on these islands, but Dr. Nelson (1887) has this to say about the haunts and habits of this subspecies:

On May 13, 1877, I landed, during a heavy gale, on the island of Akoutan, just east of Unalaska, and was making my way cautiously along the rock-strewn beach, half expecting a fall of fragments from the beetling cliffs above to join the rocky mass which had already fallen. While occupied in searching cautiously for a firm footing, a faint, wiry, note struck my ear and brought me to a sudden standstill. All about lay huge blocks of riven lava, from which arose the overhanging crags; a little back a more sloping bluff presented its face, the inequalities of which were dotted by scattered grass and other vegetation, now dead and yellow, or in spots were flecked with patches of snow. As my eye scanned this abrupt slope, the author of the notes was seen clinging to a dwarf willow bush at the very brow of the bluff, over which the wind came with great force, beating the bush back and forth as if it would uproot it.

* * * The last of September and first of October, 1881, while the Corwin lay at Unalaska, I had still further opportunities for studying this little-known species in its home. They were very common everywhere on the lower portions of the island, wherever the rank grass and other plants, combined with the stunted bushes, offered a fitting shelter. Here the birds were seen repeatedly, swinging on the projecting sprays or flitting busily from point to point, and showing a peculiar sprightliness and activity common to it and its kind.

TROGLODYTES TROGLODYTES SEMIDIENSIS (Brooks)

SEMIDI WREN

Only two specimens of this wren from the Semidi Islands, on the south side of the Alaska Peninsula, to which it seems to be confined, were available for study when Dr. Oberholser (1919) described it as similar to the Unalaska bird, "but wing, tail, and bill somewhat longer; upper parts less rufescent (more grayish) and somewhat darker; under surface paler, less deeply ochraceous, and posteriorly rather more heavily barred." He says that it differs from the Pribilof bird "in its decidedly longer bill and somewhat longer tarsus and middle toe; somewhat lighter, less rufescent upper parts; and paler, less ochraceous lower surface."

Nothing seems to have been recorded about its haunts or habits.

KODIAK WREN

This race seems to be confined to Kodiak Island. Dr. Wilfred H. Osgood (1901) named it in honor of Edmund Heller, who was with him when the type was collected. He described it as "slightly larger and paler colored than" the western winter wren, and remarked that it "is merely another illustration of the tendency of west coast birds which range as far north as Kodiak to become pale in their northern habitat."

Dr. Oberholser (1919) calls it similar to the Unalaska bird, "but smaller, especially the bill; upper surface much darker, more sooty (less rufescent) ; dark bars of lower back, rump, and upper tail-coverts more conspicuous; lower parts darker, and posteriorly more heavily dark-barred."

It is apparently one of the rarest of the subspecies, and very little seems to be known about it.

STEVENSON'S WINTER WREN

Dr. Harry C. Oberholser (1930) has split off another finely drawn race from the many recognized subspecies of Alaskan wrens, to which he has given the above name. He describes it as similar to the Unalaska wren, "but upper parts, and to a less extent, also the lower surface, more grayish or sooty (less rufescent) in both adult and juvenal plumages; posterior lower parts in adult on the average less heavily spotted with fuscous; bill and middle toe averaging slightly longer."

He says that it is found on "Amak Island and Amagat Island, Alaska; and probably also other neighboring islands and the southwestern end of the Alaska Peninsula.

"As in most of the other Alaska races of this species there is considerable individual variation in this new form; and the differences, while very readily recognizable in a series, are, of course, to some extent overlapped by individuals of the most closely related subspecies, *Nannus troglodytes petrophilus*. It is interesting, however, to note that the color differences are fully as noticeable in the juvenal plumage as in the adult, as is well shown by the series of 10 young and 5 adults from Amak and Amagat Islands that have been examined."

WESTERN WINTER WREN

PLATES 32, 33

HABITS

Baird (1864), in his original description of this wren, says: "I find, on comparing series of eastern birds with those from the Pacific slope, that the latter are considerably darker in color above, with little or almost none of the whitish spotting among the dusky bars so characteristic of eastern specimens. The under parts are more rufous, the tarsi appear shorter, and the claws decidedly larger."

Ridgway (1904) describes it as similar to the eastern bird, "but darker and more richly colored; brown of upper parts darker, more rusty, more uniform, the back, etc., much less distinctly barred, often quite uniform; color of throat, chest, etc., much deeper and brighter, more tawny-cinnamon or light russet; bill straighter and more slender."

The breeding range of the western winter wren extends along the Pacific slope from Prince William Sound, Alaska, to central California, and in the Rocky Mountan region from western Alberta to northern Colorado.

The haunts and habits of the western winter wren are similar to those of its eastern relative, though the environment is somewhat different. The eastern bird is content to make its summer home in dense forests of spruces and firs that grow to only moderate heights, while its western relative lives in the deep forests of giant conifers that so heavily clothe the northwest coast from sea level to the limit of trees, and in the deep shade of the grand redwood forests of California.

S. F. Rathbun tells me that it is one of the few birds to be found in the deep forests of western Washington, even in the densest places. He finds it in the forests bordering the beaches, at lake level inland and up to 5,000 feet in the Olympic Mountains. Referring to Mount Rainier, in Washington, Taylor and Shaw (1927) write: "The western winter wren seems as much a part of the forest floor as the mosses, huckleberry vines, huge logs, and upturned roots of his surroundings. * * * When the traveler emerges from the dark woods onto the open meadows or well-lighted brushy burns the wrens become much less numerous, for they are fond of shadows. They are often found at a considerable distance from water on some forest-covered hillside. Once, indeed, they were noted in clumps of alpine firs on an open and well-lighted hillside with a southern exposure."

Grinnell and Storer (1924) say that, in the Yosemite region, this, the smallest and most seclusive of the wrens, "lives at the middle altitudes, amid freshest-bared tangles and rootlets and accumulations of drift materials along shaded stream courses." W. A. Kent writes to me that, at the head waters of the Kern River in the Sierra Nevadas he found that the western winter wren had nested at an elevation of 11,000 feet. Dawson (1923) says: "The Western Winter Wren is one of the commonest birds in the humid coast belt of western California as far south as middle Monterey County. Not only is it the most characteristic inhabitant of rugged stream beds and romantic dells, but it may be found throughout the somber depths of the fir and redwood forests, from sea-level nearly to the tops of the northern mountains."

Courtship.—I do not know whether anyone has ever seen the courtship display of the eastern winter wren, but I have never seen it reported. Therefore, the following account of the display of the western winter wren, by Theed Pearse (1933) is of special interest:

The bird was in a bush above a tangle in which, possibly, there was a female, on a branch just clear of the tangle. First, the bird fluttered or quivered its wings, keeping them close to the body slightly drooped. Its general attitude was rather squatting, the converse of the ordinary alert up-standing posture. When quivering it looked down towards the ground (the tangle where there may have been a female) and worked its tail alternately from side to side. At times it would utter a note, a much modified and softened regular alarm note.

The climax came when the bird dropped its wings and fanned with them, bringing them forward and then backwards. The feathers carried concavely from the front, with the feathers on the back also raised between the wings. The bird "fanned" about ten times; the action was quick but easily followed. After this the bird dropped into the bush and moved away. Shortly afterwards a Winter Wren appeared in the same bush, up from below and perched there for a time bowing or bobbing.

It was when the bird had the wings held open "fanning" that it brought into prominence some white markings on the feathers that were raised on the rump. The glimpse one had, made it difficult to decide whether the white was on the secondary tertial or rump feathers, but there was sufficient to draw attention, though so inconspicuous, that I had to make sure by examining the skins in Mr. Laing's collection. We found that when the feathers on the rump were parted there were some that showed white markings or spots.

Nesting.—The nests of the western winter wren are apparently very similar, in construction and in the kinds of material used, to those of the eastern bird, but the locations chosen seem to be somewhat more varied. Dawson and Bowles (1909) say:

For nesting sites the Wrens avail themselves of cubbyholes and crannies in upturned roots or fallen logs, and fire-holes in half-burned stumps. A favorite situation is one of the crevices which occur in a large fir tree when it falls and splits open. Or the nest is sometimes found under the bark of a decaying log, or in a crevice of earth in an unused mine-shaft. If the site selected has a wide entrance, this is walled up by the nesting material and only a smooth round aperture an inch and a quarter in diameter is left to admit to the nest proper. In default of such shelter, birds have been known to construct their nests at the center of some baby fir, or in the drooping branches of a fir tree at a height of a foot or more from the ground.

Mr. Rathbun mentions in his notes a nest that was still farther from the ground: "The nest was attached very near the extremity of one of the lower limbs of a small hemlock tree at a height of 12 feet. It was almost round in shape and resembled a bunch of moss hanging from the limb, but it was too perfect in shape to deceive me."

Thomas D. Burleigh (1930) records four nests, found in north-western Washington, in four different situations; one was "2 feet from the ground in the upturned roots of a large fir at the side of a stream in a wooded ravine." Another was "2 feet from the ground in a crevice at the end of an old rotten log on a hillside in a ravine"; a third "was 3½ feet from the ground in a hole in an old rotten stump in a stretch of thick woods." The fourth nest seems most unusual "for it was 5 feet from the ground well concealed in a mass of dead leaves lodged in a clump of shoots growing from the trunk of a large alder in a short stretch of open woods."

There is a nest in the Thayer collection in Cambridge that was apparently similarly located; it was taken by F. J. Smith, of Eureka, Calif., "in woods near town, fastened to sprouts against the side of an alder tree, partly concealed by tall sword ferns."

The western winter wren is one of the species that accepted J. H. Bowles's invitation to nest in artificially prepared nesting sites; he had a pair adopt a "very old and badly broken down Creeper 'decoy' "; he tried tin cans and other devices unsuccessfully, and then says (1922): "Finally I removed a section of bark from a small dead fir stub, dug out a space about six inches in diameter, then replaced the bark and made an entrance hole about an inch and a half in diameter close to the top of the cavity." A pair of wrens took possession, a few weeks later built a beautiful nest, and laid a set of five eggs in it.

Like some other wrens, notably the long-billed marsh wren, the western winter wren builds extra nests, false or decoy nests, perhaps through super-abundant energy on the part of the male, or with the idea of appropriating all available nesting sites for possible future use. Mr. Bowles (1899) says: "The number of 'decoys' built by one pair of these birds varies from one to at least four, and on one occasion I found eight of these false nests that were strung along the edge of a stream bordered by dense growth of all sizes. These were all in a space about 150 yards long and almost in a straight line." He does not claim that all of these nests were made by one pair of birds, but only one appeared during his search. "The 'decoys' are never so well constructed as the regular nests, but a few weeks ago I was surprised to find that a pair had made over and lined one of last season and laid one egg."

Eggs.—The eggs are indistinguishable from those of the eastern winter wren. The measurements of 40 eggs average 16.4 by 12.4 millimeters; the eggs showing the four extremes measure 18.1 by 12.7, 17.2 by 13.0, and 14.0 by 12.0 millimeters.

Young.—Mrs. Wheelock (1904) says that the young "are fed by regurgitation for several days after hatching, the menu being chiefly small grubs which the busy little parents pick out of the bark of the coniferous trees. They are fed on insects and worms also. After the sixth day the food is mostly given in the fresh condition. The wren nestlings leave the nest between the seventeenth and twenty-first days."

Grinnell and Storer (1924) watched a nest containing young that was located on the edge of a small stream, only 13 inches above the water. They write:

The parent was busily engaged in feeding large green worms, millers, crane-flies, and other insects to the young. A beam of light reflected into the nest from a mirror did not seem to frighten the wrens and so it was possible to observe closely the process of feeding. The old bird made visits at intervals of 4, 9, 2, 2, 7, 8, and 3 minutes, respectively; twice, at the second and last of these timed visits, the bird carried away excrement. The young void the excrement (which is enclosed in a gelatinous sac) immediately after being fed; it is dropped by them on the rim of the nest where it lies as a conspicuous spherical white object, the size of a large bean. The old bird seizes this in her bill and in one instance carried it away fully 50 feet before depositing it in a wild currant bush. One sac fell into the small stream and as it floated slowly along the surface the bird snatched nervously at it again and again. Finally it was recovered, whereupon the bird flew off and disposed of it in the usual manner, in a place where it would give no clue to the location of the nest.

Food.—No comprehensive, detailed study of the food of the western winter wren seems to have been made, but it probably does not differ much from that of other wrens in its habitat. It seems to subsist almost wholly, if not entirely, on insects and their larvae. The items mentioned in the food of the young, above, probably constitute the bulk of its food.

Behavior.—Anyone familiar with our eastern winter wren would recognize this little westerner by its behavior. It is the same, nervous, active little mouse, dodging about near the ground, in and out of tangles and the roots of trees, and about prostrate logs, bowing and bobbing, with its short tail cocked up over its back. Grinnell and Storer (1924) say:

The bird seems to *skip* along and uses both the short wings and long legs in all its ordinary movements. It seems equally at ease on a nearly vertical twig and on a horizontal root or branchlet.

One evening just at sunset, in October, while our party was camped near Sweetwater Creek, a winter wren was watched as it came down to bathe. The bird fluttered down, half flying, half hopping, to a small pool completely screened from above. It would stay a few seconds, splashing in the water, and then move to a perch a few feet above the pool, soon to return for another brief dip. Five or six such short visits were made and then the bird returned to the perch where it stayed for a while, fluffing out all its feathers, and using its bill to press out the water. Two or three minutes sufficed to complete its toilet and then the wren made off down the creek to a brush pile.

Voice.—What has been written about the voice of the eastern winter wren would apply equally well to its western relative. The song is hardly inferior to it in any way, and its call notes are similar. Mr. Rathbun tells me that this wren has a long period of song; he has heard it as early as February 28, but it sings most incessantly from the middle of March to the end of June; he hears it also in July and early in August, but then the song, "although well rendered, seems to lack the abandon of that heard during the earlier period" and is not so frequently given. He once timed the duration of the song and found that its length varied from 8 to 17 seconds, at times up to 23 seconds; the intervals between the songs were 4 to 12 seconds; sometimes the songs were repeated without intermissions. He remarks that some of the notes have "the quality of the tones given by lightly striking the edge of a thin glass goblet."

Taylor and Shaw (1927) say: "If the observer remains quiet, and perhaps makes a squeaking sound with the lips on the back of his hand, he can easily attract the midgets to within 3 or 4 feet. Under such conditions a call note is uttered, evidently expressive of curiosity or caution, *tssss! tssss!* The usual call note is a *check! chek-chek! chek-chek!*"

Winter.—Cold weather, snow, and ice combine to drive the wrens down from the higher elevations in the mountains to the lower and milder valleys, where they seek such shelter as they can find. Even here they sometimes perish during severe winters. Theed Pearse tells me that, on Vancouver Island, they suffered a great reduction in numbers as a result of two successive cold and snowy winters, 1936–37 and 1937–38, but had recovered quite well by the winter of 1939–40.

C. E. Ehinger (1925) tells an interesting story of a winter wrens' lodginghouse in western Washington. This was a small birdbox, 6 inches square, attached to their cabin, which was surrounded with woods. During severe winter weather, in December and January, an increasing number of wrens began using this box as a night roosting place. He describes their actions as follows:

At the setting of the sun the wrens began to gather, and for half an hour they played about the bird box in the most interesting manner. Singly and in groups they would dash up to the cabin wall, cling there a moment, then with a flying leap change their position to one a little nearer to the bird box. This was continued until they could spring upon the roof of the box, from which they dropped to the little platform and entered. After a moment they would usually fly out again and circle around, only to repeat the manoeuvre. Several times, 10 to 15 wrens were counted clinging to the cabin wall at the same time, like so many great flies, when they would repeat the aforesaid manoeuvre and finally disappear silently through the tiny opening into their lodging house like little feathered mice. * * *

January 21, time 4:45 to 5:20 p. m., proved the prize record for wren lodgers. After a short period of the usual "play-antics" the birds entered rapidly until 30 were counted. Others continued to come, but the situation inside apparently seemed hopeless, and they flew around to the front of the cabin where a ledge under the eaves seemed to furnish a protected roosting place. We saw those later through a little ventilating window under the eaves and also heard them moving about. Just before complete darkness, one belated wren came to the bird box, tried to enter and failed, finding a full house; but not to be denied a warm sleeping place he stood a few moments on the little porch and made a vigorous but unsuccessful attempt to gain entrance. He heard the wrens inside chattering and moving about, perhaps trying to make room for the late comer. He finally made a third desperate attempt and, climbing over seemingly insurmountable obstacles, he gained entrance, and in a few moments all was still with 31 Winter Wrens snugly ensconced in this 6×6×6 inch apartment.

THRYOMANES BEWICKII BEWICKII (Audubon)

BEWICK'S WREN

PLATE 34

HABITS

Bewick's wren, the type race of the species, is the eastern representative of a widely distributed species that has been subdivided into 12 additional subspecies in western North America within the limits of our Check-list. Although it has the widest range and has been known for the longest time, it does not seem to have been so thoroughly studied as some of the western races. Its breeding range, according to the 1931 Check-list, is from southeastern Nebraska, northern Illinois, southern Michigan, and central Pennsylvania south to central Arkansas, northern Mississippi, central Alabama, central Georgia, and the highlands of South Carolina.

The local distribution of Bewick's wren seems to be dependent on, or limited by, the local distribution of the house wren, for the two do not seem to get along well together, as several observers have noted. Perhaps the gentle Bewick's wren is no match for the more aggressive house wren.

Dr. George M. Sutton (1930) says: "The House Wren and Carolina Wren may inhabit precisely the same region without friction; but the House Wren and Bewick's Wren, or the Bewick's Wren and Carolina Wren, or all three species, evidently do not." (See also Bayard H. Christy's 1924 paper.)

Whatever the local situations may be, or whichever wren may be the aggressor, the fact remains that Bewick's wren has been steadily extending its general range northward into the States named above, as well as in Ohio and Indiana, in regions where it was unknown 50 years ago; most of this northward extension seems to have occurred during the last decade of the last century and the first ten years of this. This movement is discussed in more detail by Leon J. Cole (1905) and more lately by W. E. Clyde Todd (1940), for those who care to study its progress.

Where Bewick's wren replaces the house wren it becomes *the* "house wren" of the community, avoiding the swampy woodlands and frequenting open woodlands, upland thickets and hills, fence rows near houses, and orchards, where it is often seen perched on telephone wires or even the roofs of houses and farm buildings, pouring out its delightful song. Ridgway (1889) says: "No bird more deserves the protection of man than Bewick's Wren. He does not need man's encouragement, for he comes of his own accord and installs himself as a member of the community, wherever it suits his taste. He is found about the cow-shed and barn along with the Pewee and Barn Swallow; he investigates the pig-sty; then explores the garden fence, and finally mounts to the roof and pours forth one of the sweetest songs that ever was heard." William Brewster (1886) says that, in western North Carolina, it was "confined almost exclusively to the towns, where it was usually one of the most abundant and conspicuous birds. * * * At Asheville it was breeding in such numbers that nearly every shed or other out-building harbored a pair."

Nesting.—Almost any suitable cavity or place of support will suit this wren for a nesting site. Dr. S. S. Dickey (Todd, 1940) writes: "Odd and wonderful are the sites that Bewick's Wren habitually chooses for its summer home. Away from the haunts of man, it selects locations suggesting its primitive habits—knotholes in fallen trees in the woods or open fields, natural cavities and woodpecker-holes in trees, or now and then the center of a dense brush heap. But civilization has provided this bird with an unusual variety of homes. Any opening of ready access invites its attention; among those used are holes in fence posts, tin cans, empty barrels, discarded clothing hung in buildings, baskets, bird boxes, deserted automobiles, oil wells, and crevices in stone, brick, or tile walls."

Ridgway (1889) adds the following:

Usually it is in a mortise-hole of a beam or joist, or some well-concealed corner. One was beneath the board covering of an ash-hopper; another, in a joint of stovepipe which lay horizontally across two joists in the garret of a smoke-house; a third was behind the weather-boarding of an ice-house, while a fourth was in the bottom of the conical portion of a quail-net that had been hung up against the inner side of a buggy shed. None of these nests would have been found had not the bird been seen to enter.

The nest is generally very bulky, though its size is regulated by that of the cavity in which it is placed. Its materials consist of sticks, straw, coarse feathers, fine chips, etc., matted together with spiders' webs, and lined with tow and soft feathers of barnyard fowls."

Myra Katie Roads writes to me of a nest that was built in a mail box and disturbed every time the mail was deposited or removed; it was destroyed before the eggs hatched. There is a set of eggs in my collection, taken by Dr. Dickey; the nest was built on top of and partly inside a last year's nest of the phoebe; this was plastered to the side of a horizontal beam against the ceiling of the lower story of a sheep shed, 8 feet above the ground.

In addition to the materials named above, nests have been found to contain green moss, dead leaves, cotton, hair, wool, and occasionally a piece of cast-off snakeskin.

On at least two occasions, a cowbird's egg has been found in the nest of this wren, according to Dr. Herbert Friedmann (1929).

A. Dawes DuBois tells me of a nest he found that "was between two sheets of loosely placed sheet iron in the flat roof of a farmer's shelter for pigs; he has another in his collection that "was in a sack hung up with seed corn in an old outhouse; there was a hole in the side of the sack and through this the wrens entered." And Aretas A. Saunders writes to me that he saw one building a nest in a wood pile.

Eggs.—The commonest numbers of eggs found in the nests of Bewick's wren run from 5 to 7; perhaps 7 might be called the average; as few as 4 and as many as 11 have been found, and sets of 8 or 9 are not very rare. The eggs are often very pretty; the ground color is white, and they are more or less irregularly spotted and dotted with reddish brown, umber, various shades of lighter brown, purplish brown, drab, or lavender. The markings are sometimes concentrated in a ring about the larger end. Some are very finely and faintly sprinkled with minute dots; and some are nearly immaculate. The measurements of 40 eggs in the United States National Museum average 16.4 by 12.7 millimeters; the eggs showing the four extremes measure 17.8 by 12.7, 16.8 by 13.2, 14.6 by 12.8, and 15.3 by 11.7 millimeters.

Young.—The period of incubation has been estimated as 10 to 14 days, but most observers agree on 14 days as the average. Probably only the female incubates, as suggested by one of the western races. The young remain in the nest about 14 days and are fed by both parents while in the nest and for 2 weeks or more after they leave it. Two broods are generally raised in a season, and sometimes three in the South. Butler (1898) says that the young return "every night to roost in the nest after they are able to fly."

M. B. Skaggs (1934) timed the feedings of a brood of four young for four periods of one hour each on three different days, with the following results:

First day: Rain almost constantly. Fed 13 times at an average of 4.61 minutes. Second day: a. m., fed 24 times at average intervals of 2.50 minutes; p. m., fed 19 times at average intervals of 3.15 minutes. Third day: fed 23 times at average intervals of 2.61 minutes. The average interval was 3.04 minutes; the longest interval was 15 minutes; the shortest interval was ½ minute.

Assuming that the feeding was done only 13 hours per day, 250 trips were made daily. If young were in nest only 12 days, this would mean about 3,072 insects were consumed in addition to what the adults ate. The food for the young seemed to consist mostly of green worms with a few moths and caterpillars. Obviously this destruction of insect life must have been very beneficial to the near-by apple orchard.

Plumages.—I have seen no very young nestlings. Ridgway (1904) describes the plumages as follows: The young in juvenal plumage are "similar to adults, but ground color of middle rectrices brown, like back, etc., feathers of chest (sometimes throat also) more or less distinctly margined or edged with grayish or dusky, and under tail-coverts more brownish and less distinctly barred." Young birds, showing the postjuvenal molt, are scarce in collections, but apparently this molt occurs in August or September, involving the contour plumage, the wing coverts and the tail, but not the rest of the wings. This produces a first winter plumage that is practically indistinguishable from the winter plumage of the adult. Ridgway (1904) says that winter adults, at least in fresh plumage, are "more brightly colored, the upper parts more chestnut-brown," than in spring birds, "middle rectrices browner (broccoli brown to light bistre), sides and flanks more strongly tinged with brown, the under tail-coverts with ground color brownish white or pale buffy brown." Wear and fading produce somewhat duller colors before spring. Adults apparently have a complete postnuptial molt in August and September.

Food.—No comprehensive study of the food of the eastern Bewick's wren seems to have been made, but it probably does not differ widely from that of the California races. It is undoubtedly an insectivorous bird, as are all the wrens. It has been credited with eating boll weevils in the South and locusts in Nebraska.

Behavior.—Bewick's wren is a gentle, confiding bird, rather courting than avoiding human society, being a familiar dooryard bird throughout most of its range. What has been said about its haunts and nesting habits illustrates this point. Mr. Brewster (1886) writes of its actions: "This species resembles other Wrens (especially *T. ludovicianus*) in habits and motions, creeping and hopping about under eaves of buildings, and along fences, entering every hole and crevice, and appearing and disappearing like a mouse. Its slender shape and long tail give it, however, a somewhat peculiar appearance—much like that of the *Polioptilae*. The tail is habitually carried above the line of the back, although its position and inclination are constantly changing. It is not moved in the usual jerky Wren-fashion, but rather slowly and deliberately. In a breezy situation it often seems quite beyond the bird's control, waving about with every passing puff of air."

Ridgway (1889) says that, as the bird hops about, its long tail is "carried erect or even leaning forward, and jerked to one side at short intervals. In its movements it is altogether more deliberate than either *T. ludovicianus* or *T. aedon*, but nothing can excel it in quickness when it is pursued."

Voice.—Bewick's wren is a fine singer. Mr. Brewster (1886) says that "the song is sweet and exquisitely tender—one of the sweetest and tenderest strains that I know.   It recalls that of the song sparrow, but is more prolonged, varied, and expressive."   A. W. Butler (1898) reports a long period of song, as heard in Indiana, from the last of March until the end of August; and once it was heard on October 14.   He says that the common alarm note is *plit;* and they have "a finer rattling note than that uttered by the Carolina Wren.   *   *   *   One song I have written *chip, chip chip, te-da-a, te-dee;* another, *cheep, cheep, che-we-e-e-e.*   A third song sounds something like *whee-to-weet, a-her, che-chee;* while one of its most familiar efforts seems to be expressed by *chick, click, for me-é, for you.*"

Ridgway (1889) says that the song is "not a voluble gabble, like the House Wren's merry roundelay, but a fine, clear, bold song, uttered as the singer sits with head thrown back and long tail pendent,—a song which may be heard a quarter of a mile or more, and in comparison with which the faint chant of the Song Sparrow sinks into insignificance."

Howell and Oldys (1907) made a careful study of various songs of this wren, and state that "in imitative ability the Bewick Wren has, apparently, no rival among our eastern birds other than the Mockingbird, by which, however, it is greatly excelled.   *   *   *   It seems to be better entitled to the sobriquet of 'Mocking Wren,' than the Carolina Wren, on which the name is sometimes inappropriately bestowed."

Francis H. Allen (MS.) writes the song as "*tzip-ta-tzee-ta-*trill-*zip,* or *pit-zee-ta-*trill, both infrequent."   And he calls the scolding note a buzzing *dzz.*   He says that the ordinary song is like a song sparrow's, but has a minor strain near the beginning suggestive of the fox sparrow, and *ends* in a trill.

Field marks.—Bewick's wren is smaller than the Carolina wren and larger than the house wren.   It has a much longer tail than either; the tail is rounded at the tip and appears broader there than at the base; the lateral tail feathers are tipped with white spots, which show when the tail is spread; the tail is frequently in motion.   There is a conspicuous white line over the eye.   The back is grayer, less reddish brown, than in the Carolina wren, the underparts are lighter colored, and the bird is more slender.

DISTRIBUTION

Range.—From the southwestern British Columbia and the Pacific coast region; and from central United States to southern Mexico.

Breeding range.—The Bewick's wren breeds **north** to southwestern British Columbia (Comox, V. I., Chilliwack, and casually to Howe Sound) through Washington and Oregon west of the Cascades, to northeastern California (Sugar Hill and Cedarville); southern Nevada (Pahrump Mountains and St. Thomas) ; southern Utah (Iron

City); southwestern Wyoming (Green River Valley); central Nebraska (Kearney); southern Iowa (Iowa City and Davenport); southern Wisconsin (Prairie du Sac); southern Michigan (Grand Rapids and Ann Arbor); and central Pennsylvania (Beaver and State College). **East** to central Pennsylvania (State College and Blue Ridge Summit); the eastern slope of the Alleghenies, south to northern Georgia (Brasstown Bald and Ellijay). **South** to northern Georgia (Brasstown Bald and Ellijay); central Alabama (Woodbiana and Prattville); northern Mississippi (Iuka and New Albany); central Arkansas (Conway and Rich Mountain); northeastern Oklahoma (Tulsa County) to central Oklahoma and Texas and to southern Mexico (Oaxaca). **West** to Oaxaca (Oaxaca); Jalisco (Lake Chapala and Guadalajara); Baja California (San Juanico and Cedros Island); north through California, Oregon, and Washington west of the Cascades to British Columbia (Victoria and Comox).

Winter range.—Bewick's wren winters **north** to southern Vancouver Island, British Columbia (Courtenay), and south through Washington and Oregon west of the Cascades to southern California (Death Valley); southern Nevada (opposite Fort Mojave); central Arizona (Prescott); southern New Mexico (Silver City and Deming); central Texas (Fredericksburg, Waco, and Dallas); central Oklahoma (Oklahoma City); central Arkansas (Hot Springs); southern Illinois (Olney); and southwestern Ohio (Xenia). **East** to southwestern Ohio (Xenia); central Kentucky (Lexington); central Tennessee (Nashville and Murfreesboro); central Georgia (Athens and Macon); South Carolina (rarely Chester County and Charleston); and northern Florida (Daytona). **South** to northern Florida (Daytona and Pensacola); the Gulf coast to southern Texas (Brownsville); and southern Mexico (Oaxaca). **West** to Oaxaca (Oaxaca); Baja California (Cedros Island); Guadalupe Island, formerly; and the Pacific coast north to Vancouver Island.

The range as outlined is for the entire species, which has been divided into 16 subspecies or geographic races. The typical race (*T. b. bewickii*) breeds from Nebraska eastward to central Ohio; the Appalachian Bewick's wren (*T. b. altus*) breeds from central Ohio and Pennsylvania through the mountains to Alabama; the Texas wren (*T. b. cryptus*) is found from central Texas to Tamaulipas and Nuevo León; Baird's wren (*T. b. eremophilus*) occurs in southeastern California, Arizona, southern Utah, and Colorado to extreme western Texas to Coahuila, Durango, and central Zacatecas; the Seattle wren (*T. b. calophonus*) is found on the Pacific slope from British Columbia to Oregon; the Nicasio wren (*T. b. marinensis*) occupies the coastal belt from southwestern Oregon to Marin County, Calif.; the Warner Valley wren (*T. b. atrestus*) occurs in southern Oregon from the Warner Valley west to Medford and Ashland; Vigor's wren (*T. b. spilurus*) is found from San Francisco Bay to northern Monterey County, Calif.; the San Joaquin wren (*T. b. drymoecus*) occurs from the lower San Joaquin Valley and the western slope of the Sierra Nevada north to northern California; the San Diego wren (*T. b. correctus*) is found in the coastal belt from San Benito and Monterey Counties, Calif., to near the Mexican boundary; the Santa Cruz wren (*T. b. nesophilus*) occupies Santa Cruz and Santa Rosa Islands, Calif.; the Catalina wren (*T. b. catalinae*) occurs on Santa Catalina Island; the San Clemente wren (*T. b. leucophrys*) occurs on San Clemente Island; the sooty wren (*T. b. charienturus*) is found in northwestern Baja California, south to latitude 30°; the Cedros Island wren (*T. b. cerroensis*) occurs on Cedros Island and the adjacent mainland; the Guadalupe wren (*T. b. brevicauda*), formerly a full species, now considered a subspecies of the Bewick's wren, occurred on Guadalupe Island but is probably now extinct.

Spring migration.—Late dates of spring departure are: Florida—Chipley, March 27. Georgia—Beachton, March 26. North Carolina—Raleigh, April 3. Mississippi—Ellisville, March 29. Louisiana—Baton Rouge, March 9. Arkansas—Delight, April 2. Texas—Bonham, April 4. Oklahoma—Oklahoma City, March 16. Arizona—Tucson, May 2.

Early dates of spring arrival are: Virginia—Lynchburg, March 14. West Virginia—French Creek, March 19. Pennsylvania—State College, April 10. Tennessee—Knoxville, February 19. Kentucky—Bowling Green, March 1. Ohio—Columbus, March 3. Indiana—Lafayette, March 17. Illinois—Urbana, March 17. Iowa—Blacksburg, March 19. Kansas—Manhattan, March 10. Nebraska—Hastings, April 6. Arizona—Tombstone, February 18. Colorado—Fort Morgan, May 4.

Fall migration.—Late dates of fall departure are: Colorado—Fort Morgan, November 17. Arizona—Tombstone, November 15. Iowa—National, October 1. Missouri—Jasper City, November 12. Arkansas—Rogers, October 30. Illinois—Rantoul, October 25. Indiana—Richmond, October 14. Ohio—Cleveland, October 24. Kentucky—Versailles, October 20. Pennsylvania—Beaver, October 2. West Virginia—French Creek, October 12. Virginia—Naruna, November 18.

Early dates of fall arrival are: Oklahoma—Oklahoma City, October 15. Texas—Bonham, September 29. Arkansas—Delight, September 18. Louisiana—New Orleans, August 28. Mississippi—Bay St. Louis, September 21. North Carolina—Raleigh, September 24. South Carolina—Summerton, October 10. Georgia—Macon, September 27. Alabama—Greensboro, September 17. Florida—Pensacola, September 29.

Casual records.—Two nests have been found near Augusta, Ga.; at Point Pelee, Ontario, specimens were taken in April of 1909 and 1917; one was collected at Appin, Ontario, on December 13, 1898; at Alton, N. H. a bird was shot on April 25, 1900; one was recorded at New Hamburg, Pa., on January 1, 1891; it was recorded on December 22, 1890, at Washington, D. C., and there are several records of occurrence there from March to November but no record of breeding.

Egg dates.—California: 120 records, March 26 to June 18; 60 records, April 17 to May 13, indicating the height of the season.

Lower California: 7 records, April 11 to May 21.

Missouri: 5 records, March 28 to June 17.

Texas: 106 records, March 17 to July 22; 54 records, April 8 to May 10.

Washington: 23 records, March 29 to June 27; 12 records, April 25 to May 4 .

West Virginia: 9 records, April 15 to June 8.

THRYOMANES BEWICKII ALTUS Aldrich

APPALACHIAN BEWICK'S WREN

One more race, an eastern one, is added to the long list of subspecies of this plastic species, to which Dr. John W. Aldrich (1944) has given the above name. He describes it as "similar to *Thryomanes bewickii bewickii*, but darker and more sooty (less rufescent). In fresh autumnal plumage: above near mummy brown instead of Prout's brown of Ridgway's 'Color Standards'. * * * There seems to be no significant size difference between this race and *bewickii*."

"The breeding range," says Dr. Aldrich, "extends: *north* to northeastern and central western Pennsylvania, and central Ohio, casually to central northern Ohio; *west* to southwestern Ohio, southeastern Kentucky, east central Tennessee, and northwestern Alabama; *south* to central Alabama, north central Georgia, and central South Carolina; and *east* to central South Carolina, central and northeastern Virginia, southern New Jersey (casually), and northeastern Pennsylvania." It winters *north* to near northern limit of breeding range; *south* to northern Florida and the Gulf coast; and *west* to northeastern Texas."

THRYOMANES BEWICKI CRYPTUS Oberholser

TEXAS WREN

HABITS

The wrens of this group, ranging from Kansas through Texas to Tamaulipas and Nuevo León, in Mexico, have been given the above name. The subspecies is described by Ridgway (1904) as "similar to

T. b. bewickii but decidedly larger, tail relatively longer (averaging equal to or longer than wing instead of distinctly shorter), and coloration grayer above (broccoli brown to a more decided brown hue), and whiter beneath, with blackish bars on under tail-coverts much narrower."

The haunts and habits of the Texas wren are not much different from those of its eastern relative. George F. Simmons (1925) includes the following in his list of its habitats around Austin, Tex.: "Usually broken country, almost always near civilization; * * * old pastures dotted with brush heaps and lined with brush fences; cut-over woods; * * * thickets and beds of cactus in mesquite and cactus country; brush heaps and thickets along creeks; dense cedar brakes on the hills; along rather open creek valleys, on slopes and hills, and in semi-open country, but never in dense bottom woods or on extreme open country; about barns, deserted houses, wood piles and brush heaps. * * * The commonest local wren, a pair in nearly every garden."

We found this wren to be a common resident about the city of Brownsville, in the rural districts surrounding it, in the open country about the ranches, and in the chaparral and pricklypear thickets. Other observers seem to have had the same experience with it there.

Edwin V. Miller (1941) says that "at Chipinque, Nuevo León, at 4,000 feet, the wrens' habitat consisted of large oaks, pines and other trees, with a thick undergrowth of brush; in the same habitat were Whip-poor-wills and Couch Jays."

Nesting.—The Texas wren builds its nest in just such a variety of situations as its eastern relative and in similar places. The only nest we saw was found beside the road as we were driving out from Brownsville; it was built behind a blind on a deserted house, and contained a brood of young on May 24, 1923. George B. Sennett (1879) says that "a pair of them built their nest between the ridge-pole and thatching of the roof of a corn-crib which we occupied in preparing our specimens, and almost over our heads. They were so tame as to hop about among the cotton, tow, papers, etc., on our benches, within a few feet of us, and take whatever pleased them." He found another nest "in a brush fence at Lomita Ranch. The nest was quite simple, being but a handful of hair, leaves, feathers, cotton, and fine bark matted together." Referring to the same general region about Brownsville, Dr. James C. Merrill (1878) says: "Its nests are placed in a variety of situations. I have found them in an old Woodpecker's nest, placed between three or four joints of the prickly pear, forming a bulky structure, and among the twigs of various thorny bushes."

Mr. Simmons (1925) says that, in the Austin region, the nest may be placed anywhere from 3 inches to 25 feet, but usually about 6 feet, above ground. He mentions a number of nesting sites similar to those chosen by Bewick's wrens elsewhere and adds a few unusual sites, such as broken bottles on shelves in sheds, old cow skulls in pastures, old hats in sheds, and old oriole and mockingbird nests. Others have found this wren nesting in old nests of the cactus wren and verdin; Harry P. Atwater (1887) has seen several such. He relates the following story: "I once told a little boy to put an old tin can in a brush heap and perhaps a bird would make a nest in it for him. About a week after I was surprised when the boy came and told me the bird had done so and laid an egg in it. * * * On finding the nest the evening before, the boy had taken the can with him to the house with the egg and bird in it, and after showing it to his folks had placed it in another brush heap close to the house. Six eggs were laid in this nest, and the can containing bird, eggs and nest taken into the house on several occasions after dark to show to people. Finally on one occasion the eggs were broken in handling and the nest deserted."

Margaret Morse Nice (1931) watched a pair of Texas wrens building their nest, in Oklahoma; she gives the following account of their activity:

On April 18, 1926, a pair of Texas Wrens were building with great enthusiasm in one of our bird boxes; in 3¾ hours they made 239 trips—slightly more than one a minute. Their best record was 20 trips in 6 minutes. Both labored most of the time. The male was so busy that he only sang 17 songs during the period I watched. Two sample minutes will give an idea of their energy. 9:49. Both wrens coming to box, one goes in with a big twig, other says, *jee, jee, jee*, gives its twig to the bird inside, leaves, is back with a rag which it pushes part way in, saying *jee, jee*, leaves. 1:57. Bird goes in with dead leaf, out again; other goes in with grass root, out; first enters with dead grass, out; other in with twig, out.

Mr. Simmons (1925) says that the nest is a "large, compact structure, top level and open above; composed of a mass of rubbish, principally cedar bark strips, small short sticks and twigs, dead leaves, bits of twine, and chicken feathers, with the occasional use of horsehair, cowhair, grass, weed stems, rootlets, oak blossoms, cast-off snake skin, cotton waste, leaf skeletons, spider webs, cobwebs, caterpillar cocoons, paper, and bits of corn husks. Cedar bark and twigs are usually interlocked and moulded into a strong, symmetrical nest with deep, well constructed cup."

Eggs.—The Texas wren sometimes lays as many as nine eggs, but the usual set consists of six or seven. These are practically indistinguishable from those of Bewick's wren, showing the usual variations; some are more heavily marked with larger and more confluent spots, especially about the larger end. The measurements of 40 eggs in the United States National Museum average 16.2 by 12.7 millimeters; the eggs showing the four extremes measure 17.8 by 13.2, 16.4 by 13.2, 14.6 by 12.0, and 15.8 by 11.7 millimeters.

The food, behavior, and voice of the Texas wren apparently do not differ materially from those of the species elsewhere. Mr. Simmons (1925) says that it "sings throughout the year, winter as well as summer." The song reminds him of the song of the western lark sparrow, in its buzzing quality. Dr. Friedmann (1929) reports that Roy W. Quillen, of San Antonio, told him that he had found eggs of the eastern cowbird in a number of nests of this wren, and that, near Brownsville, Dr. A. H. Cordier found a nest "containing three eggs of the Red-Eyed Cowbird and one of the Wren's. The female Wren was sitting on the eggs. The next day all three eggs hatched and two days later the nest and young were destroyed by a skunk."

THRYOMANES BEWICKI EREMOPHILUS Oberholser

BAIRD'S WREN

PLATE 35

HABITS

This is the desert wren of the Southwestern States and parts of Mexico, ranging from Colorado, southern Utah, southern Nevada, and southeastern California southward, through Arizona, New Mexico, and extreme western Texas, to Coahuila, Durango, and Zacatecas.

Ridgway (1904) describes this race as "similar to *T. b. cryptus*, but decidedly grayer above (hair brown, approaching broccoli brown in some winter specimens); upper tail-coverts and middle rectrices clearer gray; under parts still whiter, the sides more faintly tinged with brownish gray, the under tail-coverts more purely white and narrowly barred with black; wing and tail slightly longer, bill decidedly longer, midle toe shorter."

Referring to Moffat County in northwestern Colorado, Russell W. Hendee (1929) writes: "While frequently reported from the juniper and pinyon region of southern Colorado, the Baird Wren has seldom been recorded from the northern part of the State. However, we found this species among the commonest of the breeding birds of the junipers near the Sand-wash [a dry valley]. A few were seen among the trees on the ridges near the river, but the birds were much more numerous in the more arid region to the westward."

In Arizona we found Baird's wren in the Huachuca and Catalina Mountains, in the lower portions of the canyons up to 6,000 feet, chiefly in the live-oak associations near the mouths of the canyons and on the low foothills. It was common, also, in the mesquite forest, in the valley of the Santa Cruz River, where there were many large trees and plenty of underbrush. In New Mexico and Texas its distribution seems to be about the same, mainly between 4,000 and 6,000 feet in the mountains, rarely up to 7,000 feet.

Nesting.—We did not succeed in finding a nest of this wren in Arizona, but my companion, Frank C. Willard, told me that he once found a nest in the fold of a piece of burlap that was being used as an awning on a house in the Huachuca Mountains. Mr. Swarth (1904b) says that the nest is quite difficult to find and that he saw only three or four in this region, "all built in cavities in the trees, from six to fifteen feet from the ground."

Dr. Coues (1882) found a nest in northern Arizona that was "in the hollow end of a blasted horizontal bough" of a cedar, "about eight feet from the ground." The nest "rested upon the horizontal floor of the cavity, upon a bed of wood-mould and cedar-berries, about a foot from the ragged entrance of the hollow. It was a neat structure, about 4 inches across outside, by half as much in internal diameter, cupped to a depth of an inch and a half. Outside was a wall of small cedar twigs interlaced, and next came a layer of finely frayed inner bark strips from the same tree; but the bulk of the nest consisted of matted rabbit-fur stuck full of feathers, among which those of the Carolina Dove were conspicuous."

Mr. Hendee (1929) found two nests in northwestern Colorado, of which he says: "A fresh nest, empty, was found on May 19. The first egg was laid about a week later and the set of six was completed on May 31. The nest was composed mostly of wool and feathers and a few small pieces of paper, loosely piled in a natural cavity in a juniper tree, about 2 feet from the ground. The opening was very small. A second nest was found on June 3. It was placed in a dead juniper branch about 5 inches in diameter, the opening, caused by the breaking off of a small branch, being about an inch in diameter at the widest point. The five eggs in this nest were hatching when it was visited on the following day."

Eggs.—The eggs of Baird's wren are typical of the species, with the usual variations. The measurements of 40 eggs average 16.5 by 12.8 millimeters; and eggs showing the four extremes measure 17.8 by 13.0, 17.0 by 14.3, and 14.1 by 11.9 millimeters.

Plumages.—Dr. Oberholser (1898) says: "Young birds of *eremophilus* range in color above from a light rufescent gray, hardly distinguishable from the shade of young *cryptus*, to a very dark, dull brownish gray; averaging, however, very much darker than the Texan form. Many of the specimens are fully as deeply colored as the young af *charienturus*, though averaging rather less rufescent."

Van Tyne and Sutton (1937) found in their series of 29 adults, collected in Brewster County, Tex., between February 28 and May 26, two "well marked color phases, a gray and a brown one. * * * We cannot distinguish brown-phase Brewster County specimens from comparable Arizona and New Mexico specimens."

Enemies.—Probably these wrens are preyed upon by the usual predatory birds and mammals, but two reported cases are worth mentioning. Van Tyne and Sutton (1937) state that a "Baird's Wren was found in the stomach of a Roadrunner." And Mrs. Bailey (1928) says that Major Goldman found a dead wren "in the mouth of a rattlesnake that had just killed it."

Winter.—Dr. Grinnell (1914) found the desert Bewick wren to be common as a winter visitant in the lower Colorado Valley, in southeastern California; he says that it was "observed chiefly in the sparse brush margining the washes leading down from the desert interior. The catclaw and larger creosote bushes appeared to afford both productive foraging grounds and safe retreats. It was rarely that this wren was seen near the river, and then only as far as the salt-bush belt. The range of the western house wren in the willow association appeared to be not at all impinged upon by that of the desert Bewick wren. This again shows the local dissociation of birds of the same or nearly the same habits, even in their winter habitats. It is to be inferred that there are inherent preferences of the two species for cover of the two different sorts."

THRYOMANES BEWICKII CALOPHONUS Oberholser

SEATTLE WREN

PLATE 36

HABITS

For a comparatively short distance along the humid northwest coast, from southern British Columbia to Oregon, we find this somewhat larger and darker subspecies. It does not seem to be much darker or browner than its nearest neighbor on the coast, *marinensis*, but its size is greater.

Before Dr. Oberholser (1898) wrote his paper on this group, *spilurus* was supposed to range north to, at least, Marin County, the type locality of *marinensis.* He naturally wrote at that time, regarding *calophonus*: "It differs from *spilurus*, its nearest ally, in conspicuously larger bill, besides averaging greater in all its other measurements. The upper surface seems to be usually rather deeper and richer brown; the flanks somewhat more rufescent. From *bewickii*, *calophonus* is easily distinguished by deeper, more sooty brown above, much darker sides and flanks, wider superciliary stripe, longer bill, tarsus and middle toe."

When I was in Seattle, in 1911, these wrens were common on the partially wooded campus of the University of Washington, especially in the ravines and on the brushy slopes. We saw them almost daily in the partially cleared woodlands around Kirkland, and on the wooded islands in the lake. S. F. Rathbun says, in his notes, that the Seattle wren is "partial to a somewhat rough country, to open second growth, and about the edges of the cleared spaces among the debris on the ground, particularly if there exists a confusion of fallen limbs. A section of cleared forest in the transitory stage toward being utilized, but as yet in a quite rough condition, will be found a favorite spot for this wren, especially if open enough to admit considerable light and sunshine."

Nesting.—The only nest that I saw was found near Kirkland, Wash., on May 10, 1911; it was placed in a natural cavity in the upturned roots of a fallen tree; as it contained five young birds, almost ready to fly, it was not examined closely. Mr. Rathbun tells me that this is one of the favorite spots among a variety of sites chosen; one nest that he describes in his notes was in such a situation; it was built into the cavity left where a stone had been lifted with the roots and then fallen out; it was made outwardly of small twigs, pieces of moss, rootlets, sheep wool, fibrous strips of dead stalks of various plants, and some bits of dead leaves, some of this material being somewhat interlaced; it was lined with fine plant fibers and soft feathers, including some of the mountain quail, a few pieces of snakeskin, and a few horsehairs. The nest measured 3 inches high and 5 inches in diameter externally; the inner cavity was 2 inches in diameter and 1½ inches deep.

J. H. Bowles (Dawson and Bowles, 1909) writes:

The building sites chosen by this wren for its nests are so variable that hardly anything can be considered typical. It may be in the wildest swampy wood far removed from civilization, but it is quite as likely to be found in a house in the heart of a city. A few of the nesting sites I have recorded are in upturned roots of fallen trees, deserted woodpecker holes, in bird boxes in the city, in a fishing creel hanging on a porch, under a slab of bark that has scaled away a few inches from the body of a tree, or an open nest on a beam under a bridge.

A very complete study of this wren has convinced me that it never builds any nests except those used in raising the young. In other words, it is the only wren in the Northwest that is positively guiltless of using "decoys."

Eggs.—Mr. Bowles (Dawson and Bowles, 1909), who has had considerable experience with the Seattle wren, says: "A set contains from four to six eggs, most commonly five. These are pure white in ground color, marked with fine dots of reddish brown. The markings are variable in distribution, some specimens being marked very sparingly over all, while in others the markings are largely concentrated around the larger end in the form of a more or less confluent ring. The eggs are rather short ovate oval in shape, and average in measurements 0.68×0.54 inch.

"Two broods are reared in a season; or perhaps it would be more correct to say that fresh eggs may be found at any time between the middle of April and the middle of June."

The measurements of 27 eggs average 17.2 by 13.3 millimeters; the eggs showing the four extremes measure **18.3** by 13.2, 16.3 by **14.0, 15.7** by 13.5, and 17.7 by **12.8** millimeters.

Behavior.—Theed Pearse has sent me the following notes on the territorial behavior of this wren: "A question of territory arose between a pair of Seattle wrens that were nesting and an incoming house wren that had nested nearby for some years. The house wren on arrival investigated the garden and met the Seattle wren, both birds alighting on a dividing fence; the Seattle wren cackled, but nothing further happened; the house wrens absolutely recognized that beyond this line was the territory of the others; and, until the Seattle wrens had finished nesting operations, they never passed that line and always flew on the other side of the house." He noted once that some violet-green swallows ousted some Seattle wrens from a partially built nest.

Voice.—Mr. Rathbun tells me that this wren begins to sing as soon as winter breaks early in March, continuing well into July, intermittently in August, and at odd times in autumn; sometimes it sings on the pleasant days in winter, if the weather is mild. Early in spring it begins shortly after daybreak and will sing more or less continuously, sometimes for an hour or so. "At this time the renditions follow each other closely, spaced by a few seconds only. After this morning burst of singing wanes, the wren sings at odd times throughout the day. The song so often sung at this period is the one which has four notes, given in a chanted manner as it were."

W. L. Dawson (Dawson and Bowles, 1909) writes: "To those who are acquainted only with the typical Bewick Wren of the East, the added vocal accomplishments of our western representative come in the nature of a surprise. For the characteristic ditty of *bewickii* proper, *calophonus* has introduced so many trills and flourishes that the original motif is almost lost to sight. *Calophonus* means having a beautiful voice, or sweetly sounding, and right well does the bird deserve the name, in a region which is all too conspicuous for its lack of notable songsters."

I cannot quite agree with that last phrase, as there are many fine singers west of the Rockies.

Theed Pearse writes to me that he has heard the Seattle wren mimicking the spring note of the chickadee so correctly that he did not recognize it as mimicry until the wren broke into its regular song.

Winter.—Mr. Pearse tells me that, even as far north as Vancouver Island, this wren appears to be "very sedentary" all through the year; but the cold winters of 1937–38 and 1938–39 practically exterminated it, and not until 1941 could it be said to have recovered average numbers.

THRYOMANES BEWICKII ATRESTUS Oberholser

WARNER VALLEY WREN

Dr. Oberholser (1932) describes this wren as "similar to *Thryomanes bewickii drymoecus* from the San Joaquin Valley, California, but much less rufescent (more grayish) above; somewhat darker; and averaging larger. * * * Resident in central southern Oregon, from the Warner Valley west to Medford and Ashland, and north to Gold Hill."

"This new race," says Oberholser, "is most typical in the Warner Valley. Birds from localities west to Gold Hill, Ashland, Keno, and Klamath Falls are somewhat rufescent above, thus inclining a little toward the race occupying the coast of Oregon. Compared with *Thryomanes bewickii calophonus* the present form is so much smaller and more grayish that it needs no special comparison. Altogether a series of 20 examples has been available."

THRYOMANES BEWICKII MARINENSIS Grinnell

NICASIO WREN

HABITS

On the humid coast belt of southwestern Oregon and northwestern California, we have a wren that Dr. Grinnell (1910) describes as "similar to *T. b. spilurus* (Vigors), of the Santa Cruz faunal area south and east of San Francisco Bay, in size, but dorsal coloration brighter brown, of a vandyke tone, and flanks and light intervals on crissum strongly washed with vandyke brown. Similar to *T. b. calophonus* Oberholser, of western Washington and Oregon, but dorsal coloration brighter brown, of a less sooty tone, and size decidedly less." He gives the range as Marin and Sonoma Counties, Calif., and remarks that he had not seen any specimens from the more northern coast region of California. The range of this form is now considered to extend into Oregon. Here we have a race, intermediate in range, like its southern neighbor in size and somewhat like its northern neighbor in coloration, yet not strictly intermediate in both characters.

As it lives in a somewhat similar environment and is evidently very closely related to these two adjacent races, we could hardly expect to find much difference in its habits. Practically nothing has been published on its habits that is in any way peculiar to it.

Robert R. Talmadge writes to me: "This form of the Bewick wren is a rare breeder in Humboldt County. I have found it breeding only on the lower bars of the Eel and the Van Duzen Rivers. In both of these localities the bars have a heavy growth of alder, cottonwood, willow, blackberries, and grasses. Among this growth are many drift

logs and stumps, brought down by the high water. It is among the
tangled roots and natural cavities of these stumps that this wren
nests."

The eggs of the Nicasio wren are apparently no different from
those of the other races of this species. The measurements of 26 eggs
average 16.7 by 12.9 millimeters; the eggs showing the four extremes
measure 18.5 by 13.5, 16.1 by 13.9, 14.6 by 12.5, and 16.3 by 11.9
millimeters.

THRYOMANES BEWICKII SPILURUS (Vigors)

VIGORS'S WREN

HABITS

This was the first of the western races of Bewick's wrens to be described and named. The other races have all been separated since
about 1880; in our first Check-list, published in 1886, this and Baird's
wren were the only western races included. The above name then
covered all the wrens of this species inhabiting the Pacific slope of
the United States, Baird's wren occupying the southwestern desert
regions. This old name is now restricted to the wrens of a narrow
range in west-central California, from San Francisco Bay to northern
Monterey County.

The distinguishing characters are thus described by Dr. Oberholser
(1898): "*Thryomanes bewickii spilurus* may be distinguished from
bewickii by its duller brown upper surface, darker sides and flanks,
broader superciliary stripe, shorter wing and tail, rather longer middle toe and tarsus. It may be separated from *charienturus* by darker,
decidedly more rufescent flanks and upper parts and by shorter tail;
from *drymoecus* by the much darker color of sides, flanks and upper
surface."

Mr. Swarth (1916) says of the characters of *spilurus:* "Most nearly
like *T. b. marinensis*, whose range adjoins that of *spilurus* at the north,
but of lighter brown coloration dorsally, and of slightly greater size.
Compared with *drymoecus* it is brighter reddish above. From *charienturus* it differs in deeper red coloration, and in different proportions. In *spilurus* the tail is slightly shorter than the wing; in *charienturus* the tail is longer than the wing." He admits that it is intermediate in range and in characters between *marinensis* and *charienturus*,
both of which occupy much more extensive ranges.

Edwin V. Miller (1941) has published an interesting paper on the
habitats of several western races of this species and a long account
of the behavior of Vigors's wren, from which much of what follows has
been taken, though space will not permit as full quotations as the material warrants. He says in a general way: "There are but few features of habitat common to all the races of Bewick wrens. Thick
plant growth of a kind that will furnish the proper insect food seems

to be the chief requisite. The kinds of plants in one part of the range of the species may be totally different from those in another part. The wrens may be found in trees more than 100 feet high or in brush not more than 3 feet high. In the Upper Sonoran Life-zone they are most abundant where the plant growth is thickest. They are particularly noted for their preference for mixed brush."

It appears from his accounts, and the statements of others, that the western races are less domestic than the eastern race, and are more abundant in brushy areas away from human habitations. Chaparral covered hills abound throughout the range of Vigors's wren, and it is there that the wrens are found in greatest numbers, where they find an abundant food supply and suitable nesting sites. But they are also found to some extent in other situations. "On the north-facing slope" of Strawberry Canyon in Berkeley, "the wrens are common, being found in chaparral, mixed brush and oak, and in pure stands of Monterey cypress and Douglas fir, without underbrush. In the chaparral association, baccharis is the dominant plant, forming dense stands of 4 to 6 feet in height. In the mixed brush and oak region the height of the plant cover is anywhere from 1 to 30 or 40 feet."

Mr. Miller (1941) determined to his own satisfaction that the males establish and maintain definite territories during the breeding season, and perhaps to a less extent at other seasons; he says:

Bewick Wrens are found throughout the year either singly or in pairs. Most commonly the males appear on territories in the early spring and are mated shortly afterward. Males of *T. b. spilurus* show territorial reactions toward other males at any time of the year, although much more frequently in the spring. Females show no such reactions toward males, at least, and probably have no part in the defense of territory. Males and mated pairs have territories in the spring and may possibly have them in the winter. The territories of several wrens were mapped; they proved to be about 50 yards wide by 100 yards long. * * * The limits of these territories did not vary more than a few feet from day to day. The males of these areas exhibited strong reactions toward other males adjacent to them. When two males happened to meet on a boundary, they would stop foraging, sing, and give harsh vocal utterances, and follow each other along the edge of their territories. Males would often stop foraging and hurry to their boundaries when they heard another male nearby.

Nesting.—The same observer states that "Bewick Wrens' nests are placed in secluded cavities in or near the ground. Each nest has a well defined cup of soft materials and usually has a base of small twigs. Most nests are open above; rarely they are arched over the top. The male may develop slight nest-building instincts before he is mated, but in most instances nests are not built until the female is present. Both mates may build the nest, although the male works sporadically, and the female often builds alone. Usually only one nest is built, although some authors state that several are sometimes begun. * * * The nest may be built in 10 days and the eggs may be laid in 6 days."

Mrs. Amelia S. Allen writes to me: "The Vigors wren is perhaps, next to the California quail and the spotted towhee, the most abundant resident species in Strawberry Canyon in Berkeley. It comes back again and again to the same nest hole, which it often visits as early as the first week in February. On March 15, 1928, I found one taking the fur from a rabbit skin that had been thrown into a tree and carrying it into a hole at the very bottom of a live oak. In 1919 a pair brought up a brood in a big flicker box that stood on a wall near our front door waiting to be placed in its permanent position. In 1936 a pair nested in the same box in a position near a second-story window."

Dawson (1923) says of the nesting site: "A cranny of suitable size is the *sine qua non*, and this may be in a rock-pile, in a canyon wall, in an old woodpecker hole, in the mouth of an old tunnel of a Rough-winged Swallow, under a root, behind a sprung bark-scale, in an old shoe or a tin can, or the pocket of a disused coat." Nests have been found also in empty boxes or small baskets left lying around, in wood piles, behind the lattice on a porch, under a tile on the roof of a house, in trash piles, in cavities on cliffs, and behind bunches of sprouts or leaves on the trunk of a tree.

Dawson (1923) says the nests are made "basally of sticks, twigs, weedstems, grasses, bark, or moss; lining of fine grasses, hair, fur, or feathers." Various other materials enter into the composition of the nests, such as fine rootlets, dry leaves, wool, cotton, spider nests, horsehair, and sometimes bits of snakeskin; probably any soft pliable material will do.

Eggs.—Mr. Miller (1941) says: "Three females were observed to lay their eggs early in the morning; each female laid at about the same time each day. Two sets of eggs usually are laid, with from three to eight eggs per set; six is the most common number." The eggs are practically indistinguishable from those of the other races of the species, being white, with scattered fine dots of reddish brown or cinnamon, and sometimes a few shell markings of pale drab; some are nearly immaculate. The measurements of 40 eggs average 16.6 by 12.8 millimeters; the eggs showing the four extremes measure 18.0 by 12.5, 17.0 by 14.0, 15.2 by 12.7, and 15.2 by 12.2 millimeters.

Young.—Observations made by Mr. Miller (1941) "seem to warrant the conclusion that the female does all the incubation, at least in the early stages. She leaves the nest for short periods to forage and to be fed by the male. The male may also feed her at the nest. * * * The periods of incubation and nestling life are about 14 days each. The parents probably care for the young for about 2 weeks after the latter leave the nest. * * * The total nesting cycle is about 58 days in length."

Food.—Professor Beal (1907) examined the stomachs of 146 specimens of the California races of Bewick's wrens, taken in every month of the year. A little more than 97 percent of the food consisted of insects and less than 3 percent of vegetable matter. Six stomachs contained seeds, and one held what was supposed to be fruit pulp. Of the animal food, various bugs (Hemiptera) were the largest item, 31 percent; these included the black olive scale, a very injurious species, leaf bugs, stink bugs, shield bugs, leafhoppers, treehoppers, and jumping plant lice. Beetles (Coleoptera) amounted to over 21 percent of the food; ladybirds were the only useful beetles eaten, but they amounted to only 3 percent, against 10 percent of harmful weevils; the stomachs of two wrens contained 85 and 80 percent of engraver beetles, which live under the bark of trees and do much damage to the timber; other beetles, mostly leaf beetles, were eaten to the extent of 8 percent. Ants formed about 7 percent and wasps 10 percent of the food. Caterpillars and a few moths and some cocoons constituted a little less than 12 percent and grasshoppers 4 percent of the wren's diet. Very few flies were eaten, and spiders made up more than 5 percent of the total food.

Regarding the feeding habits of Vigors's wrens, Mr. Miller (1941) writes: "Foraging takes place on the ground and on the limbs and foliage of bushes and trees. In foraging, the birds use their bill for picking insects off leaves and branches, for flicking over leaves on the ground and, less commonly, for digging insects from cracks in bark. They do not scratch for food. They forage rapidly, and this activity takes up the larger part of their time. The method of foraging varies in accordance with the size and distribution of the plants in their habitat. In early spring the male of a mated pair forages high up in brush and trees, and his mate forages low down in brush and weeds."

Behavior.—Mr. Miller says: "The relations of Bewick Wrens to other vertebrate animals of their habitat are mostly neutral. They probably are preyed upon to a slight extent by bird-hawks and owls. Where the wrens nest about buildings in suburban areas, they sometimes have conflicts over nesting sites with House Wrens, titmice, and other small birds. Under these circumstances the Bewick Wrens usually retreat. Some individuals have been found roosting in cavities. Bathing in both dust and water occurs."

Laidlaw Williams (1941) has published an interesting paper on the roosting habits of chestnut-backed chickadees and Bewick's wrens. The wrens used two types of roosts, on the sides of buildings and beneath a canopy of fallen dead needles on a Monterey pine bough. On the side of one building the wren roosted in a vertical crack between two rustic slabs of bark, resting on a horizontal slab over a window; on four rainy nights a wren roosted on a wire under the eaves of a house and leaned against the wall. In all cases the feathers of the rump were greatly ruffed out, showing the subterminal white spots.

Voice.—The various call notes of Vigors's wren are apparently about the same as those of the eastern Bewick's wren; the song is similar, certainly not inferior, and is said to show more versatility. Mr. Miller (1941) says that "the songs of the wrens in Arizona, Texas, and northeastern Mexico differ noticeably from those of wrens along the coast of California. The songs of *spilurus* and *marinensis* are considerably more complex and varied" than those of the others. He says further:

Only the males sing. Males, at least of the race *spilurus*, do not sing throughout the year; they cease for a month or two in late autumn. * * * Wrens in Strawberry Canyon generally perch on the outer small twigs near the top of a tree or bush. * * * I once saw a wren singing from four different perches in two minutes. Most of the wrens I have observed sing in about the following position: feet spread wide apart, tail horizontal, bill tilted slightly upward, wing tips a little beyond the body and a little below the level of the base of the tail. * * * Most authors speak of the tail hanging down in the manner of a thrasher, but I have not seen them sing in this posture more than with the tail horizontal, and I have even seen the tail erect during singing.

Mrs. Amelia S. Allen says in her notes: "During the last week of July and throughout August, when most birds are silent, the Vigors wrens sing a very subdued song. After watching them for many years, I have come to the conclusion that the birds of the year begin to sing at that time. By the middle of September the full song is heard."

Winter.—At this season, Vigors's wrens, and probably others of the California races, are more widely distributed. Ralph Hoffmann (1927) says that "in the fall many Bewick Wrens move down from the chaparral slopes and inhabit shrubbery near habitations, though some stay in the canyons all winter. * * * The Bewick Wren in winter frequents the same places in the lowland which the House Wren occupies in summer; occasionally both are present at the same time."

These fall and winter wanderings, not strictly migrations, carry the wrens quite down to the coast in suitable places, such as the Point Lobos Reserve on the coast of Monterey County, where the bird is almost unknown in summer. Here, according to Grinnell and Linsdale (1936), they were seen in "considerable numbers" all through winter, becoming common in September. They were seen foraging in the lower branches of cypresses and pines, in the brush and grass, and on the ground among lupine and sage bushes. Other types of winter habitat were a "blackberry tangle along a fence; dead and living ceanothus on south-facing, chaparral-covered slope; thicket of live oak in low mat around base of pine; brush of buckwheat, monkey flower, sage, baccharis, and poison oak; and low horehound mats."

THRYOMANES BEWICKII DRYMOECUS Oberholser

SAN JOAQUIN WREN

HABITS

This subspecies occupies an extensive range in inland California, which Swarth (1916) outlines as follows: "The central portion of California; the Sacramento Valley, and northward at least to the Oregon boundary; northeast to the Warner Mountains, on the Nevada boundary; the west slope of the central Sierra Nevada, everywhere below Transition; southward over about the northern half of the San Joaquin Valley."

He gives as its distinguishing characters:

Compared with *charienturus* [now called *correctus*], *drymoecus* has the upper surface darker and more rufescent. The tail is somewhat shorter, and in different proportion to the wing. In *charienturus* the tail is slightly longer than the wing, in *drymoecus* slightly shorter. Compared with *spilurus*, the upper surface of *drymoecus* is a duller and less rich brown. In the juvenal plumage the character of intensity of rufescence of the upper surface is also apparent, young of *drymoecus* being less deeply colored than young of *spilurus* and *marinensis* on the one hand, and somewhat darker (though slightly so) than the young of *charienturus* on the other. It is noteworthy in this regard that whereas in typical *drymoecus* (Sacramento Valley birds) the adults approach *spilurus* more nearly than they do *charienturus*, the juvenal plumage is but slightly different from the same stage in *charienturus*.

Being centrally placed, this race naturally intergrades with each of the surrounding subspecies at their points of contact, making it difficult to draw hard and fast lines as to the limits of its distribution.

Not much can be said about the haunts and habits of the San Joaquin wren beyond what has been written about the adjacent races, as the California races are all much alike in these matters. Referring to the Yosemite region, Grinnell and Storer (1924) say that this wren "is common in the Upper Sonoran foothills, and some are to be found still farther to the west, in the San Joaquin Valley, in the bottom lands of the Merced and Tuolumne rivers. There are four species of wrens in the foothill country, yet no two meet each other in serious competition. The Cañon Wren is found on rocky cañon walls, the Rock Wren about earth bluffs and rocky outcrops, the House Wren in oak trees, whereas the San Joaquin Wren inhabits the mixed growths comprising small trees and brush."

John G. Tyler (1913) writes: "The nature of the country about Fresno is not such as to attract wrens of any kind in numbers. Wood sprites they are, and must have a well timbered country; so it is not surprising that the present species occurs, within the range of this paper, principally along the San Joaquin and Kings rivers and at the mouth of one or two of the creeks that lead down out of the hills. From these places they make somewhat extended visits to other parts of the valley during the winter months, and are sometimes encountered in brush piles along the canals and ditches. Here they climb over logs, dodge into brush heaps, or pry into the holes in partly dead willows, picking up from such places whatever offers in the way of food."

Four eggs of this wren in the United States National Museum measure 17.8 by 13.2, 16.5 by 12.7, 16.5 by 12.8, and 16.6 by 12.5 millimeters.

THRYOMANES BEWICKII CORRECTUS Grinnell

SAN DIEGO WREN

HABITS

The above name is the result of an unfortunate shift of names, which Dr. Grinnell (1928) found necessary. This is the race of the San Diegan region that Dr. Oberholser (1898) and Mr. Swarth (1916) called *charienturus*. Dr. Grinnell discovered that wrens from the type locality of *charienturus*, in northern Baja California, were "almost indistinguishable from the San Pedro Mártir race." This made it necessary to transfer the name *charienturus* to the wrens of the San Pedro Mártir region and adjacent portions of northwestern Baja California and to invent a new name for the wrens of the San Diegan district; he promptly "corrected" the error by naming it *correctus!* He gives the characters of *correctus*, "as compared with *T. b. drymoecus*, dorsal tone of coloration decidedly lighter, 'warmer' brown, light bars on tail paler, and tail longer."

The 1931 Check-list gives the range of the San Diego wren as, "coastal belt of California from the west side of the San Joaquin Valley, in San Benito and Monterey counties, southeast through the San Diegan district to near the Mexican boundary."

In a general way, the haunts and habits of the San Diego wren are similar to those of the surrounding subspecies, but Harry H. Dunn (1902) gives a somewhat different impression of conditions in Orange County; he says: "Wherever there are rocky canyons, particularly those which contain scattering pools of water, there will be found one or more pairs. * * * It is never found far from rocks, and, in so far as I am able to learn, never nests anywhere except in crevices of rocky ledges, interstices between boulders, or in small caves. * * * In many cases, especially where wood rats are abundant, the Wrens will select a crevice between two rocks, into which even a rat cannot go. * * * Where holes in the solid rock, as in the faces of numerous southern California cliffs, are available, however, the little pair will select a good sized cave and in its sandy floor scratch out a hole large enough to hold a loosely woven nest." Such nesting sites seem more characteristic of rock wrens or canyon wrens, but it seems hardly likely that he could have been mistaken.

Eggs.—The eggs of the San Diego wren are apparently indistinguishable from those of other races of the species. The measurements of 40 eggs average 16.7 by 12.8 millimeters; the eggs showing the four extremes measure 18.9 by 14.3, 14.6 by 12.8, and 15.8 by 11.7 millimeters.

THRYOMANES BEWICKII NESOPHILUS Oberholser

SANTA CRUZ WREN

HABITS

In naming this as a new subspecies from Santa Cruz and Santa Rosa Islands, Dr. Oberholser (1898) says: "This new subspecies may be distinguished from *charienturus* [now called *correctus*] by the darker, more rufescent coloration of the upper surface, sides and flanks; the tail also averages appreciably shorter. It is noticeably lighter and rather more grayish than *spilurus*, besides having a somewhat longer culmen. From *drymoecus* it is without difficulty separable by the noticeably darker and rather more sooty color of the flanks and upper surface. The tail also averages slightly shorter. * * * The young in first plumage are apparently not to be discriminated from those of *charienturus*, though they perhaps average more rufescent. They are usually darker than the young of *drymoecus*."

In a later review of this group, Mr. Swarth (1916) says:

The Santa Cruz Wren is apparently one of the most illy defined of any of the described forms of *Thryomanes bewicki*. The available series affords satisfactory material for comparison. * * * Judging from these specimens this island form has become but slightly differentiated from the mainland race. * * * It is perhaps noteworthy that the slight differences serving to distinguish *nesophilus* from *charienturus* [now called *correctus*] are steps in the direction of *spilurus*, the slightly more reddish dorsal coloration, darker flanks, and shorter tail, being just the characteristics encountered in birds occupying the intermediate coastal region between the ranges of *charienturus* and *spilurus*. The mainland nearest to Santa Cruz Island forms part of this intermediate region.

The only information I have on the nesting of this subspecies is from the data on a set of six eggs in the Doe collection in Gainesville, Fla. This was taken by M. C. Badger on Santa Cruz Island, March 31, 1935. It was from a nest of small twigs, grass, and plant down, well concealed and sunken into the ground beneath a fallen willow tree.

The eggs in this set measure 17.5 by 13.0, 17.5 by 12.7, 17.3 by 13.0, 17.3 by 12.7, 16.8 by 13.0, and 16.8 by 12.7 millimeters.

THRYOMANES BEWICKII CATALINAE Grinnell

CATALINA WREN

HABITS

The Bewick's wrens of Santa Catalina Island, off the coast of southern California, were named by Dr. Joseph Grinnell (1910) and described as "closely similar in color and general size to *T. b. charien-*

turus Oberholser [now called *correctus*], of the adjacent mainland, but averaging darker dorsally (more sepia and not so umber brown), and with heavier bill and conspicuously and constantly larger feet (longer toes and heavier tarsus); differs from *T. b. leucophrys* (Anthony), of San Clemente Island, in decidedly darker, less ashy coloration, and in much more heavily barred under tail-coverts; differs from *T. b. nesophilus* Oberholser, of Santa Cruz Island, in duller, less rufescent, coloration, grayer flanks, longer bill and generally larger size."

He says that it is common on Santa Catalina Island and permanently resident. It does not seem to differ in any of its habits from the mainland forms of the species.

There is a set of six eggs of this race in the collection of Charles E. Doe, of Gainesville, Fla. It was taken by J. S. Rowley on Santa Catalina Island, May 8, 1920. The nest was in a crevice of the "bark of a scrubby-like bush in the bottom of a gulch."

The eggs in this set and five more in the Philipp collection, 11 in all, average in measurements 17.6 by 13.2; the eggs showing the four extremes measure **18.3** by 13.5, 17.6 by **13.6, 16.8** by 13.0, and 17.8 by **12.7** millimeters.

THRYOMANES BEWICKII LEUCOPHRYS (Anthony)

SAN CLEMENTE WREN

HABITS

A. W. Anthony (1895a), with Dr. Edgar A. Mearns, collected a series of Bewick's wrens on San Clemente Island, off the extreme southern coast of California, from which this wren was described and named as a new species. Mr. Anthony describes it as "differing from *T. spilurus* in decided gray wash on the upper parts, in the less heavily barred under tail-coverts, and in having a somewhat longer bill." He says further:

Although the present species is obviously closely related to the mainland bird, * * * I see no reason at present for regarding it as a subspecies of that form. San Clemente Island lies 75 miles from the mainland, and it is quite evident that the species does not intergrade through the other islands of the Santa Barbara group, as the *Thryothorus* from those islands proves to be no nearer related than does the mainland form.

The differences are at once noticeable even at a glance; the longer bill, the more purely white and much more conspicuous superciliary stripe, together with the more gray upper parts are quite striking to one acquainted with the mainland bird. The species is quite common in the thick cactus and low brush on the south end of the island, but owing to its habits is quite difficult to secure.

A. Brazier Howell (1917) writes:

These wrens are evenly distributed over San Clemente, frequenting the densest thorn bushes and cactus patches, from the tops of which their loud clear song, differing but little from that of the mainland bird, is given. Before one is within good range of them they will casually hop down into the lower cactus, and it is very hard indeed to make them show themselves again. If it is in a low bush that they disappear, no amount of trampling will bring a bird forth, but as soon as one steps off the bush, out he pops and away to another one. I shot a juvenal with fully grown tail, April 2, 1915, and from then on the youngsters were not rare. The eggs have evidently never been discovered, but I believe that the nest is invariably built in the center of a dense patch of cactus. While I was trying to remove a dead bird from such a place, on March 29, and smashing the cactus as I went, I uncovered an unfinished nest, probably pertaining to this species. It was wedged under and between cactus leaves some 8 inches above the ground, a 3-inch ball formed of soft fiber, and with the entrance on one side. Two days later when I returned, some little lining had been added, but the situation had been so disturbed that it was deserted before eggs were laid.

THRYOMANES BEWICKII CHARIENTURUS Oberholser

SOOTY WREN

HABITS

This is the wren that Dr. Joseph Grinnell (1927b) described as the race inhabiting "the San Quintin subfaunal district of northwestern Lower California." It ranges south to about latitude 30°. Dr. Grinnell named it *Thryomanes bewickii carbonarius*, sooty Bewick wren, and described it as "similar to *Thryomanes bewickii charienturus* Oberholser (from western San Diego County, Calif.), but bill slightly smaller, and coloration grayer, more slaty (rather than brown), in many respects, as follows: bill, tarsus, toes and claws blackish, with no tinge of light brown; sides of neck, sides of body, and flanks clearer gray; top of head and whole dorsum darker, less warmly, brown; dark portions of webs of all flight feathers darker, more slaty."

But this first name for the race did not stand long, for Dr. Grinnell (1928) discovered that a shift of names was necessary. He found that the type of *charienturus* came from "Nachoguero Valley, in extreme northern Lower California a few miles southwest from Jacumba, San Diego County, Upper California. Fresh fall examples now at hand from exactly that locality show themselves to be, not as I had heretofore assumed they would be, of the San Diegan district race, but almost indistinguishable from the San Pedro Mártir race. Hence it becomes necessary to use the name *charienturus* for the 'Sooty Bewick Wren' of the San Pedro Mártirs and to invent a new name for the race of the San Diegan district."

This shift may be a bit confusing and therefore unfortunate, but it was perfectly logical and proper. I cannot find that anything distinctive has been published on the habits of this subspecies.

There is a set of six eggs of this wren in the Doe collection, taken by N. K. Carpenter, in the Nachoguero Valley, on April 27, 1937. The nest was in a bird box, 10 feet up in a live-oak tree, made of grass and twigs, and lined with snakeskin and feathers.

The measurements of 18 eggs in the Doe, Hanna, and Philipp collections average 17.3 by 12.7 millimeters; the eggs showing the four extremes measure 18.7 by 13.1, 16.4 by 12.6, and 16.5 by 12.2 millimeters.

THRYOMANES BEWICKII CERROENSIS (Anthony)

CEDROS ISLAND WREN

HABITS

The Cedros Island wren has a rather restricted range on the island by that name and on the neighboring mainland of Baja California, in the middle of the peninsula, between latitudes 25° and 30°.

A. W. Anthony (1897), who named and described it as a new species, writes:

The present species needs comparison with none of our western species of the genus unless it be *T. leucophrys*, from which it is very easily separated by its much shorter bill, as well as other discrepancies in size, as will be seen from the accompanying table of measurements. From specimens before me taken at Rosalia Bay, 55 miles east of Cerros Island, the new species is easily separated by much more extensively gray lower parts, less heavily barred. The lower tail-coverts, and its tail feathers have a terminal band of gray of not less than 4 millimeters, whereas the main land bird has a semiobsolete bar of about 1 millimeter. The middle rectrices are also less plainly barred in the mainland specimen, the bars becoming somewhat obsolete near the shaft.

Cerros Island Wrens were not common at any point on the island, though more were seen about the pine timber on the higher ridges.

Dr. Oberholser (1898) remarks: "The wide terminal band of gray on the tail-feathers and lower tail-coverts, which Mr. Anthony regards as a character separating the Cerros Island bird from *charienturus*, is a purely individual variation, and consequently of no diagnostic value. The same may be said of the indistinctness of the barring on the central rectrices, which is observable to a greater or less extent in all the forms of the genus." He says further, however: "The characters which separate this form from *leucophrys* are the darker upper parts, rather more deeply gray flanks, much shorter bill, appreciably shorter wing and tarsus."

Comparing it with its nearest neighbor on the mainland, Ridgway (1904) says: "Similar to *T. b. charienturus*, but slightly smaller (the bill decidedly so) and coloration slightly paler and grayer."

I can find nothing to add about the habits of this subspecies.

Four eggs in the P. B. Philipp collection measure 17.7 by 12.6, 17.1 by 12.7, 16.8 by 12.6, and 17.7 by 12.5 millimeters.

THRYOMANES BEWICKII BREVICAUDA Ridgway

GUADALUPE WREN

HABITS

This well-marked form lived and died on Guadalupe Island, off the coast of Baja California, where it is now evidently extinct. As this account is in the nature of an obituary notice, it seems worth while to quote rather freely from a historical sketch of the island and the bird, as published by A. W. Anthony (1901) ; he writes:

What may have been the zoological condition of Guadalupe Island at the time of its discovery will probably never be known, but that it was to the botanist and zoologist a spot of surpassing interest and strikingly different from the island of today cannot be disputed. It was in 1875, when visited for the first time by a naturalist, found to be wonderfully rich in both plant and animal life. Not only were the species largely peculiar to the island and quite different from their mainland representatives but botanical genera were found that have since become extinct. * * *

I have at the present writing no means of ascertaining when the domestic goat was introduced on the island but as it was placed on many of the coast islands by the early whalers it is not unlikely that this pest held sway on Guadalupe a half century or more before the richness of the flora and fauna was made known to the world by Dr. Edward Palmer in 1875. It is directly due to the despised Billy-goat that many interesting species of plants formerly abundant are now extinct, and also that one or more of the birds peculiar to the island has disappeared, and others are rapidly following.

Dr. Palmer collected only two specimens of this wren on Guadalupe, on which Mr. Ridgway (1876) named and described the species in detail, saying among other things that "this insular form is much grayer than the *T. bewicki spilurus* of California and Western Mexico." Later on (1904) he describes it as "practically identical in coloration with *T. bewickii charienturis* [now called *correctus*] except tail (the middle rectrices of which are more narrowly and much less distinctly barred), but much smaller, tail relatively shorter, and bill much longer."

Walter E. Bryant (1887) made two visits to Guadalupe in 1885, in January and December, remaining 3 months on the latter visit. He gives full description of the island which is situated 220 miles south westward from San Diego and lies between latitudes 28°45′ and 29°10′ N.; it is about 15 miles long and 5 miles wide at its widest part and is said to reach an altitude of 4,523 feet at the highest point. He collected seven specimens of this wren on February 16, 1886, four males and three females, and says: "This rare local species has become much restricted in distribution and perhaps in numbers since Dr. Palmer obtained the only two known specimens in 1875. I am informed that no collecting was done at that time among the pines on the northern portion of the island, in which place alone was I able to discover any trace of this species; and as no collecting was done by Dr. Palmer among the palms (an unlikely place for the birds to be found), I infer that the two original specimens must have been found toward the central portion of the island."

According to Mr. Anthony (1901), the restricted area in which Mr. Bryant collected his specimens consisted of a growth of straggling pines along the sharp ridge of North Head, affording a habitat of about 60 by 300 feet. He says:

Fearing the extermination of the species the balance of the colony was unmolested, but as the sheltering undergrowth was more and more constricted by the goats the birds were either blown from the island by violent gales that frequently sweep over it, or killed by cats which infest the entire island since their introduction about the time of Dr. Palmer's visit in 1875. The last week in May, 1892, Mr. Clark P. Streator, and myself paid a visit one day to the North Head.

Near the beach and directly below the pines Mr. Streator took a pair of wrens which are now in the collection of the Biological Survey. On the ridge near the spot where Bryant found them, I discovered a bird which was secured, and saw what may have been a second but was of doubtful identity. Since that date I have made several calls at Guadalupe, and though the entire top of the island was carefully searched by myself and several assistants for days at a time we never found any signs of the species which must now be classed among those that were.

The constant destruction of all low-growing vegetation by the goats still continues, not only consuming the nesting sites and shelters of Junco, Pipilo and all ground-nesting species but giving to the ever watchful cat more favorable opportunities for destroying the few birds that are left. *Pipilo consobrinus* is now nearly or quite extinct and the juncos are surely but steadily becoming scarce. Since the goats kill all of the young trees as soon as they appear above ground, and the larger trees are dying, the outlook for the future flora and fauna is not bright.

So, the Guadalupe wren probably disappeared entirely soon after 1892, and another was added to our growing list of extinct species. This sad story should serve as a lesson to conservationists, a warning against over-grazing and the release of introduced animals and of feral cats, the latter becoming a serious menace anywhere.

Nesting.—It seems that the nest of this wren has never been found; this and the eggs will remain forever unknown. Mr. Bryant and his Mexican companion made a careful and protracted search for nests during the greater part of two days, but with no success.

Plumages.—The single young bird, now in the collection of the U. S. Fish and Wildlife Service, is practically indistinguishable from the young of the San Diego wren, according to Oberholser (1898).

Food.—The stomach of one of the birds collected by Dr. Palmer "contained remnants of some small black insects which feed upon the blossoms of the White Sage" (Ridgway, 1876). And Mr. Bryant (1887) found "insects and two pine seeds" in the stomach of one of his birds.

Behavior.—Mr. Bryant (1887) says: "The birds were timid rather than shy, being alarmed by the crushing of dry branches as I worked my way amidst the dense windfalls of pines, where they were found, they fled into the thickest parts. When all was quiet they would cautiously approach until within a few feet of me, seemingly prompted by curiosity. * * * A frightened female uttered a few 'twit' 'twits' of alarm, but with this exception they were utterly silent."

THRYOTHORUS LUDOVICIANUS LUDOVICIANUS (Latham)

CAROLINA WREN

PLATES 37, 38

HABITS

In attempting to compile the life histories of the wrens of this species, I have not overlooked and shall not attempt to criticize a recent important paper on the geographical variation in the Carolina wren by George H. Lowery, Jr. (1940), in which he splits the species into eight subspecies, one of which is Mexican. This makes a rather large addition to the three races now recognized in our 1931 Check-list. Doubtless some of his races, perhaps all of them, are worthy of recognition in nomenclature. But, as the author does not claim to be a systematic ornithologist, it seems best for a work of this kind to follow the nomenclature and classification of the latest Check-list, as has been done in previous volumes.

I have always associated the Carolina wren with the sunny South, one of that happy trio of birds that are always ready to greet the northern bird lover with their loud cheery songs as he travels southward; the songs of this wren, the tufted titmouse, and the cardinal have enough in common to confuse a newcomer when he hears them for the first time, but they are really different when carefully studied; however, they are all delightful and give us a warm touch of southern hospitality, a hearty welcome to Dixie Land.

But we cannot now regard the Carolina wren as exclusively a southern bird, for it seems to have been extending its range northward during the early part of the present century. The 1931 Check-list gave as the probable northern limits of its range "southeastern Nebraska, southern Iowa, Ohio, southern Pennsylvania, and lower Hudson and Connecticut valleys" and called it "casual or accidental in Wisconsin, Michigan, Ontario, Maine, New Hampshire, and Massachusetts." Dr. Charles W. Townsend (1909) has published an interesting paper on what he calls an invasion of this wren into New England, giving a large number of records for various States; most of these are fall and winter records, but there are enough breeding records mentioned to indicate that the Carolina wren may be regarded as a rare breeding bird in at least southern New England. It has long been known to breed on Naushon Island, off the coast of southern Massachusetts; Forbush (1929) mentions several other Massachusetts breeding records, and Knight (1908) records a breeding record for Maine.

Dr. Chapman (1912) says of the haunts of the Carolina wren: "The cozy nooks and corners about the home of man which prove so attractive to the House Wren are less commonly chosen by this bird. His wild nature more often demands the freedom of the forests, and he shows no disposition to adapt himself to new conditions.   Undergrowths near water, fallen tree tops, brush heaps, and rocky places in the woods where he can dodge in and out and in a twinkling appear or disappear like a feathered Jack-in-the-box, are the resorts he chooses."

The last part of this statement is undoubtedly true, but there is plenty of evidence that he has learned "to adapt himself to new conditions."   Milton P. Skinner (1928), for example, says that, in the sandhills of North Carolina, these wrens "are dwellers in the dooryards and about houses, more even than in wilder haunts.   Almost all kinds of shrubbery attract them, but they like the thickest, thorny kind the best. While they are generally in the bushes and lower growth, they sometimes go higher into trees, even as much as thirty feet above the ground."   Arthur H. Howell (1924) says that, in Alabama, "although partial to low bottomland timber," it is "found also about farmyards and in town gardens.   Indeed, so domestic is it at times that it is often called 'house wren'."   Other observers give us similar impressions and the bird certainly shows considerable adaptability in its choice of a great variety of nesting sites about human structures.   There is no doubt, however, that it has always shown a preference for the wilder woodland thickets, preferably along watercourses and in swamps, but also in hammocks and in isolated clumps of trees and bushes on the prairies and pine barrens throughout the South.

Courtship.—I can find no information on this subject, but Mrs. Amelia R. Laskey has sent me some notes that indicate some degree of constancy.   A male banded June 25, 1934, was recaptured at intervals until January 18, 1938; and a female banded November 19, 1934, was taken at intervals until the summer of 1939.   Thus the male was at least 4½ years old, and the female at least 5 years old.   "Part of the period they are positively known to have been mates, as they wore colored plumes and were seen together in winter as well as in the nesting season."   Others have noticed that they are often seen in pairs all through winter.

Nesting.—The Carolina wren originally nested in woodlands, thickets, brushy hollows, and swamps and along the banks of streams, where it could find cover; and it still does so over most of its range, without taking advantage of the many opportunities offered in and about human structures.   In these wilder spots it may build its nest in a hole in a tree or stump, in the open crotch of a tree, in a densely branched cedar, in the upturned roots of a fallen tree, on the ground under the exposed roots of a tree or under dense undergrowth, in a hole in a bank or under its overhang among tangled roots, in a cavity in a stone wall, or even in a sheaf of grain in an open field.   Nests in such situations are hard to find and are probably not so often reported as the more obvious sites about human dwellings.

Most of the sites mentioned above are obviously at very low elevations, seldom as much as 10 feet above ground, even in trees. But M. G. Vaiden, of Rosedale, Miss., writes to me of a nest that was "30 feet up in a black walnut. This nest was extremely large and located on a partially broken-off limb growing upward and almost parallel to the main body of the tree. A few sprouts had grown out from the broken limb," which helped to prevent the nest from being blown away. "The nest was composed of dried leaves and sticks and lined with fowl feathers, forming a great ball with the entrance facing north and at the very center of the ball." Nests in such open situations in trees are usually domed or arched over, with a side entrance.

Nests of the more domestically inclined wrens have been reported in a great variety of nooks and crannies in, about, or under buildings of various kinds, under bridges, or in holes in fence posts. Almost any kind of receptacles left lying around, such as tin cans, coffee pots, pails, small baskets, pitchers, or empty boxes may be used. Old discarded hats and caps or the pockets of old clothes, coats, or overalls, left hanging in sheds or on porches, may offer acceptable nesting sites. Nests have been found in mail boxes, bird boxes, old hornets' nests, and ivy vines growing over porches; and the nest is sometimes built in an unused cupboard or on a mantel shelf inside a house. Dr. Witmer Stone (1911) writes: "In a country place near Philadelphia, a pair of Carolina Wrens entered the sitting-room through a window that was left partly open, and built their nest in the back of an upholstered sofa, entering where a hole had been torn in the back. Needless to say, they were not disturbed, and given full possession until the young were safely reared." Mr. Vaiden tells of a pair of these wrens that raised a brood of young "in the pitcher of a pitcher-pump," left in the basement of a house. "The parents came through the partly opened basement window and gave little attention to the humans that had to occasionally go into the basement."

Dr. George M. Sutton (1930) says that, in Brooke County, W. Va., "the bulky nests were found as a rule in out-buildings, and none was found in the woods far from a human dwelling. One nest was built in a rumpled paper sack which lay on a shelf in a woodshed. * * * A nest found in 1917 was built into the corner of a large drygoods box which had been nailed to the shadowy back of a barn." The cavity was far too big, but a large lot of material had been brought in and the structure was neat. "In front of the nest proper was a crude path of weed-stalks and leaves possibly eighteen inches in length. The entire nest with its approach could be lifted easily, so skilfully were the stalks and leaf stems interwoven."

Clara Calhoun (1911) tells of a most interesting nest that was built "in a bolt-rack in a busy country blacksmith shop. * * * The mother bird knew no fear, but flew boldly about, gathering shav-

ings and excelsior fairly under the smith's hands and feet, approaching the nest over a horse that was being shod, and often keeping
her place upon it when the smith worked at the vise for welding
tires, * * * undaunted by the ringing blows or showers of sparks."
A brood of five young was raised in this nest.

The Carolina wren is satisfied with almost any soft and pliable
material that is available with which to build its nest, such as grasses,
weed stalks, strips of inner bark, leaves, mosses, rootlets, and feathers;
many nests contain pieces of cast-off snakeskin, and some are partially
lined with this.   The lining generally consists of fine grass, fine rootlets, hair, feathers, and sometimes Spanish moss.   George F. Simmons
(1925) adds the following materials, used in Texas nests: Small twigs,
corn husks, pieces of paper, string, thread, wool, rags, and leaf
skeletons.

I am told that Herbert L. Stoddard has a record of a successful
nesting in a farm tractor that was in daily use.

Eggs.—The Carolina wren lays four to six eggs to a set; probably
five is the commonest number; sets of eight have been recorded.   These
are mostly ovate but often more rounded and sometimes somewhat
elongated.   The ground color is usually pure white, but often pinkish white or creamy white.   They are usually more heavily marked
with larger spots than other wrens' eggs, but not always, as some are
very sparingly and faintly marked with fine dots.   The markings may
be evenly distributed, but generally they are irregularly scattered
and often concentrated in a ring about the larger end.   The markings
are in several lighter and darker shades of reddish brown, and there
are sometimes underlying blotches in light shades of "Quaker drab"
or "lavender," producing a very pretty effect.

The measurements of 50 eggs average 19.1 by 14.9 millimeters; the
eggs showing the four extremes measure 20.8 by 15.2, 19.8 by 15.8, and
16.8 by 14.2 millimeters.

Young.—The period of incubation is said to be 12 to 14 days, and
the young remain in the nest for about the same length of time.   Evidently the task of incubation is performed wholly by the female; at
least I can find no evidence that the male ever incubates.   But both
parents work together industriously to feed the young, in the nest and
for a time after they leave it.   At least two broods are ordinarily
raised in a season and often three in the more southern localities.
McIlwraith (1894) says that even in Ontario "the Carolina Wren is
a very prolific species, the female turning over to the male the care
of the first brood before they are able to shift for themselves, while
she proceeds to deposit a second set of eggs in another nest, which
the male has prepared for their reception.   Family number two is
turned over to the male in due course, and in this way three broods
are raised during the season in a very short time."

Plumages.—Soon after hatching the young wrens are scantily decorated with slate-colored down; the juvenal *plumage* develops rapidly and they are well clothed by the time they leave the nest. In the juvenal plumage young birds look much like the adults, but they are paler in color and the plumage is softer in texture; the wing coverts are tipped with buffy white, the superciliary stripe is less clearly white, the underparts are whiter, and there is some dusky barring or mottling on the flanks and sides of the head.

The first winter plumage is acquired by a partial postjuvenal molt in August and September, involving the contour plumage, the wing coverts, and the tail, but not the rest of the wings. This plumage is darker and richer in color than the juvenal plumage, chestnut or Vandyke brown above and deep cinnamon below, with white tips on the wing coverts and a whiter superciliary stripe, young and old becoming practically indistinguishable.

Adults have a complete postnuptial molt in August and September; after this molt, in fresh fall plumage, all the colors are brighter and richer than in the worn and faded plumage seen in spring. The sexes are alike in all plumages.

Food.—In his study of the food of the Carolina wren, Professor Beal (Beal, McAtee, and Kalmbach, 1916) examined 291 stomachs, representing every month. The contents were found to consist of 94.18 percent animal matter, nearly all insects, and 5.82 percent vegetable matter, chiefly seeds. Of the animal food, beetles made up 13.64 percent, all injurious except 1.71 percent of predatory ground beetles; among the beetles found were several species of weevils, including the cottonboll weevil, 31 individuals being found in 18 stomachs; other beetles were the two cucumber beetles, the bean leaf beetle, and numerous flea beetles. Of the Hymenoptera, ants amounted to 4.63 percent and bees and wasps to about the same. Hemiptera—stink bugs, soldier bugs, leaf-legged bugs, leafhoppers, and chinch bugs—made up 18.91 percent, one of the largest items. Scale insects destructive to oranges were found in one stomach. The largest item of all proved to be caterpillars and a few moths, 21.73 percent. Orthoptera, including grasshoppers, crickets, and cockroaches and their eggs, made up 12.57 percent of the food. Flies are evidently not popular, as the average for the year was only a little over 3 percent; daddy-longlegs and craneflies were the most popular. On the other hand, spiders seem to be very attractive; they were eaten in every month, and from April to August to the extent of 16.67 percent, and the average for the year was 10.54 percent; spiders must be easily obtained in the many nooks and crannies that the Carolina wren explores. Other small items of animal food included millipeds, sowbugs, and snails. "Vertebrate animals would hardly be expected to form part of the diet of so small a bird, but the Carolina wren eats them often. Remains of lizards were found in 14 stomachs, tree frogs in 8, and a snake in 1; totaling 1.92 percent." Of the vegetable food, a little fruit pulp was found in a few stomachs, seeds of bayberry in 20, sweet gum in 10, poison ivy in 7, sumac in 4, pine in 2, weed seeds in 7, and ground-up acorns in 2.

Several observers have noted that Carolina wrens will come freely to feeding stations, if placed near brush piles, thickets, or other suitable shelter, where they will feed on ground peanuts, suet, marrow of bones, or ground hamburg steak.

Behavior.—Like others of its tribe, the Carolina wren is the embodiment of tireless energy and activity, seldom still for a moment, as he dodges in and out of the underbrush or creeps over and around a pile of logs, appearing and disappearing with the suddenness of a mouse, diving into one crevice in a wood pile, and popping out of another in some unexpected place. His movements are exceedingly quick and sudden, accompanied by frequent teetering of the body and nervous jerking of the upturned tail, chattering to himself the while, or stopping occasionally to pour out one or two strains of his joyous song, for he is a merry little chap and seems to enjoy his elusive ways. We may watch him thus, if we stand quietly, but if we move toward him, he immediately darts into the thickest cover and disappears; it is useless to pursue him, for he has a tantalizing way of keeping out of sight ahead of us and mocking us with his derisive chatter; he is more than a match for us in the game of hide and seek. C. J. Maynard (1896) says: "I have frequently seen these wrens in isolated bushes and, after seeing them vanish, have beat about the place where they disappeared, then through it without starting them, afterwards finding that the wily birds had escaped by running with great rapidity beneath the grass and weeds to the next thicket."

Although this wren does not like to be pursued, or even approached too closely, he has sufficient curiosity and boldness to do his own approaching. If we sit or stand still in some inconspicuous position, and especially if we make a squeaking noise, he will be one of the first birds to show himself and may come within a few feet of us to look us over; but a move on our part causes him to vanish immediately.

His shyness and timidity are apparent enough, especially in his woodland haunts, and it is difficult to surprise the female on her nest, from which she slips away quietly and unobserved. But the pair have often shown remarkable friendliness and confidence in human beings by building their nests in and about our premises, by coming to our feeding stations, and by roosting under the shelter of our homes. These wrens have been known to roost several times in abandoned hornets' nests; for example, Prof. Maurice Brooks (1932) writes:

Some time during the fall of 1927 my father found, and carried to the house, a verp large nest built by white-faced hornets (*Vespa maculata*). This nest was hung up in an out-building, and no attention was paid to it until late in the winter when we found, to our surprise, that a pair of Carolina Wrens had enlarged the opening, and were using it as a nightly roosting place.

The birds continued to roost there until spring; when they carefully constructed a nest of their own, in the top of the hornets' nest, away from the opening. For some reason, they later abandoned this home in favor of one in a nearby bird box.

When fall came we waited with interest to see if they would again take up their old abode. Going out to look one frosty morning before daylight, we heard them stirring in the nest, and they used it regularly from then on. This they have repeated every year until the present winter.

Another nest was placed in the same building last fall, and the resident pair, whether or not the original 1927 individuals we do not know, immediately took up quarters in the enlarged opening of the new nest. In their new home they are plainly visible, and they have allowed us to study them with flashlights. They do not seem to be in the least disturbed when we suddenly turn a light upon them. The outer bird roosts with one wing spread across the opening, and this, perhaps, shuts out most of the light.

One morning, just at daybreak, I went out to the building where the nests are hung, lighted a small gas stove, and placed before it a bucket of water over which a layer of ice had frozen. Returning in a few minutes, I found both birds perched on the rim of the bucket, as near to the fire as they could get. Whether the heat or the light was the attraction I cannot say, but they presented as charming a bird picture as I have ever seen.

In *The Migrant*, volume 14, pages 1–5, 1943, is a symposium on how birds spend their winter nights. In this the Carolina wren is reported as roosting in a pocket in a shirt that hung on a clothesline, in a fold of an old portiere hanging in a garage, and in a pocket of an old coat that hung on a porch.

Carolina wrens, like other wrens, are not much given to protracted flights; most of their short flights in their favorite retreats are erratic dartings from one perch to another or from one log to another; but in longer flights in the open, which they seldom have to make, their flights are direct and straight with rapid beats of their short wings. Most of their activity is near the ground, hopping from branch to branch with sprightly activity, or creeping over, around, and under piles of wood and always prying into every nook and crevice in search of spiders and insect food. Several observers have noted their ability to climb the trunks of trees, sometimes to a considerable height, prying into the crevices in the bark for food much after the manner of the creepers.

Voice.—The Carolina wren is one of our great singers, a beautiful singer and a most persistent singer. It is one of the few birds that sing more or less during every month in the year, though it sings most persistently and most enthusiastically during the late winter and spring months; it sings in all kinds of weather, spring sunshine, summer rains, or winter snowstorms; during the height of its song period it may be heard all through the day, from dawn to dusk. It has a varied repertoire; the songs of other birds are often suggested, or perhaps imitated, leading to some confusion at times. but it has a very distinct and characteristic song of its own, which is unmistakable.

The song is a loud, ringing combination of rich, whistling notes, given with a definite and emphatic swing and a decided accent; it can be heard for a long distance and is so pleasing in its cheering effect that it can hardly pass unnoticed by even the most casual observer. The phrases consist of two to four syllables, usually two or three, and each phrase is repeated two or three times with short intervals between the phrases. Among the 28 references to the song of this bird that I have consulted, I find an almost endless variety of interpretations, expressed in human words or in expressive syllables. I shall select only a few of the best of each which, to my mind, most clearly recall the song. Among the human words, those that please me best are "tea-kéttle, tea-kéttle, tea-kéttle"; others are "sweet heart, sweet heart," "sweet William, sweet William," "come to me, come to me," "Richelieu, Richelieu, Richelieu," "Jew-Pet-er, Jew-Pet-er," "tree- double-tree, double-tree, double-tree," "sugar to eat, sugar to eat, sugar to eat, sugar," "which jailer, which jailer," etc. All these phrases seem to suggest what is the most characteristic song of the Carolina wren; some of them may also suggest the song of the Maryland yellow-throat, but there is a great difference in the tone and quality.

Similar suggestions of the same song are found in the many different syllables used to describe it, such as *whee-udel, whee-udel, whee-udel; che-whortel, che-whortel; jo-reaper, jo-repar, jo-ree; willy-way, willy-way; túrtree, túrtree, túrtree;* and there are many other similar renderings.

There are, of course, various other songs, notably a loud whistle like that of the cardinal and one that sounds like the *peto, peto, peto* of the tufted titmouse, as suggested by some of the above syllables. Songs have been heard that resemble the rattle of the kingfisher, the call of the flicker, and songs of the pine warbler, towhee, red-winged blackbird, meadowlark, Baltimore oriole, bluebird, catbird, white-eyed vireo, scarlet tanager, and song sparrow, all of which have given the wren credit as an imitator of birds that it has heard, and it has been called the "mocking wren." Some of these songs may be actual imitations, but many of them may be only expressions of its own great versatility in song. Nuttall (1832) goes into this matter at great length, describing many songs, and adds: "Amidst these imitations and variations, which seem almost endless, and lead the stranger to imagine himself, even in the depth of winter, surrounded by all the quaint choristers of the summer, there is still, with our capricious and tuneful mimic, a favorite theme more constantly and regularly repeated than the rest."

In addition to its varied songs, the Carolina wren has a number of call, alarm, or scolding notes, among which Mr. Simmons (1925) lists "calls, with much rolling of the *r's, terrp; tierrp-tier-r-p; chier-r-r; cheerrp, tieu u u;* a slower *tieur-r-r, tieur-r-, tieur-r-r,* about a two second interval between each; *cack; clack; clink;* clinking metallic rattles; musical trills and tree-toad-like *k-r-r-r-r-ings.*"

Dawson (1903) writes: "On all occasions this nervous little creature appears to be full of a sort of compressed air, which escapes from time to time in a series of mild explosions, like the lid of a teakettle being jarred up and down by steam. When the valve is opened a little wider there follows an accelerando rattling call, which seems to be modeled after the chirr of the red squirrel; and when the throttle is held wide open the rattling notes are telescoped together into an emphatic '*kurr'r'st,*' which brings one up standing."

Aretas A. Saunders has 78 records of the songs of the Carolina wren. Following are some quotations from his notes: "In form the song is much like that of the Maryland yellowthroat, but the louder, clearer quality, lower pitch, and frequency of liquid consonant sounds make it sound quite different. Individual birds sing a great number of variations. In June 1930 I recorded eight different songs from one individual in less than half an hour. In 1928 a wren of this species lived in a locality that I visited frequently, and I recorded 36 different songs from it through the season.

"In pitch my records vary from G ' ' to A ' ' ', one tone more than an octave, and all the notes, so far as my ear could determine, lower than the highest note of the piano. The widest pitch variation in one song is four and a half tones, and the least one tone, the average about two tones.

"The length of a single song varies from about 1⅕ to 3⅕ seconds and depends mainly on the number of times the bird repeats the phrase of the song. As a rule, one phrase occupies about two-fifths of a second, except in unusual songs where a phrase is longer or shorter than usual."

Field marks.—The Carolina wren is the largest of the wrens found in eastern North America, hence the former name "great Carolina wren." It is rather a chunky bird, rich reddish brown above and buff below, except for the white chin and the barred under tail coverts. There is a conspicuous, long, white stripe over the eye. The tail is brown like the back and is barred, but it is not fan-shaped or white-tipped, like the tail of Bewick's wren.

Enemies.—This wren is annoyed by the usual external parasites that infest other birds; Harold S. Peters (1936) lists four species of ticks, two of mites, and one louse that cause some irritation. Probably some die from eating poisoned flies and other insects, and predatory mammals and birds may take their toll. The house wren is a competitor for nesting sites, but Dr. Sutton (1930) found no evidence that the house wren molested the nests of the Carolina wren, and concluded that these two species could live together with less friction than the house wren and Bewick's wren.

Dr. Friedmann (1929) gives several instances in which this wren was victimized by the cowbird; and Mrs. Nice (1931) lists 4 nests out of 16 that were so parasitized in Oklahoma.

Winter.—The Carolina wren is preferably a sedentary species; it likes to remain where it has found a suitable home throughout the year. This trait has somewhat limited the northward extension of its permanent range. Migratory birds may extend their range northward in spring and summer and retire southward before winter; they thus escape the rigors of a northern winter; but this wren does not seem to take this wise precaution. During summers and mild winters they increase in numbers throughout the middle and northern States, as illustrated by Dr. Townsend's (1909) account of the invasion of New England; these are probably unmated or young birds seeking new territory. But they are not hardy birds, and the next severe winter may result disastrously for the adventurous pioneers. Most of their food is obtained on or near the ground, and when a deep fall of snow covers the ground for a long time and is accompanied by severe cold, most of the wrens succumb to cold and starvation. As a result we have alternating periods of scarcity in the northern States and probably shall never have permanent abundance. Forbush (1929) gives the records for several such periods in New England from 1903 to 1922.

Even as far south as Washington, D. C., similar fluctuations in numbers have been noted by Dr. Alexander Wetmore (1923), who says:

Since the winter of 1917–1918, when the Carolina Wren was greatly reduced in numbers in the Washington region, this species has increased gradually until the fall of 1921 (after four breeding seasons) it was again fairly common, though still somewhat below its normal abundance. * * * A sudden heavy snowfall that continued from January 27 to 29, 1922, when the snow reached the unusual depth of twenty-six inches once more proved disastrous to the bird under discussion. The heavy blanket of snow melted slowly and not until February 3 did bare ground appear. * * * Observations during February and March show that the Carolina Wren has again decreased in this region though those that remain are somewhat greater in number than was the case in spring of 1918. The supposition advanced in my former note that decrease in this species was due not to cold but to the heavy blanket of snow that buried the normal food supply, seems substantiated.

And Prof. Maurice Brooks (1936) reports that in West Virginia, where this wren has always been one of the commonest permanent-resident birds, it practically disappeared during the severe winter of 1935–36. During late January "this section was subjected to temperatures ranging from sixteen to thirty degrees below zero, and after that the species was not again noted until April. One boy in Upshur County found five Carolina Wrens frozen to death, and there were other reports of individuals found dead."

The wrens that survive northern winters generally live in sheltered localities. The one that Dr. Townsend and I saw at Ipswich, Mass., was living in a planted thicket of spruces near a house and close to the sea on February 7, 1909, where it was seen again up to March 12. Dr. Witmer Stone (1911) writes:

In the low, flat ground bordering the tide-water creeks of southwestern New Jersey, they are particularly abundant, especially in midwinter, when it always seemed to me that most of the Cardinals and Carolina Wrens gathered in these swamps from all the country round about. Here they find food and shelter suitable to their needs, and here the winter sun seems to shine more warmly than back in the higher grounds of Pennsylvania.

The Carolina Wren, however, is not entirely confined to these low grounds in winter, but ranges well up the narrow valleys and deep ravines, and often we find him along the rocky banks of some ravine where flows a narrow, tumbling stream and here the hemlocks of the North mingle with the redbud and tulip-tree of the South.

A note recently received from Mrs. Laskey states that Nashville, Tenn., "experienced an unusually cold winter in 1940, the low temperatures and heavy snows in January were disastrous apparently to our Carolina Wrens. They were very scarce during the following nesting season. Previously, everywhere one went, its cheery song and its trills could be heard in winter. This year, 1941, they have not been so scarce, but in my observations not reaching normal numbers."

Mrs. Mary C. Rhoads (1924) tells an interesting story of a Carolina wren that spent the winter nights in her conservatory in Haddonfield, N. J. He entered each night and left each morning, at first through an open door, but eventually through a hole she made for him which he learned to use. He roosted, ate, drank, bathed, and sang there all winter, sometimes even entering the dining room to pick up crumbs; he continued to patronize the conservatory from sometime in the fall until March 24, and must have made a delightful winter guest.

Mr. Saunders writes to me from Fairfield, Conn.: "My records since I have lived in Fairfield show that this bird was not found from 1920 to 1925, but was recorded fairly frequently from 1925 to 1933. Then it disappeared again till 1939 but has been present since April of that year up to the present (November 1941)."

DISTRIBUTION

Range.—Eastern United States and northeastern Mexico; non-migratory.

The Carolina wren breeds **north** to southeastern Nebraska (Superior); southern Iowa (Des Moines and Sigourney); southern Michigan (Ann Arbor and Detroit); southern Ontario (Point Pelee, London, and Toronto); southern Connecticut (Bridgeport, New Haven, and Chester); southern Rhode Island (Middletown); and southeastern Massachusetts (Naushon). From this line the Carolina Wren is found in all the States **south** to Florida, the Gulf coast and northeastern Mexico; Tamaulipas (Ciudad Victoria); Nuevo León (Monterrey, Santa Catarina, and Linares); and Coahuila (Sabinas). **West** to Coahuila (Sabinas); central Texas (Nueces, Mason, and Abilene); Oklahoma (Wichita Mountains and Fort Reno); central Kansas (Wichita and Clearwater); and southeastern Nebraska (Superior).

The range of the Carolina wren seems to be extending northward, since there are a number of records of its occurrence **north** to South Dakota (Yankton County); Minnesota (Bigstone Lake and Minneapolis); Wisconsin (Madison and New London); Michigan (Grand Rapids and Sand Point); southern New Hampshire (Alstead and Rye Beach); and southeastern Maine (Falmouth).

The above outline is for the entire species, which has been divided into four subspecies or geographic races. The Carolina wren (*T. l. ludovicianus*) ranges south to central Texas, the Gulf States, and northern Florida; the Florida wren (*T. l. miamensis*) is found in the peninsula of Florida from Levy and Putnam Counties southward; Burleigh's Carolina wren (*T. l. burleighi*) is found at Cat, Ship, and Horn Islands, Miss.; the Lomita wren (*T. l. lomitensis*) is found in the lower Rio Grande Valley of Texas and northern Tamaulipas, Mexico. Other races occur in Mexico.

Casual records.—The Carolina wren has been observed in Burlington, Vt., from July 10 to October 5, 1936; at Center Ossipee, N. H., on August 21, 1940; one observed on June 21, 1916, at Beaver Pond, Maine; and there is one record of breeding in Maine, eggs taken at Norway Lake in June 1893.

Egg dates.—Florida: 44 records, April 1 to June 24; 24 records, April 17 to May 6, indicating the height of the season.

Georgia: 33 records, April 5 to July 3; 17 records, May 2 to June 15.

Pennsylvania: 8 records, April 8 to July 22.

Texas: 39 records, March 13 to July 9; 20 records, April 10 to May 3.

THRYOTHORUS LUDOVICIANUS BURLEIGHI Lowery

BURLEIGH'S CAROLINA WREN

In naming and describing this island race, George H. Lowery, Jr. (1940), says that it is "similar to *T. l. ludovicianus* (Latham) to which it is most closely related, but differs in being somewhat duller and more sooty above and averaging slightly paler below; color of the pileum not a great deal duller than the back; barring of the tail less

distinct than in *ludovicianus;* size not significantly different from
T. l. euronotus but easily distinguished from that race on the basis of
its lighter coloration."

Lowery gives the range of this wren as: "Resident on the islands
lying well offshore from the Mississippi Coast; known to occur on Cat
Island, Ship Island, and Horn Island. Not improbably it will be
found on certain of the islands off the Alabama and Louisiana coast
as well."

THRYOTHORUS LUDOVICIANUS MIAMENSIS Ridgway

FLORIDA WREN

HABITS

The Florida wren is a common resident in nearly all the Florida
peninsula, all but the northwestern part, or from Levy and Putnam
Counties southward, according to the 1931 Check-list. Mr. Lowery
(1940) does not subdivide this race but says that it is "typical from
Gainesville and Palatka southward."

This is the largest and darkest of all the races. Ridgway (1904)
describes it as "most like *T. l. berlandieri,* but coloration still darker
and richer, and size much greater (decidedly larger than any other
form of the species); upper parts rich chestnut to dark chestnut,
the superciliary stripe decidedly buffy (except in worn summer
plumage); under parts (except chin and upper throat) deep clay
color or tawny-ochraceous, the flanks tinged with chestnut and
(sometimes also the sides) barred with chestnut or dusky."

We found this wren everywhere that we went in Florida in the
live-oak and palmetto hammocks, in the swamps, and in dense thickets
in the river bottoms, singing more or less all winter and more often
heard than seen. We found no nests, but Mr. Howell (1932) says
that "the nests are placed on the ground in the woods, often underneath an overhanging bank, in hollow logs or stumps, or sometimes on
the sill of an outbuilding, or in a box or can within the building. The
breeding season extends from March to July, and two or more broods
are raised each season."

C. J. Maynard (1896) says:

The usual situations chosen by the wrens on Indian River were at the bottoms
of the "boots" of the palmettoes. The "boot" is the base of the dead leaf stalks
which adhere to the tree after the top has decayed and fallen off, they are quite
broad, slightly concave, and extend upward in an oblique direction leaving a
space between them and the trunk; the fronds in falling often cover the top
with a fibrous debris which is impervious to water and the cavities beneath form
a snug nesting place for the Carolina Wrens. Many more nests will be found in
these situations than elsewhere, especially in the wilderness; but I once found
one built between two palmetto leaves which had dropped over in such a position
that their surfaces were horizontal and only three or four inches apart, forming
a floor as well as a roof for the home of the Wrens. They had conveyed a large
amount of suitable material into this place and formed a cozy domicile. The

fronds were swayed by every passing breeze, yet in such a manner as not to injure the structure which was between them.

In all other respects the habits of the Florida wren seem to be very similar to those of the northern race.

Eggs.—The eggs of the Florida wren are substantially like those of the Carolina wren. The measurements of 40 eggs average 19.0 by 14.8 millimeters; the eggs showing the four extremes measure 20.5 by 14.9, 19.8 by 15.8, 16.3 by 14.9, and 18.6 by 14.2 millimeters.

THRYOTHORUS LUDOVICIANUS LOMITENSIS Sennett

LOMITA WREN

PLATE 38

HABITS

This small, dull-colored subspecies seems to occupy a rather limited range in the lower valley of the Rio Grande, in Texas and in northern Tamaulipas, in Mexico. The map published by Mr. Lowery (1940) shows decided gaps between the range of this race and the ranges of *berlandieri*, in Mexico, and his new race *oberholseri*, in southern Texas. He says: "When one views the great areas apparently uninhabited by Carolina wrens bordering the Rio Grande above and below Laredo, the isolation of *lomitensis* becomes obvious. It thus seems highly improbable that *lomitensis* comes geographically in contact with other races thereby suggesting a factor which might be responsible for its clear-cut taxonomic characters." In naming this race, George B. Sennett (1890) describes it well as follows:

Compared with *T. ludovicianus* this race is much lighter in its general appearance; the color of the back is also different, *ludovicianus* being reddish brown or bright cinnamon, while *lomitensis* is of the chocolate order of browns, fading into grayish brown during the breeding season. There is also more white on *lomitensis* than on *ludovicianus;* the barring of the tail is also different. In *ludovicianus* the bars of black are wonderfully regular, extending across both webs in a continuous line, while in *lomitensis* the bars of black are joined by a shading of white or creamy and are broken and irregular, thus giving the general mottled appearance and lighter color. The flanks, too, in all old birds of *lomitensis* show a decided tendency to barring, while in *ludovicianus* this is wanting. * * *

This new race seems to be resident in that part of the Rio Grande Valley lying adjacent to the river where the forest is heaviest, for none of the forms of this genus has been taken either above or below this timber tract. Hidalgo, where I first obtained the birds, and Lomita Ranch, where I secured the greatest number, are situated only eight miles apart on the Texas side of the river. In this locality the heavy timber is near the river, and north of it the chaparral extends for a distance of about fifteen miles; next, still northward, lies a desert of sand reaching more than fifty miles until it meets the strong vegetable growth of the valley of the Nueces River.

Mr. Sennett (1878) had collected a number of these wrens in the above locality some dozen years earlier, which he recorded under the name *berlandieri;* these specimens were puzzling for a while, until enough of the Mexican race could be obtained for comparison; so it was not until 1890 that this isolated race could be satisfactorily described and named. He says that "this bird breeds near the ground, seldom higher than 5 feet, in hollow trees, stubs, and even dead limbs lying on the ground." He could not discover that it differed in any of its habits from typical Carolina wrens elsewhere. He collected a number of eggs, which were evidently similar to those of the northern bird.

Eggs.—The eggs of this wren are indistinguishable from those of other races of the species. The measurements of 40 eggs average 19.2 by 14.6 millimeters; the eggs showing the four extremes measure **21.5** by 14.6, 20.5 by **16.2, 16.8** by 14.5, and 17.4 by **13.0** millimeters.

HELEODYTES BRUNNEICAPILLUS COUESI (Sharpe)

NORTHERN CACTUS WREN

PLATES 39–42

HABITS

CONTRIBUTED BY ROBERT S. WOODS

Best known through the abundance of its conspicuous flask-shaped nests, the cactus wren well repays a close acquaintance with its own interesting and unique personality. It is a bird that cannot easily be confused with any other North American species, either in appearance or habits.

The northern cactus wren is widely distributed through the Lower Sonoran Zone along the Mexican border from Texas to the Pacific and as far north as southern Utah and Nevada, but it is actually found only in those comparatively limited regions where thorny shrubs and trees or the more aborescent species of cactus offer nesting sites at least 2 or 3 feet above ground and capable of supporting its bulky structures. Vegetation of this type is frequently encountered on sunny hillsides, on the mesas adjacent to mountain ranges, and along gravelly watercourses. Though primarily a species of the lower country, Mrs. Florence Merriam Bailey (1928) cites records of the cactus wren's occurrence at altitudes of approximately 6,000 feet in New Mexico. W. E. D. Scott (1888a) states, however, that in southern Arizona it is "seldom found above 4,000 feet on the foothills of the several mountain chains traversing the Territory."

On the Pacific slope of southern California, suitable habitats are much less plentiful than in the more arid regions to the eastward and are steadily being reduced by cultivation and subdivision or by mere growth of population with its attendant increase in vandalism. Unlike many desert birds, the cactus wren accepts the encroachments of civilization rather graciously, and occasionally it builds its nest about houses or barns; but it is doubtful whether it would long remain in any locality after the entire removal of the native vegetation. It is easy to overestimate the abundance of these birds, not only on account of the plurality of nests built by each family but also because their vociferousness usually insures one's consciousness of their presence whenever they are near.

The geographical subdivision of this species has been attended by considerable confusion and revision, probably because of wide individual variations, and the number of races ascribed to the United States has fluctuated from one to three and back again. Dr. Edgar A. Mearns (1902b) described the subspecies *couesi* from Texas, *anthonyi* from the interior deserts, and *bryanti* from the Pacific slope, the second being distinguished from the others by generally lighter coloration, and the last by broader white stripes on the back and more white on the tail. In all these, according to Mearns, the throat is mainly black, this feature separating them from *affinis* of southern Baja California. However, a great degree of variation seems to exist in the pattern of the black throat markings; these are variously described and illustrated as spots, streaks, and occasionally as coalescent spots, but these differences have not figured as diagnostic characters. In all the adult individuals known to the present writer in Los Angeles County, Calif., the black spots of the throat have coalesced to form a conspicuous throat patch, the upper part of which usually is almost if not quite solidly black and is outlined sharply against the plain white chin. The black area extends slightly higher along the sides of the upper throat and gradually breaks up into streaks or chains of spots on the chest and the sides of the throat. In connection with this tendency in coloration, possibly there may be some significance in the apparent differences in nest-building and singing habits hereinafter noted.

Nesting.—The list of nesting sites utilized by cactus wrens is a long one. Following a study of a large number of nests near the base of the Santa Rita Mountains south of Tucson, Ariz., Mrs. Bailey (1922) wrote:

While the name Cactus Wren was justified in this locality as in others by the innumerable nests found in cholla cactus, here thorny trees and bushes especially catsclaw zizyphus (*Z. lycioides*) or lote bush, were also used extensively, while mesquite and the dense shrubby hackberry or grenjeño were used occasionally for nesting sites. It was interesting to note that zizyphus bushes containing nests generally stood under mesquite trees, so getting double protection. The protection afforded by the armament of thorns was often so complete that it was impossible to reach a nest without cutting away the obstructing branches. Even that, however, did not always satisfy the nest makers, for such bulky, conspicuous nests need to be safeguarded in every way from hawks, owls, and other enemies. Thirty-five out of sixty-four nests examined were not only protected by the entangling thorns of the surrounding branches but were built within clusters of the red-flowered mistletoe (*Phoradendron californicum*) which in many cases partially or wholly concealed them. One nest lay on a level branch covered by an unsual horizontal growth of mistletoe and showed only as a darkened mass inside, but most of them were in round ball-like masses of mistletoe, commonly at the ends of branches in terminal mistletoe rosettes, frequently so dense that it was impossible to obtain nest statistics or photographs. One of the nests without mistletoe protection was built under an umbrella-like mass of foliage.

* * * When not built inside a mass of mistletoe the nest was variously supported—by a crotch, by a horizontal branch and the trunk of the tree, or by an angle of branches.

A summary of the nests examined was appended, showing that 31 were in cholla cactus, at heights of 2½ to 6 feet from the ground, while of the 64 others, "38 were in catsclaw (29 in red mistletoe), 17 in zizyphus, 5 in mesquite (in red mistletoe), 4 in shrubby hackberry; and altogether 34 in red mistletoe. The approximate height from the ground varied from 4 to 9 feet. * * * While some of the cholla nests examined were substantial and well protected, most of them were decidedly inferior to the nests found in other bushes and trees. Being lower and more exposed to wind and storm, especially in the case of those on top of the lowest chollas, they had apparently been blown to pieces, presenting a most dilapidated appearance."

In New Mexico, says Mrs. Bailey (1928), "the bayonet-pointed heads of the tree yucca (*Yucca radiosa*) are often chosen. * * * Two nests seen were safely placed between the spears of adjoining yucca heads." F. C. Willard (1923) mentions some unusual sites in Arizona: "One pair built for several years in the hollow cornice of a schoolhouse. The entrance was through a hole cut one winter by a visiting flicker. Another site was in an old woodpecker's nesting cavity which was twenty-five feet up in a large sycamore, one of a line of these trees extending out from the foothills of the Huachuca Mountains. A broken-out cavity in a sahuaro cactus is also rather out of the ordinary for a Cactus Wren to choose as a nesting site."

In coastal southern California, the choice of acceptable nesting sites is more restricted. On the gravelly river washes, such as that of the San Gabriel River, *Opuntia parryi*, the only "cholla" (*Cylindropuntia*) present, is rather small in stature, so that only the largest specimens offer suitable situations. Most of the pricklypears (*Platyopuntia*) are procumbent in habit, but a large-jointed form (*O. occidentalis*) furnishes a few nesting sites of the required minimum height of 2 or 2½ feet. Large clumps of this latter species also occur on some of the south-fronting hillsides. Thorny trees and shrubs are absent, but nests are occasionally built in large bushes such as *Rhus laurina* and *R. ovata*, or even in orange trees in a grove, at heights of around 8 feet. One nest was placed on a four-by-four lookout under the gable of a barn roof, another between palm leaves on the roof on a pergola, and W. Leon Dawson (1923) mentions that "Mr. Frank S.

Daggett found a nest in an apricot tree, and another one, still more remarkable, on the cross arm of a power-line pole, near Azusa, at a height of 30 feet."

It would appear that cactus wrens appreciate the protection afforded by the proximity of dwellings; at any rate, they readily avail themselves of dooryard specimen cacti as nesting sites. In addition to the use of "chollas" in the writer's yard at Azusa, they have maintained a nest almost continuously for several years between the vertical columns of a good-sized *Cereus*, building a new one from time to time upon the collapsed ruins of the old.

The nest of the cactus wren is more than a mere receptacle for holding eggs and young. It serves as an actual home for the bird throughout the year, a protection against cold, rain, and enemies at night and perhaps against storms at any time. It is kept in repair and rebuilt when necessary, and each young bird, upon reaching maturity, prepares its own domicile against the coming winter. This use, of course, calls for a larger and more elaborate structure than most birds' nests. Mrs. Bailey (1922) thus describes the nests observed in Arizona:

In form, the Cactus Wren's nest suggests a retort, having a large globular chamber about 6 inches in diameter approached through a long passageway or entrance, the whole normally about 12 inches in length, the mouth of the entrance being about 3 inches above the base of the globular chamber. This nest chamber in course of years becomes a thick felted mass of gray, weathered plant fibers so hard that saucer-like sections sometimes crack off from the back showing the solid, sodden bottom of the nest. The entrance, on the contrary, is made of long straw-like plant stems which may easily get blown about and so often need replenishing.

When the old nests are repaired and ready for winter use these new straw-colored entrances often afford a striking contrast to the old gray globes, although occasionally the new material is lavishly distributed over the whole top of the nest. One nest, found on March 21, looked new, only straw-colored material showing from the few possible points of observation; but it might easily have had merely a coating of fresh material. A mass of fuzzy plant material was outside the mouth. An old gray nest fragment which might have supplied foundation material was behind the nest. Besides replenishing the straw entrance, the wrens re-line for cold weather. In one instance fur, and in many instances the small gray body-feathers of the Gambel Quail, and sometimes well-marked feathers of other species of birds, were seen in the entrances and about the mouths. One nest used for roosting purposes during the winter, when examined for eggs on April 30, had its globular chamber so thickly lined with soft feathers that it suggested a feather bed.

Considerable variation and adaptability were shown in the construction of the nests examined. Sometimes in the process of repair the angle of the entrance was changed. In one case, while the old nest faced east, the new entrance faced south by east, almost at right angles, presumably for better support for the mouth and larger twigs for perches at the mouth.

Mrs. Bailey also found that while the entrances of the nests faced in all directions, the greatest number were toward the southwest. In the San Gabriel Valley I have been unable to detect any preference in this regard. In the *Cereus* previously referred to, the successive nests have faced in various directions; and in repairing an old nest a new entrance is sometimes made in the opposite end.

It is evident that the nests of these two regions differ markedly in the type of materials used. The Los Angeles County nests are built entirely of herbaceous stems and grasses, some of them green in the early part of the year. Because of the impermanence of this material, and possibly also the greater humidity, a nest will be in a state of collapse and disintegration by the end of one year. This is no fault of the workmanship, for a recently constructed nest was found to remain quite dry inside after a 2-inch rain. New nests are invariably built in spring or summer for the raising of the broad, the old ones serving as roosts. The greatest nest-building activity occurs in September and October, as the nests that have gone through the previous winter's rains must be replaced, and even some of those built for the current year's broods are likely to be no longer habitable.

Apparently the first to discover the winter use of the nests was A. W. Anthony (1891), who thus describes his observations in southwestern New Mexico:

As these nests were usually seen in groups of from four or five to a dozen, frequently six or seven being seen in one mesquite bush, the first impression obtained was that the birds nested in colonies. As the season advanced, however, and the collections of nests were found to be used by but a single or at most two pairs of birds, a question of what the rest of the nests were for, frequently presented itself. It was very evident from even a casual examination that nearly or all the nests had been built at about the same time, and from their uniform fresh and unbroken appearance I concluded that they could not have been subjected to the driving storms that sweep that country from October until April.

It was not until the winter of 1889, however, that a possible explanation presented itself. On October 24 of that year, while hunting antelope near the Mexican boundary, I availed myself of the protection of a small thicket of mesquite scrub to observe the movements of a herd of game on the plain beyond. I had scarcely concealed myself when I saw flying toward me a cactus wren, with its mouth full of dry grass. Alighting in a bush near by it immediately entered a nest within 30 feet of me, and after a moment reappeared without the grass and started for another load. An examination showed that the grass had been used as a lining and to further thicken the walls. The long horizontal tunnel-like opening also gave evidence of having been lengthened. Five or six other nests within a radius of 50 feet all showed equal evidence of having been refitted and strengthened. Here at last was a possible clew to the many empty nests seen during the summer, and, hoping to gather further information, the locality was frequently visited until December 16. The work of rebuilding the old nests continued during pleasant weather until about the first of December. By this time all of the nests of the vicinity were so thoroughly repaired that they had every appearance of new nests. At no time was there more than one bird to be seen. I think, however, that a pair were interested in the improvements, as the notes of a second wren were heard at no great distance. During storms or cold windy weather I frequently found cactus wrens in the very near vicinity of these and other nests, and while I never succeeded in catching them in the nests I am confident that they were made use of at such times as shelters from the storm and probably also as roosting places. It would also appear that several of the nests were repaired and used during the winter by the same pair of wrens.

Upon coming to the Pacific Coast I was immediately impressed with the difference in the nesting habits of the species as seen in Southern and Lower California, and in the higher regions of New Mexico and Arizona. I am unfortunately without a series of measurements of the nests of the two regions, but am safe in saying that the bird of the coast region builds a smaller nest, especially noticeable in its much shorter covered opening, which in fine specimens from the interior (New Mexico and Arizona) frequently measures from twelve to fourteen inches in length and is supported by being built along a horizontal branch of *cholla* cactus or thorny bush. California nests are seldom or never, as far as my experience goes, found in colonies. Two or more nests are sometimes seen in the same thicket of cactus, but in such case each nest is used by a pair of birds, there being no supplementary nests to be used as lodging-houses, as would appear to be the case in the interior, nor have I any evidence of the nests in mild coast region being rebuilt for use in winter.

The last sentence illustrates the danger that lies in the drawing of negative conclusions, even by the most competent observers. Certainly these inferences are not true in all southwestern California, and in view of the general use of nests as night roosts by other species of this genus, even in tropical latitudes, as described by Alexander F. Skutch (1940), it seems unlikely that there would be local deviations from this habit. The more scattered distribution of the California nests may be in part, at least, a matter of suitable sites.

In constructing the framework of the nest, the bottom is first laid, then the vaulted upper part is fashioned, and finally the entrance tunnel is added. It is often impossible to determine exactly which direction the entrance will face until the exterior of the nest is almost finished, as the tunnel may be either straight or rather sharply curved to one side. This tunnel, whose inner end is about even with the ceiling of the nesting cavity, may be nearly horizontal, but usually it slopes more or less steeply down into the interior of the nest. In the many-branched "chollas" the tunnels are often so cleverly placed that the branches form an encircling support and a convenient doorstep. The building proceeds rapidly and would be completed in a short time were it not that the work is conducted rather spasmodically, with long intervals of apparent neglect. The lining of the nest is a more tedious process and doubtless entails extended search for suitable materials, of which feathers seem to be most favored, though kapok or cotton will be used if found. Many abortive attempts at nest-building are made, the nests being abandoned at various stages of construction when the birds apparently decide to choose another location.

Despite the accessibility of most cactus wrens' nests, a study of their family affairs is not easy. The contents of the nest are seldom visible through the entrance tunnel, which is directed toward the upper part of the nesting cavity and is often curved or bent at a right angle, while the walls are so thick and the material so tightly matted together that it would be difficult to make an opening into the nesting chamber without considerable damage to the nest. The cavity is also usually more or less filled with loose feathers. Curiosity as to the contents of cactus wrens' nests should be tempered by due caution, as I have been informed that one such investigation unfortunately resulted in the loss of an intruder's eye as the startled bird darted suddenly through its only means of exit.

In spring, nesting usually begins in March or April, according to the season. If the first brood is fledged successfully, in California a new nest is built and a second brood brought off in June or thereabouts. According to Mr. Scott (1888a), in Pinal and adjacent counties of southern Arizona, the cactus wrens raise "at least two and sometimes three broods. * * * The first eggs are laid in the Catalina region as early as March 20, and the broods vary from three to five in number."

Eggs.—[AUTHOR'S NOTE: The usual set for the northern cactus wren consists of four or five eggs, most commonly four; but as few as three may constitute a full set, and as many as six or even seven have been found in a nest. The eggs are mostly ovate in shape, some being slightly elongated or shortened. They are somewhat glossy. The ground color varies from "salmon color" or "salmon-buff" to "seashell pink," pinkish white, or rarely to nearly pure white. Usually the egg is more or less evenly covered with fine dots or very small spots of reddish browns, "rufous" to "ferruginous," sometimes nearly concealing the ground color; sometimes the markings are concentrated in a ring about the larger end. Rarely an egg seems nearly immaculate, and still more rarely an egg with a white ground is quite heavily spotted or blotched with the above browns. The measurements of 50 eggs in the United States National Museum average 23.6 by 17.0 millimeters, the eggs showing the four extremes measure 26.4 by 15.2, 24.9 by 19.1, and 19.8 by 13.2 millimeters.]

Young.—Because of the difficulty of discovering exactly what transpires in the dark, feather-filled recesses of the nest, little information is available as to the exact length of the incubation and fledging periods. Both parents seem to share the nesting duties equally, bringing insects and worms of various kinds to the young at frequent intervals. Mrs. N. Edward Ayer (1937) gives the following interesting account of the activities and difficulties of a family of cactus wrens which occupied a nest in a rather unusual situation at Pomona, Calif.:

Toward the end of April 1937, a pair of Cactus Wrens built and occupied a nest on a ledge under the corner of our tiled roof. On May 9th, a broken egg shell, creamy pink spotted with cinnamon, was found beneath the nest. For the next 3 weeks the parents were kept busy feeding four hungry mouths, bread crumbs from a nearby feeding station forming an important part of their diet. On the morning of May 29th, when we came down to breakfast, a loud chattering was heard, and we saw both parents and the four young on a nearby sycamore. One baby was caught and banded, but unfortunately 2 days later, we found it dead * * *.

Every night between 6:30 and 7, the parents led the young back to their nest for the night, and the entire proceeding, accompanied by much scolding and fussing, was a most ludicrous and lengthy performance. Not until June 11th, however, did we discover the real difficulty, which lay in the 4-inch overhang of the tile. In order to enter the nest, unless the bird could fly straight in, which the babies evidently could not—it must be reached from the roof tile which formed a hood over the nest, and this necessitated a kind of flying sortie with a quick right-about-face, which the youngsters could not easily accomplish. On June 11th, then, we saw the little family start to retire. They were at the opposite end of the house from their nest when first observed. After a prolonged inspection of a nest over the garage which the parents had built, prior to the one eventually occupied, the family started for home, hopping in stately procession across the tiled roof, single file and very sedately. Then after encouraging clucks from the parents, baby number one negotiated the difficult jump to the nest. Not so the second baby—he essayed it three times, missing the hole each time, and being obliged to cling to the house, woodpecker fashion. The fourth time, he caught a long piece of string which dangled from the nest and swung back and forth until one of his parents flew under him, and he crawled to safety over her body, just as the first baby, weary of his lonesome sojourn in the nest, flew out in the world again! And so it went on, ad infinitum.

We had several times previously seen the parent bird clinging to the side of the ledge and the babies crawling in over her, but did not realize the significance of this act until this night. The string, too, had given us much concern lest the babies become entangled in it, but now we wondered if it could have been designedly placed there—like a rope ladder.

Plumages.—[AUTHOR'S NOTE: The young cactus wren in juvenal plumage is similar to the adult, but the crown is of a duller, darker brown, the light markings of the upper parts are pale brownish buff or rusty white, instead of white, those on the wings being pinkish buff, and the black spots on the throat and chest are smaller and fainter, the throat sometimes almost immaculate; all the markings are less sharply defined.

The postjuvenal molt, which in some individuals is not finished until September, apparently involves everything but the wings. This produces a first winter plumage that is practically adult, with the light streaks on the back whiter and broader, and the flanks and posterior under parts bright "cinnamon" or "ochraceous-buff," instead of rusty white.

Adults have a complete postnuptial molt in August and September.]

When the young cactus wren emerges from the nest, its coloration is similar, though somewhat less sharply defined, to that of the adult except for the absence of the black markings on the throat, which is plain whitish or lightly flecked with darker. The full adult plumage is attained rather suddenly in the early fall, about September.

It has been conjectured by some that the varying amounts of black on the throats of individual cactus wrens might be related to the age of the birds. This, however, is not true, as the throat patches assumed by the birds in their first autumn are likely to show nearly the maximum degree of blackness; whereas in individuals having more than the usual amount of white on the throat, this character persists from year to year.

Food.—Prof. F. E. L. Beal (1907) has reported on the contents of 41 stomachs of cactus wrens "taken in the region from Los Angeles to San Bernardino, and from July to January, inclusive. They contained about 83 percent of animal matter to 17 of vegetable." Beetles and Hymenoptera ("the latter ants and wasps") each made up about 27 percent of the total, 10 percent of the former being weevils. Grasshoppers constituted 15 percent, Lepidoptera 5 percent, and bugs (Hemiptera) 5 percent, including black scale (*Saissetia*) in six stomachs. The percentage of spiders was lower than in other wrens. "A few of the long bones of a tree frog were found in 1 stomach."

The proportion of vegetable food was found to be larger than in other wrens: 13 percent was made up of fruit pulp, which in all cases where identification was possible consisted of wild species, including cactus (*Opuntia*), elderberry (*Sambucus*), and cascara (*Rhamnus*). The 4 percent of seeds consisted of *Rhus*, filaree (*Erodium*), and *Amsinckia*. Summarizing the cactus wren's diet, Prof. Beal says that "it contains but little that is useful to man, while the great bulk is made up of elements that are, or would be, harmful if present on cultivated lands."

Supplementing the mention of tree-frog bones, Dr. Tracy I. Storer (1920) reports taking a cactus wren near Mojave, Calif., that had swallowed a lizard about 2 inches in length. Aside from the edible kinds of cactus fruit, all cultivated fruits seem to be ignored. The birds do, however, greatly enjoy young sweet corn if the husks are stripped down to give them access to the grains. One will also occasionally visit a feeding-table for bread crumbs, but these are not attractive enough to them to establish a regular habit where insects are plentiful. The animal portion of the food appears to be obtained predominantly from the ground, among fallen leaves and other debris.

Behavior.—Mr. Dawson (1923) says that the cactus wren "is the most wary and secretive of the Troglodytine race." However, those that nest near human habitations soon forget their shyness and allow as close an approach as most of our dooryard birds. On one occasion I found that a pair living some distance away from any evidences of civilization refused to return to their nest and feed their young while a camera remained near; but those that nest near buildings show no such fear and will even make the camera or its tripod a way-station on their trips to and from the nest.

The demeanor of the cactus wren is that of a creature which finds ample interest and enjoyment in life; especially is this true of the immature individuals. The birds of the summer brood remain together for several weeks after leaving the nest, and in little troops of three or four they come fearlessly about houses and perform all manner of clownish antics and acrobatics, all to the accompaniment of a rollicking chatter. I have seen one start from the seat of a wicker chair, run nimbly up the back and over the top, and hang head downward on the other side; often they race back and forth along the ridge of a building with exultant squawks, perhaps clinging to the edge of the roof and twisting their necks to peer underneath. Their curiosity is insatiable; everything must be climbed over, all packages, receptacles, cracks, and crannies looked into and anything inside pulled out if possible. Though the adults lose some of the frivolity, the attitude of good humor seems to remain, and quarrels are few. The only actual battle I recall seeing resulted when one immature bird attempted to bring material to a nest being built by another.

Both the cactus wren's food and its hunting grounds are much the same as those of the thrashers, but its manner of foraging is strikingly different from the strenuous methods of the latter. The cactus wren approaches a leaf or other movable object, inserts its bill carefully under one side, and raises it up, meanwhile peering beneath in readiness to seize any small creature thus revealed. The bird runs rather swiftly but usually flies if going any considerable distance. Its flights are ordinarily comparatively short, direct, and close to the ground.

Writing of the winter birds of Palm Springs, on the western edge of the Colorado Desert, where the cacti, though abundant, are not of large stature, Dr. Grinnell (1904) includes the following note on the cactus wren: "Fairly common out on the desert; and also, as surprised me when I first found them, in Palm Canyon. In the latter locality they made themselves at home among the drooping dead leaves beneath the green heads of the lofty palms. The birds could be plainly heard rattling about inside, but were difficult to drive out. Doubtless such palm-leaf bowers afforded insect food in plenty, as well as a well-protected retreat."

Alexander F. Skutch (1935, 1940) has reported the communal roosting of the banded cactus wren (*Heleodytes zonatus*) and the hooded cactus wren (*H. capistratus*) in Central America, as many as 11 of the former having been found sleeping together in one nest. This habit does not appear to be shared by our northern species, except when the members of a recently fledged brood return at night to the nest in which they were hatched. That one or both of the parents sometimes keep them company might be inferred from the previously quoted account by Mrs. Ayer, though the quarters must be somewhat cramped.

However, the young birds lose little time in starting to build individual roosting places of their own, if the available supply is insufficient. A few resort to makeshift devices, one of them attempting, with rather indifferent success, to use as a foundation an abandoned nest of the hooded oriole among the leaves of a dracaena tree. Another, also believed to be immature, was reported by A. H. Anderson (1934b) at Tucson, Ariz., to have appropriated a verdin's nest, notwithstanding its inadequate size. Some of these roosting nests, presumably built by young birds, have little if any entrance tunnel, the entire interior being clearly visible. Aside from the recently fledged broods, I have never flushed more than one bird from a nest; on the other hand, in coastal California, where the nests deteriorate rapidly, nearly every habitable nest will contain an occupant after sunset, as indicated by the tip of a tail projecting out into the entrance tunnel.

Occasionally a cactus wren will drink from a birdbath, but in general they seem to have little need or desire for water, other than the moisture contained in the insects and cactus fruit of their ordinary diet. Rarely, one of the wrens attempts a bath, but after many timid approaches it usually succeeds only in wetting the feathers of the breast. I have never seen them roll in the dust, after the manner of some of the smaller wrens.

Voice.—The voice of the cactus wren has rather a deep, throaty quality, sometimes becoming almost a croak. The bird uses a great diversity of notes, some of them grating or ratchetlike, varied with jay-like squawks and occasional cries suggesting the plaintive demands of young birds. While foraging, a softer clucking or croaking note may be given at intervals, though the birds are often silent for long periods while so engaged.

Many of the ornithological handbooks refer to the cactus wren's enthusiasm as a songster. Mrs. Irene G. Wheelock (1904), for example, says: "He sings constantly as well as sweetly." Others speak of the typical wrenlike quality of the song. Since this is decidedly at variance with the present writer's observations in southern California, there must be differences in the singing habits of the species in various parts of its range. In Los Angeles County the cactus wren's song is not often heard, and, while it may somewhat resemble in form the songs of the smaller wrens, it can hardly be characterized as melodious. In this locality a much more frequent expression, which perhaps also partakes of the nature of a song, is the rapid repetition of a single staccato note. The quality of this note varies, but never in the same series. This type of call is usually delivered from the top of a tree, a building, or a pole, sometimes antiphonally by a pair of birds on the tops of different bushes. The most tuneful utterance that I have ever heard from these cactus wrens was a warbling song given by an immature bird, a song so soft that it could have been heard only within a distance of a few feet.

Noisy and unmusical though the California representative of the species may be, its cries are never shrill or mournful but convey a suggestion of rollicking good humor, rather pleasing than otherwise.

Field marks.—The cactus wren is easily distinguished from any other North American wren by its much greater size, as well as by the fact that it never carries its tail in the tilted position so familiar in the smaller species. The only bird with which it might be confused, by reason of size, general appearance, and arid habitat, is the sage thrasher, from which it differs, among other respects, in its longer bill and white-streaked back. When flushed, its most conspicuous feature is the white-banded tail, which is widely extended in flight.

Enemies.—In thickly populated districts the chief hazard to the cactus wren undoubtedly lies in the fact that its conspicuous, conveniently located nests offer an irresistible challenge to vandals. This is but one of the many instances in which defenses that cope successfully with natural enemies prove but traps and delusions when the human element enters. Fortunately, the greater part of the cactus wren's domain presents little allurement to colonists, so the species may well prosper for many years to come.

In other respects, the cactus wren's nesting habits must be of great advantage. In cholla cacti the viciously sharp, barbed spines, to which the birds themselves seem utterly oblivious, must very effectually bar the way to climbing predators, while the covering of the nest shields it contents from flying enemies, as well as providing shelter from the elements. In leafy bushes or trees, the nests are placed at the ends of the branches in the outer foliage, thus again making them almost inaccessible to climbers. These precautions, of course, will not avail against the California jay, and the complete disappearance of two sets of eggs in my own yard, without damage to the nests, could be ascribed only to that culprit.

Winter.—Though not truly migratory, cactus wrens may shift about somewhat when not engaged in nesting duties. In writing of this species in southern Arizona and southwestern New Mexico, H. W. Henshaw (1875) reported that "in the fall, the thickets bordering the streams are frequently resorted to by them." Perhaps such moves into denser cover have contributed to the general impression that the wrens are less common in winter. They also seem less vociferous at this time of year and hence more likely to be overlooked. Near Los Angeles, the birds are often absent from their breeding grounds in winter for days or weeks at a time, but they reappear often enough to show that they have performed no actual migration.

The paired birds seem to remain together through winter, and, aside from pursuits, no courtship demonstrations have been noted.

Range.—Southwestern United States to central Mexico; nonmigratory.

The cactus wren is found **north** to southern California (Kernville and Coso); southern Nevada (Vegas Valley and Sheep Mountains); southwestern Utah (Beaverdam Mountains and Toquerville); southern New Mexico (Carlisle, Silver City, and the mountains near Engle); and southern Texas (San Angelo, San Antonio, and Runge). **East** to central Texas (Runge and Brownsville); Tamaulipas (Jaumave); and Yucatán (Progreso and Río Lagartos). **South** to Yucatán (Progreso and Río Lagartos); Mexico (Valley of Mexico); Jalisco (Guadalajara); and Baja California (San José del Cabo). **West** to Baja California (San José del Cabo, San Quintín, and San Telmo); and southern California (Santa Paula, Tejon Pass, and Kernville).

The above outline is for the species as a whole, which has been divided into four subspecies or geographic races within our limits; other races occur in Mexico. The northern cactus wren (*H. b. couesi*) occupies the entire range within the United States and the northern part of the northern States of Mexico; Bryant's cactus wren (*H. b. bryanti*) is found on the west coast of Baja California from San Telmo south to Santa Catarina Landing; the San Ignacio cactus wren (*H. b. purus*) is found in central Baja California from about latitude 29° to latitude 25°; the San Lucas cactus wren (*H. b. affinis*) is found in southern Baja California.

Egg dates.—Arizona: 82 records, March 10 to August 6; 40 records, April 21 to May 25, indicating the height of the season.

California: 160 records, March 2 to July 5; 85 records, March 20 to April 22.

Lower California: 48 records, March 17 to August 18; 27 records, April 14 to May 15.

Texas: 25 records, March 12 to July 15; 14 records, April 8 to May 14.

HELEODYTES BRUNNEICAPILLUS BRYANTI Anthony

BRYANT'S CACTUS WREN

HABITS

As mentioned under the northern race, *H. b. couesi*, there has been some confusion in the past as to the recognizable races of this species. In his study of the cactus wrens of the United States Dr. Edgar A. Mearns (1902b) proposed the recognition of three subspecies within our borders and designated the range of this race, *bryanti*, as includ-

ing southern California west of the Coast Range.   Harry S. Swarth
(1904a) disagreed with this view and published the results of his
study, which indicate that only one subspecies, *H. b. couesi*, is found
north of the Mexican boundary, which seems to be the generally
accepted view today.

In naming this race, Mr. Anthony (1894) gives its subspecific
characters as "differing from *affinis* in very much heavier spotting of
lower parts, the black predominating, in extreme specimens, on the
throat and upper breast, and in its perfectly barred tail and slight
wash of rufous on belly and flanks; from *brunneicapillus* by heavier
spotting, especially on sides and belly, in having intermediate rectrices more or less perfectly barred, and in much less rusty wash on
lower parts."

The above description as to the barring of the tail seems to be a bit
confusing, for Mr. Anthony says that "as a rule *bryanti* exhibits a
fully barred tail as in *affinis*."   For a more detailed study of the subject, which seems beyond the scope of this Bulletin, the reader is
referred to the three papers mentioned above, as well as Ridgway's
(1904) treatment of the group.

So far as I can learn, the habits of Bryant's cactus wren do not differ
materially from those of the species elsewhere.   Mr. Anthony (1895b)
has this to say about this subspecies as observed near San Fernando,
Baja California:

Not uncommon throughout the region but everywhere noticeable for its extreme shyness.   The normal note of the Cactus Wren is quite harsh and unmusical, consisting of a series of notes rapidly uttered in a monotone, but at the
mine I once heard one give voice to a song exactly intermediate between the
normal, discordant notes of this species and the incomparable song of the Cañon
Wren.   The full, rich cadence and clear tones of *Catherpes* was very pronounced
but not more so than the characteristic *gou-gou-gou* and deeper tones of *Heleodytes*.   I was not near enough to secure the bird and before I could get within
range it flew further up the mountain where it several times repeated the song
that first attracted me.

There are two sets of three eggs each in the Thayer collection
in Cambridge.   Any of these eggs could be matched by different types
of eggs of the northern cactus wren.   In one set the eggs have a pale
pinkish ground-color and are marked with faint dots.   In the other
set the ground-color is white and the eggs are marked with distinct,
rather large spots and small blotches of pale reddish brown or
"cinnamon."

Mr. Bancroft (1930) says that the measurements of a series of 70
eggs average 24.9 by 17.1 millimeters.   Among the six eggs in Cambridge, the eggs showing the four extremes measure 27.2 by 16.7, 24.4
by 17.3, and 23.7 by 17.0 millimeters.

HELEODYTES BRUNNEICAPILLUS AFFINIS (Xantus)

SAN LUCAS CACTUS WREN

HABITS

Although this wren was originally described from the Cape region of Baja California, its range is now extended northward over more than half of the peninsula, to about latitude 29°; it apparently intergrades with *bryanti* somewhere south of San Fernando.

Ridgway (1904) gives the best description of it as follows: "Most like *H. b. bryanti* but much paler, with under parts less heavily and more sparsely marked with black; color of pileum and hindneck more reddish brown (mummy brown to chestnut-brown), the feathers often with paler terminal small spots or streaks; all the rectrices, except middle pair, with distinct white bars on both webs; under parts more purely white (distinctly tinged with buff posteriorly only in fresh autumnal plumage), the black markings on lower parts of body broadly guttate, those on throat and chest but little larger (never large and confluent as is often the case in other subspecies), but of different (irregular and variable) form."

William Brewster (1902) says of its haunts: "In the Cape Region proper the St. Lucas Cactus Wren is everywhere a common resident excepting on the higher mountains, where it appears to be wholly wanting. Its favorite haunts are the arid, cactus-grown plains near the coast and the almost equally barren and waterless foot-hills, but at San José del Cabo Mr. Frazar found it abundant in gardens and among shrubbery near or even directly over water."

Griffing Bancroft (1930) says of its distribution in the central portion of the peninsula: "These wrens, while common, are not nearly so abundant as experience elsewhere would lead one to expect. It is not easy to define their range because, in exceptional cases, they breed among the palms of the oases as well as on the lava mesas. But in general they limit themselves to areas of intermediate fertility, shunning alike heavy undergrowth and associations of scant vegetation. That leaves them the less rocky valley floors and most of the stream beds as well as the narrowing cañons and the lateral branches running into the hills. The birds are appreciably more plentiful at the higher altitudes."

Nesting.—The same observer says of the nesting habits:

In their choice of nesting sites the Cactus Wrens indulge in a wide range of individual preference. The most popular selection is the upper part of a cholla or the center of a palo verde, but nests are not at all unusual in any low cactus, in mesquite or other trees, in heavy mistletoe, in the crotches of sahuaros, or within woodpecker holes. A formidable list could be made of unusual locations. There is, with the exception of the lining, a marked uniformity in the construction of the nests. Long fine grass stems are used as the basic material. These are woven into gourd shaped structures fifteen to eighteen inches long with the nesting cavity inside. Entrance is effected through a five-inch tunnel. The lining is almost always profuse and is usually of the feathers of some larger bird. Sometimes it is of plant down and in one nest nothing was used but native cotton.

There are three nests and nine eggs of this wren in the Thayer collection in Cambridge, all collected in the Cape region, on May 1, August 3, and August 18. The nests are substantially built as described above, but one is made externally of dry grasses, dry leaves, fine twigs, rootlets, and lichens; it is lined with very fine grasses. The second one is similar. The third is made chiefly of dry grass stems, mixed with a lot of poultry feathers and a few pieces of rags, string, and cotton; it is profusely lined with feathers and white hairs; the feathers stick out all over it; evidently the wrens had secured most of their material from some farmyard.

Eggs.—Evidently the San Lucas cactus wren seldom lays more than 3 eggs, and often fewer. The three sets referred to above consist of 3 eggs each. Mr. Bancroft (1930) states that "the number of eggs laid is 2. Of the many sets examined I found but one that contained 3 eggs. Incubated singles were unusual rather than rare. The laying season begins about April 25, in a desultory way, and is not under full head until past the middle of May." J. Stuart Rowley (1935) says that "of some 35 nests examined, none contained more than 3 eggs or young, with the majority holding two."

The eggs probably show all the variations to be seen in the eggs of other races of the species. The 9 eggs referred to above vary from ovate to elliptical-ovate and are somewhat glossy; they are mostly of the lighter types of coloration. The measurements of 40 eggs in the United States National Museum average 23.7 by 17.0 millimeters; the eggs showing the four extremes measure 25.9 by 17.8, 19.8 by 18.3, and 23.4 by 15.8 millimeters.

Plumages.—Mr. Brewster (1902) writes:

Young in juvenal plumage differ from old birds in breeding plumage only in having the crown of a darker, duller brown (almost slaty brown in some specimens) ; the light markings of the back rusty white and broader, on many of the feathers taking the form of deltoid spots; the light markings of the wings, including those of the outer primaries (but not the tail), strongly rusty; the spotting of the under parts finer and somewhat fainter.

Young (and perhaps old birds also) in autumn differ from spring adults and young in juvenal plumage in having the light streaks of the back broader and whiter; the flanks, abdomen, anal region, and crissum bright cinnamon or ochraceous buff, instead of rusty white.

HELEODYTES BRUNNEICAPILLUS PURUS van Rossem

SAN IGNACIO CACTUS WREN

In describing this subspecies, Mr. van Rossem (1930) says that it "differs from all of the known races of *Heleodytes brunneicapillus* in possessing, when in relatively unworn plumage, pure black and white underparts with only very rarely the slightest traces of brown or buffy on the flanks.   Differs from *Heleodytes brunneicapillus affinis* Xantus of the Cape region in lacking the strong buffy suffusion on the under-parts and in having decidedly grayer (less reddish) upperparts. Differs from *Heleodytes brunneicapillus bryanti* Anthony of the San Pedro Martir District in less buffy underparts, broader dorsal streak-ing and from both *affinis* and *bryanti* in slightly smaller general size and in decidedly smaller bill."

The range he gives as "Middle portion of the peninsula of Lower California, Mexico, from Dolores Bay (25°05' N.) north to Mesquital (28°30' N.) and Punta Prieta (28°56' N.).   Specimens from the two latter localities are variously mediate toward *bryanti*."

TELMATODYTES PALUSTRIS PALUSTRIS (Wilson)

LONG-BILLED MARSH WREN

PLATE 43

HABITS

The name given by Wilson for this species is now restricted to the long-billed marsh wrens inhabiting a rather limited breeding range on the Atlantic slope from Rhode Island to Virginia.   Outram Bangs (1902) has shown that the wrens from this region have the extensively white lower surface, as so clearly depicted in Wilson's plate; and he has given a new name to the wrens of the interior of New England and the Middle West.

Julian G. Griggs spent a large portion of the summer of 1937 on Jamestown Island in the James River, Va., studying the habits of this wren in some detail.   He has kindly sent me his extensive unpublished manuscript, giving the results of his observations, with the privilege of quoting from it.   On this island, "about 750 or nearly one-half of the island's 1,600 acres are marshland, which occupies much of the southern part of the island.   Five narrow, parallel ridges of wooded land extend like so many fingers into the marshy area where this study was made. A narrow, branching, brackish, tidal creek extends up into the morass. Dominants in the marsh are *Peltandra* and marsh grass.   The latter dominates creek banks and other slightly raised portions, while the former, because of its greater preference for water, occupies the lower areas of the marsh.   Here and there among the grass are groups and individuals of marsh alder, groundsel-tree, knotweed, *Kosteletzkya virginica*, rosemallow, and swamp milkweed.   Cattails and longbills are usually associated together, but this is not the case at Jamestown."

In other portions of the range of this subspecies, this long-billed marsh wren *does*, occasionally at least, nest in the narrowleaf cattails (*Typha augustifolia*), notably in coastal Connecticut and coastal Vir-ginia.   Chreswell J. Hunt (1904), however, gives a somewhat different impression of the haunts of this wren; his studies were "made along the tidewater creeks which empty into the Delaware River near Philadelphia. These creeks have high and wooded banks on one side, while on the other side for the most part lie low stretches of alder swamps, covered during the summer with a rank growth of spatter-dock, calamus, wild rice, and pickerel-weed, with here and there a clump of rose-mallow or a gorgeous cardinal flower. It is here that countless numbers of these little birds find a congenial summer home."

Aretas A. Saunders writes to me: "Here in Connecticut are many bits of cattail marsh. Some contain both broad and narrow-leaved cattail, and marsh wrens. Others contain only broad-leaved cattail and no marsh wrens. They will nest where there are rushes (*Scirpus*) or reeds (*Phragmites*)."

Nesting.—The nests studied by Mr. Griggs were mainly in the marsh-grass habitat, and within this area the wren builds its nest in various plants. "The only condition necessary is that there be a place of anchorage 15 or more inches above ground. As a consequence of this, marsh alder and groundsel trees are extensively used for nesting sites. A few nests were found in *Hibiscus*, and one in some poison ivy, which happened to grow at the right angle. In a situation where alder is common, most nests are made in its branches; likewise, where marsh grass (*Spartina*) is thick a majority of nests are built among its stems. In the locality examined a majority of wren nests were fairly close to the water, because higher ground there afforded the right habitat. In a slough just north of the island, nests were found over 150 yards from the nearest water."

The average height above ground of 21 nests measured early in June was 33 inches, one was only 15 inches, and two were 72 and 78 inches up in groundsel-trees (*Baccharis*). None of the nests in the marsh grass, even later in the season when it averaged 8 feet high, were over 5½ feet above ground; but one was recorded in a groundsel-tree that was 9 feet up. The usual number of dummy nests per female varied from two to four, rather fewer than reported for some other subspecies.

Mr. Hunt (1904) says that—

along the Pensauken Creek each patch of calamus has its pair of Wrens, and each pair build, on an average four nests. In this locality the globular nests are generally built among the calamus stalks or in the crotch of an alder or elder bush. A visit to these swamps, on May 30, 1904, showed each pair of birds to have three nests almost completed, while the foundation for a fourth was in most cases already started. They seem to work on all of them at once. I watched a Wren with a piece of building material in his bill. First he carried it to one nest and started to stick it into that, then he flew away with it to another nest and finally he inserted it into the walls of the third, every little while stopping to sing a snatch of his merry song.

Robert Ridgway (1889) says of the nests that he observed in the marshes of the Potomac River, near Washington, D. C.: "Although usually fastening the nest to upright sedge—or reed-stalks, the writer has found several that were built in small willow trees, at heights varying from 6 to 15 feet above high tide." Evidently this long-billed marsh wren often differs from other races of the species else-where, in its choice of nesting sites.

The long-billed marsh wren must be added to the long list of birds that have been known to use pieces of snakeskin in their nests, for Josiah H. Clark (1899) found a nest near Rutherford, N. J., that was "lined with a cast-off snake skin, which was about a foot long."

Eggs.—This subspecies seems to lay fewer eggs, on the average, than do some other races. Mr. Griggs found that the average for 23 clutches was 4.3. Two nests had 3 eggs, 12 had 4, and 9 had 5 eggs.

I cannot see that there is any difference in the appearance of the eggs from those of the species elsewhere. The measurements of 40 eggs average 16.0 by 12.3 millimeters; the eggs showing the four extremes measure 17.3 by 13.2, 14.2 by 11.7, and 15.2 by 11.2 milli-meters. These eggs are all in the United States National Museum.

Having included so much in the life history of the prairie marsh wren, it seems unnecessary to add much more here, as the general habits of these two races are very much alike. Mr. Hunt (1904) has this to say about the midnight song of the long-billed marsh wren: "At all hours of the night the Marsh Wren's notes may be heard ring-ing across the marsh. Drifting with the tide, in an open boat, among these swamps I have heard this night song at its best. There is a pleasant surprise in store for the bird-lover who has missed it. This night song is no doubt the same as that sung in the daylight but the night gives to it a certain charm. One must hear it mingled with the quivering call of a Screech Owl and the 'quawk, quawk' of Night Herons to fully appreciate it."

Mr. Griggs adds the following items of interest: "About two-thirds of the nests studied were destroyed between the time of the laying of the first egg and the time at which the young were ready to fly. In a very few cases the nests were damaged somewhat, or a hole was torn in the bottom, but in the great majority eggs and young disappeared without the nest being damaged. About a dozen small rodents were discovered in Jamestown Island nests. One, caught inside a dummy nest, proved to be a rice rat (*Oryzomys palustris palustris*). Mr. Crook, of Williamsburg, found fragments of eggs and an adult bird, which had been eaten by some small mammal that jumped into the water at his approach. Only a few scattered feathers, the skull, leg, and wing bones of the parent bird remained."

Only about six watersnakes and about the same number of black-snakes were seen in the marsh. "At no time was a snake seen sus-piciously close to a wren nest. One blacksnake, in a bayberry bush about 15 feet from a nest, was watched for some time. His movements were accompanied by audible rustlings, but the wren never noticed him."

Wind and rain caused considerable damage to several nests, which the wrens deserted. "Nests in *Iva* or *Baccharis* were often insecurely attached. One such hung by two strands of grass for days. Young wrens were in it at the time and, although every slight breeze caused it to swing from side to side, the parent bird seemed oblivious to the precariousness of the situation."

He says that territorial boundaries were very flexible. "I have seen males fly back and forth between dummy nests spread out over a distance of a hundred yards or more. Seldom was one wren seen chasing another. At no time was a wren noticed flying after a bird of another species."

Wayne (1910) says that, in South Carolina, "this form is an abundant autumn, winter, and late spring visitor. My earliest record is September 4, 1895, and the latest May 17, 1897. During the migrations it is most abundant in October and April, when it is commonly found on the salt marshes. In winter, however, the birds prefer the freshwater marshes on the rice plantations, and I have seen more than a hundred individuals in the course of a few hours in such situations."

DISTRIBUTION

Range.—Southern Canada to central Mexico.

Breeding range.—The long-billed marsh wren breeds **north** to southern British Columbia (Chilliwack, Lac la Hache, and Springhouse); northern Alberta (Peace River Landing and the Athabaska Delta); southern Saskatchewan (Prince Albert and Indian Head); southern Manitoba (Lake St. Martin, Winnipeg, and probably Chemawawin); southern Ontario (Lake Nipissing and Ottawa); southern Quebec (Blue Sea Lake and Montreal); and New Brunswick (probably Woodstock and Midgic). **East** to New Brunswick (probably Midgic); and south through all the Atlantic Coast States to southern Florida (Eldred). **South** to southern Florida (Eldred and Charlotte Harbor); the Gulf coast to southeastern Texas (Port Arthur and Cove); southern Illinois (Horseshoe Lake); southern Missouri (Marionville); southern Kansas (Wichita); southern Colorado (Alkali Lakes and Saguache); central Utah (Marysvale); central Nevada (Ruby Lake and Carson); southwestern Arizona (Yuma); and southern California (Calipatria and Escondido). From North Carolina to Texas the species is confined almost entirely to the coastal marshes.

Winter range.—The long-billed marsh wren occasionally winters almost as far north as it breeds. The regular winter range is discontinuous. In the west it winters **north** to southwestern British Columbia (Vancouver and the Okanagan Valley). **East** to southern British Columbia (Okanagan Valley); southeastern Washington (Walla Walla); eastern Oregon (Malheur Lake); central Utah (Bear River Marshes and St. George); southern Nevada (Searchlight); southern California (opposite Yuma); Sonora (Sonoyta); and Sinaloa (Mazatlán). **South** to Sinaloa (Mazatlán); and Baja California (Santiago and San José del Cabo). **West** to the Pacific Ocean. The eastern winter range is **north** to Texas (El Paso, Del Rio, Fort Clark, and Dallas); southern Louisiana (Cameron and Mandeville); western Florida (Pensacola); eastern Georgia (Okefenokee and Augusta); and coastal North Carolina (Swanquarter and Cape Hatteras). **East** to the Atlantic Ocean. **South** to southern Florida (Royal Palm Hammock); the Gulf coast to southern Texas (Harlingen and Brownsville); and central Mexico (Veracruz, Jalapa; Hidalgo, Miraflores; and Jalisco, Ocotlán). **West** to Jalisco (Ocotlán), Chihuahua (Chihuahua), and western Texas (El Paso).

The above range includes the entire species, which has been divided into 10 subspecies or geographic races. The long-billed marsh wren (*T. p. palustris*) breeds along the Atlantic coast from Rhode Island to Virginia; Wayne's marsh wren (*T. p. waynei*) breeds on the coast of North Carolina; Worthington's marsh wren (*T. p. griseus*) breeds from South Carolina to Florida, east coast; Marian's marsh wren (*T. p. marianae*) is found along the Gulf coast from Charlotte Harbor, Fla., to Mississippi; the Louisiana marsh wren (*T. p. thryophilus*) occurs in the coastal district of Louisiana and Texas; the Alberta marsh wren (*T. p. laingi*) breeds in Alberta and western Saskatchewan; the prairie marsh wren (*T. p. iliacus*) breeds from the Great Plains and Prairie district east to Quebec, New Brunswick, and New England; the western marsh wren (*T. p. plesius*) breeds from central British Columbia, central Washington, central Oregon, and northeastern California, east to central Colorado; the tule wren (*T. p. paludicola*) breeds in the coastal district from southwestern British Columbia to southern California; and the Suisun marsh wren (*T. p. aestuarinus*) breeds in the interior of California from Napa and Solano Counties south to Tulare County.

Spring migration.—Some late dates of spring departure are: Florida—Daytona Beach, April 30. Georgia—Athens, May 24. North Carolina—Chapel Hill, May 7. Texas—Lytle, May 12.

Early dates of spring arrival are: Georgia—Macon, March 27. North Carolina—Raleigh, April 14. District of Columbia—Washington, April 17. Pennsylvania—Harrisburg, April 26. New Jersey—Cape

May, April 28. New York—Rochester, April 27. Massachusetts—Cambridge, April 23. Vermont—Burlington, May 12. Kentucky—Bowling Green, May 5. Ohio—Sandusky, April 19. Ontario—Hamilton, April 6. Indiana—Bloomington, April 7. Michigan—Ann Arbor, April 20. Illinois—Chicago, April 25. Wisconsin—Madison, April 11. Missouri—St. Louis, April 13. Iowa—Sioux City, April 17. Minnesota—Minneapolis, April 20. Manitoba—Margaret, May 3. Kansas—Harper, April 4. Nebraska—Lincoln, April 6. South Dakota—Yankton, April 23. North Dakota—Wahpeton, April 17. New Mexico—Albuquerque, April 6. Colorado—Boulder, April 3.

Fall migration.—Some late dates of fall departures are: British Columbia—Okanagan Landing, November 18. Wyoming—Laramie, October 15. Colorado—Boulder, October 22. New Mexico—Mesilla, October 16. Manitoba—Aweme, October 16. North Dakota—Argusville, October 21. South Dakota—Sioux Falls, October 26. Nebraska—Nebraska City, November 12. Kansas—Lawrence, October 22. Minnesota—St. Vincent, October 15. Wisconsin—Milwaukee, October 23. Iowa—Keokuk, November 21. Missouri—Forsyth, October 2. Michigan—Vicksburg, November 6. Illinois—La Grange, October 17. Indiana—Indianapolis, November 9. Ontario—Toronto, October 15. Ohio—Oberlin, November 19. Kentucky—Danville, October 27. Massachusetts—Boston, November 30. New York—New York, October 20. New Jersey—Elizabeth, October 20. Pennsylvania—Jeffersonville, October 29. District of Columbia—Washington, November 16. North Carolina—Raleigh, October 19. Georgia—Athens, October 11.

Early dates of fall arrival are: North Carolina—Chapel Hill, September 20. Georgia—Athens, September 24. Florida—Fernandina, September 17. Texas—Lytle, October 10.

Casual record.—A specimen was collected at Godthaab, Greenland, in May 1823.

Egg dates.—Alberta: 28 records, May 26 to July 8; 18 records, June 16 to 20.

California: 113 records, March 24 to July 22; 63 records, May 4 to 31, indicating the height of the season.

Florida: 39 records, May 2 to August 13; 20 records, May 24 to June 11.

Illinois: 48 records, May 26 to July 27; 29 records, May 30 to June 8.

Massachusetts: 31 records, May 27 to June 28; 17 records, June 6 to 18.

New York: 60 records, May 12 to August 13; 42 records, June 4 to 24.

Virginia: 37 records, April 25 to June 30; 26 records, June 6 to 26.

Washington: 31 records, March 15 to June 27; 16 records, March 15 to April 22; 10 records, June 8 to 27.

Wisconsin: 12 records, May 26 to July 14.

TELMATODYTES PALUSTRIS GRISEUS (Brewster)

WORTHINGTON'S MARSH WREN

PLATE 44

HABITS

This is the rather small, decidedly gray race of the long-billed marsh wrens that is apparently resident in the Atlantic coast region from South Carolina to northern Florida.

In naming this race, William Brewster (1893) compares it with the northern race as follows: "Black of upper parts much duller and less extended than in *palustris*, usually confined to the extreme sides of the crown and a short narrow area in the middle of the back, and in extreme specimens almost wholly absent. Brown of sides, flanks, and upper parts pale and grayish. Dark markings of the under tail-coverts, flanks, sides, and breast faint, confused and inconspicuous, sometimes practically wanting."

The haunts and habits of Worthington's marsh wren are very similar to those of the more northern coastal race. It is confined almost entirely during the breeding season, and probably for the rest of the year, to the extensive salt marshes along the tidal creeks. Wayne (1910) says that, near Charleston, S. C., when he was a boy, these "birds fairly swarmed throughout the high marshes bordering these creeks and it was not uncommon to find from 25 to 50 nests in a few hours of careful search." In Florida, according to Arthur H. Howell (1932), "the birds live in the wettest and boggiest parts of the salt marshes, chiefly on the borders of the tidal creeks, where their nests are fastened to the growing stems of the rushes, at a height of 2 or 3 feet above the water." Ivan R. Tomkins (1932) has found it along the Savannah River to about 2 miles west of Savannah, or about 17 miles inland from the outer islands, including the river ricefields, where the water is either fresh or brackish according to the height of the river.

Nesting.—Mr. Howell says that these wrens "breed in loose colonies, often of considerable size." The nests "are constructed of dead leaves of rushes and marsh grasses woven together and lined with fine grasses and down from the cattails." What few nests of this wren I have seen are similar to nests of the species I have seen elsewhere. A nest in my collection was taken by Mr. Worthington in Nassau County, Fla.; it was 3 feet above the mud, suspended amongst the grass, near the edge of a creek in a salt marsh; it held six fresh eggs on July 6, 1906.

Eggs.—What eggs I have seen are similar to the eggs of other long-billed marsh wrens, showing the usual variations. Mr. Wayne (1910), however, says: "On several occasions, between the years 1877 and

1879, I remember distinctly having found pure white eggs of this form with a speck or two of purplish shell markings at the larger end. The eggs are, however, normally chocolate color, but sometimes of a paler shade and spotted with brownish olive. From four to six eggs are laid. * * * Three broods are certainly raised, for I have taken eggs as late as August 9."

The measurements of 40 eggs in the United States National Museum average 15.4 by 11.2 millimeters; the eggs showing the four extremes measure 16.5 by 12.2, 15.5 by 12.5, and 14.1 by 11.1 millimeters.

I can find nothing in the recorded habits of this wren that is peculiar to the race. Mr. Wayne says that—

a mouse (*Hesperomys leucopus*), which lives in the marsh and builds a nest similar to that of the wren, commonly takes possession of the nest and often eats the eggs as well as the young. * * * At the present time the birds are rare and confined to a few restricted and widely separated localities, the great cyclone of August 27 and 28, 1893, having almost exterminated them. This form is non-migratory, and I understand that it is abundant on the coast of Georgia. If the birds were migratory the places of those that were destroyed by the cyclone of 1893 would be filled by migrants from Florida and Georgia. This, however, has not been the case, showing conclusively that this form is non-migratory.

TELMATODYTES PALUSTRIS MARIANAE (Scott)

MARIAN'S MARSH WREN

HABITS

Although much of the earlier literature on the status and distribution of Marian's marsh wren is decidedly confusing, it now seems safe to conclude that it is the resident, breeding form on the west coast of Florida. The 1931 Check-list gives as its range, "Gulf coast from Charlotte Harbor, Florida, to Mississippi." The latest authority on Florida birds, Arthur H. Howell (1932) calls it "an abundant resident on the Gulf coast from St. Marks south to Old Tampa Bay. * * * Marsh Wrens are not known to breed at Pensacola, and we found no breeding colonies from that point eastward until we reached St. Marks; from there southward they are abundant in suitable marshes as far as Tarpon Springs. Pennock reported a few birds seen in Charlotte Harbor, April 11 and 13, 1921, at which time he took a specimen and observed a nearly completed nest."

The Rev. H. E. Wheeler (1931) made a survey of the breeding colonies of Marian's marsh wren on the coast of Alabama, establishing the fact that this wren breeds in all suitable coastal marshes throughout the whole Gulf coast of that State, but he evidently found no breeding records for Mississippi. He, also, made an exhaustive study of the previous literature relating to this wren on the Gulf coast and to its supposed occurrence on the Atlantic coast, which is well worth reading, as an interesting history of the confusion that has existed, and to which the reader is referred, as space will permit only a few quotations from his excellent paper.

A perusal of the literature that appeared prior to 1932 will reveal some confusing statements. Dr. Louis B. Bishop (1904) made the following surprising comment: "Originally described from the west coast of Florida and believed to be resident there and restricted to that locality, it has only recently become evident that the real home of Marian's Wren is in the salt marshes that fringe the coast of North Carolina. There it is common in spring, breeds, and occasionally remains in winter, as I took one on Pea Island—30 miles north of Hatteras—on Feb. 8, 1901, and found it tolerably common there in January, 1904." He found fresh nests there in May, and, after he left, nests with eggs were sent to him from there.

Ridgway (1904) gave the range as south Atlantic coast of United States from North Carolina to South Carolina and western Florida. And the 1910 Check-list gave it as breeding on the coast of North Carolina and wintering south to South Carolina and the west coast of Florida. Arthur T. Wayne (1910) backs up Dr. Bishop by saying that "it breeds, as far as is known, only on the North Carolina coast." He records it as a migrant in South Carolina, where he says that "they are common until the beginning of November, when the great majority migrate southward, but a few winter regularly among dense reeds which grow in profusion on some of the coast islands." Strangely enough, the 1931 Check-list does not record *any* marsh wren as breeding on the coast of North Carolina!

It has since become evident that all the Atlantic coast records of supposed Marian's marsh wrens, published prior to 1930, are referable to the new dark-colored race, *Telmatodytes palustris waynei*, recently described by Dingle and Sprunt (1932). This race is so strikingly similar to *marianae* in most of its characters that the confusing of the two is not surprising. The status of *waynei* as the breeding marsh wren of the North Carolina coast has recently been confirmed by Dr. Alexander Wetmore (1941) and his assistants, as one of the results of their field work there during 1939.

In his original description of *marianae*, W. E. D. Scott (1888b) says: "The great difference between this species and *palustris* is in the conspicuous barring of the upper and under tail-coverts and the feathers of the flanks, and olive instead of rufous brown coloring throughout, with the much darker coloration of underparts." The differences between *marianae* and *waynei* are not so well marked and are much less conspicuous. Dingle and Sprunt (1932) say: "A satisfactory comparison of *Telmatodytes palustris waynei* with *marianae* is not possible on account of inadequacy of specimens of the latter. In size, *waynei* seems to be slightly larger than the Florida form; in color it is quite similar, except that there is more white on the under parts."

In order to satisfy me as to the characters that separate *waynei* from *marianæ*, James L. Peters and James C. Greenway helped me examine the series of both forms in the Museum of Comparative Zoology in Cambridge, where there are 31 specimens from the west coast of Florida and 18 specimens from North and South Carolina. It seems to me that, in the Florida birds, the sides of the head and neck average darker, the black space on the back is rather more extensive and the flanks are browner than in the Carolina birds; also, the breast, in adults at least, is more inclined to be mottled with dusky, and there is much less white on the under parts. These are only average differences and are rather slight, but the Carolina bird seems to be far enough removed geographically to warrant its recognition as a subspecies.

Ridgway (1904) gives the best description of Marian's marsh wren as follows:

Similar to *T. p. palustris*, but smaller, the coloration much darker; pileum usually entirely black or with black largely predominating; white streaks of interscapular region narrower, sometimes almost obliterated; brown of scapulars, rump, etc., darker, the upper tail-coverts (sometimes the whole rump) usually barred with dusky; sides and flanks more extensively, and usually darker, brown than in *T. p. palustris*, the chest often strongly shaded pale brown or brownish buff; frequently the chest or sides (or both) are speckled with dusky, and sometimes the sides and flanks are barred with darker brown; under tail-coverts distinctly, often broadly, barred with brown or dusky; mandible usually dusky for much the greater part of its length.

As to its haunts in the vicinity of Tarpon Springs, Fla., the type locality, W. E. D. Scott (1890) says: "I have found them most commonly on the salt water marshes at the *head* of tide water, but have detected them in the saw-grasses of the fresh water lakes and ponds that I have investigated for at least ten miles back from the coast."

Nesting.—Arthur H. Howell (1932) writes: "In the extensive salt marshes at the mouth of Pithlachascotee River, near Port Richey, we found these Wrens breeding commonly in the dense growth of *Juncus*, standing 4 to 5 feet high. On May 28, 1918, we collected several well-grown young birds. In the marsh at Elvers, June 2, 1919, D. J. Nicholson observed several nests from 5 to 9 feet above the ground in mangrove trees."

There are two sets of eggs in my collection, taken by C. J. Pennock, near St. Marks, Fla., that came from nests 2 feet above the ground in saw grass.

D. J. Nicholson wrote to Mr. Wheeler (1931) that these wrens near New Port Richey "nest among Juncus (*J. roemerianus*), a sharp-pointed rush, and principally in mangrove trees from 5 to 14 feet above the mud in salt marshes. The tree-nesting may seem strange to you and it was quite a surprise to me when I found them nesting under such odd circumstances. I think high water and rats had something to do with this nesting custom here, and it may be a comparatively recent habit." From the same source of information, Mr. Wheeler goes on to say:

Nests of *marianae* found in mangrove trees were fastened to the forks of small limbs, generally at their ends, or in the tops of small mangrove bushes. * * * Occupied nests are lined with soft shredded grasses, and sometimes with feathers, and they are so cleverly woven together that they are a complete protection against rain. None have even been found that were damp inside. Although the marsh wrens nest in colonies, the nests of *marianae* are seldom less than 40 feet apart. On the east coast of Florida Nicholson counted four to six "dummy nests" to every occupied nest of *griseus;* but in the colonies of *marianae* on the west coast near Elfers, he found only one or two bachelor nests to one that was occupied.

Referring to the coast of Alabama, he writes:

It was on the tidal flats, or rather monotypic marshes, of Heron Bayou that we found marsh wrens nesting, enough to satisfy the heart of any ornithologist. This region of vast and almost impenetrable marshes is known to the fishermen as West Heron Bay. Several narrow bayous penetrate the grass-grown region, one of them widening into a so-called lake. In such a region, in the tall bladed grasses, which grow higher than the rushes, and nearer open water, we found the marsh wrens numerous. They were singing near their neatly built nests, their entrancing songs being much in the tempo of the songs of the Prairie Marsh Wren. * * *

The nest of Marian's Marsh Wren differs in no essential way from the nest of other closely-related species or subspecies. It is globular in shape, well secured to the taller marsh grasses, and usually about 2 or 3 feet above high tide. Oftentimes the nest can be detected from a moving skiff. The bachelor nests, which are unlined, are in the proportion of four or five to one which is lined and occupied.

Eggs.—Marian's marsh wren seems to lay fewer eggs than the northern races of the species, usually three to five. These are like the eggs of the species elsewhere and show the usual variations, some being quite pale, but most of them being of a deep, rich chocolate-brown; many have a wreath of darker spots about the larger end. The measurements of 40 eggs average 15.4 by 12.2 millimeters; the eggs showing the four extremes measure **16.4** by 12.7, 16.1 by **12.9, 14.2** by 11.9, and 15.0 by **11.0** millimeters.

Behavior.—Mr. Wheeler (1931) writes: "Contrary to our expectation, we did not find these wrens particularly shy. The breeding birds were very easy to approach; and although they did not remain long on open perches they seemed quite unmindful of our invasion of their territory, singing joyously all the while, and often within 2 or 3 feet of us. Often and again the males would reappear and perch in plain view on the side of the tallest reed, and that without interruption of their song. If we could have walked through the thick vegetation at low tide with a Graflex camera, we might have gotten pictures of the birds in action."

TELMATODYTES PALUSTRIS WAYNEI Dingle and Sprunt

WAYNE'S MARSH WREN

Comment on this subspecies was made under Marian's marsh wren, to which the reader is referred. Since that account was written, the above subspecies has been accepted and will appear in the next Checklist.

Dingle and Sprunt (1932) describe it as "similar to *Telmatodytes palustris palustris*, but smaller; bill shorter and more slender; wing, tail and tarsus average shorter; upper parts darker, inclining more to olive brown; head and nape sooty black, the majority of specimens showing a short, faint median streak; black dorsal area of greater extent; tail and under tail coverts more heavily barred; flanks richer brown; these, and sides of breast with more or less barring."

"A satisfactory comparison of *Telmatodytes palustris waynei* with *marianae*," these authors say, "is not possible on account of inadequacy of specimens of the latter. In size, *waynei* seems to be slightly larger than the Florida form; in color it is quite similar, except that there is more white on the under parts."

The breeding range of this form seems to be on the coast of North Carolina, and it is found in South Carolina and Georgia in winter. See remarks under *marianae*. Its habits are apparently no different from those of the other coastal races of the species.

TELMATODYTES PALUSTRIS THRYOPHILUS Oberholser

LOUISIANA MARSH WREN

HABITS

The long-billed marsh wren of the coast region of southern Louisiana is very much like Marian's marsh wren and evidently closely related to it. Ridgway (1904) makes this comparison: "Similar to *T. p. marianae*, but paler and still smaller; pileum always extensively brown medially, often mostly brown; brown of scapulars, rump, etc., lighter, sometimes approaching broccoli brown or drab; upper tail-coverts unbarred, or with bars very indistinct; under parts never (?) speckled, but chest more or less strongly tinged with brownish buff, and sides and flanks extensively brown. Differing from *T. p. palustris* in decidedly smaller size, duller brown of upper parts, and more extensively brown under parts."

Dr. Oberholser (1938) says that "it lives in the marshes and in the high grass of the coast meadows, among the reeds, rushes, grasses, and similar kinds of vegetation," which indicates that it is similar in all its habits to the other southern coastal races.

The measurements of only five eggs of the Louisiana marsh wren are available. The eggs are in the United States National Museum. The eggs showing the four extremes measure 16.0 by 12.4 and 15.3 by 11.5 millimeters.

TELMATODYTES PALUSTRIS LAINGI Harper

ALBERTA MARSH WREN

HABITS

Dr. Francis Harper (1926) describes this wren as "nearest to *T. p. iliacus*, but paler on scapulars, rump, upper tail-coverts, and flanks; median area on forehead and crown more distinct. (*T. p. plesius* is a much browner and duller bird than *laingi*.)"

The Athabaska Delta, where the type specimen of this race was taken, is probably the northernmost point at which any long-billed marsh wrens breed. Dr. Harper gives, as the range of this subspecies in summer, Alberta and western Saskatchewan, and says that it seems to intergrade with the prairie marsh wren in south-central Saskatchewan, and that the area of intergradation "may coincide with the approximate boundary between the prairies on the east and the plains on the west."

The habits of the Alberta marsh wren are apparently similar in all respects to those of the prairie marsh wren.

There is a very pretty nest of this wren in the Thayer collection in Cambridge, taken near Fort Saskatchewan, Alberta, on June 2, 1900. It was "attached to tules in a muskeg" and was constructed chiefly of a downy substance that looks like cattail down, very compactly felted and reinforced with interwoven strips of the tules, or other marsh plants, which bound the whole structure very firmly together; its walls are so thick and solid that it must have been practically rain-proof; it is about 7 inches high and about 4 inches in diameter. There is another nest, from the Little Red Deer River, Alberta, that is more normal for the species, having been attached to the stems of bulrushes and made of the usual materials.

A. D. Henderson, of Belvedere, Alberta, writes to me of an experience that was new to him: "On July 8 I pushed my canoe into a large bed of tules where marsh wrens were singing, leaving it close to an empty nest. To enable me to find the canoe again without difficulty after wading the tule bed, I attached a bunch of white cotton to the tops of tall tules. On July 12 I returned to the same spot and found that the wren had profusely bedecked the nest with the cotton I had left nearby. It was put on quite loosely and not woven into the structure."

The eggs of the Alberta marsh wren apparently show the usual variations common to the species. The measurements of 23 eggs average 16.3 by 12.3 millimeters; the eggs showing the four extremes measure 16.8 by 12.2, 16.4 by 13.1, 15.2 by 12.7, and 15.9 by 11.9 millimeters.

TELMATODYTES PALUSTRIS ILIACUS Ridgway

PRAIRIE MARSH WREN

PLATES 45, 46

HABITS

The old familiar type name, long-billed marsh wren (*T. p. palustris*), has been restricted to the wrens of this species living on the Atlantic slope from Rhode Island to Virginia, and the birds of interior New England and the middle west are now known by the above names. Such are the vagaries of name-shifting that our old friend of the Massachusetts marshes is now called the "prairie" marsh wren, though hundreds of miles away from the nearest prairies! In describing this race, Mr. Bangs (1902) writes:

At present there are confused under the name *Cistothorus palustris* (Wilson) two quite distinct birds; one, true *C. palustris*, breeding in the salt and brackish marshes of the Atlantic coast from Connecticut southward; the other inhabiting the inland fresh-water marshes and extending north to Massachusetts, Ontario and southern Manitoba. The former, a small bird, has the chin, throat and belly pure white and the breast is usually white also, though sometimes faintly clouded with pale brownish, with the rump, upper tail-coverts and scapulars dusky brown. The latter is a decidedly larger form, in which the chin, throat and belly are buffy or brownish white, the breast much more distinctly clouded with brownish and the rump, upper tail-coverts and scapulars reddish brown.

Wilson's plate shows a decidedly white-breasted bird, to which he gave the name *palustris*; there can be no doubt, therefore, that the Atlantic coast bird should carry the type name.

The prairie marsh wren is naturally not evenly distributed throughout its wide range. Marshes of the type it requires are often widely scattered, or entirely lacking over large areas. Small, isolated marshes of less than an acre in extent are usually avoided, but where the larger marshes contain suitable vegetation the wrens may be very numerous and their nests more so.

The favorite haunts of the prairie marsh wren are the large freshwater marshes of the interior, where there is a dense growth of cattails (*Typha angustifolia* and *T. latifolia*), bulrushes (*Scirpus lacustris*), sedges (*Carex*), or wildrice (*Zizania aquatica*), which are often mixed with tall marsh grasses of various kinds, or with a scattering growth of buttonbush (*Cephalanthus*) and other small bushes. In eastern Massachusetts we sometimes find them along the banks of tidal rivers, where the water is brackish and where there is a thick growth of tall reeds and salt-marsh grasses. I have found them, also, in pure stands of wildrice bordering a sluggish inland river.

Dr. Charles W. Townsend (1905) tells of a large marsh in Essex County, Mass., in which "the growth of rushes and grasses is rank and tall, and among these a multitude of Long-billed Marsh Wrens live and build their nests. The rush-like plants in which they breed are chiefly as follows, belonging to several widely separated families: great bulrush (*Scirpus lacustris*), horse-tail (*Equisetum limonsum*), sweet flag (*Acorus calamus*), blue joint-grass (*Calamagrostis canadensis*), reed canary-grass (*Phalaris arundinacea*)."

Spring.—Very little seems to be known about the migrations of the marsh wrens. Elon H. Eaton (1914) says: "Evidently they migrate at night, and high in the air, so as to see their way and escape their enemies more successfully." They arrive in central New York from May 4 to 16.

Dr. Wilfred A. Welter (1935) has given us such a fine life history of the prairie marsh wren, based on extensive observations at Ithaca, N. Y., and at Staples, Minn., that I cannot do better than to quote from the results of his work. At both places he found that the average date for the arrival of the males was May 10 and that the females came between May 20 and 28. Males begin to select and defend their breeding territories soon after their arrival. He says:

The preferred habitat is not, as one might suppose, a dense tangled mass of dried and broken cat-tails, remnants of the preceding season, but a comparatively open area with a few tattered stalks and an abundance of some species of *Carex*.

* * * Fighting over territorial rights between males is, to a large extent, a matter of outbluffing the opponent. A male approaching too closely to the boundary of another's area is challenged by the song of the rightful owner. This is usually sufficient for the intruder, but sometimes the challenge is accepted by the visitor giving voice to his emotions and continuing to transgress upon the area in question. The first male in this case fluffs out his feathers to impress the other and, if necessary, flies at his opponent. The usurper usually reciprocates by flying at his neighbor a time or two and then, at least in all instances observed, becomes the vanquished and departs from the scene of battle.

* * * In an area 400 by 650 feet in the Renwick Marsh at the head of Lake Cayuga eight males took up residence in the spring of 1931. * * * The cat-tail-sedge association was greatly preferred to the grass association by the male birds in selecting territories. * * * *Typha angustifolia* is much preferred to *T. latifolia* as a nesting site. * * * The male territories in the favored area were noticeably smaller than in the grassy area. A single monogamous male occupied a territory of from 13,000 to 15,000 square feet, while in the grass association this was extended to approximately 30,000 square feet. The territory of a polygamous male, on the other hand, was considerably larger than that of a monogamous male nesting in the same sort of vegetation. * * * This difference in size can readily be accounted for by the fact that the female birds do not tolerate each other during the nesting season. As a result those males intent upon leading dual lives must separate the objects of their affection as widely as possible.

Courtship.—The courtship of the marsh wren is expressed in song and in display. According to Dr. Welter (1935), "song does not seem to be as important in attracting the female as display. Of course the song originally attracts the prospective mate into the territory and then display becomes first in importance. When the females begin to arrive from the south the males sing almost constantly." The songs at this time often average about 25 per minute, but during nest building the songs are less numerous and the intervals between singing periods become longer.

"The display of the male is quite simple but interesting. When the female is near he will take up his station a foot or two above her, fluff out his breast feathers and under tail coverts, and jauntily cock his tail over his back so that it almost touches. He now resembles a tiny ball of feathers perched among the reeds. As he becomes more animated he beats his partially folded wings up and down rapidly and sways his head dizzily from side to side. The female probably will fail to notice him, or at least she will not indicate any interest, and, after pursuing her and displaying for several minutes, he will burst into song and fly to another portion of the territory."

The sexual organs of the male are well developed when he arrives, but those of the female are not, so that she has to avoid him until she is ready. Dr. Welter continues:

During the period of nest construction she reaches the height of her development and is ready for the mating act. When the male approaches her at this time, singing, she climbs up a cat-tail stalk and gives the trill which has already been described. Then she beats her wings rapidly, points her bill toward the zenith, and places her tail well over her back. The male goes through the courtship display previously described. At the proper time he climbs upon the back of his mate, beats his wings rapidly as the cloacae come in contact and copulation is completed. The whole procedure takes but a few seconds. Both remain in the immediate vicinity for a short time, the male with feathers fluffed out and tail up, the female quiet and demure.

It is usually the male who tries to induce the female into copulation but on one occasion the female was observed going through the behavior leading to the mating act to entice the male. In this instance the act had been completed 25 minutes previously. The male, not giving the proper response, was chased by the female among the cat-tails and it is not known whether she was successful or not.

Dr. Welter believes that the male is "essentially polygamous while the female is not." Several of the territories were inhabited by one male and two females, and in one doubtful case it was thought that a male had three mates. There was another doubtful case of polyandry, where a female had no regular mate, and her nest was placed between the territories of two mated males.

Nesting.—The prairie marsh wren nests in wet marshes, where the water is from a few inches to 2 or 3 feet deep, along the banks of tidal rivers where the water is brackish (in Massachusetts), along sluggish inland streams, around the shores of ponds, and in inland marshes or sloughs. It seems to prefer to build its nest in the narrowleaf cattail (*Typha angustifolia*), seldom using the broadleaf species (*T. latifolia*). Early in the season, before the green flags have grown to sufficient height, I have found the nest in some thick bunch of the dead flags of the previous season, but the new green flags are much preferred. The nests are usually placed 1 to 3 feet above water, seldom higher, and are securely fastened to two or more stems of the cattails.

Nests are less often placed in bulrushes (*Scirpus*), sedges (*Carex*), wildrice (*Zizania*), tall marsh grasses, or even small bushes. In North Dakota we found these wrens nesting around the edges of the sloughs in either dead or green cattails, or in the bulrushes. Near Lake Winnipegosis, Manitoba, we found a nest firmly attached to the canes of bulrushes, 4 feet above the water; it was within 4 feet of a canvasback's nest and was lined with down from the nest of the duck. The nest is said to be shaped like a coconut, or globular, but some that I have seen have been egg-shaped with the pointed end at the bottom. The entrance is a small round hole, usually near the top.

Dr. Welter (1935) gives an elaborate account of the building of the brood nest, which is done almost entirely by the female, and which requires 5 to 8 days, beginning 6 to 15 days after her arrival. He writes:

The initial effort in building consists of lashing the supporting plants together and in this way form a cup-like foundation upon which the remainder of the nest rests. *Carex* and *Calamagrostis* are the chief materials used in this part of the structure. The outer walls which are composed for the most part of long strips of cattail leaves and stems and leaves of sedges and grasses is the roughest part of the structure. Water-soaked materials, often more than a foot long, are used here as they are more pliable and can more easily be woven together. The first strands are woven around the long axis and others, as the nest assumes shape, are put in at various angles. Some of these strands are fastened to the supporting structure by actually weaving these stems into the nest. Some of the growing leaves are also woven into the outer walls. If the support is a sedge or a grass, leaves may form a good share of the periphery. An opening is left on one side about two-thirds of the distance from the bottom of the nest. At this stage a dummy would be complete. The walls average at least a half inch in thickness and the external measurements of the entire structure approximate seven and five inches for the vertical and horizontal diameters, respectively. Inner diameters average five and three inches.

The outer shell is a small part of the completed structure, and only 2 days are required to build it. The remainder of the work is done from the inside and one must take a nest to pieces to get an idea of its arrangement. Grass and sedge leaves and small stems are used to form the second layer. This gives the walls firmness and tends to fill in the large air spaces which are necessarily present among the coarse materials of the outer walls.

The next layer to be added seems to function as an insulating region. Cat-tail down, feathers, small unidentified rootlets, entire plants of *Lemna*, and decayed fragments of *Typha* and *Carex* are the materials most often used. These are also placed into the structure in a wet condition so that, when dry, they form a compact and tight-fitting region which serves as a non-conductor of heat, cold, and moisture.

The innermost region is composed of finely shredded pieces of the vascular materials of the plants forming the outer layers. A large proportion of it is very fine strips of sedges and grasses of the preceding year. Feathers of almost any available sort are used here. Those from the following birds have been identified: Red-winged Blackbird, Virginia Rail, American Bittern, Pheasant, Ruffed Grouse, and domestic chicken. The projection at the opening is a part of this inner lining. This "door-step" or sill is always present in the female nest but is lacking in the nests of the male. It is possible, therefore, to determine the sex which built a given nest by checking for the presence of this sill. This projection forms the floor of the opening and extends farther into the nest than any other part of the lining. * * *

One wonders what the function of this door-step might be. Perhaps it serves as a protection to the eggs and young as the nest, owing to the uneven growth of the supporting plants, often assumes a distorted position which would allow the contents to roll out were it not for this structure. In like manner when the nests are placed in sedges or grasses winds alter the nests to such an extent that the young or eggs would be endangered if no sill were there to prevent the catastrophe.

Several observers have reported mud in the lining of the nests, but Dr. Welter and others have failed to note it; perhaps some mud may be brought in accidentally with material secured from the muddy floor of the marsh; it seems doubtful if the wrens every carry in mud intentionally.

The long-billed marsh wrens are notorious for building extra or dummy nests, which are almost never occupied as brood nests. These are built by the males, mainly during the 10 days or so intervening between the arrival of the males and the coming of the females. Anywhere from 1 to 10, usually not more than half a dozen, are more or less incompletely constructed by a single male within the limits of his territory. We do not fully understand the reason for these extra nests; several theories have been advanced to account for the habit, which is not wholly confined to this species, but none of the theories appears wholly satisfactory. The most plausible theory seems to be that it gives the birds an outlet for surplus energy during the period of sexual activity, for it almost always ends soon after the females arrive and mating takes place. These male nests are never as fully completed as are the brood nests; they usually do not go beyond the first stage mentioned above, and are often abandoned before they reach even that stage of completion. There is little evidence that they are ever used as brood nests, or as sleeping places for the males, or as territorial land marks.

A. D. DuBois mentions in his notes a nest that was of the "usual construction except that the top of the nest was covered by green leaves bent over and woven together over the top. All the previous nests observed here, having the green leaves woven over (nearly a dozen so noted) were empty nests."

Milton B. Trautman (1940) noted that, out of 208 nests, observed at Buckeye Lake, Ohio, 161 had their openings facing toward the south or west. There was one colony, "which was an exception, for 11 of 19 nests opened toward the northeast."

Eggs.—The marsh wren's set may consist of 3 to 10 eggs; the larger numbers are rare; 5 or 6 seem to be the commonest numbers. They are generally ovate, sometimes more rounded and rarely more pointed; they are not glossy unless heavily incubated. Marsh wrens' eggs are unique in color, the general effect being dull brownish, "Verona brown" to "snuff brown," or the color of dry, powdered baking chocolate. The ground color varies from "snuff brown" to pale "pinkish cinnamon"; it is generally evenly sprinkled with minute dots, or very small spots of darker shades of brown, often partially, or wholly, obscuring the ground color; these markings are sometimes concentrated into a ring or a cap at the large end. F. W. Braund tells me that "light or stony gray" eggs are often found in Ohio. I have seen eggs with a pinkish ground color and reddish brown spots that resembled the eggs of the house wren, but these are rare. Very rarely an egg, or a whole set of eggs, is pure white and unmarked.

The measurements of 40 eggs average 16.5 by 12.4 millimeters; the eggs showing the four extremes measure **17.8** by 12.1, 17.6 by **13.3, 15.0** by 13.0, and 17.6 by **11.2** millimeters.

Young.—The incubation period, as noted by several observers, is about 13 days, and the young remain in the nest for about the same length of time, or a day longer, if not disturbed; Dr. Welter (1935) says 14 days. Incubation seems to be performed wholly by the female, and she feeds the young while they are in the nest; the male assists in this afterward. Following are some of Dr. Welter's observations on the young:

The type of food delivered to the young by the female is determined to a certain extent by the age of the nestlings. At first this consists of very small juicy morsels such as mosquitoes and their larvae, larval Tipulids, midges, and other delicate forms. The mother brings a whole beakful of food to the nest at one time and parcels it out to the hungry occupants. * * * During the morning and evening approximately 10 trips are made per hour with food, but during midday this number is somewhat reduced.

As the nestlings grow the insects brought to the nest become appreciably larger in size. Ground, diving, and long-horned beetles, caterpillars of various assortments, sawflies and other hymenoptera, and other accessible forms now constitute the diet of the ever-hungry young. Sometimes the insect is so large that the young bird experiences difficulties in swallowing it. In such instances the female takes the hexapod to the side of the nest, chops and tears it into several smaller morsels, and then brings it back for a second trial which is usually a success. * * *

Even when the nestlings are very young, little time during the day is given to brooding. Usually after a feeding or two the young are brooded for a few minutes and then feeding is resumed. My records show a total brooding of 18 minutes per hour when the young are 2 days old. As the nestlings increase in size the brooding periods become shorter and the intervals between such periods become longer, so that, after the first week, they are discontinued during the hours of daylight. * * *

The excreta, enclosed in their envelopes, are removed by the female after feeding. These droppings are usually carried some distance from the nest and deposited, but occasionally the female has been observed eating them. * * *

When the young are small the faecal material is deposited in the bottom of the nest. As the nestlings increase in size, however, they maneuver about until they assume a position facing away from the entrance, and the dropping is ejected on the periphery of the nest. During the later period of nest life the young succeed in ejecting the excrement with such force that it is carried over the side of the nest and drops to the ground.   * *

Other waste materials, such as eggshells, infertile eggs, or any young that might die in the nest are carried away. The young increase in weight very rapidly, from about 0.87 gram at hatching to about 11.08 grams at the end of the twelfth day. Meantime the nest has become enlarged and worn as the young increase in size. The young may leave the nest on the twelfth day, if disturbed, but normally not until the fourteenth day. Occasionally one will return to the nest for shelter, but they usually spend the nights perched in the dense flags. The parents care for them for at least 2 weeks, though after the first 10 days they are able to secure some of their own food. The family group remains together through the summer and wanders about at some distance from the nesting place.

It seems to be the consensus that two broods are raised in a season, but not a third. Dr. Welter (1935) found no evidence of a third brood. "The female begins her second nest about 2 weeks after the young of the first have left the nest. The majority of the nests, then, in the regions studied would be started between July 15 and August 1, with the last week in July the most active period." Probably while the female is building the second nest the male is busy with the first brood and is not very active in building dummy nests.

Plumages.—Dr. Welter (1936) has published another excellent paper on the development of the plumage in the young marsh wren and on subsequent molts, to which the reader is referred for details; it is fully illustrated with drawings and photographic halftones. It is evident from the photographs that the young bird is practically fully feathered in the juvenal plumage before it leaves the nest, though the wings are not fully developed and the tail is still rudimentary. Dr. Dwight (1900) says that the natal down is white. In the juvenal plumage the young wren is much like the adult, but the crown is uniformly dull black, without the dividing brown area; the white streaks on the back are very faint or lacking; and the white superciliary stripe is indistinct. Dr. Dwight says that the first winter plumage is "acquired by a partial postjuvenal molt beginning about the middle of August which involves the body plumage, the wing coverts, probably the tertiaries, but not the rest of the wings nor the tail," young and old becoming practically indistinguishable. Dr. Welter (1936) differs from Dr. Dwight, as to the extent of this molt, saying: "Juvenals collected during the fall of 1931 which are now in the Cornell Collection show a molt of both rectrices and remiges." These two authorities also differ as to the prenuptial molt. Dr. Dwight says that the nuptial plumage, in both adults and young birds, "is acquired by a complete prenuptial moult as indicated by the relatively unworn condition of the feathers when the birds arrive in May." He had no positive evidence of the molt, however. Dr. Welter could "find no evidence of a prenuptial molt in the series of specimens examined." The plumage of birds living in such dense vegetation must be subjected to rather severe abrasion, which might require a renewal of plumage oftener than once a year; and it may be that the prenuptial molt takes place during the late winter or very early spring, before the birds arrive on their breeding grounds. Dr. Witmer Stone (1896) agrees with Dr. Dwight's view, and I have seen some half a dozen specimens, taken in North and South Carolina, Florida, New Mexico, and Mexico, between February 23 and March 28, that show various stages of a complete prenuptial molt. Whether these are adults or young birls I do not know.

Food.—The marsh wren feeds almost entirely on insects and their larvae, which it obtains on the marsh vegetation or on the floor of the marsh. Dr. Welter (1935) says that "much of the food is obtained near or from the surface of the water .* * * It is not unusual to observe the bird as he sights a juicy morsel fly into the air and capture it in the manner of a flycatcher. Insects as large as dragonflies are taken in this way. * * * Coleoptera and Diptera assume the highest rank while various other orders are represented to a lesser degree. Carabidae and Dytiscidae occur more frequently among the beetles than any other forms while a large percentage of the Diptera belong to the Tipulidae."

F. H. King (1883) reports from Wisconsin that "of 14 stomachs examined one ate 1 ant; one, a caterpillar; one, 3 beetles; three, 3 moths; one a small grasshopper; one, 5 grasshopper eggs; one, 1 dragon-fly; and one a small snail." Mosquito larvae are probably prominent in the food, as are larvae of other flying insects, diminutive mollusks, and aquatic insects. Forbush (1929), referring to Massachusetts, says that "in the salt marsh at high tide, it feeds on insects which crawl up on the grass and reeds, and at low tide it feeds largely on minute marine animals which it finds on or near the ground."

Behavior.—The marsh wren is much more often heard than seen. As we drift along some quiet stream bordered by extensive cattail marshes, we hear all about us the gurgling, bubbling songs, or the chattering, scolding notes of the birds, but not one is in sight in the dense jungle of flags. Perhaps one may explode into the air, rising a few feet above the cattails with an outburst of enthusiastic song and drift down again into cover; or we may see one make a longer flight from one part of the marsh to another, buzzing along on slow, direct, steady flight with rapid wing beats. If we watch quietly, curiosity may prompt one to come peering at us with furtive glances from the shelter of his retreat, clinging with feet wide apart to two

swaying stems like a little acrobat doing the "splits"; his tail is held
erect or pointed saucily forward and his head is lifted so high that
head, body, and tail seem to form a feathered circle. He climbs
nimbly up and down the reeds like a feathered gymnast, now gliding
down to the base to pick some food from the water, now gleaning along
the stems, and again swinging jauntily from a swaying top. He is
the embodiment of active energy, always in motion, never still for
a moment, and always chattering, scolding, or singing. He is a shy
and elusive little mite; if we make the slightest motion while watching his antics, he vanishes instantly into the depths of his reedy jungle.

Although most of the marsh wrens probably live in harmony with
their neighbors in the marsh, some, perhaps many, have formed the
bad habit of sucking the eggs of least bitterns and red-winged blackbirds, as reported by several observers. For example, Dr. Chapman
(1900) saw one of these wrens puncture all the eggs in two nests of
least bitterns, and he attempted to photograph the bird in the act;
the wren did not eat the contents of the eggs, though it may have
returned to do so later; it looked like a case of pure viciousness. And
Dr. A. A. Allen (1914) says that "of 51 nests of the Redwing observed
in a limited area, the eggs of 14 were destroyed" by marsh wrens,
"and it is not at all uncommon to find one or more of the eggs of a
nest with neat, circular holes in one side, such as would be made by
the small, sharp beak of a wren." One that he watched "began to
drink the contents much as a bird drinks water. After a few sips, it
grasped the eggshell in its beak and flew off into the marsh, where it
continued its feast." Dr. Welter (1935) evidently thinks that such
behavior is exceptional for he says: "Many nests of other species
of birds were under observation in the marsh and at no time were
punctured eggs found or other indications of egg eating by the Marsh
Wren observed."

Voice.—Wilson (Wilson and Bonaparte, 1832) evidently did not
admire the vocal powers of the marsh wren, saying that "it would be
mere burlesque to call them by the name of song," for "you hear a low,
crackling sound, something similar to that produced by air bubbles
forcing their way through mud or boggy ground when trod upon";
this is a fair description of some of the notes, but he apparently was
not referring to the full song, parts of which are quite musical. F.
Schuyler Mathews (1921) says that the song "ripples and bubbles
along in a fashion similar to that of the Winter or House Wren, but
with a glassy tinkle in tone not characteristic of the songs of the other
species and a tempo perceptibly more rapid than that of the House
Wren's music." Dr. Charles W. Townsend (1905) writes: "The song
begins with a scrape like the tuning of a violin followed by a trill
with bubbles, gurgles, or rattles, depending no doubt on the skill
or mood of the performer, at times liquid and musical, at other times

rattling and harsh, but always vigorous. It ends abruptly but is generally followed by a short musical whistle or trill, as if the Wren were drawing in its breath after its efforts. I have heard one sing fifteen times in a minute."

Dr. Welter's (1935) description is only slightly different; he dissects the song into three parts; first a grinding sound consisting of two to five notes with somewhat the quality of the *aac* notes of the white-breated nuthatch; then comes the more musical "warble-like" part, which reminds him "of a sewing machine of the older sort being run rapidly, but of course it is less metallic and more musical. It has much of the spontaneity of the House Wren's song but is otherwise quite distinct. This middle section begins at a low pitch, climbs upward, and then descends again." The third section he calls a trill, which is again "quite low but lacks the harshness of the beginning of the song. * * *

"This entire song is given during May and most of June. Toward the end of the month, however, the last part is often omitted and often neither the beginning nor the end is heard." The song period seems to cease entirely in August, but the full song has been heard in October, which may mean that a second song period occurs in fall.

The marsh wren is a persistent singer, chiefly during the early morning and the evening hours, but during the height of the season it sings all day and often at night. Only the male sings. He sings while clinging to the reeds or while moving among them; he indulges in his most delightful flight song while flying above the vegetation from one part of his territory to the other; or, rising in the air to a height of several feet, he flutters down to cover again in full song.

This wren also has several alarm, call, or chattering notes. According to Dr. Welter (1935) —

the *kek kek* or *tschuk* is given by the female. The male's note sometimes resembles this also but can usually be distinguished by its more grating nature and may be described as *rrek*. A series of notes is usually given together so the *rrek's* do not sound very distinct as they roll into each other producing a chattering. The *kek* notes, however, while also given together, maintain their identity. The female has a hissing sound that she gives if too closely pressed by the male. Preceding copulation the female has been heard to give a trill like that at the end of the male's song.

The call notes of the young are quite similar to those of the adult. The nestling, when the female arrives with food, gives a beady *peep* or *peet*. At first these notes are scarcely audible but as the young become older and stronger the *peet* is clearly heard. As the young leave the nest the *peet* gradually develops into a *queck*. It is much more squeaky than the adult *kek* and also lacks the woody quality. The notes of the juvenal become more and more like those of the adult until they are indistinguishable.

He says that the songs of the young males begin late in August and are entirely different from those of the adult. They reminded him at first of "the efforts of a not altogether successful Catbird," but they were "given in a more rasping manner. The grating notes of the beginning and the trill at the end are usually omitted by young birds."

Mr. Trautman (1940) "timed an isolated singing male whose territory was in a small stand of cattail and found that between 10 p. m. and 3 a. m. his average was 9 songs a minute." Another, in a similar situation, sang at the rate of 11 songs a minute between 1 :40 a. m. and 2 :50 a. m. on a moonlight night. The singing slowed down during the middle of the day, between 10 a. m. and 2 p. m., to 4 songs a minute. "The amount of singing done by these birds declined sharply after mid-August, and by September 5, only an occasional, half-hearted song could be heard."

Aretas A. Saunders writes to me: "The song of this bird is rather low-pitched and guttural, or sometimes squeaky. It consists of a series of rapid notes, so rapid as to call the result a trill, but more frequently slow enough to count the number. In 26 of my records, without trills, the number of notes varies from 8 to 16 and the average number is 12. In a majority of the songs the notes are all equal in time, but some have portions where the notes are more rapid in part of the song. These portions are sometimes the beginning and sometimes the end, or occasionally in the middle of the song.

"The pitch of the notes varies from C″ to C‴. One record is all on one pitch (B‴). A number of others are all on one pitch except the first or the final note, but others vary in numerous ways. The greatest variation in pitch in any one song is 2½ tones, and the average 1½ tones. I have occasionally seen a bird sing a flight song, when the song is somewhat more prolonged than I have described, but I have never succeeded in getting a record of this song.

"In spite of the simplicity of this song the individuals vary it considerably. I have recorded five different songs from one individual. The quality sometimes changes from guttural to squeaky in the same song. The time of songs varies from 1⅕ to 2 seconds, though flight songs are probably longer."

Field marks.—One hardly needs field marks to recognize a long-billed marsh wren, for it is wrenlike in appearance and behavior, and no other wren lives in such wet marshes. If perchance it is seen in the drier part of a marsh or meadow, it can be distinguished from the short-billed marsh wren by the blackish, unstreaked crown, the white line over the eye, and the black upper back streaked with white.

Enemies.—Hawks and owls would have difficulty in capturing these active little birds as they dive into their dense retreats. Red-winged blackbirds are often seen chasing wrens for reasons stated above. Dr. Welter (1935) mentioned three small mammals, meadow mice, jumping mice, and Bonaparte's weasels, as probably guilty of destroying some eggs and young. He says that Dr. A. A. Allen has seen bronzed grackles eating the young and has found bumble bees occupying the nests. Fleas, lice, and hippoboscid flies sometimes damage the young.

Fall.—Dr. Welter writes: "There is no marked exodus of birds from the marsh at a given time in the fall. At first the young of the year remain in family groups but, as the time of departure approaches, there is an apparent flocking together of young birds, usually near the the water's edge. At this time 25 or 30 birds may be observed together feeding near the surface of the water. * * * The first birds to leave are the adults and some of the young of the first brood." No adults were found after September 10; the birds that remain after that date are young birds, mostly those of the second brood, either in juvenal plumage or molting out of it. "As these birds complete the molt they, too, depart for their winter homes so that, by October 20, only a few scattered individuals remain. By the first of November these, also, have departed."

Elon H. Eaton (1914) describes the departure thus:

On one occasion while I was concealed in a blind watching for ducks to enter the marsh, I saw the last representative of this species leave the marshes at the foot of Canandaigua Lake. It was a cool night late in October when the moon was at the full. The little fellow uttered a feeble warble which attracted my attention and then rose from near my station, fluttering higher and higher into the air until lost at an elevation of about 300 feet, where I caught my last glimpse of him against the full moon. The following morning when I visited the marsh no more wrens were left. Evidently they migrate at night, and high in the air, so as to see their way and escape their enemies more successfully.

Winter.—Most of the prairie marsh wrens migrate in fall and spend the winter in Mexico or along the Gulf coast to western Florida. But some few individuals remain in their summer haunts all winter in the shelter of the dense cattail marshes. There are winter records for Massachusetts, Connecticut, New York, and Ohio. It may be that they are more common in winter than we realize, for they are silent and remain well hidden in the marshes, where they are hard to find.

TELMATODYTES PALUSTRIS PLESIUS Oberholser

WESTERN MARSH WREN

PLATE 47

HABITS

The western marsh wren breeds in the Great Basin regions of the western United States, from central British Columbia, Washington and Oregon, and northeastern California eastward to the Rocky Mountains in central Colorado and southward into New Mexico. Its winter range extends into Mexico.

Ridgway (1904) describes it as "very similar in coloration of upper parts to *T. p. iliacus,* but the brown averaging paler and decidedly less rufescent; upper tail-coverts usually more or less distinctly barred with dusky, and middle rectrices more distinctly barred; color of flanks, etc., conspicuously different, being pale wood brown, pale isabella color, or pale broccoli brown instead of bright buffy cinnamon or tawny-buff, the under tail-coverts usually more or less distinctly barred; wing and tail averaging decidedly longer (especially the tail), culmen averaging slightly shorter."

The haunts of the western marsh wren are evidently similar to those of the other races that breed in the fresh-water marshes and sloughs in the interior.

Nesting.—Dawson and Bowles (1909) give a very good description of the nest of this wren as follows:

The Marsh Wren's nest is a compact ball of vegetable materials, lashed midway of cat-tails or bulrushes, living or dead, and having a neat entrance hole in one side. A considerable variety of materials is used in construction, but in any given nest only one textile substance will preponderate. Dead cat-tail leaves may be employed, in which case the numerous loopholes will be filled with matted down from the same plant. Fine dry grasses may be utilized, and these so closely woven as practically to exclude the rain. On Moses Lake, where rankly growing bulrushes predominate in the nesting areas, spirogyra is the material most largely used. This, the familiar, scum-like plant which masses under water in quiet places, is plucked out by the venturesome birds in great wet hanks and plastered about the nest until the required thickness is attained. While wet, the substance matches its surroundings admirably, but as it dries out it shrinks considerably and fades to a sickly light green, or greenish gray, which advertises itself among the obstinately green bulrushes. Where this fashion prevails, one finds it possible to pick out immediately the oldest member of the group, and it is more than likely to prove the occupied nest.

The nest-linings are of the softest cat-tail down, feathers of wild fowl, or dried spirogyra teased to a point of enduring fluffiness. It appears, also, that the Wrens often cover their eggs upon leaving the nest. Thus, in one we found on the 17th of May, which contained seven eggs, the eggs were completely buried under a loose blanket of soft vegetable fibers. The nest was by no means deserted, for the eggs were warm and the mother bird very solicitous, insomuch that she repeatedly ventured within a foot of my hand while I was engaged with the nest.

A nest in the Thayer collection, taken in Lassen County, Calif., on May 10, 1910, was built in tules 2½ feet above the water. It is a large well-made nest constructed mainly of the fruiting or dry flower clusters of some marsh plant, firmly reinforced and compactly interwoven with narrow strips of tules or other marsh plants, forming a very solid and durable structure; it measures about 7 inches in height by about 4 inches in diameter.

Eggs.—The eggs of the western marsh wren are indistinguishable from those of the other races of the species. The measurements of 40 eggs average 16.1 by 12.6 millimeters; the eggs showing the four extremes measure 17.3 by 13.2, 16.6 by 13.4, and 14.5 by 11.0 millimeters.

Winter.—Harry S. Swarth (1917) makes the following interesting observation on the winter distribution of this wren in California:

The known breeding range of the western marsh wren in California is very limited, being merely the restricted northeastern corner of the State, a region which shows strongly Great Basin faunal affinities. In winter, however, *plesius* is perhaps the most abundant of any form of the species, occurring in numbers over a large part of the State. It is an especially numerous winter visitant in the San Diegan district of southern California. In this region summer is the dry season, a period of such excessive aridity that birds with the needs and proclivities of the marsh wrens are closely limited as to habitat, being restricted to extremely circumscribed areas about the few suitable permanent streams and sloughs. In winter this is all changed. Abundant rains often transform what were dry fields and pastures into ponds and marshes, while every roadside ditch is running full, and bordered with dense vegetation. In consequence, the visiting marsh wrens are enabled to scatter widely over the country.

He cites a number of records from various points along the coasts of California and Oregon, which indicate that "individuals of this form may occasionally be found in winter at any point along the coast." But he shows clearly that the center of abundance in winter is in southern California, "both on the deserts and in the San Diegan region."

TELMATODYTES PALUSTRIS PALUDICOLA (Baird)

TULE WREN

HABITS

Professor Baird (1864) was the first to name and describe a western race of this species, based on one specimen from Washington and three from California, and his name still applies to the long-billed marsh wrens of the Pacific coast district from British Columbia to southern California. His brief description gives as its characters: "Bill shorter than tarsus. Tail coverts distinctly banded all across. Bands on tail quite distinct; appreciable on the central feathers."

Ridgway (1904) gives a fuller description, based on 17 specimens, as follows: "Most like *T. p. palustris*, but tail-coverts usually barred (especially the upper), middle rectrices more distinctly barred, flanks, etc., deeper brown, bill smaller, and tail decidedly longer; agreeing with *T. p. plesius* in barred tail-coverts, more distinctly barred tail, and relatively longer tail, but decidedly smaller and with coloration decidedly darker."

The name tule wren must not be understood to imply that this wren is wholly or even mainly, confined to the tules (*Scirpus lacustris occidentalis*); although it breeds abundantly in this type of vegetation in the extensive marshes or where it grows around the shores of lakes, it also breeds commonly in the cattail marshes along the intersecting channels or the banks of quiet streams, and in the salicornia of coastal marshes where the supply of cattails is inadequate.

Dr. Gordon D. Alcorn writes to me that the tule wren is abundant in suitable localities in western Washington but says that "the wren population diminishes sharply within a few miles of the Pacific Ocean; this might be due to the scarcity of suitable swamps for nesting purposes. The swamps within this region are mostly of low-growing sedges (*Carex*), barely reaching 2 feet in height. In most of the swamps the cattails (*Typha*), of which the wrens are so fond, are scarce or entirely lacking. I regularly visit two wren areas in Grays Harbor County. The first is located on the shores of the harbor and comprises an area of approximately 5 acres. Few cattails are present, the swamp possessing mostly sedges with a few scattered willows. The area almost touches salt water, as the limits of the grounds are bounded on the south and west by the high-water line. I visit also a rather extensive swamp paralleling the ocean beach in the vicinity of Oyhut, Wash. This swamp covers a distance of about 4 miles and is composed of low sedges with a few spiraea bushes."

Spring.—Samuel F. Rathbun tells me that, near Seattle, this little wren is more or less resident in the region, although found more commonly from early spring until late in the fall. "There appears to be a movement of the species during late March and early April; for at this period birds will be heard and seen in and about small marshes or similar localities, in which they are absent during the nesting season."

Nesting.—Dr. Alcorn says in his notes that, in the localities mentioned above, the nests are usually placed within a foot or two of the water; the birds use sedge leaves for building and line the nests with willow cotton; the nests are always fragile structures; and there are not so many decoy nests as are found farther inland.

In the dense cattail swamps farther back from the coast, the nests are more substantial and more typical of the species. In the Thayer collection in Cambridge there are two distinct types of well-built nests, both collected by J. H. Bowles in Pierce County, Wash. One, built 4 feet above the water in dense cattails, where the water was 3 feet deep, is a compact, oval ball, made largely of cattail down interwoven with and firmly bound together with strips of the flags; it would have furnished a warm, dry shelter for the young. The other, "woven among coarse marsh grass" in a fresh-water marsh, is a firmly woven and well-made ball of interlaced strips of marsh grasses and reeds, a common type for the species.

Walter E. Bryant (1887) published the following note on a nest found by A. M. Ingersoll in an unusual situation: "A conspicuous nest, containing eggs, was woven among the almost leafless branches of a young willow, five feet above a fresh-water marsh."

The tule wren seems to be a prolific builder of decoy or male nests. Irene G. Wheelock (1904) says that she has examined "30 in 1 day and found but 1 occupied, and that was the oldest, most tumbledown of the lot." And Dawson and Bowles (1909) say that "in a day Mr. Bowles found 53 nests, only 3 of which held eggs or young. At least 2 broods are raised in a season." His brother, Charles W. Bowles (1898), throws some light on the use that may be made of these dummy nests: "In the spring of 1896 I found an empty marsh wren's nest, and on passing by later in the day, saw three nearly fledged young in it. There were also other nests near by, with one or more young in each. It seems to me probable that these duplicate nests are built, if the birds have a large family, for the young to roost in, at least at night, when they are too large to be all contained in one nest, but not yet able to take care of themselves."

Eggs.—The eggs of the tule wren are apparently no different from those of other long-billed marsh wrens. The measurements of 40 eggs average 16.3 by 12.8 millimeters; the eggs showing the four extremes measure **17.6** by 13.0, 16.8 by **13.5, 15.5** by 12.8, and 16.0 by **12.0** millimeters. These eggs are all in the United States National Museum.

Young.—Mrs. Wheelock (1904) writes:

Twelve days are required for incubation, and even during this short period the mother is not a close sitter. I have known her to leave the nest for 2 hours in the middle of the day, trusting to the intense heat of the sun to perform her task for her; and but for the thick, moist walls of the cradle, this same sun would have been fatal to the bird life within the shells.

As soon as the eggs hatched in the nest I was watching, I cut a slit in the top of it to look at the young. They were naked, light pink in color, with tiny heads, mere knobs for eyes and buds for wings; each nestling measured 1 inch in length. After this examination I tied up the slit, and before I was a yard away the mother entered the nest again. Four days later the eyes of the young wrens had begun to open, and looked like tiny slits, while a thin buffy down covered the top of their heads and was scattered sparsely over their bodies. As in the young of the long-billed marsh wrens, the ear openings were conspicuously large. Bill and legs had changed from pink to light burnt-orange in color. They were fed by regurgitation for the first 4 days and doubled in weight every 24 hours. When a week old they were commencing to feather, and in 3 days more were nearly ready to leave the nest. They were now fed on larvae of water insects, slugs, and dragonflies, besides other insects, and meals were served four times an hour during most of the day.

These young wrens left the nest, when examined, at an age of 12 days; they were able to glean some of their food but were fed by their parents for 2 weeks longer.

Food.—Only 53 stomachs of the California races of this species were examined by Professor Beal (1907), in which animal matter amounted to 98 percent, and vegetable matter, consisting of a few seeds of sedges and one of amaranth, amounted to 2 percent. "Beetles, wasps, ants, bugs, caterpillars, and a few miscellaneous insects, with some spiders and snails, make up the bill of fare." Bugs—assassin bugs, damsel bugs, stink bugs, leafhoppers, and treehoppers—constituted the largest item, 29 percent. Scales were found in one stomach. Caterpillars and chrysalids amounted to 17 percent, beetles (mainly harmful species) 16 percent, ants and wasps 8 percent, flies, grasshoppers, dragonflies, and a few other insects 11 percent. Spiders were eaten regularly and made up over 5 percent of the food. One stomach contained 11 small snails.

Not much more need be said about the habits of tule wren after all that has been written about the prairie marsh wren, for their habits are practically identical. Although some suspicion exists, there is no positive evidence that snakes destroy the eggs or young of these wrens, so far as I know. Dr. Gordon D. Alcorn (1931), however, published the following observation, which is at least suggestive; a pair of wrens were much disturbed by the presence of a garter snake near their nests.

The snake was slowly crawling some 2 to 5 feet above the water over the dead cattail leaves and stems in which were located a number of occupied and unoccupied wren nests. The birds remained perfectly silent, but with outspread wings and ruffled feathers darted again and again at the head of the reptile. The snake paid no attention to the birds but continued to "explore", finally approaching a wren nest and entering it. About two-thirds of the snake's body remained outside the nest while it stayed at the nest for about 30 seconds. The snake was allowed to enter several nests in a similar manner. It was then killed and the stomach examined and found to be empty but for a well-digested slug. Also each nest entered was examined and each found to be empty (undoubtedly "decoys," as each was unlined and in a conspicuous position.) * * * The snake was without doubt looking for food, either eggs or young birds, in these nests, and was not able to discriminate between occupied and unoccupied nests.

Dawson (1923) writes: "In autumn the Tule Wrens leave the sheltered precincts of the ponds, and go roaming about through dry weed patches and adjacent chaparral. Here they are as noisy and as elusive as ever, and are in nowise awed by their less usual surroundings. There is, doubtless, some invasion from the north and consequent crowding in winter."

Mrs. Amelia S. Allen tells me that "on September 24, 1941, they were abundant in a damp cow pasture inland in sedge grass."

TELMATODYTES PALUSTRIS AESTUARINUS Swarth

SUISUN MARSH WREN

HABITS

In naming this race Mr. Swarth (1917) says of its characters: "In coloration *aestuarinus* is darker than the average of *paludicola*, especially as compared with southern Californian examples of the latter. Occasional specimens of *paludicola*, however, from all parts of its range, are quite as dark colored. In dimensions, *T. p. aestuarius* differs from *T. p. paludicola* in its greater size throughout, being of about the same dimensions as *T. p. plesius*. From *plesius* it differs in its much darker coloration." This subspecies seems to be an intermediate between the two adjacent races, resembling one in color and the other in size. It also occupies a rather limited breeding range between the other two, mainly in Solano and Sonoma Counties, Calif. The 1931 Check-list gives its range as "west-central California, breeding at the confluence of the Sacramento and San Joaquin rivers, in Napa and Solano Counties, and thence south to Tulare County. In winter spreads beyond its breeding range to Oregon and southern California." Living as it does in a smilar type of country, we should hardly expect to find anything in its habits that is different from those of the neighboring races.

The eggs of the Suisun marsh wren do not differ materially from those of the species elsewhere. The measurements of 27 eggs average 16.0 by 12.7 millimeters; the eggs showing the four extremes measure 17.1 by 13.2, 16.6 by 13.4, 14.4 by 12.4, and 15.0 by 12.1 millimeters.

CISTOTHORUS PLATENSIS STELLARIS (Naumann)

SHORT-BILLED MARSH WREN

PLATES 48–51

HABITS

This tiny wren is more of a meadow wren than a marsh wren, for it shuns the wettest marshes where the long-billed marsh wren loves to dwell among the tall, dense growths of cattails or bulrushes and where the water is a foot or more deep. It prefers the drier marshes or wet meadows, where there is little water or where the ground is merely damp. These are what we call the sedge meadows, where the principal growth consists of various species of *Carex* and tall grasses, often growing in thick tufts, and various other plants that need a little moisture. Such marshes are often intersected by streams or ditches or are bordered by lower and wetter marshes where cattails and bulrushes flourish in the deeper water; the short-billed marsh wrens have often been seen among the cattails and have even been known to build their nests low down in these flags, but they much prefer to breed in the sedge and grass association. A large marsh of the latter type, near my home, has been a favorite breeding ground for these wrens for many years; there are some small willows, alders, and gray birches along the banks of the intersecting ditches; and small bushes scattered through the marsh serve as singing stations for the wrens; many flowering plants add color to the scene all through summer, and it is a glorious sight early in fall when the bur-marigold carpets the whole meadow with a blaze of yellow. A pair of marsh hawks may be seen here in spring performing their courtships; we have often seen the male in his spectacular flight and have flushed the female from her nest. This and other similar swamps in eastern Massachusetts are the favorite haunts of swamp sparrows, song sparrows, Henslow's sparrows, and northern yellowthroats.

L. McI. Terrill (1922), writing of the Montreal district, says: "In this locality the Short-billed Marsh Wren has a decided preference for sphagnum bogs—not so much the bog proper as the firmer ground about the bog margins, where there is a certain amount of free surface water and a fairly heavy growth of grasses and sedges. Here the silky tassels of the cotton-grass waving above the lesser growth, are a familiar sight and one is more apt to find swamp laurel in greater abundance than bushes of Labrador Tea, which appears to thrive better in the yielding sphagnum. Clumps of alders are also commonly found with an occasional tamarack sapling and sometimes beds of cattails, while often there is a thicket of poplars and birches in the background."

Dr. Lawrence H. Walkinshaw (1935) says that in Michigan "the favorite habitat of the Short-billed Marsh Wren is not among the large groups of cattails with several feet of standing water, but rather in the higher part of the marshes, in the intermediate portion between the bordering meadow and the deepest part of the swamp itself. There is generally very little and often no water at all where they nest." He says that "these marshes are the favorite habitat for the sandhill crane * * *, Yellow Rail * * *, Greater Prairie Chicken * * *, Savannah Sparrow * * *, Henslow's Sparrow * * *, Leconte's Sparrow * * *, Swamp Sparrow * * *, and Song Sparrow * * *." Among the plants growing in the marsh, he lists royal, sensitive, and marsh ferns, cattails, wood bulrush, showy ladyslipper, calopogon, some of the smaller willows, fringed and closed gentians, climbing wild cucumber, tall ironweed, joepyeweed, blue vervain, Canada goldenrod, beggarticks, nodding bur-marigold, New England aster, Yellow dock, and turtlehead. "In the early part of the summer grasses and sedges predominate, and later the appearance of the marsh takes on the gay colors, the yellows and blues, of the goldenrods, asters, and vervains."

Wendell Taber tells me that in a marsh in New Hampshire, at an elevation of 1,020 feet, he has found this wren in June for four seasons in succession; he usually hears olive-sided and alder flycatchers and once a winter wren singing while he was listening to the marsh wren.

The short-billed marsh wren is widely distributed over the central and eastern parts of southern Canada and a large part of the northern half of the United States. But it does not seem to be evenly distributed and seems to be rare or unknown in many portions of this wide range. It is common only where it can find suitable marshes; some of these marshes may contain only one or two pairs, while others may support populous colonies. Perhaps it is commoner in many places than is generally supposed, because of its small size and shy, retiring habits. Furthermore, the marshes where it lives are not as carefully explored by bird lovers as some other places.

Nesting.—This wren not only lives in a different type of habitat from that of the long-billed species, but its nesting habits are quite different.

It has been said by some authors to build a nest like that of the long-billed marsh wren and in similar situations; I have seen such supposed nests of this species in collections. These nests all contained white eggs and were naturally taken to be short-billed marsh wrens' nests. But, as the long-billed marsh wren sometimes lays white eggs, perhaps oftener than we realize, I suspect that some of, if not all, these nests may have belonged to the latter species.

It has been my experience, and I find that most authors agree with me, that the short-billed marsh wren builds its nest almost, if not quite, always in the types of habitat described above and not in the dense, deep-water cattail swamps; the nest is placed in sedges or grass, or other low herbage, close to the ground, mud, or very shallow water, not more than a foot or two above it at the most, and never at the heights favored by the long-billed species in cattails and bulrushes; the nest is *globular* in shape and not oval, ovate, or coconut-shaped; it is well hidden deep down in the thick sedges or grasses, very different from the conspicuous domiciles of the other species; it is a ball of dry and green grasses, with a well-concealed opening on the side; generally the growing green grasses are woven into the ball, making it inconspicuous, and often the growing grasses are arched over it, helping still further to conceal it. It is a very difficult nest to find, most easily overlooked, and the bird usually sneaks away from it without betraying its location.

Three of the nests described in my notes illustrate the slight variations I have noted in Massachusetts nests, all of which were found in fresh water marshes near Boston. One, in a marsh where the water was nearly knee deep, was in plain sight on the side of a tussock of tall grass on the edge of an open place, about 2 feet above the water; it was, however, almost invisible and could have been easily overlooked, as it was made of green grass woven into a neat ball and so placed as to blend perfectly into the surrounding grasses. Another was beautifully hidden on the side of a large tuft of tall grass, the opening looking out to the northward across a little shallow open water between the tufts; the bottom of the nest was 12 inches above the water, and the tallest grass tops were about 12 inches above the top of the nest; the concealment of the nest was made more effective by wrapping around it many blades of green growing grass, giving it the appearance of being made of green grass. The third, in a meadow that was not very wet, was placed near the base of a tuft of tall grass only a few inches from the damp ground; it was made entirely of coarse dry grasses and was lined with fine grass, feathers, and fur. One found in the same marsh by my companion, Owen Durfee, was in shorter green grass, not tufted, near a ditch; the bottom of this nest was only 4 inches above the mud.

A nest found by Mr. Terrill (1922) in the locality near Montreal, described above, was "almost resting on the [sphagnum] moss at the base of a low kalmia bush. It was very loosely fastened to the bush and was fairly well hidden by surrounding grasses. In respect of being globular and having a side entrance it resembled the nest of the Long-billed Marsh Wren. Otherwise the loose construction and composition of very old grasses and sedges recalled nests of the shrew. Also it was resting practically on the ground, or moss. It contained two newly hatched young and three addled eggs, two of which were cracked. As far as I could discover the lining consisted of down from poplar (?) catkins, a piece of fur-covered hare skin, and a few chickadee feathers."

A nest studied by Henry Mousley (1934) near St. Hubert, Quebec, in the same general region, is thus described: "The nest, an almost globular structure with a small entrance hole on one side, was composed outwardly of narrow strips of dry cattail leaves whilst the inside lining consisted of a thick layer of cattail down and five white feathers of a domestic fowl. It was only 2 inches above the ground, at the foot of a clump of the common or soft rush (*Juncus effusus*), this being the more or less general situation. Its height was 6 inches, width 5 inches, whilst the inside diameter was 3 inches." The surrounding herbage consisted principally of goldenrods, intermixed with rushes and sedges, as well as clusters of asters, spiked purple loosestrife, meadowsweet, beggarticks, and Roman wormwood.

The nests observed in Michigan by Dr. Walkinshaw (1935) were apparently similar in location and construction to the Massachusetts nests described above, "all in dense thick masses of small-leafed sedge, or in a combination of sedges and finer grasses." The birds usually build several nests, "and the used nest is often a little closer to the ground than the false ones. * * * Often the false nests of one pair will be located almost to the territory of another pair, in large meadows where they seem to congregate in colonies. In the marsh studied in Calhoun County, during 1934, in an area of about 10 acres, there were as many as 35 or 40 males singing at the same time, while in other places of smaller size only one pair could be found."

I have no firsthand knowledge of the number of false, or dummy, nests usually built by this wren, but many observers have referred to the universal habit. These nests are presumably built by the male, but this does not seem to have been definitely proved; they are usually unlined and not so well built as the brood nest. Forbush (1929) says: "It is a great nest builder. Just how many unlined nests one ambitious male will build nobody seems to know, but where there is a large colony of these wrens, the nests are 'legion,' and where few birds are breeding the occupied nests are difficult to find."

Eggs.—The commonest number of eggs in the nest of the short-billed marsh wren seems to be 7, but as few as 4 and as many as 8 have been recorded. The eggs are ovate or pointed-ovate, the shells are thin and very fragile, and the color is pure white and unmarked. The measurements of 50 eggs in the United States National Museum average 16.0 by 12.0 millimeters; the eggs showing the four extremes measure 17.3 by 12.7, 17.0 by 12.7, 14.4 by 11.3, and 15.2 by 11.2 millimeters.

Young.—The period of incubation has been stated as from 12 to 14 days, and is apparently performed by the female alone. Dr. Walkinshaw (1935) writes:

The young of the Marsh Wren remain in the nest from 12 to 14 days. They are fed by the female almost entirely but the male occasionally will stop to feed them. Excreta are carried away by the mother bird on her feeding trips to the nest.

When the weather was very warm, the young peered out through the opening, breathing very fast with mouths wide open. They showed little fear of man until they were about 12 to 14 days old, then when one approached the nest they watched very dubiously.

After they leave the nest the young move about among the sedge and bushes of the marsh like little mice, except that they occasionally move up to secure food from their parents which feed them until they are able to take care of themselves, even then they move about in small groups until migration time.

At the nest watched by Mr. Mousley (1934), "altogether, the young were fed 28 times in the 6 hours, or at the rate of once in every 13 minutes, and this by the female alone, her partner contenting himself by always singing from his favourite station on the thorn bush, whenever she approached the nest."

Several observers have stated that two broods are raised in a season. Fresh eggs have been found at such early and late dates that this seems to be indicated.

Plumages.—I have not seen the natal down. Dr. Walkinshaw (1935) describes some very young birds as follows:

The young have legs and bill pink, the latter a little darker near the tip of the maxilla. The young when they leave the nest are from 55 to 70 mm. in length. The top of the head on one specimen of 58 mm. in length, had no stripes, being dark brown changing to a lighter brown on the forehead. The back, rump and upper tail coverts were uniform hair brown, the wings a deeper brown, and the breast very similar but a little lighter, than that of the adult. The tail was 10 mm. in length, hair brown with one black band about two mm. in width at the tip. A bird 66 mm. in length had the coloration much the same, but there were indications of black on the wings and nape. In a bird 69 mm. long the head was colored the same, but the wings were barred with blackish and tipped with brown, and the back was barred with black. The breast on the sides was much more buffy and had a distinct band near the throat. The bills were decurved in these young birds.

Dr. Dwight's (1900) description of what is probably an older bird differs but slightly: "Above, dull black on the pileum and back, the nape, sepia, the rump and upper tail coverts russet; streaked anteriorly with white, barred on the rump and wings with black, white and cinnamon, palest on the primaries; the tail drab, mottled rather than barred with black. Below, including sides of the head, ochraceous buff palest on the chin and throat and washed strongly on the sides, flanks and crissum with cinnamon, the feathers whitish centrally and terminally."

He says that the first winter plumage is "acquired by a partial post-juvenal molt beginning about the middle of August which involves the body plumage and wing coverts, probably the tertiaries, but not the rest of the wings nor the tail." This plumage he describes as "similar to the previous plumage, the forehead largely sepia-brown and conspicuous white stripes on the crown. Below, the ochraceous wash is deeper including a pectoral band and a few black and white bars occur on the flanks. The tertiaries are distinctly black, edged and barred with white, russet bordered."

This plumage is practically indistinguishable from the winter plumage of the adult. The prenuptial molt of both adults and young is nearly or quite complete. Dr. Dwight says that this is proved by birds taken in Texas on April 15. "Limited material indicates that only a few of the outer primaries are renewed in some cases." Dr. Stone (1896) says: "There is a complete spring molt of the body feathers in this bird as shown in a series taken at Tarpon Springs, Fla., April 15th." Dr. Sutton (1940) took one of these wrens in southern San Luis Potosí, Mexico, on April 18, that was "in the midst of a molt involving head- and body-plumage." And he saw another, taken March 22, in Tamaulipas, Mexico, in which the rectrices were molting. Both year-old birds and adults have a complete postnuptial molt mainly in August. The fresh autumn plumage is more richly colored than the spring plumage and sometimes shows a few dusky bars on the flanks. The sexes are alike in all plumages.

Food.—No very extensive study of the food of the short-billed marsh wren seems to have been made. Dr. Walkinshaw (1935) says that the food consists of insects. "They have been observed to feed the young, with moths, spiders, mosquitoes, flies, grasshoppers, and bugs." Arthur H. Howell (1932) says: "Examination of 34 stomachs of this Wren from Florida showed its food to consist wholly of insects and spiders. The insects taken included ants, bugs, weevils, ladybird beetles, moths, caterpillars, locusts, crickets, and grasshoppers."

Behavior.—This tiny wren, one of the smallest of the family, is also one of the shiest, most retiring, and elusive. As we pass some likely meadow we may recognize its characteristic, chattering little song and perhaps see the male perched on some small bush in or near a marsh, or on the swaying top of a tall sedge or reed, singing to his hidden mate. If we approach for a closer look he dives into the nearest and thickest cover, and we may not see him again. His cousin, the longbill, might be prompted by curiosity to come sneaking through the cover of the cattails to have a sly look at us; but not so the little shortbill; his one glimpse was enough and he was interested only in keeping out of sight, and so off he goes, creeping mouselike through the dense grass. His mate is even more shy about her nest; only once have I succeeded in surprising her at home; then she dove like a flash into the grass and disappeared, but I heard her scolding notes as she moved about in the surrounding cover. Mr. Mousley (1934) succeeded in photographing the female at the nest, to which she returned within 20 minutes after he had beaten down the grasses in front of the nest and placed his camera only about 2 feet away. He writes: "As showing her apparent disregard of the camera she on one occasion perched on a leg of the tripod. * * * At times it was only the song of the male that gave me any indication that his partner was near the nest, whilst at others I was more fortunate in observing her approach, as she flew just above the top of the herbage suddenly flopping down into it at some distance from the nest, when all trace of her would be lost until the actions of the young made me aware that she had arrived in the near vicinity of the nest, but where she would actually appear was another matter."

If the male is flushed in the open marsh, which is not a difficult matter, he goes flying off close to the tops of the sedges with a straight, even, slow flight, looking like a tiny ball of feathers propelled with rapid beats of his little wings, and then suddenly drops down into the cover.

Voice.—Over 40 years ago I wrote in my notes that the song of the short-billed marsh wren is a chattering trill, resembling the sound made by striking two sticks very rapidly together; it suggests the song of the longbill but is fainter and lacks the musical, bubbling notes of the latter's song. Some others have suggested that the song sounds like striking small pebbles together or rattling a bag of marbles, not bad descriptions.

The song has been expressed in syllables, more or less differently by various observers. Ora W. Knight (1908) writes the full-length characteristic song as "chip—chip—chip—chip, chip-chip-chip-chir-r-r-r-r"; it reminded him of the song of the pallid wren tit; though "different in timbre, * * * harsh and lacking the bell like resonance of the Wren Tit's song it was uttered with the same accentuation and syllaballization." Ernest T. Seton (1890) writes the same song as "*chap—chap—chap–chap, chap, chap, chap p-p-p-r-r-r.*" In both of these cases the first four syllables are given deliberately, with pauses between them and on a lower key than the rest of the song, which runs off in a rapid, diminuendo trill.

Ralph Hoffmann (1904) says: "While the song of the Long-billed Marsh Wren resembles the House Wren's in its volubility, that of the Short-billed Marsh Wren suggests rather some species of sparrow. It may be represented by the syllables *tsip tsip tsip tsipper tsipper tsipper*, the first two or three notes staccato, the rest running rapidly down the scale. The call note is like the opening note of the song."

The song reminded Dr. Sutton (1928) "of the insect-like performance of the Dickcissel, particularly the latter portion of the song. This song might be written 'Dick, putt, jik, plick, chick-chick-chick.'" And Bagg and Eliot (1937) write it "*tsick, zwick, diddle-diddle-diddle.*"

As to the length of the song period, Dr. Walkinshaw (1935) writes:

With us the Short-bill sings from the time of arrival in the spring until the departure for the south in the fall. During the months of April, May, June, and July it sings almost continuously during the hours of daylight. During August, when many of our birds are extremely quiet, this species is still a persistent singer and even in September and October I have heard its repeated song at certain times of day.

Of the pair which nested directly back of our house in 1933, the male was heard to sing not only during the day but at nearly all hours of night. During the months of May, June, July, and August I heard this male sing at various times; from 11:30 P. M. until 2:00 a. m., and until daylight. Then he would sing all day long until 9:30 p. m. but from 9:30 to 11:30 p. m. I never heard him sing. Sometimes between the hours of 2 and 5 a. m. he would sing as persistently as during the hours of daylight.

He usually sang the song once, then paused a few seconds before repeating. During the height of the nesting season he would sing once every five seconds for a period of several minutes. Many times when he was timed, he sang twelve times a minute, while at others he would only sing six or eight times. After August 10 this bird did not sing nearly as often but he continued to sing early in the morning and late in the evening until he left on October 5. This Wren had favorite perches from which he would sing, two on willows, another on a wire fence which was about 1000 yards from the nest. The two willows, however, were only about 25 feet distant.

He says there is some variation in the song and writes the full, long song as "chap-chap-churr-churr-chur-r-r-chap-chur-chur-r." The usual song, quickly repeated, is merely the first part of the above. "After the season had progressed into the months of August and September this became much less forceful and the opening became, 'Sit-sit-sit-churr-chur-r-r,' or 'Sit-sit-sit-sit-t-t.'" He gives the scolding notes as "Churr-churr" and "Chap-churr."

Aretas A. Saunders writes to me: "The song of this bird is unmistakable when known because of its peculiar quality, not like that of any other bird I know. It is not musical or guttural, but the pitch of the notes can be determined in spite of this. It begins with two to five short notes, sounding like 'tip', and ends with a trill or a series of rapid notes all on one pitch, and one to three tones lower than the first notes. When the first notes are two or three in number they are likely to be all on the same pitch, and in even time, like the beginning of a song sparrow's song. Then the song is a simple 'tip-tip-tip-trrrrrr'. But when there are four or five notes there is likely to be a change in pitch, or a pause after the first note, giving a result like 'tip ———— tip – tap – trrrrrr'. The trill usually ends the song, but there is sometimes a still lower terminal note, making it end 'trrrrr-tup'. The pitch of my records varies just an octave, from C''' to C'''', but no one song I have recorded covers a whole octave. The lengths of songs in my records vary from 1⅜ to 2⅜ seconds."

Francis H. Allen watched one at close range, as he sang, and says (MS.): "When he uttered the first notes of his song he raised his tail, sometimes perpendicular to his back or even pointing forward, sometimes not so far, and sometimes hardly at all. With the last notes of the song, the tail would go back to a position about horizontal with the body. Often, though not always, it was jerked in time to the notes, that is a couple of emphatic jerks at its highest point, simultaneous with the two emphatic opening notes of the song, and then a quavering fall with the closing trill."

Fall.—Mr. Saunders's observations in Connecticut indicate that the fall migration begins early. He found birds singing in August in a place where he "was very sure no such bird had been the previous May and June, a tall grass area back of the salt marshes near Fairfield Beach. On July 26, 1941, I found a bird singing in a similar locality back of the beach, a place I passed or visited frequently throughout the year. In the next few days I found several birds in this general vicinity, and by August 9 the birds were abundant all through the grass areas back of the beach, and I heard the song in many different places. The birds continued abundant all through August but began to decrease early in September, and the last one was found September 20. Evidently fall migration can begin in July, at least in some years."

Field marks.—As the short-billed marsh wren is oftener heard than seen, its peculiar and quite characteristic song is the best means of identification. Its haunts are different from those of the long-billed marsh wren, and it is almost never seen in the cattail swamps. If one can get a good look at it, which is not easy, it can be distinguished from the long-billed species by the streaked crown and by the absence of the white line over the eye and the absence of the black back patch. The shorter bill is not very conspicuous in life.

Winter.—The 1931 Check-list does not extend the winter range of this wren beyond the southern border of the United States, but Dr. Sutton (1940) took one and heard others on April 18, 1939, in southern San Luis Potosí, Mexico; he also saw one in the American Museum of Natural History that was taken in Tamaulipas on March 22, 1888. Probably the species winters regularly in at least northern Mexico.

We found it common on various grassy meadows and prairies in different parts of Florida and collected specimens. Mr. Howell (1932) says of its haunts: "The Short-billed Marsh Wren, during the winter season in Florida, is found in marshes, both fresh and salt, and in old fields or prairies where there is a growth of dense, matted grass or weeds. The birds remain hidden in the vegetation most of the time, but are easily flushed by walking toward them, when they fly weakly for a short distance and drop again into the grass. At times I have heard them chattering in the marsh grass, or rarely singing a little." About Tarpon Springs, W. E. D. Scott (1890) has "taken the birds in both salt and fresh water marshes, though marshes of sedge grass where the water is brackish and the sedge not very high nor dense seem to be preferred." Wayne (1910) says that, in South Carolina, "it inhabits freshwater marshes and fields which are covered with broom grass, rarely, if ever, resorting to the salt marshes. The centre of abundance is on the rice plantations, where it is exceedingly abundant during the autumn, winter, and spring months."

Frederick V. Hebard writes to me: "The number of this abundant species to be recorded in the broomsedge fields and flats of southeastern Georgia near dusk on a winter day will only be limited by one's perseverance. Wet winter or dry winter, the 'Joren' is there in great numbers. It chirps its two-noted call *ch-chip*, frequently during the day and increases it toward dusk to almost choral frequency."

DISTRIBUTION

Range.—The species ranges from Canada south to Tierra del Fuego, southern South America, the North American race from southern Canada to northeastern Mexico.

Breeding range.—The short-billed marsh wren breeds **north** to southeastern Saskatchewan (Quill Lake); southern Manitoba (Lake St. Martin, Shoal Lake, and Indian Bay, Lake of the Woods); central Ontario (Whitefish Lake, Lake Nipissing, and Ottawa); southern Quebec (Montreal and Hatley); and central Maine (Glenburn and Bangor). **East** to central Maine (Bangor); and along the Atlantic coast to southern Maryland (Ocean City and Point Lookout). **South** to southern Maryland (Ocean City and Point Lookout); central Ohio (Columbus); central Indiana (Indianapolis); and central Missouri (St. Louis and Kansas City). **West** to western Missouri (Kansas City); eastern Nebraska (Lincoln and West Point); eastern South Dakota (Vermilion, Sioux Falls, and Petrodie); eastern North Dakota (Napoleon, Devils Lake, and the Turtle Mountains); and southeastern Saskatchewan (Quill Lake). It has been found breeding at Barbourville, Ky., and there are probably other semiisolated colonies.

Winter range.—In winter the short-billed marsh wren is confined to the coastal region of southeastern United States and northeastern Mexico from North Carolina (Cape Hatteras) **south** through South Carolina and Georgia (Savannah and Macon) to southern Florida (Royal Palm Hammock); **west** along the Gulf coast to Texas (Austin and Brownsville); and **south** to Tamaulipas (Quijano) and southeastern San Luis Potosí (Tamazunchale), Mexico.

Spring migration.—Late dates of spring departure are: Florida—Pensacola, April 25. Georgia—Athens, May 8. North Carolina—Raleigh, May 4. Texas—College Station, April 23. Kansas—Onaga, May 22.

Early dates of spring arrival are: Georgia—Athens, April 10. North Carolina—Chapel Hill, April 28. Pennsylvania—State College, April 26. New York—Rochester, April 30. Massachusetts—Wayland, May 2. Ohio—Painesville, May 2. Ontario—London, May 9. Indiana—Kendallville, May 1. Michigan—Battle Creek, April 30. Illinois—Chicago, April 21. Iowa—Grinnell, April 28. Wisconsin—Madison, May 1. Minnestoa—Duluth, May 5. Kansas—Manhattan, April 25. South Dakota—Vermilion, May 9. Manitoba—Aweme, April 29.

Fall migration.—Late dates of fall departure are: Manitoba—Aweme, October 2. South Dakota—Forestburg, October 5. Nebraska—Lincoln, September 27. Kansas—Lawrence, October 15. Minnesota—Minneapolis, October 6. Wisconsin—Racine, October 15. Iowa—Keokuk, October 13. Michigan—Detroit, October 2. Illinois—Glen Ellyn, October 17. Indiana—Waterloo, October 1. Ontario—Ottawa, October 4. Ohio—Youngstown, September 17. New York—Branchport, October 11. Pennsylvania—Carlisle, September 20. Massachusetts—Northampton, October 10. Connecticut—Fairfield, October 7. North Carolina—Chapel Hill, October 7.

Early dates of fall arrival are: Kansas—Onaga, August 7. Texas—Corpus Christi, October 6. North Carolina—Chapel Hill, August 19. Georgia—Athens, August 9. Florida—Fort Myers, September 29.

Casual records.—A specimen was taken near Camrose, Alberta, on September 19, 1927; a specimen was collected at Norway House, Manitoba, on June 20, 1900, that was possibly nesting but no nest was found; a specimen was taken at Cheyenne, Wyoming, on April 14, 1889; a specimen collected 15 miles northeast of Mosca, Colo., in the San Luis Valley, on October 23, 1907, is the first record from west of the mountains; in North Dakota several were noted in a meadow near Kenmare in July 1913, possibly a breeding colony; near Pungo, Va., several pairs were noted from May 17 to 20, 1932. Several records in winter north of the normal range are: a specimen taken at Ann Arbor, Mich., on January 15, 1938; a record from Jones Beach, Long Island,

N. Y., on December 28, 1913; and it is reported to occur occasionally in winter near Philadelphia, Pa.

Egg dates.—Massachusetts: 25 records, May 25 to July 29; 13 records, June 1 to July 7, indicating the height of the season.

New Jersey: 8 records, May 30 to August 20.

South Dakota: 2 records, June 9 and June 19.

Wisconsin: 10 records, June 1 to August 19.

CATHERPES MEXICANUS ALBIFRONS (Giraud)

WHITE-THROATED WREN

HABITS

Four races of this species were recognized in the 1931 Check-list, and five were recognized by Ridgway (1904); one of these is strictly Mexican; and recent investigations have indicated that only two forms should be included in our Check-list. The type race, *Catherpes mexicanus mexicanus*, inhabits the central and southern portions of the Mexican Plateau. According to the above authorities, *C. m. albifrons* occupies the northern portion of the Mexican Plateau and extends its range into central western Texas, near the mouth of the Pecos River. Recent faunal investigations have extended this range considerably. Van Tyne and Sutton (1937) referred to this race the canyon wrens collected in the Chisos Mountains in Brewster County; and Burleigh and Lowery (1940) collected a number of specimens of it in the Guadalupe Mountains, close to the New Mexico line. Both of these localities are far removed from the mouth of the Pecos River where it empties into the Rio Grande. It seems fair to assume that this will prove to be the breeding form throughout the whole of extreme western Texas.

According to Ridgway (1904), this subspecies is similar to the type race in size, with a bill averaging longer, but the coloration is "much paler, the general color of upper parts more grayish brown chestnut of abdomen, etc., paler, and black bars on tail averaging narrower."

The specimens collected in the Chisos Mountains were taken mainly between 5,000 and 6,000 feet elevation, and in the Guadalupe Mountains at elevations ranging from 6,000 to 8,000 feet; in the latter locality this wren "was never known to venture to the foot of the mountains."

Nesting.—The nesting habits of the white-throated wren are apparently not different from those of canyon wrens elsewhere. There is a set of four eggs, with the nest, in the Thayer collection in Cambridge that was taken in Nueva León, Mexico, on April 12, 1911, for F. B. Armstrong. It was in a snug corner of a crevice in the rock on the perpendicular wall of a canyon, about a hundred feet from the base of the cliff. The nest is made of mosses, lichens, and wool, with a few weed stems and strips of inner bark; and it is profusely lined with soft plant down and a little wool. In its present condition it measures about 4 by 4½ inches in outside and 2 by 2¼ inches in inside diameter; it is about 1¾ inches high and is cupped to a depth of 1 inch.

Eggs.—The eggs in the above set are ovate and slightly glossy. Their ground color is pure white and they are sparingly sprinkled with very small spots or fine dots of light reddish brown, more thickly distributed near the larger ends. They measure 19.1 by **14.4, 19.3** by **14.1,** 19.0 by 14.3, and **18.5** by 14.2 millimeters.

Plumages.—Ridgway (1901) says that the young of the Mexican race are "similar to adults, but upper parts more coarsely vermiculated with dusky and with few if any white specks or dots; chestnut of abdomen, etc., duller, immaculate, or with very indistinct narrow dusky bars, mostly on flanks."

Voice.—The following attractive tribute to the song of the canyon wren by Dr. William Beebe (1905) also refers to the Mexican subspecies:

The beautiful little wren-sprites of the *barranca* were the first to waken and sing, and we hardly recognized in them the Mexican Canyon Wrens of the house tops of Guadalajara. Here they were in their native haunts, and their marvellous hymn of sweetness rang out frequently in the early morning, reëchoing among the rocky cliffs. We caught the real inspiration of the wild joyous strain, which was so obscured and fitted so ill with the environment of the dusty city. It is a silvery dropping song of eight or ten clear sweet notes, becoming more plaintive as they descend, and ending in several low, ascending trills. The silvery quality is of marvellous depth and purity, and although at times the birds sang with startling loudness from the very ridgepole of the tent, there was not a trace of harshness or aught save liquid clearness. It seemed the very essence of the freshness of dawn in the cool bottom of the canyon. The little singer was not easily detected in the gray light, but at last his tremulous white throat was seen high overhead at the entrance of some dripping, mossy crevice in the rocks, his tiny body and wings of dark chocolate hue merging into the background.

As the sunlight traveled slowly downward toward us, the notes flowed more slowly from his throat, until, with the increasing warmth, only a few sleepy tones were heard—like the last efforts of the dying katydids at the time of the first frost. But the wren himself was far from sleepy. The heat had simply thawed the frozen music from his heart and he now began the serious work of the day. * * *

Of all the birds of the *barrancas* these wrens perhaps won our deepest affection; so tiny were they, and yet each morning filling the whole great gorge with their sweetness.

DISTRIBUTION

Range.—Western United States and Mexico, nonmigratory except for a slight altitudinal movement.

The canyon wren ranges **north** to central southern British Columbia

(Okanagan Valley north to Naramata); Washington (Sheep Mountain and Nighthawk); Idaho (Lewiston and Salmon River); Montana (Billings); and Wyoming (Newcastle). **East** to Wyoming (Newcastle and Laramie); Colorado (Boulder, Golden, Manitou, and western Baca County); Oklahoma (Black Mesa near Kenton and Wichita Mountains); south-central Texas (Austin, Boerne, and San Antonio); Tamaulipas (Gómez Farias); Veracruz (Chichicaxtle and Jico); Puebla (Puebla and Atlixco); and Oaxaca (Cuicatlan and Tehuantepec). **South** to Oaxaca (Tehuantepec and Santo Domingo) and Guerrero (Taxco and Chilpancingo). **West** to Guerrero (Chilpancingo); Colima (Río de Coahuayana); Baja California (La Paz Laguna Hanson, and Los Coronados Islands); California (the coast range as far north as San Francisco Bay, Escondido, Pasadena, San Jose, Baird, and Mount Shasta); Oregon (eastern slope of the Cascades, Ashland, Brownsboro, and the mouth of the Deschutes River); Washington (Wishram, Yakima, and Chelan); and British Columbia (Okanagan Valley).

The range as outlined is for the entire species, of which two subspecies or geographic races are now recognized in the United States. The typical race (*C. m. mexicanus*) is confined to Mexico; the white-throated wren (*C. m. albifrons*) occurs from central western Texas, near the mouth of the Pecos River, south over the Mexican Plateau to Zacatecas; the canyon wren (*C. m. conspersus*) occupies the rest of the range in the United States and British Columbia.

Casual records.—Two specimens were collected, adult and young, August 2 and 6, 1935, in Spearfish Canyon, S. Dak., the first record for the state; one was seen August 12, 1903 in the canyon of the White River, Sioux County, Nebraska, between Glen and Andrews; a specimen was collected on November 23, 1906, near Cheyenne Wells. Colo.

Egg dates.—Arizona: 6 records, April 18 to June 12.

California: 68 records, March 28, to July 11; 34 records, April 21 to May 17, indicating the height of the season.

Colorado: 2 records, May 8 and June 9.

Texas: 20 records, March 4 to June 19; 10 records, April 8 to 30.

CATHERPES MEXICANUS CONSPERSUS Ridgway

CANYON WREN

PLATES 52, 53

HABITS

On April 17, 1922, we drove down from the rough roads of the Catalina Mountains, Ariz., and pitched camp in the heart of Apache Canyon, one of the grandest and most beautiful of the canyons we had seen. Near our camp the floor of the canyon was broad and fairly smooth, though stony; it was watered by a clear mountain stream that flowed gently over a wide, stony bed; it was well shaded by gigantic and picturesque sycamores and by enormous cottonwoods whose lofty, spreading branches reminded us of our familiar New England elms. A zone-tailed hawk had a nest in one of the cottonwoods and greeted us with anxious cries.

Early the next morning we were awakened by the melodious songs of Arizona cardinals and by the Cassin's kingbirds' loud, striking notes, "come here, come here," as they flitted about in the big white sycamores over our heads. Above our camp we found the canyon to be heavily wooded with cottonwoods, sycamores, a variety of oaks, maples, walnuts, and other trees, in which red-tailed and Cooper's hawks had their nests. The sides of the canyons were rough and rocky, in some places very steep or even precipitous, and more or less overgrown with hackberries, thorns, mesquites, and mountainmisery, where these and small giant cacti could find a foothold. We saw or heard a long list of interesting birds, but the gem of them all was the canyon wren. Its wild, joyous strain of sweet, silvery notes greeted us as we passed some steep cliffs; they seemed to reverberate from one cliff to another, to fill the whole canyon with delightful melody and to add a fitting charm to the wild surroundings.

The above is fairly typical of the haunts of this species, for most observers seem to agree it is well named as a dweller on the cliffs or the rocky slopes of the canyons, where it can dodge in and out among the numerous cracks, crannies, and dark little caves. But it is not wholly confined to such places and has even adapted itself to living in human surroundings. George Finlay Simmons (1925) says that. in Texas, it is found about "old rock buildings in towns; less commonly, about houses and barns." It is "common in and about the city of Austin, and sings from the chimneytops with the Western Mockingbirds and Texas Long-tailed Wrens." Referring to this, Mrs. Bailey (1902) remarks that "when they do, what cool, grateful canyon memories they awaken in the midst of the town! When heard afterwards on their own native canyon cliffs it seems impossible that they could ever sing in a city, their song is so attuned to the wild mountain fastnesses." W. Leon Dawson (1923) writes: "There is no place forbidden to a Canyon Wren, no rock wall which frights him, no tunnel's mouth, nor intricacy of talus bed. He has no special predilection for the picturesque, however, as his name might seem to imply. A brush pile or a heap of old tin cans will do as well as a miner's cabin or an old Mission."

This race of the species has by far the widest range of any of the forms of the species; and, if we eliminate *punctulatus* [1] and *polioptilus*, as modern research seems to indicate that we should, *conspersus* inhab-

---

[1] See Grinnell and Behle (1935) for reasons why *C. m. punctulatus* is synonymous with *conspersus*.

its all suitable regions in western North America from the eastern edge of the Rocky Mountains to the Pacific slope, except for the restricted range of *albifrons* in Texas. It differs but little from *albifrons*, being paler and smaller.

Nesting.—We eventually found the nest of the pair we saw in Apache Canyon. It was in a small cave at the base of a rock cliff, and almost inaccessible in a crevice above a little shelf in the roof of the cave. Other nests have been found in similar situations. For example, Dr. Alexander Wetmore (1920) found a nest in a gulch near Lake Burford, N. Mex., of which he says:

> The nest was placed on a small shelf of rock in the top of a shallow cave or hollow in a sandstone cliff. This ledge was about 15 feet from the floor of the gulch, and the cave was approximately 3 feet high. * * * The nest measured 8 inches across the base and 3 inches tall. The cup containing the eggs was 2½ inches in diameter and 2 inches deep. The foundation was composed of a dozen or more small twigs upon which were placed moss and masses of spider webbing with bits of leaves, catkins and bud scales. The nest lining was composed of a heavy felting of sheep's wool, most of it white, though a few bits of dark brown wool were mixed through it. In addition, in the cavity containing the eggs, were a few feathers of Great Horned Owl, Violet-green Swallow and Cassin's Finch.

The nest has been said to resemble that of the wood pewee in shape and appearance, and W. E. D. Scott (1888a) says:

> In the Catalinas I took in all half a dozen nests that were built much like the nest of the Phoebe (*Sayornis phoebe*), the same thick, heavy walls, rather soft and covered with green moss on the outside characterizing the structure, and the inside cavity not so broad or shallow as in the case of the Phoebe. The nest is generally placed in some deserted tunnel or cave, and at times in unused buildings. It is found more frequently on some projecting ledge or shelf, and rarely in some cranny or hole that will scarcely permit the old birds to enter. The eggs are from four to six in number, and three broods are generally reared each season.

Mrs. Lila M. Lofberg (1931) has published an interesting account of a most remarkable nest of this wren, which she studied intensively. She says: "Early last spring the men in the general office of the Southern California Edison Co. at Big Creek, Fresno County, wondered where all their clips, pins and such were disappearing to, when they discovered a pair of Cañon Wrens (*Catherpes mexicanus punctulatus*) were utilizing them in the building of their nest." After the wrens had left it, she took the nest home and analyzed the wonderful collection of varied materials that entered into it; the energy and industry displayed by the birds in gathering the materials and building the nest was hardly exceeded by the patience and painstaking care shown by her in pulling it to pieces. Here is her description of it:

> The foundation, 4½ inches in height and 5 inches square at the base, contained the following items: 152 twigs and slivers of wood ranging in length from ¾ to 8¾ inches, with a diameter or breadth of from ⅛ to ½ inch; 15 lengths of

straw, 1¼ to 8¼ inches long; 43 pine catkins; 4 pieces of wire insulation material, ½ to 2¼ inches long; 14 Supreme paper clips; 1 Ideal paper clip, 3 inches in length; 628 Gem paper clips; 14 T pins; 1 2-inch safety pin; 582 common pins; 28 rubber bands; 1 three-coil spring; 1 screw top from LePage's glue container; 11 steel pen points; 19 thumb tacks; 2 small screws; 11 galvanized cuphead tacks; 1 carpet tack; 2 insulation tacks; 67 rusty nails; 2 small pieces of rawhide shoe lace; 1 3-inch darning needle; 69 Star paper fasteners; 3 small pieces of insulated wire; 27 pieces of wire (5 copper), all short; 1 steel tape tip; 87 matches (three unburnt) ; 4 toothpicks.

This grand total of 1,791 countable things, while haphazardly placed, was held firmly by a filling of ½ pound of the following: Cobwebs, lint, dust, thread, sawdust, wood shavings, bits of paper, broom straw, twine, rope, plaster board, pine needles, splinters, shreds and pieces of pine bark, and asbestos, shells, and gauzy wings of insects, an air-mail label, horsehair, small pieces of walnut shell, triangle of glass (¼ inch base and 1 inch in length), and an Eversharp pencil lead.

The nest proper was so firmly fastened to the foundation that it was not easy to dislodge. It was 4 x 5½ inches with an outside depth of 3½ inches. It was composed of very small pieces of straw, pine needles, string, rope, thread, and twigs. It was a solid mat made by clever filling of dust, lint, and dog and horse hairs. The upper 2 inches were very soft, made entirely of padding filched from mattresses. Into this was hollowed the cup for the eggs, 2½ inches across at the rim and 1¾ at the bottom, the depth being ¾ of an inch.

The nest proper weighed only an ounce, while that of the entire structure was 2⁷⁄₁₆ pounds.

Mr. Simmons (1925) says that, in the Austin region of Texas, the canyon wren nests "rarely, in holes in cedar fence posts, eaves of outhouses and rafters of barns, crevices about rock buildings, cross-braces underneath houses and cabins, under cornices of verandas, and in chimneys of uninhabited houses; before abundance of the European House Sparrow, nested in mail boxes as commonly as does the Texas Long-tailed Wren."

Mrs. Amelia S. Allen tells me of a nest that "was placed inside a crude lean-to made of rusty oil cans. The rusty red of the wren matched exactly the color of the tin."

Eggs.—The canyon wren usually lays 5 or 6 eggs to a set, sometimes only 4 and rarely more than 6. These vary from ovate to nearly elliptical-ovate. The ground color is pure, clear white. The eggs are usually very sparingly marked with fine dots of reddish brown, sometimes so faintly marked as to appear immaculate; more rarely the markings are small spots of darker brown, which even more rarely may be concentrated about the larger end. Apparently they are never as heavily marked as are other wrens' eggs. The measurements of 50 eggs of the canyon wren and the dotted wren combined average 17.9 by 13.2 millimeters; the eggs showing the four extremes measure 19.8 by 13.7, 17.7 by 14.1, 16.8 by 12.7, and 17.5 by 12.6 millimeters. These were selected at random from the large series in the United States National Museum.

Behavior.—Grinnell and Storer (1924) mention the following items that are not recorded under the other subspecies: "Like the Rock Wren, the Cañon Wren has acquired a special flatness of body structure, which is an obvious adaptation to allow it passage through *horizontal* crevices. * * * The bird's legs (tarsi) are short and are held at an acute angle with the surface on which it is travelling, so that the body is close to the substratum. At intervals of 2 to 12 seconds the hinder parts are slowly raised and then instantaneously depressed. So quickly and violently is this done that the whole body is drawn into the movement."

Young.—Dr. Wetmore (1921) says of a brood of young that he observed near Williams, Ariz.:

On July 8 a female was found feeding young in the canyon south of town. The young, three in number, though not fully fledged, had left the nest and reposed at the bottom of a cleft in the rock in a space 2 inches wide. * * * The labor of caring for them seemed to be left entirely to the female, though the male was in the vicinity. The female came and went fearlessly carrying food, in the form of brown crickets with elongated antennae, paying little attention to me as I peered in the crevice with my face barely two feet away. After feeding she carried away excrement exactly as though the young were in the nest. The young were able to climb up and down the steepest rock surfaces with no difficulty whatever. When placed in the open, they became more alert and after a minute or so clambered away toward shelter. The heat of the sun, though apparently mild, affected them severely so that they panted heavily and closed their eyes seeming almost overpowered; it is probable that never before had they felt its rays. The call note for food was a faint *tsee tsee*.

Plumages.—I have seen no very young canyon wrens. Young birds in juvenal plumage look much like the adults, but the colors are all duller; there are few if any white spots on the upperparts, which are more or less mottled or vermiculated with dusky; the rich brown of the abdominal region is paler and is immaculate rather than spotted. I have seen birds in this plumage as late as August 17 and 30, but usually the postjuvenal molt of young birds and the postnuptial molt of adults apparently occurs during the last two weeks of August and the first two weeks of September.

Food.—No comprehensive study of the food of the canyon wren seems to have been made. It probably does not differ materially from the food of other western wrens, consisting mainly, if not wholly, of insects and spiders. Its feeding habits are evidently of no economic importance in its native wilderness, and, even when living in towns, it apparently does no harm and probably destroys many troublesome insects.

Behavior.—The canyon wren is usually heard long before it is seen. We hear the loud, ringing song echoing from the walls of the canyon and scan the rocky cliffs to find the tiny source of such a soul-filling outburst of melody. We catch a glimpse of his gleaming white throat before we can make out the outlines of the bird, for the browns of body, wings, and tail blend well into the background of rocks. At first, as he creeps along some narrow ledge or dodges in and out among the loose rocks and crevices of the cliff, we may mistake him for a chipmunk or a white-throated mouse, so mouselike are his movements. Soon he stops in full view on some sharp prominence or even the crest of the cliff, throws back his head, his silvery throat swells, and out pours the delicious strain; and we are astonished to connect such a volume of sound with such a tiny bird.

The frequent outbursts of song are not allowed to interfere with the serious business of the day; much of the daylight hours must be spent in climbing over, under, and around the rocks, searching in every nook and cranny for hidden insects and spiders. The wren's feet, with their sharp claws, are well adapted for climbing, even over nearly perpendicular surfaces and over the roofs of small caves, much as a brown creeper negotiates the trunks and limbs of trees. All day long this tireless bundle of feathered energy explores it rocky domain, disappearing from sight and suddenly appearing again at some unexpected spot, jumping or flitting from one rock to another, its eyes ever alert for its tiny prey and its brown tail erect, spread or flirted to express its feelings.

The canyon wren is not particularly shy, merely somewhat elusive and busy with its own affairs. About ranches and houses it is often quite unsuspicious and friendly. W. E. D. Scott (1885), writing from Arizona, says: "During that portion of the year when we live with doors and windows open (and this is for fully 9 months), the little brown friend with silvery throat is often in the rooms of the house, hopping about and searching every 'nook and cranny' for insect life, and betimes singing as merrily as when on the faces of the perpendicular rocks in the cañons, which are ever the favorite hunting grounds he delights in." And Howard Lacey (1911), who lived in Kerrville, Tex., says that "for 2 years a pair lived with us in the ranch house and became very tame, hopping about the floor and even singing on the table while we were in the room. They nested over one of the windows."

Voice.—Many authors have given the voice of the canyon wren unstinted and well-deserved praise, for its song is one of the best and most surprising of the many delightful songs of American birds. No song is quite like it, and when heard for the first time in the wild and desolate rocky canyons, to which it is a fitting accompaniment as it echoes from cliff to cliff, it creates an impression that can never be forgotten. No description is adequate to convey this impression to the reader, but the following quotations will give some idea of it. Mrs. Bailey (1902) writes: "His voice is so powerful that the canyon fairly rings with his song. What joyous notes! They sound as if his happiness were so great that he needs must proclaim it. His song comes tripping down the scale growing so fast it seems as if the song-ster could only stop by giving his odd little flourish back up the scale again at the end.   The ordinary song has seven descending notes, but often, as if out of pure exurberance of happiness, the wren begins with a run of grace notes, ending with the same little flourish.   The rare character of the song is its rhapsody and the rich vibrant quality which has suggested the name of bugler for him,—and a glorious little bugler he surely is."   Ralph Hoffmann (1927) says: "From the bare grim walls of rock the Cañon Wren pours out a cascade of sweet liquid notes, like the spray of a waterfall in sunshine.   The opening notes are single staccato notes followed by long-drawn double notes, *tsee-i*, *tsee-i*, slower and descending in pitch, ending with still lower *tóo-ee tóo-ee tóo-ee*."   Mr. Simmons (1925) says that this wren sings from late February to November in Texas, and describes the call note as "a clear, ringing, rather measured, slightly quickened *peupp*, *peupp*, *peupp*, *peupp*, *peupp*, each slightly lower in key and pitch than the last, but never approaching a trill."   Mr. Scott (1885) says that "the female sings quite as much as the male."   Charles F. Batchelder (1885) calls the commonest winter note "a peculiar, loud, harsh, penetrating cry, not unlike the ordinary cry of the Nighthawk, and can be heard at a long distance.   Besides this note I one day heard one repeatedly utter a sharp *peá-body*, the first syllable being rather prolonged and having the principal accent."

Field marks.—The most conspicuous field mark of the canyon wren is the gleaming white throat, which extends well down onto the breast and contrasts strongly with the chestnut-brown abdomen; this latter feature will distinguish it at a glance from the rock wren, which is sometimes seen in somewhat similar surroundings.   The rock wren's tail has a conspicuous black subterminal band and whitish tips, whereas the tail of the canyon wren has no terminal bands and only a few narrow dusky bars.   The back of the canyon wren is dotted with whitish.

SALPINCTES OBSOLETUS OBSOLETUS (Say)

COMMON ROCK WREN

PLATES 54, 55

HABITS

Our northern race of the rock wrens occupies a wide range in western North America, from the western edge of the Great Plains to the Pacific slope, and through much of northern Mexico.   Allied races occur in Mexico and Central America.   Throughout its range north of the Mexican boundary its characters are remarkably stable; there seems to be no reason for attempting to split it into subspecies; this is in marked contrast with what has been done with such plastic species as the horned lark and the song sparrow. One reason for this is that its specialized habitat is remarkably uniform, as to sunshine and shadow and as to aridity and humidity, throughout its wide range.

An ornithologist is sometimes asked by a beginner where to look for birds; the answer is simple, almost anywhere and everywhere, for there are few places on this earth where we may not hope to find some species of bird. There are, of course, more species of birds and more individuals in fertile, well-watered temperate and tropical regions, but the places that seem to us most forbidding are seldom wholly birdless. The raven survives the long winter night on the icy shores of Greenland; the pipit and the rosy finches retire to the barren mountaintops to breed above timberline; the desert race of the horned lark lives on the bare, sun-baked, sandy plains of the southwestern deserts, where not another living thing appears; and the rock wren makes a living in the hardly less inviting rocky barrens of the badlands. Probably these birds have been crowded out of more favorable environment where competition was too keen and have learned to adapt themselves to new conditions and make a living where the food supply is scanty but sufficient for their needs.

During the breeding season, and largely at other times of the year, rock wrens confine their activities to bare, open, wind-swept, sunny, rocky surfaces, either steep or gently sloping, in valleys, foothills, or wide canyons, where there are piles of broken rocks or scattered boulders and generally little or no vegetation. On the open plains of Cochise County, Ariz., we found them in the dry, rocky arroyos and on the open slopes entirely destitute of rocks, where the clayey soil, baker hard by the hot, glaring sun, had been cut into miniature canyons 6 to 10 feet deep by the heavy rushing torrents of the previous rainy season.

Limestone quarries are favorite resorts, and the cliffs and caves of the deeper canyons are sometimes invaded, close to the haunts of the canyon wrens. Where suitable rocky environment can be found, they range upward in the mountains to 8,000 or 10,000 feet. Fred Mallery Packard tells me that, in the Rocky Mountain National Park, Colo., rock wrens are fairly common summer residents, arriving "at the park boundaries in mid-April, some continuing their migration to timberline nesting sites. They nest late in May and in June, the harsh song continuing until mid-July, and occasionally it may be heard in August. There may be some vertical wandering in summer, when a few have been seen above timberline. The descent from the mountains begins about August 20, and by the end of September they have left the park."

Mrs. Bailey (1902) draws the following pen picture of the rock wren in its haunts: "*Salpinctes!* To the worker in the arid regions of the west this name calls up most grateful memories. On the wind-blown rocky stretches where you seem in a bleak world of granite or lava with only rock, rock, everywhere, suddenly, there on a stone before you, stands this jolly little wren, looking up at you with a bob and a shy, friendly glance.   The encounter is as cheering as the sight of a bird at sea, and before such meetings have been repeated many times, you love the little wren as you do the barking conies that give life and a touch of companionship to the barren rock slides of the mountains."

Nesting.—Two nests that we found in Cochise County, Ariz., were built in holes in the steep, almost perpendicular banks of a little arroyo that had been cut out like a miniature canyon by running water.   The holes were not far from the top of the cut-bank and 4 or 5 feet from the bottom of the cut, and were exposed by the cutting away of the soil (pl. 54); they were probably made by gophers or some other animal long ago, for the soil was baked too hard for the wrens to have excavated them.   The holes were about 12 inches deep, and the nests were placed far back; the entrance to each nest was paved with two or three handfuls of small, flat stones, which were also found under and behind the nest.   The nests were made of grasses, straws, weed stems, and rootlets and were lined with fine grasses, horsehair, and a few feathers.

Mrs. Amelia S. Allen writes to me that she found rock wrens nesting under similar circumstances near Livermore, Calif., "in an eroded gulch 10 to 12 feet deep.   Nests were in the earthen banks of this gulch with not a rock outcropping in sight.   In Corrall Hollow itself, we found a nest near the top of an earthen cut about 15 feet high.   It was lined with sheep's wool and contained six eggs."

Frank C. Willard records several other nests in his Arizona notes. One was in a hole in the wall of an adobe building, 10 feet up; one was 2 feet up in a hole in a large conglomerate boulder in a rocky gulch, another in a hole in an old stone reservoir, and one was in the top of a window casing in an adobe wall; the entrances to all the above nests were paved with stone chips, and in one case the paving was mixed with bits of wood.   He mentions two other nests, one of which was in an old stove and the other in an old table drawer in a deserted house.

The nests are often placed in cavities and small crevices under and among loose rocks; such nests are usually far out of sight and difficult to find, as the birds give no indication of the exact spot among hundreds of possible sites in a large area.   Often the birds appear more unconcerned when the searcher is near the nest than when he is far away from it.   Nearly always the entrance to the nest is paved with small, flat stones, and, where these can be seen, the nest may be easily located.   In some cases there is no room for a paved walk to the nests, or perhaps no necessity for it; but always, so far as I can learn, these small stones are used as a foundation for the nest, or are mixed with the material of the nest. In some cases the stone walk extends 8 or 10 inches out from the nest. The stones vary in length from half an inch to 2 inches or a little more, and it seems remarkable that the slender bills of the birds are strong enough to carry them, often for a considerable distance. The reasons for this curious habit, which seems to be so universal, are not well understood. In some cases the stones are piled up so high at the entrance that only the flattened body of the wren can enter, thus possibly forming a barrier to entering enemies. Or, they may serve as direction marks to help the owners to find the home crevice. But neither of these theories seems wholly satisfactory; perhaps some day we may know the answer.

The rock wren is, I believe, the only permanently resident land bird on the Farallone Islands, where it seems to breed abundantly among the rocks. Milton S. Ray (1904) found about 20 nests there, including old and new. He says:

Whether the nest was in a niche in the cliffs, beneath a rock fence, or under a granite ledge cropping out above the surface, it was always placed among rocks firmly embedded and never amid the loose rocks that lay scattered about on the top of the ground. * * * By far the most elaborate nest I found was in the rear of the Stone House; it ran in the earth among the rocks of a rock fence. A shelf-like stone at the entrance formed a sort of veranda, and this the birds had literally covered, as well as the main corridor leading to the nest. I noticed the pavement was equally deep under the nest, and that all the tiny nooks and crevices on the way were filled. I carefully counted all the stones and other material in this earthen burrow between the bare granite boulders, and as it was situated 2 feet up in the wall the birds had undoubtedly brought all of them.

His list of materials follows: One safetypin, 2 pieces of wire, 2 pieces of a pair of scissors, 10 pieces of zinc from old batteries, 2 fish hooks, 2 pieces of glass, 1 piece of leather, 4 copper tacks, 2 pieces of limestone, 4 pieces of plaster from the walls of the house, 12 pieces of shingles (some as large as 2 by 3 inches), 9 bits of abalone shells, 20 bits of mussel shells, 106 rusty nails, 227 bits of flat rusty iron, 492 small granite stones (very regular in size), and 769 bones of rabbits, fish, and birds, as well as the usual nesting material.

He continues: "The birds in this case had easy access to all the little bits of material that accumulate around dwellings; but even then, what a vast amount of patience and labor, as well as perception, it required to find and transport the 1,665 listed objects, to say nothing of building the nest itself! This was composed of the bird's favorite substance, excelsior packing, together with a few weeds and grasses and bits of cotton and rabbit fur tucked in decoratively here and there, and measured 5¼ inches over all, while the cavity was 3 inches across by 1½ inches deep." He suggests that lining the passageway and placing stones under the nest may serve to keep them free from dampness. He noticed that more stones were used where the nests were built on earthen floors, than when built on rocks, and says that the birds line the passageway and the nest cavity before the nest is built.

Philo W. Smith, Jr. (1904), found 13 nests in an extensive limestone quarry in Texas and says that "where the nests were located at the bottom of the quarry there was no attempt at building a walk, but when the nest was situated in a crevice the walk was invariably there provided."

Eggs.—Five and six eggs are the commonest numbers laid by the rock wren, but sometimes as few as four constitute a full set, seven or eight are not rare, and as many as ten have been found in a nest. Ovate is the commonest shape. The ground color is pure, glossy white, and the eggs are sparingly and irregularly sprinkled with fine dots of reddish brown, "cinnamon-rufous," or "burnt umber." The measurements of 50 eggs in the United States National Museum average 18.6 by 14.8 millimeters; the eggs showing the four extremes measure 20.3 by 15.2, 19.6 by 15.7, 15.8, by 14.7, and 18.8 by 13.7 millimeters.

Young.—Generally two and perhaps sometimes three broods are raised in a season. As the male has been seen to assist his mate in building the nest, and to feed the female on the nest, it is fair to assume that both parents help in the feeding and care of the young.

Plumages.—I have seen no very young rock wrens, but those in juvenal plumage differ from adults in having the upperparts faintly and narrowly barred with dusky, instead of streaked, and lacking the white spots; the light brown, "vinaceous-cinnamon" rump is immaculate; and the underparts are whiter than in the adult and unspotted, with a brownish wash on the flanks and under tail coverts.

Dickey and van Rossem (1938) say of the molting of this wren in El Salvador: "Juveniles taken on the Colinas de Jucuarán as late as September 7 have only just commenced the postjuvenal body molt. Adults from the same locality show the annual molt to commence about August 1, and a specimen taken September 7 is in practically complete, fresh, fall plumage. There is no spring molt discernible in numerous specimens taken between February 26 and March 26, and it seems likely that none normally occurs."

I have seen adults molting as early as the first week in July and at other dates during that month; other adults that I have examined have been in worn breeding plumage as late as August 7, and others had completed the postnuptial molt during the first two weeks in September.

Food.—Very little seems to have been published on the food of the rock wren, no detailed analysis having been made. Living as it does in rocky barrens, its food is of little importance to the agriculturalist. Its food probably is much like that of other wrens, consisting mainly of spiders, beetles, and other insects that it finds among the rocks, it is surprising how many insects are to be found even in such unpromising places. R. C. Tate (1925) says that, in Oklahoma, its favorite food seems to be "earth worms, and grubs from the bark of trees." Junius Henderson (1927) states that Aughey includes the rock wren among the birds that feed their young on locusts in Nebraska. Knowlton and Harmston (1943) report that, of 74 stomachs of Utah birds examined, 30 contained 59 adult grasshoppers and 1 nymph.

Behavior.—The sprightly little rock wren adds a delightful spark of life to the barren rocky landscape where he chooses to make his home, a tiny bit of cheerful companionship for the lonely traveler and a charming surprise in some unlikely spot. He is a busy, active little body, dodging out of sight among the rocks, or perching for a moment on some nearby stone to look us over, for he is not particularly shy. Dr. Oberholser (1921) pictures him very well as follows:

If started up from work or rest his quick, jerky flight to the nearest point of observation preludes a sharp, harsh note of interrogation and alarm, almost startling in its suddenness and volume, which degenerates into a prolonged sputtering scold, as the bird works himself into a ridiculous frenzy of voice and of action over what he doubtless regards as a wholly unwarranted and quite reprehensible intrusion. But his is an acquaintance that may well be cultivated, for once we are in his confidence he is found to be more than ordinarily interesting; he will sing for us, and this performance is by no means monotonous or unattractive; or, confiding in our friendship, he may even lead us to the spot where, protected under an overhanging ledge or hidden away in a crevice of the rocks, is his little home. His lot, with several voracious mouths to feed in this all too barren land, might readily seem to be a hard one, but this is only apparent, for the desert yields to the patient toil of this little worker far more than falls under the gaze of the passing traveler.

As we know so little about the roosting habits of birds, the following note by R. M. Bond (1940) is of interest:

The night of October 15, 1939, two Rock Wrens (*Salpinctes obsoletus*) were found asleep in a shed near some cliffs in southern Alameda County. The wrens were perched side by side on the rough, vertical side of a mud wasp nest (*Sceliphron*, sp.) which was built on the 4 inch side of a 2 by 4 inch rafter. The position of the wrens was vertical, substantially that of a perching woodpecker or creeper (*Certhia*), with the tails jammed against the mud wasp nest for support and the feet at about mid-breast level, and far enough apart to show the outer toe on each side when the bird was viewed from behind. It was not possible to see exactly how the heads were held, but apparently they were placed with the beak pointed downward between one wing and the body. One of the birds awoke and slipped away in the beam of my flashlight, but the other did not stir. I left the birds for about 15 minutes, and returned with another observer. The wakeful bird had returned to its former position and posture, and slipped away again. The heavy sleeper was picked up by hand. It is doubtful if the birds could have been reached by any small mammal, because of the position of the roosting site.

Voice.—Comments on the musical quality of the rock wren's song vary considerably, but, whether the song be harsh or melodious, it is a delightful surprise when heard for the first time among the dreary, uninhabited rocks, and a cheery note of welcome to the traveler where he least expects to find a song bird. By contrast with its surroundings it is doubly welcome, and perhaps its quality is overrated. Mrs. Bailey (1902) gives it faint praise: "Even his song, which at first hearing seems the drollest, most un-bird-like of machine-made tinklings, comes to be greeted as the voice of a friend on the desert, and its quality to seem in harmony with the hard, gritty granites among which he lives." And Mrs. Nice (1931) likewise says: "This absurd little dweller on crags and boulders possesses a number of harsh, grating, curious vocalizations which are vastly appropriate to his environment. '*Kerée Kerée Kerée*' he says, '*Chair chair chair chair, Deedle deedle deedle deedle, Tur tur tur tur, Kerée kerée kerée trrrrrrrrr*'."

W. L. Dawson (Dawson and Bowles, 1909), on the other hand, is more appreciative, and says his song is "one of the sprightliest, most musical, and resonant to be heard in the entire West. The rock-wall makes an admirable sounding-board, and the bird stops midway of whatever task to sing a hymn of wildest exultation. *Whittier, whittier, whittier,* is one of his finest strains; while *Ka-whee, ka-whee, ka-whee* is a sort of challenge which the bird renders in various tempo, and punctuates with nervous bobs to enforce attention." Ralph Hoffmann (1927) refers to "trills and sweet notes that suggest the perfect technique and joyous vigor of a Mockingbird. The volume is much less and there is much less variety, *ti-ou, ti-ou, ti-ou, ti-ou,* is a common strain, then perhaps *flee flee flee,* or *cheep-oo cheep-oo cheep-oo,* each strain definite, and succeeded by another quite distinct with a change of pitch. The call note, often given with an energetic bob, sounds like *tick-ear.*"

I might add that, to an easterner, the song sometimes suggests the joyous spring song of the brown thrasher, with its series of couplets of distinct syllables.

Field marks.—The dull, grayish brown of the upperparts of the rock wren blends well with its rocky surroundings, but when it flies away from the observer and spreads its tail it shows its best field mark; all tail feathers except the central pair are broadly tipped with buffy white, and above that a subterminal band of black is very conspicuous. The only bird with which it is likely to be compared in a somewhat similar environment is the canyon wren, which has a conspicuous white, unspotted throat and a rich chestnut abdomen; its tail lacks the conspicuous terminal bands. In the rock wren the underparts are all dull white, with dusky spots or streaks on the chest.

Enemies.—Rockwell and Wetmore (1914) report that "a young Rock Wren just old enough to fly was taken by hand because of its weakened condition, and upon examination was found to be infested with large white grubs several of which had buried themselves deep into the bird's head and were gradually sapping its vitality. These grubs were nearly one half inch in length and were all buried out of sight under the skin." Dr. Walter P. Taylor (1912) observed one "attacking a chipmunk which was sitting on a rock, swooping at it in the same way that a mockingbird assaults a cat," which suggests that small mammals may take their toll of eggs or young. And Dr. Friedmann (1934) mentions several cases where rock wrens have been imposed upon by cowbirds.

Winter.—Rock wrens retire to some extent in autumn from their summer haunts at the higher altitudes in the mountains as these become covered with snow, though they seem reluctant to leave as long as portions of their range remain open. Many remain in their rocky retreats all winter, but some others seek their winter food in more sheltered brush lands or on open mesas. The rock wren has not yet become a dooryard bird, but it sometimes appears in the neighborhood of houses and gardens. A. H. Anderson (1934a), writes of such a case:

Here on the outskirts of Tucson, Ariz., it has been present for the last two winters around my home. The area is of typical creosote-bush mesa, shading gradually into the mesquite and catclaw border of Rillito Creek close by. Some of the land is occupied by 1-acre, suburban farm and chicken-ranch tracts.

A single Wren seems to have occupied the territory during both winters, though several times two and three birds were seen. None was seen during the summer of 1933. Usually this individual accompanied the mixed flock of birds that frequented the district, Gambel's and Brewer's Sparrows, Cactus Wrens, Palmer's Thrashers, and House Finches.

Its curiosity was very pronounced and one could easily regard the bird as tame. Sometimes I could approach as close as 5 feet as it stood bobbing upon a wood-pile, fence-post, or chicken-house. Several times it came through the open house-door, and occasionally it would climb around on the window-sill. It inspected everything in the vicinity—houses, automobiles, chicken-houses, and wells.

DISTRIBUTION

Range.—Southwestern Canada to Costa Rica.

Breeding range.—The rock wren breeds **north** to southern British Columbia (Cache Creek, Kamloops, and Shuswap); southern Alberta (Jasper House, possibly, and Red Deer); southeastern Saskatchewan (Cypress Hills, Eastend, and Wood Mountain); and North Dakota (Williston and Charlson). **East** to western North Dakota (Charlson and Mandan); western South Dakota (Pierre, Rosebud, and casually to Yankton County); central Nebraska (Valentine and Calloway); central Kansas (Rooks Creek and Ellis); western Oklahoma (Gates); central Texas (Vernon, Putnam, Kerrville, and San Antonio); through Mexico (Tamaulipas, Veracruz, and Chiapas); western

Guatemala (Quetzaltenanga and San Incas); El Salvador (San José del Sacare and Volcán de San Miguel); and Costa Rica (Hacienda El Pelon, Guanacaste). **South** to Costa Rica (Hacienda El Pelon, Guanacaste). **West** to Costa Rica; Guerrero, Mexico (Chilpancingo); Sinaloa (Los Leones and Suratata); Baja California (Cape San Lucas, Cedros Island, and Guadalupe Island); California (Santa Barbara Islands and Berkeley); east of the Cascades in northern California (Chico and Mount Shasta); Oregon (Klamath Lake and The Dalles); Washington (Yakima and Chelan); and British Columbia (Cache Creek).

Winter range.—The rock wren is resident in the southern part of its range and in winter is found **north** to northern California (west slope of Mount Lassen and Death Valley); Arizona (Fort Mojave, Grand Canyon, and Fort Verde); New Mexico (San Antonio and Las Vegas); occasionally to southern Colorado (Pueblo); and southern Texas (San Angelo, Kerrville, Boerne, and Laredo). There are records of winter occurrence somewhat north of what may be considered the normal range.

The entire species as outlined is divided into three races within our limits, others occurring in Mexico and Central America. The common rock wren (*S. o. obsoletus*) occurs south to San Luis Potosí, Zacatecas, and Baja California; the San Benito rock wren (*S. o. tenuirostris*) breeds on the San Benito Islands of Baja California; and the Guadalupe rock wren (*S. o. guadeloupensis*) is found on Guadalupe Island, Baja California.

Spring migration.—Some early dates of spring arrival are: Texas—Amarillo, March 21. Nebraska—North Platte, April 22. South Dakota—White River, April 18. North Dakota—Charlson, May 10. Saskatchewan—Eastend, May 3. Colorado—Fort Morgan, April 12. Wyoming—Laramie, April 29. Montana—Great Falls, May 5. Utah—Salt Lake County, April 11. Idaho—Pocatello, April 22. Oregon—Klamath Basin, March 28. Washington—Wallula, March 27. British Columbia—Okanagan Landing, April 26.

Fall migration.—Some late dates of fall departure are: British Columbia—Okanagan Landing, September 29. Washington—Yakima, September 13. Oregon—Weston, October 3. Utah—Toquerville, October 13. Wyoming—Laramie, October 21. Colorado—Boulder, October 2. Saskatchewan—Eastend, September 15. North Dakota—Charlson, October 3. Nebraska—Ashby, September 24. Texas—Somerset, October 19.

Casual records.—There are a number of records for the rock wren beyond its normal range. In Alberta it was recorded at Edmonton on June 29, 1898, and at Chippewyan on June 12 and 17, 1914. One was seen at Dell Rapids, S. Dak., on July 20, 1924; one was seen at Pipestone, Minn., on May 13, 1922; one was reported at Monguagon, Mich., on October 31, 1910; another was observed at Urbana, Ill., on May 26, 1926. There are several records of its occurrence in Iowa as far east as National, on September 27, 1914, and one record of its breeding near Sioux City in June 1898. Birds were seen there in other years but no evidence of breeding.

Egg dates.—Arizona: 20 records, April 14 to July 16; 11 records, May 2 to 30.

California: 77 records, February 5 to July 28; 47 records, April 3 to May 15, indicating the height of the season.

Kansas: 28 records, May 8 to July 5; 14 records, May 12 to June 1.

Baja California: 4 records, January 17, March 2 and 4, and April 5.

Texas: 3 records, April 15 to June 3.

Washington: 4 records, April 6 to May 20.

SALPINCTES OBSOLETUS GUADELOUPENSIS Ridgway

GUADALUPE ROCK WREN

HABITS

In his original description of this subspecies, Mr. Ridgway (1876) says: "The differences exhibited in these insular specimens from the continental series are quite slight, but they are so constant as to demand recognition. As to colors, there is no difference beyond slightly darker shades throughout; the lower parts being soft pinkish cream-color instead of creamy-white, the other portions of a darker shade to correspond. The differences in proportions are more decided." In his later work he (1904) describes it as "similar to *S. o. obsoletus*, but decidedly darker, wing and tail shorter, bill longer and stouter, and tarsi longer; young with upper parts much darker and more heavily barred or vermiculated."

The Guadalupe wren is confined to the island by that name off the west coast of Baja California. Walter E. Bryant (1887) says that "this species, undoubtedly the most common of the birds on the island, was distributed from the beach to the summit, but was found to be most numerous on the upper and central portions."

Nesting.—We are indebted to Mr. Bryant (1887) for practically all we know about this wren. On its nesting activities, he writes:

The weather does not seem to be taken into consideration by any of the resident species. The rock-wrens are the first to begin nesting, and endeavor to conduct their domestic affairs through the stormiest times, though not always with success. Many abandoned nests were found, some with and some without eggs, deserted, probably on account of long continued wet weather. The location of the nest, however, plays an all-important part in the success or failure of the first builders. A few birds began the construction of their nests in December, and one had her work nearly completed on the 25th of December, 1885. Four fresh eggs were found in it on January 17th. The breeding season, strictly speaking, extends from the middle of January through the month of March.

Nests were found in cavities of immense boulders, under rocks, in fallen and decayed trunks of cypress trees, the latter location being apparently a favorite one. But wherever the nests were located the passages leading to them were, with one or two exceptions, paved with flat pebbles ranging in size from a Lima bean to a half dollar. Fully a quart of these pebbles were removed from the entrance to a nest built in a boulder at a height of 4 feet, where, at some previous time, other birds had evidently built and accumulated their share of the pavement. As a rule scarcely an ordinary handful of stones are used. The nest is built in close conformity to the size and shape of the cavity which it occupies, being usually circular and varying from a shallow bed of fine dry grasses to a nest of the same material measuring 150 mm. in diameter and 60 mm. high. The egg receptacle is from 55 mm. 70 mm. in diameter, and not more than 30 mm. in depth. A lining of goat hair when obtainable is invariably used. I followed one bird fully an hundred yards from the spot where she had collected some goat hair before the nest was reached.

Eggs.—According to Mr. Bryant, "the eggs are usually 4, though sometimes 5 in number, and resemble both in color and shape those of the common rock wren." He gives the measurements of two sets and says that the average of 55 eggs is 19 by 14 millimeters. I have the measurements of 30 eggs, among which the eggs showing the four extremes measure **21.0** by 15.0, 20.0 by **16.0**, **17.0** by 14.0, and 18.4 by **13.3** millimeters.

Plumages.—Mr. Bryant (1887) describes two stages of immature plumages. One which he designates as in "first plumage," evidently a nestling, taken January 23, he says is "above lighter than the immature specimen and grayer than the adult plumage. Below, including throat, pale sulphurous white, becoming pinkish on sides, and crissum, which is unmarked." The other, evidently an older bird, taken February 19, is "above similar to adult but *much* darker, * * * the bars across middle tail-feathers dull black. The outer half of the pale cinnamon on end of tail-feathers finely mottled with dusky. Under parts pale pinkish cinnamon; the entire throat obscured with a faint dusky suffusion. Crissum darker than abdomen and unmarked."

Food.—Mr. Ridgway (1876) says that they "frequent the slaughter-yards, where goats are killed, to glean insects from the drying bones." And Mr. Bryant (1887) said: "Their food consisted mainly of caterpillars and beetles. I watched one pick to pieces and devour successively three small Carabide beetles."

Behavior.—Mr. Bryant (1887) writes:

They were by nature tamer than any birds I ever met with. While retreating, if approached, they would in turn draw quite near to a person who remained perfectly quiet. Sitting down one afternoon upon a log, I saw a Rock Wren come hopping closer and closer to where I was resting, until at length he perched upon my shoe. Then seeing a sandy spot just beyond, he availed himself of the opportunity by taking a dust-bath. So close was he to me that I could have reached him with my foot, yet constantly in motion, searching here and there among the rocks for food, he seemed entirely unconscious of my presence. Even when standing, they are seldom quiet, a nervous twitch of the tail or toss of the head bearing witness to the incessant activity so characteristic of these little creatures.

Voice.—Of the voice Mr. Bryant (1887) writes: "Seldom silent, they have, in addition to their ringing call, a considerable variety of song. I became accustomed to the variations of four or five different birds, and noticed that each had a song peculiar to himself but differing from the songs of his fellows. One little wren near camp was in the habit of beginning his song each morning at about half-past six, never varying five minutes from his self-appointed time. They are usually seen on the ground or upon a rock or stump. One remarkably foggy morning, I noticed one sitting on the top of a sage-bush, while on fine days, I have seen them mounted to the height of 20 feet on a dry cypress twig, singing their cheerful song."

SALPINCTES OBSOLETUS TENUIROSTRIS van Rossem

SAN BENITO ROCK WREN

Adriaan J. van Rossem (1943) discovered that the rock wren of the San Benito Islands, off the coast of Baja California, Mexico, has a longer bill than the familiar northern type race and gave the above name to the island bird. He says that it is "not distinguishable in color or pattern of tail markings from *Salpinctes obsoletus obsoletus.* Bill very much longer than that of *obsoletus,* but at the same time distinctly more slender in both vertical and lateral profiles."

The "very much longer" bill is a matter of about 3 millimeters on the *average;* he gives the measurements for 24 *obsoletus* as ranging from 16.5 to 20.0 and averaging 17.7 millimeters; and for 10 *tenuirostris* as ranging from 19.7 to 22.1 and averaging 20.9 millimeters; the measurements seem to overlap slightly.

Family MIMIDAE: Mockingbirds and Thrashers

MIMUS POLYGLOTTOS POLYGLOTTOS (Linnaeus)

EASTERN MOCKINGBIRD

PLATES 56–58

CONTRIBUTED BY ALEXANDER SPRUNT, JR.

HABITS

If Mark Catesby had accomplished nothing else in his pioneer work of ornithological discovery in Carolina over 200 years ago but introduce the mockingbird to science it would have been a fitting memorial. Had Linnaeus been capable of slang, he might have expressed the opinion, when receiving Catesby's notes on the species, that the collector "had something there!" Truly, that field worker of other days did have something when he heard his first mockingbird, and from his far-off day to this the bird has held primary affection in the minds of thousands who thrill to its matchless ability of song.

Audubon expatiated upon the advisability of hearing the mocker *only* amid the magnolias of Louisiana. Since he knew Carolina later, a native of the latter State would have expected Audubon to change that setting, but doubtless he never found time to rewrite his history of the bird! Seriously, however, everything in his opening paragraphs on this species, in which he dilates upon the botanical glories of the Pelican State, could have been written with equal accuracy of the Carolina Low Country. Charleston, the center of that favored region, and the mockingbird are inseparable, for that is where it was first seen and made known to science by an ornithologist.

Linnaeus described the bird from notes furnished by Mark Catesby on what the latter called the "Mock-Bird of Carolina" and whose own account of the species appears in his "Natural History of Carolina, Florida and the Bahama Islands," published in 1731, and accompanied by a drawing. Carolinians, then, have a proprietary interest in the mockingbird. Actually it occurs much farther afield, of course, but at the same time, wherever the name is mentioned, the hearer inevitably thinks of the South as the typical habitat.

Surely, this is as it should be. Can anyone visualize the gray-clad aristocrat amid snow and ice, amid spruces and hemlocks, or upon cliffs battered by the might of the north Atlantic? Can one visualize it, indeed, without mental pictures of moss-bannered live oaks or towering magnolias, where the yellow jessamine climbs aloft to burst in golden glory among the pines and cypresses and the immaculate disks of Cherokee roses reflect the moonlight? Here, along coasts fringed with semitropical jungles of barrier islands, where the slow heave of rollers out of the Gulf Stream thunders softly upon yielding sands, is the mocker's home. Here, amid the crimson clusters of cassina and holly the mocker lives, or is equally at home in a moon-drenched old city whose garden walls and graceful spires reflect the golden civilization of a vanished era. Yes, to Charlestonians and other Carolinians, the entire scope of ornithology might be summed up and typified in a single species, and that species... the mockingbird!

Spring.—Almost universally considered a southern bird, the mocker has undoubtedly been increasing its range northward and westward in recent years. It is now well known in New England and as far west as Knox County, Ill., and parts of Iowa (Monroe County). Possibly this spreading population might be considered as an "overflow" from the normal range, somewhat like certain other species that have apparently thrived upon the march of civilization and increased rather than decreased in numbers. While most mockingbird populations in the South appear to be largely stable (the writer is unable, for instance, to note any annual shifting of numbers in South Carolina), certain concentrations in parts of the southern range indicate that there may be a short migration in fall and an early return in spring.

In Florida, where the bird is abundant the year round, there are times when many more are to be seen in certain places in winter than occur in summer. This is certainly the case in the Keys, where the writer has, in winter, noted the mocker in greater abundance than anywhere else in the entire South. Through six years of fall and winter trips in the Keys he has, time and again, been impressed with the presence of the bird on Key Largo. Counting completely at random, he has seen the bird *average* seven individuals to a mile along the Overseas Highway for as much as 15 miles. All these, of course, were on conspicuous perches; no search was made, for the birds were seen from a moving car.

Increasing records from far northern points are evident. Even in Maine the mocker is now beginning to show itself, and winter records from various parts of New England are not the uncommon events they once were. Indeed, in southern New England the mocker is now resident (E. H. Forbush, 1929). One of the most remarkable northern occurrences is that of an individual seen on Mount Desert Island, Maine (Acadia National Park), by Maurice Sullivan (1940) in the winter of 1940. As an added touch of complete incongruity, an ivory gull (*Pagophila alba*) was seen at the same time, February 10. Thus, the far north and the deep south were brought together in as strange an avian mixture as perhaps has ever been noted in this country.

Definite evidence of some movement on the part of individual birds has been secured by banding. F. C. Lincoln (1939) lists an instance of a mocker banded at Haddonfield, N. J., on November 25, 1932, being found dead at Shadyside, Md., on May 25, 1935. This was a northerly banded *winter* bird found in spring some distance to the southward. Another specimen, banded at Nashville, Tenn., on May 26, 1934, was killed at Fulton, Miss., on January 29, 1936. This represents a directly westward movement.

Frank L. Farley, of Camrose, Alberta, contributes the following note : "The nesting of a pair of mockingbirds in central Alberta during the summer of 1928 was one of the most remarkable ornithological discoveries since the country was first opened to settlement. That season a pair of these southern birds nested in the garden of Mr. McNaughton, on the western edge of the town of Didsbury. This is about 200 miles north of the Montana border and roughly between 50 and 60 miles east of the Rockies. The unusual 'find' was published in the local paper, *The Pioneer*, issue of June 21, 1928. Later that summer when returning from a trip I called at Mr. McNaughton's home to get further particulars, but unfortunately the family was absent. However, I talked with neighbors who were familiar with the circumstances, and they verified the statements that appeared in the paper.   This is, I believe, the most northerly point at which the mockingbird has been recorded on the continent."

Courtship.—As might be expected in so individualistic a species as the mocker, its courtship procedure is a spectacular performance.   At least, that is what many have taken its characteristic actions to be. These have been described as a "dance" and have been witnessed by hundreds of observers all over the bird's range.   It is well described by Mrs. A. B. Harrington, of Dallas, Tex. (1923), as follows: "It was a curious and most interesting performance.   The first time they danced exactly opposite each other.   They faced each other about a foot apart, hopped up and down, moving gradually to one side, then back again, and so on.   A second pair began their dance in the same position, but first one hopped twice to one side, then the other followed the first, which hopped again sideways and the other followed, always facing each other, then they moved back in the same manner to where they started and repeated the performance.   After each dance was finished the birds flew off a short distance in opposite directions."

W. M. Tyler (MS.) describes a similar performance witnessed near Lake Okeechobee, Fla., in April 1941.   He saw "two mockingbirds in the roadway standing facing each other, close together, that is, a step or two apart, with heads and tails held up high and feathers depressed so that the legs looked very long and slim.   They made dashes at each other over and over with tense little darts, the attacked retreating a step or two each time with prim, ballet-dancer-like movements.   They gave the impressions of putting on an act.   Finally both flew off, one following the other to a tree near at hand."

In these two descriptions the dance terminated in one case by the birds flying off in opposite directions, while in the other one bird followed the other.   The writer has witnessed this nonuniformity of termination frequently, one occurring about as often as the other. Many other written descriptions of this dance are available, but all agree so closely that further repetition is without value.

The long-accepted belief that the dance is a courtship proceeding is challenged, however, by Amelia R. Laskey, of Nashville, Tenn. (MS.), who has the following to say about it: "I hope when you write about this interesting bird you will mention the 'dance' which bird books continue to describe as a part of the courtship behavior.   However, in the years since I have been using color bands for sight identification and have therefore been able to distinguish sexes, this dance has never occurred except as a territory boundary-line demonstration, when the occupants of adjoining territories are defending their respective domains.   It usually occurs between two males but may take place with a male and a female as participants when each is holding fall and winter territory.   I have never observed a mated pair performing together during the mated season or during the winter season if they remained together on a common territory. I saw it once in fall between a pair that mated for three consecutive seasons but that separated and defended individual but adjoining territories in fall and winter. The dance in the latter case seemed to be the severing of family ties for that season as they did not trespass on each other's territory. In spring, when he resumed singing, they used the two areas together."

Probably such a statement will be productive of argument. Certainly it is an original belief, but one held by an observer who has put much time and study on the species, as her "Fall and Winter Behavior of Mockingbirds" (1936) will testify. Her "territory boundary-line demonstration," however, appears never to result in actual combat, which might reasonably be expected on some occasions if an act of defense was the basis. It is difficult to see exactly how the tactics employed could be very effective in a combative sense, while it is easy to understand that the display of wings and tail, which accompanies the dance, could be an effort to impress a female with the charms of the prospective consort. Lack of actual contact in a demonstration is not, of course, conclusive by any means of the performance's not being a territory defense, but it is suggestive.

Nesting.—Domestic duties with the mocker are a serious undertaking and never marked with the slackness characteristic of some avian species. The nest is constructed by both sexes, and usually the male works as hard as the female. The materials used vary considerably, being for the most part small dead twigs. Grass and rootlets form the lining. String is frequently used and sometimes skeletonized leaves. Cotton is often found in the nest, depending on locality. The completed nest is a rather bulky affair and lasts well; old nests of two or three seasons past still retain their shape to a surprising degree. Some nests are rather small in circumference.

The site is almost invariably at low elevations, with the great majority being 3 to 10 feet above ground. The writer cannot recall any nest found by him (and he has seen them literally by the hundred) that was over 20 feet high. Nonetheless, the mocker at times breaks custom and ascends to elevations greater than 25 feet. E. H. Forbush (1929), for example, gives the range as "from 1 to 50 feet from ground." In Florida, the mocker occasionally builds in clumps of Spanish moss (*Tillandsia usneoides*), such sites being noted by A. H. Howell (1932). The writer has never seen an example of such a site in South Carolina, the nest usually occupying a small bush or tree, such as various oaks, or other stiff-twigged growth.

The mocker is strongly partial to human habitation as a nesting site. Garden vegetation, vines that climb about porches, shrubbery actually against a house, and decorative plantings in the yard are often used. It is fairly safe to say that, in parts of the South, the majority of the mockingbird population nests in towns or cities. Wild sites along open woodland edges, pastures, wood lots, and prairielike stretches, which show occasional bushes or small trees, are situations chosen away from mankind.

Nest-building consumes two days at the minimum, but probably not many nests are finished in so short a time. This would take pretty constant and unremitting toil on the part of the birds, but it certainly has been done. Incubation, as given by various authorities, differs by several days. Thus, Wilson and Bergtold (quoted by Forbush, 1929) give 14 days; F. L. Burns, 10 days. In coastal South Carolina it is usually between these two estimates, averaging 11 days. Some specific notes furnished by E. B. Chamberlain are typical of the Charleston region. He says that "a 4-foot-high spiraea bush transplanted to my yard on May 7 had a pair of mockingbirds begin building in it next morning. Both sexes built. Completed in 3 days (May 10). First egg by 8 a. m. May 11, fourth by the same time on May 14. (Thus nest built and eggs laid within a week.) Three eggs hatched between 11 a. m. and 3 p. m. May 25, the fourth between 8 a. m. and 6 p. m. May 26. On June 2 (8 a. m.) the young were on the edge of the nest or on nearby twigs. By 6 p. m. the same day all had left the bush, some to return occasionally over a period of 2 or 3 days. Thus in 26 days this pair of mockers built their nest and reared a brood to the nest-leaving stage."

On the south Atlantic coast the mocker usually begins nesting late in April or early in May. Three broods are often raised. Early and late extremes of course, occur now and then. About Charleston the earliest nesting on record concerns a nest that must have been started early in March. The writer was then connected with the Charleston Museum, and a fully fledged young mockingbird was brought to him on April 9, 1928. The bird was at least 10 days old then. If we allow a 12-day incubation period and one day for the laying of each of four eggs (average), March 15 would be the day the first egg was laid. With three days added for nest construction, March 12 results as the day the nest was begun. This is a month earlier than is customary and probably constitutes the earliest record for the State. Regarding late nesting, on September 10, 1910, a young bird just out of the nest was seen being fed by a parent in Charleston by A. S. Sloan. This is a very late date indeed.

Nesting in Florida appears to be only slightly earlier than in Carolina. A. H. Howell (1932) gives dates of fresh eggs on March 19 at Sebring and quotes F. M. Weston on a nest at Pensacola in which the eggs hatched on March 20. Both of these were begun early in March, and no doubt occasional birds nest as early as late February. Weston has furnished additional notes (MS.) as follows: "Earliest known nesting at Pensacola, Fla. (Escambia County), March 3, 1932. First egg of a set of three laid this date. This nesting *survived a low temperature of 23° F.* on March 10 and hatched in due time. Latest known nesting at Pensacola, August 13, 1923 (young birds almost ready to leave nest). Lowest known nesting site at Pensacola, a nest containing three small young in brush pile on May 24, 1928. Rim of nest only 18 inches from ground (measured).

It is not uncommon to find several mockers' nests in fairly close proximity. Two and three pairs often nest on an acre of ground. An interesting record count is furnished by M. G. Vaiden (MS.) who found 14 nests on a tract of 22 acres near Rosedale, Miss.

A detailed study of a mocker nesting at Dudley, Tenn., is given by A. V. Goodpasture of Nashville (1908). He summarizes his observations in a table as follows:

	Days
Building	2
Laying	4
Incubating	10
Care of young	5

Thus, from start of nest to flight of young was 21 days, exactly 3 weeks, being a 5-day variation in the case of the South Carolina birds noted by E. B. Chamberlain. In the notes on the Tennessee pair it was stated that "both sexes labored diligently."

Rarely, the mockingbird will use a nesting-box. It is a very uncommon procedure, however, and the writer has never seen it, but the habit must be recognized in any account of its domestic life. Illustrative of it was a nest found and photographed by H. O. Todd, Jr. (MS.), on June 9, 1940, near Murfreesboro, Tenn. The box had been erected for bluebirds but was taken by a pair of mockers and contained four eggs when found. The box had been placed on top of a fence post about 6 feet from the ground, and it was the second time that Mr. Todd had seen such a location used.

Penetrating into the Midwest one finds the mocker listed as an "uncommon breeder" by B. F. Stiles, of Monona County, Iowa (MS.). He has seen but two nests in that locality, both of these having been found at Sergeant Bluff in 1938. H. M. Holland (MS.) relates his experience with the mocker in west-central Illinois for 33 years. He states that his earliest acquaintance with it was in 1908, when two nests were found in Knox County, which "probably constitute the first local breeding records." The next 12 years passed without any more nests being found. In the early 30's, however, the birds increased and several nests were found. The westward spread of the mocker apparently dates (as far as his locality is concerned) from the late 20's. There is one record already of a bird spending the winter, and nesting pairs have become "very noticeable."

As noted above, the mocker has become an uncommon resident in southern New England and, of course, nests there.

An instance of bigamy in the mockingbird is reported by Amelia R. Laskey, of Nashville, Tenn. (MS.) She states that it is "a surprising situation in a species where both sexes are strong defenders of territory. A male that occupied one portion of our lot since 1936 had a certain mate from February 1938 until her probable death this past December (1939). She remained in his territory with him throughout the winter also. In April 1937, while she was incubating eggs across the road, he acquired another mate. He was seen carrying nesting material for the second nest, 250 feet from the other, and very close to our house. The male watched both nests, appearing at both just as soon as I went near for observation. The young of mate No. 1 were several days old and the eggs of No. 2 were due to hatch when the nest was robbed; the second female then disappeared."

Arthur T. Wayne (1910) mentions an apparent instance of a mockingbird mating with a brown thrasher (*Toxostoma rufum*), as both species were seen feeding young in the same nest. This strange occurrence was noted in Charleston County, S. C.

Frederick V. Hebard sends us the following notes on the nesting sites chosen by the mockingbird in the Okefinokee: "A decided preference was shown for the holly (*Ilex opaca*), eight nests being found in the planted hollies at Camp Cornelia. Four were found in live oaks (*Quercus virginiana*), although magnolias (*Magnolia grandifolia*), in which three were found, seem preferred if present. Other nests were found in bamboo brier (*Smilax* sp.) 2; blackberry bushes 2; saw palmetto (*Serenoa repens*) 2; waxmyrtle (*Myrica cerifera*) 1; water oak (*Quercus* sp.) 1; and unknown deciduous bushes 2. The first brood is usually raised in May and the second by the end of July. Some birds build their nests with incredible rapidity. Layton Burch saw one bird start and complete her nest on July 9; lay her eggs one a day, July 10, 11, 12, and 13; and begin incubating on July 15. The first young hatched on July 24, and hatching was completed by the next morning. The young had all left the nest by August 4.

Eggs.—[AUTHOR'S NOTE: The mockingbird lays beautiful eggs, with much variation in color and markings. Three to six eggs may constitute a set, but four or five is the usual number. The prevailing shape is ovate, with variations toward short-ovate or elongate-ovate. The ground varies from bluish white or greenish white, through various shades of bluish green or greenish blue, to some of the richer shades of blue or green; "Nile blue" is a common shade. Most of the eggs are heavily marked with spots and blotches, more or less evenly distributed, of various shades of brown, such as "hazel," "russet," "tawny," or "cinnamon." One very odd egg before me is a spotless, very pale blue, except for a dense, solid cap at the larger end of "cinnamon-rufous" overlaid with a ring of "hazel." Another is heavily capped with "Kaiser brown" over "cinnamon-rufous."

The measurements of 50 eggs in the United States National Museum average 24.3 by 18.3 millimeters; the eggs showing the four extremes measure 27.4 by 18.8, 25.9 by 19.8, 22.4 by 17.8, and 24.1 by 17.2 millimeters.]

Young.—The incubation period of the mockingbird is variously stated as from 9 to 12 days, but there is very little definite information on the subject; it is probably more than 12 days on the average.

As we found practically nothing in the literature about the nest life of this well-known bird, which was quite surprising, Mr. Bent asked Mr. Frank W. Braund, of Gulfport, Fla., to make some observations on this point and send us some information. Mr. Braund interested various members of the Gulfport Garden and Bird Club in the subject, and they made a number of observations and reported the results. Following are some extracts from Mr. Braund's report: "Of the eight nests under observation, only two records of the male entering the nest to incubate were recorded, and both of these were for a very short duration of time. H. R. Myers reports the female leaving the nest and observing the male fly from a nearby singing perch to the nest and squat in the incubating position. The female reappeared in approximately 2 minutes and drove the male from the nest. F. W. Braund observed a female leave her nest. The male, who had been singing on a nearby perch, flew to the nest and incubated the eggs until the female returned 4 minutes later and drove him off. I have, however, observed the nest and eggs unoccupied by either bird for long periods of time. I do not believe the male makes a practice of incubating when the female leaves the nest exposed.

"Robert Fredricks observed a nest on his own property. While working in the vicinity of the nest, located 8 feet up in a Mexican flamevine, both parent birds would appear with grubs in their bills and perch on a close by wire. As long as he remained in the vicinity of the nest the parents made no effort to feed. When he moved away from the nest, one parent would leave the perch and feed, the other following to feed when the first parent left."

F. C. Clayton and Mr. Braund both noted that the young were fed by both sexes; the latter reports: "I watched for several hours over a period of 10 days through 3x glasses both parents feeding the young in the nest. At times one would be at the nest feeding when the second parent would appear with food. This latter parent would patiently wait until its mate finished feeding, then fly to the nest to deposit its contribution.

"Robert Fredricks reports observing the parents feeding a green and brown larva. F. C. Clayton states that the parents follow the rake or the cultivator, picking up crickets, grasshoppers, and grubs, and carry them to the nest and feed them to the young. Observing through 3x glasses I have seen them feed cutworms and cabbage worms at a ratio of six cabbage worms to one cutworm. I have also observed them feeding crickets and grasshoppers. The legs are removed from the latter two before the insects are carried to the nest. The amputation is performed usually on the alighting perch, which in this case was a white fence between cottages."

The length of time that the young remain in the nest was not so easily determined, but he obtained two records on this point. Mrs. D. M. Morrison gave him the following data from her notes: "Nest of mockingbird started March 13, 1931. March 25, 2 eggs; March 27, 4 eggs; April 7, first downy young. April 8, 4 downy young; April 21, young left the nest." In this case the nest life of the young was 13 days.

In 1942, Mr. and Mrs. H. R. Myers and Mr. Braund watched a nest closely. "This nest contained four eggs, one of which did not hatch. All young hatched between 9:00 p. m. on June 6 and 11:00 a. m. on June 7. The young were dry at this latter time. One of the young left the nest at 4:00 p. m. on June 20, the second at 5:00 p. m. on June 20, and the third at 9:00 p. m. on June 20. Deep twilight was at 9:00 p. m., Eastern War Time. Using the 11:00 a. m. June 7 date would establish the nest-life cycle of these young at 13 days 6 hours, 13 days 6 hours, and 13 days 10 hours, respectively."

William G. Fargo writes to Mr. Bent from Pass-a-Grille, Fla., that a pair of mockingbirds, nesting in his seagrape, began incubating on a set of five eggs during the morning of April 7, and that the eggs were hatched on the morning of April 19, showing an incubation period of about 12 days. He never saw any evidence of more than one bird incubating, but Dr. Eugene E. Murphey, of Augusta, Ga., states (MS.) that "he has seen the male relieve the female at the incubation duties, and take his turn at sitting on the eggs."

Mr. Braund (MS.) reports the following interesting observation, made at the residence of L. A. Kosier in Gulfport: "On April 19, 1942, the nest with four eggs and the parent bird incubating were reported by Miss Kosier. We visited the nest daily until April 24, when a painter appeared to paint the cottage and the birds abandoned the nest. The nest was visited each day to April 30. The adult birds were not seen; the eggs were cold. On May 6 Braund returned to the nest to collect the abandoned eggs. This revisitation disclosed a fifth egg in the nest and either the same pair or another pair of mockingbirds about the location. On May 7 the nest contained six eggs, May 8 seven eggs and a parent bird incubating the eggs at 3:00 p. m. This nest was visited each day to May 27, a period of 19 days, when the parent birds again abandoned the nest. The nest was watched each day to May 30, when the eggs were collected and blown. All seven eggs were found infertile."

Plumages.—[AUTHOR'S NOTE: I have not seen the natal down, but Dr. Dwight (1900) describes it as pale sepia-brown. Unlike most of the family, the young mockingbird in juvenal plumage is quite unlike the adult. The upper surface is browner, grayish "sepia" rather than deep "smoke gray," with indistinct streaks of darker brown on the back; the wings and tail are much like those of the adult, but the greater wing coverts and secondaries are broadly edged with pale "wood brown"; the most conspicuous difference is on the underparts, where the chest, breast, sides, and flanks are spotted with dusky.

A partial postjuvenal molt, which involves the contour plumage and the wing coverts, but not the rest of the wings and tail, takes place mainly in September. This produces a first winter plumage which is practically adult. Adults have a complete postnuptial molt at about the same time, but no spring molt; the nuptial plumage is acquired by wear and is paler and grayer than the fall plumage.]

Food.—The diet of the mockingbird is the one phase of its existence that does not entirely redound to its credit, at least in the opinion of some. Until detailed studies were made of its food there was considerable doubt as to which side of the economic scale was tipped by it. The whole question hinged on the bird's fondness for fruit. In the southern orange groves and vineyards, much complaint from growers of citrus and grapes was directed against the mocker, and many took it into their own hands to reduce the species about their own particular properties. It is to be hoped, however, that the grape grower mentioned by G. C. Taylor (1862) as having killed 1,100 mockingbirds at his place near St. Augustine, Fla., is exceptional. This man was said to have buried the bodies of that many birds at the roots of his grapevines!

The report of extensive stomach analyses by Prof. F. E. L. Beal (Beal, McAtee, and Kalmbach, 1916) still stands as the most complete study on record. Recent attempts to obtain more up-to-date information have proved that there is little, if anything, that can be added to it in the files of the Fish and Wildlife Service. Therefore, for a general digest of the food habits over the main part of the range the Beal report is summarized as follows:

Stomachs of 417 specimens were available for study, and these proved that 47.81 percent animal matter and 52.19 percent vegetable matter were consumed. Most of the animal matter is taken in May, amounting to 85.44 percent. December and January are the greatest vegetable-consuming months, with 86.55 percent each. The proportion of beetles and grasshoppers appearing in the insect list shows that the bird feeds to a considerable extent on the ground. This habit must have been noted by anyone who has watched the bird much, or indeed, even casually. Six stomachs contained nine specimens of the cotton-boll weevil. Ants form 4.48 percent of the animal food and were found in 75 stomachs, another ground-feeding proof. Bees and wasps composed 3 percent. Though only two stomachs contained that notorious pest the chinch bug, Professor Beal says that "any bird which eats this pest deserves honorable mention." Grasshoppers composed 14.85 percent of all animal food and are eaten every month in the year. Caterpillars were a monthly diet except for October and made up 9.48 percent. Among "a host of others" appeared the cotton-leaf wörm, spiders, crawfish, sowbugs, and snails. Peculiar items were a few lizards (3) and a small snake.

In the vegetable line wild fruit is *the* item. It is eaten every month and totals 42.58 percent, more than four-fifths of all vegetable matter. Maximum consumption occurs in October, amounting to 76.91 percent. Wild fruit was found in 246 stomachs, and 76 contained nothing else. Thirty-five species were identified, and among the most frequently eaten were various kinds of holly, smilax, woodbine, blackberry, pokeberry, elderberry, mulberry, and sourgum. Domestic fruit comprised only 3.35 percent, the bulk of it being either raspberries or blackberries. Since both of these grow wild in abundance, the berries eaten by mockers "are as apt to be taken from thickets and briar patches as from gardens." Figs were found occasionally. A few grapes, which might have been wild species, were identified. As long as wild fruits are available the mocker will probably never do much harm to cultivated varieties. Certainly, the above would indicate that the mocker is not a heavy consumer of domestic fruit, as was thought by many. Professor Beal sums up his account by the statement that "there appears to be nothing to prove that the Mockingbird eats domestic fruit to an injurious extent."

A. H. Howell (1932) gives some interesting information in regard to the mocker's diet in Florida. He adds to the berry list above the sumac, poison ivy, Virginia-creeper, red cedar, black alder, and bayberry, by which last is probably meant the waxmyrtle, as it is abundant in the Southeast and the bayberry is not. He quotes C. J. Maynard (1896), as saying that at Key West mockers eat the fruit of the pricklypear cactus (*Opuntia*) extensively in fall and winter. H. H. Bailey (1925) says that the fruit of the wild fig and seagrape (*Coccolobis*) are eaten. He was told by the late Charles Torrey Simpson that mockers at Lemon City (near Miami) consume the berries of a nightshade (*Solanum seaforthianum*) and become intoxicated therefrom. D. J. Nicholson found the birds feeding on berries of the waxmyrtle (*Myrica cerifera*) and French mulberry (*Callicarpa*) as well as those of the cabbage palm (*Sabal palmetto*). This last is a frequent food item on the South Carolina coast, where the writer has often seen the mocker as well as numerous other avian species indulging on it. The ring-billed gull (*Larus delawarensis*) also often eats the berries of the palmetto!

Lester W. Smith (MS.) writes that about Sarasota, Fla., he has found mockers eating the pods of the yucca, or Spanish bayonet. They "feed on the upper ripe pods while the lower mass, still green, is untouched." Miss Clara Bates (1940), of Fort Pierce, Fla., writes that "like all birds, the Mockingbird is partial to the small red pepper (*C. frutescens*)."

Behavior.—As individualistic as the mocker is, its actions and behavior are replete with vigor and vivacity. There seems to be no condition under which the bird does not appear keenly alive. One of its marked traits is its alert defense of territory against all comers, and in this it rivals the kingbird (*Tyrannus tyrannus*) in attacking anything that violates it. At times it seems that a spirit of innate pugnacity prompts attacks, for these are by no means limited to the nesting season, or even winter territorial defense. Encounters among themselves are frequent and as many as six, eight, or even more birds will indulge in a battle royal. The writer once saw a group of 12 in his yard engaged in a pitched combat of determined proportions, this being the largest avian "mass attack" of which he has knowledge.

The spirit of play appears well developed in the mocker also. It is somewhat reminiscent of the duck hawk (*Falco peregrinus anatum*) in this respect. It seems to delight in bedeviling dogs and cats and puts either to flight. A neighbor of the writer in Charleston maintained a kennel of hunting dogs for some years, and the mockers of the neighborhood would often "dive-bomb" these dogs, plunging upon them as they slept, or else they roamed about the enclosure and frequently drove them to the shelter of the kennels, tails between legs! At times they would actually alight on a dog's back and peck savagely. M. G. Vaiden (MS.), of Rosedale, Miss., says that "I have seen the mockingbird ride my Belgian shepherd's back more than once, near the nesting site, and usually the dogs find some other places to ramble than those near a mocker's nest." It often attacks snakes also, and an instance of this is related by Mrs. J. L. Alley (1939), of Tavernier, Fla. She states that she witnessed an attack on a coachwhip snake (*Masticophis flagellum*) near St. Petersburg in the summer of 1939. The bird repeatedly alighted on the head of the snake and pecked it viciously. The encounter was watched for a considerable time, the snake finally seeking sanctuary under some bushes.

The flight of the mocker is well sustained but appears somewhat labored at times, particularly in heavy winds, probably on account of the long tail. It is often the case that, when alighting on the ground, where it spends much time, the bird elevates its wings and holds them high, after the manner of some of the shorebirds, before folding them.

Also it will often continue such behavior with a series of opening and closing the wings, fanning them gently, running a few feet then stopping abruptly with head high. This may be done as many as five or six times, the whole performance illustrating the trim, alert character of the bird. When two or three are going through such actions it reminds one of a sort of avian gymnastic drill. It is thought by some that these performances are indulged in to startle unseen insects into betraying their whereabouts, but this needs more definite study and proof than are now available.

Though a low-ranging species generally, as regards feeding and nesting, the mocker often selects an elevated perch for singing, or even resting. Telephone wires, chimney tops, or the top twigs of trees are frequently used. To watch one atop a tall yucca, outlined against the sky, amid the sand dunes of a barrier beach, or the flaming colors of a city garden, is as characteristic a sight as anything could be in a southern State. When the bird chooses a chimney for a singing perch, the effect of its song coming down into the rooms below is a most striking auditory experience, muted as it is by perhaps two or more floors of flues. This is often heard on moonlight nights, when it is the more remarkable.

The ready willingness of the mocker to attack anything about its nest or territory is proverbial. Occasionally, however, it meets a match in such species as the loggerhead shrike (which it superficially resembles). In the files of the Charleston (S. C.) Museum are some notes by Francis M. Weston as follows: "March 3, 1907, St. Andrew's Parish, S. C. Mockingbird chased by Loggerhead." Again, on March 17, same year, the same observation was made at 4-Mile House, Charleston County. On the other side of the ledger appear such notes from the same observer as: "Dec. 24th, 1906, Pee Dee River, S. C. Mocker chasing Phoebe" and "Dec. 27th, 1906, Pee Dee River, S. C. Mocker chasing Red-bellied Woodpecker." H. R. Sass, of Charleston, notes that a mocker was "worrying Robins" in his garden on January 9, 1906.

As is the case with several other species the mocker frequently attacks its own image in polished, reflecting surfaces. This has been commented on by numerous observers. M. G. Vaiden (MS.) writes: "In June 1933, my car was parked at the side door of the residence when I observed a mockingbird pecking at the highly polished radiator. I scared the bird away and returned to the house; the bird came back and again started pecking and occasionally striking with wings, whereupon I concluded that it was fighting its shadow (reflection) in the radiator. This continued for an hour or more until I moved the car. The next day I noticed the bird doing the same thing and covered the radiator with a towel to prevent any possible damage to the mocker."

A friend of the writer had much the same experience near Georgetown, S. C., when a mocker made persistent attacks on its own image in the surface of a car's hubcap. The owner of the car finally covered the cap with moss when he parked it! A mockingbird living in the yard of the writer fought itself literally for days in the window of the cellar, which was almost on a level with the ground. This is almost certainly a territorial defense action, as the image is taken by the bird for an intruder on its domain and treated accordingly.

The immense popularity of the mocker throughout its range has resulted in its being chosen as State bird by no less than five commonwealths!

Voice.—There is no possibility of doubt that the vocal attainments of the mockingbird are its primary characteristic. Its voice overshadows its every other trait, habit, and even appearance. Recognition of it is evident in both the common and the scientific name of the species, and neither could be more appropriate. Though its amazing powers of imitation were not known to Linnaeus except second-hand, his designation of *Mimus polyglottos* as its name was well chosen, for as a "many-tongued mimic" the mockingbird stands alone. Catesby's name of "Mock-bird" is practically the same as its present-day appellation. Some years ago Herbert R. Sass, of Charleston, S. C., referred to the mockingbird in one of his inimitable nature articles as "Mimus the Matchless," and it has always seemed to this writer that no more descriptive adjective could be used in connection with it. Truly, that is the word for the mocker. . . . matchless!

It is evident, of course, that there are remarkable performers among the so-called song birds of this country, and each has enthusiastic partisans. However, whatever can be said about each one of them can be said of the mockingbird, plus. Always plus, because if given the opportunity, the mocker can deliver the song of any other bird as well as the species itself, plus the fact that it has a wonderfully beautiful song of its own!

Ample proofs that the writer is not hopelessly biased in his statements regarding the mocker's vocal ability are numerous. Illustrative of what others think are quotations that follow. Baird, Brewer, and Ridgway (1874) say:

"The vocal powers of the Mockingbird exceed, both in their imitative notes and natural song, those of any other species. Their voice is full, strong and musical, and capable of an almost endless variation in modulation. * * * In force and sweetness the Mocking bird will often improve upon the original." A. H. Howell (1932) states that "the song of the Mocker is easily the most prominent and best loved of southern bird voices."

John Burroughs (1895) is less qualified in his approbation than the conservative Howell and joins with Ridgway in enthusiastic praise. He termed the mocker "Our nightingale" and goes on to say that it is "famed mostly for its powers of mimicry, which are truly wonderful, enabling the bird to exactly reproduce and even improve upon the notes of almost every other species of songster. * * * Here is the lark and the nightingale in one."

In connection with the reference to the nightingale, probably the most famous of Old World songsters, an amusing story is even yet related in Florida connected with this species and the mocker. It seems that Edward Bok, who created the well-known Singing Tower near Lake Wales, had several nightingales imported and confined there in cages. When the strangers had settled down and had begun to voice their famous song abroad across the orange groves, great satisfaction was felt, of course. Before long, however, nightingale songs were heard all over the surrounding territory! Here, there, and yonder the foreign strains were echoing, but all the captives remained in their cages. The mockingbirds of the area had taken charge and were broadcasting nightingale melodies over the countryside! It is said that the European performers were put to silence and soon refused to sing at all. Particularly apropos of this is R. W. Shufeldt's symposium on the mockingbird in Newton's "Dictionary of Birds," for he says there: "I believe were he successfully introduced into those countries where the Nightingale flourishes, that princely performer might some day wince as he was obliged to listen to his own most powerful strains poured forth * * * by this king of feathered mockers." It has happened.

The mocker begins its performance at an early age. Amelia R. Laskey (MS.) says that they start "when very young but these songs are very soft-toned, 'whisper' songs that cannot be heard unless one is very close to the performer. Four young birds under observation started singing at the following ages: 30 days, 34, 57, and 73 days." This whisper song is also indulged in by the adult and is an exquisite thing—soft, appealing, and infinitely tender in its cadences.

Aretas A. Saunders (MS.) says that "the song is long continued, consisting of phrases with pauses between them. The mocker differs from the catbird and the brown thrasher in a tendency to repeat a phrase four or five more times in succession, in a richer quality, in greater frequency of singing, tendency to sing at night, especially when moonlight * * * frequently in fall * * * frequently on the wing. The greatest number of different phrases I have recorded from one bird is 30, but I have no doubt that it uses many more than that."

That gifted ornithological writer Edward H. Forbush (1929), speaking as a New Englander, gives the mockingbird one of the finest of tributes when he says that "the Mockingbird stands unrivaled. He is the king of song. * * * He equals and even excels the whole feathered choir. He improves upon most of the notes that he reproduces, adding also to his varied repertoire the crowing of chanticleer, the cackling of the hen, the barking of the house dog, the squeaking of the unoiled wheelbarrow, the postman's whistle. * * * He even imitates man's musical inventions."

T. Gilbert Pearson (1909) writes that he has "sometimes thought that they must be conscious of the power of their numbers. * * * The bird revels in the glory of his vocal strength, and shouts his ringing challenge to the trees, the flowers, the very sky itself. * * * However, it is at night that the Mockingbird is at his best. If he is the music-prince of the grove by day, he is the song-king of the lawn on moonlight nights."

It is not surprising that, in such a species, particular individuals have become known for particular powers of rendition and imitation. One of these is mentioned by Frank M. Chapman (1912), a specimen heard by Leverett M. Loomis near Chester, S. C. This mocker imitated 32 different birds in a space of 10 minutes. Of it Chapman says, "This was a phenomenal performance, one I have never heard approached, for in my experience many Mockingbirds have no notes besides their own, and good mockers are exceptional." In an observer and student of the wide knowledge and experience of Dr. Chapman, this seems a strange statement. The writer, during a lifetime with the mocker, would observe that there is little, if any, difference in the individual powers of this bird. One is as capable as another. It would be difficult to assign any reason why this should not be the case. Why would one be especially gifted and another not?

As remarkable as was the performance of the South Carolina specimen, however, its record has been eclipsed since Dr. Chapman gave it prominence. E. H. Forbush (1929) quotes W. L. Dawson as saying that the latter heard a mockingbird change his tune *87 times in 7 minutes* and that he was able to recognize 58 of the imitations given! Forbush had such unqualified belief in the mocker's powers that he says, "Perhaps there is no song-bird * * * that the Mockingbird cannot imitate to perfection."

Despite all the foregoing, it would be reprehensible not to mention that amazing bird that has come to be known as the Arnold Arboretum Mocker, of Boston. It has been written of at length and in great detail by C. L. Whittle (1922). In summarizing its astounding vocal powers, it need only be said that Mr. Whittle lists its imitations of 39 bird songs, 50 bird calls, and the notes of a frog and a cricket!

A. V. Goodpasture, of Nashville, Tenn. (1908), says:

The most obvious charms of his song, however, are the infinite variety and range of his round, full, distinct notes, and the rapidity and enthusiasm with which he trills his marvelous medley. * * * Four observations of his song, taken at different times, will convey some idea of his performance: (1) In ten minutes he changed his song of from one to four notes, forty-six times, and repeated each from one to nine times—an average of 3.41 times. (2) In three minutes he changed his song twenty-eight times, repeated each from one to nine times—average four times. (3) In one minute he changed thirteen times, repeated from one to nine times—average 6.3 times. (4) In ten minutes he changed 137 times, repeated from one to twelve times—average 3.18 times.

The call notes of the mockingbird have none of the melodious quality of its song; indeed the tone is quite the opposite. There is a grating harshness about them more suggestive of the bird's fighting temper than of any quality of musical sweetness. Rendered into words (never satisfactory, of course) the call note has been described as "a harsh, grating 'chair'" by R. Hoffmann; a "chuck" or "chick" and a harsh, scolding note (almost veery-like) "whee-e-e" by J. A. Farley. A. H. Howell calls it a "harsh chuck."

There has doubtless been speculation on the ability of *memory* on the part of the mocker in reproducing the songs of other birds. Since there is very little in the literature concerning it, the following notes from F. M. Weston (MS.) are of extraordinary interest:

"March, 1912, Charleston, S. C. Mockingbird heard giving 'tucky-tuck' call of summer tanager (*Piranga rubra*), then tanager song, then call again, showing definite association of those two sounds. Tanager had not yet arrived in spring migration, and recollection was at least of 6 months' duration.

"May 25, 1925, Pensacola, Fla. A mockingbird that has been singing in the neighborhood all spring imitates the full song of the field sparrow (*Spizella pusilla*) more than that of any other species. He is so persistent about it that I can recognize him by that feature of his performance. During my 10 years' residence here, I have yet to hear the song of the field sparrow in this region. That particular mockingbird has spent some earlier period of his life in some other region, and his memory is at least eight months long."

Field marks.—Even its most ardent admirers could hardly call the mockingbird handsome. It is trim, alert, and clean-cut but not striking in plumage and is quite plain in appearance. At rest, the long tail is diagnostic, and the conspicuous white wing patches show to advantage in flight and can also be seen while the bird is perched. There is a decided general resemblance to the loggerhead shrike (*Lanius ludovicianus*), which had led to the latter's being known in some localities as the "French mockingbird." However, the mocker is a darker gray and lacks the sharply contrasting pattern of the loggerhead, as well as the black line through the eye.

Albinism is not rare in mockingbirds, and the writer has seen specimens ranging from totality to only a few feathers in wings or tail. A totally albino bird was reported to the writer on May 29, 1940, as occurring in the grounds of a resident of a Charleston (S. C.) suburb for several days. Two or three specimens were brought into the Charleston Museum during the years the writer was connected with that institution, and the late A. T. Wayne had at least one specimen in his collection.

Enemies.—The mockingbird is probably as free from natural enemies as any passerine bird could be. Because of its pugnacious tendencies it, like the kingbird (*Tyrannus tyrannus*), takes the offensive rather than the defensive against all avian enemies, although, of course, it would be and sometimes doubtless is a victim of such predatory species as the accipitrine hawks.

In regard to man it is fortunate in holding a high place in public sentiment and affection. If a census could be taken regarding the bird most beloved by the public generally throughout the entire country, the result would probably be a close race between the mockingbird and the robin. Even the small boy, who must be classed as a predatory animal of dangerous proportions at one stage of his development, usually directs his slingshot, airgun, or .22 rifle at some other avian target than this general favorite.

Years ago the mocker figured largely as a cage bird in many parts of the South at least, but this practice is now all but nonexistent except in the most remote regions where the laws governing it are not well known. The bird's attacks on fruit orchards and groves are not serious, and few are done away with on such accounts.

Dr. Friedmann (1934) cites only two cases in which the mockingbird has been imposed upon by the cowbird.

E. B. Chamberlain (MS.) records a very interesting occurrence that took place in the yard of his residence near Charleston, S. C. He had been watching the nest of a mockingbird in a small oak, where it was built near the end of a limb and only 4 feet from the ground. On the afternoon of July 7, 1942, it held four pinfeathered young. As he came into the yard that afternoon, a Cooper's hawk rose from the nest, bearing one of the young in its claws. It stopped in a larger oak nearby but escaped out of the far side before it could be shot. An hour later there was an outcry from the mockers and on rushing out, Chamberlain saw the hawk making away with a second youngster. I "cut loose," he says, "just for the noise effect as I had no chance to hit the hawk." The next day passed without a repeat visit from the hawk, but on the following day (9th) "again I met the spectacle of the hawk leaving the nest, the third young in its talons." The adult mockers gave chase to the marauder as it flew out over the adjacent marshes. While at the supper table that same evening, at 7:45 p. m., Chamberlain witnessed the return of the hawk and the departure of the last of the young by "the same well worn route." He then closed the account with the statement that "I was interested to note that by 8:15 p. m. the adult male (?) mocker had recovered enough to burst into song on a nearby perch. Perhaps he had forgotten the tragedy already."

DISTRIBUTION

Range.—The United States and southern Canada, to southern Mexico and the West Indies: generally nonmigratory.

The mockingbird occurs with some regularity, generally breeding, **north** to northern California (Corning and Chico); southeastern Oregon (an isolated colony in the Blitzen Valley, Harney County); southern Nevada (Oasis Valley and Pahranagat Valley); southern Utah (St. George and Zion National Park; occasional or local north to Great Salt Lake and the Uinta Basin); southern and eastern Colorado (Grand Junction, Salida, Denver, and Loveland); southeastern Wyoming (Laramie and Douglas); Nebraska (Sioux County, rare, Greeley, and Omaha); Iowa (Sioux City and Grinnell); northern Illinois (Chicago, rare); northern Indiana (Elkhart and Fort Wayne); northern Ohio (Toledo, Sandusky, and Stanhope); southwestern and southeastern Pennsylvania (Hickory, Finleyville, Harrisburg, and Philadelphia); central New Jersey (Barnegat); and sporadically to central New York, Massachusetts, and southern Maine. **East** to the Atlantic coast of the United States, the Bahamas (Abaco and Inagua Islands); the Greater Antilles to the Virgin Islands (St. Thomas and St. Croix). **South** to the Virgin Islands (St. Croix); Hispaniola (Ciudad Trujillo); Jamaica (Port Royal); Grand Cayman; Cuba (Isle of Pines); the Gulf coast of the United States and Mexico to Veracruz (Orizaba); and southern Oaxaca (Santa Efigenia). **West** to Oaxaca (Santa Efigenia and Oaxaca); Guerrero (Acapulco); the Pacific coast of Mexico and throughout Baja California (Cape San Lucas, Santa Margarita, and Ensenada; accidental on Guadalupe Island); and the coast of California (including the Santa Barbara Islands) to the San Francisco Bay region and the Sacramento Valley (Willows and Corning).

The above range is for the species as a whole, of which two subspecies or geographic races are recognized in the United States. The eastern mockingbird (*M. p. polyglottos*) occurs in the northern Bahama Islands and the eastern United States, west to the edge of the Plains in eastern Nebraska and Kansas; the western mockingbird (*M. p. leucopterus*) is found from western Nebraska and Kansas westward and south to Baja California and Oaxaca.

Since the law was passed prohibiting the caging of native birds, the mockingbird has increased in numbers and has pushed its normal range northward. There are also many records of occurrence (often in winter) and of breeding far north of what may be considered the normal range. Some of these records may belong to the "casual" list, but it is difficult to separate them. During the winter of 1922 one appeared at Ferndale, Humboldt County, Calif., where it remained for several weeks. There are two records for Vancouver Island, British Columbia; one observed at Port Alberni on June 7, 1931, and a specimen collected at Duncan, on January 20, 1940. Apparently the only record for Alberta is of a pair that nested at Didsbury in June 1928. One was observed at Piapot, southwestern Saskatchewan, on May 2, 1927, and a specimen was collected at Eastend on June 4, 1928. In 1934 a nest was reported 35 miles south of Regina, and on May 7, 1936, one was observed in Regina. In Manitoba, the first report was from Hillside Beach, in May 1928, and one was observed from November 15, 1939, to January 2, 1940, near Winnipeg. The mockingbird has nested in two localities in Ontario—at Point Pelee in 1909 and at Nanticoke in 1924—besides which there are a number of records of its occurrence at all times of the year as far north as Ottawa and at Moose Factory on June 4, 1928. It was recorded at Gaspé, Quebec, on November 5, 1938, and a specimen was taken on Anticosti Island on August 8, 1902. Three specimens have been collected at Grand Manan, New Brunswick, all in fall and winter. A specimen was taken on Sable Island, Nova Scotia, on September 3, 1902. Casual records previous to 1900 are usually open to question as being possibly escaped cage birds.

In some sections the mockingbird appears to be migratory, but there does not seem to be any definite and regular migration. The movements of mockingbirds seem to be local or individual. Banding returns indicate that some individuals travel considerable distances.

Introduction.—In 1893, six pairs of eastern mockingbirds were liberated in Bermuda, and some were still to be found there in 1914.

Egg dates.—Arizona: 52 records, April 12 to August 2; 26 records, May 18 to June 15, indicating the height of the season.

California: 94 records, February 16 to September 2; 50 records, April 18 to May 21.

Florida: 56 records, March 25 to August 12; 28 records, April 24 to May 21.

Georgia: 26 records, April 14 to July 9; 16 records, May 10 to June 6.

Oklahoma: 11 records, May 2 to June 23.

Texas: 94 records, March 10 to July 20; 48 records, May 2 to 27.

MIMUS POLYGLOTTOS LEUCOPTERUS (Vigors)

WESTERN MOCKINGBIRD

PLATES 59, 60

HABITS

The western mockingbird is a larger bird than its eastern relative, with a *relatively* shorter tail; its general coloration is paler, with the underparts more washed with buffy; the white at the bases of the primaries is more extended and the white tips of the wing coverts are broader; and the wing feathers are tipped with white; *leucopterus* is an appropriate name. It was long considered to be a bird of the southwestern States and Mexico, but either it has extended its range or we have extended our knowledge of its distribution during recent years. Even the 1931 Check-list seems to limit its northward range to central California, southern Wyoming, and northwestern Nebraska. Laurence B. Potter, of Eastend, Saskatchewan, writes to me: "In Canada generally, the mockingbird is considered a rare visitant anywhere. This fact makes all the more remarkable the irruption of mockingbirds into the prairie provinces, with nesting records in Alberta and Saskatchewan. The first bird was noted in 1927, the last about 1937, a period of about ten years. Since then mockingbirds have appeared on Vancouver Island. P. A. Taverner (1934) says that the western mockingbird is probably the one that has wandered to southern British Columbia, but that "the subspecific identity of the prairie occurrences is doubtful."

The western mockingbird is a more or less permanent resident in the hot Lower Sonoran valleys of the southwestern States, but it retires in winter from the northern portions of its range and from the foothills farther south, where it is common up to 5,000 feet in summer. John G. Tyler (1913) says of its haunts in the Fresno region of California, which are typical: "The writer has observed Mockingbirds in a small orchard surrounding a ranch house, far out on the plains near Wheatville, among the tangle of swamp growths below Riverdale, and along one or two of the creeks that lead down from the foothills; but the center of their abundance seems to be the most highly cultivated and thickly settled tracts in the valley. Orchards, hedgerows, fig-bordered vineyards, and shade trees around dwellings are favorite haunts of this famous vocalist; and from the tops of windmills, the topmost branches of trees, or the roofs of buildings, they pour forth their wonderful repertoire of song." And Ralph Hoffmann (1927) adds: "It is one of the surprises of a bird student on his first visit to the Coast to see Mockingbirds singing from the chimneys of a hotel, flirting their long tails on the curbing of city streets or pursuing one another in and out of city traffic. All they ask are yards about the houses, a bit of lawn to feed on and vines or thick bushes in which to nest."

Territory.—Harold and Josephine R. Michener (1935) made an intensive study of the territorial behavior of a number of western mockingbirds in the immediate vicinity of their home in Pasadena, Calif., covering a period of over a year, from January 1, 1933, to February 15, 1934. Their interesting report covers 44 pages in *The Condor*, to which the reader is referred, for space will permit the inclusion of only a few extracts here. The birds were trapped and marked with colored bands, for identification. The area under observation is a lot, 100 by 317 feet, within a mile of the center of Pasadena and surrounded by the city on all sides.

The territories occupied by the five mated pairs varied from approximately 3,750 to 60,000 square feet in an environment that was especially favorable; probably average territories elsewhere are much larger. They think that the birds have two general types of territories, summer territories and winter territories:

The summer and winter territories of an individual or a pair may or may not be identical areas. The summer territory is the family home, held and defended by the male and occupied solely by him until the female joins him, unless his mate of the previous year has remained with him.

The female rarely takes part in the defense of the summer territory.

The winter territory centers about the food supply and is defended by both the male and the female, in case the pair remain together, or by the lone male or female occupant. * * * The defense of the winter territories seems much more vigorous than that of the summer territories. This may be because the invaders in the winter are much more numerous than in summer and because the territory holder has many other things to do in the summer while in winter the defense of the food supply is the only important activity.

The so-called "dance," so well described under the courtship of the eastern mockingbird, and the display, which I refer to below, may both be used as part of the boundary defense demonstration, as strongly suggested by Mrs. Laskey (MS.). I doubt if it is often necessary for the birds to enter into actual physical combat; the demonstration is generally sufficient warning to the trespasser. Even the song may be all that is necessary.

Courtship.—On April 21, 1929, I saw what I believe was a courtship display. A mockingbird, presumably a male, was running along on our lawn at Pasadena, flirting his spread tail up and down, making a soft cooing sound and occasionally lifting both his wings high above his back and spreading them so as to show the conspicuous white areas.

At San Diego, on June 21, 1929, Frank F. Gander (1931) saw a pair of western mockingbirds in copulation. The female was feeding on the ground under some shrubbery. He says:

The male was singing from the top of a tall flagpole nearby. Suddenly he dropped from his perch. In full song, he shot down into the shrubbery about

15 feet beyond the female.   As he sped past her, the female crouched a little and begun to quiver her wings.   She continued in this as the male, singing excitedly and with tail and wings half spread, advanced toward her with dancing steps. As he neared her his excitement grew but his approach was stately and un-hurried.   As he came near he seemed to be floating along just over the ground and he rose gradually and settled upon her back.   All this time he had been pour-ing forth impassioned melody.   The act lasted several seconds and was accom-panied by much fluttering of wings.

Nesting.—The western mockingbird will build its nest in almost any of the many varieties of bushes, small trees, or tangles of vines found within its habitat, including such western plants as sagebushes, pricklypear cactus, or the different chollas.   Dense shrubbery or the thickly leaved branches of trees are preferred.   The nest may be placed anywhere from 1 foot to 40 feet above ground, though most of them are 6 feet up or less.   George F. Simmons (1925) says that, in Texas, the nests are sometimes placed in a hollow in the top of a "cedar fence post, in brush piles, on stumps, or in corners of rail fences."   F. W. Braund has sent me the data for seven nests in his collection; one was in a vine in an open field, three were in bushes, and three were in chollas; the heights varied from 3 to 5 feet above ground.   The foundation of the nest is made of coarse and fine twigs, often thorny, mixed with coarse grasses and weed stems; sometimes bits of rags or cotton, string, paper, or other trash are added.   The lining usually consists of fine grasses, but sometimes fine rootlets, horsehair, or plant down is used.

Eggs.—The eggs of this western race are indistinguishable in every way from those of the eastern mockingbird, showing the same range of beautiful variations.   The measurements of 50 eggs in the United States National Museum average 24.6 by 18.6 millimeters; the eggs showing the four extremes measure **27.4** by **19.8, 21.8** by 17.8, and 23.4 by **17.3** millimeters.

Young.—The period of incubation is said to be 10 to 14 days; probably the latter figure is approximately correct.   The young are said to remain in the nest 9 to 12 days; perhaps nearly 2 weeks would be the normal time, if the young are not disturbed.   Probably in-cubation is shared by both sexes, but the literature seems to be very silent on this point and on the care and development of the young. Two broods are regularly raised in a season, and rarely three.

As to the care and feeding of the young, Mrs. Wheelock (1904) gives us the only account I can find; she writes:

Both male and female Mockers flit through the green like silent shadows hunting insects under the leaves, earthworms on the ground, or berries in the garden.   These are all swallowed first and delivered to the infant Mockers by regurgitation for the first few days, or until the babies' eyes open.   After that, the number of earthworms, butterflies, etc. devoured by those nestlings rivals the story of the young robins who in 12 hours ate 40 percent more than their own weight.   There seems to be no limit to their appetite and scarcely any to their capacity. Even after they leave the nest and are nearly as large as the adults, they follow the overworked father about, begging with quivering wings.

Food.—Professor Beal (1907) says: "No serious complaints of the bird's depredations in this State [California] have yet been made, but this perhaps is due to the fact that mocking birds are rare in sections where cherries and the smaller deciduous fruits are grown. Where mockers are most abundant, citrus fruits are the principal crop and the birds do not appear to molest them."

He examined 33 stomachs, taken between July 18 and August 18, which contained 23 percent of animal matter and 77 percent of vegetable. Of the animal food, "beetles of several families formed a little less than 1 percent. Hymenoptera, largely ants, were eaten to the extent of somewhat more than 10 percent. Grasshoppers constituted the largest item of animal food, and amounted to 11 percent of the whole. A few caterpillars and spiders made up the other 1 percent of the animal food." Most of the vegetable food was fruit, some of it wild, "but blackberries or raspberries, grapes, and figs were found in many stomachs. Many of the birds were taken in orchards and gardens, and some were shot in the very act of pilfering blackberries. * * * The only species of wild fruits that were identified were elderberries, which were found in a few stomachs." Seeds of poison oak were conspicuous; one stomach was entirely filled with them. Nineteen other stomachs were examined, taken in nine other months; they contained much similar material. One, taken in March, contained a lizard; three, taken in September, contained "a few wasps"; the only useful insect eaten was a carabid beetle.

Robert S. Woods has sent me a photograph of a mocker feeding on the fruit of the pricklypear cactus (*Opuntia*). Mockers will come freely to feeding stations that are supplied with cultivated or wild fruits and berries. They also eat the berries of the peppertree.

Voice.—The behavior and voice of the western mockingbird are so similar to these attributes of its gifted eastern relative that it seems sufficient to say that it is just as marvelous a singer, equally versatile, and just as welcome a visitor to town and rural gardens. Many observers have referred to its versatility as a mimic. Mr. Simmons (1925) says that, in Texas, it "imitates the excited twittle of the Scissor-tailed Flycatcher, the song of the Wood Thrush, calls of the Roadrunner, the Southern Blue Jay, the Sennett Titmouse, the Chuck-will's-widow, the Howell Nighthawk, and countless others, even the Migrant Shrike, the Blue-gray Gnatcatcher, and some of the smaller warblers; an individual bird frequently has as many as three dozen imitated songs. Utters each imitation two or three times, and then takes up another, which it treats in the same way; frequently such repetition is the only thing that distinguishes the imitation from the song mimicked."

Mr. Sennett (1878) several times heard the screeching call of the chachalaca coming from a mocker. Mrs. Bailey (1928) adds the *killy-killy* of the sparrow hawk, the *ja-cob* of Mearns's woodpecker, and the notes of the pinyon and Woodhouse's jays, the western kingbirds, the green-tailed towhee and the Rocky Mountain nuthatch. Mrs. Nice (1931) includes the yap of the English sparrow, the scold of the robin, the *chebec* of the least flycatcher, and the notes of the scaled quail, lark sparrow, canyon towhee, Bullock's oriole, western kingbird, and house finch. In addition to those named above, C. H. Richardson, Jr. (1906), lists the following imitations heard in the vicinity of Pasadena: Western gull, killdeer, valley partridge, sparrow hawk, California woodpecker, red-shafted flicker, ash-throated flycatcher, Say's and black phoebes, western wood pewee, western flycatcher, California jay, western meadowlark, Arizona hooded oriole, Bullock oriole, Brewer's blackbird, San Diego song sparrow, black-headed grosbeak, western tanager, purple martin, cliff swallow, phainopepla, California shrike, western gnatcatcher, dwarf hermit thrush, and western robin.

Following are some of the Micheners' (1935) remarks on the songs:

The males have a set of summer songs and a set of winter songs and some songs that seem to be the same in both summer and winter. * * * As probably the first indication of revival of activity after the molt, about the middle of September, the males at mid-day from low thick bushes sing a soft, faint, varied and beautiful song having no imitations in it. * * * The females are quiet in the summer season. They join in the *hew-hew* notes and the rasping notes of the pair in early summer. Beginning about mid-September, as the depression of the molt wears away, the females sing a soft, faint song which can scarcely be distinguished from the song of the immatures. * * * The young birds sing a faint, soft song quite without imitations of other bird songs but distinctly a mockingbird song. They seem absorbed in the production of song and sing, usually at mid-day, for several days and then disappear. While singing the birds perch in low, thick shrubbery, mounting higher as the days go by but never do they sing from tree tops or other such high perches. At least some individuals sing before, during, and after the molt.

Enemies.—There seems to be no information available on the natural enemies of the western mockingbird, which are probably as numerous as those of other passerine birds. It has served as host for the eggs of the dwarf cowbird on several occasions, according to Dr. Friedmann (1934).

DUMETELLA CAROLINENSIS (Linnaeus)

CATBIRD

PLATES 61–65

HABITS

CONTRIBUTED BY ALFRED OTTO GROSS

The catbird is a stable species; throughout its extensive nesting range from British Columbia to Quebec and south to the Gulf States and the Bermuda Islands not a single subspecies has been recognized.

Outram Bangs and Thomas S. Bradlee (1901) described the smaller
Bermuda birds, which have narrow and shorter tail feathers and
primaries as *bermudianus*, but this species was never accepted by the
A. O. U. committee on nomenclature.

It is almost universally known as the catbird, but in the south this
recognized singer and mimic is sometimes locally called the black
mockingbird, and in Bermuda where there are no resident Icteridae
the natives have named it the blackbird. The name catbird though
a misnomer is destined to remain. It probably originated from
some casual listener who gave ear only to the short, grating, catlike
call and did not hear or was not impressed by its pleasing and varied
song. As a boy the name prejudiced me against this bird until I
learned to know its true worth and the high place among our native
birds it now holds in my estimation.

Though modestly colored the catbird is exquisitely tailored and
always presents a trim appearance. He is intelligent and friendly
and possesses a lively and restless temperament, ever ready to be help-
ful to others of its kind in trouble of any sort, often coming to the aid
of distracted parents in the defense of their homes and little ones.
He is very playful, full of droll pranks and quaint performances. He
is also an accomplished singer as well as a mimic and possesses many
other admirable qualities that endear him to the bird lover who has
learned to know his interesting personality.

Spring.—In Florida the catbird is an abundant migrant, but it is
also a fairly common winter resident and a few breed in the central
and northern parts of the State. According to A. H. Howell (1932),
the spring migration begins very early, as indicated by the record of
25 catbirds seen flying north at Sombrero Key on the night of January
26. Two others were seen there on January 28. However, the majority of the migrants pass through the State about the middle of April,
with belated stragglers migrating as late as the first two weeks of May.
In Alabama the catbirds appear as migrants at various parts of the
State from April 6 to April 19. Likewise in Louisiana and Texas the
mass of catbird migrants passes through during the first weeks of
April. They reach Pennsylvania and Ohio about April 27. At Cape
May, N. J., the average date of 18 years of first arrival records made
by Witmer Stone (1937) is April 25. The average date of first arrivals
at Minneapolis, Minn. (T. S. Roberts, 1932), is May 5, the earliest
April 27, 1921. In New York, New England, and southern Canada
the catbirds may be expected the first week of May.

In general the great bulk of migrants arrive about a week after the
first birds of the season are seen. The migratory wave of catbirds requires about a month in traveling from the southern part of the United
States to the northern and western section of their nesting range.

The spring migration northward is regular, and the date of arrival varies but little from year to year. Even during times of unseasonably cold weather the catbird does not seem to halt its movements to await for warmer days but usually proceeds on schedule.

The catbird travels chiefly at night and is so quiet that its great flights are seldom detected, but on arrival at their breeding grounds their presence is announced by their delightful songs. Each spring during the first week of May I am awakened by the first catbird song from a friendly individual who sings from his perch in the catalpa tree just outside my window. He seems eager to let us and everyone else in the neighborhood know that he is here for the season. He also informs his neighbors that the syringa bushes, lilacs, and arborvitae about the catalpa tree are his territory and that he is ready to challenge any intruder.

Courtship.—After a few days the female arrives and an animated courtship begins. This is carried on largely in the seclusion of the dense shrubbery and evergreens which cover much of the backyard. Often they may be seen dashing in and out of the thick cover, the male in hot pursuit of his elusive mate. Frequently he pauses for an outpouring of song, with his plumage raised and tail lowered he bows with his bill toward his perch. He slides about in a curious manner, or struts in a fantastic fashion with his wings lowered and tail erected, and sometimes he wheels about displaying the only bit of color he possesses: the contrasting chestnut patch on his under tail coverts. After a few days of arduous courtship nest-building begins, with the song period of the male reaching its climax. He sings almost continuously during the early morning and evening hours and sometimes well into the night. As he sings he seems to be well aware that he is an accomplished and versatile vocalist. He gives a distinct impression of a bird that likes to show off; he wishes to be heard and seen by everyone. His self-consciousness and vanity at such times are most amusing. Not only does the male sing vigorously but also he is ever on the alert to protect his territory against all intruders whether it be the gray squirrel that comes to the feeding shelf nearby or the Baltimore oriole that builds its nest on a pendent limb of the tall elm bordering the street.

Nesting.—The catbird usually chooses low dense thickets, tangles of vines, or small bushy trees for its nesting site. Often it is in vegetation bordering marshes, streams, or forests. In all cases the nest is well concealed by foliage. It is an adaptable species and may seek the habitations of man to build in hedgerows or cultivated shrubs of the gardens. At Brunswick, Maine, there is a pair that builds each year in a mass of shrubbery within a few yards of the house where the frequent presence of members of the household fails to disturb their normal activities. The catbird is characteristic of the country home, and I have vivid memories of a pair that regularly built in the blackberry briers that bordered our vegetable garden of a central-Illinois farm. The old apple orchard was also a favorite nesting place of a pair of them. Witmer Stone (1913a) writes as follows: "Every old garden has somewhere about it a shady thicket of lilacs, mock-orange, or some similar shrubbery in a niche by the back porch, perhaps, or behind the greenhouse, or over in the corner where the fences come together; and it is with such a spot that the Catbird is most closely associated in my mind."

All the nests I have examined have been placed relatively low, ranging from 2 to 6 feet above ground. A. D. DuBois has sent us details of 16 nests that he found located in osage-orange hedges, willows, a small elm, thorn trees, elderberry, and various bushes and shrubs. These nests ranged from 3 to 10 feet above ground.

In Maine the catbird sometimes resorts to coniferous trees, and I have found the nests in low thick spruce and fir trees. R. T. Morris (1923) reports a pair of catbirds that built in a pine tree on his place at Stamford, Conn. The nest was at an elevation of 20 feet above ground. Two broods were reared, but he could not be sure the same nest was used for the second brood, as the branches were too thick to allow climbing for investigation. Catbirds are not adverse to wet situations, and some of them have been found nesting in cattail marshes and inland swamps. C. R. Stockard (1905) states that in the east-central portion of Mississippi he has found nests of the catbird in bushes bordering lakes in which the nests were suspended over the water.

As might be expected, individual catbirds may depart from the usual nesting sites. M. B. Trautman (1940) studied 35 catbird nests in the region of Buckeye Lake, Ohio, of which two were built on the ground in spite of the fact other more favorable places were available. At the other extreme Pearson and the Brimleys (1910) reported a nest located 50 to 60 feet above the level of the ground. W. N. Colton (1889) reports finding a catbird's nest in a natural cavity of a dead apple tree. The birds had filled up a cavity almost 9 inches deep with nesting materials. These nesting sites represent unusual conditions, and we should not allow them to confuse our conception of the usual nesting site of the catbird.

The nest has a substantial and bulky foundation of coarse sticks, weed stems, grasses, leaves, and twigs. It is rather rough and straggly-appearing outwardly but neatly lined with skeleton leaves, pine needles, fine shreds of bark, and more often with dark fibrous rootlets. In the Midwest, nests are sometimes provided with a horsehair lining. Some of the nests, especially those built near the habitations of man, have in addition to the usual materials bits of paper, cotton, tow, strings, and rags. W. L. McAtee (1940a), who analyzed the materials used in the construction of 12 catbird nests, reports as follows:

"Twelve nests were made of the following materials, the frequency of use of which is indicated by the numbers in parentheses. Foundation: coarse weed stalks (11), leaves (7), paper (7), coarse twigs (5), red-cedar bark (4), grass (3), chestnut bark (1), and lumps of dirt (1). Lining: in each case (12) made exclusively of rootlets."

Both birds share in the work of carrying sticks to the nest, but the female does the major part of the construction and the shaping of the structure. If the male finds the female at the nest when he brings nesting material, he hands it over to the female for her to manipulate into the nest. On the other hand, if the male is at the nest when the female arrives, he immediately gives her right-of-way. The male accompanies the female on many of her journeys for nesting material, but a considerable portion of his time is taken up by singing and defending his territory.

About 5 or 6 days are required to complete the nest, and in one case under observation the first egg was laid during the morning of the day after the nest was finished. One egg was added each morning thereafter until a set of four was complete. During the first few days the female did not incubate continuously but was away from the nest at irregular intervals of time. Thereafter she seldom left her eggs and was fed on the nest by the male.

On coming to the nest and settling down on the eggs she shifted her body from side to side, working the feathers of the breast and belly around the eggs and permitting them to come in direct contact with naked aptera to receive the heat from her body needed for incubation. The nest is usually so deeply cupped that her long tail is thrust upward at an angle nearly perpendicular to the axis of her body, and likewise the head is generally thrown back.

Eggs.—The number of eggs per set varies from two to five. R. C. Harlow (1918), who examined 110 nests of the catbird in Pennsylvania and New Jersey, determined the average to be 4 with a variation of from 3 to 5. Exceptional sets of 6 eggs have been reported by various observers. M. B. Trautman (1940) found a nest at Buckeye Lake, Ohio, on June 24, 1927, that contained 6 eggs. Nests with only 1 or 2 well-incubated eggs have been reported.

The eggs are a deep glossy greenish blue or bluish green, much deeper in tone than those of the robin or wood thrush. They are almost always without markings, but there are a few rare exceptions. John Nichols has seen the eggs spotted with red. Sage, Bishop, and Bliss (1913) and E. D. Wintle (1883) also reported catbirds as laying spotted eggs.

The measurements of 50 eggs in the United States National Museum average 23.3 by 17.5 millimeters; the eggs showing the four extremes measure **26.4** by 17.8, 24.1 by **18.8**, **21.3** by 17.8, and 21.8 by **15.8** millimeters.

Incubation.—Mrs. Helen G. Whittle (1923) studied a pair of cat-birds that built near her home in Peterboro, N. H. She writes:

The male took no share in incubating, nor did he ever, I think, make any attempt to brood the young. If he came to the nest and found the female absent, during incubation, he would fidget on a nearby twig in a helpless, wor-ried fashion, but apparently never thought of taking her place. * * * Dur-ing incubation, the male sang very infrequently within my hearing, and brought food to the female so seldom that I wondered how she could survive. There was however, evidence that the male of this pair was an inexperienced bird, possibly young, and this his first family.

The female, left to do all the incubating, was very faithful to her task and sat patiently day after day through an extremely rainy period, which con-tinued with only brief respites, all through June and early July in southern New Hampshire. One afternoon there was a severe hailstorm, and the female on the nest with feathers drawn close, bill pointing straight up and eyes shut, made as good a watershed of herself as possible, while hailstones the size of large peas pelted her unmercifully.

The incubation period of the catbird as reported by various observers is 12 or 13 days.

Young.—Ira N. Gabrielson (1913) describes the details of the hatching of the eggs in two catbirds' nests as follows, the observations being made by Arthur F. Smith:

At 4:55 a. m. one more egg was pipped, evidently by the old bird, as it was chipped inward and directly around the center of the egg. The egg hatched at 5:55 p. m., the young bird forcing the shell open by rolling and plunging gently and by some use of the feet and wings. At 6:45 the female carried away half of the shell and returned at 6:48 with something in the bill which she swallowed, tho I could not determine whether it was the crushed shell or food. She left the nest at 6:53 only to return at 6:55 and take away the remaining shell.

In nest C the first egg was pipped at 9:00 a. m. on July 20 and at 7:00 p. m. all three were pipped in practically the same place. The first break in each shell came from within and was a little beyond the center of the egg toward the larger end. It was simply a slight bulging evidently produced by a blow from the beak of the young bird. A series of cracks radiated in all directions from this place. The next thing noticed was the extension of a series of these bulges around the egg at right angles to the long axis. At 11:30 a. m. July 21 one egg had hatched and the shell had been removed. The two other eggs had four of these breaks extending half way around the shell. From this time until 3 o'clock there was no change in appearance altho a number of times the female picked gently at the cracked places. On these occasions I could not see that she took anything away although she undoubtedly broke the shell a little by these actions. At 3:00 p. m. she left the nest and was hardly out of sight when the egg she had been picking began to hatch. A dark line appeared around the shell and enlarged in a series of tiny jerks until I could see the young bird kicking and twisting within. The crack grew steadily wider until it was fully half an inch wide on the top of the egg, tho it had hardly opened at all on the side next the nest. At this point the female returned and immediately commenced picking at the shell membrane which still held the two pieces of shell together. As it came away a bit at a time, she swallowed it, repeating the process until the two pieces had fallen apart. She then seized the smaller piece (the big end of the egg and the one that had contained the head of the nestling) and carried it away, leaving the nestling still in the remaining piece. In less than a minute she returned and seized the membrane still attached to the shell. As she pulled on the membrane, the nestling was lifted clear of the nest but fell back without injury. On the second attempt it pulled loose and tumbled the young one into the nest. The membrane was quickly swallowed and the remaining shell carried away. She returned immediately and picked the small bits of shell from the bottom of the nest, devoured them and commenced to brood. The actual process from the time the crack appeared until the last bits of shell were taken from the nest did not exceed 10 minutes.

At 9: 28 the next morning (July 22) the female partly rose from the nest displaying the separating halves of the last egg. The process was practically the same as that previously described. The parent again took the smaller piece of the shell first. She then returned and picked at the remaining piece two or three times and brooded for 12 minutes before any other move was made. At the end of that time she rose in the nest, picked the bird up in the shell and then let it down again. The shell then came away from the nestling and was removed, the small pieces being picked carefully from the nest as before.

In these three instances the hatching process seems to have been the same. In each case it was due to the combined efforts of the parent and the young bird within the egg. In the first case the initial movement may have come from the female while in the last two it originated with the young. In all three the female assisted by pecking at the egg and by removing the broken shell from the nestling much sooner than it would have been able to free itself from the pieces.

Dr. Gabrielson found that the catbirds brooded the young very closely during the first days of nest life, but when the young became older they were brooded only about 30 percent of the observation time. The conditions of the weather were an important factor in the determination of the time spent by the female in brooding the young, but in general the brooding time resolved itself into three distinct periods:

The first period [was] from 4: 30 a. m. to 7: 30 a. m.; the second from 10: 30 a. m. to 2: 00 p. m.; and the third from 6: 30 p. m. until dark. The first period was undoubtedly as a protection against the chill of the early morning. During the second period the sun's rays fell directly into the nest and the brooding at this time was for the protection against the heat. * * * The brooding in the evening was possibly merely preliminary to settling down on the nest for the night and was the most variable of the three. * * * The position assumed in brooding depended on its purpose. In protecting the nestlings from rain or cold the positions were the same. The female settled down on the nest until it was completely covered and the feathers of the breast were well down over the young. It was also noticed that she generally faced the wind. In brooding as a protection from the heat, she stood on the edge of the nest, with her back to the sun, wings spread, feathers of the breast ruffled and mouth open. From this study the brooding time seems to depend on three factors, viz.—temperature, rainfall, and age of the young. The temperature factor will of course be modified by the length of time the nest is shaded by the surrounding vegetation. As the young become older the brooding becomes less intense for heat or cold but remains about the same as a protection against rain.

The catbird is scrupulous in the sanitation of the nest. The excreta is rarely allowed to touch the nest but is taken from the young and immediately eaten or removed. During the observations at the nest Dr. Gabrielson states: "The excreta was removed 125 times, 88 times from the nestling last fed, 20 times from some other one and in 17 instances it was not determined. * * * Up to the sixth day the excreta was always devoured * * * and the remainder carried away. The proportion carried away, increased to the end of the study."

Dr. Gabrielson observed the departure of one of the young as follows: "His departure was accomplished very simply. At about 11:15 a. m. he climbed to the edge of the nest and attempted to jump to a twig a short distance away. He fell short and tumbled to the ground without injury. At this time the parents appeared and coaxed him off into the thick underbrush in the ravine. The next morning both of the others were gone from the nest."

R. W. Shufeldt (1893) observed the details of the nesting of a pair of catbirds that built their nest in a honeysuckle vine under the roof of his veranda. The young remained in the nest 10 days, and he records their departure as follows:

At 6:45 p. m. on June 5, all the birds left the nest together. No one was near it at the time, and there appeared to be no special disturbing cause. There was threatening weather, to be sure, and low rumbling thunder at the time, but no lightning nor loud reports. We were dining at that hour, and my first knowledge of their having left the nest was my attention being called to a young one near the open dining-room door, which led out on the veranda. All the young were easily made prisoners on the ground, and I consigned them to a comfortable cage, which I hung up under the roof close to the nest. Here the parents faithfully fed them through the cage wires until noon of June 8, at which time any one of them could fly 50 or 60 feet with considerable vigor. Fearing that something might happen to them in the cage, at the time just mentioned I took them all down to the lower end of my garden and let them go in the dense underbrush that was overshadowed by numbers of second growth oaks and other trees.

Mrs. Helen G. Whittle (1925) determined by banding that a pair of catbirds remained mated for both the first and second broods of the season of 1924. They both appeared the following May and again reared their broods. S. E. Perkins, 3d (1928) banded a pair of catbirds on June 6, 1926, when they were nesting, and on July 11, 1926, they were retrapped, when they were still mates at the second nest. The following year on June 24, 1927, the same pair were mated and using a nest built within 5 feet of both 1926 nests. J. D. Black (1929) states that five consecutive broods were raised in the same rosebush. The first nest was built late in the summer of 1927. In 1928 the birds built a few inches from the 1927 nest and reared two young catbirds. As soon as the young left, a second nest almost touching the first was built and four young were reared. The third nest of the year and the fourth in the bush was built, and two birds again were raised. The chain was broken with the flying of the first 1929 brood. The adults built a second in another rosebush 20 feet away. As far as I know Mr. Black did not band the birds, and one cannot be certain that the adults of the six nestings were the same individuals, but presumably they were. These three cases indicate a constancy of catbirds to their territory and to their mates.

Geoffrey Gill (1935, 1936a) obtained somewhat different results with catbirds banded at Huntington, Long Island. In 12 cases he studied not a pair remained mated for two broods in a single season. Considerable variation was exhibited by the birds in their return to the same territory. One male was constant to one territory for four consecutive summers and six nestings. This male had six different mates in 5 years, but in the last 2 years, as he grew older, he had only one nest each season and during this period was faithful to the same mate. The catbirds that Mr. Gill studied frequently changed their territory for different nestings. It is evident that there is considerable individual variation in the constancy of catbirds to their mates and territory.

An anonymous writer (1887) reports from Laramie, Wyo., that he found a catbird living on intimate terms with a shrike; both pairs of birds built their nests in the same bush, but each seemed to hold undisputed possession of their particular side of the bush. Mrs. Kenneth B. Wetherbee (1930) reports a unique case of the interrelationship of a pair of catbirds and a pair of robins, which built their nests in the same clump of lilacs. The robin and catbird took turns in incubating the catbird eggs, and when the young hatched they were brooded by both robins and catbirds. The robin's nest was a few feet above that of the catbird and was not discovered until the young catbirds had left their nest. It would be interesting to know whether the catbirds assisted the robins in their household duties.

Catbirds have been known to care for the young of other birds. Earl Brooks (1922) writes of a brood of orphaned cardinals that were fed and mothered by a catbird, and W. J. Hayward (1937) reports a case where a mother catbird fed a half-grown flicker that had been dislodged from its nest and separated from its parents during a severe storm. The feeding instincts are strongly developed in catbirds, and if they have lost their own young through some misfortune they will readily adopt the offspring of others.

In contrast to the behavior described above the catbird occasionally destroys the eggs of other birds, but this habit is not characteristic of the species. J. B. W. (1884) reports he saw a catbird destroy an egg of the wood pewee before the latter succeeded in driving it away from its nest. Edwin Dixon (1930) states that a catbird was found robbing a chipping sparrow's nest. It ate the contents of one egg and picked holes in the other two. Proof that the egg was eaten was obtained by shooting the catbird. Leda W. Chace (1931) saw a catbird glide into a locust tree outside her window where a robin's nest was located. The catbird was seen to thrust its bill into one of the eggs and lift it clear

of the nest. Later another of the robin's eggs was found on the ground
with a punctured side as if a large needle had pierced it.

Plumage.—In the juvenal plumage of the catbird the pileum is a
dull sooty brown, many shades lighter than that of the adult. The
wings and tail are nearly black as in the adult, the primaries and
secondaries edged with smoke gray, the coverts browner edged, the
tail with indistinct barring; the interscapular region brownish ashy,
shading into pale mouse gray indistinctly mottled with clove brown
or rufous, the throat and sides faintly tinged with sepia, the crissum
pale, dead cinnamon or mars brown. Bill and feet dusky pinkish
buff becoming black.

The first winter plumage, according to Jonathan Dwight (1900)—

is acquired by a partial postjuvenal moult, beginning early in August, which
involves the body plumage and the wing coverts, but not the rest of the
wings nor the tail, young and old become practically indistinguishable. Similar to the previous plumage but much grayer and no mottling. Everywhere
clear slate-gray, much paler below and on the sides of the head and neck;
the pileum black; the crissum deep chestnut.

The first nuptial plumage acquired by wear which produces little obvious
change.

The adult winter plumage acquired by a complete post-juvenal moult in
August. Practically indistinguishable from the first winter; the wings and
tail perhaps averaging blacker and with grayer edgings. The adult nuptial
plumage acquired by wear as in the young bird.

According to Chapman (1916) "some females have the crown and
upperparts slightly browner than in the male but they vary too
little to make the sexes certainly distinguishable. The catbird shows
no geographic variation throughout its wide range."

Some individuals present a variation in the relative amount of the
chestnut coloring of the crissum. Lincoln (1920) reports that a
specimen captured at Washington, D. C., had an extreme restriction
of the chestnut. "Basally," he says, "there was no trace of chestnut
which was present only in the form of a very narrow edging (in no
place as much as a sixteenth of an inch in width) beginning about
midway of the feathers and continuing around the tips."

Alexander Wetmore (1936) has determined the number and
weight of the contour feathers of many of our passeriform birds.
In a catbird obtained June 4, 1933, weighing 35.6 grams, there were
1,733 contour feathers weighing 2.3 grams.

Albinism is of relatively common occurrence in the catbird; many
both pure and partial albinistic forms have been reported of which
the following are representative. Mrs. F. L. Battell (1941) writes
of seeing two albino catbirds that appeared with the parent catbirds at Ames, Iowa, during the summer of 1940. Although nearly
full grown they were still fed by the adults. The young were pure
white, even the feathers of the crissum being without a trace of

color. R. Deane (1879) reports an immature catbird collected at Hyde Park, Ill., on July 21, 1878, and pure white albino with pink eyes captured alive at Trenton, N. J. R. J. Middleton (1936) trapped a nearly pure white specimen at Norristown, Pa. The underparts of this specimen were grayish white with a tinge of reddish brown on the under tail coverts; the back was gray and the head about the color of the back of normal specimens. Annie T. Slosson (1883) writes of a partial albinistic catbird that she kept in captivity at Hartford. This bird had a band of white across the tail, about an inch from the tip. There was also one white feather in the wing, but otherwise the coloration was normal. The band in the tail was very conspicuous especially when the tail was spread.

Food.—Unfortunately the food habits of the catbird are not entirely beneficial from the standpoint of the interests of man. Bitter complaints of damage, perhaps in some instances greatly exaggerated, have come from the growers of berries and owners of orchards.

To obtain a true picture of its food habits it is well to examine not only the records of the stomach-content analyses of representative specimens taken over the entire range of distribution but also the numerous field observations that have been made concerning the food of this important and attractive bird.

VEGETABLE FOOD: According to Sylvester Judd (1895), who examined the stomach contents of 213 catbirds, only 13 of the birds had eaten strawberries and 20 had taken cherries. However, Judd calls our attention to the fact that though the bird may eat the bulk of only one strawberry or cherry a score may have been pecked, and the injury of a single grape in a bunch detracts from the value of the whole bunch. F. E. L. Beal (1918), reporting on the stomach contents of 645 catbirds, states that 56 percent of the food was vegetable; one-third of which consisted of cultivated fruits or those that may be cultivated such as strawberries, raspberries, and blackberries. The remainder of the vegetable matter was mostly wild fruit, such as wild cherries, dogwood, sourgum, elderberries, greenbrier, spiceberries, black alder, and sumac. C. C. Purdum (1902) in the examination of 192 stomachs found 18 percent of the food to be cultivated fruits, 35 percent wild fruits, and 2 percent miscellaneous vegetable matter, making a total of 55 percent, practically the same as the determinations made by Beal.

That the catbird can subsist on a purely vegetable diet, even under adverse conditions, is shown by the large number of reports of this bird wintering in the north as far as the New England States, a time when no insects are to be found but when an abundance of berries is present in their winter haunts. C. E. Moulton (1921) observed a catbird at frequent intervals at Lynn, Mass., from January 10 until April 6. This individual fed chiefly on the berries of the buckthorn.

It remained within the limits of a little swamp among the hills which was completely surrounded with woods. The bushes were overrun with catbrier filled with berries. There was an abundance of mountain-ash and bittersweet, which furnished a full larder for this wintering bird. W. H. Ball (1927) observed a catbird near Washington, D. C., during December and January 1925–26, which he found was subsisting chiefly on the berries of the honeysuckle vines. A. W. Schorger (1926) collected a catbird at Madison, Wis., on December 20, the stomach of which was filled with the fruit of the climbing bittersweet. Witmer Stone (1913b), in presenting the records of William Bartram, cites the record of a catbird that was seen and heard singing in Bartram's garden on January 8, 1820. On the next day it was seen feeding on the berries of *Sideroxylon;* although a violent storm raged on January 10 and the snow covered the ground the bird still remained, evidently attracted by the berries. P. A. Taverner (1919) states that the catbirds observed by him in the Red Deer River district, Alberta, fed chiefly on buffaloberries. Otto Widmann (1907) states that the late migrants in fall congregate in the region of St. Louis to feed on wild grapes. H. Brackbill (1942) studied the food habits of a catbird at Baltimore, Md., from November 3, 1940, until February 23, 1941. Feeding was observed on 23 days, during which five foods were eaten, including the Japanese honeysuckle, which was eaten on 21 days from December 1 through February 23. The latter was eaten in great quantities, at one time he saw the bird eat 30 of the berries in 22 minutes in addition to other food. It was also seen to eat the haws of the cockspur thorn, frost grapes, and seeds of poison ivy and sumac.

In Florida, where the catbird is a regular though not abundant winter resident, various observers have reported the birds subsisting on holly, poke, and smilax berries, balsam apples, and Barbados cherries, and stomachs of catbirds collected at Micco, Fla., were found to contain the seeds of the saw palmetto. It is obvious from the foregoing representative reports that the catbird can adapt itself to a purely vegetable diet, and this accounts for the surprising number of winter records over a wide range, even in sections of the country where cold weather and snow prevail.

From an economic standpoint the vegetable diet of the catbird as a whole does not represent a serious loss. Under certain conditions the growers of berries, grapes, cherries, and other fruits do have a just grievance. According to F. E. L. Beal (1897), most of these complaints come from the Mississippi Valley where fruit-bearing shrubs, which afford such a large part of the bird's food, are conspicuously absent. With the settlement of the region comes the extensive planting of orchards, vineyards, and small fruit gardens, which furnish shelter and nesting sites for the catbird and other species. There is in consequence a large increase in the number of birds, but no corresponding gain in the supply of native fruits upon which they are accustomed to feed. Under these circumstances, what is more natural than for the birds to turn to cultivated fruits for their food? Cultivated fruits can be protected by planting the wild species, which are preferred by the birds. For example, the Russian mulberry is preferred to all varieties of cutivated fruits, and the planting of a number of these trees will solve the problem of devastation by the catbird and at the same time preserve this bird, which at certain seasons is a useful destroyer of insects. That the catbirds are attracted by wild berries and fruits is shown by the experience of Geoffrey Gill (1936a), who by planting Scotch pine for cover and wild blackberry canes and other berry-bearing shrubs for food at his banding station in Huntington, Long Island, increased the number of catbirds from 72 individuals in 1931 to 183 in 1935.

In New England few complaints are ever lodged against the catbird. For example, F. E. L. Beal, of Lunenburg, Mass., says: "On my farm in Massachusetts I have raised strawberries, blackberries, and raspberries by the acre, with grapes, pears, and apples in abundance, and although the farm was nearly surrounded by woods and was adjacent to a swamp where the catbirds and thrashers abounded, I never knew one of them to touch a single fruit, though perhaps they have taken a few. I thought no more of accusing the catbirds or robins of fruit stealing than I would the swallows in the barn."

ANIMAL FOOD: The damage done by the catbird in its depredations on cultivated fruits is compensated for by the injurious insects eaten at other seasons of the year. The animal food contained in the stomachs of 645 catbirds as reported by F. E. L. Beal (1897) constitutes 44 percent of the entire contents. The animal food is chiefly insects, most of which are serious pests to crops. Ants, beetles, caterpillars, and grasshoppers make up three-fourths of the animal food, the remainder consisting of miscellaneous insects and spiders. In the examination of 192 stomachs of the catbird C. C. Purdum (1902) found that ants constituted 10 percent of the entire food, beetles 24 percent, caterpillars 5 percent, grasshoppers 4 percent, bugs 2 percent, spiders and thousandlegs 4 percent, and miscellaneous animal food 5 percent. According to S. D. Judd (1895), in May when the catbird arrives from the South two-thirds of its food is animal matter made up chiefly of ants, thousandlegs, May beetles, predaceous ground beetles, and caterpillars. For the first part of June the May-ratio of the animal to vegetable matter is sustained, but during the latter part of the month the proportion of vegetable food increases. Early in the season the catbirds eat few grasshoppers and crickets, but by the end of June these insects constitute 10 percent of their food. Five catbirds examined in June contained an average of 30 grasshoppers each. After June the

number of grasshoppers dwindles to insignificance. The number of
May beetles eaten increases from the first to the twentieth of June,
but after this time they are also replaced by fruits. By August the
percentage of insects eaten drops to 1 percent but rises again in September. The examination of 213 stomachs reveals that beetles and
ants form the most important food of the catbird, though smooth caterpillars play no insignificant part. Crickets and grasshoppers are
relished and come next in importance. The less important though
constant parts of the fare are thousandlegs, centipeds, bugs, and
spiders. In addition to the insects revealed by stomach examinations,
field observations indicate that many and diverse kinds of insects are
eaten.

J. C. Wood (1905) observed catbirds catching and eating the large
cecropia, prometheus, and sphinx moths, which were also fed to the
young. H. B. Wood (1930) reports seeing a catbird capture and eat a
large number of honeybees that had invaded a summer cottage. Henry
Mousley (1932) found the catbird to be one of the most important
destroyers of Japanese beetles. E. H. Forbush (1907) states that he
saw catbirds eating plant lice for hours at a time. He also reports
seeing them feed extensively on gypsy and browntail moth larvae.
R. S. Deck (1928) observed them feeding on dragonflies. Jennie K.
Macoubrie (1932) gives an interesting account of a catbird that entered a basement laboratory through an open window to feed on
museum pests, dermestid beetles. For a period of two weeks it made
frequent visits in and out, each time carrying one of the beetles to its
young. Perhaps the most unusual departure from the usual food habits of the catbird was reported by Dr. John C. Phillips (1927), who saw
the birds wading in shallow water at the Sutton fish hatchery, where
they were deftly catching and swallowing trout fry about 1½ inches
long. According to the superintendent of the hatchery it was a common habit among several pairs of catbirds that nested close by. W. L.
McAtee (1926a), in his study of the relation of birds to woodlots, mentions the following insects eaten by the catbird that have not been
previously mentioned. "Among the ants are numerous carpenter ants
which are given to hollowing out trees. The beetles include numerous forms detrimental to the forest, as leaf chafers, goldsmith beetles,
junebugs, nut weevils, bark beetles, and other weevils. * * *
Other injurious beetles taken are the round-headed wood borers, including the ash borer (*Necolytus capraea*), leaf beetles, including the
grapevine flea beetle (*Fidia viticida*) and the locust leaf miner
(*Odontota dorsalis*). Plant lice, leaf hoppers, tree hoppers, psyllids,
cicadas, sawflies, and white ants are additional enemies of trees that
the Catbird consumes." Francis H. Allen has observed the catbird
feeding among the dead leaves on the ground. Quoting from his correspondence: "Catbirds throw the leaves aside with their bills. The

motion is much like a sidewise rooting, but sometimes I have seen clearly that the leaf was picked up in the bill and thrown very quickly to one side or the other or behind. A leaf will often go a foot or a foot and a half, and sometimes one will drop on the bird's tail."

Various observers have reported the catbird's fondness for such food as cheese, bread, raisins, currants, milk, corn flakes and puffed wheat soaked in milk, mushrooms, garbage, boiled potato, fried fish, beef stew, peanuts, and beef soup. E. G. Holt and G. M. Sutton (1926) report that a catbird ate bits of meat of skinned specimens that they were preparing at Gator Lake, Fla. Indeed the food eaten is so diversified in nature that the catbird can be considered omnivorous in its food habits. Few birds are more adaptable in eating any kind of food that chances to be readily accessible.

Perhaps the most useful eating trait of the catbird in its relation to man's interest is its frequent concentration on certain destructive insects that become abundant during severe infestations. It is at such times that the catbird arises to the situation and renders great service in keeping the ravages of the pests in check. S. A. Forbes (1883) has vividly described the important action of catbirds on the orchard infestations of cankerworms in Illinois. W. L. McAtee (1920) tells how the periodic abundance of cicadas almost entirely diverted the attacks of catbirds from cultivated fruits. Phoebe Knappen (1933) reports that catbirds which discovered a sawfly infestation of an ash tree fed on the larvae exclusively as long as the insects were in evidence. During the great plague of armyworms in New Jersey, New York, and New England States of the summer of 1914 there were many reports of catbirds as well as other birds, which fed ravenously on these pests. Edward A. Gill Wylie (1914) wrote: "The present plague of armyworms, * * * provides a severe example to us of one of the many reasons why the number of insectivorous birds should not only be conserved but materially increased. A horde of these pests suddenly came to light on a small place about 4 acres large. * * * Immediately the birds of the neighborhood deserted their usual haunts and assembled on these four acres. They ate so many [of the armyworms] that often a bird would disgorge and proceed to make a fresh start, * * * at least one-half of the worms were consumed by them (catbirds and others) in the 2 days that elapsed before the spraying by experts commenced to destroy what was left." E. H. Eaton (1914) writes of a plague of cankerworms in the orchards of Monroe County, N. Y., in 1898. The orchards were practically denuded by the worms. He observed the catbirds and other birds swallowing the larvae at the rate of 15 to 40 a minute.

FOOD OF THE YOUNG: S. D. Judd (1900) examined the stomach contents of 14 young nestlings of the catbird and 11 adults mainly the parents of the young. The old birds had taken 91 percent of their food in fruits—buckthorn, catbrier, cherries, raspberries, and blackberries. The nestlings, however, had eaten fruit to the extent of only 4 percent of their food, and the remainder of their diet was principally ants, beetles, caterpillars, spiders, and grasshoppers.

Dr. I. N. Gabrielson (1913) made detailed observations of the food fed by adult catbirds to their nestlings. Practically all the food delivered consisted of insects, and it was only during the last 2 days that food in the form of raspberries and gooseberries was fed to the young. Out of 596 feedings observed there were 99 flies, 55 beetles, 52 larvae, 42 mayflies, 40 grasshoppers, 35 moths, 21 measuring-worms and 21 worms of various species, 17 spiders, 11 crickets, 9 katydids, 8 caterpillars, 8 raspberries, 6 dragonflies, 5 wireworms, 3 butterflies, and 1 each of mosquito, small frog, and gooseberry. There were 161 unidentified morsels chiefly insects too small or too crushed to determine with accuracy. Dr. Gabrielson's observations reveal the great variety of insects and the comparatively small amount of fruit that is delivered to the young when insect life is abundant, as it was in the vicinity of the nests he studied.

If all these varied food habits are considered from a purely economic standpoint the catbird will be found to have much in its favor to counteract the less than 20 percent of its food that consists of cultivated fruits useful to man.

Behavior.—Although the catbird usually establishes itself in a well-defined territory to which it challenges all intruders, it does at times live in harmony with other birds. E. A. Doolittle (1923) writes of a catbird nest containing four eggs that was built in a little thornbush hardly 3 feet high. Less than 4 feet from the catbird's nest and on the same level was a nest and five eggs of the yellow warbler. Apparently the catbirds made no effort to disturb their smaller neighbors and were indulgent with their presence.

The catbird is not so adaptable in solving unusual situations with which it may be confronted, as some other birds. Dr. A. A. Allen (1912) found that if a cloth is placed over a phoebe's nest, the bird with a single glance grasped the situation and immediately removed the obstacle. The catbird, however, was at a total loss as to what to do under a similar situation.

During the first 10 minutes that the cloth was in place upon the nest, the female bird inspected ten times at fairly regular intervals, usually peering from the rear of the side. The first and eighth times, however, she walked around the edge of the nest. After the tenth inspection, an interval of 4 minutes ensued before she returned. She then passed around the nest, but inspected its edges more than the rag. The feathers of the nape were usually raised during inspection. After an interval of 1 minute, she approached the nest from the side, crouching and ruffling the feathers as if about to incubate. She then left for 4 minutes. Appearing again, she started to incubate on the thick mat of twigs and leaves at one side of the nest, remaining in this position with the feathers ruffled for 30 seconds. The next time she stayed away 9 minutes and returned only to inspect from the rear. Intervals of 6 and 7 minutes followed, the bird apparently taking less and less interest in the nest. Realizing this, I became anxious for the safety of the eggs and removed the cloth. In 3 minutes more she was back in the bush but did not inspect the nest. Ten minutes later, however, she returned apparently to stay, inspected the eggs and began at once to incubate.

* * * What light this throws on the natures of the two birds. The one, with changing conditions, has been able to adapt itself, the other has remained ever the same. Surely this foreshadows the future. At present both are among our common birds. The phoebe will become more and more so as he copes with new conditions, the catbird rarer and rarer as time goes on.

Voice.—The catbird at its best stands high in the ranks of our American bird singers. Each year one appears in my backyard, and immediately upon his arrival his song is the most delightful feature of the chorus of the multitude of bird voices. A good catbird song needs no apology. The bird sits on some tall spray rising above the general tangle of shrubs, its tail depressed and body held low to the perch, and pours forth its medley of song. Phrase follows phrase in rapid succession, and snatches of all the bird songs in the neighborhood appear intermixed with occasional harsher notes, which are given with as much care and finish as the more melodious ones. When an intruder is detected approaching, the outpour stops with a sudden squeak, the tail flies up, and the bird comes to attention. No matter how many years we may listen to his performance there is always something new and interesting to be learned from his varied renditions. The catbird is individualistic, and while one bird may be unusually versatile and of prima-donna rank others may be quite ordinary in their ability to imitate and very mediocre in the quality of their voice.

"The song in general," as analyzed in notes by A. A. Saunders, "is long-continued and of phrases that are greatly varied with pauses between them. It differs from both the mockingbird and the brown thrasher in that phrases very rarely consist of repetitions of certain notes. The quality is not quite so full and rich as that of the mockingbird or thrasher. In my records pitch ranges three tones more than an octave, from $A^{b'\prime}$ to D'''''." According to Albert R. Brand (1938), who has determined vibration frequencies of many of the passerine bird songs by recordings on motion-picture film, the song of the catbird has a frequency ranging from the lowest note of 1,100 to the highest of 4,375. The approximate mean of the recordings of the catbird's song was determined to be 3,000 vibrations.

Winsor M. Tyler (MS.) describes the usual song of the catbird as a "series of quick, bright widely varying phrases, which is continued sometimes for 5 minutes or more. In form it is like the brown thrasher's song but is more disjointed and does not run on with the regular beat of the thrasher, but is interrupted by pauses and marred by the interpolation of harsh, squeaky, or squawking notes. The phrases may consist of three or four syllables or may be reduced to a single high peep. As we listen we hear such phrases as '*eweet, twit-twit-twit, cherooeekoo, tereet, erokeet,*' involving a wide range of pitch. In tone of voice the song sometimes suggests a vireo in some of its phrases but is much more lively. It has a pleasant whistled quality and at its best approaches the rich tone of the talented robin.

"When singing, the catbird as a rule is half hidden in the shrubbery, but he sometimes mounts on the top of a bush to sing. He stands with wings drooped, tail hanging low, rump feathers elevated, and body somewhat humped up. Often he turns his head from side to side, and as he sings he opens his bill wide. As he goes on he seems to be trying experiments, perhaps for his own amusement, but we sometimes get an impression that his song is addressed to an audience, perhaps to ourselves, for he often glances over his shoulder as if to say, 'How's that?' There appears to be a bit of the clown in the catbird's nature."

At times the song has a soft ventriloquial character, seeming to come from everywhere about; again it is loud and easily traced to its source. At the approach of any disturbing element the song ceases and the angry catlike mew is uttered, a note that has given origin to the unfortunate name. This note, a petulant cry or snarl, an impolite whine, lazy and drawling, is long-drawn-out with a falling inflection at the end. This call is one of the most outstanding characteristics of its varied song. Often we may be in doubt as to the identity of a certain song if the singer is hidden from view, but when the catbird interrupts its musical phrases with this catcall it at once dispels all uncertainty.

Another note of the catbird is a harsh, sharply enunciated chatter, rather wrenlike. We may hear this note suddenly rattle out with startling effect from the shrubbery where a bird is hiding or sometimes from the air as he flies away. E. P. Bicknell (1884) describes one of its characteristic vocal accomplishments as a short crackling sound like the snapping of small fagots. E. A. Samuels (1872) writes: "The alarm note is a rattling cry, like the sound of quick breaking of several sticks: it is perhaps well expressed by the syllables *trat-tat tat tat* uttered very quickly."

Still another note we hear issuing from the catbird's tangle is a low, mellow chuck, like the soft quack of a duck giving the impression of being uttered way back in the throat—a note of minor alarm. R. Hoffmann (1904) describes notes resembling a mellow cluck and occasionally a grating chatter, *kak-kak-kak.*

Associated with the courtship is a whistled monosyllable, *peer,* suggestive of the notes of the pine grosbeak.

A. A. Saunders (1929a) writes:

The catbird during courtship sings a song that differs from the territory song chiefly in intensity. It is low and soft and almost in a whisper and is usually sung with the bill closed. One must be near the singer to hear the song. The bird closes its bill and sings the familiar carol so softly that it is audible only a short distance; at times the catbird accompanying them with a grotesque display, spreading the wings and tail and fluffing out the feathers.

It is not always certain, however, that peculiar songs at the height of the mating season are stimulated by the presence of the female. At times they may be due to the presence of a rival male, for bird song is used in battle as well as in courtship. It is not uncommon to see birds fighting in the season of courtship and mating. Whether the battle be over mates, or over territory it is often accomplished by song.

During the summer of 1910 the catbirds were abundant about Fairyland Place, Bermuda Islands. A pair of them had built their nest in a cedar tree about 4 feet above ground and just outside my window. The song of unusually high musical quality, pleasing and indescribably beautiful, was sung frequently throughout the day and sometimes well into the night. One of this pair was seen and heard to sing while on the nest, a curious behavior, which would seem to advertise the location of the nest to possible enemies lurking in the neighborhood. This trait is not peculiar to the Bermuda catbird residents, for O. W. Knight (1908) writes: "I have known the male bird to engage in song while on the nest and to keep it up for some minutes at a time." Several observers have seen the female catbird singing while on the nest. Helen G. Whittle (1923) writes: "One day as I sat close to the window, within 3 or 4 feet of her, I was amazed and delighted to hear her, while sitting on the nest, take up the strain her lord was singing. She followed it in all of its intricacies, perfectly and beautifully, but in a 'whisper' voice. On a later day she did a similar thing, though in briefer, less brilliant fashion."

On June 28, 1907, I was camping on the Ohio River near Shelterville, southern Illinois. About midnight I was awakened by a chorus of bird voices. It was a gorgeous, clear, moonlit night, so bright that it was almost like day. When I strolled outside the camp I heard the songs of the yellow-breasted chat, the mockingbird, the Carolina wren, and the catbird, in this unusual medley of moonlight serenaders. They all seemed at their best, but had it not been for the fact that I could see the singers it would have been difficult to identify some of the performers. Both the mockingbird and catbird were giving a full series of imitations and at times were carrying the parts of the chat and wren of this musical quartet.

In correspondence received from Francis H. Allen he writes: "On May 19, 1923, nearly 2 hours before sunrise, I heard the nocturnal song from a catbird. He sang for some time very sweetly but slowly, the phrases coming much farther apart than in the usual daytime singing." Mrs. Marie A. Commons (1930) has beautifully and graphically described the nocturnal song of the catbird as follows: "And at night, when white flowers in the garden shine faintly luminous in the world of shadows and ipomoeas on the pergola gleam like pale moons, caressing the air with fragrance, it is then that our cavalier is transformed into a celestial singer, as soul-stirring as the nightingale in the Old World gardens or the mockingbird in southern climes."

Many observers have heard and reported the "whisper" songs of several species of birds, but this trait is most pronounced in the catbird. It seems to be heard most frequently in autumn, but it may be given at all seasons. J. W. Lloyd (1914) gives an account of the whisper song of the catbird he heard on September 14, 1908, well after the nesting season: "A catbird, not over 4 or 5 feet from me, sitting trustfully on a stick among the weeds, quite unconcerned, and singing in such a low, fine voice that I could only just hear him. * * * His throat merely, trembled, and occasionally the bill parted just a trifle. Yet his song seemed the full repertoire of the catbird, including * * * two faint mews. The whisper song was heard in the autumn on subsequent years which may or may not have been the same individual. Penelope Baldwin (1929) tells of her experience in hearing this song in the spring as follows: "I saw a catbird * * * in the plum tree just outside my window. There was no sound of his song, but I could see that he was singing. Quietly I opened the window. In came the smell of plum blossoms, in came humming of a thousand bees, in came the whispered song of the catbird, tranquil and clear, indescribably lovely."

The catbird possesses a remarkable talent in mimicking the calls and songs of other birds—in fact any sound it may hear whether it be a cackling hen, an agonizing squeak of an ungreased wagon wheel, or the musical song of its bird neighbors. Some individual catbirds are extremely versatile, yet you may listen to others throughout the season and never hear a recognizable imitation. There is also a variation in the quality of the song.

There are so many reports from reliable observers of the mimicking ability of the catbird that we must conclude that it approaches a very close second to that expert the mockingbird. E. H. Forbush (1929) writes: "It is somewhat startling * * * to hear the catbird's sweetest song interrupted by a perfect imitation of some harsh cry such as that of the great crested flycatcher, the squawk of a hen, the cry of a lost chicken or the spitting of a cat. * * * He is inclined to attempt to imitate the most common sounds, such as the croaking of the frogs and the utterances of barnyard fowls, but also sometimes succeeds in reproducing unusual musical sounds."

Marie E. Hegler (1923) gives an interesting account of her experience in teaching a catbird a whistled call. The bird did not respond the first summer, but in the following spring it was heard to utter the whistle followed by a series of catcalls, when it first arrived. Thereafter it was frequently heard throughout the summer.

Mary M. Russell (1929) gives an account of hearing a catbird imitate the call of a whippoorwill. The imitation was short, staccato, with a happy lilt, but very, very real. At one time when the catbird, perched in the branches of a cherry tree, was singing his song, Miss Russell began to whistle the whippoorwill call. He continued singing but was deaf to her call. She went closer and continued to whistle the notes. After many repetitions the catbird suddenly stopped short, perked up his head to one side, and after a moment of complete silence sang *whip-poor-will* four times.

Winton Weydemeyer (1930) writes of an unusual case of mimicry by a catbird. A wandering male bobolink appeared at his ranch in Montana where these birds are not common but in recent years have been extending their range to the State. For at least half an hour during the morning of May 31, when the bobolink first arrived, a catbird from a nearby brushy flat perched on fence posts near the flying bobolink and mimicked its song. In many of its imitations it repeated the entire song of the bobolink, without introducing foreign notes or phrases. Another interesting feature of the performance was the persistence of the catbird in repeating the imitation so many times without the interspersion of other singing. On July 22 Mr. Weydemeyer was astonished to hear what sounded like a typical flight song of the bobolink. He then saw a catbird fly out and upward until it reached a height of about 30 feet above the brush; then while descending at an angle, its flight slow and jerky, but not fluttering, it gave a strikingly realistic rendition of the bobolink's flight song. This is the first case of combined song and flight mimicry that the observer had ever noted in the catbird.

Dr. C. W. Townsend (1905) says for a moment he was deceived by a catbird that swooped down one July day and flew across the Ipswich River with a perfect kingfisher rattle and action. Later Dr. Townsend (1924), in his excellent account of mimicry of voice in birds, wrote:

> He appears to be constantly trying some new combination of notes, and some of his improvisations are very sweet and musical. These he occasionally repeats in a manner of the brown thrasher, particularly when a musical phrase appears to tickle his fancy. Thus I once heard a catbird rolling off a delightful phrase which sounded like *Peter-boro, Peterboro*. This he repeated five or six times, then *mewed* and tried something else. If the catbird would suppress his love of bazarre and harsh notes, and of buffoonery and horseplay—for I suspect he has a sense of humor—and would devote himself more continually to his musical repertoire, he would rank among our best singers.

Dr. Townsend gives us an imposing list of catbird imitations of bird songs or their calls from his own experience and that of other observers. The list includes blue jay, bobwhite, flicker, robin, barn swallow, goldfinch, rose-breasted grosbeak, veery, wood thrush, red-eyed, yellow-throated, and solitary vireos, brown thrasher, greater yellowlegs, least flycatcher, crested flycatcher, wood pewee, cowbird, chewink, scarlet tanager, and black-polled warbler. A. A. Saunders (MS.), who has given particular attention to the imitations of the catbird, lists many of the above and in addition the red-shouldered hawk, killdeer, phoebe, bluebird, blue-headed vireo, redstart, the yellow, magnolia, black-throated blue, black-throated green, chestnut-sided, and prairie warblers, western meadowlark, and cardinal. He has also heard the catbird imitate the tree frog (*Hyla versicolor*). Many other imitations have been reported. It is apparent that the range of its imitations are limitless. This enterprising bird is ever on the alert and is constantly experimenting in the mimicking of any note, song, or sound that it may hear. However, only a comparatively few are so versatile, and not every individual catbird indulges in such extensive mimicry.

The song of the catbird has never impressed me as conveying the expression of sadness, yet that is the way it appealed to the Chippewa Indian naturalist who named it *Ma-ma-dive-bi-ne-shi*, meaning the bird that cries with grief.

In correspondence received from Francis H. Allen he writes: "Catbirds vary more than most birds in their powers of song. One year I had one on my place in West Roxbury, Mass., that hardly ever sang anything more than one, two, or three short phrases at a time, usually only two, which I memorized as *William-see-me*. Sometimes it was *William* and nothing more. Again my catbird another year may be one with an astonishing repertoire, including sweet phrases of his own and a number of striking imitations. One of these accomplished musicians imitated the crested flycatcher, wood pewee, blue jay, towhee (song), scarlet tanager (song), red-eyed vireo (song), black-poll warbler (song), brown thrasher, and robin. Sometimes a catbird will surprise one with a wholly original and unexpected vocal performance. On May 15, 1942, the catbird that had sung fairly steadily near my house for some days was silent almost all day but in the afternoon broke his silence with a succession or raucous, quite unmusical, and uncatbirdlike notes of varied character but always high-pitched and often repeating the same note or phrase many times in succession. These notes were delivered in the manner of a song, the bird being stationary and with no other bird nearby. Sometimes the bill was open and sometimes to all appearances closed, but the pulsations of the throat were always plain to be seen. It was as if this bird had lost his voice, but later I heard some ordinary catbird strains from him.

"Catbirds can utter uncatbirdlike notes on occasions of excitement as well as calm. On May 29, 1916, in West Roxbury, I heard from a thicket a curious harsh note, that I did not recognize, repeated several times. It suggested a jay's scream with a little of a downy-woodpecker quality. This was followed by a sweet warbled phrase given three or four times; then came the strange harsh notes again. My first thought was of a chat, and I was surprised when I found the notes came from a catbird that was flying about closely pursued by another. The birds kept up the performance for 10 minutes or so before I left them. The singer discontinued the harsh notes soon but kept up the sweet warbling notes and gave from time to time other song notes of a catbird character besides the *mew*, the *chatter*, and the sharp *chip*. The song notes were uttered disconnectedly, except that one might be given two or three times in succession, and were frequently given on the wing, perhaps oftener on the wing than when the bird was alighted. The pursuing bird would sometimes almost strike the singer and alight beyond him and sometimes would stop 5 or 10 feet short of him. This one was silent, but once when it alighted near me I saw it opening and shutting its bill in a threatening manner. The two were on the wing most of the time, the stops being very short, and they dodged hither and thither among the branches, flying pretty swiftly, but kept inside an area perhaps 30 or 40 feet square. Whether this was courtship or territory defense I cannot say, but it evidently was not a combat *à outrance*.

"Again, on May 12, 1938, in West Roxbury, at about 8 p. m. with the temperature about 45° F., I heard a strange medley of squawks and discordant cries interspersed with repetitions of high-pitched phrases of a more melodious character coming from a wet spot in the woods. Again I could think only of the yellow-breasted chat, but again I found that catbirds were responsible. In this case there were three or four of them flitting about low in the trees and bushes. After keeping up this performance for some time, during which not a single one of the notes suggested a catbird to me, they separated, and at least two and I think three of them sang normal songs for a short time. The strange notes were various in character, some having a jarring quality. The high-pitched notes were usually, if not always, repetitions of a single phrase over and over again."

The catbird sings from the time of its arrival in spring until late in July or August but with decreasing regularity toward the end of this period. According to A. A. Saunders (MS.), "some individuals cease singing about the time the last egg is laid, and do not resume singing again till the young are out of the nest several days." Saunders says further:

In some cases the second or third nest is built before the young of the previous nest are out and in such cases the song is not resumed. The average date for cessation of song in 14 years in Allegany State Park, N. Y., is July 28 with the latest date August 11, 1940. In Connecticut it seems to last a little longer and in the Adirondacks I did not hear it after July 4. This bird rarely sings in the fall, and then the song is generally primitive, that is, faint, whispered, and rather indefinite in form. I have heard it October 22, 1927, September 24 and October 9, 1932, September 3 and 5, 1937, and October 8, 1939.

Francis H. Allen writes (MS.) that in September he has heard a catbird utter a note resembling *chip-tit*, the last syllable very short and fainter than the other, coming like a sort of echo of the first. Mr. Allen has also recorded the notes of the young as follows: "From young able to fly well, a sharp high-pitched chippering note with something of a thrill to it at times. It suggests a familiar note of the slate-colored junco. Also from the young a coarse *chip* suggestive of the scarlet tanager. They utter a very warblerlike *pssp* when begging for food, a note that changes from day to day to a *chip* or *hick*. Then again they utter a high pitched *fee*."

Enemies.—Because of the nature of the usual nesting site, a situation in low dense often marshy thickets and usually near the ground, the catbird frequently becomes a victim of various species of snakes. C. J. Clarke (1915) relates an experience at Lenox, Mass., in which a milksnake was found to have swallowed a newly hatched catbird, which it had taken from a nest. The victim was rescued and, though rather the worse for its adventure, was still alive and was carefully returned to the nest. The next day the youngster was still alive, with a third fledgling in the place of one of the eggs he had noted the day before. Hugh Spencer (1928) writes of the persistence of a blacksnake in taking the young from a catbird's nest at Chester, Conn. A member of the family called his attention to a blacksnake that was robbing the nest. He arrived just in time to see the big snake departing while the parents and several other birds cried and scolded. He was unable to get to the nest, which was in a low swamp huckleberry bush surrounded by a thicket of wild-rose brambles. Two young remained. He returned to his work, and in a short time the clamor arose again, but by the time he reached the nest another young had been taken. The experience was repeated, but the snake was frightened, leaving the last young dying on the ground. R. T. Morris (1925) writes of seeing a blacksnake suspended loosely among the branches of a tree with its head within a few inches of a catbird's nest. It was being violently attacked by four catbirds, two kingbirds, a male oriole, and a wren that had come to help the catbirds in distress. The bird mob won the battle, and the snake was driven away. The catbirds continued to harass the snake until it was 100 feet away at a place where it was finally shot by Mr. Morris. G. M. Sutton (1928) reports two cases of catbirds' eggs destroyed by blacksnakes at Pymatuning Swamp, Pa. There are many reports of eggs and young that have been ravaged by snakes, indicating that the latter rank as one of the worst enemies of nesting catbirds. Catbirds that build their nests in the yards and gardens near the homes of man are subject to attacks by the domestic cat. E. D. Nauman (1912) relates an experience in which a pair of nesting catbirds were being molested by a cat at 11 o'clock at night. He was attracted to the nesting site by the fluttering and distress calls of the adults. The cat had climbed the nesting boxelder tree and was within 2 feet of the nest when it was violently driven away by the use of a club. The pair was not molested again and succeeded in rearing their young.

Rats also may be a factor in the lives of the catbirds. In correspondence received from Hervey Brackbill he writes as follows: "Less than 10 minutes after a young bird, on its first day out of the nest, had fluttered from a bush to the ground and hopped off into a little wood lot, a rat appeared, slowly nosing its way in the same direction. Quickly one of the catbirds came on the scene and, perching on one thing and another—twigs and a wire fence—just above the rat, followed it along, *queuh-ing* continuously. The rat paid no attention, but went into the brush pile about 25 feet short of the young bird. The parent then perched here and there on the brush pile, still calling, until finally the rat reappeared and began working slowly back the way it had come. Now the adult catbird actually dropped to the ground and hopped after the rat, sometimes only a foot or two behind, *queuh-ing*, and even held its ground when once the rat half turned and gazed at it for a second or more. Only when the rat had gone about 25 feet from the young bird did the parent's alarm subside; then it stopped calling and flew back to the fledgling."

Catbirds nesting in more remote situations along forest fringes are subject to prey by predaceous mammals and birds. P. L. Errington (1935) found that Midwest foxes include the catbird in their food.

W. J. Breckenridge (1935) in his ecological study of Minnesota marsh hawks found the catbird among other birds in the food eaten by these birds. A. H. Howell (1932) states that the duck hawk feeds on the catbird. Etta M. Morse (1923) found the remains of a catbird in the stomach of a long-eared owl that had molested a brood of catbirds she was observing near her home in Woonsocket, S. Dak. These representative records indicate that predaceous birds and mammals take their toll of catbirds.

There have been instances in which the catbird has been molested or evicted from their nests by other passerine birds. Mrs. George W. Trine (1935) states that the eggs of a catbird were destroyed by bronzed grackles. W. L. Burk (1938) relates a case of a catbird that built a nest and laid one egg. A brown thrasher removed the egg, appropriated the nest, and reared its brood. W. M. Orford (1929) writes that a pair of cardinals that appeared in a thicket containing a newly built nest of a pair of catbirds repeatedly chased the rightful owners away and took possession of the nest. The cardinals added new nesting material and apparently settled down to use the structure. When the nest was visited 2 days later it contained a single egg of the cowbird and was deserted.

Casualties.—H. B. Wood (1934) and others report catbirds being killed on the highways by speeding motor cars. H. F. Lewis (1927) reports that catbirds were killed by flying into various lighthouses during the time of migration. Several of the lighthouse keepers along the coast of Maine have told me that catbirds are frequent victims at their stations during the migratory flights. Robert Overing (1938), in reporting on the 1937 fall migration at the Washington Monument, mentions the catbird as being killed by flying into the structure. These instances lend support to the view that the catbird flies chiefly at night during its migration and spends the daytime resting and feeding in preparation of the next leg of its journey. Weather also proves to be a factor in the mortality of the species. A. T. Wayne (1899) writes that a large number of birds including the catbird perished during the great cold wave of February 13–14, 1889. Mrs. G. W. Trine (1940) states that catbirds were killed by a terrific wind and hailstorm at Red Cloud, Nebr., on June 22, 1940.

Diseases and parasites.—Bird banders who have trapped catbirds have found them subject to certain diseases. T. E. Musselman (1930), in his banding operations at Quincy, Ill., trapped a catbird that had both legs badly diseased up to the tarsal joints. He writes: "Heavy cellular proliferation resulting in grayish crusts and knots nearly doubled the size of the bird's legs. So burdensome were the incrustations that the bird could fly only with great effort and walking was practically an impossibility." H. A. Allard (1930) writes concerning a catbird with a deformed bill observed in his garden at Arlington, Va. The bill was deformed in such a way that the upper mandible did not close upon the lower in a normal manner. The bend of the upper mandible was somewhat past the middle toward the nares and formed an angle of about 45° with the plane of the lower mandible, exposing much of the inside of the mouth and tongue. He did not see it feed but the bird appeared well nourished and lively.

The majority of catbirds are infested by a few and some by many external parasites. H. S. Peters (1933, 1936) reports the catbird to be host to the louse *Myrsidea incerta* (Kell.) ; the two bird flies *Ornithomyia avicularia* (Linn.) and *O. anchineuria* Speiser; the two mites *Liponyssus occidentalis* Ewing and *L. sylviarum* (C. & F.), and the two ticks *Haemaphysalis leporis-palustris* Packard and *Ixodes brunneus* Koch.

The catbird is subject to parasitism by the cowbird. A. C. Bent has informed me of a catbird's nest that he found in an ash tree about 6 feet above the ground, in Nelson County, N. Dak., on June 14, 1901. The catbird was incubating four cowbird's eggs and one of its own. Mr. Bent states that the cowbird's eggs were of two different types, suggesting that they had been laid by two different individuals.

Dr. Herbert Friedmann (1929), the foremost authority on the cowbird, states that the catbird is an uncommon victim and that as far as he knows the cowbird has never been definitely reported to be successful with this bird. The few published records range from Maine, New York, and Pennsylvania to Indiana and North Dakota. Experiments were tried to see whether the catbird could distinguish her own eggs from the eggs of other species. In every case the foreign eggs were ejected by the catbird. Nuttall (1903) also states: "On placing an egg of this species [cowbird] in the Catbird's nest it was almost instantly ejected." It is obvious that the catbird is very intolerant of foreign eggs. "It is worthy of note," says Dr. Friedmann," that while the catbird seems to know enough to distinguish between its own and other eggs and to get rid of the unwelcome additions to its nest, if a leaf is laid lightly over the nest it does not seem to know enough to get rid of it but will sit on the leaf as though trying to incubate through it."

The eggs of the Nevada or sagebush cowbird (*Molothrus ater artemesiae*) as well as those of the eastern cowbird (*Molothrus ater ater*) have been found in nests of the catbird.

The yellow-billed cuckoo sometimes lays its eggs in the nests of other birds of which the catbird is a known victim. Nuttall (1903) in writing of the yellow-billed cuckoo stated: "Careless in providing comfort for her progeny, the American Cuckoo, like that of Europe seems at times inclined to throw the charge of her offspring on other birds. Approaching to this habit, I have found an egg of the Cuckoo in the nest of a Catbird; yet though the habitation was usurped, the intruder probably intended to hatch her own eggs." O. Widmann (1882) writes of a similar experience as follows: "I was not a little astonished to find last Saturday, June 4, 1881, an egg of a Yellow-billed Cuckoo in a Catbird's nest. The Catbird's nest contained only one egg of its rightful owner; another Catbird's egg was found broken on the ground. The Cuckoo's egg was fresh, but the Catbird's egg was incubated." Robert Dresser (Webster, 1892) took a catbird's nest on May 20, 1892, which contained four eggs of the catbird and one egg of the yellow-billed cuckoo.

H. Miller (1891) reports a most astonishing mixup in which a catbird's nest containing two eggs of the catbird and two eggs of the cowbird were incubated by a brown thrasher. There were no eggs of the thrasher.

Banding and longevity.—Many catbirds have been banded, but with relatively few exceptions the hundreds of returns have been made at or near to the places where they were originally banded. Among some of the exceptions Lincoln (1939) reports a catbird banded at Schoharie, N. Y., on May 24, 1927, that flew into a house at Tela, Honduras, on October 25, 1929. Another catbird banded at Northville, S. Dak., on September 20, 1936, was killed at Tuxpam, Veracruz, Mexico, about January 1, 1937.

A number of longevity records of the catbird have been reported. Miss Marion A. Boggs (1935) reports two catbirds banded at her station at Waynesville, N. C., which were at least 7 years old when last seen. One adult banded July 7, 1924, returned each year until May 25, 1930. The other a female banded on July 2, 1926, also returned each year; the last date of trapping was April 22, 1932. A catbird banded at Demarest, N. J., on May 25, 1926, was retrapped at the same place on May 23, 1934, and again on May 8, 1935, a longevity record of 9 years (F. C. Lincoln, 1939). That the above records may be unusual is emphasized by the work of Geoffrey Gill (1940), who has presented the analysis of returns of catbirds banded at his station at Huntington, Long Island, N. Y., over a 10-year period. Mr. Gill banded 1,134 catbirds of which 489 were adults, 579 immatures, and 66 fledglings. At the time of his report 99 individuals had made a total of 158 returns to his station. Of the 99 birds to return 63 were banded as adults, 35 as immatures, and only 1 as a fledgling. In regard to the longevity of the birds Mr. Gill writes as follows:

Of the 58 individuals returning which were banded previous to 1936, only 2 are known not to be less than 5 years old. Of 75 returning individuals handed previous to 1937, only 15 are known to have lived at least 4 years, while of 86 returning birds banded previous to 1938, 36 are known to be at least 3 years old.

Taking the age of the oldest banded bird recorded at this station and assuming that this age divided by two, would give the average life-span of a catbird, it would place the average at around 2½ years. Such a theory is substantiated to a degree by banding records, but, due to the large element of chance in the trapping of wild birds, a large number must be banded and must return to the same traps before any conclusions can be drawn.

Winter.—There are so many winter records of the catbird that its occurrence in the North during the time of cold weather and snow does not seem unusual. Some of the individuals have been reported as being numbed or stupefied by extremely low temperature, but others seem to live successfully under the adverse conditions of a northern winter. Some of these records have been mentioned under the section pertaining to food and need not be repeated here.

The catbird is a common winter resident in the southern States, but many of them continue on to Central America as far south as Panama.

H. H. Kopman (1915) states that the catbird reaches southern Louisiana about September 10 and becomes abundant shortly after September 20. By the early part of November most of them have passed on. C. W. Beckham (1887), writing of the catbird at its winter home in Louisiana, states that it is of retiring habits and exclusively a denizen of the woods and dense thickets and so few know of its presence.

William Brewster (1882b) states that in the South the local birds do not mix with the strangers. When seen the catbirds occur in flocks in the timber.

During January 1928 I saw two catbirds on a banana plantation at Monte Verde, Costa Rica, and it gave me a real thrill to see these friends so far from home. They seemed preoccupied in searching for food as they worked through and about the vegetation in the neighborhood of the plantation house. The catbirds were seen for several days, but at no time did I hear them sing or even utter a simple note. They seemed to keep aloof of the resident birds of that tropical environment.

DISTRIBUTION

Range.—Southern Canada to Panama.

Breeding range.—The catbird breeds **north** to southern British Columbia (Bella Coola and Soda Creek); central Alberta (Belvedere and Edmonton); Saskatchewan (Carlton House and Prince Albert); southern Manitoba (Lake St. Martin, Shoal Lake, and Lake of the Woods); southern Ontario (Kenora, Sault Ste. Marie, Lake Nipissing, and Ottawa); southern Quebec (Blue Sea Lake and Quebec); New Brunswick (Woodstock and Fredericton); possibly Prince Edward Island (Stewarts Mill); and Nova Scotia (Wolfville and Pictou). **East** to Nova Scotia (Pictou and Halifax) and the Atlantic Coast States south to North Carolina (Raleigh and Wilmington); western South Carolina (Spartanburg and Greenwood; two records from Charleston); and Georgia (20 miles above Savannah). **South** to central Georgia (20 miles above Savannah, and Macon); central Alabama (Montgomery); also a few in north-central Florida (Wakeenah, Gainesville, and Dade City); Mississippi (Jackson and Edwards; also occasionally on the coast); northern Louisiana (Monroe and Shreveport); northeastern Texas (Huntsville, Corsicana, and Dallas); Oklahoma (Norman and Kenton); northern New Mexico (Santa Fe). **West** to central northern New Mexico (Santa Fe and Rinconado); western Colorado (Fort Lewis and Grand Junction); central northern Utah (Provo and Ogden); eastern Oregon (Frenchglen, Harney County, La Grande, and Weston); Washington (Prescott, Pullman, and Lake Chelan; also has occurred at Bellingham); and British Columbia (Chilliwack and Bella Coola). The catbird is resident in Bermuda.

Winter range.—In winter the catbird is found **north** to southern Texas (Brownsville, Matagorda, and Cove, rarely to Giddings); southern Louisiana (Cheniere au Tigre and Southport); Mississippi (Edwards and Biloxi); Alabama (Mobile); southern and eastern Georgia (Fitzgerald, St. Marys, and Savannah); eastern South Carolina (Aiken and Charleston); and eastern North Carolina (Washington and Lake Mattamuskeet). **East** to North Carolina (Lake Mattamuskeet and Ocracoke); the Bahamas (Abaco and Wattling Islands); western Cuba (Habana, Santiago de los Banos, and Isle of Pines); Cayman Islands, Nicaragua (near Bluefields); Costa Rica (Limón and Cauita); and western Panama (Almirante, and casually to the Canal Zone). **South** to Panama. **West** to Panama (Almirante region); eastern Costa Rica (Guacimo); central Nicaragua (San Rafael del Norte); central Guatemala (Los Amates and Coban); Tabasco (Frontera); Veracruz (Mirador); Nuevo León (near Linares); and Texas (Brownsville and Giddings).

The catbird has been found in winter occasionally as far north as southern New Hampshire, southern Michigan, northern Iowa, and Salt Lake County, Utah.

Migration.—Some late dates of spring departure from the winter home are: Panama—Almirante, April 23. Nicaragua—Bluefields, April 17. Honduras—Tela, April 22. Guatemala—Oaxactum, April 27. San Luis Potosí—Tamazunchale, April 28. Cuba—Habana, May 1. Bahamas—Berry Island, April 20. Texas—Somerset, May 9. Louisiana—New Orleans, May 13. Mississippi—Biloxi, May 20. Florida—Daytona Beach, May 3.

Some early dates of spring arrival are: Alabama—Birmingham, April 15. Georgia—Savannah, March 14. South Carolina—Columbia, April 5. North Carolina—Winston-Salem, March 29. Virginia—Lexington, April 6. District of Columbia—Washington, March 21: West Virginia—French Creek, April 17. Pennsylvania—Beaver, April 21. New York—Rochester, April 18. Massachusetts—Dennis, April 3. Vermont—Rutland, April 27. Maine—Lewiston, May 2. Nova Scotia—Wolfville, May 12. Quebec—Quebec, May 10. New Brunswick—Scotch Lake, May 13. Arkansas—Helena, April 12. Tennessee—Knoxville, April 5. Kentucky—Bowling Green, April 9, Missouri—St. Louis, April 6. Ohio—Oberlin, April 13. Ontario—Toronto, April 22. Indiana—Terre Haute, April 23. Michigan—Ann Arbor, April 12. Iowa—Ames, April 25. Wisconsin—Madison, April 23. Minnesota—Duluth, May 1. Manitoba—Winnipeg, May 5. Oklahoma—Tulsa, March 13. Kansas—April 25. South Dakota—Vermilion, April 29. North Dakota—Cando, May 16. Saskatchewan—Indian Head, May 3. Colorado—Boulder, May 9. Wyoming—Cheyenne, May 12. Montana—Great Falls, May 5. Alberta—Camrose, May 12. British Columbia—Summerland, May 16.

Some late dates of fall departure are: British Columbia—Okanagan Landing, September 8. Alberta—Camrose, September 14. Montana—Bozeman, September 26. Wyoming—Laramie, September 24. Saskatchewan—Eastend, September 18. North Dakota—Fargo, October 17. South Dakota—Sioux Falls, October 10. Nebraska—Lincoln, October 3. Kansas—Clearwater, October 6. Oklahoma—Tulsa, October 17. Manitoba—Aweme, October 1. Minnesota—Minneapolis, October 5. Iowa—Sioux City, October 1. Missouri—Kansas City, October 12. Wisconsin—Racine, October 10. Illinois—Lake Forest, October 14. Michigan—Grand Rapids, October 30. Ontario—Ottawa, October 7. Ohio—Columbus, October 28. Tennessee—Nashville, October 18. Quebec—Montreal, October 3. Nova Scotia—Wolfville, October 3. Maine—Portland, October 13. New Hampshire—Concord, October 9. Massachusetts—Boston, November 9. New Jersey—Elizabeth, October 28. District of Columbia—Washington, November 13. Virginia—Lawrenceville, October 13. North Carolina—Raleigh, October 15. Georgia—Athens, October 13.

Some early dates of fall arrival are: Florida—St. Augustine, September 25. Mississippi—Bay St. Louis, September 11. Louisiana—New Orleans, August 15. Texas—Brownsville, October 1. Cuba—Habana, October 10. Honduras—Tela, October 25. Nicaragua—Bluefields, October 28. Costa Rica—Guacimo, September 11. Panama—Cocoplum, Boco del Toro, October 24.

Some interesting notes on the migration of the catbird are found in the recoveries of banded birds, only a few of which can be cited. Three birds banded in Massachusetts were found the following winter in North Carolina, South Carolina, and Georgia, respectively. One banded in New York was found two years later at Tela, Honduras. One banded in Wisconsin was found in Kentucky during fall migration, and one from Ohio was taken in Mississippi. A catbird banded at Lansing, Mich., on September 24 was found near Slidell, La., on October 31 of the same year. One banded at St. Petersburg, Fla., in January was found the following June in Westchester County, N. Y.

Casual records.—The northernmost record for the catbird is a specimen collected at Hazelton, British Columbia, on June 10, 1921. A specimen collected on the Farallon Islands on September 4, 1884, is the only record for California. There are two records for Nevada—a specimen from Cave Spring, Esmeralda County, on June 18, 1928, and one observed at Alamo, on May 1, 1924; also two specimens from Arizona—one collected at Springerville on June 7, 1915, and one from Tunitcha Mountains, June 25, 1927. On May 5, 1930, one was observed near Alfalfa, El Paso County, Tex. There is a single record from Haiti, a specimen collected on Tortue Island, on February 5, 1917. On March 22, 1932, a specimen was collected at Paracoté, Panama, on the Pacific slope. The southernmost record is of a specimen taken at Ciénaga, Colombia, on March 23, 1917.

A specimen was collected on October 28, 1840, on the island of Helgoland, in the North Sea.

Egg dates.—Colorado: 5 records, May 6 to July 3.

Illinois: 58 records, May 18 to July 11; 33 records, May 26 to June 10, indicating the height of the season.

Massachusetts: 76 records, May 3 to August 15; 50 records, May 24 to June 5.

Minnesota: 21 records, May 12 to June 28; 11 records, June 2 to 13.

Washington: 4 records, June 15 to 28.

West Virginia: 51 records, May 4 to June 22; 40 records, May 11 to 31.

TOXOSTOMA RUFUM RUFUM (Linnaeus)

BROWN THRASHER

PLATES 66–70

HABITS

The well-known and popular brown thrasher occurs over a wide range in eastern North America, from southern Canada to the Gulf coast and Florida, and from the base of the Rocky Mountains to the Atlantic coast. The 1931 Check-list extends its breeding range southward to central Florida, but now it is known to breed occasionally, if not regularly, as far south as Miami. It breeds abundantly as far south as Georgia.

Its haunts, its habits, and to some extent its disposition vary somewhat in different portions of its range. These variations were first called to our attention by Miss Althea R. Sherman (1912), who published an interesting paper on the subject; the points that she suggested will be referred to farther on.

During some 60 years of acquaintance with the brown thrasher in eastern Massachusetts, I have formed a somewhat different impression of it from that gathered from the published accounts of it in more western and southern regions. Ever since I was a small boy, the catbird has lived and raised its young in my father's yard, and more recently in my own yard, every year, and this close to the center of the city of Taunton, almost within a stone's throw of brick and mortar. But the thrasher never has nested here, and only on rare occasions have I seen a straggler in my yard. And my experience has been similar to that of other observers. Here the thrasher is essentially a bird of the rural, woodland, and farming districts, living in bushy pastures, sproutlands, brier patches, tangles along fences, dry thickets, brushy hillsides, and the edges of woodlands, almost always far from human habitations. On large estates and in parks or reservations, where there are scattered woodlands and plenty of shrubbery, the

brown thrasher may find a congenial home, and here it may build its
nest close to a house; but such cases are exceptional in New England,
so far as I can learn; as a rule, our thrashers are shy, retiring birds
of the more open countryside.

Miss Sherman (1912) writes:

In eastern Massachusetts it is said to be a nesting bird of the woodlands,
rarely coming close to the homes of men to build its nest. This may in part
be due to the pruned, trimmed and shaven condition of trees, shrubs and lawns.
I remember once seeing a pair nesting in a hedge quite near a house at Quaker
Hill in eastern New York. It is a bird that seeks a bit of thick and tangled
growth in which to build, but in Iowa it finds such places to its taste in the
man-planted trees and shrubs that grow upon prairie soil, usually not far
from human homes. It is eminently a house-yard bird, although it sometimes
nests in patches of bushy second growth that have sprung up on clearings made
in the woods.

Dr. W. G. Erwin (1935) made his extensive studies of the brown
thrasher on the campus of George Peabody College for Teachers, in
Nashville, Tenn., where several pairs nested near the buildings and
in the shrubbery, in spite of much human activity. At Fairmount
Hill, a suburb of Wichita, Kans., Dwight Isely (1912) found this
bird "in large numbers all over the city, and in the parks. Its nests
are very abundant in osage orange hedges. In May and June the old
birds, followed by the young, may be seen on the lawns everywhere,
pulling worms out of the ground. They feed also in the fields and a
few follow the plow." And, in Kansas City, Mo., according to Harry
Harris (1919), "they breed freely within the city in the same districts
and in the same kind of brushy cover as the Catbird. The two species
do not nest close together, however, as they are mortal enemies during
the breeding season and have been known to battle to the death over a
disputed nesting site." Similar habitats are frequented in other western and southern States, which are quite different from our conception
of the haunts of the brown thrasher in New England; perhaps, if we
had more neglected brush heaps and tangles of unkempt shrubbery
and vines about our grounds, we might tempt the thrasher to be
more sociable and nest near our homes.

Spring.—Many of the early-spring birds, the bluebird, the robin, the
phoebe, the grackle, and others, have come to Massachusetts during
March and the early April days; they have advanced and they have
retreated as gentle spring struggled to overcome relentless winter;
but, during the last 10 days of April, when the pussy willows are
decorated with golden tassels, the swamp maples are glowing with
bright red blossoms, and the shadbush and the cherry trees are in full
bloom, it seems as if spring had really come, with nature awakening
all about us. Then we may look for the coming of the brown thrasher.
As we walk along some country road on a bright spring morning,
warmed by the rising sun and the soft south wind, we may see him

perched in the top of some wayside tree or on some tall bush on the border of the woods, pouring out his delightful song, with his head held high, his bill wide open, his long tail drooping, and his whole frame vibrating with the ecstasy of his song. We may imagine that he is telling the farmer in the adjacent plowed lot how to plant his corn; at least, his words seem to say so; but, more likely, it is just an outburst of joy, to announce that he has found his summer home, a warning to any rival that he claims this territory, or an invitation to an expected mate to come and join him in his homemaking. What a thrill of springtime pleasure such a scene must give to the appreciative mind! I pity the sordid soul that can pass it by unheeded, for he misses much of the beauty in the world about him.

Territory.—Each pair of thrashers has a definite breeding territory, which it defends during the nesting season. The male arrives some days in advance of the female and begins at once to look the region over with a view to selecting his territory; at first he is furtive and quiet but soon announces his choice in his loud outburst of song, an invitation to his mate. The actual nesting site, probably selected by the female, may or may not be very near the singing tree. Aretas A. Saunders writes to me: "In the spring of 1923 I noted during early morning walks that a brown thrasher sang daily from a small tree along a roadside in Fairfield, Conn. The bird sang from April 27 to May 13. On the 14th, not hearing the song at first, I soon discovered the bird in a tangle of weeds and blackberry almost directly beneath the singing tree. Another bird, evidently the female, was with him and he was following her around on the ground, singing constantly a song like the normal one in form but so faint I could not have heard it had I not been very close to the birds. After that time I no longer heard this bird in song and did not see it or its mate again until May 22, when I discovered the nest with four eggs and a bird incubating them. The nest was in almost the exact spot where I had observed the courtship and almost directly beneath the singing tree of late April and early May."

Another experience of his was quite different. On a small hill near his house was a dense thicket of sumacs, rambler roses, and other shrubs, in which for a succession of years a pair of song sparrows and later a pair of catbirds had nested. "The catbirds nested there until 1938. That spring the male catbird arrived and sang as usual, and a week or so later his mate arrived. On May 18, when the catbirds were just beginning to gather nesting material, a pair of brown thrashers arrived rather suddenly; they at once took over the thicket and started nest-building. I saw no fighting between them and the catbirds. The latter simply retired to a neighboring yard.

"I had heard no thrasher song anywhere near my home, and I did not hear it now. The birds had simply moved in from elsewhere after

they had become mated. The nest was soon finished and the eggs laid.
During the period of incubation, I heard the male thrasher sing a few
notes one day, but that was all the song I heard from the bird that
summer. They produced a brood of young successfully.

"I believe that both the brown thrasher and the catbird are territorial in nesting behavior. But in this region the catbird is extremely
abundant and the thrasher only fairly common. For catbirds territory is scarce, but for thrashers it is abundant. Evidently a pair of
thrashers can have their pick of territory, once they are mated, by
simply taking that of the catbirds. So they often move elsewhere
after the mate arrives, whereas catbirds must stick to the territory
they have selected.

"So, it seems from this observation that the male thrasher does not
always select the nesting territory, but merely one to which it first
attracts a mate by its singing. The nesting territory, in some cases at
least, is selected after the mating has taken place, and then it would
seem likely that the female would have more to do with the selection
than her mate."

From Dr. Erwin's (1935) studies of the territorial behavior of the
brown thrasher on Peabody College campus, "it seems that the male
Thrasher selects a desirable area immediately after arrival, and remains in this area for 10 or more days before beginning his song. The
author was unable to secure data which would indicate whether territorial fights occurred within this interval or not." He continues:

An effort was made to locate the boundaries of the territories of each pair of
Thrashers on Peabody Campus. The method used was the observation of the
limits of their feeding grounds and the locations and results of territorial fights.
* * * There seemed to be a definite tendency for the Thrashers to adopt
buildings, driveways, walks, and shrubbery rows for boundaries in many cases.
After a territory was established, the activities of the particular pair of Thrashers seemed to be almost entirely confined to this area. All nests of the season
were built within this territory. * * *

Thrashers almost always object to the presence of other Thrashers in their
territory, although they usually do not object to the presence of birds of other
species so long as they do not go near their nest, or do not interfere with their
feeding activities.

Courtship.—The loud, tree-top song of the male is the first step in
the courtship performance, the curtain raiser, as it were. It will be
noted from the above account that the male does not begin to sing
immediately on his arrival but waits until he can expect the arrival
of a possible mate, a matter of perhaps 10 days or 2 weeks. Then he
issues his loud invitation, which, under favorable circumstances, may
be heard at a long distance. This song is also a challenge to rival
males, and territorial fights between the rivals may occur during the
early stages of courtship. When the male and the female finally come
together, the song of the male becomes so subdued and soft that it is

almost inaudible, as the pair play about close together under the shrubbery. Dr. Erwin's (1935) records show that the male "sang very
softly when the female was nearby, but when she flew away he also
[as did another] began to sing much louder, as if to call her back, and
at one time followed her a short distance, singing on the wing."

The more intimate part of the courtship is not easily seen, as it
usually takes place under dense cover, but Dr. Erwin has published the
following account of it in his excellent paper:

April 29, 9:00 a. m., both male and female were observed under the shrubbery
at the right of the exit. The female hopped out in the grass away from the
shrubbery about 10 feet and began to dig in the ground with her bill. After
about 5 minutes the male came out a distance of about a foot from the shrubbery.
The female picked up a small twig in her bill and hopped back to the male,
fluttering her wings as she went, after which she dropped her twig and fluttered
her wings vigorously, giving soft chirps. No further activities were observed as
they searched for food among the leaves for 8 minutes. Then the female hopped
out on the grass, again secured a twig, and began to flutter her wings and give
soft chirps as before. The male picked up two dead leaves and hopped toward
her, whereupon she fluttered her wings even more vigorously and issued chirps
a little louder. Both dropped the materials held in their bills and engaged in
coitus. Both birds then hopped down the shrubbery row, the female gathering
twigs and fluttering her wings several times, after which both went under the
shrubbery.

He did not see any show of display or strutting in this or other
courtship antics. Audubon (1841b), however, says: "The actions of
this species during the period of courtship are very curious, the male
often strutting before the female with his tail trailing on the ground,
moving gracefully round her, in the manner of some pigeons, and
while perched and singing in her presence, vibrating his body with
vehemence."

Brown thrashers do not always remain mated through even one
breeding season. Samuel Elliott Perkins, 3d (1930), has shown this
to be so in at least some cases by banding and recovering adult
thrashers during the rearing of their first and second broods. He
reports "a case of a pair of birds changing mates 2 months after they
had raised a brood together, under conditions which proved that it
was not the seeking of a new mate after the death of the previous one."
In this case, each of the original pair was trapped and found to be
paired with a new mate. He continues: "We have had four other
pairs of Brown Thrashers in the same area under observation, where
only one of each pair was a banded bird. The inference seems
irresistible that after each brood is raised there is a complete shuffling
of mates among the Brown Thrashers." Apparently the brown
thrasher is no more constant in its marital relations than is the house
wren. Arthur T. Wayne (1910) was told by a man he considered
reliable of a female brown thrasher being mated with a male mockingbird.

Nesting.—I have been surprised to read in the literature and in contributed notes that, throughout the western and southern portions of
its range, the brown thrasher very seldom builds its nest upon the
ground, for that is certainly not the case in New England, or at least
in eastern Massachusetts. Miss Sherman (1912) writes:

In Iowa I have never found a nest nearer than 18 inches or 2 feet of the
ground, one of these being in the lower branches of a spruce tree, the other in a
brush pile. Another was found built in a brush pile, but farther from the
ground, these are the only nests thus situated that have been found, but brush
piles on prairie land are rare. The next locations nearest the ground are where
nests are built in such bushes as gooseberry, lilac, and syringa, when they are
from two to three feet above the ground. The highest nest situation found was
one in a tame crabapple tree about ten feet up; other trees frequently used are
spruce, willow, apple, and plum trees in which a majority of the nests are about
five feet from the ground.

A. Dawes DuBois has sent me his data on 19 nests, found in Illinois,
only one of which was on the ground "under a large, cattle-eaten bush
in a pasture"; he remarks that this is the only nest he ever found on
the ground. His other nests were mostly in bushes, hedges, or low
trees; one was 3 feet from the ground in a large osage-orange hedge,
and one was in the top of an apple tree.

Frank W. Braund's data sent to me show five nests, found in Ohio,
all 2½ to 4 feet up in bushes or small trees. One nest found near
Jackson, Tenn., but not collected, was of rather unusual construction,
being made of coarse grasses, with a few leaves, and lined with fine
grass.

There is a set of six eggs in my collection, taken by W. L. Griffin
in Pulaski County, Ky., that came from a nest 15 feet from the
ground in a gum tree; the eggs were evidently laid by two females,
as two of them were more heavily marked than the other four; furthermore, three adult birds appeared and made the usual demonstration while the eggs were being taken.

Evidently none of the nests studied by Dr. Erwin (1935) at Nashville, Tenn., was on the ground; his lowest nest was a foot from the
ground in a thick growth of smilax; one pair of thrashers started a
nest 14 feet up on a horizontal branch of a maple but never completed it. Of the 59 nests examined, nearly 80 percent were between
2 and 7 feet above ground; only nine were higher and three lower.
"The most common locations for nests on Peabody Campus were
Golden Bell (*Forsythia* sp.) and Privet (*Ligustrum* sp.). Other
shrubs and smaller trees were occasionally used."

W. Leon Dawson (1903), referring to Ohio, writes: "Nesting sites
are various, but the bird shows a decided preference for those which
are naturally defended by thorns. Nearly every full sized Crategus
(thorn apple) has at one time harbored a nest. Hedges of osage-

orange are well patronized—almost exclusively so * * * further west—and the honey-locust tree is not forgotten. Next after these come wild plum thickets, grapevine tangles, brush heaps, fence corners, and last of all, the ground." He shows a photograph of a nest in a corner of a Virginia rail fence.

H. O. Todd, Jr., tells me that out of 109 nests found in Tennessee, only one was on the ground.

It is rather unusual for a thrasher to build its nest close to a house, but several such cases have been reported; E. S. Cameron (1908) reports a nest built close to a window in his house on his ranch in Montana; and E. D. Nauman (1930a) writes: "While myself and family were living on a farm near Thornburg, Iowa, some years ago, we had a thriving rose bush standing directly in front of the kitchen window and close up; so close in fact that some of the foliage and roses touched the glass. One season the Brown Thrashers (*Toxostoma rufum*) made their home in the rose bush. Their nest was twenty inches from the window glass." The birds were not in the least disturbed by activities within the house.

The only report I can find of any considerable number of brown thrasher nests on the ground in the Middle West comes from Edmonde S. Currier (1904) in Minnesota. He says: "Several nests seen, and *all* of them were sunken in the ground after the manner of a Towhee's. In Iowa I have seen the nest thus placed, but it is very unusual, and it is strange that the Leech Lake bird should prefer such a situation, though there must be a reason."

On the contrary, ground nests are common in New England. One half of the nests in southeastern Massachusetts, as recorded in my field notes, were on the ground under bushes, trees, or thickets. The others were in bushes, small trees, or brush heaps; the highest nest I find recorded was only 4 feet from the ground in an arborvitae. Frederic H. Kennard's notes for the vicinity of Boston record 23 nests, 10 of which were on the ground. All authorities seem to agree that, in this region, ground nests are of common occurrence, especially on the higher lands, where the ground is warm and dry and where the thrasher evidently prefers to nest.

Eggs of the brown thrasher have been found in the nests of other birds. There is a set of eggs in the American Museum of Natural History, in New York, taken by H. B. Bailey on June 5, 1886, near South Orange, N. J. It was taken from a wood thrush's nest, which contained four eggs of the thrush, incubated about 7 days, and two fresh eggs of the thrasher. Thrasher eggs have also been found in nests with those of the mockingbird, the robin, and the cardinal. Dr. W. C. Herman (1923) tells of a remarkable dual nest, in which "the foundation was typical of that of the thrasher, while the center was that of the robin, both nests being well made and complete in every detail." His photograph of it shows four eggs of the thrasher and one of the robin. The thrasher was on the nest, which was afterward destroyed by some unknown enemy. E. D. Nauman (1930b) found a thrasher incubating on its nest, with two of its own eggs and two of the cardinal under it. The cardinal's eggs were evidently deposited about a week after incubation had begun on the thrasher's eggs, for the next time he visited the nest it contained two young thrashers and two eggs of the cardinal, on which the latter bird was incubating. This nest also came to grief.

Dr. Erwin (1935) gives a very full account of the building of the nest, in which both birds take part, and a good description of the composition of the nest:

The later nests were more poorly constructed than the earlier ones. Five to seven days were usually required for the construction of the earlier nests, while only three to four days were required for the later ones. It also seemed that the type of location of the nest had something to do with the amount of materials used.

Twenty-three nests were carefully examined to discover the architecture and materials of construction. The nests were composed of four concentric layers, or baskets. The first basket was composed entirely of twigs, usually from four to twelve inches long and from $\frac{1}{16}$ to $\frac{1}{4}$ of an inch in diameter. The second basket was composed principally of dead leaves. A few pieces of paper, thin bark, and tiny twigs were sometimes used. The third basket was composed of tiny twigs and grass stems. In a few of the later nests this basket was almost completely lacking. The fourth basket, or lining, was usually composed of well-cleaned rootlets, mostly from grasses. In a few cases petioles of the Honey Locust were used exclusively.

He gives an account of the building operations in too great detail to be quoted here. The birds had considerable difficulty in carrying the twigs through the thickly entwined branches of the shrubbery; often the twigs were left hanging where they were caught, and sometimes they were recovered but sometimes not. When the female apparently discovered a desirable place, "with her bill she pushed the twigs closer together, then got on the thickly matted stems and began the movements in which many birds engage during nest building. She intermittently lowered her head, relaxed her wings, and with rapid jerks shifted her feet sidewise." This method of nest-shaping was continued with each of the successive layers. At one nest he noted that the female made 28 and the male 21 trips to the nest between 2:45 and 4:40 P. M.

Soon after the young have left the first nest, the female starts building a second nest, leaving the male to care for the first brood of young. At one nest the young left the nest on May 5, and on May 10 the female was discovered putting the lining into the second nest. Another female was seen completing a second nest 11 days after the young had left the first nest. Mr. Saunders tells me that a pair that he watched "produced a brood of young successfully, which left the nest on June 15. On June 17 they began a second nest. Incubation of the second set began on June 24."

Nesting sites in the South are apparently similar to those in the Midwest—hedges, shrubbery, brush heaps, thickets, grapevine tangles, vines, and trees. A. H. Howell (1932) states that "Nicholson found a number of nests at Orlando [Florida] in oak and orange trees, 8 to 20 feet above the ground." Frederick V. Hebard mentions in his notes from southeastern Georgia a nest in a "sea-myrtle bush about 20 inches above ground. This nest was badly constructed of dried grass supported by twigs, one of which was over 14 inches long. Corn husks were in the nest. The nest had an inside diameter of 3¾ inches, an inside depth of seven-eighths inch, and an outside depth of 3¾ inches." Another nest was in a camphor tree, 7 feet above ground.

Eggs.—Nearly all the nests of the brown thrasher of which I have record contained either 4 or 5 eggs, generally 4; the one set of 6 eggs in my collection was evidently the product of 2 females. Eggs were laid in 52 of the nests examined by Dr. Erwin (1935) in Tennessee; 31 contained 4 eggs, 13 contained 3 eggs, 7 contained 5 eggs, and one contained only 2 eggs. Six eggs have been recorded.

The eggs are not handsome, but they show considerable variation in color and shape; they are usually ovate, but some are somewhat elongated and some are short-ovate. The ground color is very pale blue, bluish white, or white, with sometimes a greenish tinge. They are usually rather evenly covered, more or less thickly, with very small spots or fine dots of reddish brown or duller browns. Sometimes the markings are so small, scarce, and faint as to make the egg appear almost white. Very rarely a set of eggs is immaculate. Occasionally the markings are grouped in a ring around one end. A rare and handsome type has a darker green ground color, with bright reddish spots. The measurements of 50 eggs in the United States National Museum average 26.5 by 19.4 millimeters; the eggs showing the four extremes measure 30.2 by 19.8, 26.7 by 21.3, and 21.3 by 16.3 millimeters.

Young.—The period of incubation is stated by several observers to vary from 11 to 14 days, according to weather temperatures and other conditions. Dr. Erwin (1935) says: "Of the 32 nests in which eggs were laid on Peabody Campus, only 17 were successfully incubated. Nine of these required a period of 13 days, six 12 days, one 11 days, and one 14 days. The set of eggs which required 14 days was in an early nest." Both sexes shared in the duties of incubation. During a period of 14 hours 15 minutes, the female incubated 9 hours 11 minutes; and the male sat 3 hours 51 minutes, about 27 percent of the total time, perhaps to give the female a chance to feed. "For 12 successful nests on Peabody Campus, the average nestling period was

11 days. Two of the nests had young with a nestling period of 13 days. Both of these nests were early. The nestling period for one nest was 12 days, for four, 11 days, for four, 10 days, and for one, 9 days."

He noted that both parents helped to feed the young in the nests. A total of 8 hours 6 minutes on parts of five days was spent in observation of the feeding process at two nests. He says:

During this period, the different females made a total of 40 trips to the nest with food, and the males, 31 trips. This food consisted almost entirely of white grubs, soft caterpillars, and earth worms. A small part of the time was spent in brooding, this duty being shared both by male and female. Most of the periods of brooding occurred in the early morning when the weather was cool and the young still were without a full coating of feathers. On one occasion the female, being unable to cover the five young, used her bill to pull them toward her. Both male and female always inspected the nest for excreta before going on to brood. Excretion always occurred immediately after the nestling, or nestlings, were fed. The excreta was encased in a transparent bag, which prevented it from soiling the nest while being removed. The excreta from the very young birds was almost always eaten, while that from the older nestlings was usually carried away and dropped. * * *

In cases where a second nest was built after young were successfully brought off the preceding nest, the female remained to help care for the young only a few days, after which she built the second nest without assistance of the male, his duty being to care for the nestlings. There were only two nests in which this occurred during the year. The other nestlings were brought off too late, due to previous failures, for the adults to build another nest. In two instances where the female did not build another nest after the young were brought off, the young were divided, the male taking a part of the young, and the female the remainder. Also in these two instances, the territory was also divided. * * * After the first brood of young became independent, it seemed that the male returned to assist the female in the care of the second brood.

Dr. Ira N. Gabrielson (1912) made a careful study of a brood of young brown thrashers in Iowa; the nest was on the ground, which he remarked was unusual; when it was discovered, on June 17, it held four young, "not more than 24 hours old," and an addled egg; a blind was set up near the nest and observations began on June 23 and continued until the young left the nest on June 28. He says:

[On June 23] the afternoon was hot and sultry and the nest was in such a position as to be exposed to the hot rays of the sun. One or the other of the old birds brooded almost all of the time. During the afternoon, the male brooded once for a period of 26 minutes and the female for 20 minutes, but the periods as a rule were short, being from 2 to 5 minutes in length. At about 2 o'clock the shadow of an oak tree was thrown on the nest and the old birds ceased brooding. * * * There was a marked difference in the position assumed by the male and female in brooding. The male sat on the edge of the nest with his feathers ruffled up, or stood in the nest in much the same posture, affording very poor protection for the young as compared with that given by the female. She spread her wings, ruffled her feathers, and stood in such a position as to completely shade the nest.

He made a careful record of the food given to the young and published a long list of insects, larvae, spiders, and worms supplied. "The four insects consumed in the largest quantities were found to be as follows: grasshoppers 247, Mayflies 425, moths 237, and cutworms 103. Two of these, at least, are positively destructive insects; and in the summer of 1911 the grasshoppers were almost a plague in parts of northern Iowa. Many fields of grain were destroyed and many more were cut green to prevent destruction, making the oats light weight and poor quality. The grasshoppers stripped the oats from the straw by cutting the stem of each grain. This was done while the grain was in the milk, so it was a total loss."

A record was kept of the number of feedings by each parent each day; the longest and largest record was made on June 27; from 3:30 a. m. to 9:00 p. m. the male fed the young 98 times and the female fed them 186 times, or a total of 286 feedings, including twice that the young were fed without the sex of the parent being known. In order to determine the quantity of food received by each nestling, the young birds were marked with green, orange, blue, and white thread. "From June 26 at 4:11 p. m., until Green left the nest on the 28th, at 12:19 p. m., he was fed 152 times; Orange 142 times; White 169 times; and Blue 133 times. Orange was a small and active bird; White was large and inactive, but seemingly possessed of plenty of strength; Blue was weak and timid." The total amount distributed during this time, parts of 3 days, was 976 insects, or an average of 219 to each young bird. Gabrielson continues:

Sometimes it seemed as if chance determined which individual would receive the morsel, and at other times looked as if there were other factors. There seemed to be a tendency to feed the one nearest the parent bird, and, as the old birds almost invariably approached the nest from the south, it would follow that the nestling on that side would get the most food. However that may be, the young were constantly trying to get to that side of the nest. One would no sooner got into place on that side than another would crowd him out. This was not always the case, for at times the parents would reach over and feed those on the farther side. Again it seemed as if the nestling that made the greatest disturbance received the food.

The nest was kept scrupulously clean through the efforts of both parents; on June 27, from 3:30 a. m. to 9:00 p. m., the nest was cleaned 18 times by the male and 38 times by the female.

Three interesting facts were noted in connection with the passage of the excreta: viz., the young birds made no attempt to void the excreta except when one of the parent birds was present; second, only one of the nestlings voided the excreta at any one visit of the parent birds; and third, almost always the bird fed, or if two were fed, one of the two voided the excreta. * * * The results of these observations seem to indicate that the feeding may possibly be the direct stimulus to the voiding of the excreta, as out of a possible 112 times 104 sacs of excreta were removed from the nestling receiving the food at that visit, while only eight were removed from different birds. The parents always stopped a few seconds after feeding, possibly waiting for the appearance of an excreta sac. In the case of the nestling voiding the excreta, there were usually some premonitory signs: viz., general uneasiness, ruffling the feathers, and flirting the tail. Then followed the elevating of the posterior end of the body, and as the sac came away the parent bird seized it and either devoured it or carried it away. * * * It would seem * * * that about the eighth or ninth day the old birds ceased devouring the excreta and commenced to carry it away. * * *

At about noon, June 28, the young birds became very restless, especially Green and Orange. They were continually crawling out of the nest and back again. At 12:30 p. m. Green crawled out of the nest and sat chirping for a short time. He then spread his wings and made an attempt to fly, but only succeeded in going a few inches. Immediately on falling he commenced to hop rapidly away; stopping a short interval at a fence about 10 feet distant. One of the old birds returned at this time and coaxed him along until he reached the top of a little hill some 60 yards away. * * * At 2:10, Orange left the nest in much the same way. The male went with him and by coaxing him a short way at a time soon had the second nestling on the little knoll occupied by Green. The male busied himself the rest of the day caring for these two while the female fed White and Blue in the nest.

The next morning White started away at 7:07 and was coaxed along by the female for about 30 yards. Blue remained alone in the nest until 7:45, being fed only once in the interval, though White was fed three times. 7:45 Blue left the nest, but no parent bird returned to aid in the journey as long as the observations were continued. At 8:15, when the observations ceased, Blue was still alone in the grass. Later all four of the fledglings were found in the ravine nearby. They were noticed here several times, July 25 being the latest date on which they were positively indentified.

Amelia R. Laskey tells me that "a fledgling fed by hand, but given freedom, was noted singing a very soft song on July 24, when 44 days old. This song was similar to the autumn singing heard each year in August and September in the garden."

A. L. Pickens sends me the following note on the method used by a thrasher in coaxing its young from the nest: "The young had been hatched in a rose vine at the edge of our front porch and were at that stage where they could clamber out of the nest and perch in the surrounding vines. They could not fly, but the old bird seemed anxious to have them leave a spot so frequently examined by human eyes. Coaxing having failed, the parent resorted to strategy. She came to the nest with a small piece of paper so folded and compressed together as to resemble, especially in size, the morsels of food usually brought to the young. This she held temptingly first above one young one's mouth, then above another's. But as the young beaks were expectantly extended she raised or withdrew the bogus morsel still farther away. Then she flew away to a short distance still temptingly holding the bit of paper. At last one of her offspring, fluttering and clambering, dropped to the ground, and she began leading it along a route that led through the yard and grove, evidently to the denser growth of a small wood nearby. Fearing for the young's safety I captured it and brought it back to the nest amid angry protests from the parent. In this outburst she dropped her imitation morsel, and I took particular pains to carefully retrieve and examine it.

Plumages.—I have not seen any young brown thrashers in natal down. The juvenile plumage is softer and looser, less compact, and easily recognized. It resembles the adult plumage in pattern but is paler and duller throughout; the top of the head is darker and the rump lighter, and all of the upper surface is more or less streaked or spotted with dusky; the wing bars are buffy, and the tertials are edged and tipped with buffy; the underparts are dull white, the streaks and spots being more numerous and less sharply defined. The iris in the young bird is gray.

A postjuvenal molt occurs late in summer or early in fall, beginning the last of July, and involving the contour plumage and most of the wing coverts, but not the rest of the wings or the tail. This produces a first winter plumage, which is practically indistinguishable from that of the adult at the same season.

Adults have one complete annual molt, the postnuptial, in July and August. In fresh fall plumage the colors are darker and richer than they are in spring, the upper surface being deep cinnamon-rufous, and on the lower surface the throat, sides, and crissum are washed with ochraceous-buff; the wing coverts are cinnamon-rufous, and the wing bands are buffy white. There is no evidence of a spring molt, but wear and fading are considerable, the buffy shades disappearing and the whole plumage becoming more or less ragged before midsummer. The sexes are alike in all plumages.

Food.—E. H. Forbush (1929) gives a very good account of the food of the brown thrasher, based largely on Prof. Beal's (Beal, Mc-Atee, and Kalmbach, 1916) report:

An examination of 266 stomachs of the bird from various parts of the country was made by Prof. F. E. L. Beal of the Biological Survey, and it showed that the food consisted of 37.38 percent vegetal and 62.62 percent animal food, the latter nearly all insects. The insect food was rather evenly divided among the various orders. Beetles were eaten regularly the year round. Such pests as May beetles, white grubs, twelve-spotted cucumber beetles, many weevils, including the cotton-boll weevil, curculios, snap-beetles and wire-worms, rose-beetles, strawberry-crown girdlers and wood-boring beetles, caterpillars, including canker-worms, army-worms, cut-worms and hairy caterpillars such as the tent and gipsy caterpillars, also bugs of many kinds, especially those that eat berries, also leaf-hoppers, tree-hoppers and cicadas, quantities of grasshoppers and locusts and many crickets are eaten, also many of the ants that destroy timber. A small proportion of beneficial ground-beetles are taken, and very few wasps and bees; daddy-long-legs, sow-bugs, small batrachians, lizards and snakes are taken more or less.

Professor Beal (Beal, McAtee, and Kalmbach, 1916) says that beetles form the largest item in the thrasher's food, 18.14 percent; caterpillars come next, 5.95 percent; other insects are eaten in much smaller quantities, as are also spiders, myriapods, crawfish, snails, and angleworms. "Bones of lizards, salamanders, and tree frogs (in all, 0.92 percent) were found in 11 stomachs." He gives the thrasher credit for destroying only 2.43 percent of grasshoppers and crickets for the year, with a maximum of 8.5 percent in September, whereas Dr. Gabrielson (1912) says that, at the time of his study in Iowa, 20 percent of the food of old and young thrashers consisted of grasshoppers.

Of the vegetable food, Professor Beal (1916) writes:

The vegetable food of this bird is nearly equally divided between fruit and a number of other substances, of which mast is the most prominent. Wild fruit, the largest item in the vegetable portion (19.94 percent), was eaten every month in varying quantities, the month of maximum consumption (45.69 percent) being September; January and February, with dried-up fruit from the last summer's crop, stand next. Altogether about 30 species of wild fruits or berries were identified in the stomachs. Those most eaten are blueberries, huckleberries, holly berries, elderberries, pokeberries, hackberries, Virginia creeper, and sour gum. Some seeds not properly classified as "fruit" were found, as bayberry, sumac—including some of the poisonous species—pine, and sweet gum.

Domestic fruit, or what was called such, was found in nine months, from April to the end of the year, most of it (53.19 percent) in July. Raspberries or blackberries, currants, grapes, cherries, and strawberries were positively identified by their seeds, but as all of these grow wild, it is probable that much that is conventionally termed domestic fruit is really from uncultivated plants. The aggregate for the year is 12.42 percent.

Mast, principally acorns, was estimated at 23.72 percent for the year, and grain only 2.57 percent. "The grain was nearly all corn, with a little wheat, but from the season in which it was taken most of it evidently was waste." The thrasher has been accused of pulling up planted corn, but this is probably local and restricted to a few individual birds.

W. L. McAtee (1926a) mentions some additional insects, eaten by the thrasher, that are injurious to wood lots, such as nut weevils, the wild cherry-leaf weevil (*Epicaerus imbricatus*), oak weevil (*Eupsalis minuta*), and the yellow-necked caterpillar (*Datana ministra*); and, also to the above lists, he adds the Japanese beetle, clover-root weevil, billbugs, and the chinch bug, as of more interest to the agriculturalist.

The brown thrasher spends most of its time on or near the ground and obtains the greater part of its food there. One may often be seen foraging among the fallen leaves on the ground under trees or shrubs, or in more open spaces. It apparently seldom scratches for its food, as do the fox sparrow and the towhee, but uses its long, strong bill much as a haymaker uses a pitchfork in spreading hay; thus, with powerful sidewise strokes, it sends the leaves flying in all directions, and then stops to pick up what desirable morsels it finds beneath them. In this way it works diligently over considerable ground, occasionally picking up a leaf to cast it aside but more often pitching them away with its closed bill. Some writers have suggested that his name may have come from this habit of thrashing about among the leaves and rubbish; another suggestion is that his habit of thrashing large insects or other prey on the hard ground to kill or mutilate them has suggested the name; a still more fanciful notion came from someone who had been thrashed by the bird in the defense of its nest.

Milton P. Skinner (1928) writes of its feeding habits in North Carolina:

One was seen that picked the ground for a time and then alternated its picking strokes with some sidewise scoops of its bill. Later it ran swiftly along for 6 feet and caught an insect that was flying low. Another Thrasher was seen making flycatcher-like sallies from the ground, and later from well up in an oak. They sometimes chase lively, erratic insects through the grass, and at other times adopt the Flicker method of digging down a good inch and a half into the sandy soil, probably for grubs. Brown Thrashers sometimes pick up acorns and carry them away in their bills, and later open them as the Jays do. But they are ground birds, unlike the Jays, and when they try to split the shell from an acorn by pile-driver blows, they often drive the acorn down into the soft ground. In spite of this difficulty, they persevere and the shell eventually flies off. I have seen one eat a shelled acorn in a few bites. Apparently, acorns are an essential part of their winter food.

He says that thrashers "occasionally fly up on the weed stalks and pluck the seeds direct" and also that they are very fond of sumac berries; one "ate for some minutes, quite stripping the head of all fruit; then rested a few minutes before eating another score of the berries." He adds that they sometimes eat persimmons and smilax berries but found that sumac berries were a favorite food in December.

Behavior.—As suggested by Miss Sherman (1912) and as mentioned in the first part of this account, there seems to be some variation in the general behavior and in the disposition of the brown thrasher in New England from what has been noted in the Midwest and South. In Massachusetts I have always regarded it as a shy, retiring, and somewhat unfriendly bird, shunning human society and especially hostile to the intruder near its nest. In other parts of the country, it seems to be more sociable, more friendly, and more inclined to make its home in parks in towns and villages, or even cities, in gardens, orchards, and close to human dwellings. These are not, however, hard and fast rules, for there are exceptions in both cases.

The thrasher is one of the most valiant and aggressive defenders of its nest and young among all our small birds, exhibiting the greatest bravery and boldness. While the late Herbert K. Job and I were photographing birds near West Haven, Conn., on June 5, 1910, we found a thrasher brooding her young in a nest 5 feet from the ground in a thick bush. She allowed Mr. Job to stroke her on the nest before she left and then set up a loud cry of protest and defiance, which soon brought her mate to join in the attack. As I attempted to examine the young, both birds flew at me and attacked me savagely; they flew at my face, once striking a stinging blow close to my eye and drawing blood; within a few seconds I was struck on the side of my head, and we decided to withdraw from the scene of the battle, leaving the brave birds masters of the situation. Mr. Job had had a similar experience with fighting thrashers a few years previously; they attacked his hands, when he attempted to touch the young, and scratched and bit holes through the skin.

Mrs. Amelia R. Laskey, of Nashville, Tenn., writes to me: "Almost all brown thrashers show much concern when I look into the nest or remove young for banding. Most of them scold or squeal excruciatingly as if suffering intense pain. I have found several individuals that were very pugnacious in attacking me and very bold in their close approach. One bird struck the top of my head with great force, apparently striking with both feet. Another made a swift stab at my temple, striking with its beak with such force as to draw blood. Another attacked the hand, removing and replacing the young for banding purposes, with such venom that drops of blood stood on several fingers from jabs made by its beak."

Mr. DuBois tells me of one that attacked him, alighting on his back and swooping down repeatedly to strike his hat. And there are other published reports of similar behavior toward human and other enemies. Dr. B. H. Warren (1888) writes: "When their home is invaded by a black snake, they assail such intruder in a most vigorous manner. I once saw a dog, which had upset a nest containing young Thrushes, forced to make a speedy retreat when attacked by the old birds, who flew at his head and struck him in the eyes." Dr. T. M. Brewer wrote to him as follows:

I found a nest containing three eggs, which I removed, leaving in their places three Robin's eggs, and retired to wait the issue. In a few moments the female approached, gave the contents of the nest a hasty survey, and immediately flew off. She returned in a short time in company with her mate, and both flew to the nest apparently in the greatest rage, took each an egg in their *claws*, and dashed it against the ground at a distance of more than a rod from the nest, the female repeating the same to the other egg. This done, they continued for some time to vent their rage on the broken eggs, tossing them about, and at the same time manifesting their displeasure in every possible way. They afterwards forsook the nest.

But not all thrashers are too shy, hostile, or vindictive. In regions where they are closely associated with human activities, notably in the Midwest, some individuals have become quite tame and friendly, come freely to feeding stations, bathe in bird baths, and have on rare occasions been induced to feed from human hands (see Bird-Lore, vol. 10, p. 253, and vol. 20, p. 299). Sidney E. Ekblaw (1918) reports the following interesting experience:

It was in the latter half of June that the brown thrasher first appeared at our home near Rantoul, Ill. My mother and sister were at work on the back porch when the bird alighted on the ground. Its apparent tameness attracted their attention, and when it flew to a nearby fence-post my sister went out to it. When she approached, the bird flew to her shoulder, where it stayed contentedly for at least 3 minutes.

For 2 days it stayed about the place, not in the least afraid, in no wise concerned about household activities carried on about it. It allowed the various members of the family to pet it, while it perched upon an arm or shoulder; it ate cherries that my brother fed it, while he held it in his hand; and it showed not the least objection to having its picture taken. The second day it disappeared and we saw it no more.

The brown thrasher lives in the lower levels of the trees and shrubbery, except when it mounts to the top of some outstanding tree to sing its springtime challenge. It is especially at home upon the ground, where it probably spends most of its time, walking or running with short easy strides, or hopping about when in no hurry. If necessary it can run quite fast to catch some insect prey; or it can cover considerable ground with a series of long high hops, where walking or running is not convenient. The use of its strong bill to obtain its food is explained in the section headed Food (p. 363).

Its flight is rather slow and, apparently, heavy; its short wings are not adapted for swift or protracted flight; it usually flies low and not for any great distances unless in crossing an open field or a river. We often see the long, brown bird in the middle of a country road, taking a dust bath in some dusty hollow, or picking up the grain in scattered horse droppings; when thus disturbed, it spreads its long, handsome tail, makes a short low flight, and disappears in the roadside shrubbery or glides over the top of a half-hidden stone wall and swoops down into cover. It is equally at home in the thickets, running to cover when approached and dodging skillfully through the brier tangles to escape.

Mr. Skinner (1928) says: "They are very fond of bathing, especially when the weather gets warm in spring. In earthenware saucers, they will bathe when it is as cold as 55° F., and when it is warmer they bathe regularly twice a day. But they do not stop taking shower-baths just because artificial baths are available. They are even out in steady rains, thoroughly shaking themselves as the heavy raindrops soak their plumage."

We do not know yet quite how long birds may live, as we have not been banding birds long enough, or extensively enough, to be sure that we have trapped the oldest bird. Several brown thrashers have been reported as from 8 to 10 years old, but the oldest one seems to be the bird reported by Miss Marion A. Boggs (1939) which, on the eleventh return, was at least 13 years old.

Voice.—The brown thrasher is one of our best and most spectacular singers; his loud, striking spring song, once heard, can never be forgotten. Almost every writer on American birds has commented on it and mostly favorably.

Dr. Winsor M. Tyler has given me his impression of it as follows: "The song of the brown thrasher is a brilliant performance, equaled, if judged solely by its technical skill, by few North American birds, and surpassed by perhaps only one, the mockingbird. Indeed, it is sometimes difficult to distinguish the song of a thrasher, if an exceptionally fine singer, from that of mockingbird.

"The thrasher's song is made up of a long series of short, sparkling phrases given rapidly, sometimes repeated two or three times in quick succession, but as the song goes on it displays a great variety of phrases. To sing, the thrasher mounts to a conspicuous perch where, with the tail pointing to the ground, a characteristic pose of the wrens while singing, he devotes himself to his song, pouring out his loud, spirited concert, like a vocalist singing a solo.

"In Massachusetts the thrasher sings from its arrival late in April, with marked diminution during the nesting season, to the first week in July. After this time it becomes silent and inconspicuous, and we see it chiefly as a flash of cinnamon as it retires into the shrubbery."

Dr. Charles W. Townsend (1924) writes the following appreciative note on the thrasher's song:

The Brown Thrasher, a near relative of the Mockingbird, has a more continuous song and, at its best, one of great beauty and power not marred by harsh or disagreeable notes. His song consists of a series of couplets with here and there an enthusiastic triplet or even a quadruplet. It is an inventive song. He is consistently improvising, but there is often the suggestion of mimicry as the song wanders on and new phrases appear and are repeated. It is rare, however, that one can recognize the source of the mimicry. I have detected the call of the Bob-white and the melody of the Robin, the Bobolink and the Veery, but mimicry is not needed to complete the perfection of his song. He generally avoids vulgar plagiarism, but doubtless profits by the musical suggestions of other birds.

W. L. McAtee (1940b) says: "I was much interested in the opportunity afforded me near Vienna, Va., in June 1940 to make observations on a mimicking thrasher (*Toxostoma rufum*). On a few occasions the song, beginning with imitations of some shrill-noted species suggested that of a Mockingbird until it lapsed into the gutturals and more deliberate phrasing characteristic of the thrasher's music. The birds that were imitated were all species commonly heard on the spot and included the Flicker, Cardinal, Tufted Titmouse, Crested Flycatcher, Yellow-breasted Chat, and Wood Thrush."

Aretas A. Saunders (MS.) says: "The thrasher does not imitate birds frequently, and I believe only a few individuals do so, whereas many catbirds and practically all mockingbirds do so. I have heard the thrasher imitate the phoebe, robin, wood thrush, white-eyed vireo, red-winged blackbird, Baltimore oriole, vesper sparrow, and field sparrow.

"The song of the brown thrasher is similar to those of the mockingbird and catbird. Although the songs of the three eastern species are much alike in form, there are great differences in the seasons of song. The brown thrasher has the shortest period of all. The song ceases, according to my records, on an average date of July 11. The earliest date is July 6, 1921, and the latest July 18, 1940. When nesting begins individuals stop singing, so that the song is never so abundant late in May and in June as it is late in April and early in May. Birds usually sing until the eggs are laid and then cease until the young are out of the nest. Sometimes the second-brood nesting follows the first so quickly that there is no singing between broods.

"The limits of pitch in the songs in my records are B $'$ $'$ to C $'$ $'$ $'$ $'$, one octave and three tones, and curiously just a half tone lower, in both lowest and highest limits, than my catbird records.

"Alarm notes about the nest consist of a loud call much like the sound of a kiss, a whistled call like *teeola*, and a series of harsh, slurred calls, like *teea teea*, repeated six to ten times, gradually becoming higher in pitch and louder." The kiss note is a loud smack, or sucking kiss, something like the sound made by the clicking of a heavy pair of pruning shears, a most startling sound for a bird to make and perhaps effective in frightening away small enemies. The thrasher also makes a local hissing sound about its nest.

Amelia R. Laskey writes to me from Tennessee: "There are lovely 'whisper' songs given in both spring and autumn. The late songs of the season are given in August and September. For September 10, 1935, I have the following note: A brown thrasher sang almost an hour in very soft tone. It consisted mostly of low warblings but often contained phrases similar to spring songs, all very clear, but inaudible a few feet away from the singer. September 14: The 'whisper' songs continue. The bird was perched today in shrubs about 3 or 4 feet from the ground. It sang with closed beak. The song had overtones with undertones of soft warbling, giving the impression at times of a duet."

The soft courtship songs, given while the birds are hunting nesting sites, have been referred to under "Courtship." Mrs. Laskey has observed this twice when she could see both birds.

There are very few birds whose songs can be well expressed, or accurately recalled to mind, by the use of human words or phrases, but it seems to me that the brown thrasher is one of them. The oft-quoted words, "drop it, drop it—cover it up, cover it up—pull it up, pull it up, pull it up," first written, I believe, by Thoreau in his "Walden," as fancied advice to a farmer planting his corn, recall to my mind most vividly the theme and the tempo of the thrasher's song, and I fancy that I can see him perched on the top of a tall birch tree beside the plowed lot.   Many other wordings have been attributed to this versatile bird, but there is not room to quote them all here. One of the most elaborate versions is given by Mrs. H. P. Cook (1929) as one end of a telephone conversation, like this: "Hello, hello, yes, yes, yes, Who is this? Who is this? Well, well, well, I should say, I should say, How's that? How's that? I don't know, I don't know, What did you say? What did you say? Certainly, Certainly, Well, well, well, Not that I know of, Not that I know of, Tomorrow? Tomorrow? I guess so, I guess so, All right, All right, Goodbye, Goodbye."   F. Schuyler Mathews (1921) suggests the following advice to the farmer: "Shuck it, shuck it; sow it, sow it; Plough it, plough it; hoe it, hoe it."   All these interpretations seem to suggest the song that Forbush (1929) describes as "a succession of phrases of two to four syllables, loud, clear, rich, musical and of great variety, each one delivered as a positive statement complete in itself, and unrelated to the rest, with a brief pause after it."   Mrs. Nice (1931) made the following careful observation: "An April 1, 1926 I noted the number of times a Thrasher repeated each phrase and found the scheme less regular than I had suspected; it went thus: 2, 1, 2, 3, 2, 1, 2, 2, 2, 1, 1, 1, 1, 1, 1, 2, 3, 3, 1, 2, 2, 2, 3, 1, 3, 4, 2, 3, 1, 3, 4, 2, 3, 2, 2, 2, 2, 2, 1."

Tilford Moore, of St. Paul, Minn., tells me that, on April 30, 1941, he saw a thrasher singing as it flew between two perches; it did this twice.

Field marks.—A brown thrasher could hardly be mistaken for any other bird within its range.   It is a long, slim bird with a long tail, bright reddish brown above, with two whitish wing bars on each wing, whitish beneath, streaked with blackish, a long bill and glaring, yellow eyes.

Enemies.—Nesting as it does on or near the ground, the eggs and young of the thrasher are particularly vulnerable to the attacks of prowling predators, such as dogs, cats, foxes, raccoons, skunks, weasels, probably squirrels, and snakes.   Crows, blue jays, and perhaps grackles may rob the nests, if they can find them.   Hawks, especially the accipiters, may kill a few adults, though the thrashers are quite expert in dashing into thick bushes and hiding.   I have several records of cowbirds' eggs in thrasher nests, but Dr. Friedmann (1929) calls the thrasher "a decidedly uncommon victim of the Cowbird. This species is the largest passerine bird affected by the parasite, and is the largest bird definitely known to have hatched and reared a young Cowbird. J. A. Allen saw a female Brown Thrasher feeding a nearly full grown Cowbird in Western Iowa in 1868. * * * As far as I know, the late Dr. Allen's observation has remained unique to this day."

Tilford Moore (MS.) saw a thrasher feeding three young cowbirds.

Audubon's spirited plate shows a thrasher's nest being attacked by a blacksnake, with several thrashers rallying to the rescue. He (1841b) reports that the snake was finally killed and one injured bird rescued. I once saw a pair of thrashers making a great fuss around a bunch of oak scrub, where I soon discovered the cause of their anxiety; a large blacksnake was coiled about their nest and had evidently swallowed the eggs or young, as the nest was empty. I tried to kill the snake, but the underbrush was too thick and it escaped.

Thrashers are not immune from parasites, even while still in the egg. Bagg and Eliot (1937) publish the following note from Lewis O. Shelley:

The Thrasher is an uncommon summer resident here [Westmoreland, N. H.], and it is a curious fact that, of all the nests I have seen, each one harbored one or more "wormy" eggs. Outwardly seeming in perfect shape and condition, an egg turned over might reveal a neat round hole, one mm. in diameter, bored in the under side, or more than one such hole. I found that, if blown, the egg-shell crumbled after a short time, due to the lining being eaten together with the yolk and albumen. By dissecting two eggs from a nest of half-fledged young, I found the grubs to be small white oval shapeless forms capable of great elongation when feeding and very closely resembling, while smaller, the *Tachinids* that so commonly sting larvae of various *Saturniidae* caterpillars; but the mature insect is more closely akin, in form, to the *Hymenoptera* or membranous-winged flies, with well-developed maxilliæ, probably the organ wherewith the parasite drills an exit through the egg-shell when the time arrives. It is notable that this parasite differs from the *Tachinids* in that it emerges at perfection and not as a grub.

Harold S. Peters (1936) lists three species of lice, five of mites, two of ticks, and one fly, as external parasites on the brown thrasher.

Winter.—The brown thrasher is a permanent resident throughout the southern portion of its range, but more or less migratory through the greater part of it. Most of the thrashers leave New England during fall, mainly in October, but there are a number of wintering records as far north as Massachusetts.

Henry Nehrling (1893) gives a very good account of its migration and winter haunts:

Unobserved, silent usually from thicket to thicket, and in bushes along streams and rivers, the Brown Thrush migrates southward, ordinarily during October. The Southern States, especially those bordering on the Gulf of Mexico, are the Brown Thrasher's winter quarters. I have found the bird in southeastern Texas from December to March. They usually remain near the water where thicket succeeds thicket. They are especially common where the magnolia, cherry-laurel, holly, dense blackberry and Mexican mulberry bushes, Cherokee roses, and vines of many species, grow. The ground swarms with insects of many kinds, the old leaves cover larvae and snails, and the bushes are rich in berries. In these thickets the Brown Thrush leads a very secluded existence, in company with the Hermit Thrush, Towhee Buntings, White-crowned and White-throated Sparrows, and others. It is here so shy and knows so well how to screen itself from view that it is but rarely seen.

Here, its call-notes are seldom heard. In the dense hammock woods of Florida, it is one of the most abundant winter birds. These woods usually consist of large deciduous and evergreen trees, with an undergrowth of low saw-palmettos, sparkleberry bushes, hollies, smilax, Carolina jasmine, and a host of other tropical species.

DISTRIBUTION

Range.—Southern Canada and the United States.

Breeding range.—The brown thrasher breeds **north** to southeastern Alberta (Red Deer region and Rossyth); southern Saskatchewan (Wiseton and Quill Lake); southern Manitoba (Brandon, Portage la Prairie, and Shoal Lake); southern Ontario (Lake Nipissing and Ottawa); southern Quebec, probably (has bred at Montreal, recorded from Blue Sea Lake); and southwestern Maine (Waterville; has occurred at Dover). **East** to southwestern Maine (Waterville and Portland); and throughout the Atlantic Coast States to southern Florida (Miami and Cutler). **South** to southern Florida (Cutler and Fort Myers); and the Gulf coast to southeastern Texas (Houston). **West** to eastern Texas (Houston, Weatherford, Vernon, and Canadian); eastern Colorado (Colorado Springs, Denver, Loveland, and Walden); eastern Wyoming (Wheatland and Douglas); eastern Montana (Kirby, Billings, and Great Falls); and southeastern Alberta (Warner and Red Deer).

Winter range.—The brown thrasher withdraws in winter to the southern part of its range. At that time it is found **north** to northeastern Texas (Decatur); eastern Oklahoma, rarely (Oklahoma City and Tulsa); Arkansas (Van Buren and Tillar); western Tennessee (Memphis and Nashville, rarely); northern Georgia (Atlanta and Athens); northern South Carolina (Greenwood and Spartanburg); eastern North Carolina (Raleigh and Louisburg); and southeastern Virginia (Bowers Hill, Norfolk County). The species also migrates somewhat southwestward in Texas, reaching Victoria, San Antonio, Kerrville, Austin, and Waco.

Individual birds sometimes spend the winter well north of the normal winter range of the species, and have been found at that season as far north as Laramie, Wyo., southern Michigan, southern Ontario, Montreal, Quebec, and Massachusetts.

The above ranges as outlined apply to the whole species, which has been divided into two subspecies or geographic races. The eastern brown thrasher (*T. r. rufum*) breeds west to Manitoba, eastern Kansas, and Texas; the western brown thrasher (*T. r. longicauda*) breeds from Alberta and Saskatchewan to Colorado and western Kansas.

Migration.—Some early dates of spring arrival are: North Carolina—Hendersonville, March 21. Virginia—Lynchburg, March 20. West Virginia—French Creek, April 7. District of Columbia—**Wash-**

ington, March 19. Pennsylvania—Pittsburgh, April 11. New York—Rochester, April 11. Connecticut—Hartford, April 18. Vermont—Rutland, April 27. Maine—Portland, April 27. Quebec—Montreal, May 8. Ohio—Columbus, March 28. Ontario—Toronto, April 25. Indiana—Bloomington, March 17. Michigan—Detroit, April 7. Illinois—Olney, March 11. Wisconsin—Milwaukee, April 12. Missouri—Kansas City, March 13. Iowa—Iowa City, April 14. Minnesota—St. Cloud, April 13. Manitoba—Winnepeg, May 1. Oklahoma—Caddo, March 8. Kansas—Topeka, April 5. Nebraska—Omaha, April 11. South Dakota—Vermilion, April 27. North Dakota—Charlson, May 10. Saskatchewan—Regina, May 4. Colorado—Denver, May 4. Wyoming—Torrington, May 3. Montana—Great Falls, May 13.

Some late dates of fall departure are: Montana—Big Sandy, September 7. Wyoming—Wheatland, September 15. Colorado—Yuma, September 28. Saskatchewan—Eastend, September 21. North Dakota—Fargo, October 3. South Dakota—Yankton, October 3. Nebraska—Lincoln, October 7. Kansas—Hays, October 30. Manitoba—Aweme, September 21. Minnesota—St. Paul, October 6. Iowa—Sioux City, October 16. Missouri—Columbia, November 9. Wisconsin—Madison, October 14. Illinois—Chicago, October 20. Michigan—Grand Rapids, October 18. Ontario—Ottawa, October 20. Ohio—Toledo, October 26. Kentucky—Danville, October 19. Maine—Winthrop, October 1. Vermont—Wells River, October 3. Massachusetts—Boston, October 16. New York—New York, October 30. Pennsylvania—Germantown, October 23. District of Columbia—Washington, October 15. West Virginia—Bluefield, October 2. Virginia—Lexington, October 10.

Recoveries of banded birds throw some light on individual migrations. The following records are of birds taken during fall and winter in the winter range, all of which had been banded the previous summer on the breeding grounds! Of four taken in North Carolina, two came from Massachusetts and one each from Long Island and New Jersey. The two found in South Carolina came from New Jersey and Maryland. The three found in Georgia were one each from Massachusetts, Long Island, and New Jersey. In Alabama nine have been recovered as follows: one from Ohio, three from Indiana, three from Illinois, and two from Tennessee. The four in Mississippi were: one from South Dakota and three from Illinois. Only two have been recovered in Arkansas, both of which had come from Illinois. The 12 recoveries in Louisiana show the diversity of banding locality: one from New Jersey, one from North Carolina, one from North Dakota one from Wisconsin, one from Indiana, five from Illinois, one from Iowa and one from Tennessee. In Texas have been found one from

Saskatchewan, two from South Dakota, one from Indiana, three from Iowa, and one from Missouri.   An adult banded on Long Island in May 1932 was caught in a rat trap in Texas in March 1940.

Casual records.—An individual was closely studied on August 20, 1940, at Klamath Lake, Oregon.   There are 4 records for California: one at Clear Lake, Lake County, in September 1870; one present at Altadena from December 1, 1932, to late March 1933; one near Hollywood from January 13 to April 17, 1939; and one at Pomona in March and April 1940.   A specimen was collected on December 9, 1935, at Zion Canyon, Utah, after the bird had been observed for several days.   In Arizona a specimen was collected on October 5, 1907, in the foothills of the Huachuca Mountains.   On November 24, 1938, a specimen was collected a few miles north of Albuquerque, N. Mex.   The brown thrasher has been recorded twice at Grand Manan, New Brunswick, and a specimen has been taken at Hamilton, Bermuda.

Egg dates.—Florida: 20 records, March 25 to July 9; 10 records May 3 to 25, indicating the height of the season.

Georgia: 25 records, April 16 to June 20; 18 records, April 22 to May 5.

Illinois: 114 records, April 22 to July 5; 65 records, May 12 to 30.

Massachusetts: 40 records, May 18 to July 8; 26 records, May 20 to 31.

Oklahoma: 16 records, May 4 to 29.

South Dakota: 20 records, April 29 to June 19; 13 records, May 31 to June 8.

TOXOSTOMA RUFUM LONGICAUDA (Baird)

WESTERN BROWN THRASHER

The familiar brown thrasher is one of comparatively few birds whose name has always stood on our list as a binomial, in spite of the fact that the apparent existence of a western race was called to our attention nearly 90 years ago.   Professor Baird (1858) wrote, long years ago: "Among the series before me are several specimens (5651, 5652, 4703) differing in some noticeable points.   They are considerably larger than Pennsylvania ones, with decidedly longer tail and wings. The under parts are more decidedly rufous white; the white band on the wings tinged with the same.   The concealed portion of the quills (including the shafts) is much darker brown, and the shafts of the tail feathers are dark brown, conspicuously different from the vanes. The spots on the breast are considerably darker, showing little, if any, of the reddish brown.   *   *   *   As a strongly marked variety, at least, it may be well to call it *H. longicauda.*"

The type specimen was taken in western Kansas, but the range extends to eastern Colorado and northward to Alberta and Saskatchewan; it winters from Tennessee to Mississippi, Louisiana, and Texas.

It is rather strange that it remained so long unrecognized until Dr. Oberholscr (1938) included it as a "rare winter resident" in Louisiana, and Dr. Wetmore (1939) listed it from Tennessee.

TOXOSTOMA LONGIROSTRE SENNETTI (Ridgway)

SENNETT'S THRASHER

PLATE 71

HABITS

Sennett's thrasher was once supposed to be a variety of our common brown thrasher, which it superficially resembles, but it is now recognized as a northern race of a Mexican species. Its range covers northeastern Mexico, the lower Rio Grande Valley, and as far north along the southern coast of Texas as Nueces County. It differs from our brown thrasher in having the upperparts darker and duller and the sides of the head and neck more grayish. It is somewhat larger than the type race of southeastern Mexico.

We found this thrasher to be an abundant bird in Hidalgo and Cameron Counties, in southern Texas. It was common in the mesquite and cactus chaparral, but still commoner in the dense forests along the resacas or stagnant watercourses near Brownsville; these forests were made up of some large trees, mesquite, huisache, ebony, palms, etc., with a thick undergrowth of many shrubs and small trees, such as granjeno, persimmon, coffee bean, and bush morning-glory.

Nesting.—Dr. Herbert Friedmann (1925) found 25 nests of this thrasher near Brownsville, containing either eggs or young, "pretty evenly scattered through the month" of May. We found a nest there, containing young on May 25, about which the old birds were very solicitous. Two days later, May 27, 1923, in the same dense thickets along a resaca, we found three nests with young and one with three eggs; all these nests were over 4 feet from the ground, and the last was 10 feet up; the nests were very much like those of our common brown thrasher.

George B. Sennett (1878), for whom this thrasher was named, found numerous nests in the above region; he secured a score or more sets of eggs and examined many that he did not take. He writes: "Of those taken, the lowest was 4 feet from the ground and the highest some 8 feet, averaging, I think, 5½ feet. I found their nests in a variety of places—prickly-pear cactus, Spanish bayonet, chaparral, and most commonly in the dense undergrowth under the heavier timber. I saw no nest of this bird in an exposed position 'above the upper branches'. Its usual position is in the very heart of the tree or plant selected, and, like most of the nests of this region, not capable of being detached from the thorny bushes without falling to pieces." He was unable to detect any difference in position or structure between the nests of this species and those of the mockingbird and curve-billed thrasher.

There are four sets of eggs of Sennett's thrasher in my collection, one of which is said to have come from a nest in a mesquite bush, made of thorny twigs and lined with grass and straws.

Eggs.—Sennett's thrasher apparently lays anywhere from two to five eggs to a set, four being the commonest number. What eggs I have seen are practically indistinguishable from those of the brown thrasher; they are ovate in shape and finely sprinkled with "cinnamon" over a bluish-white or greenish-white ground. Mr. Sennett (1878) says: "The usual complement of eggs is four; in fact, I found only one clutch of five. * * * The typical egg has a ground-color of the faintest greenish-white, and is finely speckled all over with brown, the dotting being thickest at the larger end. Several sets were obtained with the ground-color yellowish-white, and so thickly speckled as to have a general color of ochre. One set is nearly pure white, speckled thickly only in the form of a wreath at the larger end, otherwise very sparsely and faintly marked." He says elsewhere (1879) that four eggs "were usually laid in the first clutch in April, while second clutches, late in May, contained generally three."

Dr. J. C. Merrill (1878) writes: "The usual number of eggs is three, often two, more rarely four: the ground-color varies from greenish to reddish-white, more or less thickly sprinkled with reddish and brownish dots and spots. One set is sparingly covered with large clouded blotches, giving the eggs an appearance unusual in this genus."

The measurements of 50 eggs average 27.3 by 19.8 millimeters; the eggs showing the four extremes measure **30.0** by 20.3, 29.5 by **21.3,** 24.4 by 18.8, and 27.4 by **18.3** millimeters.

Plumages.—The sequence of molts and plumages is evidently the same as with the brown thrasher. The young bird in juvenal plumage is much like the adult, but the rump is paler and indistinctly streaked with dusky; the blackish streaking on the under surface is less clearly defined; and the whole body plumage is softer and looser.

Food.—Cottam and Knappen (1939) analyzed the stomach contents of three Sennett's thrashers and reported the following items: Antlions, 4 percent (one bird had consumed eight larvae of these peculiar insects); termites 1 percent; grasshoppers, locusts, etc., 5 percent (some obtained by each bird); stink bugs, 9 percent; miscellaneous true bugs, 6.67 percent, formed a part of each meal; beetles, 30 percent; Tenebrionidae, 30 percent; ants, 13.33 percent; other Hymenoptera, 1 percent; moths, 11.67 percent; miscellaneous insects, 2.67 percent; spiders, 2.67 percent; centipedes, 1.67 percent; fragments of a small frog, 1.33 percent; fruit of hackberry, 7.33 percent; undetermined plant fiber, 2.66 percent. One bird made 23 percent of its last meal on hackberries.

Mr. Sennett (1879) says that "it feeds upon the como and other berries, as well as insects and larvae."

The behavior, voice, and other habits of Sennett's thrasher seem to be similar to those of the brown thrasher, to which it is so closely related. According to Dr. Friedmann (1929), it has occasionally been imposed upon by both the dwarf cowbird and the red-eyed cowbird.

DISTRIBUTION

Range.—Southern Texas and northeastern Mexico.

The range of the species is **north** to southern Texas (Del Rio, Fort Clark, Encinal, and Corpus Christi). **East** to the Gulf coast of Texas (Corpus Christi and Brownsville); Tamaulipas (Altamira); and Veracruz (Jalapa and Córdoba). **South** to central Veracruz (Córdoba and Orizaba); and Mexico (Mexico City). **West** to Mexico (Mexico City); Hidalgo (Jacala); Querétaro (Jalpan); San Luis Potosí (Angostura); Coahuila (Sabinas); and Texas (Del Rio).

The typical subspecies, the long-billed thrasher (*T. l. longirostre*), is found only in Mexico from Querétaro and Veracruz southward. Sennett's thrasher (*T. l. sennetti*), the race occurring in the United States, is found from Texas to San Luis Potosí and Tamaulipas.

Casual record.—A specimen was collected at Barr, Colo., in May 1906.

Egg dates.—Texas: 135 records, April 2 to June 24; 82 records, May 6 to 23, indicating the height of the season.

Mexico: 13 records, March 18 to July 7.

TOXOSTOMA CINEREUM CINEREUM (Xantus)

SAN LUCAS THRASHER

HABITS

John Xantus (1860) described and named this species, which he says is "very similar to *Mimus montanus* [sage thrasher], with longer and more curved bill. The upper parts are grayish brown or cinereous with a faint trace of rufous on the rump. Beneath white with a tinge of brownish yellowish towards the vent; the breast and sides with sharply defined sagittate or subtriangular spots of brown, scarcely elongated on the sides, the shade of brown similar to, but darker than that of the back. The lateral tail feathers are tipped with white, the outer one sometimes edged with the same. There are two narrow dull whitish bands on the wings."

This, the type race of the species, occupies about the southern half of the peninsula of Baja California, ranging north to about latitude 28°. Another race, *mearnsi*, is found farther north on the peninsula, and there is another race in southern Mexico.

William Brewster (1902) says: "It is resident and rather generally distributed in the Cape Region, where, however, it does not seem to occur at elevations much exceeding 3,000 feet. Mr. Frazar found it common in the neighborhood of La Paz and San José del Rancho, somewhat less numerous at Triunfo, and 'very scarce' at San José del Cabo."

Griffing Bancroft (1930) writes: "These thrashers are relatively common wherever there is any considerable growth of small cactuses. Their distribution is in direct proportion to the density of the required growth. It is, therefore, peninsula-wide and unaffected by altitude or climate except in so far as those factors determine the abundance of the cactus. That growth is most dense near the ends of the cross section. It comes to an abrupt termination, together with the habitat of these thrashers, where the sand dune association begins."

In some notes recently sent to me Bancroft says: "Beginning at the northern limit of the Vizcaino Desert the habitat of the San Lucas and Mearns's thrashers skirts the foothills of Sierra San Pedro Mártir, on the westerly side, and just below San Quintín, swings abruptly to the east. South of the Sierra, it reaches both the Pacific and the Gulf coasts, and includes the whole interior, wherever there are suitable associations.

"The territory described is coincidental with the Lower Sonoran Zone in Lower California, except for the extension of the Colorado Desert faunal area. The latter occupies the northeastern corner of Lower California, from the international boundary south to the eastern side of Sierra San Pedro Mártir. It is important to notice that in the entire region occupied by *cinereum*, there is also to be found *Lophortyx californica*. Where that quail is replaced by *Lophortyx gambeli*, there are none of these thrashers.

"It was remarked that, within the area specified, these thrashers are to be found wherever associations are suitable. These might be defined as semiriparian—and that in a country wholly without streams. The birds do not find what they need in or along river beds that are scoured by flash storms. They do like what perhaps are extinct stream beds with a poor apology for soil and with broken lines of scattered mesquite, palo verde, and ironwood; but always a certain amount of minor vegetation.

"On the whole, *cinereum* is probably more closely associated with cholla and garambullo than with any other form of vegetation—and this despite the fact that the bird will follow these cacti up cañon walls, but not onto the open mesa above, and despite the fact that, in many semiriparian associations, the thrasher is nearly as common as it is anywhere in regions totally devoid of any form of cactus."

Nesting.—Mr. Bancroft (1930) says of the nesting habits of this race:

It builds about half its nests in or under mistletoe, therefore most often in mesquite. It uses cholla frequently, the crotch of a cardon, or an arrow tree or other thorny growth. The same pair may utilize, in successive seasons, three or four types of sites. If in a scrub tree it may be anywhere from the heart to the outer branch tips. It will on the average be perhaps ten feet above the ground.

The nests themselves are not very dissimilar though those of the Vizcaino Desert average somewhat larger and they are more substantial than the others. A good understructure of rather short and fine twigs holds a hemispherical cup. This is thicker and deeper than that of the jays and is built of thread-like rootlets. It is of the same material throughout, the only suggestion of a lining being an occasional feather, or bit of lizard skin, or perhaps a pinch of cotton.

Baird, Brewer, and Ridgway (1874) state that, according to Xantus, "their nests were flat structures, having only a very slight depression in or near their centre. They were about 5 inches in diameter, and were very little more than a mere platform."

Since the above was written, Mr. Bancroft has sent me the following notes: "In choosing nesting sites in cholla the Mimidae, as a family, display little individuality. They select healthy plants, apparently to prevent their nests being destroyed by falling segments. They usually, though by no means always, build in the lower half of the bush and make a definite effort to get well inside. They are much more interested in protection from the top and sides than from below. I have noticed virtually no differences in the technique of *cinereum*, *lecontei*, and *curvirostre*.

"The garambullo is a globe-shaped echinocactus typically about 6 feet in diameter. It is composed of innumerable arms 2 or 3 inches thick and spaced about twice that far apart. The thrasher we are discussing usually places its nest halfway from the center to the outside of the bush, and about two-thirds the distance from the bottom to the top. There may be easily six or eight old nests in one plant. It is not at all unusual to find the nest of a wood rat and an occupied thrasher nest in the same garambullo. The inference, of course, is that the rats do not disturb the birds.

"In an ironwood the nest is apt to be 5 or 6 feet above ground, according to the thickness of the foliage, and placed directly against the trunk. In mesquite it usually is placed in the ubiquitous mistletoe and may be easily 15 or 20 feet high.

"It is an old trick, in hunting for the eggs of any thrasher, to follow up the lead given by old nests. Where these are found a search in the vicinity will often reveal the new one. If I should discover an old *cinereum* nest in, for instance, a cholla, I probably will locate other old nests in the immediate vicinity, also in cholla. If so, it would be a waste of time to look through the garambullo or any other growths

in the neighborhood. The particular pair of birds in which I am
interested have a cholla complex which they stubbornly maintain.
Similarly, if my old nests are in garambullo, it would be foolish to
work in cholla, or, if they were on a hillside, it would be useless to
scour the valley. But, until the first of the old nests is noticed, I
have little reason to prefer one form of vegetation over another.

"Nearly all my thrasher sets have been taken either from cholla,
garambullo, or ironwood. I have found the bird nesting, however,
in flatleaf cactus, pitahaya, and mesquite, on the arm of a cardón, in
frutilla, and in other unusual sites. Individually the birds are very
consistent; racially quite the reverse."

Eggs.—Mr. Bancroft (1930) writes:

Nothing has been published contrasting the breeding habits of the two forms
of San Lucas Thrasher, though a comparison should be of interest. The Mearns
San Lucas Thrasher (*Toxostoma cinereum mearnsi*) reaches the height of its
breeding season 6 weeks to 2 months earlier than does *T. c. cinereum.* That
means March and April for one and May and June for the other. They lay
either two or three eggs; I have one record of four for each. The more northerly
bird lays three much more often than two; the converse is true of the other
thrasher. The eggs themselves are not distinguishable. They resemble those
of the Bendire Thrasher (*Toxostoma bendirei*) so closely that identification is
possible only from averages of color and sizes.

Baird, Brewer, and Ridgway (1874) say: "The ground color is
greenish-white, profusely marked with spots of mingled purple and
brown. In others the ground color is bluish-green. In some specimens the spots are of a yellowish-brown, and in some the markings
are much lighter."

The only three eggs that I have examined are ovate, somewhat
elongated, and have a very slight gloss. The bluish-white ground
color is more or less evenly covered with spots and blotches of pale
browns, pale "cinnamon-buff" or very pale "clay color," and with
shell spots of "pale ecru-drab." They are totally unlike the eggs
of other thrashers, except Bendire's, which they closely resemble;
this is not strange, as the two species are closely related. Other observers have noticed this resemblance and their resemblances to eggs
of the mockingbird.

Mr. Bancroft (1930) gives the average measurements of 92 eggs as
27.3 by 19.5 millimeters; among the measurements of 39 other eggs
before me, those showing the four extremes measure **31.0** by **27.0**,
23.9 by 18.8, and 26.7 by **18.0** millimeters.

Plumages.—Ridgway (1907) describes the juvenal plumage as much
like that of the adult but "pileum, hindneck, and back light buffy
grayish brown (between broccoli brown and wood brown), passing
into cinnamon on rump and upper tail-coverts; middle and greater
wing-coverts tipped with cinnamon-buff, the tertials margined ter-

minally with the same; markings on underparts much smaller, more linear."

The markings on the underparts are also more numerous on young birds than on adults. I have no information on the molts, which are probably similar to those of the other desert thrashers. Mr. Brewster (1902) says: "Autumn birds are much more ashy above and buffy beneath than spring specimens. In some of the former, the wing coverts are tipped with rusty, and the flanks, abdomen, crissum, and under tail coverts with light rusty ochraceous. As the season advances, these colors gradually fade, until by April the upper parts become dull ashy brown, while the abdomen and crissum are only faintly tinged with rusty. In June the plumage is excessively worn and faded, and the underparts are essentially uniform soiled white."

Field marks.—Birds of this species are somewhat like sage thrashers in general appearance and behavior, but the sage thrasher is not likely to be seen in Baja California except in winter and is not very common then. The San Lucas thrasher is a much larger bird than the sage thrasher, has a much longer and more curved bill, and has somewhat less white on the tips of the lateral tail feathers.

Enemies.—Mr. Bancroft says in his notes: "The life problem of *cinereum* consists far more in obtaining food than it does in escaping enemies. There is little evidence that the depredations of the latter are a serious deterrent to an increase in the number of birds; if the contrary were true, I am sure that we who are familiar with Lower California would have sensed it. Sharp-shinned and pigeon hawks definitely are not factors. Nor are nocturnal birds of prey, in my studied opinion. I do not see how owls can catch thrashers in appreciable numbers. Certainly not without leaving traces which we could hardly have failed to detect. This same line of thought applies to predatory animals. Furthermore, though there are quite a few varieties, individually their relative number is small and all are utterly dependent on other than avian prey for maintenance.

"The worst offender is the gopher snake, *Pituophis vertebralis.* Occasionally I have found one that has climbed into a garambullo, or even a cardón, in apparent search for eggs or nestlings. However, if these reptiles often met with success, they would leave traces that are noticeably absent, records plain enough for all to read. As a matter of fact, snakes are not at all abundant on the southern deserts; three times only have I seen one engaged in one of these forays."

DISTRIBUTION

Range.—Baja California; nonmigratory.

The species ranges **north** in Baja California to a little north of latitude 31° (San Antonio del Mar and San Telmo). **East** to central

Baja California (San Telmo, San Fernando, and San Jubier) south-ward to about latitude 28°30′ N., thence eastward to the coast of the Gulf of California (Santa Rosalia, San José Island, and La Paz). South to the end of the peninsula (Cape San Lucas). West to the Pacific Ocean (Cape San Lucas, Todos Santos, San Juanico Bay, Santa Catarina Landing, and San Antonio del Mar).

The above range is for the species as a whole, which has been divided into two subspecies. The San Lucas thrasher (*T. c. cinereum*) is found across the peninsula from about latitude 28° 30′ southward; the Mearns's thrasher (*T. c. mearnsi*) occupies the Pacific coast strip, between latitudes about 31° and 28° 30′.

Egg dates.—Baja California: 115 records, March 20 to August 23; 56 records, April 6 to 30, indicating the height of the season.

TOXOSTOMA CINEREUM MEARNSI (Anthony)

MEARNS'S THRASHER

HABITS

A. W. Anthony (1895c) named this northern race and described it as "differing from *H. cinereus* in much darker upper parts, the rump vandyke brown in contrast, more rusty flanks and crissum, much larger and more intensely black spots on the lower parts and in the less curved bill."

The range of this subspecies, so far as known, seems to be confined to the Pacific slope of northern Baja California, from latitude 28°30′ to latitude 31°.

Nesting.—In comparing the nesting (see above) and other habits of the two Lower California forms of this species, Griffing Bancroft (1930) says:

The nesting of the two birds presents the strongest antitheses. The Mearns, with but two exceptions noted, builds in cactus. There are many varieties of this plant within its range, and they are used indifferently, flat leaf, cholla of two or three species, and especially the pitahaya and garambulla. It is to be noted, however, that a given individual pair of these birds adheres uncompro-misingly to one species of cactus. If, in the breeding season, you find an old thrasher nest and search the surrounding country you are apt to find another old nest in every satisfactory plant of the species which contained the first. If you have sufficient patience and luck you will also find an occupied nest in the same kind of plant. The normal site is on the lower and outer branches, say of a cholla, well protected from above and 3 feet off the ground. In pitahaya such sites are impracticable but are approximated as closely as possible.

Eggs.—He says that the eggs, more often three than two, are indis-tinguishable from those of the San Lucas thrasher or Bendire's thrasher. The measurements of his 47 eggs average 28.1 by 19.9 milli-meters. J. Stuart Rowley (1935) gives the measurements of the largest and the smallest egg in his series as 32.0 by 21.0 and 25.0 by

20.0 millimeters. The measurements of 40 eggs before me average 27.7 by 19.7 millimeters; the eggs showing the four extremes measure 32.0 by 21.0, 27.1 by 21.1, 24.3 by 19.1, and 27.6 by 18.6 millimeters.

Behavior.—Comparing the behavior of the two races, Mr. Bancroft (1930) says: "In its conduct in the field the Mearns Thrasher is more shy, by far. It seldom allows a close approach and I have never known one to betray its nest. The Cape bird depends more on concealment and is not notably wary. It frequently hovers about its nest, and on many occasions I have flushed sitting birds at a range of a few feet. These characteristic traits harmonize with the preferred associations."

Mr. Anthony (1895c) also found the northern race remarkably shy, making it almost impossible to secure specimens. He writes: "On June 13 I was stalking a herd of antelope on the San Carlos mesa, near the coast, and had prostrated myself under a large cholla cactus to wait for the game, which was slowly feeding toward me; and in this uncomfortable position I spent about half an hour, during which not less than half a dozen of these usually shy Thrashers took up stations on adjoining cacti, within 15 yards, showing great curiosity and making frequent remarks, uncomplimentary, no doubt, on the new species of lizard they had found, but always ready to drop out of sight at the first movement on my part."

I can find no further information on the behavior of either race of this species, and nothing at all on their food or voices.

TOXOSTOMA BENDIREI (Coues)

BENDIRE'S THRASHER

PLATES 71–73

HABITS

Bendire's is one of several species of thrashers that breed in our southwestern deserts. The Southwest is rich in species and subspecies of this genus, but they all occupy rather limited ranges, as compared with our wide-ranging and homogeneous brown thrasher. Bendire's thrasher is one of the most limited in its range, breeding only in southeastern California, Arizona, southwestern New Mexico, and northern Sonora. And, according to my experience, it is not very common anywhere, except perhaps in the low, flat country around Tucson and the foothills of the southern Catalinas. It has been reported as locally common in the Lower Sonoran valleys in other parts of Arizona and western New Mexico and in some places up to 4,000 or even 6,500 feet in the mountains. There are scattering records from northeastern and northwestern Arizona.

Spring.—W. E. D. Scott (1888a) writes: "On the plains about Tucson and to the southward, this species is resident, but even here there seems to be a very considerable migration, as the birds are much more common in the spring and during the breeding season than during the late fall and winter months. * * *

"In the foothills of the Catalinas the birds were not resident but were present for about 8 months of the year, and were quite common during the breeding season, though they did not range above 4,000 feet. Here they arrive early in March, the 7th of that month being the earliest record made, and begin mating and nesting almost at once."

Herbert Brown (1901) says: "During the winter months an occasional one can be found in their usual habitat, but, as a whole, they go south bodily on the first fall storm of wind and rain. The return migration is more gradual, but always of uncertain date. I have known the difference of a full month to exist in their homecoming in two succeeding years. This was probably due to climatic conditions further south." He gives February 9 as the earliest known date of arrival, when "they were gathered in small flocks and were not mated."

Nesting.—Our experience with the nesting of Bendire's thrasher in Cochise and Pima Counties, Ariz., was limited to three nests, one found April 26, 1922, with young, and two, found on May 23 and June 11, with eggs. So I prefer to quote from some of the excellent accounts that have been published. Herbert Brown (1901) gives the fullest account; he says: "The first week in March will frequently find them nesting, and the middle of April preparations for a second brood are well under way, but, taken over a long series of years, the beginning of April generally sees them busy with their first house making. I have never been able to fully determine the exact number of families raised by one pair of birds during a season. Of two there can be no question, but a third is in doubt, although I have known the nesting season to last three full months and a half. To be more exact, February 24 is the earliest and July 18 the latest I have in mind for 1 year.".

He has measured at least 200 nests and gives these measurements and other data on 17 of them; the highest of these, there recorded, was about 12 feet from the ground in a mesquite; of the others, in tasajas and chollas, two were 5 feet, one only 22 inches, and the remainder between 3 and 4 feet above the ground; the measurements of these 17 nests varied greatly; the diameter of the nest proper was 6 to 7 inches, but as much as 11 or 12 inches over-all, including the foundation twigs; the inside diameter varied $2\frac{1}{4}$ to $3\frac{1}{2}$ inches, the inside depth $1\frac{1}{2}$ to $3\frac{1}{2}$, and the over-all depth 3 to 9 inches. He observed that—

the larger portion of the nests are in tasajas. This is a species of cactus for which, for the want of a better name, I am obliged to use that of the Mexicans. The word means "dry or jerked beef" which in color and shape the tasaja somewhat resembles. The spines, although innumerable, are short and the branches spreading and open. The cholla is the characteristic cactus of the desert. It is a mass of barbed spines and is the favorite nesting place of *H. palmeri*, but not of *H. bendirei*. Taking 50 nests in succession 34 of them were placed in tasajas, 11 in chollas, 3 in tesota bushes, 1 in a mesquite tree and one in a willow tree. These results are from the Fort Lowell district. In other sections of country less characteristic of the cacti I have found them largely inclined to tree nesting, but never at any great height from the ground. This was Capt. Bendire's experience also. The highest I ever saw one placed was in a willow about 20 feet up. I also saw one in a tasaja the bottom of which was not more than 6 inches from the ground. * * *

The nest is small and daintily constructed by comparison with those of other thrashers. It is less compactly built than that of *H. palmeri*, but the manner of construction is common to all Arizona thrashers. There is an external nest of sticks, few or many, the nest proper of grass and lined with any soft material conveniently obtainable.

M. French Gilman (1909) has published a comprehensive paper on the thrashers of Arizona, in which he says of this species:

A great range in choice of nesting sites was noticed. Of the thirty-nine nests, thirteen were in *Lycium* bushes; three in mistletoe, in mesquite and catsclaw (*Acacia greggii*); three in palo verde, two in catsclaw, two in *Sarcobatus*, one in screw-bean, and one in a salt-bush. The average height was 5 feet, and the extremes 3 feet and 10 feet. Two nests, deserted as far as the thrashers were concerned, were found, each containing an egg of Gambel Partridge. * * *

The nests are much finer in material and workbirdship than those of most thrashers. They are smaller, more compactly built and very symmetrical in their cupped shape. Finer twigs are used in the outside and they are fitted closely together. The lining is variously composed of horse-hair, thread, twine, pieces of cloth, grass, weeds, rootlets, fine bark, wool and cotton from bed-quilts, etc., etc. Most of them contain more or less horsehair, and if near an Indian home, as is often the case, twine and material from the bed covers enters largely into the lining. One nest I noticed was built against a Verdin's nest, the wall of the latter in fact forming part of one side of the thrasher's nest. Both nests contained eggs, so the proprietors were on very neighborly terms, even tho I could discover no doorway between the apartments.

F. W. Braund has sent me the data on a nest he found near Tucson on May 7, 1935, that was lined with creosote blooms, weed stems, and seed pods.

Dr. Friedmann (1934) mentions only one case where Bendire's thrasher has been a host to the dwarf cowbird.

Eggs.—Mr. Brown (1901) has seen so many eggs of Bendire's thrasher, that I cannot do better than to quote his full description of them as follows:

With rare exceptions four eggs are the maximum number laid. I have examined probably 500 nests, two only of which contained more. They had five eggs each. Four is not an unusual number, but three is a normal set. * * *

The ground color in the majority of the 148 specimens varies from a pale gray green to a greenish white, the former predominating. In a single set it is a clear pale green with a bluish tinge. Most of the eggs are irregularly spotted and blotched with well-defined markings of tawny ecru drab, fawn color and vinaceous buff. These markings are generally heaviest about the larger end of the egg; in some specimens the spots run longitudinally. In this type about three-fourths of the eggs examined can be included. They resemble, in the style of marking, the eggs of *Mimus polyglottos*, somewhat, although the eggs themselves look quite different. In about 20 percent the ground color is somewhat clouded over and partially obscured by the markings, which are finer, less pronounced, giving the egg a uniform pearl gray and pale greenish gray appearance till closely looked at. In an occasional specimen, the markings are simply fine pinpoints, as in the smaller spotted eggs of *Harporhynchus rufus*.

In about 5 percent of the eggs, the ground color is grayish or pinkish white with scarcely a trace of green, and the egg is heavily and uniformly spotted with longitudinal markings of pale salmon color and lavender, bearing a striking resemblance to some eggs of *Myiadestes townsendi*, excepting in size. A single egg has a distinct wreath about the larger end.

The shape of these eggs varies a great deal, the most common form being an elongate ovate, varying from this to ovate, short ovate, and elliptical ovate.

The measurements of 50 eggs in the United States National Museum average 25.6 by 19.1 millimeters; the eggs showing the four extremes measure 29.7 by 19.6, 28.5 by 21.8, 23.4 by 18.8, and 25.4 by 17.8 millimeters.

Young.—No one seems to have determined the period of incubation for this thrasher or the length of time that the young remain in the nest, though Bendire's probably does not differ materially from other desert thrashers in these matters. This species is so shy about its nest that the care and feeding of the young are not easily observed, and nothing seems to have been recorded on this subject. As mentioned above, two broods in a season seems to be the rule, with sometimes a third brood. Mr. Gilman (1915) noted that one pair of birds brought off a brood of young about the first of May, a second brood left the nest on July 6, and on July 25 the female was incubating on a third set of eggs.

Mr. Scott (1888a) says: "The young birds, as soon as they are fully grown, begin to congregate in companies, often being associated with one or two *H. curvirostris palmeri* and *H. crissalis*. I have seen forty or fifty young Thrashers, mostly *bendirei*, together in such a flock in late May and early June. At such times the birds seek a somewhat higher altitude, as high as five thousand feet, and effect thickets of low oaks and juniper."

Plumages.—Young Bendire's thrashers in juvenal plumage differ from the breeding adults, which are then quite worn and faded, in having the upper parts, especially the rump, tinged with reddish brown, the secondaries and tertials broadly edged and tipped with buffy brown, the greater wing coverts broadly tipped with "cinnamon-buff," and the tail feathers (except the central pair) tipped with buffy brown. In very young birds the underparts are more or less tinged with "cinnamon-buff," most strongly on the flanks and crissum, which fades out to dull white in older birds; there is much individual variation in the amount and distribution of the grayish brown spots or streaks on the under parts; in some these markings cover all the breast and abdomen, while in others they are confined to the breast or only to the sides.

The time at which the postjuvenal molt takes place varies with the dates on which the two broods were hatched, but a partial molt, involving the contour plumage and the wing coverts, produces a first-winter plumage practically indistinguishable from that of the fall adult.

Adults have a complete postnuptial molt, beginning late in July and continuing through August. Adults in fresh fall plumage are darker and grayer above and the spots on the chest are darker than in spring birds; wear and fading produce paler spotting on the underparts, the spots becoming faint in many cases before summer.

Food.—No very comprehensive study of the food of Bendire's thrasher seems to have been made and very little has appeared in print about it. Like other thrashers, it evidently lives largely on insects, such as beetles, caterpillars, and other larvae and pupae, which it obtains mainly on or near the ground. William L. Engels (1940) says: "The Bendire thrasher, like the brown, spends much time on the ground while foraging. Near Coolidge, Arizona, one was watched from an automobile as it searched for food on the shoulder of the road, hammering vigorously at the ground with its relatively short, slightly curved bill. Another, seen in a cultivated field beside a patch of mesquite in which its nest was situated, was running along between plant rows, occasionally jumping up into the air as if catching insects." Two that he shot, a pair coming to their nest, were "found to be carrying small, green, wormlike larvae."

Behavior.—Mr. Scott (1888a) regarded this thrasher as "at all times shy and wary and difficult to approach, even when nesting." But Mr. Gilman (1915) says: "The Bendire Thrasher is one bird that from all indications takes kindly to settlement. These birds nest near houses, on which they perch to sing, come into the yards, and seem fearless if not molested. If their natural shelter is cleared up they take kindly to artificial or planted growth and I believe will persist in the face of civilization. All this of course, provided that they receive some measure of protection and encouragement."

Mr. Engels (1940) gives us some information on the general behavior of this thrasher on the ground and in the air. One that he watched on a creosote-bush flat was followed for several hundred yards:

It walked or ran along, now slowly, now rapidly, in and out among the creosote bushes, sometimes flying up into a low bush, then directly down again to the ground. Gait and carriage in these birds were essentially as in the brown thrasher.

Most Bendire thrashers seen, when not perched, were moving on the wing in smooth easy flight.   A. H. Miller (MS field notes, 1936) finds their flight remindful of that of mockingbirds.   Flight is their usual method of locomotion; time and again they were seen flying from tree to tree at heights of from 25 to 50 feet, and, once, for a distance of more than a quarter-mile.   This behavior was especially noticeable when the bird was being pursued; before I could maneuver myself into shotgun range, the bird would fly off to some more distant perch.   A bird suddenly approached, while on the ground, flew directly up into the top of an adjacent mesquite about 30 feet high.

Voice.—Like all the thrashers, Bendire's is no mean singer; it is almost equal to the brown thrasher and suggestive of even the mockingbird.   Mr. Gilman (1909) praises it in the following words:

As for singing, the Bendire has them all beaten.   The others are fine singers indeed, but their repertoire is limited.   Not so with Bendire.   No two seem to sing exactly alike and some of the songs are quite distinct from others.   Not only in variety of notes but in arrangement, are differences noticed.   He is a more constant singer than the others and I frequently discovered a nest by the song of the bird.   The earliest date of singing was January 3, and I could hardly believe at first that Bendire was the performer.   It was a low warbling song with a decided sparrow "burr" to it.   I approached as near as the bird would allow, but could not be sure that he was the singer as no throat movement could be detected.   When the bird flew, the song ceased and began again after he perched on a post.   I repeated this maneuver several times before I was convinced that Bendire was warbling.   Next evening I walked under a mesquite tree containing the singer and obtained a good close view of him and his performance.

As the breeding season approached they sang more often, the song becoming louder and with less of the burr, in fact more like the typical thrasher song, if such there be.   The songs were all very pleasing, but the variations were often puzzling at first.   Whenever I heard a new strain I said, "only another Bendire tuning up."   They kept up the music till late in June and occasionally a song could be heard all summer and up to the last of September.

Field marks.—Bendire's might easily be confused with Palmer's thrasher in the field, but the former is browner above, the spots on the chest are smaller and more distinct, and there is more white on the tail tips.   Mr. Gilman (1909) says that Bendire's has a smoother, evener flight than the somewhat jerky flight of Palmer's thrasher. Bendire's can be distinguished easily from the crissal and LeConte's thrashers by its comparatively short, straight bill and by the grayish-brown spots on its breast; the latter two have much longer, curved bills and unspotted breasts.

Winter.—Authorities seem to differ as to the extent of the migration and the winter range of Bendire's thrasher.   Probably there is usually a short migration in fall from most of the range of the species. Some individuals evidently remain on or near their breeding grounds all winter, but they seem to be very scarce or entirely absent from many of their summer haunts at that season.   Their migration route is not long, and they are absent for only a short period late in fall and early in winter.   Their winter range extends only as far south as southern Sinaloa.

Range.—Southwestern United States and northwestern Mexico.

Breeding range.—The Bendire's thrasher breeds **north** to southern California (Victorville, Cima, and Rock Spring); central and northeastern Arizona (Beale Spring, Klethla Valley, Navajo County, and Chin Lee). **East** to northeastern Arizona (Chin Lee and St. Michaels); extreme western New Mexico (Catron County, 25 miles east of Springerville, Arizona, and Rodeo, Hidalgo County); and northwestern Chihuahua (Sierra Carrizalillo). **South** to northwestern Chihuahua (Sierra Carrizalillo); and central Sonora (Tecoripa and Guaymas). **West** to western Sonora (Guaymas, Artiz, and Santa Ana); Arizona (Menager's Dam, Gunsight, Gilabend, and Congress Junction); and southern California (Palm Springs and Victorville).

Winter range.—The winter range of the Bendire's thrasher cannot be exactly defined on the basis of available records. It withdraws from the northern part of its range, but is resident in southern Arizona, probably north about to the Gila River (the northernmost winter record is Phoenix). It moves southward to southern Sonora (Camoa, Tesia, and Alamos) and to southern Sinaloa (Escuinapa).

Casual records.—In a suburb of Los Angeles, Calif., an individual was picked up on September 10, 1912. The only record for Nevada is of two individuals seen and one collected on May 16, 1939, near Delmar, Lincoln County. There are three records for Utah; a nest and eggs from the shore of Utah Lake south of Lehi on April 26, 1932; a single bird seen and collected 10 miles southeast of Escalente, Garfield County, on May 9, 1937; and two specimens collected and other birds seen on July 4, 1927, in Monument Valley where they may be of regular occurrence. A specimen was collected in El Paso County, Colo., at Austins Bluffs, on May 8, 1882.

Egg dates.—Arizona: 143 records, February 21 to August 1; 76 records, March 16 to April 15, indicating the height of the season.

TOXOSTOMA CURVIROSTRE PALMERI (Coues)

PALMER'S THRASHER

PLATES 74–77

HABITS

When I did my field work in southern Arizona, in 1922, Palmer's thrasher was regarded as the breeding form of this species all across the southern part of the State. At that time, J. Eugene Law (1928) had not called attention to the fact that the form breeding east of the Santa Rita Mountains in southeastern Arizona and southern New Mexico is *celsum* and not *palmeri*. But, as our field work covered much of both Cochise and Pima Counties, we were able to make the acquaintance of both forms.

Harry S. Swarth (1929) confirms Mr. Law's diagnosis by saying: "Differences between the two lots, east and west of the Santa Ritas, are, in most cases, fairly apparent, especially so in the freshly assumed fall plumage. The eastern birds (*curvirostre*) are rather more slaty above, have fairly well marked white wing bars, have sharply defined white tips to the outer rectrices, and the breast spots are large and fairly well defined. The western birds (*palmeri*) are browner above, lack the wing bars, have the tail spots obscurely indicated or else entirely wanting, and have the breast spots less distinct."

The range of Palmer's thrasher covers a large part of southern and western Arizona, in the Lower Sonoran Zone, north to the central western part, east to the Santa Rita and Catalina Mountain region, and south to Sonora and northern Chihuahua in Mexico, mostly below 3,000 feet elevation. It is one of the most abundant and characteristic birds of these arid plains, where the hard, sun-baked soil supports only a scattered, open growth of small mesquites, greasewood and creosote bushes, salt bushes and other thorny shrubs, with an occasional ironwood tree, a screwbean, or a paloverde, gorgeous in spring with its solid mass of yellow blossoms. But the most interesting features of these desert mesas are the varied forms of cacti that are scattered through this open growth of unattractive, low shrubs that nowhere hide the bare ground. There are several species of chollas, or closely allied forms, of varied shapes and colors with blossoms of different hues, the huge barrel cactus that may someday slake a traveler's thirst, the long, slender stems of the ocotillo with their flaming tips, and, here and there, the picturesque, towering candelabra of the saguaros punctuate the landscape. Here the Palmer's and Bendire's thrashers find a congenial home, make their nests in the spiny chollas, and vie with the other desert dwellers for the scanty living that such a forbidding region affords.

But these thrashers are not wholly partial to the open desert mesas; we frequently saw them about the ranches and often near houses, where they could find a solitary cholla in which to build their nest. Mr. Swarth (1920) says that "about Phoenix and Tempe it is, perhaps, the most abundant single species of bird, and it even ventures into the towns where sheltering brush piles or thickets remain in vacant lots or along roadsides. Cultivated farm lands hold little attraction for the thrasher, however, and it is rarely seen about such places."

Courtship.—Palmer's thrashers are permanent residents in southern Arizona and are probably more or less permanently mated; at least the pairs seem to remain together during winter. Their courtship seems to be a very simple affair just preceding nest-building. Earle F. Stafford (1912) has published an interesting account of a pair that spent the winter about his ranch. On February 14, an appropriate date, he noticed signs of courtship: "One sidled along the fence, and the other followed at a respectful distance, singing a little, *sotto voce.* They were constantly in company after this, having little pursuits and 'tiffs,' and the male, after two weeks of silence, sang oftener and with greater force than before." On the 16th they started gathering nesting material, but they went about it in an "easy and desultory fashion." When he left the ranch on March 9, no eggs had been laid, though the female had been seen on the nest repeatedly.

Nesting.—All the nests we found, with one exception, were in chollas, 3 to 5 feet above ground; one was in that dense woolly cholla *Opuntia bigelovii,* the most thickly branched and most densely covered with vicious, barbed spines of all the chollas; how the birds can pick their way into it and out again is a mystery. In one nest, we were surprised to find three eggs of Gambel's quail. The only nest that was not in a cholla was placed 5 feet from the ground between the three branches of a soapweed yucca. The nests were all made of coarse and fine thorny twigs, rather loosely laid, and were lined with fine grasses and in some cases with a little horsehair. Sometimes there were one or more old nests in the same cholla with the new one; M. French Gilman (1909) shows a photograph of a cholla only 5 feet high that had been a favorite nesting site, for it contained five old cactus wrens' nests and four old nests and one new nest of Palmer's thrasher. W. L. Dawson (1923) states that his son counted as many as 14 old nests, or their remnants, in one bush.

We were not the only ones to find eggs of Gambel's quail in the old nests of Palmer's thrasher; Mr. Gilman (1909) reports a nest that held 13 eggs of this quail; and F. C. Willard (1923) found a quail sitting on a set of 17 eggs, and shows a photograph of the nest and eggs.

In this same paper Mr. Willard states that he saw a Palmer's thrasher fly from a hole 15 feet up in a large sycamore, where he found a nest full of young thrashers.

All observers seem to agree that the favorite nesting sites of Palmer's thrasher are in chollas. Mr. Gilman (1909) says:

Of 27 nests found, 11 were in the cholla; 7 in the jujube, about as spiny as any cactus; 4 were in mistletoe of mesquite and cottonwood; 2 in Lycium, 2 in mesquite, and 1 in a clematis vine trailing over a shrub. The average distance from the ground was 6½ feet, and the extremes were 2½ feet and 10 feet. * * * The nest is a bulky affair but well built. The nest proper is 3 or 4 inches deep, inside measurement, and above this is a superstructure or rim from 2 to 3 inches high. Several nests seen measured over 6 inches deep. Rather coarse twigs are used in the construction and the lining is mostly of rootlets, though some fine bark, hair or feathers may also be seen in some of the nests. The bird is not too proud to use a foundation already laid, as three nests were found built right on top of old Cactus Wrens' nests.

Herbert Brown (1892) refers to the thorny protection of the thrasher's nest, probably in *Opuntia bigelovii,* that exceedingly bristling cholla, as—

ten million of cambric needles, set on hundreds of loosely jointed spindles, woven so closely together as to apparently defy the penetration of a body however small, but the thrashers go in and out and up and through them with the ease of water running through a sieve. In some convenient fork, on a limb against the bole of the bush, or in a cavity formed by the pendent stems of the plant, the nest is most commonly built. All the spines in the vicinity of the nest are pulled off for the better protection of the young. This does not, however, always save them as I have found them once in a while, tangled and dead in the terrible burs. * * *

One nest was built on the ruins of three others and probably represented as many successive broods, and gave the interior of the cholla the appearance of having been solidly filled in with dead sticks. Exterior diameter of the nest 20 inches, depth 36 inches, cavity across the top 4½ inches, bottom 3 inches, depth 6 inches, but lined only about 4 inches up with baling rope, hog bristles and grass. * * * In the spring of 1889 I noted several nests made almost entirely of flowering weeds. This came from the nature of the vegetation in the immediate vicinity of the cholla belt in which the nests were placed.

Eggs.—Most Palmer's thrashers' nests contain three eggs, the usual complement, but four are not rare, two are frequent, and sometimes a single egg is incubated and hatched. Fourteen of 27 nests examined by Mr. Gilman (1909) contained three eggs each, two had four eggs, and the rest held two or one. There are 21 sets of eggs of this thrasher in the J. P. Norris collection, 15 of three, 5 of four, and 1 of two.

The eggs vary in shape from ovate to short-ovate or elliptical-ovate, and they are not glossy. There is very little variation in color or markings; the ground color varies from pale bluish green, "dull opaline green," to pale greenish blue, "etain blue," or even to paler shades of these colors. The markings usually consist of minute specks or fine pinpoints of pale brown, "cinnamon-rufous," evenly distributed over the entire egg, but rarely more thickly at the larger end. Still more rarely there are somewhat larger spots of darker brown, such as "burnt umber." There is considerable variation in size; the measurements of 40 eggs, in the United States National Museum, average 29.3 by 20.2 millimeters; the eggs showing the four extremes measure **32.5** by 20.0, 31.0 by **25.5**, **25.9** by 19.8, and 26.4 by **18.3** millimeters, a variation of about seven millimeters, or nearly 25 percent, in both length and breadth.

Young.—The period of incubation is said to be about 13 days, and the young remain in the nest 14 to 18 days. The male shares with his mate the duties of incubation and the care of the young; they are a devoted pair and equally devoted as parents. Almost always two broods, and sometimes three, are raised in a season. If the eggs are taken from a nest, a second set will be laid within about two weeks; and within two or three weeks after the first brood leaves the nest, either the same nest, or another nearby, will be used to start the second brood. Although the nesting season is a long one, it seems unlikely that a third nesting would be attempted, unless one of the earlier attempts had been broken up.

A. L. Rand (1941) has published a most interesting and very extensive paper based on his studies, near Tucson, Ariz., of a large number of young thrashers of this species, both in the wild and in captivity, from the time of hatching until about 90 or 96 days old. The reader is referred to this paper for details, as only a few of the many interesting facts and reactions can be mentioned in the limited space available here. He says that "in common with most passerine birds the young thrasher hatches in a blind, nearly naked condition; has a tendency to keep right side up and open its mouth for food in response to a wide variety of stimuli; it is utterly dependent on the adult. In the course of 5 or 6 weeks its physical equipment and its behavior develop so that it can survive independently, finding its own food and escaping its enemies."

He gives a detailed account, day by day, of the physical growth and the development of behavior of the young bird during the 18 days that it is in the nest. For the first 5 days the young are blind and helpless. On the sixth day, the eyes can be widely opened and the contour feathers are just breaking the skin; the rectrices are beginning to break out of their sheaths. On the fourteenth day the young bird is well feathered, and may leave the nest on or before the eighteenth day. "Two young of one nest, usually one a day older than the other, often leave the nest a day apart, the stimulus causing one young to leave not causing the other to do so. Their physical equipment is such that they can hop and run well, but their wings only help them to flutter down at a steep angle. * * * When young thrashers in captivity were beginning to feed themselves to a considerable extent (after about 30 days), they still begged occasionally. * * * By the 40th day they became completely independent and somewhat shy of persons."

He conducted a number of interesting experiments to determine the reaction of young thrashers to various stimuli, including mammals, predatory birds, and reptiles introduced in the cages. The thrashers usually showed mild interest and sometimes fled, but they apparently had not learned to recognize dangerous enemies. This section of his paper is well worth reading.

Plumages.—The Brewster collection, in the Museum of Comparative Zoology in Cambridge, contains a large series of specimens of this thrasher, including several in juvenal plumage. I cannot improve on Mr. Brewster's (1882a) own words in describing some of them. One young bird, "although well feathered, has the wings and tail undeveloped, and was taken from the nest. Its entire upper plumage is rusty brown with a chestnut tinge which deepens on the rump

and outer webs of the secondaries to decided chestnut brown. The
general coloring of the under parts is pale fulvous with a strong tinge
of rusty chestnut across the breast, along the sides, and over the anal
region and crissum. The breast is obsoletely spotted, but the plumage
elsewhere, both above and below, is entirely immaculate."

Several other young birds, somewhat older, show varying degrees
of intensity of the rusty tinge and its distribution, and considerable
variation in the amount and distribution of the spotting on the breast.
He continues:

> Several of these young birds are so nearly similar to specimens of *H. bendirei*
> in corresponding stages that they can be separated only with great difficulty. The
> stouter bill and entirely black lower mandible of *palmeri* may, however, always
> be depended upon as distinguishing characters; and, moreover, the pectoral
> spotting of *bendirei* is usually (but not invariably) finer and sharper, and the
> rusty tinge above paler and less extended.
>
> The adults present a good deal of variation, most of which is apparently
> seasonable. Winter specimens have the lower abdomen, with the anal region and
> crissum, rich rusty-fulvous, while the markings beneath are similar in character
> to those of true *curvirostris* and the spots equally distinct, numerous and widely
> distributed. With the advance of the season, and the consequent wear and tear
> of the plumage, the spots gradually fade or disappear. Indeed some of the June
> specimens are absolutely immaculate beneath, although most of them, like
> Mr. Ridgway's types have a few faint markings on the abdomen. In this
> condition the general coloring is also paler and grayer, and the fulvous of the
> crissum and neighboring parts often entirely wanting.

The postnuptial molt of adults, and apparently the postjuvenal
molt of young birds, begins late in July and continues through August;
old birds look very much worn, bedraggled, and faded at this season.

Food.—The food of Palmer's is very similar to that of the other
thrashers, including numerous insects and their larvae as well as
various fruits and berries. Its feeding methods remind one of our
eastern brown thrasher. It is fond of water and comes freely to
bird baths and other places where it can find water about houses, as
well as resorting to open water holes. Florence Merriam Bailey
(1923) writes:

> One was seen drinking from a dripping faucet and another seen perched on
> top of a viznaga reaching down with its long curved bill digging out the shining
> black seeds and the moist pulp which the House Finches had also found a ready
> source of both food and moisture. A Thrasher accidentally caught in a trap,
> January 28, had an empty crop but a gizzard full of seeds of cactus (*Opuntia*
> sp. ?), and the shrubbery hackberry (*Celtis pallida*), a few oat shells, one
> grain, a few insect remains, apparently ants, and some gravel. One of the
> birds was seen, February 3, walking in the mesquite pasture, flipping up cow-
> chips as he went, evidently looking for insects or other toothsome morsels below—
> a scorpion had been found under one of them.

Mr. Stafford (1912) says: "I have seen my birds spend much time
in the yard half squatting, with braced feet, digging holes of considerable depth (some as deep as 2½ inches) with quick, powerful blows of

their sickle-like beaks; or casting aside the mould and parched soil with nervous sidewise thrusts, in search of grubs. On those parts of the desert, too, affected by the birds the ground usually shows plentiful signs of their probing."

Mr. Brown (1892) says that "they press their tails firmly against the ground, after the manner of the woodpecker; if the earth be dry and sandy, a perfect fusillade of dirt is kept up. The force of the blow is downward and toward the body, but occasionally to clean the sand out they strike sideward blows, and dirt flies for a foot in all directions."

Behavior.—One cannot watch a Palmer's thrasher long without being impressed with its decided resemblance to the brown thrasher in all its movements. It runs rapidly or hops lightly over the ground, or skims swiftly through the air from one low bush to another, seldom rising high in the air, and, if pursued, flies away or dashes to seclusion in the thickest shubbery it can find. Its method of foraging on the ground is much like that of our eastern bird, as it tosses the leaves and litter aside with its bill while hunting for food under trees and bushes.

Mr. Engels (1940) writes:

The gait of the Palmer thrasher is not smooth, but rather jerky; the bird gives the appearance of being set back on its haunches and of being stiff legged. The jerkiness of the gait is most in evidence when the bird is moving directly toward or directly away from the observer; the stiff-leggedness and the peculiar set of the body on the legs are best observed in profile. I do not mean to intimate that the Palmer thrasher is not at ease on the ground, but only that in its walking and running its action is not so smooth as that of other thrashers. * * *

The Palmer thrasher is entirely like the brown and the Bendire in frequency of flight. In 16 days on the Arizona deserts in 1936, I saw at least 100 Palmer thrashers and followed many of them. Their reaction to pursuit was invariably the same; they moved away by flying, at a good height and often for rather long distances. On a cut-over mesquite flat one bird was followed for more than a half-mile, and in the course of its flight it entered and left four or five mesquites in succession without once descending to the ground. Brooding birds were repeatedly flushed from their nests in the cholla cactus; they always left on the wing and continued in flight to some distant perch.

Some observers have referred to this thrasher as shy, and it may be so in its wilderness haunts, though we did not notice that it was any more shy than the average wild bird; and in the defense of its nest and young it is sometimes quite bold and fearless. About the ranches, where it is not molested, it even becomes rather tame. Mr. Gilman (1909) says:

The Palmer and Bendire seem naturally much tamer than the others and come about homes quite frequently. All summer I placed pieces of watermelon in the shade of a school building—vacation time and no children about—and both these thrashers came freely and ate with a family of scolding Cactus Wrens. But never a Crissal appeared. The Palmer and Crissal dug in the garden and also ate wheat planted nearby, and frequented the barn and well. They would come and drink from an iron kettle placed on the ground for the chickens. At the Casa Grande ruins the custodian had a large can placed so water from it dripped onto a milk and butter cooler. This was against a window under the porch roof and a pair of Palmers would come and catch the drops of water as they fell. At a post trader's store near Blackwater the Palmer would come into a porch and drink from the drip of an olla or water cooler. Both Palmer and Bendire frequently sing from the tops of Indian homes and sometimes from the school house. * * * This thrasher is a close sitter and when disturbed leaves the nest, but soon returns showing much concern. Both parents usually show up, approaching as near as 6 feet and uttering the usual two-syllabled call, tho sometimes using the guttural scolding note.

Commenting on the fearlessness of these thrashers about his ranch in January, Mr. Stafford (1912) wrote in his notes: "Last night as we sat motionless on the porch one of the Thrashers approached by stages to within 5 feet of us, caught a moth beneath the umbrella trees, flew up into one of the trees just before me, and then to the tap and bent over again and again for the drops of water that collected just within the mouth of the faucet. All of these acts he performed utterly unconscious of us as living and observing creatures."

He gives an interesting account of their nightly roosting habits in the cholla containing their nest. On January 27, 1912, he wrote in his notes:

At about sunset, and while it was yet quite fully light, I took a small chair and seated myself almost within arm's reach and in full view of the cholla cactus back of the sheds. For 20 minutes nothing appeared save a troop of Desert and Brewer's Sparrows flying by, cheeping, to their roost in the low mesquites. As yet there was no sign of the Thrashers. Suddenly, as the gloom was faintly beginning to gather, one of the birds, without previous warning, arrived from the east and lighted on a fence post near me. I sat motionless, but he evidently regarded this unwonted object near his home with suspicion. I felt that he was examining me. Then he uttered, fairly in my ear, a volley of his whip-like whistles, which, after a moment, was loudly answered upon a sudden from the second bird, which seemed to come from the south. The two, thus joined for the night, flew about in the chollas, though not yet to them, singing and purring softly to each other. One sat just beyond a bush in front of me, on the ground, for 10 or more minutes. It was still so light that I contented myself with glances through nearly closed lids. * * *

At length I heard them enter the chollas close at hand, uttering low notes; and then silence. I looked and saw one perched crouched, I think on a certain de-spined branch above the nest. The other I could not see. For a half hour the bird sat, facing the sunset, and motionless, and I could see its long curved beak and slim body outlined against the sky. As it grew darker I opened my eyes more freely, and I imagined it regarding me the while. At length it moved, and turned about—I thought it had detected me and was on the point of flight—but instead it slid gently down into the big nest and disappeared in its ample cup.

On other occasions he noted that "after sunset and before sunrise every day a few sharp whistles from the direction of the chollas announced the roost-going and the waking of the thrashers with precise punctuality." And he concludes by saying: "As far as I can conclude, then, two Palmer's thrashers, having mated for life, select a suitable cholla and build a nest that shall serve indefinitely with such yearly repair as it requires, for the rearing of young in the breeding season, and for sleeping quarters the rest of the year." It will be noted that his roosting observations were made in January, that no signs of court-ship were seen until February 14, and that nest-repairing did not begin until 2 days later.

Additional evidence on this method of roosting is furnished by Josiah H. Clark (1898), who says: "In one instance I saw a series of five half completed nests built around the central stalk of a cholla cactus and resting on the branches that grew out from the main stalk; they were all connected, and made a platform 2 feet in diameter, and only about a foot and a half from the ground. It was built during the winter and used only for a roosting place. The nest that was used as a breeding place was built 5 feet away in the top of a small cholla."

Voice.—As a singer Palmer's thrasher is somewhat inferior to Bendire's and decidedly inferior to the mockingbird and even the brown thrasher. Mr. Stafford (1912) writes: "The song of this species suggests that of the eastern Thrasher, but lacks its variety and separa-tion into distinct phrases, and is more in the nature of a loud, inter-rupted carol, clear, and melodious. Its two or three note call is sharp and startling, like the 'sing' of a whip stroke echoing upon itself. These, together with low trills and Wren-like chatters, uttered at times when the birds are together, were the only notes I heard; and the song is not to be confused with the feverish, rollicking music of the Ben-dire's (*Toxostoma bendirei*)—a bird nearly as common in this region as *palmeri*."

Mr. Brown (1892) says: "Palmer's thrasher may never be classed as a musical prodigy, but nevertheless among Arizona birds he is rivalled only by that king of American songsters, *Mimus polyglottos*. Morn-ing, noon and evening, perched on the topmost branch of a cholla, he is always in tune, and while his notes may perhaps be less varied than his more favored kinsman, it is none the less bold and commanding, and but for the ubiquity of his rival in song would be in demand as a cage bird."

Mrs. Bailey (1923) writes: "The three-syllabled liquid *tee-dle-lah* was heard commonly all winter and the loud strident call occasionally, and on the morning of January 12, while the ground was still covered with white frost, a soft low song was heard coming from one of the birds sitting fluffed up in the cold. The song was heard again on January 19 and February 3, and on March 4, one was heard singing loudly from the peak of a tent at Continental."

Field marks.—Palmer's thrasher might easily be confused with Bendire's; both have the typical thrasher build, long and slender, with a particularly long tail, and a rather long bill; both are dull, earthy brown on the upper surface, matching the desert floor, and faintly spotted on the breast; there are no conspicuous, distinguishing marks

on either. Bendire's is a little smaller than Palmer's, is a little more
definitely spotted on the breast, and has a shorter and less curved bill.
The songs of the two are somewhat different; and the flight of Bendire's is smoother, less jerky, than that of Palmer's.

Winter.—This thrasher is a permanent resident in Arizona and
apparently remains paired during winter. Mr. Stafford (1912) makes
the statement that "after the young are launched, the old pair, while
remaining inseparable, lapse into a condition of conjugal camaraderie,
and that the male quietly courts his mate anew each spring in anticipa-
tion of nesting."

Mr. Brown (1892) says: "During the winter months they leave the
mesas for the more sheltered bottoms where they frequent the brush
fences, pomegranate and willow hedge rows bordering the ploughed
fields, and then, literally, they are in mud to their eyes."

TOXOSTOMA CURVIROSTRE CELSUM Moore

PLATEAU THRASHER

HABITS

The distribution of this race of the species is now understood to
extend from southeastern Arizona, east of the Santa Rita Mountains,
and southern New Mexico, through western Texas and into Mexico
through Chihuahua and Durango, east of the Sierra Madres. This
is the form that we found breeding abundantly in Cochise County,
Ariz., which we supposed at that time to be *palmeri*. The haunts
and the habits of the two were similar as far as we could see. The
characters in which these two forms differ are explained under the
foregoing subspecies, as noted by H. S. Swarth (1929). In New
Mexico, according to Mrs. Bailey (1928), it is a common breeder on
the cactus mesas and up to 6,000 and sometimes 7,000 feet on some
of the mountains. Josiah H. Clark (1904) found this thrasher breeding commonly in the State of San Luis Potosí, Mexico, where the elevation is about 8,000 feet and Palmer's thrasher in Sonora at an elevation
of 1,200 feet, where chollas, common to both localities, served as the
most common nesting sites.

Nesting.—With the exception of one nest, all the nests of this
thrasher that we found in Cochise County, Ariz., were in chollas and
not different in location and construction from those of Palmer's
thrasher found farther west. The one exception was a nest with
young found in Rucker Canyon, in the Chiricahua Mountains, on
April 25, 1922; it was placed in a large soapweed yucca that stood
close to the house at Moore's ranch; the old bird was unusually tame.

Mr. Clark (1904), who has examined over 100 nests of the two
races of this species in Mexico, writes:

The nests of both birds are the same, made of thorny twigs; in fact, nothing grows there without thorns on it, so they can get nothing else. These sticks are 6 to 10 inches long, and form the outside of the nest, which is lined with wire grasses; sometimes horse hair is used in place of the grass, or with it. The nests are externally about 10 inches in diameter and 8 inches deep; internally about 3½ inches, both in diameter and depth. * * *

The new nest of both birds is generally near the old one, usually in the same cactus, and sometimes the old nest made over.

Sometimes the nest is completed 2 or 3 weeks before the eggs are laid. Then again, if the nest and eggs are taken the birds will have another nest and eggs in from 12 to 15 days, and the new nest is usually about 50 feet from the one taken, but if the first nest is not disturbed the new nest will usually be about 5 feet from the old one.

Of 58 nests of this thrasher, "40 were in cholla cactus, 16 in nopalo cactus, and 2 in palma trees."

Eggs.—Three eggs seems to be the usual number; of 10 sets, of which he gives the measurements, 8 were sets of three, 1 of two, and 1 of four. The eggs are apparently indistinguishable from those of Palmer's thrasher, showing similar variations in colors and markings. The measurements of 50 eggs in the United States National Museum average 27.3 by 19.8 millimeters; the eggs showing the four extremes measure 30.8 by 20.8, 28.2 by 20.8, 23.4 by 18.8, and 24.4 by 18.0 millimeters.

Plumages.—Van Tyne and Sutton (1937) report that the natal down on a young nestling, taken from a nest, "was Chaetura Drab above and whitish on the chin and ventral tracts, the lining of the mouth was Yellow Ocher." The sequence of molts and plumages is doubtless similar to those of the species elsewhere, though the postnuptial molt of adults seems to come somewhat later, mainly in September and early in October.

Nothing that is peculiar to it seems to have been published on the food of this subspecies, and apparently it does not differ materially in any of its habits from other races of the species.

DISTRIBUTION

Range.—Southwestern United States and Mexico.

The species ranges **north** to central Arizona (Hackberry, Big Sandy Creek, Fort Verde, Salt River Wildlife Refuge, and Clifton); southern New Mexico (Pleasanton, Elmendorf, Capitan Mountains, and Carlsbad); and southern Texas (Comstock, Uvalde, San Antonio, and Runge). **East** to southern Texas (Runge, Corpus Christi, and Brownsville); Tamaulipas (Matamoros, Xicotencatl, and Tampico); Veracruz (Orizaba); Puebla (Techuacán); and Oaxaca (Oaxaca). **South** to Oaxaca. **West** to Oaxaca; Guerrero (Chilpancingo); Michoacán (Tancitaro); Jalisco (Tuxpan); Nayarit (Tepic); Sinaloa (Escuinapa and Altata); Sonora (Obregon, Guaymas, Tiburón Island,

Altar, and Sonoyta); extreme southeastern California (Bard); and
Arizona (Castle Dome Mountains, Harqua Hala Mountains, and Hackberry). An isolated colony has become established in the Black Mesa
near Kenton, Cimarron County, Okla.

The range as outlined is for the entire species, three subspecies of
which occur within the United States. Palmer's thrasher (*T. c.
palmeri*) is found in southern Arizona and Sonora; the plateau
thrasher (*T. c. celsum*) occurs from extreme southeastern Arizona,
southern New Mexico, and western Texas, south to northeastern Jalisco
and northwestern Guanajuato; the Brownsville thrasher (*T. c.
oberholseri*) occurs in extreme southern Texas and northeastern
Mexico; Coahuila to Tamaulipas.

The species occurs in winter throughout its range but some individuals apparently withdraw from the northern sections.

Casual records.—A specimen was collected at Spur, Tex., on November 12, 1931; from April 19 to May 4, 1936, from 1 to 5 were seen at
North Platte, Nebr., and a specimen collected on May 2; one was seen
daily from June 5 to 11, 1932, near Pensacola, Fla., and it was collected
on the latter date.

Egg dates.—Arizona: 7 records, April 19 to May 24.

Texas: 110 records, March 12 to August 1; 60 records, April 24 to
May 23, indicating the height of the season.

Mexico: 38 records, March 1 to July 24; 20 records, April 8 to
May 28.

TOXOSTOMA CURVIROSTRE OBERHOLSERI Law

BROWNSVILLE THRASHER

HABITS

In naming and describing this subspecies, J. Eugene Law (1928)
says: "The white terminal spots of the lateral rectrices combined
with the near-equal length of wing and tail differentiate *oberholseri*
from *palmeri, occidentalis* and *maculata* of the Pacific watershed.
From *curvirostris*, its nearest neighbor, of the continental highlands,
oberholseri only differs in shorter length of wing and tail. * * *
The material at hand does not carry this small race [the smallest of
the species] out of the lowlands of southern Texas and of northeastern Mexico (Tamaulipas, Nuevo Leon and Coahuila). More than
75 percent of the stations recorded on the labels of the series examined are under 500 feet altitude; none apparently is over 2,000 feet."

We found this thrasher rather common in Cameron and Hidalgo
Counties in southern Texas, especially in the more open growth of
chaparral where there was a scattered growth of prickly pear cactus. George B. Sennett (1879) says: "This species, like the Long-
billed, is usually more fond of dense cover than the Mockingbird, and
while not often found, in the heaviest timber, yet will be found in the
thickets common on the edges of such tracts. In open woodland,
where clumps of tall thorny bushes and cacti surround the scattered

trees, it is always found, and usually in company with the Long-billed Thrush."

Dr. Herbert Friedmann (1925) says that, near Brownsville, this bird is called "Field Thrasher," as it is found in open fields.

Nesting.—Mr. Sennett (1879) says of the nesting haunts of this thrasher:

In nesting, the habits of this species vary to suit the locality. In districts where chaparral covers the country, there is no respectable growth of timber, but now and then openings, principally occupied by prickly-pear cactuses and stunted mesquite trees, and here their nests will be found in cactuses more frequently perhaps than in trees. But at Lomita I found five nests in trees to one in cacti. * * * At Lomita Ranch, close by a large and much frequented gateway, stands a young ebony-tree, from which, in plain sight, and some 12 feet from the ground, I took a nest and four eggs in April * * * and on May 20 I took a nest and three fresh eggs, at a height of 14 feet, in a large ebony, close by a pathway on the edge of a cornfield. These were the highest nests found, and in both instances the birds were as tame as Robins. Nests are seldom found lower than 4 feet from the ground.

Elsewhere, referring to the same region near Brownsville, he (1878) writes:

The first nest secured was at Hidalgo, April 17. Its location was beneath the roof in the broken side of a thatched outhouse in the very heart of the village. A more exposed place for human view could not be found, nor was there in the village a yard more frequented by children; yet I could not imagine a safer retreat from its more natural enemies. * * * The average size of nest was about that of an ordinary 4-quart measure, although, from its irregular shape, it would not set into one. Its depth outside was fully 6 inches, with an inside depth of 2 so that when the bird was on, though only 6 feet from the ground, nothing but its head and tail could be seen. The nest was composed of twigs from the size of a leadpencil down, and lined with dry grasses. * * *

On May 10th, while on horseback, I came upon a prickly-pear cactus, wonderful to me for its size and tree-like shape. Its trunk was the size of a man's body, and some of its branches were above my head as I sat on my horse. Its general form was that of a wine-glass. While peering about and poking the stalks with my gun, I discovered in the very heart of the great cactus a nest and four eggs of this Thrush. It was about 5 feet from the ground, perfectly exposed above, yet nothing could be more secure from all sides.

Dr. J. C. Merrill (1878), writing about the same region, says:

"The nests are usually placed among the fleshy joints of the prickly pear, or in some of the many thorny and almost impenetrable bushes found in Southern Texas; they are often seen in the dense prickly hedges that surround most Mexican *jacals*. They are, as a rule, readily distinguishable from those of the Texas Thrasher and Mocking-bird by the almost invariable lining of yellow straws, giving a peculiar appearance to the nest. They are also more compactly built, are well cupped, and often have the edges well guarded by thorny twigs."

George B. Benners (1887) found a nest in an old woodpecker's hole in a live oak tree on the bank of the Rio Grande near Laredo, Tex.;

the nest was "composed of dry grass, lined with feathers," and contained four eggs.

Eggs.—Four eggs seems to be the usual set for the Brownsville thrasher, though some of the sets consist of only three; this, if true, is quite at variance with the custom of the species elsewhere. The eggs are evidently indistinguishable from those of Palmer's thrasher, and show the same variations in size, shape, and markings. The measurements of 40 eggs average 27.1 by 19.7 millimeters; the eggs showing the four extremes measure 32.3 by 20.5, 26.5 by 22.5, 22.5 by 19.0, and 25.0 by 17.5 millimeters. Note that the greatest breadth and the least length are the same, a most unusual variation! The next shortest egg measures 24.9 and the next broadest 21.6.

There is little more to be said about the habits of the Brownsville thrasher, which seem to be quite similar to those of the species elsewhere. Mr. Sennett (1879) says:

It is resident where found, commences to breed in March on the Rio Grande, and rears several broods in a season. The first is hatched in April, and generally numbers four. By the middle or latter part of May, clutches for the second brood are full, and consist nearly always of three eggs. I have taken, however, a few sets of four from the second laying. * * * By the 1st of April, the plumage becomes faded and worn; and, by the latter part of May, moulting begins. About this time, also, the small black fruit or berry of the como-tree, upon which the bird feeds, ripens, and it becomes almost impossible to shoot and prepare a specimen without the plumage becoming stained with the purple juices which issue from the mouth and vent. * * * Were the country thickly settled, this bird might become as domestic as the Mockingbird or Robin.

Elsewhere (1878) he says: "I do not remember hearing its song, but I am told by the residents of the country that it sings very sweetly in secluded places, but never in confinement." Dr. Merrill (1878), on the other hand, says: "I cannot confirm the praises of the song of this bird given by Couch and Heerman: it seems to me to be one of the most silent of the song Thrushes. Its alarm note is a sharp *whit-whit.*"

R. D. Camp told Dr. Friedmann (1929) that he had found this species, near Brownsville, to be imposed upon by the dwarf cowbird. This is, I believe, the only case recorded for any of the races of this species.

TOXOSTOMA REDIVIVUM REDIVIVUM (Gambel)

CALIFORNIA THRASHER

PLATES 78–80

CONTRIBUTED BY ROBERT S. WOODS

HABITS

The California thrasher is appropriately named, as it is one of a number of birds of various families that, while common and widely distributed in California, are almost exclusively confined to that

State, with its faunal extension, the northwestern portion of Baja California. The range of the species extends from the western slopes of the Sierra Nevada and the higher mountains of southern California to the Pacific, and from the head of the Sacramento Valley to about latitude 30° in Baja California.

As pointed out by Dr. Joseph Grinnell (1917), it is predominantly a species of the Upper Sonoran Zone, being most abundant along the bases of the mountains, where it ascends the brushy southerly and westerly slopes to an altitude of at least 5,000 feet in the southern part of the State, but never enters the Transition Zone coniferous forests. Its lower limits, however, are less strictly defined, especially toward the south, where it follows the brush-bordered watercourses down into the Lower Sonoran. Dr. Grinnell suggests that a certain degree of atmospheric humidity may also be a requisite for this species, as it fails to follow the Upper Sonoran Zone around the southern end of the Sierra Nevada into apparently suitable territory on the eastern slope of the range.

The California thrasher has occasionally been found nesting on the desert side of the San Gabriel, San Bernardino, and San Jacinto Mountains, in the territory of the crissal and LeConte's thrashers, but in general both high mountains and deserts constitute effective barriers to its spread. As to its ecological relationships, Dr. Grinnell (1917) says:

The California Thrasher is a habitual forager beneath dense and continuous cover. Furthermore, probably two-thirds of its foraging is done on the ground. In seeking food above ground, as when patronizing cascara bushes, the thrasher rarely mounts to an exposed position, but only goes as high as is essential to securing the coveted fruits. The bird may be characterized as semi-terrestrial, but always dependent upon vegetational cover; and this cover must be of the chaparral type, open next to the ground, with strongly interlacing branch-work and evergreen leafy canopy close above—not forest under-growth, or close-set, upright stems as in new growth willow, or matted leafage as in rank-growing annual herbage.

In these favored haunts throughout its range the thrasher is associated with two other birds of rather similar coloration, the brown towhee and the wren-tit. Like the towhee, the thrasher holds no prejudice against civilization but becomes a common and by no means shy dooryard resident of the foothill towns.

In comparing the species of this genus, William L. Engels (1940) writes: "The California * * * thrasher appears to have few characters in common with the brown thrasher: the bill is very long and markedly decurved, sicklelike; the bird's upper parts are grayish brown and the underparts somewhat lighter in color, but without the dark streaks so distinctive of the brown thrasher. The migratory brown thrasher, in its daily rounds, progresses predominantly by flight; the nonmigratory California thrasher is a swift and skillful runner and makes little use of its wings in moving about. Other species of the genus are intermediate in various respects between these two extremes."

He also finds that the three species occurring regularly in California, *redivivum*, *lecontei*, and *dorsale*, form a group distinguished from the more eastern members of the genus not only in their plain coloration and longer, more curved bills, but also in their reluctant flight and their strong digging propensities. Furthermore, when on the ground, according to Mr. Engels, "the tail is held low in *rufum*, *bendirei* and *curvirostre;* it is carried up at a sharp angle in *redivivum*, *dorsale* and *lecontei*."

The typical form of the California thrasher occupies the southern portion of the territory, as far north as Monterey and Placer Counties. It differs from the northern subspecies in the more grayish brown of the general plumage and the white rather than buffy color of the throat.

Nesting.—The nesting habits of the California thrasher offer little of divergence from those of others of its genus and family, aside from the notable length of its breeding season. The birds apparently remain mated throughout the year, and Mrs. Grace Tompkins Sargent (1940) mentions one brood having been brought off in Pasadena during the month of November 1935. Other occupied nests have been reported for each subsequent month up to at least July. February and March, however, are more usual months for the opening of the nesting season, the raising of the second brood often lasting well into summer.

The nests are usually placed within a few feet of the ground, well inside a large bush or scrubby tree. Dense masses of foliage are avoided, but the sites are usually well screened from outside view. In its construction the nest closely resembles that of mockingbirds building in the same locality, except of its slightly larger size and coarser materials, in proportion to the sizes of the birds. The foundation and body of the structure are composed of stiff, rough twigs, with a lining of rootlets, fibers, grasses, or other flexible material.

When incubating or brooding, the thrashers often show little fear when approached, and W. Leon Dawson (1923) tells of picking up one of the birds and turning it around on its nest so that it would face his camera! They are, nevertheless, cautious in their approach to the nest, as Mr. Engels (1940) mentions: "Of two pairs of California thrashers whose nesting activities I observed, I never saw a bird approach the nest in any way but through the bush, working up from the base after coming to it on the ground. One nest was about 4 feet above ground in a bush, and the birds here often left in the same manner in which they had come—except when frightened off, when they flew down to the ground." By this habit of approaching the nest from the ground, and by the reluctance of the sitting bird to be flushed, the thrasher guards well the secret of its nesting site.

Eggs.—[AUTHOR'S NOTE: The California thrasher lays two to four eggs to a set, apparently oftener three than four and only rarely two. These are mostly ovate, with variations toward elliptical-ovate or short-ovate. They are only slightly glossy. The ground color is "Nile blue," "pale Nile blue," or even paler blue. They are more or less evenly covered with small spots, flecks, or fine dots of pale browns; these are often very faint and sometimes much scattered; they are very rarely conspicuously spotted, or even dotted with darker browns.

The measurements of 50 eggs in the United States National Museum average 30.1 by 21.2 millimeters; the eggs showing the four extremes measure **34.0** by 21.3, 30.5 by **22.9, 26.4** by 20.8, and 30.9 by **19.8** millimeters.]

Young.—According to Mrs. Irene G. Wheelock (1904), "both sexes assist in the construction of the bulky nest, and both brood on the eggs. In 14 days the naked pink young emerge from the shells and are fed by regurgitation for 4 days, or until their eyes open." And from the same source: "The young thrashers leave the nest when 12 to 14 days old, but are fed by the adults for some time after. I have found the male caring for a fully fledged brood, while his mate was sitting on a nestful of eggs; and after this second series were hatched, he at once began to feed them as faithfully as he had fed the first."

In refutation of the theory that "a parent bird is moved to feed its young only by that young bird's opening its mouth," Ernest I. Dyer (1939) cited the behavior of this species, stating that "in the case of *every one* of the 15 or 20 nests of the California Thrasher which [the writer] has had under observation at his home, at 'reading distance,' there have been innumerable instances of one or the other of the parents' persistently trying to induce a totally unresponsive chick, by cluckings and bill-proddings, to open its mouth to receive food."

The bills of the nestlings are proportionately shorter and much less curved than those of the adults. After the young appear fully mature in other respects, their bills are still noticeably short. Since the maximum sicklelike development of the bill is seen in comparatively few individuals, it might be surmised that the growth of this member continues through a part, at least, of the adult life.

Plumages.—[AUTHOR'S NOTE: According to Ridgway (1907), the young are "essentially like adults but browner above, with larger wing-coverts and tertials margined terminally with lighter cinnamon-brownish, the rectrices more or less rusty brownish terminally; chest less grayish (more brownish), sometimes only slightly different from general color of under parts."

The postjuvenal molt of young birds occurs mainly in July, and the

The late-summer molt of the thrasher is perhaps more noticeable than that of any other California land bird. In this it contrasts strongly with the mockingbird, which is seldom seen in a disheveled state. During this period following the end of the nesting season, individuals can always be seen in smooth, neat plumage, and others in a very ragged condition. The latter birds show no inclination to seek seclusion, but pursue their usual activities.]

Food.—In an examination of 82 stomachs of this species, Prof. F. E. L. Beal (1907) found vegetable food to exceed animal in the ratio of 59 to 41. Carabidae constituted 3.8 percent, other beetles 6 percent, the most numerous being darkling beetles (Tenebrionidae) and May beetles (Scarabaeidae). "But very few weevils or other species that live on trees or foliage were found. Of all the insects, Hymenoptera are the most abundant, as they are also the most constant element of the thrasher's food. About half of these are ants, the rest wasps and bees. * * * Together they make up something more than 12 percent of the food of the year. Two specimens of worker honey-bees (*Apis mellifera*) were found in one stomach." Caterpillars, cocoons, and moths amounted to 8 percent, mostly eaten during winter, probably while hibernating; spiders and myriapods formed 6 percent.

Of the vegetable food, Prof. Beal found 18 percent represented by fruit, "probably not of much value." Seeds of blackberries or raspberries, elderberry, cascara, and manzanita were present. The seeds of poison oak and other species of *Rhus* formed 14 percent. "They were not found in many stomachs, but appear to be eaten in considerable quantities when eaten at all." The miscellaneous part of the vegetable food, amounting to 26 percent, consisted of mast, weed seed, galls, and rubbish. Professor Beal concludes: "It is not probable that the California thrasher will ever become of special economic interest unless under very exceptional circumstances. In the meantime it performs its part in the great work of reducing the vast numbers of insects."

The thrashers will eat figs and cactus fruit, such as that of the cultivated "spineless" *Opuntia,* but as a rule they show little interest in any kind of fruit too large to be swallowed whole; obviously the shape of the bill is not well adapted to biting. They are very fond of grapes, especially the small seedless varieties, and display great persistence in finding openings through any sort of net that may be put over them. They relish also the berrylike grains of the pomegranate, available to them after the splitting of the hard rind. As with many other birds, offerings of crumbs and table scraps seem to be most acceptable in cool weather, or when there are families to be fed. At times California thrashers will visit a feeding-table regularly and eat quantities of dry bread crumbs, a food which the mockingbird only occasionally deigns to notice; in general, however, the food preferences of the two species are similar.

Behavior.—Prominent among the characteristics of this species is its adaptation and preference for the terrestrial mode of life. On the ground it is swift, efficient, and at ease; but when forced to take to the air, its jerky flight, accomplished by labored beating of its short wings, and with awkwardly drooping head and tail, offers the greatest possible contrast to the graceful buoyancy of its relative and frequent neighbor the mockingbird. The thrasher's usual gait is a brisk run, even when proceeding a very short distance. In moving only a step or two, it may either walk or hop. While the bird is running, the tail is tilted upward, but when perching it is held in line with the body or drooping slightly.

The California thrasher, in its native haunts, has frequently been referred to as a shy bird; perhaps, however, this is mainly due to the nature of its usual surroundings, which make keeping out of sight an easy matter. In our dooryards it is one of the least timorous of birds, paying not the slightest attention to any unusual paraphernalia, such as a camera and tripod, and showing no aversion to lawns and other open spaces. In its attitude toward other birds it is bold and confident, and the California jay, of equal size, deems it prudent to defer to the thrasher at the feeding-table. Among themselves the thrashers are not quarrelsome; sometimes they are seen chasing one another about on the ground, but this often seems to be in a spirit of play.

In its territory the thrasher is unique in its method of foraging. Most of its animal food is obtained by raking away fallen leaves or by digging in the soil. In the words of Dr. Grinnell (1917), "The bird's most conspicuous structural feature, the long curved bill, is used to whisk aside the litter, and also to dig, pick-fashion, into soft earth where insects lie concealed. Ground much frequented by Thrashers shows numerous little pits in the soil surface, less than an inch deep, steep on one side and with a little heap of earth piled up on the opposite side." In the Point Lobos Reserve, according to Grinnell and Linsdale (1936), "the most suitable foraging situation was the accumulation of leaf litter beneath the ceanothus bushes." Flower beds also are favored resorts, and in their entirely laudable search for cutworms and other pests, the birds are apt to annoy gardeners by digging up newly planted bulbs and seeds. On the technique of digging, Mr. Engels (1940) writes:

The food which it obtains from the ground and surface debris beneath the chaparral cover is procured entirely by means of the long, curved bill. The feet are never employed for scratching, but ground spiders, grubs, and crickets are dug out of the ground; the curved bill is struck into the ground with rapid strokes of the head and neck, and the dirt "hooked" back and out with a powerful pull of the neck. Side-to-side sweeps of the bill are also frequent in the digging operation, but most of the dirt is thrown backward. Rather large objects may be thus moved; I once saw a California thrasher toss a clod of dirt half the size of my fist a distance of nearly 2 feet.

The bill is not always kept closed during the digging operation; the mandibles are frequently separated by a few millimeters, being then driven into the ground like a two-pronged fork rather than a single pick. This was seen more often in the "hooks" and "pulls" than in the "lateral sweeps". Once an opening is made in the ground surface, many direct downthrusts or pokes are made. When digging, the bird frequently stops, cocks its head far to one side, bringing one eye to bear directly on the work, and seems to peer into the excavation.

* * * All parts of the body except the wings are brought into play in this operation, each contributing its share to the sum of the forces which produce the powerful digging strokes and the return of the body to an easy, balanced position.

That the use of the bill for opening nuts may involve a possible hazard is indicated by a manuscript note from Mrs. Amelia S. Allen, of Berkeley: "One came to the tray with a hazelnut stuck on its beak. It tried to knock it off by striking it against the tray; then flew to the ground and pecked; then to a branch where it rubbed the shell against its foot. It disappeared in the brush with the shell still on its beak."

Though most of the habitat of this species is deficient in water, the thrashers make frequent use of it in hot weather if it is provided. They appear to drink very copiously, but it may be merely that the shape of the bill makes drinking a tedious process. In view of the fact that wasps are reported to make up a considerable portion of their diet, it is strange to note the almost ludicrous attitude of alarm induced by the arrival of one of these insects at a bird bath where a thrasher is drinking. In cooler weather, water is utilized for bathing, which is done in a practiced and thorough manner.

Under only one circumstance does the California thrasher forget its affinity for the earth and its inclination to remain as close to it as possible. When it feels the urge to sing it seeks the most conspicuous position available, the topmost twig of a large bush or small tree. The song ended, it spreads its wings and glides back to earth. At no time does it share the fondness of many other ground-foraging birds for the roofs of buildings.

Voice.—The California thrasher is not ordinarily a voluble bird, nor are its call notes varied. As it goes about its usual business it occasionally utters a flat and unmusical *chack*, or more rarely a harsh note of alarm. It is only when it mounts to the top of a bush or tree and pours out its rich song that its vocal abilities may be appreciated.

At its best, the song of the thrasher is one of the finest of bird songs, probably less fluent than that of the mockingbird, but deeper and richer. Its quality varies greatly, probably both with the ability of the individual and the mood of the singer. Mrs. Sargent (1940) found that a female which she watched for more than a year also sang on certain occasions, sometimes "loudly and sweetly," and says that in January the mated pair once sang together for about 15 minutes and for shorter periods at other times. While winter and early spring seem to be the seasons of greatest vocal activity, the thrasher's song may be heard intermittently at almost any time of year.

Like the mockingbird, the California thrasher often interpolates into its song the utterances of other birds, including, according to John Van Denburgh (1899), the flicker, house finch, quail, goldfinch, and black-headed grosbeak. Ornithologists differ in their estimates of the thrasher's ability as a mimic, most of them ranking it below the mockingbird. My experience, however, has been the reverse, and it seems probable that there are individuals in both species that are outstandingly proficient. One midwinter day I was surprised to hear the unmistakable buglelike notes of Bullock's oriole, a summer visitant, and traced them to a California thrasher singing on the top of a bush. Again, late in summer, the song of a thrasher contained notes resembling those of the robin, a winter visitor here. These incidents seem to indicate that the thrasher's memory is at least several months long.

Another striking demonstration of mimicry, perhaps by the same thrasher, was the reproduction of the short howl or wail of the coyote. Such was the ventriloquial effect and the perfection of the rendition that even as I watched the bird singing on the top of a nearby bush, it would have been difficult to believe that I was not actually hearing a coyote in the distance had not the wails fitted perfectly between the phrases of the song.

Mrs. Allen (MS.) has noted the following imitations by thrashers at Berkeley: long-tailed chat, red-tailed hawk, robin, ruby-crowned kinglet, olive-sided flycatcher, titmouse, house wren, willow goldfinch, California jay, quail, purple finch, European blackbird, frog, and postman's whistle. Most of these were recorded in September. In eight different years she found the song period marking the completion of the molt to begin in August; in 11 years the starting of territorial song ranged from December 21 to February 22.

Field marks.—The California thrasher's long, decurved bill is sufficient to distinguish it from any other bird ordinarily seen within its territory. When its bill is not visible, it might be mistaken for a brown towhee, but the tail is appreciably longer and is often tilted up. In and around the passes leading from the Pacific slope to the desert, the range of this species is said to slightly overlap the territories of the crissal and LeConte's thrashers. From LeConte's the California thrasher is distinguished by its darker color and somewhat longer, more curved bill; with the crissal it agrees rather closely in size, coloring, and shape of bill, the identification being based principally on the color of the under tail coverts, cinnamon in the California thrasher, cinnamon-

rufous in the crissal.   In the California and LeConte's thrashers, the
iris is always brown; in the crissal it is usually represented as light
yellow, though Ridgway (1907) described it as brown; in other species
of the genus the iris is yellow or orange.

Enemies.—Hearing a succession of frenzied shrieks in the yard one
day, I hastened out to find a thrasher in the grip of a sharp-shinned
hawk.   Upon seeing me the hawk immediately flew away, leaving its
intended victim apparently little the worse for the encounter.   In
this instance the thrasher's vocal chords had proved its best defensive weapon.

From the nature of its habits the thrasher would seem to be especially
vulnerable to terrestrial enemies, but it is undoubtedly a bird of more
than average sagacity, and I have seen no indication that many of the
adults fall victim to cats or other prowlers.   Because of the scant
height at which the nest is usually placed, there must be a considerable
loss from semiterrestrial nest-robbers, such as skunks, banded racers,
and perhaps alligator lizards, as well as from the California jay.

Dr. Grinnell (1917) surmises that in view of the thrasher's dull
brown coloration, swiftness of foot, and poor flight, the chaparral cover
may be quite as valuable in its protective effect as it is in furnishing a
suitable foraging ground.

DISTRIBUTION

Range.—California and northwestern Baja California; nonmigratory.

The California thrasher is found **north** in California to extreme
southern Humboldt County (Thorn); central Trinity County (Hay-
fork); Shasta County (Baird); and Tehama County (Manton).
East to Tehama County (Manton); the western slope of the Sierra
Nevada (Grass Valley, Placerville, Murphy, El Portal, and Walker
Pass); western San Bernardino County (Hesperia and Redlands);
Riverside County (Palm Springs); eastern San Diego County
(Jacumba); and northwestern Baja California (Hanson Laguna,
Sierra San Pedro Mártir, and San Fernando).   **South** to northwest-
ern Baja California (San Fernando and Rosario).   **West** to the
Pacific Ocean in Baja California (Rosario, San Quintín, and En-
senada); and California (San Diego, Los Angeles, Santa Barbara,
Monterey, Nicasio, Ukiah, Cummings, and Thorn).

The range as given for the entire species is divided into two subspecies.   The Sonoma thrasher (*T. r. sonomae*) occurs in the northern
part of the range south to Eldorado, San Joaquin, and Santa Cruz
Counties; the California thrasher (*T. r. redivivum*) occupies the
range from there southward.

Egg dates.—California: 132 records, December 15 to June 27; 72
records, March 20 to May 8, indicating the height of the season.

TOXOSTOMA REDIVIVUM SONOMAE Grinnell

SONOMA THRASHER

HABITS

This northern race of the well known California thrasher is described by Dr. Joseph Grinnell (1915) as "similar to *T. r. redivivum*, but size slightly greater and back, chest and sides less 'warm' in tone of brown; similar to *T. r. pasadenense*, but size, especially of foot, greater, and coloration throughout darker, less ashy."

He says that it is a "fairly common resident of the Upper Sonoran zone around the upper end of the Sacramento Valley and thence west through the inner coast ranges north of San Francisco Bay." It probably intergrades with the more southern race in the vicinity of Placer County. It has been recorded from Shasta, Marin, Mendocino, and Solano Counties.

I cannot find in the literature, or in contributed notes, anything to indicate that this thrasher differs at all in its habits from the closely related California thrasher, which has been so well treated by Mr. Woods.

In the Lassen Peak region, Grinnell, Dixon, and Linsdale (1930) found this thrasher living mainly in the scrub-oak chaparral. One nest was found in an isolated clump of buckbrush, and other nests were seen in clumps of scrub oaks.

The eggs are indistinguishable from those of the California thrasher. The measurements of 25 eggs average 31.2 by 21.5 millimeters; the eggs showing the four extremes measure **33.1** by 22.2, 31.9 by **22.7, 29.2** by 21.2, and 31.3 by **19.5** millimeters.

TOXOSTOMA LECONTEI LECONTEI Lawrence

LECONTE'S THRASHER

PLATES 81–83

HABITS

For many years after its discovery LeConte's thrasher was considered one of the rarest and most elusive of the desert birds. Dr. Edgar A. Mearns (1886) gives a brief historical sketch of it, from which I quote as follows:

"This Thrasher is at once the oldest and least known species of the genus in Arizona. Originally described by George N. Lawrence in 1851, from a specimen taken at the mouth of the Gila River, near Fort Yuma, it was not again met with by naturalists for a decade, when Dr. Cooper added it to the avifauna of California, stating that it was not uncommon in certain portions of the route between the Colorado Valley and the coast slope of California. * * * In 1865, Dr. Coues took a fourth specimen, in the month of September, near the Colorado River above Fort Mojave. * * * The fifth specimen was taken by Mr. F. Stephens, on February 21, 1880, in central Arizona."

Thus, in a period of nearly 30 years after its discovery, only five specimens were collected! During the next 5 years much hard work on the part of Mr. Stephens, Dr. Mearns, and others brought the total number of specimens up to about two dozen. During that time and since then much has been learned about its habits and distribution, and much has been written about its elusiveness and the difficulty of collecting it.

LeConte's thrasher lives mainly in the lowest, barrenest, and hottest desert plains and valleys of southwestern Arizona and southeastern California, where, according to Frank Stephens (1884), "the thermometer gets to 100° in the shade in April, and even to 130° in July and August." The sun beats down with torrid fury on the white sand; the climate is so excessively dry that it is dangerous to travel without a good supply of water; and one's mouth, throat, and nostrils soon become uncomfortably dry and parched, as the terrific heat dries up all the natural moisture in the body. Then, too, I found that the ground was so hot that the soles of my feet became blistered and pealed, if I wore thin shoes.

Dr. C. Hart Merriam (1895) describes this desert region very well as follows:

The great Colorado River, emerging from the marvellous cañons of northern Arizona, bends southward to traverse a vast, inhospitable desert, parts of which, below the level of the sea, surpass the deserts of India, Arabia, and even the great Sahara in heat, aridity and desolation. * * *

These deserts receive little water: the rainfall is meagre, the streams from the surrounding mountains soon disappear in the hot sands, and the broad Colorado itself hurries on to the sea as if in a conduit, without imparting verdure to even its immediate banks save in a few favored spots. The vegetation is scanty and peculiar: the sandy gravel slopes are covered with the resinous *Larrea* or creosote bush, more or less mixed with cactuses, yuccas, daleas, ephedras and other desert forms, while the alkaline and saline clay soils are dotted here and there with greasewoods and fleshy saline plants.

Near the Gila River Dr. Mearns (1886) found that the desert "country was bare of grass, sandy, and covered with scattered sagebrush and cacti (*Opuntia, Echinocereus, Cereus,* and *Echinocactus*), with occasional bare areas of white sand, where the sun's reflection was terrible."

I made my acquaintance with LeConte's thrasher on the Mojave Desert in southeastern California, where it seems to be as abundant as anywhere. Driving out eastward from Victorville, we passed through the rocky ramparts of Deadman's Point, among the picturesque Joshua-trees, or tree yuccas, of that section, onto the broad level plain of the desert, bordered on the north by numerous rough,

rocky hills or low mountains and on the south by the then snow-capped
San Bernardino Mountains. The floor of the desert was dry and hot,
sparsely covered with a scattered growth of creosote bushes, so widely
separated that we could easily drive anywhere among them on the
hard, sandy floor and so scantily branched as to afford a minimum of
shade beneath them. A few stunted mesquites relieved the monotony,
and there were scattered clumps or more often individual bushes of
chollas (*Opuntia echinocarpa*, the branching cholla, *Opuntia bigelovii*,
the white cholla, or *Opuntia ramocissima*, the long-spined species). As
we wended our way in and out among the scattered desert vegetation,
we frequently saw these sandy-colored thrashers running rapidly
ahead of us or dodging in low flight among and under the creosote
bushes.

There are two northward extensions of the breeding range of Le-
Conte's thrasher in California, in Owens Valley and in the San Joaquin Valley, where the surrounding mountain ranges shut off hot and
arid valleys. While driving from Bakersville to the Kettleman Hills,
through Kern County, we saw a number of LeConte's thrashers on
the arid, sagebrush plains and noted some of their old nests in these
bushes; my host, J. R. Pemberton, told me that they nest regularly in
the sagebushes in this region.

Of the haunts of this thrasher in the San Joaquin Valley, Dr. Joseph
Grinnell (1933) writes:

The most conspicuous element in the perennial vegetation about was a
species of salt-bush. Fragments saved have been identified for me by Dr. H. F.
Copeland, of the Herbarium, University of California, as *Atriplex polycarpa*.
* * * The bushes of it grow small and far-scattered on exposed, high terrain;
but in low places, in ravines and along gullies, washes, or arroyos the bushes grow
eight or ten feet in diameter, and five feet or more high, and may crowd together
here or there along a favorable draw to form a continuous thicket. It is the
presence of this more luxuriant growth of atriplex that, together with much
open ground between the scattering bushes nearby, and the general climatic
conditions of high temperature and low humidity, appears to form the final
requirement controlling the presence and relative numbers of the LeConte
Thrashers in the San Joaquin Valley."

Nesting.—The nests that we saw in the Mojave Desert were all
alike and similarly placed in the chollas (*Opuntia echinocarpa*, *O.
bigelovii*, or *O. ramocissima*). The birds seemed to select the densest,
most thickly branched chollas, where the nests could be located but not
easily seen; in many cases it was necessary to chop away several
branches before the nest could be clearly seen, or even before the hand
could be safely inserted among the many bristling spines (see pl. 81).
The nests were very bulky, often filling a large central space among
the sprawling branches, to which they were insecurely attached but
safely supported and guarded. The bulk of the nest consisted of a
great mass of thorny twigs and sticks, filling most of the space, on which

was firmly imbedded a thick mass of the flower clusters of a fine, gray, woolly plant that grew abundantly on the surrounding desert; this formed the lining of the nest proper and made a soft bed for the eggs or young; this silvery gray lining was charcteristic of all the nests, distinguishing them from the nests of all other desert birds, at least in that locality. The nests were easy to find, as they were generally in isolated chollas, and it was only necessary to drive over the smooth desert floor, in and out among the small, scattered creosote bushes, and look at each likely looking cholla. The chollas were not large specimens, and the nests averaged about 3 feet above ground. We saw a number of old nests, which in that dry climate persist for several years, though the soft lining rots and becomes a sodden mass.

The nesting habits and the nests of LeConte's thrasher are somewhat different in other localities. As already stated, we found the old nests in sage bushes on the more arid plains of Kern County and the upper San Joaquin Valley in California. G. Holterhoff, Jr., was the first man to discover a nest of this thrasher, or at least the first to publish an account of it. He published a brief account of it in the *American Naturalist* for March 1881, and the following fuller account in the Bulletin of the Nuttall Ornithological Club (1883). The nest was found near Flowing Wells, in the heart of the Colorado Desert.

The country thereabout is a barren, sandy desert, broken by an occasional dry arroyo or river bed, scarce worthy of the name, as they are only rivers when bearing off the deluge from some fortuitous cloud-burst. Scattered sparingly along the course of these fickle streams is a stunted growth of mesquite and palo-verde trees. * * * [The nest was in a thick palo-verde tree.] The nest, situated about 5 feet from the ground, was a very bulky affair, set so loosely and carelessly amid the branches that a considerable foundation had been thrown together before the structure was firm enough to bear the nest proper. This was composed of the thorny sticks and twigs of mesquite, loosely intercrossed, and the interior rather neatly lined with reddish fibres and rootlets. The external dimensions were about 9 inches in depth and 6 inches in width at the top; interior, depth 3 inches and width about 4 inches. The cavity was deep enough to conceal the sitting bird, except as to its projecting tail.

M. French Gilman (1904) says that of 28 nests, found between Banning, Calif., and Salton Sea, "all but 4 were in the cholla cactus, the others being as follows: 1 in a mesquite, 1 in an unidentified desert shrub and 2 in thorn trees, about as bad as the cholla." He continues:

Climatic variations in the seasons appear to have an effect on the numbers of the birds. In seasons of more than normal rainfall they seem more numerous and nest more than in dry seasons. The spring of 1895 was a very favorable one, the desert enjoying heavy spring rains, and consequently an abnormal growth of vegetation, making the desert wastes a perfect flower garden. The sand hills were covered with desert primroses, acres of country were tinged pink with the sand verbenas or abronias and other acres were flaming with the yellow annual encelias. Insect life fairly swarmed and birds, especially Leconte thrashers and mockingbirds, were more numerous than before or since. I found eight Leconte's nests on one trip near Palm Springs and saw many of the birds.

The next 3 years were dry on the desert and I saw only six nests, though frequently in their territory.

A nest found by Dr. Mearns (1886) between Casa Grande and Sweet Water was "placed in a mesquite, at a height of 6 or 8 feet. It rested upon a fork and received additional support from a neighboring branch. It was composed of fine grasses and weeds, the inner nest resting upon a mass of large sticks, loosely placed. The nest-lining was of grass and a few feathers."

The nests found by Dr. Grinnell (1933) in the San Joaquin Valley were all in saltbushes (*Atriplex polycarpa*). Of the first nest he says: "The nest bush was one of a row of large-sized atriplex bushes growing irregularly along the edges of a meandering gully in the bottom of a shallow draw. * * * The nest was not in the center of the bush, but was situated in the dense tangle of twigs about 700 mm. east of its axis, resting among the complexly branching stems which varied in slant from nearly horizontal to nearly vertical." The nest was 550 mm. below the crown of the bush and 670 mm. above the ground. Grinnell continues:

The substructure * * * consisted of straggling, dry twigs, long and varyingly slender, hardly distinguishable at the periphery from the surrounding dense leafless twiggery of the bush itself. How the bird could have managed the construction of this basal shell in such close quarters, so as to provide the proper space for the nest-proper, it was difficult for me to imagine. The inside diameter of the nest cup was 95 mm., depth from its solid rim, 60 mm. The entire inside cup was astonishingly firm, almost as if made of mud; it consisted of atriplex leaves and weathered bits of newspaper packed together so as to be of almost the firmness of pulp-board. Possibly the rains of the preceding month had had something to do with yielding this result; but even so, there was no resemblance at all to the porous, open-work, inner lining of a California Thrasher's nest—nothing for the young birds to clinch their toes and claws through. In this nest there was also a sharply distinguishable intermediate layer, of long fine grass stems and slender twigs; but none of this material reached the inner wall.

At San Felipe, Baja California, Laurence M. Huey (1927) found occupied nests "in ocotillo, cholla cactus, fruitea, smoke bush and ironwood trees, while old nests were found in nearly all the species of brush, trees or cactus that offered size enough for protection."

Eggs.—Two to four eggs constitute a full set for LeConte's thrasher. Mr. Gilman (1904) says that the "usual set contains three eggs but four are not uncommon and two are sometimes found. Of the records made I find 6 sets of 4 eggs, 12 of 3, and 4 of 2—complete sets as advanced incubation showed." They vary in shape from ovate to short ovate, or elongate ovate, and are sometimes somewhat pointed at the smaller end. They have a very slight gloss.

The eggs are somewhat similar to those of the California thrasher or those of Palmer's thrasher; they are smaller than the former and about the size of the latter; but they are usually less heavily marked than either. The ground color is light greenish blue or light bluish

green, "pale Nile blue," or "beryl blue," or "pale turquoise green."
These colors fade considerably in collections, as well as in the nests;
fresh eggs in the nest may be somewhat more deeply colored than as
above indicated.

The markings are usually fine pinpoints, or very small spots, more
or less evenly distributed over the whole egg or concentrated about
the larger end, sometimes forming a ring; some eggs are nearly immaculate.   The markings are in shades of pale brown, reddish brown,
or yellowish brown, Dr. Grinnell (1933) says from "Mars Brown"
(darkest) to "Pale Purple Vinaceous" [lightest].   Rarely, the spots
are large enough to be called blotches.   Dr. Mearns (1886) says that
one egg "has large blotches of yellowish-brown and lavender sparingly
scattered over the egg, a few extending nearly to the small extremity."

The measurements of 50 eggs average 27.6 by 19.7 millimeters; the
eggs showing the four extremes measure 29.9 by 21.2 and 24.3 by 18.3
millimeters.

Young.—The period of incubation for LeConte's thrasher does not
seem to have been determined, and we apparently do not know just
how long the young remain in the nest.   But we do know that both
the male and the female help to build the nest and share in the incubation of the eggs, and both work in the feeding and care of the young.
The breeding season is a long one, and at least two broods are ordinarily raised in a season.

Plumages.—Ridgway (1907) says that the juvenal plumage is "similar to the spring and summer adult plumage but slightly paler,
especially on rump; under parts more buffy with under tail-coverts
much paler buff; upper tail-coverts pale wood brown or isabella color."
In spring and summer adult plumage the upper parts are between
"drab-gray" and "ecru-drab," and the under tail coverts are deep
buff or "pale ochraceous-buff."   In fall and winter plumage adults
have the "color of upper parts deeper and grayer (soft drab-gray);
chest (broadly) light drab-gray, strongly contrasted with the white
of the throat, and breast and upper abdomen duller, more buffy
whitish."   I have seen specimens in full juvenal plumage as early
as April 7, and one taken May 16 that was beginning the postjuvenal
molt.   I have examined adults in full postnuptial molt on July 5 and
on August 7.

Food.—The stomach of a specimen sent to William Brewster (1882a)
is said to have "contained a small species of katydid and some ants."
This seems to be the only published item on the food of this species.

Behavior.—LeConte's thrasher is a decidedly terrestrial species.   As
we drive across the level floor of the desert, we may see a long, slim,
dull, clay-colored bird running swiftly ahead of us or dodging out
of sight among the low creosote bushes, or perhaps making short
zigzag flights close to the ground or just over the tops of the bushes,

trying to keep out of sight but always able to outdistance us even in the open. Its speed is hardly less swift than that of the swift-footed lizards that scurry away from us. It suggests a miniature roadrunner in behavior, than which it is hardly less fleet of foot or less adept at hiding among the scanty vegetation. It sometimes carries its long tail straight out behind as the roadrunner does, but more often it is cocked up at a sharp angle, showing its buff under-tail coverts.

Dr. Mearns (1886) says: "When flying they dropped low down, and performed a part of each flight in a tortuous course under cover of the sage brush, ascending to the top of a mesquite like a Shrike. * * * Their speed when running upon the ground is truly wonderful. A pair of them were running upon the railroad, and for a little way kept ahead of our trotting horses with ease."

Frank Stephens (1884) worked hard to collect his specimens of this thrasher, which he found most elusive and exasperating; he tells the following story of one of his attempts which illustrates this point and was quite typical of the bird's behavior:

I heard a low song, and standing still and looking about me I saw *H. lecontei* number four sitting on a low bush not far away. He observed me about the same time, and went off to another low bush. As he flew along I dropped among the weeds, meaning to do my best to get him. I crept along among weeds that were not large enough to hide me, but could get no better cover. I soon saw that he was watching me, and concluded that my game was up, but worked along, flattened as close to the ground as I could get, for several yards, when I came to a wash a few feet wide and a foot or so deep. I meant to try to reach and cross it, and fire from the opposite side, though it was long range. He watched me closely until I got down in the wash, where I swung my gun around and slowly raised it to fire, when I saw that he had absconded. I didn't swear, oh, no! You wouldn't either under such circumstances, would you? The "confounded fool" had watched me as long as he could see me, and when I hid in the wash he evidently thought it was time for him to go. Perhaps he was not such a fool after all.

Voice.—I never had the pleasure of hearing the song of LeConte's thrasher, but those who have heard it have praised it, as a very sweet song much like the songs of other thrashers. Vernon Bailey, in Mrs. Bailey's Handbook (1902), writes: "After a cool night on the desert in March, when the morning is loaded with the fragrance of abronias, yuccas, and primroses, and the crimson and gold cups of the cactus are brilliant among the creosote bushes, the thrashers are heard fairly splitting their throats from the mesquite tops, and seen running about chasing each other over the bare stretches between the bushes. Later in the day they rest in the shade of the chaparral."

While singing, the bird sits in thrasher fashion, with its tail hanging down, its head thrown back, and its long, curved bill wide open. After silence during the intense heat of midday, he sings again in the evening coolness, sometimes far into the clear, starry, desert night. Mr. Gilman (1904) writes:

While standing one evening on a high-drifted hill of white sand about 2 miles west of the rim of ancient Salton sea I heard the sweet strains of a new bird song and began to look for the singer. I expected to find a mocking bird whose individuality had been developed by the desert solitudes and who had learned a new song. On an adjoining sand hill, perched on the exposed tip of a sand buried mesquite I saw the singer—a LeConte thrasher. Perhaps environment enhanced the music for the spot was a most lonesome, God-forsaken one, near an ancient Indian encampment and burial ground, but I have heard no sweeter bird song and the memory still lingers. Since then I have heard the song a few times but not oftener than once or twice a year, though I have been frequently among the birds. Not only do they seldom sing but the whistling call note is not often heard. They appear to be silent, unsociable creatures, never more than a pair being found together, unless a brood of young birds and parents, and then only until the former can shift for themselves.

Dr. Mearns (1886) says: "The Thrashers were heard singing during the early morning. Their song is remarkable for its loud, rich tone, and is at least as fine as that of any other of the genus. * * * One would sing so loudly that it could be distinctly heard for more than a mile." He also mentions an alarm note, a "sharply reiterated *whit*, or *quit*." Ralph Hoffmann (1927) says that "the common call is a low whistled *hew-eep*."

Field marks.—Over most of its range on the open desert, LeConte's is the only thrasher likely to be met with. Here, a slender, clay-colored bird with a long, curved bill and a long, rather blackish tail held up at an angle, as it runs, showing its rusty brown under tail coverts, is almost sure to be this species. In a limited portion of its range it overlaps somewhat with the California thrasher and more so with the crissal thrasher. Both of these species are darker colored and the latter has deeper brown under tail coverts than LeConte's. The haunts and behavior of all three are different.

DISTRIBUTION

Range.—Southwestern United States and northwestern Mexico.

The LeConte's thrasher is found **north** to southern California (Coalinga, Huron, Kernville, Walker Pass, Owens Valley north to Benton, and Death Valley); southern Nevada (Ash Meadows, Charleston Mountains, Las Vegas, and the Virgin River Valley); and southwestern Utah (Beaverdam Mountains and the vicinity of Zion Park). **East** to southwestern Utah (near Zion Park); western and southern Arizona (Beale Spring, Fort Whipple, Phoenix, and Picacho Peak); and northwestern Sonora (Port Lobos). **South** to northwestern Sonora (Port Lobos); and northeastern Baja California (San Felipe Bay); also in western Baja California from 40 miles north of Punta Prieta south to San Juanico Bay. **West** to the Pacific Ocean from about latitude 26° to 29° N. in Baja California and northeastern Baja California (San Felipe Bay and the west side of the Laguna Salada);

and California east of the coastal mountains (Julian, Banning, Buena Vista, Lake McKittrick, and Coalinga).

The entire species as outlined is divided into two subspecies. Le-Conte's thrasher (*T. l. lecontei*) is found in the United States, Sonora, and northeastern Baja California; the desert thrasher (*T. l. arenicola*) is found in central western Baja California.

Egg dates.—Arizona: 9 records, February 21 to June 24.

California: 124 records, January 22 to June 11; 41 records, March 18 to April 11; 30 records, February 10 to 28.

TOXOSTOMA LECONTEI ARENICOLA (Anthony)

DESERT THRASHER

PLATE 84

HABITS

A. W. Anthony (1897) described this race from a series of 16 specimens collected at Rosalia Bay, Baja California. He gives its subspecific characters as "differing from *H. lecontei* in upper parts being darker and grayer, tail blacker and breast gray, tail shorter (?)." He sent a specimen to Mr. Ridgway, who wrote to him: "A specimen of the same sex of *H. lecontei* from the Mojave River, California, has a shorter wing and *very much* longer tail than your bird."

The range of the subspecies, as given in the 1931 Check-list, includes the Pacific coast strip between latitudes 26° and 29°.

Mr. Anthony (1897) writes of its haunts and habits: "The region immediately back from the beach at Rosalia and Playa Maria Bays is a series of wind-swept sand dunes, with scarcely any vegetation. A few hardy shrubs and yuccas struggle for existence and afford shelter for quite a number of Thrashers. A series of 16 was secured with little effort, though the present race well maintains the reputation of the species for shyness. On several occasions they were seen on the beach, and a few were found inland, where *H. cinereus mearnsi* was more common. They were nowhere so plenty as in the sand dunes near the surf. Nests were found in the thickest shrubs, that were probably the present race, proving that they are resident."

Griffing Bancroft (1930) gives us a somewhat similar impression of the bird in its haunts, as follows:

There comes a break in the topography of the country where the cactus and other typically desert associations give way to low sand dunes and thornless vegetation. A marginal strip of irregular width, nowhere exceeding a few miles, reflects the direct influences of the ocean. This littoral is the home of the so-called Desert Thrasher. A better understanding of its habitat may be had by appreciating how misleading is its customary name. *T. l. lecontei* is the desert dweller of the species. The "Desert" Thrasher does not wander at all into what we conceive to be the desert.

A study of old nests reveals the fact that the breeding season is long past by the middle of May. It does not begin, however, until well into March. The sites chosen are, of necessity, in small bushes, but there is a consistent preference for those which afford the maximum protection. That desire satisfied, the birds indifferently build in the heart of the shrub or near its outer edges. The foundation is composed of thorny twigs from 3 to 6 inches in length. They support a cup which, in thickness and size, is midway between that of the shrike and that of the San Lucas Thrasher. The inside walls and especially the bottom of the cavity are padded rather than lined .

The habitat of these thrashers harmonizes well with their dull gray backs and lighter underparts. They are decidedly ground-loving birds, skulking from bush to bush and seldom flying. When alarmed, unless the fright is too sudden, they run from danger. This they do with surprising speed, taking to the air only as a last resource. The southern shore of San Ignacio Lagoon is their metropolis in our cross section, but even there the birds are quite rare. In 3 days we saw not more than a dozen.

The eggs of the desert thrasher are like those of LeConte's thrasher. The measurements of 10 eggs average 26.8 by 19.3; the eggs showing the four extremes measure **29.0** by **20.0**, **25.4** by 19.3, and 26.4 by **18.7** millimeters.

TOXOSTOMA DORSALE DORSALE Henry

CRISSAL THRASHER

PLATES 85, 86

HABITS

Although the range of the crissal thrasher coincides in a very general way with much of the ranges of the three other desert thrashers, its haunts and chosen habitats are quite different from those of the others, and they seldom overlap to any extent. LeConte's thrasher lives in the hottest, driest, and most open deserts; Bendire's and the curve-billed thrashers are found on the slightly more fertile deserts and valleys, where there is more vegetation, and about the ranches; but the crissal thrasher seldom ventures out onto the desert and prefers the more fertile valleys, canyons, and hillsides, where it can hide among the more abundant vegetation and in the dense thickets, often in the vicinity of water.

What few crissal thrashers we saw in southern Arizona were found in the belts of small mesquites, creosote bushes, and sagebrush that grew along the arroyos, in low bushy underbrush in the valleys, in the willows along a ditch in the San Pedro Valley, and on the rough sides of the Dragoon Mountains, where mesquites, junipers, and straggling bushes grew among the rocks. They were not very common and were always shy and retiring.

Frank Stephens told Mr. Brewster (1882a) that "he found the Crissal Thrasher in copses in valleys, and along streams. It was especially fond of well-shaded undergrowth, and spent much of its time on the ground, searching for food under the bushes. It never occurred among cactuses, and the only place where he saw it actually associating with Bendire's and Palmer's Thrashers, was at Camp Lowell, where the latter species, with other desert birds, came to drink at a water-hole and thus occasionally mingled with the Crissal Thrashers, which inhabited the neighboring thickets."

M. French Gilman (1902) says that, on the California side of the Colorado River, "great numbers of them can be found in the dense thickets of mesquite and screw-bean in the depressed portion of the desert near the Salton sink," which is from 10 to 260 feet below sea level.

Nesting.—We found only two nests of the crissal thrasher in southeastern Arizona in 1922. Near Fairbank, in the San Pedro Valley, on May 27, a nest containing one egg was seen about 8 feet above ground in a vine-covered willow in a row of these trees growing along an irrigation ditch. The other nest, found on June 1 near Tombstone, was placed 3 feet from the ground in a dense sagebush on the edge of an arroyo, where it was well hidden (pl. 85) ; it was made of thorny twigs with a lining of fine bluish fiber; it held three eggs.

Dean Amadon (MS.) reports a nest, found near Tucson on June 24, 1938, that was placed on a branch of a willow next to the trunk and about 8 feet above ground; this was near a ditch leading away from a pond in a brushy area; at that date it contained one young bird, perhaps a week old, and two unhatched eggs. A set of two eggs in the F. W. Braund collection, taken near Phoenix on March 17, 1896, came from a nest in a catsclaw bush on the desert.

A nest found by Dr. Mearns (1886) near Fort Verde, Ariz., on February 18, 1886, was described as follows: "The nest was saddled upon the fork of a mesquite-bush, about 4 feet from the ground, in part supported by the thorny branches of a neighboring bush. It rested upon a pile of sticks, and was surrounded by a bristling array of spiny 'haw' and mesquite twigs of moderate size; within this barricade the nest proper was placed; it is bowl-shaped, and, with the exception of a few feathers, composed entirely of vegetable substances very neatly felted into a compact, warm nest. The principal materials are fine withered grass, stems of plants, and shreddy inner bark. Externally it measures 150 mm. in height by 300 mm. in width; the internal depth, 45 mm.; internal diameter, 90 mm."

Mr. Gilman (1902) writes of the nests found in the Colorado desert:

On March 18 and 19 we found 10 nests containing eggs or young. With one exception they were all built close up to an over-hanging limb making it difficult to insert the hand. All but one were also in the densest part of the mesquite and rather hard to see. And hard to get at too as anyone who has crawled through a mesquite thicket can testify. The nests were from 2½ to 6 feet from the ground—the average being about 3½ feet and only one

6 feet. * * * From brief observation I should say that individual birds nest near the same spot year after year. Nearly every nest found was near from one to three old nests, probably belonging to the same bird as no new nests were ever found close to each other. In one case three nests were found in the same tree—one new and two old ones.

Nests have also been found in other bushes, such as atriplex, greasewood, wild currant, and ironwood, but never, I believe, in cactus; and they are generally in thick bushes and well concealed. Mr. Gilman (1909) says of the many nests he has noted, 27 were in mesquites, "one was on top of a stump but hidden by dense, sprouting twigs. Eleven were in 'squawberry' bushes, four in greasewood, one in a palo verde, one in a mistletoe, and one in a low brush fence."

Eggs.—The complete set of eggs for the crissal thrasher may consist of two, three, or four, most commonly two or three. These vary from ovate to elliptical-ovate and have very little gloss. They look much like robin's eggs, darker and greener when fresh in the nest and fading to paler shades of bluish green or greenish blue when older. Eggs that I have seen in the cabinet are usually a pale shade of robin's-egg blue, "pale Nile blue," or "beryl blue." They differ from all other thrashers' eggs in being entirely unmarked. The measurements of 50 eggs in the United States National Museum average 26.8 by 19.2 millimeters; the eggs showing the four extremes measure 30.5 by 19.8, 28.5 by 20.8, 24.3 by 19.7 and 25.9 by 17.8 millimeters.

Young.—Both sexes share the duties of incubation and care of the young. The long breeding season, from February to June or July, indicates that at least two broods are reared in a season. Mr. Gilman (1909) watched a nest from the time that the two eggs were laid until the young birds left the nest, a nesting period of 30 days. "The set was completed April 6. At 6 a. m., April 20, one young was just out of the shell and the other egg pipped. At 6 p. m., the same date, both young were opening their mouths and trying to swallow my finger. No eggshell could be found. May 6th both young birds left the nest."

Mrs. Wheelock (1904) writes: "The young Thrashers hatch in 14 days. They are naked, except for the faintest suggestion of down on head and back, and are fed by regurgitation until four days old. On the ninth day the young are feathered all but the wings and tail, which still wear their sheaths, and the featherless tracts which are on all young birds. The iris of the eye is white at this time, but gradually becomes straw-color like that of the adult. Unless startled into an earlier exit, the Thrasher nestlings do not leave the cradle until 11 or 12 days old, and even then they hide in the bushes for many ensuing days, helplessly waiting to be fed by the adult."

Plumages.—Young crissal thrashers in juvenal plumage are very similar to the adults in spring plumage but browner throughout, the rich chestnut-brown of the under tail coverts being only slightly duller; the rump and the broad tipping on the tail are brownish chestnut; the bill is shorter and smaller, and the plumage is softer and looser.

After the postjuvenal molt, which involves the contour plumage but not the wings and tail, the young bird becomes indistinguishable from the adult in fall plumage; the date of this molt probably varies with the date on which the young bird was hatched. Adults have a complete postnuptial molt during July and August; the fresh fall plumage is slightly darker and grayer than the faded spring plumage. The sexes are practically alike in all plumages.

Food.—Very little seems to have been published on the food of this bird. Dr. Mearns (1886) says that it is "omnivorous. It feeds largely upon berries and wild grapes. A thorny species of 'haw' is plentiful along the Rio Verde, which bears an abundance of berries, of green, red, and dark glaucous-blue colors, according to the degree of maturity; upon these the Thrashers delight to feed. Insects constitute an important article of their diet at all seasons."

It is said to eat juniper berries and other wild fruits. The stomach of one of the birds collected for Mr. Brewster (1882a) "contained insects and a *small lizard.*"

Behavior.—The crissal thrasher is a shy, retiring bird: all one usually sees of it is a fleeting glimpse as it darts away skillfully into or under the brushy thickets. William L. Engels (1940) says that they are much like the California thrasher in their behavior:

They prefer, likewise, dense and continuous cover, such as that afforded by mesquite thickets, to which they are almost exclusively restricted, as the California thrasher is to the chaparral. Beneath the cover of the dense mesquite they move quickly along, in and out, with long, graceful strides, head forward, tail high, stopping here and there to dig or to whisk the litter aside in search of food. They are likewise agile in scrambling about in the thorny trees, working their way up toward the tops, the favored singing posts.

Crissal thrashers, too, are little given to flight. In the field, one's most common sight of them is a sudden, brief glimpse of a bird abruptly dropping from a bushtop to the ground in a short swoop, wings outspread. Pursued, they make off rapidly on the ground, turning and twisting among the bushes, only occasionally taking to wing. Sometimes one may fly for 20 to 30 yards. One of the few crissals I saw in flight is thus described in my field notes: ". . . its long tail held straight out behind, the head extended forward, it would make a few rapid wingbeats; then with outstretched wings, which looked ridiculously short, it would sail on, only for a few feet, and then repeat."

Mrs. Bailey (1928) says that, "when tempted by water, the thicket-loving bird may come to drink with the chickens and dig in the garden, the strong pickaxe bill and large feet characteristic of the Thrashers making effective implements." Mrs. Wheelock (1904) also refers to his fondness for water, saying: "Rarely will you find him nesting at any great distance from water, and one of the first lessons he gives his brood is to take a morning splash. It is well worth rising at 4 a. m. to see him plunge so eagerly into the cold water and splash it in a shower of sparkling drops. The bath over, he flies up to the top of a tall bush to preen his wet feathers and fill the air with melody."

Voice.—Like most of the other thrashers, the crissal is a gifted songster. Dr. Mearns (1886) pays the following tribute to its music:

One of the first traits that we noticed about it was that it possessed a song of very remarkable scope and sweetness, having all the power of the Mockingbird, and an evenness and perfect modulation which that bird may well envy. It is one of the few birds that truly sing; and it shares, in this Territory, this rare gift with its three congeners—Bendire's, Palmer's and LeConte's Thrashers. It is no warbler of pretty ditties, nor yet a medley singer like the Eastern Thrasher or the Mockingbird, but discourses pure, natural music from the top of the tallest bushes, where it perches, with its tail hanging down, in precisely the same attitude as the Brown Thrasher of the East. Its season of song is more protracted than that of any other species with which I am familiar. Its best efforts are put forth during the mating season, in February, March, and April; but, except during July and August, when the heat becomes intense and the Thrasher's plumage is bleached almost to whiteness, and worn to tattered shreds amongst the thorny chaparral in which it finds food and some shelter from the sun, it sings commonly throughout the year. The warm sunshine of a winter's day suffices to bring out its full song, which perchance has been hushed by a cold snap and flurry of snow. At first come a few notes of doubtful confidence, barely sufficing to remind one that it *can* sing; then a thoughtful, somewhat desultory song, till the power of the tropical sun asserts itself, or the genial influence of its mate is felt, when the harmonious soliloquy grows into a serene and dignified performance that challenges attention and excites admiration. The Crissal Thrasher is a shy bird, and only sings when it fancies itself secure from intrusions upon its solitude; but, about ranches, where it associates with man, it loses some of its wildness and becomes more confident and trusting.

After the autumnal moult, when berries, grapes, and other acceptable food is plentiful, there is a distinct revival of song in this species. It has no loud call-note like the other species.

Mrs. Wheelock (1904) remarks that "every note is sweet, true, and perfect, but the whole lacks the spasmodic brilliancy we are accustomed to expect in his family. It has a more spiritual quality but less dash."

Mrs. Bailey (1928) mentions "its call notes '*queety-queety*' and a scolding '*cha.*'" W. L. Dawson (1923) refers to "a solicitous note, *pichoory, pitchoory,* or *pitchree*'"; also, "one very earnest fowl, near Tucson, remarked, *Pichoori karrik', pichoori karrik'* in quite a brisk manner."

Field marks.—The crissal thrasher was formerly called the red-vented thrasher, on account of the deep reddish brown of the under tail coverts and crissum, from which, also, the name crissal was derived. This color, which is darker and richer than in any of the other thrashers, is one of the best field marks when it can be seen. The crissal somewhat resembles the California thrasher, with a similar, long, curving bill, but it is somewhat smaller and their ranges do not overlap, except in a small section of southeastern California. It is not likely to be confused with LeConte's thrasher, for the latter is much paler in coloration and the habitats of the two do not overlap; the crissal almost never ventures out onto the open desert, and LeConte's is not likely to be seen in the shady thickets where the crissal lives. Mr. Gilman (1909) has this to say about recognizing the three species that are most likely to be seen in the same habitat:

In the field it is somewhat difficult to be sure in distinguishing the three species, Palmer, Bendire and Crissal. At close range, or if the birds are near enough together to compare, it is easy enough; but at a distance a single bird may puzzle.

In general it may be said that Crissal is darkest, has more curve to his bill and has a bobbing, jerky flight quite similar to that of the California thrasher. Palmer is a little larger, apparently at any rate, is lighter in color and has much of the same jerky flight. Bendire is smallest and lightest of the three and has a smooth, even flight. Both Palmer and Bendire have obsolete spots on the breast and light tips to outside tail feathers, but Bendire has the more distinct spots and whiter tail tips.

The crissal thrasher has no spotting on the breast, even when young. "At close range, say on the nest, the eye is indicative. Crissal has a straw-colored iris; Palmer, orange; and Bendire, orange red."

Winter.—Crissal thrashers are apparently permanently resident throughout their range, with only altitudinal migrations in spring and fall, up to about 5,000 feet in summer and fall and down to the warmer valleys in winter. Dr. Mearns (1886) says of these movements in Arizona:

The Verde Valley here has an altitude of 3,500 feet, and a much warmer climate than the bordering mesas and foothills, which in winter are often deeply covered with snow. Although they may be occasionally met with in the snow belt, most of them descend into the warmer valleys in severely cold weather. I have seen numbers of them feeding upon the bare sand upon the edge of the Verde River after a snowstorm. Making proper allowance for their being more conspicuous in winter on account of the absence of foliage, the species is undoubtedly far more plentiful in the Verde Valley during the winter season than in summer, when many of those which winter here move upward into the zone of scrub oaks, in which they breed in abundance wherever they can find water within a convenient distance. The exodus takes place about the end of February, after which the species becomes comparatively scarce; and by the middle of March nearly all those remaining are settled and occupied with domestic affairs.

DISTRIBUTION

Range.—Southwestern United States and northern Mexico; non-migratory.

The range of the crissal thrasher is **north** to southeastern California (Palm Springs, Indio, and the Providence Mountains); southern Nevada (Cottonwood Spring in the Charleston Mountains, Vegas Valley, St. Thomas, and Bunkerville); southwestern Utah (St.

George); central Arizona (Fort Whipple, Camp Verde, and Pinal Mountains); and southern New Mexico (Carlisle, Cliff, Bosque del Apache, Tularosa, and Carlsbad). **East** to southern New Mexico (Carlsbad); western Texas (Guadalupe Mountains, Glass Mountains, Marathon, and Boquillas); southern Coahuila (Saltillo and Diamante Pass); and Hidalgo (Portezuelo). **South** to Hidalgo (Portezuelo); southwestern Texas (Lajitas, Chisos Mountains, and Fort Hancock); northern Chihuahua (Colonia Diaz); and northern Sonora (Guaymas). **West** to northwestern Sonora (Guaymas, Rancho Costa Rica, and Kino Bay); northeastern Baja California (El Valle de la Trinidad, west side of the Laguna Salada, and Gardners Laguna); and central southern California (Alamorio, Martinez, and Palm Springs).

The entire species as outlined has been divided into three subspecies or geographic races. The crissal thrasher (*T. d. dorsale*) occupies the range in the United States and northern Mexico from Chihuahua to extreme northeastern Baja California; the Trinidad thrasher (*T. d. trinitatis*) occurs in El Valle de la Trinidad between the Sierra Juárez and the Sierra San Pedro Mártir; another race occurs in Mexico.

Egg dates.—Arizona: 88 records, February 18 to July 3; 44 records, April 2 to May 21, indicating the height of the season.

California: 56 records, February 10 to June 10; 28 records, March 11 to April 6.

Baja California: 6 records, May 8 to June 10.

TOXOSTOMA DORSALE TRINITATIS Grinnell

TRINIDAD THRASHER

HABITS

Dr. Joseph Grinnell (1927a) described and named this thrasher, based on a series of six specimens collected by Chester C. Lamb in the Trinidad Valley in northwestern Baja California. He says that it is similar to the crissal thrashers of California and Arizona, "but bill longer and distinctly more curved (as seen in lateral profile), and tone of coloration darker, more slaty. This latter qualification applies to both upper and lower surfaces, and particularly to the wings and tail, which are between fuscous and fuscous-black (of Ridgway, 1912), rather than near mummy brown. The bill, feet and claws also average blacker."

This subspecies evidently is isolated in a very restricted range, for he says that it is known only from the vicinity of the type locality in the Trinidad Valley. "This is a rather extensive, east-west valley which separates the Sierra San Pedro Martir immediately on the south, from the Sierra Juarez on the north. The Trinidad Valley is thus part of an intermountain pass, and through it many desert-side plants and animals have gone more or less distance onto the Pacific side, and

certain Pacific-side species have extended in the opposite direction."
Its habits are probably similar to those of the northern race.

The measurements of 17 eggs average 27.1 by 19.6 millimeters; the eggs showing the four extremes measure **30.2** by 20.0, 25.2 by **20.2**, and **24.9 by 18.7** millimeters.

OREOSCOPTES MONTANUS (Townsend)

SAGE THRASHER

PLATES 87–90

HABITS

The above scientific name and the old common name, mountain mockingbird, are both misnomers, as this is not a mountain bird and is not a mocker. But sage thrasher is a most appropriate name, for it designates the bird's habitat and its relationship to the true thrashers. It is the characteristic bird of the vast sagebrush plains, and its distribution is limited almost entirely to the semiarid regions where immense areas are clothed with practically nothing but a waving sea of pale, gray-green sage (*Artemisia tridentata*). Only the great sagehen, now rapidly disappearing, seems to show such partiality for the sagebrush plains. Though confined mainly to the valleys and mesas, this thrasher extends its range in many places up into the foothills, where the sage gives way to other bushes, junipers and mahogany woods, up to 4,000 feet or even 6,000 feet at some places; this is as near as it comes to being a mountain bird.

The 1931 Check-list gives its range as north to southern British Columbia and central Montana. It has evidently extended its range more or less irregularly during the past ten years. We did not record it in southern Saskatchewan in either 1905 or 1906, but Laurence B. Potter, of Eastend, of the same general region in which we worked, has sent me several notes on its occurrence there from 1933 to 1939. He says: "Sage thrashers made their first known appearance in this southern part of Saskatchewan during the long period of drought, lately ended, and the first specimen was secured in 1933. Rather unexpectedly, it has continued to migrate north since the wet seasons have set in. The sage thrasher is generally associated with the hot, arid plains, and it seemed strange to find it singing lustily on a cold, wet morning, as on May 8, 1938." He wrote to me on September 23, 1934, that his friend Charles F. Holmes took a breeding male in 1933 and the next year shot a breeding female and found a nest with eggs. On June 12, 1934, Fred Bard found a nest with a set of five eggs and took both birds; later on he found two more nesting pairs. The thrashers came there quite early in May in 1938 and 1939. Whether this is to be a permanent extension of the breeding range remains to be seen.

Courtship.—The first mention of the courtship activities of the sage thrasher is from the notebook of Robert Ridgway, dated April 9, 1868, at Carson City, Nev. Dr. Elliott Coues (1878) quotes from it as follows: "The Sage Thrasher is now one of the most common birds in this vicinity. To-day a great many were noticed among the brush-heaps in the city cemetery. Its manners during the pairing season are peculiar. The males, as they flew before us, were observed to keep up a peculiar tremor or fluttering of the wings, warbling as they flew, and upon alighting (generally upon the fence or a bush), raised the wings over the back, with elbows together, quivering with joy as they sang."

Ralph Hoffmann (1927) gives this slightly different account of it: "In April and May when the birds are mating, the male Thrasher gives vent to his ardor, not by mounting in the air like many ground birds, but by flying in a somewhat clownish zigzag low over the sage. At the end of this flight the bird lights with wings upraised and flutters them for an instant."

Nesting.—Mr. Ridgway's notes contain the first description of the nest of this thrasher that I can find. The sagebushes in the cemetery had been pulled up and piled in a heap; one of the nests was so well hidden in one of these brush heaps that much of it had to be removed before the nest could be seen. Other nests were found in sagebushes on the open plain, but also well concealed.

An early description of an interesting nest is given by Henry W. Henshaw (1875):

Its nest, a bulky and inartistic structure of coarse twigs, lined with grasses and fine rootlets, is sometimes placed in a sage shrub; but more often the bird selects one of the higher bushes, which, armed with sharp, stiff thorns, serves as an admirably secure platform for the clumsy nest, and affords additional security from its winged and four-footed enemies. A nest, which I examined near Fort Garland, was thus placed, and some 8 inches above it was a device, which, though it may have been the result of mere accident, certainly seemed to me to bear in the method of its construction, the evidences of design, and, if the supposition be true, would argue for the designers no small degree of intelligence. This was a platform of twigs, so placed as to screen the setting bird from the rays of the almost tropical sun. The material of which it was composed was precisely similar to that used in the construction of the nest, and it had been made at about the same time.

Mrs. Bailey (1928) says that, in New Mexico, the nest may be on the ground or in low bushes, "especially sagebrush; bulky, made largely of coarse plant stems, twigs of sagebrush and greasewood, dry sage shreds and sage bark; lined with fine rootlets and sometimes hair and fur."

In southwestern Colorado, M. French Gilman (1907) found six nests, four of which were in sage and two in greasewood bushes, all 2 to 2½ feet from the ground. One of these had "a distinct arch or platform of dry twigs just above it." This was probably similar to that described by Henshaw. Dr. Jean M. Linsdale (1938) reports some five nests found in Nevada; two of these were in sagebrush, one in rabbitbrush, one in a greasewood, and one in a horsebrush (*Tetradymia*); these were all very low nests, ranging from 5 inches to 2 feet above ground, only one above 1 foot. There is a set of eggs in the F. W. Braund collection from New Mexico that came from a nest 2 feet up in a juniper. There are two sets in my collection that came from Utah; the nests were in greasewood bushes and were lined with sheep wool and horsehair.

Eggs.—The usual set for the sage thrasher consists of four or five eggs; six eggs are found occasionally and seven have been recorded by Gilman (1907). The average shape is ovate, with variations toward short-ovate or elongate-ovate. They are often quite glossy. They have been said to resemble mockingbirds' eggs, but they can generally be recognized by the deeper and richer colors. The ground color is a deep, rich blue, or greenish blue, sometimes almost as dark as catbirds' eggs and sometimes almost as pale as the darker shades of mockingbirds' eggs, "Nile blue" or "lumiere blue." They are boldly spotted with large well-defined spots or small blotches, which are not confluent and are sometimes elongated. These markings are usually in the darker shades of rich brown, or reddish brown, such as "chestnut" or "chestnut-brown"; but sometimes the markings are in paler shades, such as "cinnamon-rufous" or "vinaceous-tawny"; sometimes there are a few shell markings of "plumbeous."

The measurements of 50 eggs in the United States National Museum average 24.8 by 18.0 millimeters; the eggs showing the four extremes measure 29.5 by 19.3 and 22.6 by 17.3 millimeters.

Young.—The period of incubation does not seem to have been determined for this species. Apparently both sexes incubate the eggs, for Dr. Walter P. Taylor (1912) says that "one of the birds frightened from a nest proved to be a male, indicating that the male takes part in incubation." Probably two broods are sometimes raised in a season, but perhaps not regularly.

Plumages.—Dr. Linsdale (1938) describes three small young as "covered with tracts of blackish down." I have not seen any small young, but Mr. Ridgway (1907) says that, in the juvenal plumage, the upper parts are "light grayish brown (decidedly browner than in summer adults), the pileum, back, scapulars, and rump rather broadly streaked with much darker grayish brown; streaks on under parts less sharply defined than in adults."

The postnuptial molt of adults occurs in August and September and is complete. In fresh fall plumage, the upper parts are grayer than in spring, the tertials are margined terminally with white, and the underparts are washed with buff.

Food.—The examination of 10 stomachs of the sage thrasher by

E. R. Kalmbach (1914) showed that, where the sagebrush areas approach the borders of alfalfa fields, this bird makes itself useful by destroying alfalfa weevils. In bulk, this weevil—

formed about an eighth of the food and was present in 7 of the stomachs. The best work appeared to be done in June, when the insect was eaten at the rate of 3 adults and 6 larvae per bird. One bird had eaten 3 adults and at least 34 larvae, which composed 44 percent of the stomach contents.

Ground beetles were present in all but two of the stomachs examined and formed about 30 percent of the food in June and a lesser amount in April and July. These beetles and a trace of an ant formed the entire contents of one stomach. Darkling beetles of the genera *Blapstinus* and *Eleodes* also were frequently eaten, composing a fifth of the food. Hymenoptera, spiders, and caterpillars were other important ingredients. The only vegetable food was a quantity of currants found in one stomach.

Ira La Rivers (1941) gives the sage thrasher credit for being one of the three species that "fed most destructfully" on the Mormon cricket (*Anabrus simplex*). "Eggs as well as adults were consumed. From my observations, the thrasher played nearly as important a role in the destruction of cricket egg-beds as did the more conspicuous Western Meadowlark. * * * The cricket, actually a long-horned grasshopper, yearly causes damage in Elko, Eureka, Lander, and Humboldt counties, Nevada, by destroying large quantities of range and field forage, crops, and garden stuffs." He found this thrasher feeding not only on the migrating crickets, in company with mice and shrews, "but also digging up crickets from partly-finished wasp burrows. One individual was surprised in the act of eating a black wasp (*Chlorion laeviventris*) which had been left by a marauding shrew."

Mrs. Bailey (1928) says that it also eats locusts, and gives one record of 62 percent grasshoppers. In a considerable tract of gooseberry brush, Dr. Taylor (1912) noted that "hundreds of sage thrashers, in company with large numbers of Brewer sparrows, green-tailed towhees, and fox sparrows, were feeding on the berries."

Mr. Dawson (1923) writes: "At the close of the season, or when the young are able to fly well, the birds, all absolutely silent now, resort in numbers to the hillside springs and brushy draws to feed on berries,—wild currants, wild gooseberries, and to lesser extent, service berries. This fondness for small fruit has betrayed the birds into conspicuous mischief in the case of isolated ranches and pioneer reclamation projects. Almost devoid of fear, the birds troup into the gardens in late July and August to strip the currant bushes or blackberries, and later the grapevines."

Clarence Hamilton Kennedy (1911) reports serious damage to small fruits and grapes on his ranch in the Yakima Valley, Wash.:

During the latter half of May, families of Sage Thrashers drift down into the irrigated ranches and begin their season of fruit-eating with the black-cap raspberries, which are then beginning to ripen. * * * During the entire summer's observation I have heard no call of any kind and on but two occasions during this period have I heard a short burst of song. Their shyness also leaves them. They become as approachable as Robins in an eastern dooryard. They will sit and without fear eat berries within a few feet of pickers.

Immediately following the raspberries come the blackberries. Both are devoured with equal readiness. Sour red berries are eaten as readily as the riper black ones. The berries are eaten whole and because of their size many of those picked off fall to the ground and are lost. After the blackberry season there is a period of 2 or 3 weeks when no small fruits are ripe. During this time the Thrashers stay about the ranches but content themselves with an insect diet.

At the end of this interim, the latter part of July, the early grapes begin to color. At first they pass unnoticed but by the time one-half of the clusters are purple the Thrashers have commenced to peck them. Usually they break the skin and sip the juice but occasionally a grape is eaten whole. After the feeding on grapes commences the vineyard is never free from Thrashers, which fly up from the vines to near posts and silently watch any intruder. * * *

On this ranch there are 140 vines of Campbell's Early. The actual loss in weight of grapes through bird damage was 25 percent, but the loss in profits was not less than 50 percent because of the large item of labor in trimming damaged clusters, and the loss in fancy value through the unattractive appearance of the trimmed bunches.

Dr. George F. Knowlton writes to me: "During the past several years I have collected 24 sage thrashers in the Snowville area of Box Elder County, Utah. Examination of the stomach contents revealed 21 to contain a total of 65 grasshoppers, 1 field cricket, and 1 snowy tree cricket. One dragonfly was contained. Eighty-six Hemiptera in the stomachs included 54 adult and 13 nymphal false chinch bugs, 9 mirids, and 3 pentatomids. The 20 Homoptera included 7 beet leafhoppers and 8 psyllids. The 40 Coleoptera were made up of 5 alfalfa weevils, 1 clover leaf weevil, 2 click beetles, and representatives of various other families. There also were contained 2 larval Lepidoptera, 7 Diptera, 41 Hymenoptera of which 35 were ants, besides 2 spiders and 35 seeds, most of these being black-currant seeds. Many of the birds were taken along a one-eighth-mile fencerow of black currants, very attractive to birds of many species."

Behavior.—The sage thrasher may have been called the mountain mockingbird, or the sage mockingbird, because it impressed some of the early observers with its resemblance to that famous songster in some of its mannerisms. It uses its tail in much the same manner as the mocker, frequently raising it rapidly and then lowering it slowly while perched on a post or the top of a bush, moving its head nervously from side to side as it views the intruder. Again, while running on the ground, the tail is held high and daintily as the mocking bird is wont to do; its pose and flight are also suggestive of the relationship. But its terrestrial habits mark it as a thrasher, for it much prefers running to flying; it runs on the ground much like a robin, when not frightened; when alarmed, it is apt to dash thrasherlike into a bush and escape by running away under cover, or by low flight close to the ground, disappearing among the bushes and perhaps showing itself again on some distant bushtop.

On its breeding grounds it is rather shy and often difficult to approach, but it is tame enough about the ranches and gardens, where it comes in summer and fall in search of berries and grapes and where it is fairly bold and fearless.   Mr. Potter writes to me from Saskatchewan: "The sage thrasher, according to the books, is a shy bird, but I have found it, like the brown thrasher, a mixture of shyness and boldness, or rather confidence.   In 1937 I watched a thrasher singing on the top branch of a dead willow, about 10 feet from the ground.   I stole up by degrees in full view until I was hardly 20 feet away and stood there watching it for some time."

Cottam, Williams, and Sooter (1942) timed the flight speed of the sage thrasher in Oregon and Utah by comparing it with the speed of an automobile; their four records showed speeds of 22, 25, 28, and 29 miles an hour.

Voice.—To appreciate fully the song of the sage thrasher, the poet of the lonesome sagebrush plain, one should visit him in his haunts in the gray of early dawn, before the chilly mists of night have lifted from the sea of gray-green billows that clothe the mesa farther than one can see in the still dim light of the coming day.   As the veil lifts with the rising sun, the mists roll away, the shadowy bushes take definite form, the vast plain is spread out before us in all its soft colors, and, scarcely visible in the distance, a gray-brown bird mounts to the top of a tall sage and pours out a flood of glorious music, a morning hymn of joy and thanksgiving for the coming warmth of day.   It may not be the finest bird song that we have ever heard, perhaps not equal to that of the mockingbird, or even that of some other thrashers, but in the solitude of such drab surroundings it is soul-filling, satisfying, and inspiring.

In pure sweetness of tone the song is fully equal to that of the mockingbird; it is full of melody and tenderness.   It is suggestive of the song of the solitaire, but is more like that of the brown thrasher, with the frequent repetition of the phrases but without the pauses between them.   Like this thrasher, it sings from the top of some prominent perch, with head raised and tail hanging downward.   But its song is really its own and quite unique.

Laurence B. Potter writes to me: "The song of the sage thrasher is of the highest quality and, like that of the European skylark, is uttered without break or periods, as the brown thrasher.   I have timed the song with my watch and have known it to continue 2½ minutes at a stretch.   The sage thrasher also sings in flight in the manner of the western meadowlark."

Dr. Wetmore (1920) describes the song very well as follows: "At its beginning the song is somewhat like that of a grosbeak.   As the notes wander on, to change and become more intricate, burring calls, that while harsh are not unmusical, creep in as an accompaniment to clearer whistled notes that are varied and pleasing. Low trills and changing combinations mark the song, reminding one of the improvisation of some gifted musician who, playing apparently at random, brings forth tones that follow one another in perfect harmony."

Ralph Hoffmann (1927) says: "Its song, given from the top of the sage or from a fence post along the road, is a long succession of warbling phrases with very little range of pitch and with constant repetition of one accented note. The bird's alarm note is a *chuck, chuck* suggesting a blackbird, and a sweet high *wheurr.*"

Field marks.—Though there is a fancied, superficial resemblance to the mockingbird in behavior, the illusion is soon dispelled when the bird takes to the air, for the conspicuous white areas in the wings of the mocker are lacking in the thrasher. The sage thrasher can be recognized as a plain brownish gray bird above, with a darker tail tipped with white on the outer feathers, with a short, straight bill, and with a breast distinctly streaked with black. None of the other thrashers need be confused with it.

Fall.—The sage thrasher is a decidedly migratory species, retiring in fall from nearly all its breeding range and spending the winter near or beyond the southern boundary of the United States. Its migration is well marked and its numbers are sometimes impressive. Harry S. Swarth (1924) gives a good illustration of this, as observed in Arizona. The birds were "first seen September 11; a few days later this became the most abundant bird species in the piñon-juniper belt. The Sage Thrashers were obviously migrating, and some days all the birds seen would be rapidly moving southward, an advancing army really impressive in numbers. Scores were in sight at once on the ground, running from bush to bush, others were taking short flights through the trees, and still others were in scattered companies overhead, almost like flocks of bluebirds in flight. The usual call-note is a harsh *chuck*, suggestive of that of a blackbird, but some thrashers were heard giving fragments of their striking song from perches in the junipers.

"By the middle of October the number of Sage Thrashers had markedly diminished. On the 20th none were seen, but on the 23d two appeared, the last observed."

DISTRIBUTION

Range.—Central southern British Columbia to northern Mexico.

Breeding range.—The sage thrasher breeds **north** to central southern British Columbia (Keremeos, Similkameen Valley, and the Okanagan Valley as far north as Okanagan Landing); central Idaho (Junction); southern Montana (Hillside, Fort Custer, and Miles City); and southwestern Saskatchewan (Eastend). **East** to southeastern Saskatchewan (Eastend); eastern Montana (Miles City and Tongue River); eastern Wyoming (Midwest, Douglas, and Laramie); northwestern Nebraska, possibly (Sioux County); Colorado east to the Plains (Loveland, Golden, and Fort Garland); and extreme western Oklahoma (the Black Mesa region of Cimarron County). **South** to western Oklahoma (Cimarron County); northern New Mexico (Santa Fe, Albuquerque, and Mount Taylor); northern Arizona (Navajo, Apache County, and Fredonia); southern Nevada (Charleston Mountains); and southern California (San Bernardino and Lockwood Valley). **West** to California, southern and eastern parts of the State (Lockwood Valley, Bakersfield, Inyo Mountains, Mono Lake, Eagle Lake, and McDoel, Siskiyou County); Oregon, east of the Cascades (Spring Lake, Fort Klamath, and John Day River Valley); central Washington (Kiona, Yakima, and Ellensburg); and southern British Columbia (Keremeos).

Winter range.—In winter the sage thrasher is found **north** to southern California (San Fernando, Twenty-nine Palms, sometimes to Coalinga, Fresno County, and Death Valley); southern Arizona (Sascaton and Tucson); southern New Mexico (Silver City and Mesilla); and southern Texas (El Paso, Fort Clark, and Kerrville). **East** to Texas (Kerrville, Uvalde, Laredo, and rarely Brownsville); and northern Tamaulipas (Nuevo Laredo and Camargo). **South** to Tamaulipas (Camargo); northern Chihuahua (Colonia Diaz and Chihuahua); northern Sonora (El Doctor, Sonoyta, and Punta Penascosa); and Baja California (Cape San Lucas). **West** to Baja California (Cape San Lucas, the Pacific coast, and occasionally Guadalupe Island), and California (San Diego and San Fernando).

Migration.—Late dates of spring departure are: Chihuahua—Palomas Lakes, April 7. Texas—Somerset, April 12. Arizona—Tucson, April 7.

Some early dates of spring arrival are: Texas—Somerset, February 10. New Mexico—Silver City, March 22. Arizona—Williams, March 31. Colorado—Walden, March 10. Utah—St. George, April 13. Wyoming—Laramie, March 27. Idaho—Rupert, March 31. Montana—Billings, May 1. Oregon—Klamath Lake, April 6. Washington—Yakima, April 10. Saskatchewan—Eastend, May 2.

Some late dates of fall departure are: Saskatchewan—Eastend, August 18. Washington—Yakima, September 15. Idaho—Meridian, September 21. Wyoming—Douglas, October 3. Colorado—Fort Morgan, October 4. New Mexico—Zuni, November 26.

Some early dates of fall arrival are: Arizona—Fort Verde, August 29. New Mexico—Carlsbad, August 6. Chihuahua—Chihuahua, October 5.

Casual records.—On June 4, 1940, at Gleeson, Cochise County, Ariz., a bird still in juvenile plumage was collected; this is more than 250 miles south of the southernmost known breeding record for the State. A sage thrasher was recorded at Portland, Oreg., on August 12, 1924. There are two sight records for North Dakota: one at Medora on June 16, 1918, and one on April 24, 1930, in Woodbury Township, Stutsman County. A specimen was collected July 29, 1913, in Buffalo Valley, southwest Stanley County, S. Dak. One specimen was collected and four other birds seen on January 2, 1926, in Cameron Parish, La., only about 100 yards from the coast. On April 12, 1942, a specimen was collected near Braddock Bay, Monroe County, N. Y.

Egg dates.—California: 24 records, April 19 to July 18; 12 records, April 19 to May 19; 9 records, June 4 to 25.

Utah: 44 records, April 30 to June 11; 22 records, May 13 to 31, indicating the height of the season.

Washington: 22 records, April 14 to May 20; 11 records, April 24 to May 9.

LITERATURE CITED

ALCORN, GORDON DEE.
1931. Does the tule wren egg or nestling form part of the diet of the garter snake? Murrelet, vol. 12, p. 58.

ALDRICH, JOHN WARREN.
1944. Geographic variation of Bewick wrens in the eastern United States. Occ. Pap Mus. Zool. Louisiana State Univ., pp. 305–309.

ALLARD, HARRY ARDELL.
1930. Bill deformity in a catbird. Auk, vol. 47, p. 93.

ALLEN, AMELIA SANBORN.
1921. Food of western house wrens. Condor, vol. 23, p. 166.

ALLEN, ARTHUR AUGUSTUS.
1912. Phoebe vs. catbird. Bird-Lore, vol. 14, pp. 269–274.
1914. The red-winged blackbird: A study in the ecology of a cat-tail marsh. Abstr. Proc. Linn. Soc. New York, Nos. 24–25, 1911–1913, pp. 43–128, pls. 1–22.
1929. Nuthatch. Bird-Lore, vol. 31, pp. 423–432.

ALLEN, CHARLES SLOVER.
1892. Breeding habits of the fish hawk on Plum Island, New York. Auk, vol. 9, pp. 313–321, pls. 4, 5.

ALLEN, FRANCIS HENRY.
1912. The white-breasted and red-breasted nuthatches. Bird-Lore, vol. 14, pp. 316–319, 1 col. pl.
1932. The song of the red-breasted nuthatch. Auk, vol. 49, pp. 482–484.

ALLEY, Mrs. JESSE L.
1939. Mockingbird fights coach-whip. Florida Nat., vol. 13, p. 26.

AMERICAN ORNITHOLOGISTS' UNION.
1910. Check-list of North American birds. Ed. 3.
1931. Check-list of North American Birds. Ed. 4.
1946. Twenty-first supplement to the American Ornithologists' Union Check-list of North American Birds. Auk, vol. 63, pp. 428–432.

ANDERSON, ANDERS HAROLD.
1934a. Notes on the rock wren. Bird-Lore, vol. 36, pp. 173–174.
1934b. A cactus wren roosting in a verdin's nest. Bird-Lore, vol. 36, p. 366.

ANGUS, H. L.
1934. An unusual nest of the house wren. Wilson Bull., vol. 46, p. 116.

ANONYMOUS.
1887. The catbird of the West. Ornithologist and Oologist, vol. 12, p. 93.

ANTHONY, ALFRED WEBSTER.
1889. New birds from Lower California, Mexico. Proc. California Acad. Sci., ser. 2, vol. 2, pp. 73–82.
1891. Notes on the cactus wren. Zoe, vol. 2, pp. 133–134.
1893. Birds of San Pedro Martir, Lower California. Zoe, vol. 4, pp. 228–247.
1894. Notes on the genus *Heleodytes*, with a description of a new subspecies. Auk, vol. 11, pp. 210–214.

ANTHONY, ALFRED WEBSTER—Continued

1895a. A new species of *Thryothorus* from the Pacific coast. Auk, vol. 12, pp. 51–52.

1895b. Birds of San Fernando, Lower California. Auk, vol. 12, pp. 134–143.

1895c. A new subspecies of *Harporhynchus* from Lower California. Auk, vol. 12, pp. 52–53.

1897. New birds from the islands and peninsula of Lower California. Auk, vol. 14, pp. 164–168.

1901. The Guadalupe wren. Condor, vol. 3, p. 73.

ARNOLD, CLARENCE M.

1908. A brown creeper's mistake. Bird-Lore, vol. 10, p. 81.

ARNOLD, WILLIAM W.

1906. Western house wren's nest. Bird-Lore, vol. 8, pp. 172–173.

ATWATER, HARRY PHILEMON.

1887. Nesting habits of Texas birds. Ornithologist and Oologist, vol. 12, pp. 103–105.

AUDUBON, JOHN JAMES.

1841a. The birds of America, vol. 2.

1841b. The birds of America, vol. 3.

AVERILL, CHARLES KETCHUM, Jr.

1888. Feeding habits of *Sitta canadensis*. Auk, vol. 5, p. 118.

AYER, Mrs. NATHAN EDWARD.

1937. Difficulties of a cactus wren family. News from the Bird Banders, vol. 12, p. 31.

BAGG, AARON CLARK, and ELIOT, SAMUEL ATKINS, Jr.

1937. Birds of the Connecticut Valley in Massachusetts.

BAILEY, FLORENCE MERRIAM.

1902. Handbook of birds of the western United States.

1922. Cactus wrens' nests in southern Arizona. Condor, vol. 24, pp. 163–168.

1923. Birds recorded from the Santa Rita Mountains in southern Arizona. Pacific Coast Avifauna, No. 15.

1928. Birds of New Mexico.

BAILEY, HAROLD HARRIS.

1925. The birds of Florida.

BAIRD, SPENCER FULLERTON.

1858. Reports of explorations and surveys to ascertain the most practicable and economical route for a railroad from the Mississippi River to the Pacific Ocean, part 2. Birds. Vol. 9.

1864. Review of American birds, in the museum of the Smithsonian Institution, pt. 1. Smithsonian Misc. Coll., No. 181.

BAIRD, S. F.; BREWER, THOMAS MAYO; and RIDGWAY, ROBERT.

1874. A history of North American birds. Land birds, vol. 1.

BALDWIN, PENELOPE.

1929. Whispered bird songs. Bird-Lore, vol. 31, p. 112.

BALDWIN, SAMUEL PRENTISS.

1921. Recent returns from trapping and banding birds. Auk, vol. 38, pp. 228–244.

1922. Adventures in bird banding. Auk, vol. 39, pp. 210–224, pls. 8, 9.

BALDWIN, S. PRENTISS, and BOWEN, WILFRID WEDGWOOD.

1928. Nesting and local distribution of the house wren (*Troglodytes aëdon aëdon*). Auk, vol. 45, pp. 186–199.

BALDWIN, S. PRENTISS, and KENDEIGH, SAMUEL CHARLES.

1927. Attentiveness and inattentiveness in the nesting behavior of the house wren. Auk, vol. 44, pp. 206–216, pls. 10–13.

BALL, WILLIAM HOWARD.
    1927. The catbird (*Dumetella carolinensis*) at Washington, D. C., in winter.
        Auk, vol. 44, p. 256.
BANCROFT, GRIFFING.
    1930. The breeding birds of central Lower California. Condor, vol. 32, pp.
        20–49, figs. 10–20.
BANGS, OUTRAM.
    1898. Some new races of birds from eastern North America. Auk, vol. 15,
        pp. 173–183.
    1902. A new long-billed marsh wren from eastern North America. Auk, vol.
        19, pp. 349–353.
BANGS, OUTRAM, and BRADLEE, THOMAS STEVENSON.
    1901. The resident land birds of Bermuda. Auk, vol. 18, pp. 249–257.
BARROWS, WALTER BRADFORD.
    1912. Michigan bird life
BATCHELDER, CHARLES FOSTER.
    1885. Winter notes from New Mexico. Auk, vol. 2, pp. 238–239.
BATES, CLARA.
    1940. Florida's State bird : Most familiar and best loved of all [mockingbird].
        Florida Game and Fish, vol. 1, No. 5, pp. 10–11.
BATTELL, HARRIET CHAPMAN (Mrs. F. L. BATTELL).
    1925. A bit of evidence. Bird-Lore, vol. 27, p. 242.
    1941. Albino catbirds and a robin roost. Iowa Bird Life, vol. 11, No. 1, p. 13.
BAYLISS, CLARA KERN.
    1917. A remarkable case of bird-feeding. Auk, vol. 34, pp. 90, 91.
BEAL, FOSTER ELLENBOROUGH LASCELLES.
    1897. Some common birds in their relation to agriculture. U. S. Dept. Agr.
        Farmers' Bull. 54.
    1907. Birds of California in relation to the fruit industry. U. S. Dept. Agr.
        Biol. Surv. Bull. 30.
    1918. Some common birds useful to the farmer. U. S. Dept. Agr. Farmers'
        Bull. 630, rev. ed.
BEAL, F. E. L.; MCATEE, WALDO LEE; and KALMBACH, EDWIN RICHARD.
    1916. Common birds of Southeastern United States in relation to agriculture.
        U. S. Dept. Agr. Farmers' Bull. 755.
BECKHAM, CHARLES WICKLIFFE.
    1887. Additions to the avi-fauna of Bayou Sara, La. Auk, vol. 4, pp. 299–306.
BEEBE, CHARLES WILLIAM.
    1905. Two bird-lovers in Mexico.
BENNERS, GEORGE BARTLESON.
    1887. A collecting trip in Texas. Ornithologist and Oologist, vol. 12, pp. 49–52.
BICKNELL, EUGENE PINTARD.
    1884. A study of the singing of our birds. Auk, vol. 1, pp. 126–140.
BISHOP, LOUIS BENNETT.
    1904. The eggs and breeding habits of some comparatively little known North
        American birds. Abstr. Proc. Linn. Soc. New York, Nos. 15, 16, pp.
        48–61.
BLACK, JOHN DAVID.
    1929. A catbird bush. Oologist, vol. 46, p. 96.
BLAKE, EMMET REID.
    1942. Mexican dipper in the Huachuca Mountains, Arizona. Auk, vol. 59,
        pp. 578–579.
BLAKE, SIDNEY FAY.
    1928. Field notes on certain California birds. Condor, vol. 30, pp. 249–250.

BOGGS, MARION ALEXANDER.
    1935. Some age-records of catbirds, brown thrashers, red-eyed towhees, white-
        throated sparrows, and song sparrows. Bird-Banding, vol. 6, pp.
        134–135.
    1939. Some age-records of the brown-thrasher, eastern song sparrow and
        indigo bunting, at Waynesville, North Carolina. Bird-Banding, vol.
        10, p. 42.
BOLLES, FRANK.
    1891. Land of the lingering snow.
BOND, RICHARD MARSHALL.
    1940. Sleeping posture of the rock wren. Condor, vol. 42, p. 122.
BOULTON, [WOLFRID] RUDYERD, [Jr.].
    1927. Ptilosis of the house wren (Troglodytes aedon aedon). Auk, vol. 44,
        pp. 387–414, 12 figs.
BOWLES, CHARLES WILSON.
    1898. Duplicate nests. Osprey, vol. 3, p. 46.
BOWLES, JOHN HOOPER.
    1899. Decoy nests of the western winter wren. Bull. Cooper Orn. Club, vol.
        1, p. 72.
    1908. The tawny creeper in western Washington. Condor, vol. 10, pp. 27–29.
    1922. The bird trapper of the twentieth century. Murrelet, vol. 3, No. 1,
        pp. 9–12, figs. 1–3.
BRACKBILL, HERVEY.
    1942. Catbird wintering in Maryland. Auk, vol. 59, pp. 112–113.
BRADBURY, WILLIAM CHASE.
    1919. Nesting notes in the Rocky Mountain creeper. Condor, vol. 21, pp.
        49–52, figs. 12–15.
BRAND, ALBERT RICH.
    1935. A method for the intensive study of bird song. Auk, vol. 52, pp. 40–52.
    1938. Vibration frequencies of passerine bird song. Auk, vol. 55, pp. 263–268.
BRANDT, HERBERT.
    1945. A new wren from Arizona. Auk, vol. 62, pp. 574–577.
BRECKENRIDGE, WALTER JOHN.
    1935. An ecological study of some Minnesota marsh hawks. Condor, vol. 37,
        pp. 268–276, figs. 51–53.
BREWER, THOMAS MAYO.
    1879. The American brown creeper. Bull. Nuttall Orn. Club, vol. 4, pp. 87–90.
BREWSTER, WILLIAM.
    1879. Breeding habits of the American brown creeper (Certhia familiaris
        americana). Bull. Nuttall Orn. Club, vol. 4, pp. 199–209.
    1882a. On a collection of birds lately made by Mr. F. Stephens in Arizona.
        Bull. Nuttall Orn. Club, vol. 7, pp. 65–86.
    1882b. Impressions of some southern birds. Bull. Nuttall Orn. Club, vol. 7,
        pp. 94–104.
    1886. An ornithological reconnaissance in western North Carolina. Auk,
        vol. 3, pp. 173–179.
    1891. Descriptions of seven supposed new North American birds. Auk, vol.
        8, pp. 139–149.
    1893. Description of a new marsh wren, with critical notes on Cistothorus
        marianae Scott. Auk, vol. 10, pp. 215–219.
    1902. Birds of the Cape region of Lower California. Bull. Mus. Comp. Zool.,
        vol. 41, pp. 1–241, 1 map.

BREWSTER, WILLIAM—Continued
    1906. The birds of the Cambridge region of Massachusetts. Mem. Nuttall
        Orn. Club, No. 4.
    1936. October Farm.
    1938. The birds of the Lake Umbagog region of Maine, pt. 4. Bull. Mus.
        Comp. Zool., vol. 66. Compiled by Ludlow Griscom.
BRIDGE, LIDIAN EMERSON.
    1911. The story of two house wrens. Bird-Lore, vol. 13, pp. 141–142.
BROOKS, EARL.
    1922. Cardinal and catbird. Bird-Lore, vol. 24, pp. 343–344.
BROOKS, MAURICE.
    1932. Carolina wrens roosting in abandoned hornets' nests. Auk, vol. 49,
        pp. 223–224.
    1936. Winter killing of Carolina wrens. Auk, vol. 53, p. 449.
BROWN, HERBERT.
    1892. The habits and nesting of Palmer's thrasher. Zoe, vol. 3, pp. 243–248.
    1901. Bendire's thrasher. Auk, vol. 18, pp. 225–231.
BROWN, NATHAN CLIFFORD.
    1878. A list of birds observed at Coosada, central Alabama. Bull. Nuttall
        Orn. Club, vol. 3, pp. 168–174.
BRYANT, WALTER (PIERC)E.
    1887. Additions to the ornithology of Guadalupe Island. Bull. California
        Acad. Sci., vol. 2, pp. 269–318.
    1888. Unusual nesting sites. II. Proc. California Acad. Sci., ser. 2, vol. 1,
        pp. 7–10.
BURK, WALTER L.
    1938. Brown thrasher evicts catbird. Iowa Bird Life, vol. 8, p. 55.
BURLEIGH, THOMAS DEARBORN.
    1921. Breeding birds of Warland, Lincoln Co., Montana. Auk, vol. 38,
        pp. 552–565.
    1927. Notes from La Anna, Pike County, Pennsylvania. Wilson Bull., vol. 39,
        pp. 159–168.
    1930. Notes on the bird life of northwestern Washington. Auk, vol. 47,
        pp. 48–63.
    1931. Notes on the breeding birds of State College, Center County, Penn-
        sylvania. Wilson Bull., vol. 43, pp. 37–54.
    1935. Two new birds from the southern Appalachians. Proc. Biol. Soc.
        Washington, vol. 48, pp. 61–62.
    1941. Bird life on Mt. Mitchell. Auk, vol. 58, pp. 334–345.
BURLEIGH, T. D., and LOWERY, GEORGE HINES, Jr.
    1940. Birds of the Guadalupe Mountain region of western Texas. Occ.
        Pap. Mus. Zool. Louisiana State Univ., No. 8.
BURNS, FRANKLIN LORENZO.
    1915. Comparative periods of deposition and incubation of some North
        American birds. Wilson Bull., vol. 27, pp. 275–286.
    1921. Comparative periods of nestling life of some North American Nidi-
        colae. Wilson Bull., vol. 33, pp. 90–99.
BURROUGHS, JOHN.
    1895. Birds and poets with other papers.
BUTLER, AMOS WILLIAM.
    1898. The birds of Indiana. Indiana Dept. Geol. and Nat. Res., 22d Ann.
        Rep., 1897, pp. 515–1197, pls. 21–25.

Butts, Wilbur Kingsley.
    1927. The feeding range of certain birds. Auk, vol. 44, pp. 329–350.
    1931. A study of the chickadee and white-breasted nuthatch by means of
        marked individuals. Part 3: The white-breasted nuthatch (*Sitta
        carolinensis cookei*). Bird-Banding, vol. 2, pp. 59–76, 1 map.
Calhoun, Clara.
    1911. Carolina wrens in a blacksmith shop. Bird-Lore, vol. 13, p. 142.
Cameron, Ewen Somerled.
    1908. The birds of Custer and Dawson Counties, Montana. Auk, vol. 25,
        pp. 39–56.
Catesby, Mark.
    1731. The natural history of Carolina, Florida and the Bahama Is-
        lands . . ., vol. 1.
Chace, Leda W.
    1931. Catbird robs robin's nest. Oologist, vol. 48, p. 102.
Chadbourne, Arthur Patterson.
    1905. Nesting habits of the brown creeper as observed in Plymouth County,
        Massachusetts, with description of a nest from North Scituate. Auk,
        vol. 22, pp. 179–183, pls. 6–9.
Chapman, Frank Michler.
    1900. Bird studies with a camera. With introductory chapters on the out-
        fit and methods of the bird photographer.
    1912. Handbook of birds of eastern North America, rev. ed.
    1916. Notes on the plumage of North American birds. Bird-Lore, vol. 18,
        p. 172.
    1925. [Editorial on the house wren.] Bird-Lore, vol. 27, p. 203.
Christy, Bayard Henderson.
    1924. Bewick's wren in Allegheny County [Pa.]. Cardinal, vol. 1, No. 3, pp.
        12–15.
Clark, Austin Hobart.
    1945. Animal life of the Aleutian Islands. *In* Collins, Clark, and Walker,
        "The Aleutian Islands: Their People and Natural History," Smith-
        sonian Inst. War Background Studies No. 21, pp. 31–61.
Clark, Josiah Huntoon.
    1898. Notes on the nesting of Palmer's thrasher at El Plomo, Sonora, Mexico.
        Auk, vol. 15, pp. 272–274.
    1899. Nest of long-billed marsh wren lined with a snake skin. Auk, vol. 16,
        p. 281.
    1904. Curve-billed and Palmer's thrashers. Auk, vol. 21, pp. 214–217.
Clarke, Charles J.
    1915. Jonah, the catbird. Bird-Lore, vol. 17, p. 382.
Cole, Leon Jacob.
    1905. The occurrence of Bewick's wren, *Thryomanes bewickii* (Aud.) at
        Grand Rapids. Bull. Michigan Orn. Club, vol. 6, pp. 8–10.
    1930. The laying cycle in the house wren. Wilson Bull., vol. 42, p. 78.
Colton, Will N.
    1889. An unusual nesting site; peculiar eggs. Oologist, vol. 6, p. 9.
Commons, Marie Andrews.
    1930. In the garden with the bird bander. Bull. Garden Club America, ser.
        4, No. 8, pp. 16–21.
Cook, Mrs. H. P.
    1929. Translating notes into words. Bird-Lore, vol. 31, pp. 257–259.
Cooke, Wells Woodbridge.
    1884. Bird nomenclature of the Chippewa Indians. Auk, vol. 1, pp. 242–250

COOPER, JAMES GRAHAM.
   1876. Nesting habits of the California house wren (*Troglodytes aedon* var. *parkmanni*). Bull. Nuttall Orn. Club, vol. 1, pp. 79–81.
CORDIER, ALBERT HAWES.
   1927. Some observations on the water ouzel. Auk, vol. 44, pp. 169–178, pls. 6, 7.
COTTAM, CLARENCE, and KNAPPEN, PHOEBE.
   1939. Food of some uncommon North American birds. Auk, vol. 56, pp. 138–169.
COTTAM, CLARENCE; WILLIAMS, CECIL SLOAN; and SOOTER, CLARENCE ANDREW.
   1942. Flight and running speed of birds. Wilson Bull., vol. 54, pp. 121–131.
COUES, ELLIOTT.
   1875. Ornithology of the Prybilov Islands. *In* A report upon the condition of affairs in the Territory of Alaska, by Henry W. Elliott, pp. 168–212.
   1878. Birds of the Colorado Valley. U. S. Geol. Surv. Terr. Misc. Publ. 11.
   1882. Nesting of the white-bellied wren (*Thryothorus bewicki leucogaster*). Bull. Nuttall Orn. Club, vol. 7, pp. 52–53.
CURRIER, EDMONDE SAMUEL.
   1904. Summer birds of the Leech Lake region, Minnesota. Auk, vol. 21, pp. 29–44.
DALEY, FLORENCE KAISER (Mrs. EDWIN WOOD).
   1926. Rearing young red-breasted nuthatches. Auk, vol. 43, pp. 528–531.
DAWSON, WILLIAM LEON.
   1903. The birds of Ohio.
   1910. Rouge et noir. Condor, vol. 12, pp. 167–170.
   1923. The birds of California, vols. 1–3.
DAWSON, W. L., and BOWLES, JOHN HOOPER.
   1909. The birds of Washington. Vol. 1.
DEANE, RUTHVEN.
   1879. Additional cases of albinism and melanism in North American birds. Bull. Nuttall Orn. Club, vol. 4, pp. 27–30.
DECK, RAYMOND S.
   1928. A catbird family. Bird-Lore, vol. 30, pp. 101–105.
DICE, LEE RAYMOND.
   1918. The birds of Walla Walla and Columbia Counties, southeastern Washington. Auk, vol. 35, pp. 40–51.
DICKEY, DONALD RYDER, and VAN ROSSEM, ADRIAAN JOSEPH.
   1938. The birds of El Salvador. Publ. Field Mus. Nat. Hist., zool. ser., vol. 23.
DINGLE, EDWARD VON SIEBOLD, and SPRUNT, ALEXANDER, Jr.
   1932. A new marsh wren from North Carolina. Auk, vol. 49, pp. 454–455.
DIXON, EDWIN.
   1930. Catbird robs chipping sparrow. Oologist, vol. 47, p. 126.
DOOLITTLE, EDWARD ARTHUR.
   1923. The disposition of the catbird. Bird-Lore, vol. 25, p. 252.
DRAKE, MRS. GILBERT.
   1931. A queer wren's nest. Nature Mag., vol. 17, p. 212.
DRESSER, ROBERT.
   1892. Brief notes. Ornithologist and Oologist, vol. 17, p. 95.
DUNN, HARRY H.
   1902. Vigor's wren. Oologist, vol. 19, pp. 33–34.
DUTCHER, WILLIAM.
   1906. Remarkable flight of red-breasted nuthatches. Bird-Lore, vol. 8, pp. 209–210.

DWIGHT, JONATHAN, Jr.
    1900. The sequence of plumages and moults of the passerine birds of New
        York. Ann. New York Acad. Sci., vol. 13, pp. 73–360, pls. 1–7.
DYER, ERNEST I.
    1939. More observations on the nesting of the Allen hummingbird.   Condor,
        vol. 41, pp. 62–67.
EATON, ELON HOWARD.
    1914. Birds of New York.   New York State Mus. Mem. 12, pt. 2.
EDSON, WILLIAM LLOYD GARRISON, and HORSEY, RICHARD EDGAR.
    1920. Rare or uncommon birds at Rochester, N. Y.   Auk, vol. 37, pp. 140–142.
EHINGER, CLYDE ERNST.
    1925. A winter wren's lodging house.   Murrelet, vol. 6, pp. 37–39.
    1930. Some studies of the American dipper or water ouzel.   Auk, vol. 47,
        pp. 487–498.
EKBLAW, SIDNEY EVERETTS.
    1918. A tame brown thrasher.   Wilson Bull., vol. 30, p. 92.
ENGELS, WILLIAM LOUIS.
    1940. Structural adaptations in thrashers (Mimidae: genus *Toxostoma*) with
        comments on interspecific relationships.   Univ. California Publ.
        Zool., vol. 42, pp. 341–400, 24 figs.
ERICKSON, MARY MARILLA.
    1938. Territory, annual cycle, and numbers in a population of wren-tits
        (*Chamaea fasciata*).   Univ. California Publ. Zool., vol. 42, pp. 247–
        334, 16 figs., pls. 9–14.
ERRINGTON, PAUL LESTER.
    1935. Food habits of mid-west foxes.   Journ. Mamm., vol. 16, pp. 192–200.
ERRINGTON, P. L.: HAMERSTROM, FRANCIS; and HAMERSTROM, FREDERICK N., JR.
    1941. The great horned owl and its prey in north-central states.   Agr. Exp.
        Stat. Iowa State Coll. Agr. Bull. 277,   pp. 759–850.
ERWIN, WILLIAM GRADY.
    1935. Some nesting habits of the brown thrasher.   Journ. Tennessee Acad.
        Sci., vol. 10, pp. 179–204.
EVANS, CONROY.
    1918. A winter house wren.   Bird-Lore, vol. 20, p. 159.
FISHER, ALBERT KENRICK.
    1893. Hawks and owls of the United States, in their relation to agriculture.
        U. S. Dept. Agr. Biol. Surv. Bull. 3.
FORBES, STEPHEN ALFRED.
    1883. The regulative action of birds upon insect oscillations.   Bull. Illinois
        State Lab. Nat. Hist., vol. 1, pp. 3–32.
FORBUSH, EDWARD HOWE.
    1907. Useful birds and their protection.
    1916. Ninth annual report of the State ornithologist for the year 1916.
    1929. Birds of Massachusetts and other New England States, pt. 3.   Land
        birds from sparrows to thrushes.
FRIEDMANN, HERBERT.
    1925. Notes on the birds observed in the lower Rio Grande Valley of Texas
        during May, 1924.   Auk, vol. 42, pp. 537–554, pls. 25–29.
    1929. The cowbirds.
    1934. Further additions to the list of birds victimized by the cowbirds.
        Wilson Bull., vol. 46, pp. 25–36.
    1938. Additional hosts of the parasitic cowbirds.   Auk, vol. 55, pp. 41–50.

GABRIELSON, IRA NOEL.
　1912. A study of the home life of the brown thrasher, *Toxostoma rufum* (Linn.). Wilson Bull., vol. 24, pp. 65–94, figs. 1–6.
　1913. Nest life of the catbird. Wilson Bull., vol. 25, pp. 166–187.
GANDER, FRANK FORREST.
　1931. The mating of the western mockingbird. Wilson Bull., vol. 43, pp. 223–224.
GIGNOUX, CLAUDE.
　1924. Nesting of pygmy nuthatches at Lake Tahoe. Condor, vol. 26, pp. 31–32.
GILL, GEOFFREY.
　1935. The constancy of catbirds to mates and to territory. Wilson Bull., vol. 47, pp. 104–106.
　1936a. Further notes on the constancy of catbirds to mates and to territory. Wilson Bull., vol. 48, pp. 303–305.
　1936b. The concentration of catbirds at the close of the nesting season. Wilson Bull., vol. 48, pp. 38–40.
　1940. An analysis of catbird returns over a ten year period. Bird-Banding, vol. 11, pp. 21–22.
GILMAN, MARSHALL FRENCH.
　1902. The crissal thrasher in California. Condor, vol. 4, pp. 15–16.
　1904. The LeConte thrasher. Condor, vol. 6, pp. 95–98.
　1907. Migration and nesting of the sage thrasher. Condor, vol. 9, pp. 42–44.
　1909. Among the thrashers in Arizona. Condor, vol. 11, pp. 49–54.
　1915. A forty acre bird census at Sacaton, Arizona. Condor, vol. 17, pp. 86–90.
GODARD, A. H.
　1915. The house wren and dry sticks. Bird-Lore, vol. 17, pp. 211–212.
GOELITZ, WALTER ADOLPH.
　1918. A unique wren nest. Bird-Lore, vol. 20, p. 295.
GOODPASTURE, ALBERT V.
　1908. A mocking bird's June. Bird-Lore, vol. 10, pp. 201–204.
GRIMES, SAMUEL ANDREW.
　1932. Notes on the 1931 nesting season in the Jacksonville region. Florida Nat., vol. 5, pp. 57–63.
GRINNELL, JOSEPH.
　1900. The intermediate wren-tit. Condor, vol. 2, p. 86.
　1904. Midwinter birds at Palm Springs, California. Condor, vol. 6, p. 40–45.
　1907. Nesting of the Sierra creeper. Condor, vol. 9, p. 59.
　1908. The biota of the San Bernardino Mountains. Univ. California Publ. Zool., vol. 5, pp. 1–170, pls. 1–24.
　1910. Two heretofore unnamed wrens of the genus *Thryomanes*. Univ. California Publ. Zool., vol. 5, pp. 307–309.
　1913. Call-notes and mannerisms of the wren-tit. Condor, vol. 15 ,pp. 178–181.
　1914. An account of the mammals and birds of the lower Colorado Valley, with especial reference to the distributional problems presented. Univ. California Publ. Zool., vol. 12, pp. 51–294, 9 figs., pls. 3–13.
　1915. A distributional list of the birds of California. Pacific Coast Avifauna, No. 11.
　1917. The niche-relationships of the California thrasher. Auk, vol. 34, pp. 427–433.
　1918. Seven new or noteworthy birds from east-central California. Condor, vol. 20, pp. 86–90, fig. 11.

GRINNELL, JOSEPH—Continued
    1926. A new race of the white-breasted nuthatch from Lower California.
        Univ. California Publ. Zool., vol 21, pp. 405–410, 1 fig.
    1927a. A new race of crissal thrasher, from northwestern Lower California.
        Condor, vol. 29, p. 127.
    1927b. Six new subspecies of birds from Lower California.   Auk, vol. 44, pp
        67–72.
    1928. Notes on the systematics of west American birds.   II. Condor, vol.
        30, pp. 153–156.
    1933. The LeConte thrashers of the Jan Joaquin.   Condor, vol. 35, pp. 107–
        114, fig. 21.
GRINNELL, JOSEPH, and BEHLE, WILLIAM HARROUN.
    1935. Comments upon the subspecies of *Catherpes mexicanus*.   Condor, vol.
        37, pp. 247–251, fig. 46.
GRINNELL, JOSEPH; DIXON, JOSEPH; and LINSDALE, JEAN MYRON.
    1930. Vertebrate natural history of a section of northern California through
        the Lassen Peak region.   Univ. California Publ. Zool., vol. 35, pp.
        1–594, 181 figs.
GRINNELL, JOSEPH, and LINSDALE, JEAN MYRON.
    1936. Vertebrate animals of Point Lobos Reserve, 1934–35.   Carnegie Inst.
        Washington, Publ. No. 481.
GRINNELL, JOSEPH, and STORER, TRACY IRWIN.
    1924. Animal life in the Yosemite.   Contr. Mus. Vert. Zool., Univ. California.
GRINNELL, JOSEPH, and SWARTH, HARRY SCHELWALD.
    1926. New subspecies of birds (*Penthestes, Baeolophus, Psaltriparus,
        Chamae*) from the Pacific coast of North America.   Univ. California
        Publ. Zool., vol. 30, pp. 163–175, 2 figs.
HARDY, MANLY.
    1878. Nesting habits of the red-bellied nuthatch.   Bull. Nuttall Orn. Club,
        vol. 3, p. 196.
HARLOW, RICHARD CRESSON.
    1918. Notes on the breeding birds of Pennsylvania and New Jersey.   Auk,
        vol. 35, pp. 136–147.
HARPER, FRANCIS.
    1926. A new marsh wren from Alberta.   Occ. Pap. Boston Soc. Nat. Hist.,
        vol. 5, pp. 221–222.
    1929. Spring bird notes from Randolph County, Georgia.   Wilson Bull., vol.
        41, pp. 235–240.
HARRINGTON, ALICE BOWERS.
    1923. Observations on the mockingbird at Dallas, Texas.   Bird-Lore, vol. 25,
        pp. 310–312.
HARRIS, HARRY.
    1919. Birds of the Kansas City region.   Trans. Acad. Sci. St. Louis, vol. 23,
        pp. 213–371.
HARRIS, LUCIEN.
    1927. An unusual nest of the white-breasted nuthatch.   Wilson Bull., vol.
        39, pp. 41–42.
HART, R. E.
    1941. Blitzed birdhouse.   Nat. Hist., vol. 48, p. 256.
HARVEY, G. V.
    1902. The lodging of the white-breasted nuthatch in winter.   Amer. Orn.
        vol. 2, pp. 170–171.

HATHAWAY, HARRY SEDGWICK.
  1911. A house wren driven from its nest by spiders. Wilson Bull., vol. 23, p. 128.
  1913. Notes on the occurrence and nesting of certain birds in Rhode Island. Auk, vol. 30, pp. 545–558.
HAYWARD, W. J.
  1937. Incidents in bird behavior. Wilson Bull., vol. 49, p. 47.
HEATH, HAROLD.
  1920. The nesting habits of the Alaska wren. Condor, vol. 22, pp. 49–55, figs. 7–9.
HEGLER, MARIE ELLIS.
  1923. The whistling catbird. Bird-Lore, vol. 25, pp. 252–253.
HEMPEL, KATHLEEN M.
  1919. Notes on nesting bluebirds and house wrens. Bird-Lore, vol. 21, pp. 173–174.
HENDEE, RUSSELL WILLIAM.
  1929. Note on birds observed in Moffat County, Colorado. Condor, vol. 31, pp. 24–32, figs. 9–11.
HENDERSON, GRANT.
  1931. Incompatibility of house and Carolina wrens. Wilson Bull., vol. 43, pp. 224–225.
HENDERSON, JUNIUS.
  1908. The American dipper in Colorado, Bird-Lore, vol. 10, pp. 1–7.
  1927. The practical value of birds.
HENSHALL, JAMES ALEXANDER.
  1901. American dipper. Amer. Orn., vol. 1, pp. 175–179.
HENSHAW, HENRY WETHERBEE.
  1875. Report upon the ornithological collections made in portions of Nevada, Utah, California, Colorado, New Mexico, and Arizona during the years 1871, 1872, 1873, and 1874. Wheeler's Rep. Expl. Surv. West 100th Merid.
HERMAN, WILLIAM CEPHAS.
  1923. Dual nest of the robin and brown thrasher. Bird-Lore, vol. 25, pp. 127–128.
HILLS, VICTOR GARDINER.
  1924. A house wren adopts a family of young black-headed grosbeaks (Denver, Colorado). Auk, vol. 41, pp. 615–616.
HOFFMAN, EDWARD CARLTON.
  1925. House wrens and arsenate-dusted currant bushes. Wilson Bull., vol. 37, p. 224.
HOFFMANN, RALPH.
  1904. A guide to the birds of New England and eastern New York.
  1927. Birds of the Pacific States.
HOLT, ERNEST GOLSAN, and SUTTON, GEORGE MIKSCH.
  1926. Notes on birds observed in southern Florida. Ann. Carnegie Mus., vol. 16, pp. 409–439, pls. 39–44.
HOLTERHOFF, GODFREY, Jr.
  1881. A collector's notes on the breeding of a few western birds. Amer. Nat., vol. 15, pp. 208–219.
  1883. Nest and eggs of Leconte's thrasher (*Harporhynchus redivivus lecontii*). Bull. Nuttall Orn. Club, vol. 8, pp. 48–49.

HOWELL, ALFRED BRAZIER.
   1917. Birds of the islands off the coast of southern California. Pacific
      Coast Avifauna, No. 12.
HOWELL, ARTHUR HOLMES.
   1924. Birds of Alabama.
   1932. Florida bird life.
HOWELL, A. H. and OLDYS, HENRY.
   1907. The Bewick wren in the District of Columbia, with a description
      of its song. Auk, vol. 24, pp. 149–153.
HUEY, LAURENCE MARKHAM.
   1927. Birds recorded in spring at San Felipe, northeastern Lower Cali-
      fornia, Mexico, with description of a new woodpecker from that
      locality. Trans. San Diego Soc. Nat. Hist., vol. 5, pp. 11–40.
HUNT, CHRESWELL JOHN.
   1904. That feathered midget of our tide-water swamps—the long-billed
      marsh wren. Cassinia, No. 8, pp. 14–16.
   1907. A brown creeper's spiral flight. Wilson Bull., vol. 19, p. 31.
HUNTER, LAWRENCE E.
   1935. Some bird tragedies. Wilson Bull., vol. 47, pp. 74–75.
INGRAHAM, SYDNEY ELEANOR (MRS. OLIN INGRAHAM).
   1938. Instinctive music. Auk, vol. 55, pp. 614–628, pls. 24, 25.
ISELY, DWIGHT.
   1912. A list of the birds of Sedgwick County, Kansas. Auk, vol. 29, pp.
      25–44.
JONES, MRS. A. H.
   1930. Pygmy nuthatches and wrens. Bird-Lore, vol. 32, pp. 426–427.
JONES, LYNDS.
   1913. Some records of the feeding of nestlings. Wilson Bull., vol. 25, pp.
      67–71.
JUDD, SYLVESTER DWIGHT.
   1895. Four common birds of the farm and garden. U. S. Dept. Agr. Yearbook
      for 1895, pp. 405–418.
   1900. The food of nestling birds. U. S. Dept. Agr. Yearbook for 1900, pp.
      411–436, figs. 48–56, pls. 49–53.
KALMBACH, EDWIN RICHARD.
   1914. Birds in relation to the alfalfa weevil. U. S. Dept. Agr. Bull. 107.
KENDEIGH, SAMUEL CHARLES.
   1934. The role of environment in the life of birds. Ecol. Monogr., vol.
      4, pp. 299–417.
   1940. Factors affecting length of incubation. Auk, vol. 57, pp. 499–513.
   1941. Territorial and mating behavior of the house wren. Illinois Biol.
      Monogr., vol. 18, No. 3, pp. 1–120, figs. 1–32.
KENDEIGH, S. C., and BALDWIN, SAMUEL PRENTISS
   1928. Development of temperature control in nesting house wrens. Amer.
      Nat., vol. 62, pp. 249–278.
KENNARD, FREDERIC HEDGE, and MCKECHNIE, FREDERIC BRIGHAM.
   1905. The breeding of the brown creeper in eastern Massachusetts. Auk,
      vol. 22, pp. 183–193, pls. 10–12.
KENNEDY, CLARENCE HAILTON.
   1911. Notes on the fruit-eating habits of the sage thrasher in the Yakima
      valley. Auk, vol. 28, pp. 225–228.
KING, FRANKLIN HIRAM.
   1883. Economic relations of Wisconsin birds. Geology of Wisconsin, vol. 1,
      pp. 441–610.

KNAPPEN, PHOEBE.
    1933. Birds eating sawfly larvae. Auk, vol. 50, pp. 451–452.
KNIGHT, ORA WILLIS.
    1908. The birds of Maine.
KNOWLTON, GEORGE FRANKLIN, and HARMSTON, F. C.
    1943. Grasshoppers and crickets eaten by Utah birds. Auk, vol. 60, pp. 589–591.
KOPMAN, HENRY HAZLITT.
    1915. List of the birds of Louisiana, pt. 7. Auk, vol. 32, pp. 183–194.
LACEY, HOWARD [GEORGE].
    1911. The birds of Kerrville, Texas, and vicinity. Auk, vol. 28, pp. 200–219.
LANGILLE, JAMES HIBBERT.
    1884. Our birds in their haunts.
LA RIVERS, IRA.
    1941. The Mormon cricket as food for birds. Condor, vol. 43, pp. 65–69.
LASKEY, AMELIA RUDOLPH (Mrs. F. C. LASKEY).
    1936. Fall and winter behavior of mockingbirds. Wilson Bull., vol. 48, pp. 241–255.
LAW, JOHN EUGENE.
    1928. *Toxostoma curvirostris:* 1. Description of a new subspecies from the lower Rio Grande. Condor, vol. 30, pp. 151–152.
    1929. Down-tree progress of *Sitta pygmaea*. Condor, vol. 31, pp. 45–51, figs. 13–21.
LEWIS, HARRISON FLINT.
    1927. Destruction of birds by lighthouses in the provinces of Ontario and Quebec. Can. Field-Nat., vol. 41, pp. 75–77.
LINCOLN, FREDERICK CHARLES.
    1920. A peculiarly marked example of *Dumetella carolinensis*. Auk, vol. 37, p. 593.
    1939. Migration of American birds.
LINSDALE, JEAN MYRON.
    1938. Environmental responses of vertebrates in the Great Basin. Amer. Midl. Nat., vol. 19, pp. 1–206.
LLOYD, J. WILLIAM.
    1914. The whisper song of the catbird. Bird-Lore, vol. 16, pp. 446–447.
LOFBERG, LILA MCKINLEY.
    1931. "Office aids" in nest building. Condor, vol. 33, pp. 245–246.
LOWERY, GEORGE HINES, Jr.
    1940. Geographical variation in the Carolina wren. Auk, vol. 57, pp. 95–104.
MACOUBRIE, JENNIE K.
    1932. A useful bird. Bird-Lore, vol. 34, p. 390.
MACOUN, JOHN, and MACOUN, JAMES M.
    1900. Catalogue of Canadian birds.
MAILLIARD, JOSEPH.
    1902. Wren-tit building in a tree. Condor, vol. 4, p. 95.
MARSHALL, JOE T., Jr.
    1942. Food and habitat of the spotted owl. Condor, vol. 44, pp. 66–67.
MARX, EDWARD J. F.
    1916. A bold winter wren. Bird-Lore, vol. 18, p. 109.
MASON, EDWIN A.
    1936. Parasitism of birds' nests by *Protocalliphora* at Groton, Massachusetts. Bird-Banding, vol. 7, pp. 112–121.
MATHEWS, FERDINAND SCHUYLER.
    1921. Field book of wild birds and their music. Rev. ed.

MAYNARD, CHARLES JOHNSON.
  1896. The birds of eastern North America. 2d ed.
McATEE, WALDO LEE.
  1920. Abundance of periodical cicadas, diverting attacks of birds from cul-
      tivated fruits. Auk, vol. 37, pp. 144–145.
  1926a. The relation of birds to woodlots in New York State. Roosevelt Wild
      Life Bull., vol. 4, pp. 1–152.
  1926b. Judgment on the house wren. Bird-Lore, vol. 28, pp. 181–183.
  1940a. An experiment in songbird management. Auk, vol. 57, pp. 333–348.
  1940b. Mimicry by a brown thrasher. Auk, vol. 57, p. 574.
McCLINTOCK, NORMAN.
  1909. A successful failure. Bird-Lore, vol. 11, pp. 198–204.
McILWRAITH, THOMAS.
  1894. The birds of Ontario.
MEAD, E. M.
  1903. The return of the nuthatch. Bird-Lore, vol. 5, pp. 12–13.
MEARNS, EDGAR ALEXANDER.
  1886. Some birds of Arizona. Auk, vol. 3, pp. 289–307.
  1890. Observations on the avifauna of portions of Arizona. Auk, vol. 7, pp.
      251–264.
  1902a. Descriptions of three new birds from the southern United States.
      Proc. U. S. Nat. Mus., vol. 24, pp. 915–926.
  1902b. The cactus wrens of the United States. Auk, vol. 19, pp. 141–145.
MERRIAM, CLINTON HART.
  1895. The LeConte thrasher, *Harporhynchus lecontei*. Auk, vol. 12, pp. 54–60.
  1899. Results of a biological survey of Mount Shasta, California. North
      Amer. Fauna, No. 16.
MERRILL, JAMES CUSHING.
  1878. Notes on the ornithology of southern Texas, being a list of birds ob-
      served in the vicinity of Fort Brown, Texas, from February, 1876,
      to June, 1878. Proc. U. S. Nat. Mus., vol. 1, pp. 118–173, pls. 1–3.
MERRITT, MAUDE.
  1916. Wren notes. Wilson Bull., vol. 28, pp. 92–94.
METCALF, E. I.
  1919. Is the house wren a bigamist? Bird-Lore, vol. 21, p. 303.
MICHAEL, CHARLES WILSON.
  1934. Nesting of the red-breasted nuthatch. Condor, vol. 36, p. 113.
MICHENER, HAROLD, and MICHENER, JOSEPHINE R.
  1935. Mockingbirds, their territories and individualities. Condor, vol. 37,
      pp. 97–140, fig. 23.
MIDDLETON, RAYMOND JONES.
  1936. Interesting albinos. Auk, vol. 53, p. 101.
MILLER, EDWIN VANCE.
  1941. Behavior of the Bewick wren. Condor, vol. 43, pp. 81–99, figs. 25–27.
MILLER, H.
  1891. Of interest to oologists. Oologist, vol. 8, pp. 183–184.
MILLER, RICHARD FIELDS.
  1914. The red-bellied nuthatch (*Sitta canadensis*) feeding among weeds.
      Auk, vol. 31, pp. 253–254.
MORRIS, ROBERT TUTTLE.
  1923. Unusual nesting-sites. Bird-Lore, vol. 25, p. 316.
  1925. Do birds sometimes win in a fight with snakes? Bird-Lore, vol. 27,
      pp. 253–254.

MORSE, ETTA M.
1923. A summer with a catbird family. Bird-Lore, vol. 25, pp. 251–252.

MOULTON, CHARLES E.
1921. A catbird in winter at Fays. Bull. Essex County Orn. Club, vol. 3, No. 1, p. 71.

MOUSLEY, WILLIAM HENRY.
1932. Further notes on the birds, orchids, ferns and butterflies of the Province of Quebec, 1931. Canadian Field-Nat., vol. 46, pp. 171–173.
1934. A study of the home life of the short-billed marsh wren (*Cistothorus stellaris*). Auk, vol. 51, pp. 439–445, pl. 14.

MUIR, JOHN.
1894. The water-ouzel. In "The Mountains of California," pp. 276–299.

MUNRO, JAMES ALEXANDER.
1924. Notes on the relation of the dipper (*Cinclus mexicanus unicolor*) to fishing interests in British Columbia and Alberta. Can. Field-Nat.. vol. 38, pp. 48–50.

MURPHEY, EUGENE EDMUND.
1937. Observations on the bird life of the middle Savannah Valley, 1890–1937. Contr. Charleston Mus., No. 9.

MUSSELMAN, THOMAS EDGAR.
1930. Two additional foot disases on birds. Bird-Banding, vol. 1, pp. 33–35, 1 pl.

NAUMAN, EMIL DANTON.
1912. A tragedy narrowly averted. Bird-Lore, vol. 14, pp. 294–296.
1930a. Intimate nestings of the brown thrasher. Wilson Bull., vol. 42, p. 137.
1930b. Cardinal vs. brown thrasher. Bird-Lore, vol. 32, pp. 274–275.

NEHRLING, HENRY.
1893. Our native birds of song and beauty.

NELSON, EDWARD WILLIAM.
1887. Report upon natural history collections made in Alaska. U. S. Signal Service, Arctic ser., Publ. No. 3.

NELSON, E. W., and PALMER, THEODORE SHERMAN.
1894. Descriptions of five new birds from Mexico. Auk, vol. 11, pp. 39–45.

NEWBERRY, WALTER CASS.
1916. A chapter in the life history of the wren-tit. Condor, vol. 18, pp. 65–68, figs. 27, 28.

NEWTON, ALFRED.
1893–96. A dictionary of birds.

NICE, MARGARET MORSE.
1931. The birds of Oklahoma. Rev. ed. Publ. Univ. Oklahoma, vol. 3, Biol. Surv. No. 1.

NORTHCUTT, CHARLES E.
1937. The Bedford wrens. Bluebird, vol. 4, No. 3, pp. 19–20.

NUTTALL, THOMAS.
1832. A manual of the ornithology of the United States and of Canada. Land birds.
1903. A manual of the ornithology of the United States and of Canada. Land birds. (Revised by Montague Chamberlain.)

OBERHOLSER, HARRY CHURCH.
1898. A revision of the wrens of the genus *Thryomanes* Sclater. Proc. U. S. Nat. Mus., vol. 21, pp. 421–450.
1919. Notes on the wrens of the genus *Nannus* Billberg. Proc. U. S. Nat. Mus., vol. 55, pp. 223–236.

OBERHOLSER, HARRY CHURCH—Continued

1921. Glimpses of desert bird life in the Great Basin. Ann. Rep. Smithsonian Inst., 1919, pp. 355–366.

1930. Another new subspecies of *Nannus troglodytes* from Alaska. Proc. Biol. Soc. Washington, vol. 43, pp. 151–152.

1932. Descriptions of new birds from Oregon, chiefly from the Warner Valley region. Sci. Publ. Cleveland Mus. Nat. Hist., vol 4, No. 1, pp. 1–12.

1934. A revision of the North American house wrens. Ohio Journ. Sci., vol. 34, No. 2, pp. 86–96.

1938. The bird life of Louisiana. Louisiana Dept. Conserv. Bull. 28.

ORFORD, W. McLEOD.

1929. Cardinal vs. catbird. Bird-Lore, vol. 31, p. 263.

OSGOOD, WILFRED HUDSON.

1901. New subspecies of North American birds. Auk, vol. 18, pp. 179–185.

OVERING, ROBERT.

1938. The 1937 fall migration at the Washington Monument. Wilson Bull., vol. 50, p. 146.

PEABODY, PUTNAM BURTON.

1906. Rocky Mountain nuthatch. Warbler, vol. 2, pp. 50–55, figs. 3, 4.

PEARSE, THEED.

1933. Display of winter wren (*Nannus hiemalis pacificus*). Murrelet, vol. 14, p. 45.

PEARSON, THOMAS GILBERT.

1909. The mockingbird. The National Association of Audubon Societies. Educational leaflet No. 41. Bird-Lore, vol. 11, pp. 274–277, 1 col. pl.

PEARSON, THOMAS GILBERT; BRIMLEY, CLEMENT SAMUEL; and BRIMLEY, HERBERT HUTCHINSON.

1919. Birds of North Carolina. North Carolina Geol. and Econ. Surv., vol. 4.

PERKINS, SAMUEL ELLIOTT, 3d.

1928. Catbirds remain mated. Wilson Bull., vol. 40, p. 207.

1930. The matings of the brown thrasher. Wilson Bull., vol. 42, p. 221.

PETERS, HAROLD SEYMORE.

1933. External parasites collected from banded birds. Bird-Banding, vol. 4, pp. 68–75.

1936. A list of external parasites from birds of the eastern part of the United States. Bird-Banding, vol. 7, pp. 9–27.

PHILLIPS, JOHN CHARLES.

1927. Catbirds and robins as fish-eaters. Bird-Lore, vol. 29, pp. 342–343.

PHILP, GILBERT.

1937. The effect of smudging on birds. Condor, vol. 39, p. 125.

PIERCE, WRIGHT McEWEN.

1907. Notes on the pallid wren-tit. Condor, vol. 9, pp. 151–152.

PIERS, HARRY.

1898. Remarkable ornithological occurrences in Nova Scotia. Auk, vol. 15, pp. 195–196.

POOLE, EARL LINCOLN.

1938. Weights and wing areas in North American birds. Auk, vol. 55, pp. 511–517.

PREBLE, EDWARD ALEXANDER, and McATEE, WALDO LEE.

1923. A biological survey of the Pribilof Islands, Alaska. North Amer. Fauna, No. 46.

PURDUM, CHARLES CHRISTOPHER.

1902. The food supply of the meadowlark. Oologist, vol. 19, pp. 8–9.

RAND, AUSTIN LOOMER.
    1941. Development and enemy recognition of the curve-billed thrasher, *Toxostoma curvirostre*. Bull. Amer. Mus. Nat. Hist., vol. 78, pp. 213–242.
RAY, MILTON SMITH.
    1904. A fortnight on the Farallones. Auk, vol. 21, pp. 425–442.
    1909. Birds of the Big Basin. Condor, vol. 11, pp. 18–22.
RHOADS, MARY CAWLEY.
    1924. Our winter guest. Bird-Lore, vol. 26, pp. 172–175.
RICHARDSON, CHARLES HOWARD, Jr.
    1906. Birds whose notes are imitated by the western mockingbird. Condor, vol. 8, p. 56.
RIDGWAY, ROBERT.
    1876. Ornithology of Guadeloupe Island, based on notes and collections made by Mr. Edward Palmer. Bull. Hayden Surv. Terr., pt. 2, pp. 183–195.
    1877. United States geological exploration of the fortieth parallel. Part 3: Ornithology.
    1889. The ornithology of Illinois, vol. 1, pt. 1.
    1904. The birds of North and Middle America. U. S. Nat. Mus. Bull. 50, pt. 3.
    1907. The birds of North and Middle America. U. S. Nat. Mus. Bull. 50, pt. 4.
    1912. Color standards and color nomenclature.
ROBERTS, THOMAS SADLER.
    1932. The birds of Minnesota. Vol. 2.
ROCKWELL, ROBERT BLANCHARD, and WETMORE, ALEXANDER.
    1914. A list of birds from the vicinity of Golden, Colorado. Auk, vol. 31, pp. 309–333, pls. 31–33.
ROWLEY, JOHN STUART.
    1935. Notes on some birds of Lower California, Mexico. Condor, vol. 37, pp. 163–168, figs. 32–33.
RUSSELL, MARY MERRICK.
    1929. One catbird. Bird-Lore, vol. 31, pp. 192–193.
SAGE, JOHN HALL; BISHOP, LOUIS BENNETT; and BLISS, WALTER PARKS.
    1913. The birds of Connecticut. State of Connecticut Public Doc. No. 47, State Geol. and Nat. Hist. Surv.
SAMUELS, EDWARD AUGUSTUS.
    1867. Ornithology and oölogy of New England.
    1872. Birds of New England and adjacent States.
SARGENT, GRACE TOMPKINS.
    1940. Observations on the behavior of color-banded California thrashers. Condor, vol. 42, pp. 49–60, figs. 15–17.
SAUNDERS, ARETAS ANDREWS.
    1921. A distributional list of the birds of Montana. Pacific Coast Avif., No. 14.
    1929a. The summer birds of the northern Adirondack Mountains. Roosevelt Wild Life Bull., vol. 5, pp. 327–499, figs. 93–160.
    1929b. Bird song. New York State Mus. Handb. 7.
    1935. A guide to bird songs.
SCHORGER, ARLIE WILLIAM.
    1926. Notes from Madison, Wisconsin. Auk, vol. 43, pp. 556–557.
SCHWAB, L. H.
    1899. An odd nesting site. Bird-Lore, vol. 1, p. 166.
SCLATER, WILLIAM LUTLEY.
    1912. A history of the birds of Colorado.

SCOTT, WILLIAM EARL DODGE.

1885. Early spring notes from the mountains of southern Arizona. Auk, vol. 2, pp. 348–356.

1888a. On the avifauna of Pinal County, with remarks on some birds of Pima and Gila Counties, Arizona. Auk, vol. 5, pp. 159–168.

1888b. Supplementary notes from the gulf coast of Florida, with a description of a new species of marsh wrens. Auk, vol. 5, pp. 183–188.

1890. A summary of observations on the birds of the gulf coast of Florida. Auk, vol. 7, pp. 114–120.

SELOUS, EDMUND.

1901. Bird watching.

SENNETT, GEORGE BURRITT.

1878. Notes on the ornithology of the lower Rio Grande of Texas. Bull. U. S. Geol. and Geogr. Surv., vol. 4, pp. 1–66.

1879. Further notes on the ornithology of the lower Rio Grande of Texas. Bull. U. S. Geol. and Geogr. Surv., vol. 5, pp. 371–440.

1889. *Troglodytes aedon*, house wren, breeding in a sand bank. Auk, vol. 6, p. 76.

1890. A new wren from the lower Rio Grande, Texas, with notes on Berlandier's wren of northeastern Mexico. Auk, vol. 7, pp. 57–60.

SETON, ERNEST THOMPSON.

1890. The birds of Manitoba. Proc. U. S. Nat. Mus., vol. 13, pp. 457–643, pl. 38.

SHAW, HENRY SOUTHWORTH, Jr.

1916. Some experiences in attracting birds—The nesting of a red-breasted nuthatch. Bird-Lore, vol. 18, pp. 166–170.

SHERMAN, ALTHEA ROSINA.

1912. The brown thrasher (*Toxostoma rufum*) east and west. Wilson Bull., vol. 24, pp. 187–191.

1925. Down with the house wren boxes. Wilson Bull., vol. 37, pp. 5–13.

SHUFELDT, ROBERT WILSON.

1893. Nesting habits of *Galeoscoptes carolinensis*. Auk, vol. 10, pp. 303–304.

SILLOWAY, PERLEY MILTON.

1907. Stray notes from the Flathead woods. Condor, vol. 9, pp. 53–54.

1923. Relation of summer birds to the western Adirondack forest. Roosevelt Wild Life Bull., vol. 1, No. 4, pp. 397–486.

SIMMONS, GEORGE FINLAY.

1925. Birds of the Austin region.

SIMPSON, CHARLES TORREY.

1923. Out of doors in Florida.

SKAGGS, MERIT B.

1934. A study of the Bewick wren. Bird-Lore, vol. 36, p. 365.

SKINNER, MILTON PHILO.

1922. Notes on the dipper in Yellowstone National Park. Condor, vol. 24, pp. 18–21.

1928. A guide to the winter birds of the North Carolina sandhills.

SKUTCH, ALEXANDER FRANK.

1935. Helpers at the nest. Auk, vol. 52, pp. 257–273, pl. 12.

1940. Social and sleeping habits of Central American wrens. Auk, vol. 57, pp. 293–312, pl. 5.

SLOSSON, ANNIE TRUMBULL.

1883. Birds in confinement. Ornithologist and Oologist, vol. 8, p. 55.

SMITH, PHILO W., JR.

1904. Nesting habits of the rock wren. Condor, vol. 6, pp. 109–110.

SMITH, WILBUR FRANKLIN.
    1911a. The friendly house wrens. Bird-Lore, vol. 13, pp. 135–140.
    1911b. A strange partnership. Bird-Lore, vol. 13, pp. 303–304.
SPENCER, HUGH.
    1928. Blacksnakes and birds. Bird-Lore, vol. 30, pp. 108–110.
SPRUNT, ALEXANDER, JR.
    1931. Certain land birds observed at sea. Auk, vol. 48, pp. 133–134.
STAFFORD, EARLE F.
    1912. Notes on Palmer's thrasher (*Toxostoma curvirostre palmeri*). Auk, vol. 29, pp. 363–368.
STEIGER, J. A.
    1940. Dipper, wilderness dweller. Bird-Lore, vol. 42, pp. 10–14.
STEPHENS, FRANK.
    1884. Collecting in the Colorado desert—Leconte's thrasher. Auk, vol. 1, pp. 353–358.
STEVENSON, JAMES.
    1933. Experiments on the digestion of food by birds. Wilson Bull., vol. 45, pp. 155–167.
STOCKARD, CHARLES RUPERT.
    1905. Nesting habits of birds in Mississippi. Auk, vol. 22, pp. 273–285.
STONE, WITMER.
    1896. The molting of birds with special reference to the plumages of the smaller land birds of eastern North America. Proc. Acad. Nat. Sci. Philadelphia, 1896, pp. 108–167.
    1011. The Carolina wren. The National Association of Audubon Societies Educational leaflet No. 50. Bird-Lore, vol. 13, pp. 167–170, 1 col. pl.
    1913a. The catbird. The National Association of Audubon Societies Educational leaflet No. 70. Bird-Lore, vol. 15, pp. 327–330, 1 col. pl.
    1913b. Bird migration records of William Bartram. Auk, vol. 30, pp. 325–358.
    1937. Bird studies at old Cape May. Vol. 2.
STONER, DAYTON.
    1932. Ornithology of the Oneida Lake region: With reference to the late spring and summer seasons. Roosevelt Wild Life Ann., vol. 2, Nos. 3, 4.
STONER, EMERSON AUSTIN.
    1938. Creeper nesting in Solano County, California. Condor, vol. 40, p 86, fig. 29.
STORER, TRACY IRWIN.
    1920. Lizard eaten by cactus wren. Condor, vol. 22, p. 159.
SUCKLEY, GEORGE, and COOPER, JAMES GRAHAM.
    1860. The natural history of Washington Territory and Oregon.
SULLIVAN, MAURICE.
    1940. Ivory gull from Mount Desert Island, Maine. Auk, vol. 57, p. 403.
SUTTON, GEORGE MIKSCH.
    1928. The birds of Pymatuning Swamp and Conneaut Lake, Crawford County, Pennsylvania. Ann. Carnegie Mus., vol. 18, pp. 19–239, pls. 3–10.
    1930. The nesting wrens of Brooke County, West Virginia. Wilson Bull., vol. 42, pp. 10–17.
    1940. Winter range of the short-billed marsh wren. Auk, vol. 57, p. 419.
SWALES, BRADSHAW HALL, and TAVERNER, PERCY ALGERNON.
    1907. Recent ornithological developments in southeastern Michigan. Auk, vol. 24, pp. 135–148.

SWARTH, HARRY SCHELWALD.

1904a. The status of the southern California cactus wren. Condor, vol. 6, pp. 17–19.

1904b. Birds of the Huachuca Mountains, Arizona. Pacific Coast Avifauna, No. 4.

1916. The Pacific coast races of the Bewick wren. Proc. California Acad. Sci., ser. 4, vol. 6, pp. 53–85.

1917. A revision of the marsh wrens of California. Auk, vol. 34, pp. 308–318.

1920. Birds of the Papago Saguaro National Monument and the neighboring region, Arizona.

1924. Fall migration notes from the San Francisco Mountain region, Arizona. Condor, vol. 26, pp. 183–190.

1929. The faunal areas of southern Arizona: A study in animal distribution. Proc. California Acad. Sci., ser. 4, vol. 18, pp. 267–383, pls. 27–32.

TATE, RALPH C.

1925. Favorite foods of some Oklahoma birds. Univ. Oklahoma Bull., vol. 4, pp. 33–35.

TAVERNER, PERCY ALGERNON.

1919. The birds of the Red Deer River, Alberta. Auk, vol. 36, pp. 248–265.

1934. Birds of Canada. Dept. of Mines, National Museum of Canada, Bull. No. 72, biol. ser. No. 19.

TAVERNER, P. A., and SWALES, BRADSHAW HALL.

1908. The birds of Point Pelee. Wilson Bull., vol. 20, pp. 107–129.

TAYLOR, GEORGE CAVENDISH.

1862. Five weeks in the peninsula of Florida during the spring of 1861, with notes on the birds observed there. Ibis, vol. 4, pp. 127–142.

TAYLOR, JOHN W.

1905. Incidents among birds. Bird-Lore, vol. 7, pp. 209–210.

TAYLOR, WALTER PENN.

1912. Field notes on amphibians, reptiles and birds of northern Humboldt County, Nevada, with a discussion of some of the faunal features of the region. Univ. California Publ. Zool., vol. 7, pp. 319–436, pls. 7–12.

TAYLOR, W. P., and SHAW, WILLIAM THOMAS.

1927. Mammals and birds of Mount Rainier National Park.

TEACHENOR, DIX.

1927. Snakes' sloughs as nesting material. Auk, vol. 44, pp. 263–264.

TERRILL, LEWIS MCIVER.

1922. The short-billed marsh wren in the Montreal district. Auk, vol. 39, pp. 112–115.

TODD, WALTER EDMOND CLYDE.

1940. Birds of western Pennsylvania.

TOMKINS, IVAN REXFORD.

1932. Worthington's marsh wren in the vicinity of Savannah, Georgia. Wilson Bull., vol. 44, p. 40.

TORREY, BRADFORD.

1885. Birds in the bush.

1904. Nature's invitation.

TOWNSEND, CHARLES WENDELL.

1905. The birds of Essex County, Massachusetts. Mem. Nuttall Orn. Club, No. 3.

1909. A Carolina wren invasion of New England. Auk, vol. 26, pp. 263–269.

1913. Some more Labrador notes. Auk, vol. 30, pp. 1–10.

1924. Mimicry of voice in birds. Auk, vol. 41, pp. 541–552.

TRAUTMAN, MILTON BERNARD.
    1940. The birds of Buckeye Lake, Ohio. Univ. Michigan Mus. Zool., Misc.
        Publ., No. 44.
TRINE, Mrs. GEORGE W.
    1935. The case against the bronzed grackle. Nebraska Bird Rev., vol. 3,
        pp. 54–55.
    1940. Some June bird notes from Red Cloud, Webster County. Nebraska
        Bird Rev., vol. 8, p. 91.
TURNER, LUCIEN McSHAN.
    1886. Contributions to the natural history of Alaska. U. S. Signal Service,
        Arctic ser., Publ. No. 2.
TYLER, JOHN GRIPPER.
    1913. Some birds of the Fresno district, California. Pacific Coast Avifauna,
        No. 9.
TYLER, WINSOR MARRETT.
    1914. Notes on nest life of the brown creeper in Massachusetts. Auk, vol.
        31, pp. 50–62.
    1916. A study of a white-breasted nuthatch. Wilson Bull., vol. 28, pp. 18–25.
VAN DENBURGH, JOHN.
    1899. Notes on some birds of Santa Clara County, California. Proc. Amer.
        Philos. Soc., vol. 38, No. 160, p. 177.
VAN ROSSEM, ADRIAAN JOSEPH.
    1929. The races of *Sitta pygmaea* Vigors. Proc. Biol. Soc. Washington,
        vol. 42, pp. 175–178.
    1930. Four new birds from northwestern Mexico. Trans. San Diego Soc.
        Nat. Hist., vol. 6, pp. 213–226.
    1931. Description of new birds from the mountains of southern Nevada.
        Trans. San Diego Soc. Nat. Hist., vol. 6, pp. 325–332.
    1936. Birds of the Charleston Mountains, Nevada. Pacific Coast Avifauna,
        No. 24.
    1943. The horned lark and the rock wren of the San Benito Islands, Lower
        California. Condor, vol. 45, pp. 235–236.
VAN TYNE, JOSSELYN, and SUTTON, GEORGE MIKSCH.
    1937. The birds of Brewster County, Texas. Univ. Michigan Mus. Zool. Misc.
        Publ. No. 37, pp. 5–115, pls. 1–5.
VORHIES, CHARLES TAYLOR.
    1921. The water ouzel in Arizona. Condor, vol. 23, pp. 131–132.
WALKINSHAW, LAWRENCE HARVEY.
    1935. Studies of the short-billed marsh wren (*Cistothorus stellaris*) in
        Michigan. Auk, vol. 52, pp. 362–369, pl. 17.
WARREN, BENJAMIN HARRY.
    1888. Report on the birds of Pennsylvania.
WAYNE, ARTHUR TREZEVANT.
    1899. Destruction of birds by the great cold wave of February 13 and 14,
        1889. Auk, vol. 16, pp. 197–198.
    1910. Birds of South Carolina.
WEBSTER, FRANK BLAKE.
    1892. Brief notes. Onithologist and Oologist, vol. 17, p. 95.
WELLMAN, GORDON BOIT.
    1933. The courtship flight of the red-breasted nuthatch. Auk, vol. 50, p. 112.

WELTER, WILFRED AUGUST.
    1935. The natural history of the long-billed marsh wren. Wilson Bull., vol.
        47, pp. 3–34, figs. 1–4.
    1936. Feather arrangement, development, and molt of the long-billed marsh
        wren. Wilson Bull., vol. 48, pp. 256–269.
WETHERBEE, Mrs. KENNETH BRACKETT.
    1930. Coöperative parents. Bird-Lore, vol. 32, p. 202.
WETMORE, ALEXANDER.
    1920. Observations on the habits of birds at Lake Burford, New Mexico.
        Auk, vol. 37, pp. 393–412.
    1921. Further notes on birds observed near Williams, Arizona. Condor,
        vol. 23, pp. 60–64.
    1923. Present status of the Carolina wren near Washington, D. C. Auk,
        vol. 40, pp. 134–135.
    1936. The number of contour feathers in passeriform and related birds.
        Auk, vol. 53, pp. 159–169.
    1939. Notes on the birds of Tennessee. Proc. U. S. Nat. Mus., vol. 86, pp.
        175–243.
    1941. Notes on the birds of North Carolina. Proc. U. S. Nat. Mus., vol. 90,
        pp. 483–530.
WEYDEMEYER, WINTON.
    1930. An unusual case of mimicry by a catbird. Condor, vol. 32, pp. 124–125.
    1933. Zonal range of the red-breasted nuthatch in northwestern Montana.
        Condor, vol. 35, pp. 32–33.
WHEELER, Mrs. A. L.
    1933. Brown creepers as guests. Bird-Lore, vol. 35, p. 268.
WHEELER, HARRY EDGAR.
    1931. The status, breeding range, and habits of Marian's marsh wren.
        Wilson Bull., vol. 43, pp. 247–267.
WHEELOCK, IRENE GROSVENOR.
    1904. Birds of California.
    1905. Regurgitative feeding of nestlings. Auk, vol. 22, pp. 54–70.
WHITTLE, CHARLES LIVY.
    1921. Sociable water ouzels. Auk, vol. 38, pp. 118–119.
    1922. Additional data regarding the famous Arnold Arboretum mocking-
        bird. Auk, vol. 39, 496–506.
    1930. An old white-breasted nuthatch. Bird-Banding, vol. 1, p. 83.
WHITTLE, HELEN GRANGER.
    1923. Recent experiences with nesting catbirds. Auk, vol. 40, pp. 603–606.
    1925. Catbird history. Bull. Northeastern Bird-Banding Assoc., vol 1, pp.
        48–49.
    1926. Recent history of a pair of white-breasted nuthatches, nos. 117455♂
        and 117456♀. Bull. Northeastern Bird-Banding Assoc., vol. 2,
        pp. 72–74.
WIDMANN, OTTO.
    1882. Cuckoos laying in the nests of other birds. Bull. Nuttall Orn. Club,
        vol. 7, pp. 56–57.
    1907. A preliminary catalogue of the birds of Missouri.
WILLARD, FRANCIS COTTLE.
    1912. Nesting of the Rocky Mountain nuthatch. Condor, vol. 14, pp. 213–215.
    1923. Some unusual nesting sites of several Arizona birds. Condor, vol.
        25, p. 121, figs. 41–43.

WILLIAMS, HELEN PATTERSON.

1931. Modern steel construction. Nature Mag., vol. 17, p. 167.

WILLIAMS, LAIDLAW ONDERDONK.

1941. Roosting habits of the chestnut-backed chickadee and the Bewick wren. Condor, vol. 43, pp. 274–285, figs. 77–81.

WILLIAMS, ROBERT WHITE.

1918. My nuthatch tenants and a pair of red-headed ruffians. Bird-Lore, vol. 20, pp. 217–218.

WILSON, ALEXANDER, and BONAPARTE, CHARLES LUCIEN.

1832. American ornithology. Vol. 1.

WINTLE, ERNEST DOUGLAS.

1883. Ornithological notes. Can. Sportsman and Nat., vol. 3, p. 200.

WOOD, HAROLD BACON.

1930. Bee-eating catbird. Bird-Banding, vol. 1, p. 43.

1934. Death on the highway. Oologist, vol. 51, p. 128.

WOOD, JOHN CLAIRE.

1905. Some Wayne County, Michigan, notes, 1905. Auk, vol. 22, pp. 423–424.

WOODCOCK, ARTHUR ROY.

1902. Annotated list of the birds of Oregon. Oregon Agr. Exp. Stat. Bull. No. 68.

WYLIE, EDWARD A. GILL.

1914. [Letter quoted in "Birds and the Army-worm."] Bird-Lore, vol. 16, p. 400.

W., J. B.

1884. [Note on catbird at nest of wood pewee.] Young Oologist, vol. 1, p. 56.

XANTUS, JOHN.

1859. Description of supposed new species of birds from Cape St. Lucas, Lower California. Proc. Acad. Nat. Sci. Philadelphia, 1859, pt. 1, pp. 297–299.

INDEX

aculeata, Sitta carolinensis, 12, 13, 14, 17, 20, 21.

aëdon, Troglodytes, 179.
  Troglodytes aëdon, 113, 140.

aestuarinus, Telmatodytes palustris, 239, 264.

affinis, Heleodytes brunneicapillus, 220, 231–233, 235.

alascensis, Troglodytes troglodytes, 159, 163.

Alaska wren, 159, 163.

alba, Pagophila, 297.

Alberta marsh wren, 239, 247.

albescens, Certhea familiaris, 69, 72, 79.

albifrons, Catherpes mexicanus, 276, 278, 280.

Alcorn, G. D., on California creeper, 77.
  on tule wren, 261, 264.

Aldrich, John W., on Appalachian Bewick's wren, 183.

Aleutian wren, 159, 161.

alexandrae, Sitta carolinensis, 12, 20.

Allard, H. A., on catbird, 345.

Allen, A. A., on catbird, 355.
  on prairie marsh wren, 256.
  on white-breasted nuthatch, 5.

Allen, Amelia S., on California thrasher, 408, 409.
  on canyon wren, 281.
  on common rock wren, 286.
  on dipper, 102.
  on Gambel's wren-tit, 92.
  on pygmy nuthatch, 45.
  on tule wren, 264.
  on Vigors's wren, 194, 196.
  on western house wren, 144.

Allen, C. S., on eastern house wren, 119.

Allen, Francis H., on Bewick's wren, 180.
  on brown creeper, 63.
  on catbird, 333, 338, 341–343.
  on eastern winter wren, 156.
  on red-breasted nuthatch, 28–30.
  on short-billed marsh wren, 273.
  on white-breasted nuthatch, 3, 6, 9.

Allen, J. A., 370.

Alley, Mrs. J. L., on eastern mockingbird, 307.

altus, Thryomanes bewickii, 181, 183.

Amadon, Dean, 99.
  on crissal thrasher, 421.

americana, Certhia familiaris, 56, 69, 71, 77.

anatum, Falco peregrinus, 307.

Anderson, A. H., on common rock wren, 291.
  on northern cactus wren, 229.

Angus, H. L., on eastern house wren, 119.

Anthony, A. W., on Bryant's cactus wren, 232.
  on Cedros Island wren, 202.
  on desert thrasher, 419.
  on Guadalupe wren, 203, 204.
  on Mearns's thrasher, 382.
  on northern cactus wren, 223.
  on San Clemente wren, 200.
  on San Pedro wren-tit, 96.
  on white-naped nuthatch, 55.

anthonyi, Heleodytes brunneicapillus, 220.

Apache wren, 146.

Appalachian Bewick's wren, 181, 183.

arenicola, Toxostoma lecontei, 419.

Argue, Arthur, on brown creeper, 68.

Arnold, C. M., on brown creeper, 54.

Arnold, W. W., on western house wren, 143.

atkinsi, Sitta, 12, 13.
  Sitta carolinensis, 17.

atrestus Thryomanes bewickii, 181, 191.

Atwater, H. P., on Texas wren, 185.

Audubon, J. J., 296, 371.
  on brown creeper, 57.
  on brown thrasher, 355.

Aughey, S., 52, 59, 103.

Averill, C. K., Jr., on red-breasted nuthatch, 27.

Ayer, Mrs. N. Edward, on northern cactus wren, 225, 228.

Badger, M. C., 199.

Bagg, A. C. and Eliot, S. A., Jr., on brown thrasher, 371.
  on short-billed marsh wren, 272.

Bailey, Florence M., on Baird's wren, 188.
  on black-eared nuthatch, 47, 54.
  on canyon wren, 279, 283.
  on common rock wren, 285, 290.
  on crissal thrasher, 423, 424.
  on dipper, 97.
  on northern cactus wren, 219–222.
  on Palmer's thrasher, 394.
  on plateau thrasher, 398.
  on Rocky Mountain creeper, 71.
  on Rocky Mountain nuthatch, 15.
  on sage thrasher, 428, 430.
  on western mockingbird, 320.

Bailey, H. B., 357.

Bailey, H. H., on eastern mockingbird, 306.
  on Florida nuthatch, 13.

Bailey, Vernon, on LeConte's thrasher, 417.

461

Thrasher, LeConte's, 411, 419.
  Mearns's, 380, 382.
  Palmer's, 389, 400.
  plateau, 398, 400.
  sage, 377, 427.
  San Lucas, 377, 382.
  Sennett's, 375.
  Sonoma, 410, 411.
  Trinidad, 426.
  western brown, 372, 374.
Thrashers, 295.
Thryomanes bewickii, 188, 190, 192, 199.
  bewickii altus, 181, 183.
  bewickii atrestus, 181, 191.
  bewickii bewickii, 176, 181, 183, 184.
  bewickii brevicauda, 182, 202.
  bewickii calophonus, 181, 188, 191.
  bewickii carbonarius, 201.
  bewickii catalinae, 182, 199.
  bewickii cerroensis, 182, 202.
  bewickii charienturus, 182, 187, 192, 198, 199, 201-203.
  bewickii correctus, 182, 198-200, 203.
  bewickii cryptus, 181, 183, 186, 187.
  bewickii drymoecus, 182, 191, 192, 197-199.
  bewickii eremophilus, 147, 181, 186.
  bewickii leucophrys, 182, 200, 202.
  bewickii marinensis, 181, 188, 191, 192, 196.
  bewickii nesophilus, 182, 199, 200.
  bewickii spilurus, 182, 188, 191, 192, 199, 200, 203.
thryophilus, Telmatodytes palustris, 239, 246.
Thryothorus ludovicianus, 179.
  ludovicianus berlandieri, 217-219.
  ludovicianus burleighi, 216.
  ludovicianus euronotus, 217.
  ludovicianus lomitensis, 216, 218.
  ludovicianus ludovicianus, 205, 216, 218.
  ludovicianus miamensis, 216, 217.
  ludovicianus oberholseri, 218.
Todd, H. O., Jr., 357.
  on eastern mockingbird, 301.
Todd, W. E. Clyde, on Bewick's wren, 176.
Tomkins, I. R., on Worthington's marsh wren, 241.
Torrey, Bradford, on brown creeper, 67.
  on eastern winter wren, 155.
  on red-breasted nuthatch, 31.
Townsend, C. W., 32.
  on brown thrasher, 368.
  on Carolina wren, 205, 214, 215.
  on catbird, 340.
  on prairie marsh wren, 248, 256.
  on red-breasted nuthatch, 28.
  on white-breasted nuthatch, 6.
townsendi, Myiadestes, 386.

Toxostoma bendirei, 383, 394, 397.
  cinereum cinereum, 377, 382.
  cinereum curvirostre, 379.
  cinereum lecontei, 379.
  cinereum mearnsi, 377, 380, 382, 419.
  curvirostre, 390, 394, 400.
  curvirostre celsum, 389, 398, 400.
  curvirostre oberholseri, 400.
  curvirostre palmeri, 385, 386, 389, 398, 400.
  dorsale, 404.
  dorsale dorsale, 420, 426.
  dorsale trinitatis, 426.
  lecontei arenicola, 419.
  lecontei lecontei, 404, 411, 419.
  longirostre sennetti, 375.
  redivivum pasadenense, 411.
  redivivum redivivum, 402, 410, 411.
  redivivum sonomae, 410.
  rufum, 302, 357.
  rufum longicauda, 372, 374.
  rufum rufum, 351, 372.
Trautman, M. B., on catbird, 323, 324.
  on prairie marsh wren, 252, 258.
Trine, Mrs. George W., on catbird, 344, 345.
Tringoides, sp 54.
Trinidad thrasher, 426.
trinitatis, Toxostoma dorsale, 426.
troglodytes, Nannus, 161.
Troglodytes aëdon, 179.
  aëdon aëdon, 113, 140.
  aëdon baldwini, 140, 146.
  aëdon parkmanii, 113, 140, 141.
  brunneicollis cahooni, 146, 147.
  brunneicollis vorhiesi, 146.
  domestica, 113.
  domestica baldwini, 114.
  domesticus, 146.
  domesticus baldwini, 146.
  domesticus domesticus, 146.
  domesticus parkmanii, 146.
  troglodytes alascensis, 159, 163.
  troglodytes helleri, 159, 170.
  troglodytes hiemalis, 148, 159.
  troglodytes kiskensis, 159, 163.
  troglodytes meligerus, 159, 161, 163.
  troglodytes pacificus, 159, 170.
  troglodytes petrophilus, 159, 169.
  troglodytes pullus, 159, 161.
  troglodytes semidiensis, 159, 169.
  troglodytes stevensoni, 159.
  troglodytes tanagensis, 159, 168.
Troglodytidae, 113, 127.
Tule wren, 239, 261.
Turner, L. M., on Aleutian wren, 162.
Tyler, John G., on San Joaquin wren, 197.
  on Sierra creeper, 76.
  on western mockingbird, 316.
Tyler, W. M., on brown creeper, 56, 60, 61, 65.
  on brown thrasher, 368.
  on catbird, 336.
  on eastern house wren, 131.
  on eastern mockingbird, 298.

PLATE 1

Ithaca, N. Y.   Adult.   A. A. Allen.

Warwick, R. I., May 17, 1900.   Nesting site.   H. S. Hathaway.

WHITE-BREASTED NUTHATCH.

PLATE 2

Taunton, Mass., June 4, 1941.   Grice & Bent.

YOUNG WHITE-BREASTED NUTHATCHES.

PLATE 3

Ithaca, N. Y.   A. A. Allen.

Intimidation display.

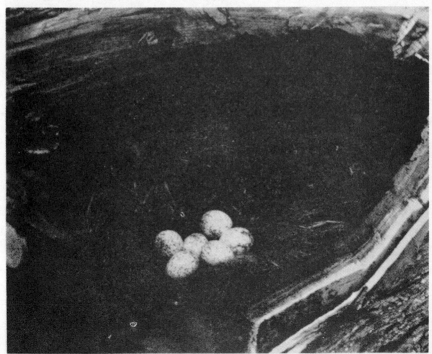

Harford County, Md., May 14, 1899.   W. H. Fisher

Nest and eggs.

WHITE-BREASTED NUTHATCH.

PLATE 4

Toronto, Ontario. H. M. Halliday.

Ottawa County, Mich., January 1940. B. W. Baker.

WHITE-BREASTED NUTHATCHES.

PLATE 5

S. A. Grimes.

Duval County, Fla., April 1932.

S. A. Grimes.

NESTING SITE OF FLORIDA NUTHATCH.

Duval County, Fla., March 26, 1932.

PLATE 6

Duval County, Fla., April 7, 1935.   S. A. Grimes.

Nesting site indicated by arrows.

S. A. Grimes.

Adult chiding young.

FLORIDA NUTHATCHES.

PLATE 7

Ashland, Oreg., May 10, 1920. J. E. Patterson.

NEST AND EGGS OF SLENDER-BILLED NUTHATCH.

PLATE 8

E. C. Aldrich.

Pinnacle National Monument, Calif., April 1934.

SLENDER-BILLED NUTHATCH.

PLATE 9

Near Arnprior, Ontario.　　　　　　　　　　　　　C. Macnamara.

NEST SITE OF RED-BREASTED NUTHATCH.

PLATE 10

Near Arnprior, Ontario.   C. Macnamara.

RED-BREASTED NUTHATCH AT NEST.

PLATE 11

J. E. Patterson.

Fort Klamath, Oreg. May 15, 1926.

Nest in quaking aspen.

Cordelia J. Stanwood.

Young.

RED-BREASTED NUTHATCH

PLATE 12

Duval County, Fla., April 1937.   S. A. Grimes.

Duval County, Fla., April 1933.   S. A. Grimes.

ADULT AND NEST OF BROWN-HEADED NUTHATCH.

PLATE 13

Pinehurst, Oreg., May 3, 1924.   J. E. Patterson

Huachuca Mountains, Ariz., May 7, 1922.   A. C. Bent.

NESTING OF BLACK-EARED NUTHATCH.

PLATE 14

Cordelia J. Stanwood.

O. Durfee.

Canton, Mass., May 16, 1904.

NESTING SITE AND NEST AND YOUNG OF BROWN CREEPER.

PLATE 15

A. A. Allen.

Ithaca, N. Y.   Adult at nest.

V. Burtch.

Potter Swamp, N. Y., May 20, 1915.   Nesting site.

BROWN CREEPER

PLATE 16

Courtesy Colorado Mus. Nat. Hist.

Nest found by R. J. Niedrach in Colorado.

ROCKY MOUNTAIN CREEPER.

PLATE 17

Huachuca Mountains, Ariz., May 15, 1922.

A. C. Bent.

Arizona.

F. C. Willard.

NESTING OF MEXICAN CREEPER.

PLATE 18

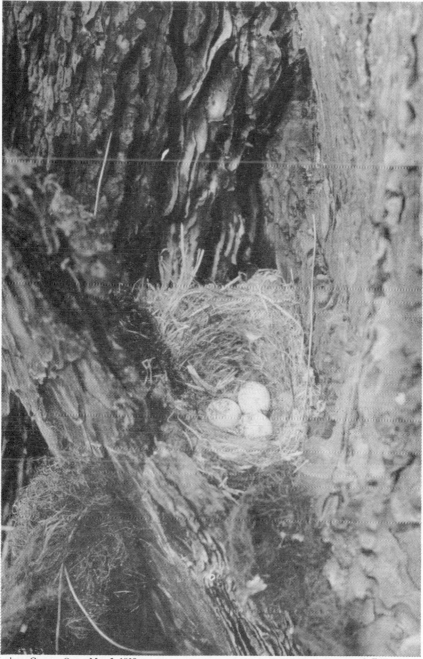

Jackson County, Oreg., May 5, 1920.

J. E. Patterson.

NEST OF SIERRA CREEPER.

PLATE 19

Berkeley, Calif., May 6, 1931.

Mary M. Erickson.

Roosting bush of male.

Berkeley, Calif., August 4, 1933.

Mary M. Erickson.
Courtesy of Mus. Vert. Zoology.

NESTING OF GAMBEL'S WREN-TIT.

PLATE 20

Azusa, Calif., October 6, 1936.   R. S. Woods.

PALLID WREN-TIT.

Berkeley, Calif.   Mary M. Erickson.
                                    Courtesy Mus. Vert. Zoology.

GAMBEL'S WREN-TITS.

PLATE 21

Santa Clara County, Calif. Gayle Pickwell.

GAMBEL'S WREN-TITS

PLATE 22

Logan Canyon, Utah.   A. A. Allen.

A. H. Cordier.

DIPPERS.

PLATE 23

Jenny Creek, Oreg., April 1923.   J. E. Patterson.

NEST AND EGGS OF DIPPER.

PLATE 24

ADULT DIPPER AT NEST.

Santa Clara County, Calif.

PLATE 25

Ithaca, N. Y.   A. A. Allen.

EASTERN HOUSE WREN AND NEST.

PLATE 26

Hennepin County, Minn., June 28, 1941.   A. D. DuBois.

NATURAL NEST SITE OF EASTERN HOUSE WREN.

PLATE 27

W. E. Shore.

EASTERN HOUSE WREN.

Near Toronto, Ontario, June 29, 1942.

PLATE 28

Coeur d'Alene, Idaho.   H. J. Rust.

Pinehurst, Oreg., May 5, 1924.   J. E. Patterson.

WESTERN HOUSE WRENS.

PLATE 29

Kingston, R. I., May 24, 1908.   A. C. Bent.

Nest in upturned roots.

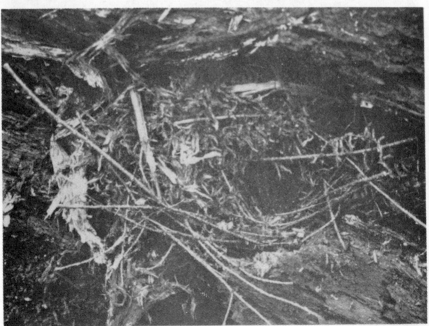

Near Ithaca, N. Y.   A. A. Allen.

Nest in fallen log.

NESTS OF EASTERN WINTER WREN.

PLATE 30

Lancaster, N. H., May 20, 1904.

Owen Durfee.

Branchport, N. Y., May 28, 1915.

C. F. Stone.
Courtesy of Verdi Burtch.

NESTING SITES OF EASTERN WINTER WREN.

PLATE 31

Harold Heath.

St. George Island, Bering Sea.

NEST AND EGGS OF ALASKA WREN.

PLATE 32

W. L. & Irene Finley.

WESTERN WINTER WREN FAMILY.

PLATE 33

W. L. & Irene Finley.

Nesting site.

WESTERN WINTER WRENS.

Adult and young.

Portland, Oreg.

PLATE 34

Hocking County, Ohio.   E. S. Thomas.

BEWICK'S WREN.

PLATE 35

R. J. Niedrach.

R. W. Hendee.
Courtesy Colorado Mus. Nat. Hist.

Bacon County, Colo., May 1914.

Colorado.

NESTING OF BAIRD'S WREN.

PLATE 36

W. L. & Irene Finley.

YOUNG SEATTLE WRENS.

Portland, Oreg.

PLATE 37

Duval County, Fla., June 1931.   S. A. Grimes.

Arkansas City, Kans., July 15, 1929.   Walter Colvin.

NESTS OF CAROLINA WREN.

PLATE 38

Jackson County, Ohio.   E. S. Thomas.

Nest in an old stove.

CAROLINA WREN.

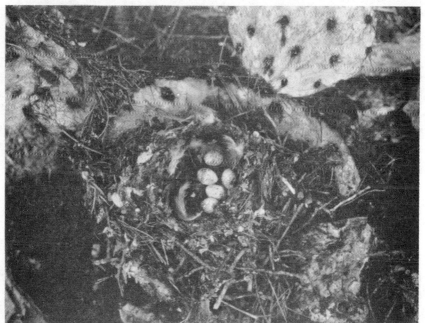

Brownsville, Tex., May 5, 1924.   Herbert Friedmann.

NEST OF LOMITA WREN.

PLATE 39

Cochise County, Ariz., April 24, 1922.   A. C. Bent.

NESTS OF NORTHERN CACTUS WRENS.

PLATE 40

Azusa, Calif., April 12, 1940.   R. S. Woods.   Arizona.   W. L. & Irene Finley.

Nest in dooryard *Cereus*.   Young.

NORTHERN CACTUS WRENS.

PLATE 41

Near Claremont, Calif., April 17, 1916.   W. M. Pierce.

Near Claremont, Calif., April 1, 1916.   W. M. Pierce.

NEST AND YOUNG OF NORTHERN CACTUS WREN.

PLATE 42

Eliot Porter.

NORTHERN CACTUS WREN.

Arizona, April 22, 1941.

PLATE 43

J. G. Griggs.

NESTING OF LONG-BILLED MARSH WREN.

Jamestown Island, Va.

PLATE 44

Duval County, Fla., July 1937.   S. A. Grimes.

Duval County, Fla., June 9, 1934.   S. A. Grimes.

NESTING OF WORTHINGTON'S MARSH WREN.

PLATE 45

A. A. Allen.

Adult at nest.

NESTS OF PRAIRIE MARSH WREN.

Section showing "door sill."

Ithaca, N. Y.

PLATE 46

Buckeye Lake, Ohio.   E. S. Thomas.

PRAIRIE MARSH WREN.

PLATE 47

J. E. Patterson.

Klamath County, Oreg.

NEST OF WESTERN MARSH WREN.

PLATE 48

Nesting meadow.

Canton, Mass., June 17, 1903.

A. C. Bent.

Well-concealed nest.

NESTING OF SHORT-BILLED MARSH WREN.

PLATE 49

A. A. Allen.

SHORT-BILLED MARSH WRENS.

Near Ithaca, N. Y.

PLATE 50

L. H. Walkinshaw.

SHORT-BILLED MARSH WREN.

Near Battle Creek, Mich., July '6, 1933.

PLATE 51

Illinois, June 16, 1942.   Eliot Porter.

SHORT-BILLED MARSH WREN.

PLATE 52

Catalina Mountains, Ariz., April 18, 1922.　　　　　　　　　　A. C. Bent.

Nesting cave.

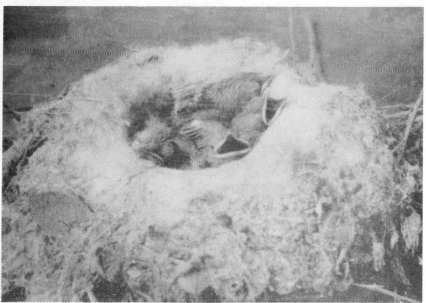

Arizona.　　　　　　　　　　　　　　　　　　　　　　　　　F. C. Willard.

Nest and young.

CANYON WRENS.

PLATE 53

Southern California.

W. L. & Irene Finley.

Fledged young.

Santa Clara County, Calif.

Gayle Pickwell.

Adult and nest.

CANYON WRENS.

PLATE 54

Huachuca Mountains, Ariz., April 14, 1922.   A. C. Bent.

Tombstone, Ariz., April 28, 1922.   A. C. Bent.

Note stone pavings.

NESTING HOLES OF COMMON ROCK WREN.

PLATE 55

Inyo County. Calif., April 4, 1926.   J. S. Rowley.

O. W. Howard at nesting site.

Arizona.   F. C. Willard.

Excavated nest.

NESTING OF COMMON ROCK WREN.

PLATE 56

Duval County, Fla., April 16, 1933.   S. A. Grimes.

Duval County, Fla., April 1935.   S. A. Grimes.

NESTS OF EASTERN MOCKINGBIRD.

PLATE 57

Manywings, Fla.   A. D. Cruickshank.

St. Cloud, Fla.   A. A. Allen.

EASTERN MOCKINGBIRDS.

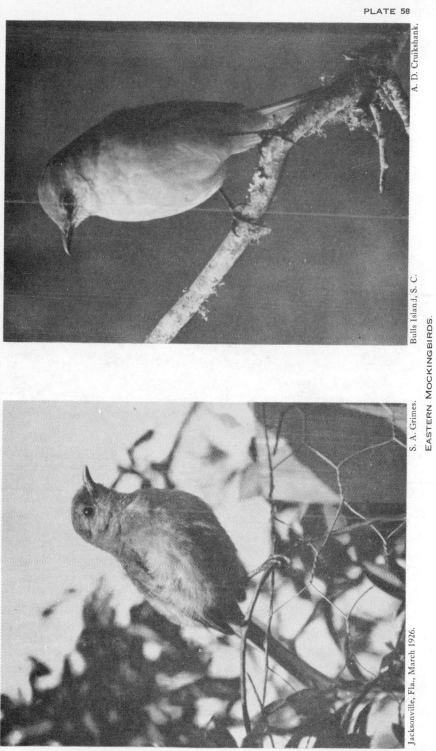

PLATE 58

A. D. Cruikshank.

Bulls Island, S. C.

S. A. Grimes.

EASTERN MOCKINGBIRDS.

Jacksonville, Fla., March 1926.

PLATE 59

Stanislaus County, Calif., April 18, 1936.

J. E. Patterson.

NEST OF WESTERN MOCKINGBIRD.

PLATE 60

Azusa, Calif., February 26, 1933.   R. S. Woods.

Azusa, Calif., September 27, 1923.   R. S. Woods.

Eating *Opuntia* fruit.

WESTERN MOCKINGBIRDS.

PLATE 61

Warwick, R. I., June 2, 1899.   H. S. Hathaway.

Wyoming County, N. Y., June 1928.   S. A. Grimes.

NESTS OF CATBIRDS.

PLATE 62

White Plains, N. Y.   A. D. Cruickshank.

Hennepin County, Minn., May 28, 1938.   A. D. DuBois.

CATBIRD

PLATE 63

CATBIRD INCUBATING.

PLATE 64

H. M. Halliday.

CATBIRD FEEDING YOUNG.

Near Toronto, Ontario.

PLATE 65

A. D. Cruickshank.

CATBIRD.

PLATE 66

Hennepin County, Minn., April 1929.   S. A. Grimes.

Knox County, Ill., May 24, 1938.   H. M. Holland.

GROUND NESTS OF BROWN THRASHER.

PLATE 67

BROWN THRASHER ON NEST.

Murfreesboro, Tenn., April 27, 1941.

PLATE 68

Oyster Bay, Long Island, N. Y., January 1942.   R. T. Peterson.

BROWN THRASHER IN WINTER.

PLATE 69

Eliot Porter.

BROWN THRASHER.

Illinois, May 28, 1942.

PLATE 70

A. D. Cruickshank.

BROWN THRASHER.

PLATE 71

Pima County, Ariz., May 24, 1922. A. C. Bent.

NESTING SITE OF BENDIRE'S THRASHER.

Brownsville, Tex., May 17, 1924. Herbert Friedmann.

NEST OF SENNETT'S THRASHER.

PLATE 72

Arizona.   W. L. & Irene Finley.

NEST OF BENDIRE'S THRASHER.

PLATE 73

W. M. Pierce.

NEST OF BENDIRE'S THRASHER.

Near Victorville, Calif.

PLATE 74

Pima County, Ariz., May 24, 1922.   A. C. Bent.

Catalina Mountains, Ariz., May 23, 1922.   A. C. Bent.

NESTING OF PALMER'S THRASHER.

PLATE 75

Arizona.

W. L. & Irene Finley.

NEST OF PALMÉR'S THRASHER.

PLATE 76

Arizona.   F. C. Willard.

Tucson, Ariz.   W. L. & Irene Finley.

NEST AND YOUNG OF PALMER'S THRASHER.

PLATE 77

Eliot Porter.

PALMER'S THRASHERS

Arizona, May 6, 1941.

PLATE 78

Palo Alto, Calif., April 4, 1927.   J. E. Patterson.

Azusa, Calif., May 4, 1922.   R. S. Woods.

NESTS OF CALIFORNIA THRASHER.

PLATE 79

Near Claremont, Calif., May 24, 1913.   W. M. Pierce.

NEST OF CALIFORNIA THRASHER.

PLATE 80

Azusa, Calif., September 15, 1932.   R. S. Woods

Los Angeles, Calif.   Loye Miller.

CALIFORNIA THRASHERS.

PLATE 81

Mojave Desert, Calif., March 11, 1929.   A. C. Bent.

Mojave Desert, Calif., April 17, 1929.   W. M. Pierce.

The author chopping out a nest.

NESTING SITES OF LeCONTE'S THRASHER.

PLATE 82

Mojave Desert, Calif., May 8, 1916. W. M. Pierce.

Mojave Desert, Calif. W. M. Pierce.

YOUNG AND NEST OF LECONTE'S THRASHER.

PLATE 83

Note padded lining.

NEST OF LeCONTE'S THRASHER.

PLATE 84

E. N. Harrison.

San Rosalia Bay, Baja California.

HABITAT OF DESERT THRASHER.

PLATE 85

Cochise County, Ariz., June 1, 1922.   A. C. Bent

Arizona.   F. C. Willard.

NESTS OF CRISSAL THRASHER.

PLATE 86

YOUNG CRISSAL THRASHERS.

PLATE 87

Siskiyou County, Calif., May 10, 1924.   J. E. Patterson

NEST OF SAGE THRASHER.

PLATE 88

Klamath County, Oreg., May 10, 1924.

J. E. Patterson.

NEST OF SAGE THRASHER.

PLATE 89

Bailey & Niedrach.

SAGE THRASHER.

Canyon City, Colo., May 14, 1931.

PLATE 90

Bailey & Niedrach.

SAGE THRASHER.

Canyon City, Colo., May 14, 1931.

DATE DUE